T0321689

Contemporary Research on Intertextuality in Video Games

Christophe Duret
Université de Sherbrooke, Canada

Christian-Marie Pons
Université de Sherbrooke, Canada

A volume in the Advances in Multimedia and
Interactive Technologies (AMIT) Book Series

An Imprint of IGI Global

Published in the United States of America by
>   Information Science Reference (an imprint of IGI Global)
>   701 E. Chocolate Avenue
>   Hershey PA, USA 17033
>   Tel: 717-533-8845
>   Fax: 717-533-8661
>   E-mail: cust@igi-global.com
>   Web site: http://www.igi-global.com

Library of Congress Cataloging-in-Publication Data

Names: Duret, Christophe, editor. | Pons, Christian-Marie, 1954- editor.
Title: Contemporary research on intertextuality in video games / Christophe
   Duret and Christian-Marie Pons, editors.
Description: Hershey PA : Information Science Reference, [2016] | Includes
   bibliographical references and index.
Identifiers: LCCN 2016010965| ISBN 9781522504771 (hardcover) | ISBN
   9781522504788 (ebook)
Subjects: LCSH: Video games. | Intertextuality.
Classification: LCC GV1469.3 .C6464 2016 | DDC 794.8--dc23 LC record available at https://lccn.loc.gov/2016010965

This book is published in the IGI Global book series Advances in Multimedia and Interactive Technologies (AMIT) (ISSN: 2327-929X; eISSN: 2327-9303)

British Cataloguing in Publication Data
A Cataloguing in Publication record for this book is available from the British Library.

All work contributed to this book is new, previously-unpublished material. The views expressed in this book are those of the authors, but not necessarily of the publisher.

For electronic access to this publication, please contact: eresources@igi-global.com.

Advances in Multimedia and Interactive Technologies (AMIT) Book Series

Joel J.P.C. Rodrigues
Instituto de Telecomunicações, University of Beira Interior, Portugal

ISSN: 2327-929X
EISSN: 2327-9303

MISSION

Traditional forms of media communications are continuously being challenged. The emergence of user-friendly web-based applications such as social media and Web 2.0 has expanded into everyday society, providing an interactive structure to media content such as images, audio, video, and text.

The **Advances in Multimedia and Interactive Technologies (AMIT) Book Series** investigates the relationship between multimedia technology and the usability of web applications. This series aims to highlight evolving research on interactive communication systems, tools, applications, and techniques to provide researchers, practitioners, and students of information technology, communication science, media studies, and many more with a comprehensive examination of these multimedia technology trends.

COVERAGE

- Audio Signals
- Digital Watermarking
- Multimedia Streaming
- Digital Communications
- Mobile Learning
- Web Technologies
- Social Networking
- Internet Technologies
- Multimedia technology
- Digital Games

IGI Global is currently accepting manuscripts for publication within this series. To submit a proposal for a volume in this series, please contact our Acquisition Editors at Acquisitions@igi-global.com or visit: http://www.igi-global.com/publish/.

Titles in this Series

For a list of additional titles in this series, please visit: www.igi-global.com

Emerging Perspectives on the Mobile Content Evolution
Juan Miguel Aguado (University of Murcia, Spain) Claudio Feijóo (Technical University of Madrid, Spain &
Tongji University, China) and Inmaculada J. Martínez (University of Murcia, Spain)
Information Science Reference • copyright 2016 • 438pp • H/C (ISBN: 9781466688384) • US $210.00 (our price)

Emerging Research on Networked Multimedia Communication Systems
Dimitris Kanellopoulos (University of Patras, Greece)
Information Science Reference • copyright 2016 • 448pp • H/C (ISBN: 9781466688506) • US $200.00 (our price)

Emerging Research and Trends in Gamification
Harsha Gangadharbatla (University of Colorado Boulder, USA) and Donna Z. Davis (University of Oregon, USA)
Information Science Reference • copyright 2016 • 455pp • H/C (ISBN: 9781466686519) • US $215.00 (our price)

Experimental Multimedia Systems for Interactivity and Strategic Innovation
Ioannis Deliyannis (Ionian University, Greece) Petros Kostagiolas (Ionian University, Greece) and Christina Banou
(Ionian University, Greece)
Information Science Reference • copyright 2016 • 378pp • H/C (ISBN: 9781466686595) • US $195.00 (our price)

Design Strategies and Innovations in Multimedia Presentations
Shalin Hai-Jew (Kansas State University, USA)
Information Science Reference • copyright 2015 • 589pp • H/C (ISBN: 9781466686960) • US $225.00 (our price)

Cases on the Societal Effects of Persuasive Games
Dana Ruggiero (Bath Spa University, UK)
Information Science Reference • copyright 2014 • 345pp • H/C (ISBN: 9781466662063) • US $205.00 (our price)

Video Surveillance Techniques and Technologies
Vesna Zeljkovic (New York Institute of Technology, Nanjing Campus, China)
Information Science Reference • copyright 2014 • 369pp • H/C (ISBN: 9781466648968) • US $215.00 (our price)

Techniques and Principles in Three-Dimensional Imaging An Introductory Approach
Martin Richardson (De Montfort University, UK)
Information Science Reference • copyright 2014 • 324pp • H/C (ISBN: 9781466649323) • US $200.00 (our price)

www.igi-global.com

701 E. Chocolate Ave., Hershey, PA 17033
Order online at www.igi-global.com or call 717-533-8845 x100
To place a standing order for titles released in this series, contact: cust@igi-global.com
Mon-Fri 8:00 am - 5:00 pm (est) or fax 24 hours a day 717-533-8661

Editorial Advisory Board

Table of Contents

Section 3
Hypertextuality

Section 4
Architextuality

Detailed Table of Contents

Section 1
Transmediality/Intermediality

Chapter 1

Luke Arnott, The University of Western Ontario, Canada

This chapter presents a model that explains how the epic is a narrative genre that has become popular across a variety of new media. It demonstrates how the Arkham series of Batman video games – Batman: Arkham Asylum (Rocksteady Studios, 2009), Batman: Arkham City (Rocksteady Studios, 2011), Batman: Arkham Origins (Warner Bros. Games Montreal, 2013), and Batman: Arkham Knight (Rocksteady Studios, 2015) – is constructed as an epic narrative within the larger Batman media franchise. The Arkham series aspires to epic status by eclipsing competing Batman texts or by assimilating those texts into its continuity. The series is an example of how video games now influence the evolution and cross-adaptation of derivative and parallel works such as comics, movies, and other paratexts. The chapter concludes by observing how games like the Arkham series relate to representation and theories of postmodernism.

Chapter 2

Clara Fernandez-Vara, New York University, USA

The video game adaptation of *Blade Runner* (1997) exemplifies the challenges of adapting narrative from traditional media into digital games. The key to the process of adaptation is the fictional world, which it borrows both from Philip K. Dick's novel *Do Androids Dream of Electric Sheep?* (1968) and Ridley Scott's film *Blade Runner* (1982). Each of these works provides different access points to the world, creating an intertextual relationship that can be qualified as transmedia storytelling. The game utilizes the properties of digital environments in order to create a world that the player can explore and participate in; for this world to have the sort of complexity and richness that gives way to engaging interactions, the game resorts to the film to create a visual representation, and to the themes of the novel. Thus the game is inescapably intertextual, since it needs of both source materials in order to make the best of the medium of the video game.

Michael Fuchs, University of Graz, Austria

In many respects, *Alan Wake* reminds of a typical postmodernist text: it draws on various sources, integrates other texts into its textual body, and is highly self-conscious both about its construction and the recipient's role in generating meaning. However, *Alan Wake* is not a postmodernist novel, but a video game. This chapter explores the ways in which this video game incorporates other cultural artifacts and argues that its cannibalistic incorporation of other media transforms *Alan Wake*'s textual body into the game text's true, Gothic monster.

Mehdi Debbabi Zourgani, Paris 5 Descartes, France
Julien Lalu, UFR SHA Poitiers, France
Matthieu Weisser, UFR SHA Poitiers, France

This chapter proposes to study intermediality in video games in order to highlight media interactions. The purpose is to analyze some intermedia processes to illustrate how intermediality can create signification. The chapter is focused on the survival horror game *Silent Hill 2* (Konami, 2001). More specifically, it is about, but not only, two protagonists: James Sunderland and Eddie Dombrowski. Analyses follow three different intermediality levels that can be applied in video games to get a better comprehension of it. The co-presence shows what is played between the media included in the game. The transfer has an interest to the links between video games and other objects in order to find how its language is created. *Silent Hill 2*, as a Japanese production, includes many Japanese symbols. The emergence reveals what creates the specific identity of the video game as a medium by observing the interactions between the different media composing it.

Section 2
Intertextuality

Andréane Morin-Simard, Université de Montréal, Canada

Given the pervasiveness of popular music in the contemporary media landscape, it is not unusual to find the same song in multiple soundtracks. Based on theories of intertextuality and communication, this chapter seeks to define the relationship which develops between two or more narrative and/or interactive works that share the same song, and to understand the effects of such recontextualizations on the gamer's experience. The media trajectory of Blue Öyster Cult's "Don't Fear the Reaper" is mapped as a network to categorize the many complex intersections between video games, films and television series which feature the song. Three video games are analyzed to propose that the song's previous associations with other works may positively or negatively interfere with the music's narrative and ludic functions within the game.

This chapter examines the popular 2007 video game *BioShock* and its relation to the work of Objectivist author Ayn Rand. Using Jacques Rancière's model of emancipatory learning and Polanyi's concept of tacit knowledge, the authors explore how video games can instill transferable skills and knowledge by forming intertextual connections to other media. Including an interview with *BioShock* creator Ken Levine, the authors discuss how players may learn about works such as Rand's *Atlas Shrugged*, forming opinions, criticisms, and applications of her philosophy, without ever receiving explanations of it in the game. They conclude the chapter by demonstrating the potential for such forms of learning to become more prominent in video games, while also acknowledging the inherent limitations of the medium.

This chapter explores the intertextual nature of video games. Video games are inherently intertextual and have utilized intertextuality in profound ways to engage players and make meaning. Youth who play video games demonstrate complex intertextual literacies that enable them to construct and share understandings across game genres. However, video game literacy is noticeably absent from formal education. This chapter draws from bi-monthly meetings with a group of youth video gamers. Video game sessions focused on exploring aspect of video game play such as learning and civic engagements. Each session was video recorded and coded using You Tube annotation tools. Focusing on intertextuality as an organizing construct, the chapter reports on five themes that emerged that were then used to help explore the use of video games as teaching tool in a grade 11 Language Arts class. A critical concept that emerged was the idea of complex intertextual literacy that frames and enables adolescents' engagement with video games.

This essay posits two crucial elements for the representation of digital games in film: intertextuality and player control. Cinematically, the notion of player-agency control is influenced greatly by this intertextuality, and player control has been represented in a number of films involving video games and digital worlds. This essay looks at the use and representation of player-agency control in films that focus on action within digital games. There are three elements that are essential to this representation: 1) there is a separation between the virtual and the real; 2) the virtual world is written in code, and this code is impossible for player-agents to change, though they can manipulate it; 3) the relative position of the player to the player-agent, is one of subservience or conflict. I argue that the notion of player-agency control is essential to the cinematic representation of video games' virtual worlds.

Chapter 9

Enrique Uribe-Jongbloed, Universidad del Norte, Colombia
Hernán David Espinosa-Medina, Universidad de La Sabana, Colombia
James Biddle, University of Georgia, USA

This chapter addresses the relationship that exists between intertextuality and cultural transduction in video game localization. Whereas the former refers to the dual relationship established between texts and previous texts available to the potential readers and the bridges that are consciously or unconsciously established between them, cultural transduction refers to the conscious process of transforming audiovisual content to suit the interests of a given cultural market. Three case studies are presented to explore the relationship that exists between the place of production, the internal cultural references to other texts within the games and the intended market where the video game is distributed: Finally, the importance of intertextuality as part of the cultural transduction process is highlighted.

Chapter 10

Christopher Totten, American University, USA

This chapter explores art history to establish parallels between the current state of the game art field and historical art and architectural periods. In doing so, it proposes methods for both making and studying games that subvert the popular analysis trends of game art that are typically based on the history of game graphics and technology. The chapter will then demonstrate the use of art and design history in game development by discussing the Atelier Games project, which utilizes the styles and techniques of established artists and art movements to explore the viability of classic methods for the production of game art and game mechanics.

Section 3
Hypertextuality

Chapter 11

Kristin M. S. Bezio, University of Richmond, USA

This chapter examines Crystal Dynamics' 2013 *Tomb Raider* reboot, arguing that the game makes use of intertextual references to the original Core Design *Tomb Raider* (1996) and popular culture archaeology in an effort to revise the original franchise's exploitative depiction of both Lara Croft and archaeological practice. Framed by a theoretical understanding of Orientalism and the constraints of symbolic order and the recognition that video games in general and the Tomb Raider franchise in specific are "games of empire," it becomes clear that the 2013 *Tomb Raider* ultimately fails to escape the constraints of imperial procedural semiotics.

This chapter is based on the analysis of previous cross-media game adaptations, on empirical research, and on reflection on practice with the design of a game concept for a fantasy book. Book-to-game adaptations are particularly interesting examples of cross-media adaptation. They not only weave the literary source text with intertexts from the game medium, but also require a modal transposition from the realm of words to a visual, interactive, multimodal medium where narrative and ludic logics intersect. This study proposes to look at different layers of cross-media intertextuality in the process of adaptation - at the level of specific texts, at the level of medium conventions, and at the level of genre conventions. It draws on crowd-sourcing research with readers to demonstrate that collaboration operates through multi-layered processes of collective intertextuality through which the intertextual repertoires of individuals meet to weave a final text.

Section 4
Architextuality

Intertextuality is present in most digital games since their beginnings. However, despite its importance for understanding games, research about the theme tends to be disproportionally rare and limited to representational aspects (text, images, audio, etc.), leaving out games' most distinctive characteristics, namely, their rules and mechanics. Since the classic concept of intertextuality does not account for this dimension, the authors propose a concept that is to games what intertextuality is for texts, combining principles of intertextuality with the theory of procedural rhetoric, which deals with the construction of meaning in digital games. This concept, interprocedurality, describes the explicit or implicit inclusion of other games' rules and mechanics in a given game. As a way to exemplify its presence in a specific game, this chapter presents a brief analysis of the interprocedurality occurring in the digital game Deus Ex: Human Revolution and the findings it generated.

Even though literary genres are instrumental for the study and analysis of video games, we should also take into consideration that, nowadays, the boundaries of literature have been crossed and we have to deal with a broader transmedia reality. Approaching it can be quite challenging and, in addition to the already existing genre theory, it requires the implementation of appropriate analytic tools, both adaptable to different languages and media and able to reconstruct and motivate the isotopies woven into the net.

In the authors' opinion, semiotics is particularly suitable for this task, for many reasons. The aim of this chapter, then, is to propose a semiotic methodology, oriented toward the analysis of the architextual aspects of video games. Two case studies will be taken into consideration, in order to shed some light on the inner working of architexts featuring video games, as one of their most relevant components: the horror genre and the high fantasy genre.

Section 5
Paratextuality

Chapter 15

This chapter examines paratext as an active element within video games. Paratext, as taken from Gérard Genette's works has often been cited within the context of video games, but not examined in detail. Current scholarship focuses on epitext, but not peritext, which is Genette's primary focus. Mia Consalvo and Peter Lunenfeld's work discuss the epitextual importance of paratext within video games, with only a hint towards the importance of peritext. Through a brief exploration of paratext's history in both literature and games, this chapter will reveal a need for deeper analysis within video game studies. Focusing on in-game, in-system and in-world types of paratexts this paper will attempt to formalise the unaddressed issue of paratext in video games.

Chapter 16

This chapter provides a revised framework of paratextuality which deals with some of the limitations of Gérard Genette's concept while keeping its focus on the relationship between a text and socio-historical reality. The updated notion of paratextuality draws upon Alexander R. Galloway's work on the interface effect. The proposed revision is explained in a broader context of intertextuality and textual transcendence. Regarding Genette's terminology, this chapter rejects the constrictive notion of a paratext and stresses that paratextuality is first and foremost a relationship, not a textual category. The new framework is then put to the test using four sample genres of official video game communication – trailers, infographics, official websites of video games and patch notes.

Preface

Intertextuality is present in all types of media, from serial literature to television series, from comics to cinema. It accounts for a significant proportion of the enjoyment experienced by the reader/viewer in the consumption of these media, but also for the richness of textual productions of the latter, which extends into a vast network of quotations, open or covert references, influences and parodies.

The notion of intertextuality has changed considerably through its 80-year history. As part of a process of socio-historical definition of the poetics of the novel through dialogism (Bakhtin, 1978), or a semanalysis approach (Kristeva, 1969, 1970) and, more broadly, poststructuralism (Barthes, 1974; Sollers, 1968), pointing alternately to hermeneutical (Riffaterre, 1979, 1982) (Barthes, 1973), poetic (Genette, 1979, 1982), genetic (Le Calvez, 1997; Pickering, 1997; Rastier, 1997), sociodiscursive (Angenot, 1989), and sociocritical (Duchet & Maurus, 2011) phenomena or, more recently, to adaptation (Hutcheon 2013), transmediality (Jenkins 2006), and transfictionalization (Saint-Gelais 2011), this notion is somewhat polysemic and polemic. A vast collective assembly of specification and deconstruction of the terms "intertextuality" and "intertext" has taken place during this long history, and today, they refer to a constellation of textual relations and various texts known as co-texts (Duchet & Maurus, 2011), metafictions (Hutcheon, 1984), transfictions (Saint-Gelais, 2011), transmedia storytelling (Jenkins, 2006), adaptations (Hutcheon, 2013) autotextuality (Dällenbach, 1976) intertextual irony (Eco, 2003), general or limited intertextuality (Ricardou, 1986/1974), external or internal intertextuality (Ricardou, 1971), allusion, plagiarism, pastiche, charge, forgery and parody (Genette, 1982), quotation (Compagnon, 1979), interimage (Duffy, 1997), prescriptive intertextuality (Vetters, 2011) and doctrinal intertextuality (Suleiman, 1983), metatextuality and hypertextuality (Genette, 1982), architextuality (Genette, 1979), paratextuality (Genette, 1987), and so on. In practice, intertextuality has become functional, saved from the danger that awaited it of becoming a catch-all concept that could fit everything and its opposite.

Despite the pervasiveness of the concept of intertextuality in digital games and a longstanding tradition associated to it, only a handful of game scholars have used it or one of its derivative terms in their research (see Bonk, 2014; Consalvo, 2003; Dormans, 2006; Duret, 2015; Egliston, 2015; Jones, 2008; Krzywinska, 2006, 2008; Krzywinska, MacCallum-Stewart & Parsler, 2011; Love, 2010; Poor, 2012; Schrader, Lawless & McCreery, 2009, Scodari, 1993; Weise, 2009) and this book is the first to be entirely dedicated to it.

What might explain the absence of this concept in the game studies field? Since the early 2000s, there has been a shift from intertextuality (or, more broadly, of transtextuality, a near-synonym of the term for some authors) to transfictionality and transmediality in the study of fictional works (novels, comics, digital games, films, graphic novels, etc.), with the researches of Jens Bonk (2014), Kristy Dena (2009), Henry Jenkins (2003; 2006), Marsha Kinder (1991), Lisbeth Klastrup and Susana Tosca (2013),

Marie-Laure Ryan (2008; 2013), Richard Saint-Gelais (2000; 2011), Carlos Alberto Scolari (2009), and Jan-Noël Thon (2009), among others. This shift implies a change in object of study and, consequently, the level of analysis: after the text, the attention of researchers focuses more readily on the spatiotemporal universes of the works (known as the cosmos, diegesis, fictional world, storyworld, heterocosm, transfictional world, and so forth), the plots that occur within these universes and the characters inhabiting them. In other words, the focus is on the fiction rather than the texts that convey it.

In digital games, transfictionality is a widespread phenomenon and justifies the growing number of researchers interested in it. But this interest for transfictionality should not be allowed to obscure the intertextual/transtextual nature of the digital games, the contribution of exogenous texts (pastiches, parodies, quotations, allusions, metatexts, hypertexts, paratexts, and so forth) strongly contributing to their depth. In other words, the concepts of transfictionality and transmediality do not call into question the relevance of intertextuality. On the contrary, some of the collaborations in this book illustrate the relevance of addressing the digital game object by combining the two perspectives, especially when it comes to analyzing its procedural dimension.

More broadly, the richness and scope of the contributions presented here attest to the topicality of intertextuality and its usefulness with regard to the field of game studies. This research will allow us to better map the vast textual ecosystems that feed digital games and which are fed back from them.

ORGANIZATION OF THE BOOK

This book is organized around five topics: transmediality and intermediality (chapters 1 to 4); intertextuality *stricto sensu* (chapters 5 to 10), with the first three chapters focusing on the role played by gamers in the intertextual process; hypertextuality in the Genettian sense, in reference to reboots and adaptations (chapters 11 & 12); architextuality (chapters 13 & 14); and finally, paratextuality (chapters 15 & 16).

A brief description of each chapter follows.

Transmediality/Intermediality

Chapter 1

In "Arkham Epic: *Batman* Video Games as Totalizing Texts", Luke Arnott describes the *Arkham* series of Batman video games as an epic narrative. Four levels of analysis are proposed (the textual, paratextual/intertextual, symbolic, and socio-historical levels, respectively) in order to illustrate how the series can be critiqued as a cohesive epic within the Batman franchise, with which it shares a relationship of both continuity and competition. The chapter concludes by demonstrating how, as totalizing texts, the *Arkham* games are a representation of the postmodern space.

Chapter 2

In "The Inescapable Intertextuality of *Blade Runner - The Video Game*", Clara Fernández-Vara examines how *Blade Runner - The Video Game* is part of a larger transmedial narrative, including Philip K. Dick's novel *Do Androids Dream of Electric Sheep?* and Ridley Scott's film, *Blade Runner*, as it utilizes the properties of interactive environments in order to create an interactive world that the player is invited to explore. *Blade Runner - The Video Game* retains the themes and the fictional world of the novel, as well as the conventions of *noir* detective stories, which are adapted in accordance with the procedural, participatory, spatial, and encyclopedic characteristics of the digital game medium. By doing so, the game presents itself as "inescapably intertextual."

Chapter 3

Many critics contend that the narrative complexity of *Alan Wake*, a game that boasts a profusion of storyworlds-within-storyworlds, comes at the expense of its gameplay, which some consider simplistic and repetitive. In "A Different Kind of Monster: Uncanny Media and *Alan Wake*'s Textual Monstrosity", Michael Fuchs argues, however, that this alleged weakness with regard to gameplay, as well as the confusion between and conflation of different storyworlds, reinforces the game text's meaning in accordance with its self-reflexivity toward the Gothic tradition and its meta-reflexivity concerning the relationship between video games and other media. The author suggests that the uncanny effects produced by *Alan Wake*'s Gothic narrative are more likely attributable to the elements of intermediality and remediation that are found in the game rather than the monsters that the players are pitted against. *Alan Wake* is thus seen as a monstrous text that cannibalizes other media.

Chapter 4

In "Intermediality and Video Games: Analysis of *Silent Hill 2*", Mehdi Debbabi Zourgani, Julien Lalu, and Matthieu Weisser analyze the *Silent Hill 2* video game from an intermedial perspective and, more specifically, the relationship that unites two of the main protagonists of the game. To this end, three levels of intermediality are used: co-presence, transfer, and emergence.

Intertextuality

Chapter 5

In "Gamers (Don't) Fear the Reaper: Musical Intertextuality and Interference in Video Games", Andréane Morin-Simard examines the intertextual relationship that links video games together when they share the same song. The media trajectory of the song *Don't Fear the Reaper* is then mapped in order to understand how its recontextualization in the *Ripper*, *Roadkill* and *Prey* video games impacts the gamer's experience. In doing so, the author shows how the association of the Blue Öyster Cult's song with previous works interferes with its functions regarding the gameplay and the narrative of the games.

Chapter 6

In "*BioShock* and the Ghost of Ayn Rand: Universal Learning and Tacit Knowledge in Contemporary Video Games", Chris Richardson and Mike Elrod examine the *BioShock* video game and its relation to the work of the Russian-born American philosopher Ayn Rand. More specifically, the authors put Jacques Rancière's model of emancipatory learning and Michael Polanyi's concept of tacit knowledge in dialogue with the concept of intertextuality in order to show how the players benefit from transferable skills and knowledge by forming connections to other media without receiving explanations from within the game.

Chapter 7

In "Exploring Complex Intertextual Interactions in Video Games: Connecting Informal and Formal Education for Youth", Kathy Sanford, Timothy Frank Hopper, and Jamie Burren use a complexity theory framework and propose the concept of complex intertextual literacy in order to explain how adolescents are provided incentives through video games like *BioShock Infinite, Gone Home, L.A. Noire,* and *The Stanley Parable* to make connections to a wide array of texts. The authors consider the potential of these games to form a critical space to engage students in meaning-making.

Chapter 8

In "'You can't mess with the program, Ralph': Intertextuality of Player-Agency in Filmic Virtual Worlds", Theo Plothe examines the representation of player-agency control in films that focus on action within digital games. This representation relies on three essential elements: a separation between the virtual and the real; a written code underlying the virtual world that the player can manipulate, but not effectively change; a relationship based on subservience or conflict between the player and the player-agent. The films analyzed in this chapter are *Tron, Tron: Legacy, The Matrix, The Matrix Reloaded, The Matrix Revolutions, The Lawnmower Man, eXistenZ, Avalon, Spy Kids 3-D: Game Over*, and *Wreck-it Ralph*.

Chapter 9

In "Cultural Transduction and Intertextuality in Video Games: An Analysis of Three International Case Studies", Enrique Uribe-Jongbloed, Hernán David Espinosa-Medina, and James Biddle address the question of video game localization through the convergence of the concepts of intertextuality and cultural transduction. To this end, three case studies are presented, namely *El Chavo Kart, South Park: The Stick of Truth*, and the *Kingdom Rush* series.

Chapter 10

In "Moving Forward by Looking Back: Using Art and Architectural History to Make and Understand Games", Christopher Totten demonstrates how the field of game art could benefit from the history of art and architecture and finds new opportunities for game production. As an alternative to the most popular ways of analyzing game art, which are based on the history of game graphics and technology, artistic intertextuality and architextuality are useful tools for researchers and developers to understand and make new game types. The author analyzes various indie games such as *Dys4ia, Dominique Pamplemousse, A Duck Has an Adventure*, and *Lissitzky's Revenge*.

Hypertextuality

Chapter 11

In "Artifacts of Empire: Orientalism and Inner-Texts in *Tomb Raider* (2013)", Kristin M.S. Bezio examines Crystal Dynamics' 2013 *Tomb Raider*, the reboot of the original Core Design *Tomb Raider* from

1996. She draws on Edward Said's concept of Orientalism, Julia Kristeva's constraints of the symbolic order, as well as Nick Dyer-Witheford and Greig de Peuter's conception of video games as "games of empire," to demonstrate how the *Tomb Raider* reboot, constrained by both its inter- and inner-texts, failed to escape the constraints of imperial procedural semiotics.

Chapter 12

In "Weaving *Nature Mage*: Multi-layered Intertextuality in a book-to-game adaptation", Claudio Pires Franco analyzes, from the point of view of a researcher and creator, a case of cross-media adaptations, namely the book-to-game adaptation of a teen fantasy series called *Nature Mage*, by Duncan Pile. The study examines three layers of cross-media intertextuality: the level of specific texts, medium conventions, and genre conventions. In addition, the author describes the use of readers' involvement and co-creation implied in the adaptation process as a form of collective intertextuality "through which the intertextual repertoires of individuals meet to weave a final text."

Architextuality

Chapter 13

In "Interprocedurality: Procedural Intertextuality in Digital Games", Marcelo Simão de Vasconcellos, Flávia Garcia de Carvalho, and Inesita Soares de Araujo prefer the procedural dimension of intertextuality (i.e. rules, mechanics) to the representational one (e.g.: text, images, audio). When used jointly with Ian Bogost's procedural rhetoric, the concept of intertextuality becomes "interprocedurality," which is defined as "the explicit or implicit inclusion of other games' rules and mechanics in a given game." The authors illustrate their concept by analyzing the *Deus Ex: Human Revolution* video game.

Chapter 14

In "Architextuality and Video Games, a Semiotic Approach", drawing on Algirdas Greimas' schema of actantial and thematic roles and Yuri Lotman's theory of the semiosphere, Mattia Thibault and Maria Katsaridou study the horror and high fantasy genres by making use of a semiotic methodology oriented toward the analysis of the architextual aspects of video games. The authors use a broad definition of architextuality that implies intertextuality and hypertextuality in order to take into account the notion of genre in complex phenomena such as transmedia storytelling. They defend their argument by analyzing the tabletop role-playing game *Dungeons & Dragons* and the *Warcraft*, *Silent Hill,* and *Resident Evil* video game series.

Paratextuality

Chapter 15

In "Paratext: The In-Between of Structure and Play", Daniel Dunne notes the lack of attention concerning the Genettian concept of peritext in the game studies field, when compared with that of epitext.

After discussing prior works on the topic by game scholars such as Mia Consalvo, Peter Lunenfeld, and David Jara, he remedies the situation by offering a new definition of paratext that focuses on peritextual analysis with the help of a model considering three levels of video games where paratext can be found: in-game, in-system, and in-world.

Chapter 16

In "'Footage Not Representative': Redefining Paratextuality for the Analysis of Official Communication of Video Games", Jan Švelch draws on Alexander R. Galloway's work on interfaces in order to put forward a revised definition of paratextuality. This redefinition takes into account the relationship between a text and its socio-historical reality and its links to wider textual ecologies. The author then examines paratextuality in four sample genres of official video game communication: trailers, infographics, official websites, and patch notes.

Christophe Duret
Université de Sherbrooke, Canada

Christian-Marie Pons
Université de Sherbrooke, Canada

REFERENCES

Angenot, M. (1989). *1889, un état du discours social*. Longueuil, Canada: Le Préambule.

Bakhtine, M. (1970). *La poétique de Dostoïevski*. Paris, France: Seuil.

Bakhtine, M. (1978). *Esthétique et théorie du roman*. Paris, France: Gallimard.

Barthes, R. (1973). *Le plaisir du texte*. Paris, France: Seuil.

Barthes, R. (1974). Texte (théorie du). *Encyclopædia Universalis*. Retrieved from http://www.universalis-edu.com/encyclopedie/theorie-du-texte

Bonk, J. (2014). Finishing the fight, one step at a time: Seriality in Bungie's *Halo*. *Eludamos (Göttingen)*, *8*(1), 65–81. Retrieved from http://www.eludamos.org/index.php/eludamos/article/view/vol8no1-5

Compagnon, A. (1979). *La seconde main ou le travail de la citation*. Paris, France: Seuil.

Consalvo, M. (2003). *Zelda 64* and video game fans: A walkthrough of games, intertextuality, and narrative. *Television & New Media*, *4*(3), 321–334.

Dällenbach, L. (1976). Intertexte et autotexte. *Poétique*, (27), 282-296.

Dena, C. (2009). *Transmedia fictions: Theorizing the practice of expressing a fictional world across distinct media and environments* (Unpublished doctoral dissertation). University of Sydney, Sydney, Australia.

Dormans, J. (2006). The world is yours: Intertextual irony and second level reading strategies in *Grand theft auto*. *Game Research*, [En ligne] http://game-research.com/index.php/articles/the-world-is-yours-intertextual-irony-and-second-level-reading-strategies-in-grand-theft-auto (Page consultée le 20 septembre 2011).

Duchet, C., & Maurus, P. (2011). *Un cheminement vagabond: Nouveaux entretiens sur la sociocritique*. Paris, France: Honoré Champion.

Duffy, J. (1997). Claude Simon, Joan Miro et l'interimage. In E. Le Calvez & M.-C. Canova-Green (Eds.), *Texte(s) et intertexte(s)* (pp. 113–139). Amsterdam, Netherland; Atlanta, GA: Rodopi.

Duret, C. (2015). Écosystème transtextuel et jeux de rôle participatifs en environnement virtuel: Le sociogramme de l'ordre naturel dans les jeux de rôle goréens. In F. Barnabé & B.-O. Dozo (Eds.), *Jeu vidéo et livre*. Liège, Belgium: Bebooks.

Eco, U. (2003). Ironie intertextuelle et niveaux de lecture. In *De la littérature* (pp. 269–298). Paris, France: Grasset et Fasquelle.

Egliston, B. (2015). Playing across media: Exploring transtextuality in competitive games and eSports. In *Proceedings of DiGRA 2015: Diversity of play: Games – cultures – identities*. Retrieved from http://www.digra.org/digital-library/publications/playing-across-media-exploring-transtextuality-in-competitive-games-and-esports/

Genette, G. (1979). *Introduction à l'architexte*. Paris, France: Seuil.

Genette, G. (1982). *Palimpsestes: La littérature au second degré*. Paris, France: Seuil.

Genette, G. (1987). *Seuils*. Paris, France: Seuil.

Hutcheon, L. (1984). *Narcissistic narrative: The metafictional paradox*. London, UK; New York, NY: Routledge.

Hutcheon, L. (2013). *A theory of adaptation*. London, UK; New York, NY: Routledge.

Jenkins, H. (2003). *Transmedia storytelling: Moving characters from books to films to video games can make*. Retrieved June 3, 2015, from http://www.technologyreview.com/news/401760/transmedia-storytelling/

Jenkins, H. (2006). *Convergence culture: Where old and new media collide*. New York, NY: New York University Press.

Jones, S. E. (2008). *The meaning of video games: Gaming and textual strategies*. London: Routledge.

Kinder, M. (1991). *Playing with power in movies, television, and video games: From Muppet Babies to Teenage Mutant Ninja Turtles*. Berkeley, CA: University of California Press.

Klastrup, L., & Tosca, S. (2013). *Transmedial worlds: Rethinking cyberworld design*. Retrieved May 17, 2015, fromhttp://www.itu.dk/people/klastrup/klastruptosca_transworlds.pdf

Kristeva, J. (1969). *Sēmeiōtikē: Recherches pour une sémanalyse*. Paris, France: Seuil.

Krzywinska, T. (2006). Blood scythes, festivals, quests, and backstories: World creation and rhetorics of myth in *World of warcraft*. *Games and Culture*, *4*(1), 383–396.

Krzywinska, T. (2008). World creation and lore: *World of Warcraft* as rich text. In H. G. Corneliussen & J. W. Rettberg (Eds.), *Digital culture, play, and identity: A World of Warcraft reader* (pp. 123–142). Cambridge, MA: The MIT Press.

Krzywinska, T., MacCallum-Stewart, E., & Parsler, J. (2011). *Ringbearers: The Lord of the rings online as intertextual narrative*. Manchester, UK: Manchester University Press.

Le Calvez, E. (1997). La charogne de *Bouvard et Pécuchet*: Génétique du paragramme. In E. Le Calvez & M.-C. Canova-Green (Eds.), *Texte(s) et intertexte(s)* (pp. 233–261). Amsterdam, Netherland; Atlanta, GA: Rodopi.

Love, M. C. (2010). Not-so-sacred quests: Religion, intertextuality and ethics in video games. *Religious Studies and Theology*, *29*(2), 191–213.

Pickering, R. (1997). Écriture et intertexte chez Valéry: Portée et limites génétiques. In E. Le Calvez & M.-C. Canova-Green (Eds.), *Texte(s) et intertexte(s)* (pp. 219–232). Amsterdam, Netherland; Atlanta, GA: Rodopi.

Poor, N. (2012). Digital elves as a racial other in video games: Acknowledgment and avoidance. *Games and Culture*, *7*(5), 375–396.

Rastier, F. (1997). Parcours génétiques et appropriation des sources: L'exemple d'Hérodias. In E. Le Calvez & M.-C. Canova-Green (Eds.), *Texte(s) et intertexte(s)* (pp. 193–218). Amsterdam, Netherland; Atlanta, GA: Rodopi.

Ricardou, J. (1971). *Pour une théorie du nouveau roman*. Paris, France: Seuil.

Ricardou, J. (1974). "Claude Simon", textuellement. In J. Ricardou (Ed.), *Lire Claude Simon* (pp. 7–38). Bruxelles, Belgium: Les Impressions Nouvelles. (Original work published 1986)

Riffaterre, M. (1979). *La production du texte*. Paris, France: Seuil.

Riffaterre, M. (1982). L'illusion référentielle, In Littérature et réalité (pp. 91-118). Paris, France: Seuil.

Ryan, M.-L. (2008). Transfictionality across media. In J. Pier & J. A. Garcia (Eds.), Theorizing narrativity (pp. 385-417). Berlin, Germany: de Gruyter.

Ryan, M.-L. (2013). Transmedial storytelling and transfictionality. *Poetics Today*, *34*(3), 361–388.

Saint-Gelais, R. (2000). *La fiction à travers l'intertexte: Pour une théorie de la transfictionnalité*. Retrieved July 25, 2015, from http://www.fabula.org/forum/colloque99/PDF/Saint-Gelais.pdf

Saint-Gelais, R. (2011). *Fictions transfuges: La transfictionnalité et ses enjeux*. Paris, France: Seuil.

Schrader, P. G., & Kimberly, A. Lawless, & McCreery, M. (2009). Intertextuality in massively multiplayer online games. Handbook of Research on Effective Electronic Gaming in Education, (3), 791–807.

Scodari, C. (1993). Operation desert storm as "wargames": Sport, war, and media intertextuality. *Journal of American Culture, 16*(1), 1–5. Retrieved from http://onlinelibrary.wiley.com/doi/10.1111/j.1542-734X.1993.1601_1.x/pdf

Scolari, C. A. (2009). Transmedia storytelling: Implicit consumers, narrative worlds, and branding in contemporary media production. *International Journal of Communication, 3*, 586–606.

Sollers, P. (1968). Écriture et révolution. In *Tel quel: Théorie d'ensemble*. Paris, France: Seuil.

Suleiman, S. R. (1983). *Le roman à thèse ou l'autorité fictive*. Paris, France: PUF.

Thon, J.-N. (2009). Computer games, fictional worlds, and transmedia storytelling: A narratological perspective. In: J. R. Sageng (Ed.), *Proceedings of the philosophy of computer games conference 2009* (pp. 1-6). University of Oslo, Norway. Retrieved August 18, 2015, from http://www.hf.uio.no/ifikk/english/research/projects/thirdplace/Conferences/proceedings/Thon%20Jan-No%C3%AB1%202009%20-%20Computer%20Games,%20Fictional%20Worlds,%20and%20Transmedia%20Storytelling%20A%20Narratological%20Perspective.pdf

Vetters, C. (2011). Quand le Sam Spade de Dashiell Hammett devient celui de John Huston: Hammett revu et corrigé par Hays et Warner. Médiation et Information, n°33, Littérature & communication: la question des intertextes, p. 49-58.

Weise, M. (2009). The rules of horror: Procedural adaptation in *Clock Tower, Resident evil* and *Dead rising*. In B. Perron (Ed.), *Horror video games: Essays on the fusion of fear and play* (pp. 238–266). Jefferson, NC: Macfarland.

Acknowledgment

The editors would like to acknowledge the help of all the people involved in this project and, more specifically, to the authors and reviewers that took part in the review process. Without their support, this book would not have become a reality.

First, the editors would like to thank each one of the authors for their contributions. Our sincere gratitude goes to the chapter's authors who contributed their time and expertise to this book.

Second, the editors wish to acknowledge the valuable contributions of the reviewers regarding the improvement of quality, coherence, and content presentation of chapters. Most of the authors also served as referees; we highly appreciate their double task.

Additional thanks are due to Nolan Bazinet (Université de Sherbrooke) for his assistance during the linguistic revision process.

Christophe Duret
Université de Sherbrooke, Canada

Christian-Marie Pons
Université de Sherbrooke, Canada

Section 1
Transmediality/Intermediality

Chapter 1
Arkham Epic:
Batman Video Games as Totalizing Texts

Luke Arnott
The University of Western Ontario, Canada

ABSTRACT

This chapter presents a model that explains how the epic is a narrative genre that has become popular across a variety of new media. It demonstrates how the Arkham series of Batman video games – Batman: Arkham Asylum (Rocksteady Studios, 2009), Batman: Arkham City (Rocksteady Studios, 2011), Batman: Arkham Origins (Warner Bros. Games Montreal, 2013), and Batman: Arkham Knight (Rocksteady Studios, 2015) – is constructed as an epic narrative within the larger Batman media franchise. The Arkham series aspires to epic status by eclipsing competing Batman texts or by assimilating those texts into its continuity. The series is an example of how video games now influence the evolution and cross-adaptation of derivative and parallel works such as comics, movies, and other paratexts. The chapter concludes by observing how games like the Arkham series relate to representation and theories of postmodernism.

INTRODUCTION

I shall provide him with plans for the greatest asylum the world has ever known... – Cyrus Pinkney, Batman: Arkham Origins (Warner Bros. Games Montreal, 2013)

Arkham is a looking glass. And we are you. – The Mad Hatter, Arkham Asylum: A Serious House on Serious Earth (Morrison & McKean, 1989)

According to Dictionary.com's list of "The Worst Words of 2012," the descriptor "epic" – as a mere synonym for "great" or "incredible" – was already so overused that it had topped popular lists of banished words for three years running. "But," the site notes, "epic refuses to be banished." (Dictionary. com, 2012) For anyone versed in the study of the classical epics of antiquity, this resurgence of the term was at once validating and depressing. On the one hand, it described fascinating new digital works such as Dan Sinker's *The F***ing Epic Twitter Quest of @MayorEmanuel*, which is a print collection of a

DOI: 10.4018/978-1-5225-0477-1.ch001

two-thousand-post Twitter feed that periodicals such as *Wired* and *The Economist* have mooted as "the first real work of digital literature" (A. T., 2011). On the other hand, the term "epic" has been slapped on other works, such as the video games *Kirby's Epic Yarn* and *Disney's Epic Mickey*, which are perhaps epic only in the popular sense lamented by the curators of Dictionary.com.

Despite this renewed popular awareness, the epic as it has been conventionally understood has often been considered a dead, or hopelessly antiquated, genre. This has been a tradition in literary scholarship going back as far as the *Poetics*, in which Aristotle (1951) argued that the seriousness of Homer's poetry had already, by the fifth century BC, been supplanted in Greek culture by tragic drama. But, here too, the epic refuses to be banished. Not only have there been notable revivals of the classical epic poem in the hands of such geniuses as Virgil or Milton, but other literary forms, such as the novel, and even other media, such as film, have vied to be the inheritors of epic storytelling. (Harrigan & Wardrip-Fruin, 2009; Bates, 2010; Phillips, 2012; Elliott, 2014) What makes all of these disparate works somehow, almost intuitively, "epic"? Is there some critical need that narratives of great scope fulfill across cultures? What does the epic look like in the twenty-first century, and what are the implications of its contemporary forms?

This chapter will briefly outline a genre theory of the epic that is as applicable to the traditional epic as it is to narrative works in new media, ranging from film and television to comic books and video games. This theory will enable a definition of epic that allows critics to consider it on four separate levels of analysis, from the textual to the socio-historical. The chapter will then deploy this definition to show how a particular video game series, *Batman: Arkham Asylum* (Rocksteady Studios, 2009) and its sequels, can be critiqued as a cohesive epic. The *Arkham* series reveals processes of intertextuality and paratextuality that are particular to video games, and the complexities of adapting narrative material both to and from video games and films, novels, and comics. Furthermore, the chapter will argue that the *Arkham* games reveal the role of video games within contemporary, transnational capital, and that they are a compelling way of modeling postmodern notions of space.

BACKGROUND

A Theory of Genre across Media

Genres are not stable. Pierre Bourdieu (1993) has noted how they are in a constant state of flux within what he calls the "field of cultural production"; the status of particular works or authors, according to Bourdieu, is determined partly by their "position-takings" within that field in relation to the other works and authors, and these positions influence the positions taken by works and authors that will follow. More recently, critics have noted similar shifts in video game genres (Arsenault, 2009), and even entire media forms jockey for cultural supremacy within a dialectical logic of remediation. (Bolter & Grusin, 1999) Therefore, before dealing specifically with the epic, a few general observations about genre are in order: how genres can evolve over time, and how a genre that develops within a particular socio-historical context can be extrapolated into other, sometimes vastly different, cultural contexts. This can also help account for how generic categories are transferred across different media.

Norman Fairclough's (2003) critical discourse analysis offers a model for understanding genre along these trans-media lines. Fairclough considers genres as types of discourse within social contexts, and this definition accords well with more traditional approaches from literary criticism that see genre as a type of speech act. (Nagy, 1999) Fairclough divides genres into three levels of increasing abstraction: first, the situated genre; second, the disembedded genre; and third, the pre-genre.

Figure 1 illustrates these levels using the concept of "epic" as an example. According to Fairclough, a situated genre is specific to a discoursal context, and this is often where a particular genre finds its origin. This is, in the case of the epic, the long, heroic poem that arises from an oral culture, with the paradigmatic example being the *Iliad* or the *Odyssey*. Although the literary tradition looks back to the works of Homer, it is easy to see this arising independently in similar contexts, as in the earlier *Epic of Gilgamesh* or the later *Beowulf*. In any event, this very specific type of epic can then become "disembedded" from its origin to encompass a different type of practice. An example would be an "epic narrative," which would still be discoursal, but would include, in addition to heroic poetry, prose works such as novels, and even new media such as films, comic books, and video games. This process of dis- and re-embedding accounts for the fact that, for instance, nineteenth- and twentieth-century novels were felt by many critics to have taken up the work of the classical epic (Bakhtin, 1981; Lukács, 1971). Finally, at the level of the pre-genre, the concept can be considered as an abstract idea that includes even predominantly non-discoursal activities and events. This explains the current popular use of the term "epic" as anything that is generally big, important, or otherwise impressive: the epic battle, the epic football game, the "epic fail."

A Theory of Epic and Its Symbolic Content

If this is how genres move from one culture and one medium, from being situated in one context to becoming re-embedded in a new one, what features of the epic, in its original social context, have moved from ancient oral cultures into globalized, postmodern digital media? Although literary critics since

Figure 1. Illustration of Norman Fairclough's three levels of genre, using "epic" as an example
Source: The Author.

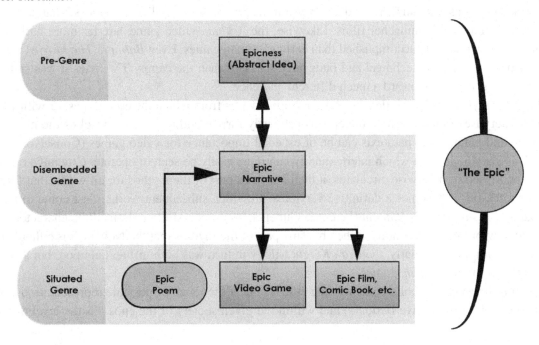

Aristotle have disagreed about the forms and uses of the epic, a number of similar ideas about what makes up the epic have recurred whenever the matter is debated (Arnott, in press-b, 2015): for instance, the epic is often noted for its "seriousness," high formal quality, and broad range of action (Aristotle, 1951); it has greater meaning for a certain community (Lukács, 1971); it struggles for dominance over other, competing works (Bakhtin, 1981; Bourdieu, 1993; Moretti, 1996); and it concerns itself with the deeds of exceptional, but still mortal actors (Frye, 2000). A synthesis of these commonalities can provide a working definition of the epic: the epic is a disembedded, totalizing genre of narrative text; it aspires to a qualitatively elevated style, and in its themes it looks beyond individual concerns to the concerns of a community. Although commonly fictive, an epic narrative must draw upon and allude to a greater body of symbolic material, which might be variously mythic, fictive, or historical. (Arnott, in press-b, 2015) The epic strives to include as much of this material as possible – but, inevitably, it never quite can. This explains the encyclopedic tendency of epic, as noted by various critics (Havelock, 1963; Moretti, 1996; Frye, 2000). Epics aspire to be the definitive expression of their subject, and therefore they necessarily attempt to represent or to create a totality, to encapsulate an entire culture or subculture within their narrative scope.

Because of the epic's ambitious range, it is useful to examine it at four distinct levels of analysis, from the narrowest to the broadest: these might be called the epos, the mythos, the ethos, and the cosmos. (Arnott, in press-b, 2015) Figure 2 outlines these levels, using groups of Batman texts and their relationships to each other as examples.

First, there is the epos, namely the epic work itself as it is generally understood. It is a narrative text, of whatever medium, and it is constructed so that it fulfills certain formal criteria. It is highly complex and cohesive when compared to similar works in the same medium. It is regarded to be "high quality," and the formal criteria determining that quality are specific to the affordances of the work's particular medium and production context. The "bigger" and "better" a work is, relative to its peers, the more "epic" it generally is. For example, the *Dark Knight* film trilogy – consisting of *Batman Begins* (Thomas et al., 2005), *The Dark Knight* (Roven et al., 2008), and *The Dark Knight Rises* (Thomas et al., 2012) – is far longer than previous Batman films, and its story continues across its installments more so than the 1990s Tim Burton and Joel Schumacher films. Likewise, the *Arkham* video games are far more narratively ambitious and technically accomplished than earlier Batman games. Even *Batman: The Movie* (Dozier, 1966) aspires to a higher technical and budgetary standard than the campy TV series it was spun off from, even if it is geared toward a much different audience.

Next, the mythos: this includes the other narrative works from which the epos draws, or with which it must otherwise contend. Where the epos is primarily formal and textual, the level of the mythos is historical and paratextual; paratexts can be of especial importance for video games (Consalvo, 2007), and this is also the level at which intertextuality can most easily be seen to operate. Crucially, once an epos is published or otherwise circulates, it then becomes part of the mythos for all works that follow: if it is successful, it becomes a definitive version with which subsequent works must come to terms. For example, Tim Burton's *Batman* (Peters & Guber, 1989) successfully redefined the character away from the previous campy versions; it then became part of the mythos that the Nolan films either had to incorporate or reject. Similarly, the *Dark Knight* trilogy in turn was both influential upon, but also differentiated from, the *Arkham* games.

The third level of symbolic content is the ethos. This is the range of possible representations, both within the world of narrative fiction(s) and within the given society of the epos. As the level that lies

Figure 2. Four levels of analyzing the epic, showing the relationship between selected Batman texts
Source: The Author.

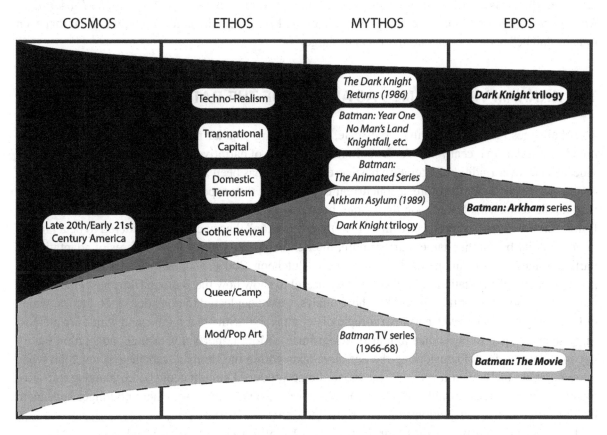

between the literalism of media texts and external reality, the ethos also plots the gap between the world and our understanding of it, and is as such ideological. (Althusser, 2001) The ethos is therefore the space within which the very definition of what constitutes a "legitimate" narrative or medium within a particular social context is contested. For instance, the ethos of Batman includes certain notions of justice (e.g., Batman does not kill) that are shared amongst all versions, but not every version can encompass all possible types of representation. Compare the camp sensibilities of the 1960s *Batman* or Schumacher's *Batman and Robin* (MacGregor-Scott, 1997) with the earnest, hyper-masculine Batman of the *Dark Knight* films or *Arkham* games.

Finally, the broadest level of analysis is the cosmos. This is the "totality" which the epos represents (or is believed to represent); it is the level of culture as that term is broadly understood. An epic can be an epic of an entire civilization, or of a small subset of a particular society. The former is, for obvious reasons, much harder to create successfully, especially considering the much greater scope and larger population of the contemporary world when compared to ancient societies. It is therefore possible to conceive of various different scales of totality as required, defined by a particular time and place; the greater this totality, the more "epic" the work is. In the case of the *Dark Knight* trilogy or the *Arkham* series, the cosmos is early-twenty-first century America, with Gotham City as a fictionalized stand-in for the contemporary urban environment. Although the fan base for Batman films and games is necessarily less than the population as a whole, sales figures for tickets and discs of each entry number in the tens of millions. When one considers that it is possible that more people went to see *The Dark Knight Rises* in movie theatres than the entire population of the Roman Empire at its height, it is clear that even today's "niche" audiences can be significantly large.[1]

THE *ARKHAM* VIDEO GAMES AS AN EPIC OF THE BATMAN MEGATEXT

The challenges raised by studying large-scale, long-running popular media franchises have been well noted by scholars in recent years. As the cultural dominance of narrative media such as film, comics, and video games over traditional literature has increased, there has been an ever-greater expansion of what counts as a "text," and, therefore, a concurrent expansion in the scope of "intertextuality" within those new-media texts. This has not, on the whole, been conceptually problematic; as Allen (2011) argues, frameworks such as Bolter and Grusin's (1999) "remediation" theory can be considered to be a kind of intertextuality by another name. Furthermore, intertextuality can illuminate processes of adaptation of particular narratives from one medium to another (Hutcheon, 2006), and, as Brooker (2012, p. 50) has noted, theories of adaptation can be particularly useful to show how the Batman films have drawn from many earlier sources for their plots. Yet these analyses have neglected to consider video games, which only recently have achieved a narrative complexity comparable with older media, and which are increasingly seen as equal to those media in artistic legitimacy. More importantly, though, adaptation theory becomes less useful for considering the narrative texts within the Batman franchise as a whole; when large numbers of Batman texts in all media are being produced simultaneously, exchanging narrative elements within a recognizable but often contradictory fictional "universe," there no longer appears to be a linear process of adaptation from an original to derivative works.

In a discussion of the various *Star Trek* series, Daniel Bernardi has described that franchise as a "mega-text," namely, "a relatively coherent and seemingly unending enterprise of televisual, filmic, auditory, and written texts." (1998, p. 7) This concept of the megatext, originally mooted in rather different form as the shared assumptions of science fiction literature (Le Guin & Attebery, 1993), is quite similar to the concept of mythos as defined in the sections above, and is perhaps a useful middle ground between individual texts in a particular narrative universe and texts from the broader culture that may nevertheless have an intertextual relation to them. The curation of such a megatext is an example of what Henry Jenkins would later call "transmedia storytelling," the process of telling related narratives across diverse media, ideally without redundancies and with each medium playing to its supposed strengths. (2006, pp. 95-96) However, the longevity and sheer number of Batman comics alone – other media notwithstanding – have long since made this process of complex storytelling cumbersome, even when it is planned and executed well. The recent spate of remakes, reboots, and resets of entire fictional universes in many media franchises speaks to the challenges of constantly producing more and more new stories. However, this narrative turnover also provides more opportunities for new epics to appear and to challenge the definitive status of earlier works. For this reason, the remainder of this chapter will focus on the *Arkham* video game series as only the latest attempt to corral the Batman "megatext" into a cohesive shape, showing how it achieves a kind of epic status, according the model outlined above, and what some of the implications that has for issues of representation and industry practice.

The *Arkham* Series as a Video Game Epos

The *Arkham* series consists of four main games: *Batman: Arkham Asylum*, *Batman: Arkham City* (Rocksteady Studios, 2011), *Batman: Arkham Origins* (Warner Bros. Games Montreal, 2013), and *Batman: Arkham Knight* (Rocksteady Studios, 2015), each released for PC and most major video game consoles. In the *Arkham* games, players control Batman across his career, from his first clash with his arch-nemesis the Joker in *Arkham Origins*, to the Joker's apparent death and its aftermath in *Arkham City* and *Arkham Knight*. The history of Arkham Asylum, which houses many of Batman's criminally insane adversaries, plays an important role throughout the series: it is the setting for the first eponymous game, and the theme of the madhouse as a metonym for Gotham City runs throughout the series. The idea is even made literal in *Arkham City*, in which part of Gotham is walled off to become a super-prison of that name run by private security. Each game in the series progressively has greater ambitions in its depiction of the storyworld and space of Gotham: *Arkham Asylum* is limited to the Asylum itself and its surrounding grounds, but *Origins* and *Knight* allow players to roam freely over an open-world version of much of Gotham City proper. This stands in marked contrast from previous Batman video games, which were mostly platformer adaptations of Batman movies and TV series, beginning with the 1989 Tim Burton film.

In terms of gameplay and interface, the Arkham series also vastly outclasses its predecessors. Play is balanced between various modes: a complex hand-to-hand combat system that is easy to progress along but difficult to master, stealth encounters in which Batman stalks and evades his enemies, and free-roaming that requires spatial exploration and puzzle-solving. In all these gameplay modes, players are encouraged to use the full range of Batman's trademark gadgetry, from Batarangs to grappling guns; *Arkham Knight* adds combat with the Batmobile as well. Only the video game adaptation of *Batman Begins*, released concurrently with the film in 2005, comes close to the *Arkham* series' range of activity. Moreover, the *Arkham* games, like contemporary series such as *Mass Effect* or *Assassin's Creed*, deploy a blend of cinematics, gameplay, and pseudo-historical codices to tell its story fully (as well as to provide some redundancies or references for more casual players). In this way it represents an effective attempt at merging what Lev Manovich considers the "natural enemies" of narrative and database in one medium, the video game (2001, p. 225). Indeed, the *Arkham* games fulfill some of the specific conditions under which Marie-Laure Ryan has argued that database and narrative can be reconciled; these include revisiting familiar storylines, using modular narratives, foregrounding the setting of the story, and employing transparent design (2006, p. 149). Thus the *Arkham* series, in encompassing not only the largest story of any Batman game to date, but doing so with the greatest technical ambitions, can be considered an epos of the Batman megatext.

The *Arkham* games have, on the whole, been recognized as succeeding at these ambitions of scope and quality. *Arkham Asylum* was highly praised, and many in the gaming press called it the greatest Batman game and even the best game based on any comic book (Reiner, 2009; Miller, 2010); *Arkham City* was lauded even more, with many reviewers ranking it not only among the best games of the year, but of all time. (Whishnov, 2011) *Arkham Origins*, made by a different developer, received mixed reviews on account of some technical issues and the fact that some felt it was more of a re-tread of the previous entries. (Kollar, 2013) However, despite being "an incremental installment, not a transformative one," (Narcisse, 2013) it was still considered a worthy entry in the series, with sales comparable to *Arkham Asylum*, but less than *Arkham City*. (Martin, 2013) Initial reactions[2] to *Arkham Knight*, meanwhile, described the final game in the series as a return to form in both scale and technical achievement, "an epic and satisfying conclusion to a groundbreaking series that proved a pop-culture icon could be thrillingly brought to life in a virtual world" (Lang, 2015); nevertheless, critics expressed some reservations about the storyline and the militarization of the Batmobile (Maiberg, 2015) or the relative emptiness of Gotham when compared to the environments of other open-world games. (Walker, 2015)

The Complex Mythos of the *Arkham* Games

The *Arkham* games could not hope to encompass all the preceding Batman stories in comics and other media, but what they do include, and how successful they are in doing so, speaks to the series' epic status. The first game expands on the premise of Grant Morrison and David McKean's graphic novel *Arkham Asylum: A Serious House on Serious Earth* (1989). In that story, the Joker takes over Arkham Asylum (on April Fool's Day, no less), forcing Batman to traverse the grounds and interact with many of his classic adversaries. Via a wealth of literary allusions and postmodern psychology, Batman's journey is presented as an extended metaphor of his own psychological problems. Although Morrison and McKean do not get an in-game credit, *Batman: Arkham Asylum*'s writer, Paul Dini, has acknowledged that their work, along with that of other seminal Batman artists Neal Adams and Frank Miller, was an influence on the game. (LeTendre, 2009) More generally, the *Arkham* series also includes much narrative material from current DC Comics continuity, such as characters, like Bane, who have been introduced relatively recently, or revamped versions of long-established villains, like the Penguin.

Paul Dini's work scripting the first two *Arkham* games is also significant because Dini first made his name as one of the main writers on *Batman: The Animated Series* (Radomski et al., 1992), the 1990s TV show which itself was a landmark in the Batman franchise and set a new standard for superhero cartoons. But it is not just Dini's presence that lends added credibility to the *Arkham* games: actors Kevin Conroy and Mark Hamill reprised their *Animated Series* roles as Batman and the Joker, respectively[3]; even though they were replaced by younger-sounding voice actors in *Arkham Origins*, their now-iconic interpretations were closely imitated. Conroy returned for *Arkham Knight*, and so did Hamill, in a surprise reprise despite the Joker's apparent death in *Arkham City*.

Other elements of the *Arkham* games aim to incorporate a wide range of material into a new, definitive synthesis. The series' music, for example, recalls previous Batman film scores and other incidental pieces to good effect. Nick Arundel and Ron Fish's music for the first two games blends stylistic features from both the Nolan and Burton films: the use of rhythmic, string-based ostinatos recalls Hans Zimmer's music, while the motifs are reminiscent of the alternatingly brooding and triumphant choral melodies of Danny Elfman's music. Arundel's title theme for *Arkham City* is perhaps the clearest example of this: it begins with a brass phrase expanded from the two-note motif for Batman from the *Dark Knight* trilogy, and crescendos with a phrase similar to the ascending major chord which begins Batman's theme in (and finishes the finale of) the 1989 film. Christopher Drake's music for *Arkham Origins*, which *Rolling Stone* praised as an "epic score" that "rivals anything from the films" (Brukman, 2013), continued in that tradition; it also expanded the Batman soundscape with allusions to classics like "The Carol of the Bells" and "The Thieving Magpie" (in a fight scene recalling Stanley Kubrick's *A Clockwork Orange*).

So the *Arkham* series clearly takes from a wide variety of previous Batman films, comics, and other media. But another measure of its success as an epos of Batman is how much of an influence it has already had on the mythos of later works. The character of Harley Quinn, the Joker's sidekick/abused girlfriend, is a cogent example of this. Quinn is unusual in that she first appeared not in the comics, but in

Batman: The Animated Series – another measure of the influence of that series. She appeared in *Arkham Asylum* and *Arkham City*, voiced again by Arleen Sorkin, the actress who had originated the character. But instead of the traditional harlequin's costume that Quinn had worn on television and in subsequent comic-book appearances through the 2000s, in the *Arkham* series her look was radically redesigned. Quinn sported dyed pigtails and a punk aesthetic, and this became her new look across multiple media, from the regular DC Comics continuity to her appearance in the spin-off film *Suicide Squad* (Johns et al., 2016). This new version revived interest in the character, although it also alienated some longtime fans with what some considered pandering to the tastes of teenage boys. (Riesman, 2015) Yet regardless of whether her video game appearance is simply "edgier" or is symptomatic of a double standard of female representation in AAA video games, it is clear that the *Arkham* series has already left a mark on the Batman texts that have come in its wake.

The games have also spawned tie-in comics and spin-off games that flesh out the backstory surrounding the main installments of the *Arkham* series, in a textbook example of Jenkins' transmedia storytelling theory. The motivations in this case are primarily promotional and commercial. Each game has had at least one comic book prequel story published in the lead-up to its release; *Arkham City*, in particular, has had three separate miniseries, and there has even been a direct-to-video animated film, *Batman: Assault on Arkham* (Melniker et al., 2014), which was set between the events of *Arkham Origins* and *Arkham Asylum*. A number of *Arkham*-branded mobile games have been released, as well as *Arkham Origins Blackgate* (Armature Studio, 2013), which was made for handheld consoles like the Nintendo DS and Playstation Portable. What is interesting here is how all these new texts support the "main" *Arkham* games: they are supplementary works not only because they are meant to stoke interest in the AAA releases, but because they do not aspire to the scope or qualitative standard of epics in their own right, regardless of what their medium of origin is. The comics are mostly digital-only releases, by less well-known writers and artists, while the games are not as technically advanced as the main *Arkham* games, featuring simplified gameplay and more rudimentary storylines.

The *Arkham* Ethos and Its Limits

The corpus of narrative texts that inform the *Arkham* series, and which are in turn generated by it, still has its limits. This is the ethos of the *Arkham* games, or the range of their representational possibilities. The concept is useful for anticipating innovations and original content that might appear outside of the established mythos, as well as explaining why certain older material is either left out or actively suppressed.

Many stories about superheroes have a similar ethos, and lend themselves easily to works of epic scale, because of how the relationship between the hero and his or her world must be represented. Northrop Frye's theory of modes defines this relationship rather well, and it can help explain why modern comic-book superheroes have supplanted the figures of ancient mythology in terms of their cultural relevance. Frye outlines how fictions can be classified by "the hero's power of action," and this is the third of his five classifications of that power:

If superior in degree to other men but not to his natural environment, the hero is a leader. He has authority, passions, and powers of expression far greater than ours, but what he does is subject both to social criticism and to the order of nature. This is the hero of the high mimetic mode, of most epic and tragedy, and is primarily the kind of hero that Aristotle had in mind [in the Poetics]. (2000, pp. 33-34)

Clearly, Batman himself fits this description, and his pre-eminence as a superhero without any "superpowers" as such makes him perhaps the most famous example of this paradigm in mainstream comics and film. Moreover, in the medium of the video game, this relationship is easily replicated, and even mirrored by the player-avatar's parallel relationship to the algorithmic logic of the game. In action-adventure games like the *Arkham* series, the player's skill increases with each challenge that is overcome and the possibility of more complex and virtuosic play increases as more bat-gadgets and combat moves are unlocked. Ideally, this occurs in a smooth progression, maintaining a state of "flow" (Csikszentmihalyi, 1990), as the avatar never outclasses his on-screen enemies to a degree that would make the game too easy. The player only exerts total control over the avatar's environment (if at all) once all tasks and side-missions are exhausted, once every villain is defeated. The end of the game's narrative thereby coincides with the player's complete freedom to maneuver throughout the designed gamespace. This is in marked contrast with games that facilitate a contest between players or teams of players, as in *Super Smash Bros.* or *League of Legends*, or with simulation games that give the player godlike powers over the gamespace, such as *The Sims*. The player's range of action within the world of a narrative-based video game makes the medium particularly fertile ground for the telling of large-scale stories with heroic protagonists, and why even popularizing critics at some level recognize the "epic" potential of video games (McGonigal, 2011, p. 98).

In a more narrow sense, the ethos of the *Arkham* games overlaps in many ways with the *Dark Knight* film trilogy. For instance, in the *Arkham* games there is a heavy emphasis on technology, which, though not always "realistic" as such, is at least plausible or logically extrapolated from currently available technology. Forensic DNA analysis, computer hacking, and infrared tracking are all parts of the series' gameplay, and the storyworlds of both the games and the films highlight issues of wealth inequality in the distribution of transnational capital and the prosecution and incarceration of domestic terrorists. On the other hand, the *Arkham* series – in keeping with its comic-book progenitors – includes within its representational possibilities elements of Gothic revival architecture, something more in keeping with the look of the Burton films than the more recent Nolan interpretations. Because of this, side-missions such as solving the "murder" of Cyrus Pinkney, the nineteenth-century architectural wunderkind responsible for the look of the *Arkham* series' Gotham, do not feel out of place, despite being an original contribution to the overall Batman mythos.

And yet *Arkham*'s ethos rejects other representations. Will Brooker has noted that Batman texts have for decades fluctuated between the "dark," gritty representations of the character and the "rainbow," camp versions (2012, pp. 215-216), and *Arkham* falls squarely into the former category. This is evident throughout the games, but it is particularly notable when the available character "skins" are considered. For the first playthrough of each game, the Batsuit hews closely to the look of the "darker" comics and films, with some variations – for instance, in *Origins* and *Knight* Batman more closely resembles the armored version of the *Dark Knight* trilogy, while in *Arkham Asylum*, his suit has longer "ears" in keeping with the more Gothic-inflected comics. However, in each game, various alternate Batsuits from a variety of eras and media can be unlocked, either as in-game rewards or purchase incentives, and these are therefore presented as "good" objects within the *Arkham* ethos. Thus players can dress their avatar in such "classic" outfits as the 1970s Neal Adams Batman or the 1980s Frank Miller Batman; even cartoon skins, such as those mimicking the look of *Batman: The Animated Series* and *Batman Beyond*, are available, as they still seem, despite their vastly different graphic style, to be in keeping with the representational possibilities of the *Arkham* world. Missing, however, are the "camp" Batsuits: there is no opportunity to play as Batman from the Joel Schumacher films, wearing the sculpted-rubber Batsuits notorious for their conspicuous nipples and codpieces. But, as Brooker notes (2012, p. 216), the repressed elements of the broader Batman megatext still resurface, and that is the case even here: relegated only to a Playstation-exclusive add-on pack, the 1960s Adam West Batsuit was recently made available as a skin for *Arkham Origins* and *Arkham Knight*. But it is important to note that Batman still appears as much more "realistic" and muscular than West ever did, and that the skin's face does not use the actor's likeness. Thus even at the representational fringes of the *Arkham* series, its ethos cannot quite break free of certain limitations.

Arkham and Mapping the Postmodern Cosmos

There is of course much else that exists beyond the representational world of the *Arkham* series, but like any epic, the games provide resonance within their social context and reflect broader hermeneutic trends. In particular, the *Arkham* games exhibit many features common to postmodern texts, both in ways particular to the games themselves and also in ways that are shared by other video games that aim to represent the totality of contemporary, global life.

Postmodernism as a concept has had a long and contradictory history, meaning different things in various academic and artistic contexts. Most useful for the present purpose is the work of those critics who view postmodernism as a particular "condition" (Harvey, 1990) or dominant cultural logic (Jameson, 1991); according to this view, postmodernism describes the tendency among cultural productions across a wide range of media, starting around the 1960s and 1970s, to model a new experience of space and time as the result of the spread of transnational capital. Postmodern texts tend, among other things, to create pastiches of historical material, to encourage endless plays of signification, and to appeal to fragmented, dispersed, and hybrid audiences. More broadly, there is a greater emphasis in such works on conceptual space to the detriment of coherent, historical time. The *Arkham* series serves as an exemplary model of how this construction of space works; one example is the quintessentially postmodern re-use, by developer Warner Bros. Games Montreal, of real Montreal graffiti to create mashed-up intertexts on the buildings of Gotham in *Arkham Origins*. (Sinervo, 2015) But, more significantly, the *Arkham* series also serves as a model for players to interpret the world outside the game. As such, it becomes one way of cognitively mapping postmodernity for its players.

The "cognitive map" was originally a psychological concept (Tolman, 1948), but it has been adapted by other disciplines over the last several decades. It appears to have come into particular vogue in the 1980s, most notably in Fredric Jameson's *Postmodernism, Or The Cultural Logic of Late Capitalism* (1991), but also, for example, in Robert Jackall's classic study of corporate management, *Moral Mazes* (2010); not coincidentally, cognitive mapping has even been deployed in various forms specifically to critique Batman texts over the past twenty-five years. (e.g., Collins, 1991; Taylor, 2010) Thus the cognitive map seems to fulfill a function that conventional representation has recently appeared less and less capable of doing. For Jameson, cognitive mapping is the key to any possible "political art" in postmodernism, because such mapping can, at least in principle, begin to make sense of the enormous complexity of contemporary culture and social organization. (1991, p. 54) It serves as a way to give coherent meaning to increasingly fragmented and disjointed experiences.

All the *Arkham* games require their players to engage in a kind of cognitive mapping in order to progress through and complete the story. First, mapping in the literal sense takes place: as the player explores Arkham Island or the districts of Gotham, the in-game map expands, aiding navigation and automatically marking locations and goals. This auto-mapping feature is common in most contemporary games and can be traced back to early 1990s landmarks such as *Doom* (id Software, 1993) and *Super Metroid* (Nintendo R&D1 & Intelligent Systems, 1994). In addition to this, though, the *Arkham* series also requires that players examine their environment through two contrasting kinds of third-person view: Batman's regular vision, and "detective mode," a kind of combination x-ray vision, infrared, and heads-up display. This mechanism of switching between viewing modes, with no mode complete or exhaustive in itself, also has its roots in the *Metroid* series, most notably in *Metroid Prime* (Retro Studios, 2002) and its sequels. (Arnott, in press-a) Thus no single way of looking at Batman's surroundings is sufficient, whether it is for finding hidden entryways, or for tracking and disabling multiple enemies. Moreover, the blending of these playing modes seems far less contrived than in other games, not least because the logic behind Batman's premise (a hero in the high mimetic mode, both physically and technologically) is so congruent with such a treatment of space and the hero/avatar's movement within it. When the various viewing modes are considered in addition to the repeated referral to maps, it becomes clear that something akin to Jameson's cognitive mapping is at work: it is the representation of a totality, intelligible only in discrete, incomplete, and yet complementary semiotic systems, which are then deployed as a kind of postmodern triangulation. The conquest of conceptual space is the ultimate goal – the game is only complete when the player has visited, scanned, and mastered every available environment.

It is not a coincidence that in Batman media since the 1990s, Gotham City has been depicted as a series of islands – that is to say, physically fragmented and isolated spaces. Likewise, Arkham Asylum began, from its introduction in the 1970s comics through to the mid-1990s, as a country estate on the outskirts of Gotham, but it has regularly been depicted in recent years as located on its own island adjacent to the city: this happens in, for example, *Batman Begins*, and it continues through to the current Fox TV series *Gotham*. Figure 3 shows how *Batman: Arkham Asylum* is mapped as an island connected to Gotham by a bridge in keeping with this trend. Thus Arkham, long since a microcosm of the ills of Gotham, also serves as a spatial metonym for the city, especially since each game in the series features an increasingly larger, yet still insular, gamespace that serves as a figurative madhouse. In *Arkham City*, the eponymous super-prison is on another of Gotham's islands, as shown in Figure 4. In *Arkham Origins*, two islands of Gotham are again presented as the playground of super-criminals, and still more islands are added in *Arkham Knight*. The construction of video game worlds as islands, often necessary given the technological limitations of (ironically-named) open-world games, has long been noted (Juul, 2005), and it is most spectacularly evident in *Grand Theft Auto V*'s (Rockstar North, 2013) city of Los Santos and the surrounding Blaine County. But this feature of current large-scale games can have a deeper meaning and reveal some possibilities for different ways of understanding the wider world.

When fictional narratives are considered as a kind of representational experiment, connected and subject to multiple articulations even as they are isolated from the totality of lived experience, the "space" of Gotham becomes newly illuminating. The *Arkham* games become one possible layer on a cognitive map of our world. Fredric Jameson's work is instructive again in this context, specifically his writings on the idea of Utopia in science fiction and its connection to imagining political projects. Science fiction, in its depiction of utopias and dystopias alike, is especially suited to this kind of mapping; it is no coincidence that the growth of science fiction as a literary genre roughly parallels the social disruption of industrialization and post-industrial organization, nor is it coincidental that Batman narratives have for decades flirted with science-fiction elements. For Jameson in *Archaeologies of the Future* (2005), any new global Utopia must still be represented in some way, since "representability, or the possibility of mapping, is a very significant matter for practical politics" (p. 221). Jameson describes how certain

Figure 3. Map of Arkham Island and its buildings
Adapted from Batman: Arkham Asylum (Rocksteady Studios, 2009). Source: The Author.

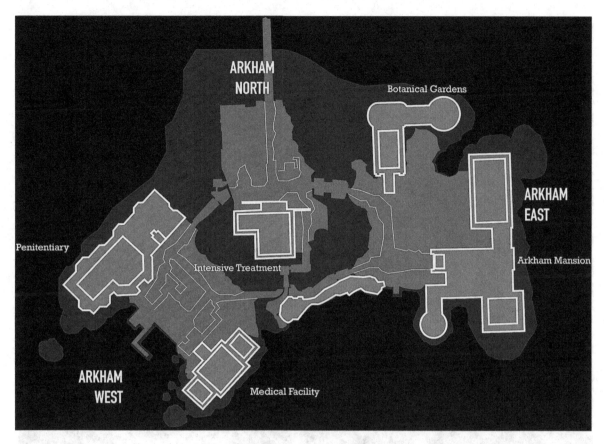

utopian visions require absolute mobility between non-communicating communities. The best way to imagine this in spatial terms is as a chain of islands:

I therefore propose a more accessible or visualizable form of this imagined global system, about which we must remember that its novelty as a Utopian mechanism consisted in the non-communicability or antagonism inherent in its component parts, a novelty which had the immediate effect of excluding rhetorics of communication, multiculturalism and even empire (in the recent sense of Americanization). In this spirit, I propose to think of our autonomous and non-communicating Utopias – which can range from wandering tribes and settled villages all the way to great city-states or regional ecologies – as so many islands: a Utopian archipelago, islands in the net, a constellation of discontinuous centers, themselves internally decentered. At once this metaphorical perspective begins to suggest a range of possible analogies, which combine the properties of isolation with those of relationship. (p. 221)

Gotham-as-archipelago seems to work as a small-scale, representational version of this same utopian principle: a way to imagine and map possible social arrangements. In Jameson's discussion of the utopian archipelago, communities must be related – insofar as people must have the ability to move between them as they like; but the communities must be isolated too, so that they can evolve into distinctly different

Figure 4. Map of Arkham City and its boundaries
Adapted from Batman: Arkham City (Rocksteady Studios, 2011). Source: The Author.

possibilities – mobility between identical choices would be meaningless. Likewise, if the "visions" of Gotham are to have utility as maps of urban possibilities, they must strike this balance between closure and porousness. They must connect to real lived experience to some extent, for if they were purely fantastic, they would have no practical or political use. So, to mention just one possibility, the version of the Batman universe of which the *Arkham* series is the epos allows specific artistic reflection about the roles of incarceration, mental health, and surveillance that other Batman epics might downplay or ignore. The use of the insane asylum, or city-as-asylum, as one cognitive map of the postmodern world fits squarely into a contemporary tradition of other video game "islands" that critique and parody models of social organization; these range from the failed Objectivist utopia of Rapture in *BioShock* (2K Boston, 2007), to the multinational corporate ruin of Sevastopol Station in *Alien: Isolation* (The Creative Assembly, 2014).

SOLUTIONS AND RECOMMENDATIONS

Considering the *Arkham* series as an epic, as defined in the framework outlined earlier, is useful for a number of reasons. First, deploying and testing a more flexible and nuanced definition of the epic genre helps give added theoretical credibility to claims that certain popular, mass-produced works – not only video games, but also comic books, TV shows, and so on – should be considered as legitimate narrative epics (for some examples, see Harrigan & Wardrip-Fruin, 2009). Such a definition can also help critique dubious cases and rule out outliers; it might explain, to cite one example, why Jane McGonigal's (2011) argument that games such as *Halo 3* are "epic" in large part because of the scale of their online leaderboards is not a terribly convincing claim. Indeed, the gratuitous inclusion of online and multiplayer elements to traditionally single-player games has become quite common in recent years, and it is no guarantee of favorable reception – recall that *Arkham Origins*, the least-successful of the *Arkham* games, was the first in the series to offer an online multiplayer option. Scale is a necessary, but not sufficient, criterion for lasting success.

The second reason that this framework of epic is useful is that it pays close attention to the intertexts and paratexts of particular large-scale works. For an epos like the *Arkham* series to be seen as a success, it must draw upon and generate a rich mythos of narratives in a variety of media. It is also important, however, that those who seek to create works on an epic scale understand the competencies of their audience: the *Arkham* series appears to do this quite well, drawing upon the larger Batman megatext but at the same time offering some fresh interpretations and not becoming bogged down in lore. This is especially important when considering the spin-off paratexts that the *Arkham* series has generated. Knowledge of the derivative works is not essential to understand or enjoy the main series, unlike, for instance, the works released in conjunction with the *Matrix* films (see Jenkins, 2006), which some fans suspected of being more of a cynical marketing ploy than a legitimate expansion of an established narrative universe. Although outright pandering to fan expectations can stifle the originality necessary to create successful new works, this discussion of the *Arkham* games suggests that historical precedents and long-term audience reception of narrative epics should not be overlooked. They too are important conditions for lasting artistic and commercial acclaim.

FUTURE RESEARCH DIRECTIONS

This chapter has examined the *Arkham* series as one epic of the Batman megatext, but the theoretical framework is also applicable to other key works within the Batman franchise, such as the *Dark Knight* film trilogy (see Arnott, 2015), or other series within the DC animated universe. It will be interesting to see how successful the more recent challengers to these Batman texts, starting with the *Gotham* TV series and the Suicide Squad and Batman-Superman crossover films, will be over time – not only with respect to the Batman texts that have come before them, but also with respect to the highly-successful Marvel cinematic universe that they increasingly take as a model.

The ethos of the *Arkham* games is in many ways quite suited to the traditionally-masculine world of ancient epics, but this theory of epic certainly does not preclude the possibility of female characters in the high mimetic mode as the subjects of large-scale narratives. Even in video games, there are good examples of this, such as the recent *Tomb Raider* series reboot or the *Mass Effect* trilogy. At the same time, more investigation is required to determine exactly why, despite the ratio of female to male gamers approaching that of the general population, female representation within epic games (and within the industry itself) remains disproportionate.

CONCLUSION

This chapter began by considering the renewed appearance of "epic" as a generic term in reference to large-scale narrative texts in a variety of new media. By examining the way in which genres change over time, and by considering some of the historical continuities between epic texts that appear to be much more constant, it put forth a more nuanced definition better suited for identifying (and discarding) possible epic narratives. One such new epic is the *Batman: Arkham* video game series, which aspires to high quality on a large narrative scale, even as it takes from and gives back to a rich and varied Batman megatext. The *Arkham* series' representational limits and possibilities provide insight about how players interpret postmodern spaces, and it serves as a model for other transmedia franchises to imitate as they adapt their complex narratives to and from video games.

REFERENCES

A. T. (2011). *Twitter and epic poetry: The first real work of digital literature?* Retrieved June 30, 2015, from http://www.economist.com/blogs/prospero/2011/10/twitter-and-epic-poetry

Allen, G. (2011). *Intertextuality* (2nd ed.). London, UK: Routledge.

Althusser, L. (2001). 1971). Ideology and ideological state apparatuses. In *Lenin and philosophy, and other essays* (B. Brewster, Trans.). New York, NY: Monthly Review Press.

Aristotle, , Butcher, S. H., & Gassner, J. (1951). *Aristotle's theory of poetry and fine art: With a critical text and translation of the Poetics*. New York, NY: Dover.

Armature Studio. (2013). *Batman: Arkham origins Blackgate*. New York, NY: Warner Bros. Interactive Entertainment.

Arnott, L. (2015). *Narrative epic and new media: The totalizing spaces of postmodernity in The Wire, Batman, and The Legend of Zelda.* (Unpublished doctoral dissertation). The University of Western Ontario, London, Canada.

Arnott, L. (in press). -a). Mapping *Metroid:* Narrative, space, and *Other M. Games and Culture.* doi:10.1177/1555412015580016

Arnott, L. (in press). -b). Epic and genre: Beyond the boundaries of media. *Comparative Literature.*

Arsenault, D. (2009). Video game genre, evolution and innovation. *Eludamos (Göttingen), 3*(2), 149–176.

Bakhtin, M. M. (1981). Epic and Novel. In M. Holquist (Ed.), *The dialogic imagination: Four essays* (M. Holquist & C. Emerson, Trans.). Austin, TX: University of Texas Press.

Bates, C. (Ed.). (2010). *The Cambridge companion to the epic*. Cambridge, UK: Cambridge University Press. doi:10.1017/CCOL9780521880947

Bernardi, D. (1998). *Star Trek and history: Race-ing toward a white future*. New Brunswick, N.J.: Rutgers University Press.

Bolter, J. D., & Grusin, R. (1999). *Remediation: Understanding new media*. Cambridge, MA: The MIT Press.

2K. Boston. (2007). *BioShock*. Novato, CA: 2K Games.

Bourdieu, P. (1993). *The field of cultural production: Essays on art and literature*. New York, NY: Columbia University Press.

Box Office Mojo. (2015). *The dark knight rises (2012)*. Retrieved June 14, 2015, from http://www.boxofficemojo.com/movies/?id=batman3.htm

Brooker, W. (2012). *Hunting the dark knight: Twenty-first century Batman*. London, UK: I. B. Tauris.

Brukman, J. (2013). *Inside the Batman: Arkham Origins soundtrack*. Retrieved June 1, 2015, from http://www.rollingstone.com/culture/news/inside-the-batman-arkham-origins-soundtrack-20131018

Collins, J. (1991). *Batman: The Movie*, narrative: The hyperconscious. In R. E. Pearson & W. Uricchio (Eds.), *The many lives of the Batman: Critical approaches to a superhero and his media* (pp. 164–181). New York, NY: Routledge.

Consalvo, M. (2007). *Cheating: Gaining advantage in video games*. Cambridge, MA: The MIT Press.

Csikszentmihalyi, M. (1990). *Flow: The psychology of optimal experience*. New York, NY: Harper & Row.

Dictionary.com. (2012). *The worst words of 2012*. Retrieved June 1, 2015, from http://blog.dictionary.com/worst-words-of-2012/

Dozier, W. (Producer), & Martinson, L. H. (Director). (1966). *Batman: The movie*. [Motion Picture] Twentieth Century Fox.

Elliott, A. B. R. (Ed.). (2014). *The return of the epic film: Genre, aesthetics and history in the twenty-first century*. Edinburgh, UK: Edinburgh University Press. doi:10.3366/edinburgh/9780748684021.001.0001

Fairclough, N. (2003). *Analysing discourse: Textual analysis for social research*. London, UK: Routledge.

Frye, N. (2000). *Anatomy of criticism: Four essays*. Princeton, NJ: Princeton University Press.

Harrigan, P., & Wardrip-Fruin, N. (Eds.). (2009). *Third person: Authoring and exploring vast narratives*. Cambridge, MA: The MIT Press.

Harvey, D. (1989). *The condition of postmodernity: An enquiry into the origins of cultural change*. Oxford, UK: Blackwell.

Havelock, E. A. (1963). *Preface to Plato*. Oxford, UK: Blackwell.

Hutcheon, L. (2006). *A theory of adaptation*. New York: Routledge.

id Software. (1993). *Doom*. New York, NY: GT Interactive.

Jackall, R. (2010). Moral mazes: The world of corporate managers (20th anniversary ed.). Oxford, UK: Oxford University Press.

Jameson, F. (1991). *Postmodernism, or, the cultural logic of late capitalism*. Durham, NC: Duke University Press.

Jameson, F. (2005). *Archaeologies of the future: The desire called utopia and other science fictions*. New York, NY: Verso.

Jenkins, H. (2006). *Convergence culture: Where old and new media collide*. New York, NY: New York University Press.

Johns, G., Snyder, Z., Snyder, D., & Wilson, C. (Producers), & Ayer, D. (Director). (2016). *Suicide squad*. [Motion Picture] Warner Bros.

Juul, J. (2005). *Half-real: Video games between real rules and fictional worlds*. Cambridge, MA: The MIT Press.

Kollar, P. (2013). *Batman: Arkham origins review: Knightfall*. Retrieved June 1, 2015, from http://www.polygon.com/2013/10/25/5026574/batman-arkham-origins-review-knightfall

Lang, D. J. (2015). *Review: An epic final flight for Batman in Arkham Knight*. Retrieved July 1, 2015, from http://www.salon.com/2015/06/23/review_an_epic_final_flight_for_batman_in_arkham_knight/

Le Guin, U. K., & Attebery, B. (Eds.). (1993). *The Norton book of science fiction: North American science fiction, 1960-1990*. New York, NY: W.W. Norton.

LeTendre, B. (2009). *Paul Dini talks Batman: Arkham Asylum*. Retrieved June 1, 2015, from http://www.comicbookresources.com/?page=article&id=20931

Lukács, G. (1971). *The theory of the novel: A historico-philosophical essay on the forms of great epic literature*. Cambridge, MA: The MIT Press.

MacGregor-Scott, P. (Producer), & Schumacher, J. (Director). (1997). *Batman & Robin*. [Motion picture] Warner Bros.

Maiberg, E. (2015). *Batman: Arkham Knight review roundup*. Retrieved June 22, 2015, from http://www.gamespot.com/articles/batman-arkham-knight-review-roundup/1100-6428357/

Manovich, L. (2001). *The language of new media*. Cambridge, MA: The MIT Press.

Martin, L. (2013). *Batman: Arkham Origins tops charts, sales half those of Arkham City*. Retrieved June 1, 2015, from http://www.digitalspy.co.uk/gaming/news/a526846/batman-arkham-origins-tops-charts-sales-half-those-of-arkham-city.html#~peyO0GRzxv0823

McGonigal, J. (2011). *Reality is broken: Why games make us better and how they can change the world*. London, UK: Jonathan Cape.

Melniker, B., Register, S., Tucker, J., & Uslan, M. (Producers), & Oliva, J. & Spaulding, E. (Directors). (2014). *Batman: Assault on Arkham*. [DVD] Warner Bros.

Miller, G. (2010). *Batman: Arkham asylum (game of the year) review*. Retrieved June 1, 2015, from http://ign.com/articles/2010/05/27/batman-arkham-asylum-game-of-the-year-review

Moretti, F. (1996). *Modern epic: The world-system from Goethe to García Márquez*. London, UK; New York, NY: Verso.

Morrison, G., & McKean, D. (1989). *Arkham asylum: A serious house on serious earth*. New York, NY: DC Comics.

Nagy, G. (1999). Epic as genre. In M. H. Beissinger, J. Tylus, & S. L. Wofford (Eds.), *Epic traditions in the contemporary world: The poetics of community* (pp. 21–32). Berkeley, CA: University of California Press.

Narcisse, E. (2013). *Batman: Arkham Origins: The Kotaku review*. Retrieved June 1, 2015, from http://kotaku.com/batman-arkham-origins-the-kotaku-review-1451970358

Nintendo R&D1 & Intelligent Systems. (1994). *Super metroid*. Kyoto, Japan: Nintendo.

Peters, J., & Guber, P. (Producers), & Burton, T. (Director). (1989). *Batman*. [Motion Picture] Warner Bros.

Phillips, C. N. (2012). *Epic in American culture: Settlement to reconstruction*. Baltimore, MD: Johns Hopkins University Press.

Radomski, E., Timm, B., & Burnett, A. (Producers). (1992). Batman: The animated series. [Television Series] New York, NY: Warner Bros.

Reiner, A. (2009). *Batman: Arkham Asylum: The best Batman game ever made*. Retrieved June 1, 2015, from http://www.gameinformer.com/games/batman_arkham_asylum/b/xbox360/archive/2009/09/27/review.aspx

Retro Studios. (2002). *Metroid prime*. Kyoto, Japan: Nintendo.

Riesman, A. (2015). *The hidden story of Harley Quinn and how she became the superhero world's most successful woman*. Retrieved June 1, 2015, from http://www.vulture.com/2014/12/harley-quinn-dc-comics-suicide-squad.html

Rockstar North. (2013). *Grand theft auto V*. New York, NY: Rockstar Games.

Rocksteady Studios. (2009). *Arkham asylum. London, UK: Eidos Interactive; Warner Bros*. Batman: Interactive Entertainment.

Rocksteady Studios. (2011). *Batman: Arkham city*. New York, NY: Warner Bros. Interactive Entertainment.

Roven, C., Thomas, E., & Nolan, C. (Producers), & Nolan, C. (Director). (2008). *The dark knight*. [Motion Picture] Warner Bros.

Scheidel, W. (2006). Population and demography. Princeton/Stanford Working Papers in Classics.

Sinervo, K. A. (2015). *Mapping Gotham*. Retrieved July 1, 2015, from http://www.firstpersonscholar.com/mapping-gotham/

Taylor, P. A. (2010). *Žižek and the media*. Cambridge, UK: Polity.

The Creative Assembly. (2014). *Alien: Isolation*. Tokyo, Japan: Sega.

Thomas, E., Nolan, C., & Roven, C. (Producers), & Nolan, C. (Director). (2012). *The dark knight rises*. [Motion Picture] Warner Bros.

Thomas, E., Roven, C., & Franco, L. (Producers), & Nolan, C. (Director). (2005). *Batman begins*. [Motion picture] Warner Bros.

Tolman, E. C. (1948). Cognitive maps in rats and men. *Psychological Review, 55*(4), 189–208. doi:10.1037/h0061626 PMID:18870876

Walker, A. (2015). *Superheroes, cities, and empty streets*. Retrieved July 25, 2015, from http://www.giantbomb.com/articles/superheroes-cities-and-empty-streets/1100-5241/

Warner Bros. Games Montreal. (2013). Batman: Arkham origins. New York, NY: Warner Bros. Interactive Entertainment.

Wishnov, J. (2011). *Batman: Arkham City review*. Retrieved June 1, 2015, from http://www.g4tv.com/games/xbox-360/63090/batman-arkham-city/review/

KEY TERMS AND DEFINITIONS

Cognitive Map: A psychological concept that has been extended to describe attempts at representation and meaning-making in postmodern culture. Cognitive mapping can be characterized by the use of a number of discrete hermeneutic tools in combination to model concepts for which traditional representation may be deficient.

Cosmos: The social and physical totality that an epos is trying to represent; an entire culture. The cosmos of an epos can vary in scale depending on the size of the community for whom the epos has meaning.

Disembedded Genre: A genre that has become freed from its context of origin, and which can be appropriated in another time and place. An example is "epic narrative," which has been disembedded from the original context of epic as oral poetry.

Epos: The text of a narrative epic, which can be in any medium, from poetry or prose, to comics or video games. The epos aspires to high formal quality and broad narrative scope, especially in relation to other similar texts.

Ethos: The representational limits of a particular epos. The ethos includes possible, but not-yet-realized, representations and therefore accounts for original innovations that go beyond an epos' mythos.

Mythos: The other earlier narratives and paratexts which an epos draws upon, seeking either to include or to surpass them. The mythos can be historical, fictional, or a combination of the two. In the case of media franchises, this often takes the form of a complex and generally coherent "megatext" of stories across many different media.

Postmodernism: The contemporary cultural condition and logic of production by which texts are often pastiches characterized by endless plays of signification and appealing to fragmented, dispersed, and hybrid audiences. Postmodern texts tend to emphasize conceptual space to the detriment of coherent, historical time.

Pre-Genre: The most abstract and vague level of genre. Genre as a concept not attached to any medium or cultural practice. An example is "epic" as general synonym for importance and bigness.

Situated Genre: A genre that is specific to a particular medium and discoursal context. An example is an epic narrative video game.

ENDNOTES

[1]   The worldwide box-office gross for *The Dark Knight Rises* was over one billion dollars. (Box Office Mojo, 2015) Assuming an average ticket price of between ten and twenty dollars, this means that approximately 50 to 100 hundred million tickets were sold for the film. This range is consistent with the estimated total population of the Roman Empire (Scheidel, 2006), although in both cases exact figures are impossible to determine.

[2]   *Arkham Knight* was released in June 2015, as this chapter was being written.

[3]   Conroy and Hamill had previously been featured in the 2001 game *Batman Vengeance*; this multi-platform title was based on *The New Batman Adventures*, the show that succeeded *Batman: The Animated Series*, and reunited much of the TV voice cast.

22

Chapter 2
The Inescapable Intertextuality of *Blade Runner: The Video Game*

Clara Fernandez-Vara
New York University, USA

ABSTRACT

The video game adaptation of Blade Runner *(1997) exemplifies the challenges of adapting narrative from traditional media into digital games. The key to the process of adaptation is the fictional world, which it borrows both from Philip K. Dick's novel* Do Androids Dream of Electric Sheep? *(1968) and Ridley Scott's film* Blade Runner *(1982). Each of these works provides different access points to the world, creating an intertextual relationship that can be qualified as transmedia storytelling, as defined by Jenkins (2006). The game utilizes the properties of digital environments (Murray, 2001) in order to create a world that the player can explore and participate in; for this world to have the sort of complexity and richness that gives way to engaging interactions, the game resorts to the film to create a visual representation, and to the themes of the novel. Thus the game is inescapably intertextual, since it needs of both source materials in order to make the best of the medium of the video game.*

INTRODUCTION

Philip K. Dick did not get to see *Blade Runner* (1982), the film based on *Do Androids Dream of Electric Sheep?* (1968) He did see a twenty-minute reel showcasing its visual effects in a private screening. According to Sammon (1996, p. 284), Dick had strong reservations about the capacity of Hollywood studios to adapt his novels up to that point and was rather unimpressed with the scripts he had read so far. What he saw on the screen, however, surprised him so much he told Ridley Scott, the film director, that he had managed to show the world the way Dick had pictured it in his head. "I recognized it immediately. It was my own interior world. They caught it perfectly." (Boonstra, 1982). A few months before he died, Dick wrote to the Ladd Company, producers of the film, to express his enthusiasm about another segment he had seen on television, remarking that *Blade Runner* would revolutionize what people thought

DOI: 10.4018/978-1-5225-0477-1.ch002

science fiction was (Dick, 1981). Initially, the film was a commercial flop (Redmond, 2008, p. 8), but time proved Dick right in yet another example of his capacity as a visionary. *Blade Runner* is a landmark in the history of film and a constant in every list of the best films of science fiction of all time.

Adapting Philip K. Dick's novel to the screen was a challenge. It is a complex work with many characters and interweaving themes, and several of the key scenes are difficult to narrate visually. It took two writers (Hampton Fancher and David Peoples) to write the screenplay, along with constant input from the director, Ridley Scott. Reportedly, Scott never finished reading the original novel, and Peoples did not read it at all; Dick was not involved in the process and publicly expressed his outrage at Fancher's first script (Sammon, 1996, pp. 51-70). The process was contentious all throughout, although the final version of the screenplay pleased the novelist, the screenwriters and the director.

It was the visual presentation of the world that convinced the author that the final result may be worthwhile. In his letter to the Ladd Company, he demonstrates little concern with the adaptation of the story—audiences could now really see the world he had created. In his prose, Dick was a master of world building, creating characters and conflicts, as well as unstable and ambiguous ontologies. The visual descriptions, however, were not always relevant to his world. While Fancher was writing his version of the script, Scott encouraged to him to look at what lay outside the windows (Sammon, 1996, p. 53), thus turning the attention to where the characters lived in order to understand them better. *Blade Runner* revealed the key to adapting science fiction to film – and to interactive media – by focusing on the world.

Blade Runner's influence has also extended beyond film—the first video game inspired by it came out a couple of years after the film's release. *Blade Runner* (1985) took the music soundtrack by Vangelis as the basis of its inspiration, since they could not acquire the rights to the film itself ("On the Tail of Replidroids", 1986). It took a further fifteen years, and the release of the Director's Cut of the film in 1992, for *Blade Runner* to have a worthy video game adaptation. *Blade Runner*, the video game (1997), was revolutionary at the time because of how it turned Ridley Scott's film into an interactive environment. Unfortunately, the game has been somewhat forgotten by video games history because there have been no re-releases of the game for current operating systems.[1]

Blade Runner – the game – shows how the challenges of adapting Dick's novel also extend to digital media in general, and to video games in particular. It also shows a productive strategy to adapt narrative from traditional media to video games, by focusing on the fictional world instead of the plot structure. In the process, the game draws strong ties to both the film version and the original novel in order to create that world and as part of the attractive to play it, creating an inescapable intertextuality that players participate and revel in.

Part of the game's appeal derives from the knowledge the player may have of the original sources, since the game combines Philip K. Dick's novel *Do Androids Dream of Electric Sheep?* with its filmic counterpart, *Blade Runner*. These two sources help generate the game world and the challenges that the player has to face. Because of the strong and purposeful connections between the game and its sources, we could consider their relationship an example of transmedia storytelling, as each medium provides access to interconnected narratives based on the same fictional world.

Intertextuality as the Foundation to World Building

The term *intertextuality* is generally attributed to Julia Kristeva (1980), who combined the systematic approach to language of Ferdinand de Saussure with Mikhail Bakhtin's ideas of language within their social context. The term itself invokes the intersection between content (subject), reader (addressee) and context (pp. 65-66). The text itself – which she refers to as *utterance* (p. 113) – can have diverse meanings depending on how the reader maps the relationship between what they are reading, other texts – including texts within the same genre – and the socio-historical context in which they are reading. Kristeva defines these relationships as a system, identifying patterns of signification in an almost mathematical manner (pp. 37-41).

Going back to this foundational definition of intertextuality, although abbreviated, draws renewed attention to two aspects that will be fundamental in the following pages. First, the concept does not only refer to the interrelationship between texts, but their intersection, the spaces where they enter in contact. Second, and related to Saussure's approach to semiotics, the intersecting texts make up a system where each component in connection with the rest creates the meaning as interpreted by the addressee. This article considers film and video games as multimodal texts, where audiovisual representations as well as cues for interaction can all be read as sets of signs.

The systematic nature of intertextual relationships allows us to understand how different narratives can result from the same fictional world. A fictional world is an imaginary construct that relates a set of locations, characters, props and events; the world also follows a set of rules, from its socio-economic workings to its physics (e.g. whether there is magic or the level of technological advancement). Thus worlds can be interpreted as systems, where characters and events follow the rules that define the world. A fictional world can give way to narratives in different media – novels, films, comics, toys, video games, even theme parks – all of which are different texts. The world thus becomes the intersection of these texts, while exploring their relationships is the core subject of study of this article, which provides one of the many possible exegeses of those relationships.

Expansive fictional worlds are not a recent phenomenon, although the theorization of narrative in terms of fictional worlds is. Mark P. Wolf (2012) studies the features of imaginary worlds and world building as a practice of storytelling from *The Odyssey* in the 9ᵗʰ century B.C. to the present. Saler (2012) examines the fictional worlds of Arthur Conan Doyle's Sherlock Holmes, J.R.R. Tolkien's Middle Earth and H.P. Lovecraft's mythos as "virtual worlds" that readers inhabited, and recreated, discovering how the drive to immerse oneself in a fictional world is inherent to certain types of storytelling. The worlds selected by Saler are also essential referents of world building in the sense that they have been imitated, transformed and re-appropriated in narratives across the media, so they become keystones to the intertextual relationships between these other narratives.

Transmedia Storytelling and the Properties of Digital Environments

The concept of transmedia storytelling has been popularized thanks to the work of Henry Jenkins (2006), who defines it as "a story that unfolds across multiple media platforms, with each new text making a distinctive contribution to the whole" (pp. 95-96). Transmedia storytelling can start with a novel and be extended through films, television shows, comics, and video games, as well as toys and theme parks. Before the concept of transmedia became popular, this concept was known as *media franchises*, a term still used today. Franchises become a brand that is licensed to producers in different media to develop different stories. The difference between franchises and transmedia storytelling is that transmedia stories aim at keeping a coordinated narrative coherence, so that each media incarnation provides a different point of view or plot line, but always within the same narrative world and contributing to the whole. Jenkins analyzes the multiple texts from the film *The Matrix* (1999) as an example of transmedia, where the original film gave way not only to two sequels but a series of animated shorts, *The Animatrix*, and three video games (*Enter The Matrix*, *The Matrix: Path of Neo*, and *The Matrix Online*). In each medium, the viewer/reader/player can follow a different part of the story. In the animated shorts, for example, we learn about the antecedents to the events in the original film, while the games let the audience become the collaborator of the protagonists in the movie.

In terms of narratives that expand across different media, classic mythology prefigured the possibilities of transmedia storytelling, as Jenkins affirms, since the adventures of the gods on Mount Olympus were performed in theatre plays, recounted in poems, embodied in statues, and pictured in paintings and decorations, each one representing the aspects of mythology with the affordances of the specific medium used to the best effect (Jenkins, 2006, pp. 119-120). In modern terms, each medium can specialize in specific narrative aspects. While written fiction allows for introspection or using sensorial descriptions such as smell or taste, film can display information visually and allows for juxtaposing concepts through editing.

Video games best allow the player to participate, manipulate and experiment within a fictional world. More specifically, they partake of the characteristics of digital environments according to Murray (2001): They are procedural, participatory, spatial, and encyclopedic (p. 71). *Procedural* means that they behave according to a set of rules, which Murray attributes to the computing capabilities of the platform. *Participatory* means that the user / player can introduce an input and the system will respond accordingly—it is a more sophisticated way to refer to interactivity, since Murray explains to how the participation can evoke previous knowledge of, for example, genre conventions or other stories. By invoking the *spatiality* of digital environments, Murray points to how digital environments represent a space that the player moves into and navigates, while the *encyclopedic* properties refer to the storage capacity of computers, which can keep and give access to enormous amount of information. The sections below will demonstrate how these properties help making the *Blade Runner* game an example of a transmedia text.

Blade Runner as Transmedia Storytelling

The novel *Do Androids Dream of Electric Sheep?*, along with its film version and the video game *Blade Runner*, exemplify how each access point into a fictional world can enrich the narrative without following the kind of unifying strategy of transmedia described by Jenkins, since each text was created in conversation with the others but by different people and at different points in time. The intertextual relationships create a conversation between each text as a direct consequence of the complexity of the world.

Before providing further details on how these texts constitute an example of transmedia storytelling, let us describe the fictional world in more detail, and map their intertextual relationships and their themes to demonstrate their complexity.

The novel takes place in a post-apocalyptic world after a nuclear war. Part of Earth's population has escaped to colonies on other planets, while those who have been exposed to nuclear radiation are banned from leaving the planet. Technology is advanced to the point that androids are practically indistinguishable from human beings. The only unequivocal way to identify an android is to perform a bone marrow analysis, a costly and time-consuming method. As a more affordable alternative, there are a series of questionnaires that help determine the levels of empathy of the subject; the latest questionnaire to identify the most recent android models is called Voigt-Kampff. This way, androids can be detected through an interview instead of a chemical test. Because of nuclear fallout, most animals are on the brink of extinction or have already become disappeared—therefore most of them are synthetic. Having a real animal is a status symbol, both because they are scarce but also because having one demonstrates a capacity for empathy, a quality that also seems to be on its way to extinction. The scarcity of empathy is represented by Mercerism, the cult of the figure of Wilbur Mercer. His claim to divinity is that he walks uphill forever while an invisible hand throws stones at him. The worshipers of Mercer share his pain through an empathy box, which make those holding its handles feel his pain and the emotions of other members who are connected to the Mercerism network.

The story in the novel focuses on Rick Deckard, a bounty hunter who has to *retire* – the euphemism used to refer to the assassination of androids – six Nexus 6 androids, the latest model. Deckard is married, and part of his motivation is to earn money to buy a real animal, since he only owns a synthetic sheep in order to cater to his wife's social aspirations. A parallel storyline follows John Isidore, a special, the term used to identify those with an inferior intellect as a result of nuclear exposure. Isidore meets the Nexus 6 androids and assists them before Deckard appears. The different storylines explore what it means to be human and to have empathy. Although initially the lack of empathy is what sets androids apart, the novel also highlights the lack of empathy of the bounty hunters when it comes to retiring androids without remorse.

The film starts from the fictional world created by Philip K. Dick, leaving out Mercerism and focusing on the issues pertaining to human nature. Rather than a bounty hunter, Deckard is a *blade runner*, a term Ridley Scott borrowed from Alan E. Nourse's novel *The Bladerunner* (1974). Deckard is divorced, while Isidore becomes J.F. Sebastian, an engineer who works on android technology for the Tyrell Corporation. Sebastian does not have any intellectual impairment, but rather he suffers from a genetic illness that makes him age prematurely, facing the possibility of dying prematurely, just as the replicants – the term the film uses to refer to androids – have a time limit of four years. Synthetic animals are still part of the world; the film, however, does not make references to the status achieved by owning a real animal—only to how expensive they can be.

The film takes the novel's premise and expands through the use of other texts, in order to create a world that has a history and gives a sense of depth. Unlike other science fiction films where the future is idealized and spotless, such as *Logan's Run* (1976) or the television show *Star Trek* (1966-69), *Blade Runner* takes place in a future Los Angeles that is dank and dirty, where old buildings have been patched and appropriated for new uses. This corresponds to the concept of *retrofitting*, which Ridley Scott intended as the main aesthetic of the movie (Sammon, 1999, p. 79), by which the film uses visual aesthetics for the past to create a dystopian future—an intertextual strategy to create new and distinct fictional world. As Scott himself put it, "This is a film set forty years hence, made in the style of forty years ago" (Scroggy, 1982, p. 3). For example, Union Station becomes a police station, while the Bradbury Building, an icon of L.A. architecture, becomes a damp and decayed apartment building. The screenplay does not have to explain this is a post-apocalyptic world—every frame demonstrates it is an inhospitable and hostile environment.

The concept of retrofitting also serves to invoke noir cinema, perhaps the most transformative use intersecting texts that is also key to the game. Alain Silver (2005) identifies it as a piece of neo-noir (pp. 125-30), referring to the films within the genre produced from the 1970s onwards like *Chinatown* (1974). Sammon's book title identifies the film as "future noir" (1996) as a shorthand to indicate the hybrid between science fiction and the noir film tradition. *Blade Runner* uses images and icons of the past in order to create a dystopian future, from the replicant Rachael's victory rolls hairdo to the chiaroscuro of the cinematography. Deckard is not a hitman who retires replicants; rather, he is a detective who has to locate his objective. This was overtly stated by Ridley Scott, who referred to the fictional world of the film as "a familiar atmosphere… a Philip Marlowe-Sam Spade environment" (Scroggy, 1982, p. 3). The action has been moved from San Francisco in the novel to Los Angeles, the quintessential dramatic ground of film noir (Silver, p. 12), which becomes a character in the story. Los Angeles is a sprawling urban jungle that the detective explores and masters thanks to his flying car, the spinner. Powerful replicants roam around freely in the city; the detective needs to face them with his gun, his instinct and his wits. The combination between science fiction and noir is an example of the dialogic nature of literature that Bakhtin discussed (Kristeva, 1980, pp. 67-68), only transposed to film. According to Bakhtin, literary discourse is always in transformation because literary works and their authors are in constant dialogue with each other. *Blade Runner* gave way to a new and evocative world by incorporating this dialogue in the creation of its fictional world.

The intersection of genres is one of the key concepts in understanding the rich intertextuality of the world of *Blade Runner*—genre fiction, both in film and literature, is characterized by a mastery in creating fictional worlds. In the case of science fiction, it creates parallel worlds where technology marks the contrast with our own world; in the case of noir detective stories, the city becomes a character and represents the hostility that the investigator faces, since he can never be sure who is on his side or who to trust.

This last aspect is essential to connect the themes of the novel with noir film, given that it is one of the fundamental themes of both the novel and the film. According to Patricia Warrick, the novel explores a key issue in Philip K. Dick's work: How do we tell the authentic human from that which only masquerades as a human? (as cited in Robb, 2006, p. 71-72). In the novel, empathy is too complex an emotion to determine whether someone is synthetic or not. In the film, replicants can appear more humans than those they copy, and humans can be as ruthless as replicants. To complicate things, the ambiguity is increased by the uncertainty of whether Deckard is a replicant, a question that is not directly answered in the film. However, discerning audience members could figure out the solution after watching the Director's Cut (1992) and the so-called Final Cut (2007)—these versions show that Deckard dreams of a unicorn scampering in a forest. This shot, omitted from the original version, changes the meaning of the final scene, where Deckard picks up the origami unicorn that Gaff, another blade runner, leaves for him. The film director himself has solved this riddle in an interview (Greenwald, 2007): Deckard is a replicant, and Gaff knows what he dreams because he has seen it in a report, in the same way Deckard knows about the dreams of Rachael, his replicant love interest, after talking to her creator, Tyrell.

The use of voice-over in the 1982 version of the film needs discussion too, since it will be relevant to the analysis of the video game. It is well documented that Deckard's narration was not Ridley Scott's idea, but something that the film producers decided on as they were editing the film without Scott's input (de Lauzirika, 2007). The producers believed that the film was too weird for the general public, so they included a voice-over to explain what happened on the screen. After all, first-person narration is a film noir convention to reinforce the point of view of the detective. The final result is boring and redundant in the way it explains the action, and also because the film actually changes the point of view character several times to show what the replicants are doing. To top it all off, Harrison Ford, who plays Deckard, was contract-bound to record the voice-over; he did a sloppy job on purpose because he thought it was a terrible idea, in the hope that they would drop the narration (Sammon, p. 291). But this was not the case, and the film was originally released with a stale voice-over. When Ridley Scott re-edited the film in 1992, the voice-over was the first thing to go.

These are the source texts that the 1997 game is based on. The goal of the game is to recreate the world of the film for players to revisit and interact with it, as well as to reprise some of the most memorable moments of the film. The *Blade Runner* game is an example of how video game adaptation needs to focus on world building and intertextuality rather than a sequence of events, first because the process is different from how traditional media are translated to one another, but also because the game also resorts to content from the novel in order to flesh out a world that players can explore and manipulate.

THE CHALLENGE OF VIDEO GAME ADAPTATION

Adapting a story from a medium such as literature or cinema to video games is a challenge, primarily because there is still a limited understanding of games as a narrative medium. In the early days of game studies, the core discussion was about whether games could be studied from the standpoint of narratology (see for example Juul, 2001), since there are narrative elements that may be difficult to translate. The assumption is that the sequence of events in a video game is the result of the player's interactions and is always variable, while in traditional narratives it is the author who determines a specific sequence of events to achieve satisfactory storytelling.

Discussing why this concept of narrative in video games is limited and unproductive is beyond the scope of this article. Instead, let us propose a concept of adaptation that is more relevant to video games which partakes of the dialogic approach afforded by focusing on intertextuality. Rather than limiting the narrative to reproducing a sequence of events to adapt the original text, video game adaptation can take advantage of the elements that work best in the target medium, which is one of the principles of transmedia storytelling, and also establishes a dialogue with its source texts. This section analyzes the principles of adaptation at a high level, while the specific elements pertaining to the game will be tackled in the following section.

The film version of *Do Androids Dream of Electric Sheep?* already demonstrates that adapting a story is not limited to copying the story's events from one medium to another. As discussed in the previous sections, the novel and the film share a premise, but the story is different and many of the characters change, and yet the film is a worthy adaptation of the novel because it appropriates and expands on the central themes of the novel, using visual narratives to tell the story in the film medium.[2]

In the same way, *Blade Runner* as a video game does not try to reproduce all the events of the film or the book to the letter. The game deliberately stayed away from the conventional retellings that had become common in adventure games. Louis Castle, Executive VP of Westwood Studios, explained like this: "We didn't want to re-tell the film [...] I quickly tire of point-and-click, tree-structured re-tellings of movies. It's like painfully reading a book, where I can only read three or four pages, and then I have to do a crossword puzzle before I'm allowed to read more" (Bates, 1997). The solution to avoid retelling and to bring innovation to the game design was to recreate the fictional world and its spaces and characters, taking advantage of the properties of the medium. Some moments of the film are evoked at specific times, as the following section unpacks, but recreating the film from beginning to end as an interactive experience would not make sense.

The film version, as discussed above, blends science fiction with noir film and detective stories. The detective story is not only one of the key intertextual references of the film and the game, but also shapes the types of interactions that the player carries out in the game. The relationship between games and detective stories has been established by Suits (1985), who argued that detective stories created a game-like relationship between the author posing the mystery and the reader who tries to figure it out as they read. Game-like detective work lays the foundation of the interactions, which consist of getting information from witnesses, examining crime scenes and analyzing evidence in depth. Since the game involves solving a mystery, rather than just shooting down replicants, it would be pointless to have the same plot; if the player has seen the film or read the novel, they would probably know the solution to the mystery already, rendering the efforts of the player/detective irrelevant. Thus the player controls a new blade runner, whose quest is different from Deckard's character in both the novel and the film.

The game creates a narrative game world, which needs to allow the player to explore and interact with it. When an environment is created in digital media, there are aspects of the fictional world that become prevalent through the defining features of the medium, which Murray discussed. As a procedural environment, the game has to understand how the fictional world works in order to simulate it. This has been referred to as *procedural adaptation* (Weise, 2009), because it uses the rules of a genre or a world as the foundation to produce a digital narrative instead of reproducing a series of events. The participatory properties invite the player to become part of the world of the game, which in order to be created needs to first make the space navigable and allow for manipulation of its objects, thus taking advantage of the spatial properties. Finally, in order to create a fictional world that feels alive and complex, the game refers to both the film and the book to provide the characters, objects and situations that give cues for dramatic interaction, thus resorting to intertextuality to best utilize the encyclopedic properties of digital environments.

Each aspect of a digital environment requires the game to appropriate and adapt content and themes from the source texts, so that intertextuality becomes inescapable. Part of the pleasure of playing the game is precisely to map the relationship between all the texts, where they connect and they differ; participating in activities familiar to the player through previous media artifacts. The texts here intersect but also introduce substantial variations to become independent stories, which allows us to state that this is an example of transmedia storytelling and not merely an adaptation.

The *Blade Runner* game also takes transmedia storytelling a step further, letting the core theme of the novel and the film – who is an android and who is not – determine the events of the game. The following sections tackle how the game interprets whether the player is acting like a replicant or not depending on how the player behaves toward certain characters, which lends an ontological instability that parallels the ambiguity found in the film and the novel.

Let us examine in more detail how the *Blade Runner* game incorporates it source texts.

World Building and Intertextuality as Adaptation Strategies

Blade Runner the game starts by presenting itself as a faithful interactive adaptation of the film through its paratexts, as defined by Genette (1997). Paratexts are the texts that surround the core text and help introduce and situate it, such as the name of the author, the title, or the preface (pp. 1-4); in this case, the packaging of the CD-ROM and the opening videos work as the paratexts of the game. The box of the game features a font type very similar to the one in the film poster, above the image of a Deckard look-alike. When the game starts, the player can see a grid that selects a set of coordinates on the screen, zooms into the image to reveal the name of the developer, Westwood Studios, and then cuts to the title of the game with the same slamming sound that starts the film. The next cut is to the passage that also opens the movie, and which describes the core conflict of the fictional world—the hunt for replicants.

After this introduction, the action cuts to a bird's-eye view of L.A. in 2019, the same year as the film (1992 in the novel). The darkening sky glows orange, and the black outline of buildings extends to infinity. Darkness is only pierced by the fire bursts from the chimneys lacing the horizon. An eye watches the fires and blinks. This is the computer version of the opening shots of the film, which uses a tracking long shot approaching the location to tell the player/spectator that they are entering a new world. The scene is a statement of purpose; the game does have filmic aspirations, and aims at being faithful to Ridley Scott's portrayal.

Right after these images pass, the player realizes that, even though she may be in the same world, she is going to be a participant in a different story—this is the interactive sequel to the film. The action cuts to Runciter's pet shop.[3] Two people break into the shop and kill all the animals, their modus operandi being very similar to that of replicants Roy Batty and Leon Kowalski, who attack the eye-maker, Chew in the film. The situation is similar, but it is now obvious how this is a different story that poses new challenges to the player; Chew himself appears later in the game. This cutscene is the crime that sets off the action of the game.

When the cutscene ends, the player takes over the controls. The player character is Ray McCoy, a blade runner who dresses very much like Deckard in the film. The game manual tells us that he is a rookie who has just been promoted to blade runner and is now licensed to retire replicants. The trope of making the player character a novice creates a narrative justification of the player's mistakes, which can now be explained as the result of the character's inexperience. The name does seem to be a pun on "the real McCoy," probably an ironic reference since the character may turn out to be human or replicant depending on the behavior of the player.

This is how the game sets up the action, providing the player with something to do right away—the player needs to figure out who attacked the pet shop. To do so, she needs to explore the city and find witnesses who may provide information. The player is introduced to the world at the same time that the themes of the novel are reinstated, since the dead animals were all real and presented as a luxury item. The dialogue points out that replicants are the only ones who could have committed such a vile crime, since they lack empathy towards other living creatures. As the player investigates the case and become familiar with the digital version of L.A. in 2019, new attacks take place and the player meet characters that complicate the mystery that needs to be solved.

Rather than recount the events from beginning to end, which would be complicated due to the branching plot of the game, the analysis will focus on the elements drawn from the source texts to create the game world. These elements are the recreation of locations, use of props for interaction, micronarratives and evoking the themes of the source texts.

Recreation of Locations

As mentioned above, the creation of digital spaces in which the player can participate is inherent to digital environments; here the locations also become one of the principal intertextual connections between the game and its source texts. The first striking aspect of the game is the attention to detail in the visual representation of the world, which aims at reproducing the film settings faithfully. Compared with the capacity of modern computers, the 3D graphics seem rather poor; to make things worse, the resolution of screens these days renders images that now look pixelated. However, *Blade Runner* had cutting-edge graphics for the late 1990s, and the developers were very proud of what they had achieved visually (Bates, 1997).

The game recreates many of the film locations in astounding detail—for instance, the police station is presented using the same long shot as in the movie. Other locations include Chinatown, one of the first places the player needs to visit and recognizable for the dragon in neon lights that decorates one of the food stalls and its characteristic buzzing; Animoid Row, the market for synthetic animals, the iconic offices of the Tyrell Corporation; and J.F. Sebastian's apartment in the Bradbury Building, where the climax of the movie takes place.

McCoy navigates the space in his spinner; the transitions between locations recreate the shots where Deckard travels from one place to another in the movie. The player has a map with which she can see the different areas of L.A. that she can visit, thus creating a geographic coherence that reinforces the importance of the city, both as the video game space and as a characteristic of the noir genre.

The game developers appear proud of the creation of these localizations and their faithfulness to the movie (Bates, 1997), perhaps in a rather impractical way. Each location is presented with a fixed camera, something common in other state-of-the-art 3D games of the time, such as *Resident Evil* (1996) or *Metal Gear Solid* (1998). The camera point of view imitates those of the shots in the film, but is limited to long shots. The shots of exterior locations are carefully composed, which allows us to see how McCoy traverses the space. However, this point of view does not allow for seeing the characters in a close-up unless it is a cutscene. Some of the cross-questioning involving McCoy is displayed from a distance, as if the player were a spy following McCoy who cannot get close to the action. As a result, the excessive focus on recreating the locations over getting close to the characters spoils the cinematic aspirations of the game.

Props as the Key for Interaction

Another connection between the game and the source texts is the use of the film props. They are more than just backdrops; they give cues to the player to recreate the actions of the movie in the context of the story of the game, since every object has a series of behaviors associated with them. In the field of game studies, the use of objects to initiate imaginative play is a foundational concept (Walton, 1990); this property exports to video games without much hassle, since it relates to the procedural nature of the digital medium that Murray describes.

The previous sections have already introduced the spinner, the flying car designed by Syd Mead for the film. As a prop, it is essential for the player to become familiar with the environment, as well as reinforce the idea that McCoy is a blade runner just like Deckard.

McCoy's gun, based on another design by Mead, is another key item, although its design can only be appreciated in some of the cutscenes and the cover of the game. The gun is the main tool the blade runner uses to retire replicants, so the game includes some mini-games that test the player's marksmanship with the mouse. Skills, however, are not the most important feature – whether to shoot or not is what is meaningful in the game. If the player chooses not to shoot somebody, it demonstrates empathy towards the character, whereas if the player kills a human by mistake, McCoy will be chased by the police, which makes the game much harder to traverse.

The game provides a new device, the KIA (Knowledge Integration Assistant), a portable computer – or tablet in the modern sense – which allows the player character to record every piece of new information, such as events, evidence, and people's profiles; it organizes them and allows to make deductions based on their connections. As Tosca (2005) notes, however, the player does not really have to figure out the connections herself, and it is the character who is doing the deductive work; the KIA is there more for the player's reference than to pose a challenge. Although the device does not appear in the novel or the film, it is an example of how the game aims at facilitating investigation and detective work. The KIA helps navigate the database created as the player advances in the game.

Another essential work tool is the Esper, the image analyzer that allows the player to zoom in and even move the point of view within an image, since it treats a two-dimensional photo as if it were a holographic space that has depth.[4] In the film, Deckard speaks the coordinates in the image to expand it; in the game, the player clicks on the area she wishes to examine. Although the game does not reproduce the screen and buttons of the original design, it does manage to invoke the film by using the same sound effects. This is one of the most memorable technologies featured in the film, which allows Deckard to see what may be around the corner or examine small details. It also becomes one of the most satisfying objects to use in the game, since the player can feel like Deckard when carrying out their investigation.

Another key technology is the Voight-Kampff machine, which helps determine if someone is a replicant or human. The novel describes it as a machine that combines a series of polygraphic instruments, an adhesive disk with wires that stick to the subject's cheek, and a beam of light that measures the fluctuations of tension within the eye muscles. (Dick, 2008, p. 46). The device is presented like a futuristic lie detector, while in the movie it becomes a threatening technology, since it can determine whether someone lives or is retired. Ridley Scott wanted the device to seem alive, which is why it features a large bellows that make it look as if it was breathing. Instead of a wire mesh, the device features "a triangular lens piece rises cobra-like on a levered arm system, focusing on the subject's eye" (Scroggy, 1982, p. 52).

When the player uses the Voight-Kampff machine, she can see the dials as well as a close-up of the subject. Neither the novel nor the movie explain the specifics of how the machine works, so the game designers came up with its mechanics. Interpreting the information displayed on the dials is essential to determining whether someone is a replicant or not. The goal is to be able to complete a ten-question test; if the questions are too intense or uncomfortable for the subject, they may stop the test and refuse to continue, in which case the player misses the chance to determine whether they are human or not. Deciding whether to use the machine has consequences in the story, since it is a sign that the player suspects the subject may be a replicant. As in the case of the gun, using it or not demonstrates empathy (or lack thereof) towards the subject.

Each prop has specific affordances, as the descriptions above indicate. These examples demonstrate how each one of these objects allows the player to behave like a blade runner. The visual similarities are only the surface; the props also facilitate the actions that define the player-controlled character.

The props also generate the specific jargon of the fictional world. Some of the terms come from the film (spinner, Esper); the game also recovers some of the terms from the novel to give the world depth and take advantage of the encyclopedic nature of the medium. One of these terms is *kipple*, which refers to useless objects that accumulate, such as junk mail or gum wrappers, (Dick, 2008, p. 65) and which seem to multiply out of nowhere, perhaps due to nuclear fallout. In the novel, there is an institutional concern about controlling the expansion of kipple; this concern is voiced in the newscasts that the player can listen to in the game; McCoy also mentions kipple whenever he enters an abandoned or decaying building.

The use of jargon to refer to specific objects is one of the foundations of the world, since it evokes a larger population that makes up and shares terminology to describe their reality. The world feels lived in and seems to have a past thanks to the use of this specific vocabulary.

Micronarratives

Blade Runner – the game – becomes part of transmedia storytelling by the events in the game taking place in parallel to the events in the movie, as well as creating explicit intersections between the game and its source texts. These events constitute *micronarratives*, another term coined by Henry Jenkins (2004). Micronarratives are brief moments that evoke personal stories, and in this case help interweave the story of the game with that of the source texts.

The game starts the same day as the film, so that Deckard's and McCoy's steps crisscross but never meet. It is the first day on the job for both, their hurried appointment probably due to Dave Holden, one of the blade runners, having been attacked by a replicant, and which has caused an apparent shortage of staff. Deckard's name appears last on the scoreboard of the shooting range; his score is the lowest of all characters, thus revealing he is not very experienced—or perhaps hinting at Deckard being a replicant who just joined the police.

In one of the most memorable moments, McCoy is welcomed by Rachael right before meeting Tyrell, the creator of the replicants. The visit reprises Deckard's first meeting with Rachael, in a room reminiscent of an Egyptian temple filled by the light of the setting sun. The scene is very similar to the one in the movie; Rachael explains that Tyrell has already spoken to a blade runner that same day and explained how the Nexus 6 model works. Tyrell appears soon after to talk to McCoy, mentioning Deckard by name and offering McCoy the chance to test his Voight-Kampff machine with Rachael, just as in the film. Tyrell utilizes her again to teach a blade runner how to detect a Nexus 6 replicant; at this point, she seems oblivious to the fact that she is also synthetic.

The space also makes more subtle references through the digital set design. For example, J.F. Sebastian's apartment is a rather faithful reproduction of the film set, with the same automata roaming around the space. If the player examines the items carefully, she can see a chess table with a game in progress. This is a reference to the game that Sebastian uses as an excuse to visit Tyrell late at night, bringing in the replicants who will then execute their creator. Thus a single object can evoke events from the original texts without the need to retell them.

Evoking the Themes of the Source Material

The game uses more sophisticated strategies to connect the different texts, not only recreating moments but also rehearsing some of the themes. Some of these strategies are only evident if the player is also familiar with the novel and the film, however. The game uses first-person narration any time McCoy enters a new scene, evoking again the conventions of noir film while providing information about the motivation and the goals of the game. On the one hand, this is an elegant way of relating the narrative of the game with the opportunities for interaction. On the other, this convention is as inconsistent as in the film, since the game also changes points of view occasionally to show the player what the replicants are doing, in the same way that the film follows both the detective and his targets.

The thematic references are the most subtle form of intertextuality in the game, evoking themes through dialogue or descriptions as well as interactions. The main thematic parallel is how the player's decisions determine the player character's empathy towards replicants or humans. As mentioned above, carrying out a Voight-Kampff test or shooting someone (or not) reflect the attitude of the player toward the characters in the game. For example, the game introduces Crystal Steele, a blade runner who explains how the game measures the player's empathy levels as part of the narrative.

Depending on the player's decisions, Steele may imply that McCoy is an android if he lets one of the replicants go; McCoy's response to her is that he may have "too much empathy." This paradox also appears in the novel, which explains that the androids have empathy toward each other but not toward humans, which leads them to rebel. For example, Roy Baty (sic) in the book has a wife, Irmgard, while Pris refers to them as her best friends. Both of these examples show how androids care about each other. On the other hand, it becomes clear that a blade runner can also feel attracted to a replicant, as is the case for Deckard in the novel and the film. According to one of the novel's characters, blade runner Phil Resch, the solution to this internal conflict is to sleep with the replicant to satisfy one's desire, and then retire them (Dick, 2008, p. 143-44).

Other moments in the game allow us to understand the film from a new point of view, resorting to intertextual connections to examine the themes that both have in common. For example, one of the key themes of the film is vision (Bukatman, 1997, pp. 15-16). Eyes are used as a symbol that distinguishes humans from replicants in the film, from the eye that watches the skyline of L.A. in the opening shots of the movie, to the eyes examined with the Voight-Kampff test. The replicants' view of the world is constantly highlighted visually: their dilated eyes have a red sheen, as seen in Tyrell's synthetic owl or Rachael's eyes. The person Roy and Leon visit to learn more about their nature is Chew, who makes synthetic eyes for the Tyrell Corporation. Finally, in his famous speech before dying, Batty reminisces about the celestial wonders he has seen and whose memory will die with him. The eyes are the window to the replicant's soul.

Two additional moments in the game provide further insight on Tyrell's death. In the first, Clovis attacks Tyrell, who does not recognize this replicant as one of his creations. In a moment of dramatic irony, Tyrell states that he does not think his children will ever come back to attack him; McCoy, who knows Clovis is a replicant, warns him he may be wrong. And that is the case: in the film, Roy Batty kills Tyrell by squeezing his eyes out and breaking his skull with his own hands after Tyrell explains that there is no remedy to the replicants' age limit. Later in the game, the player meets two Siamese twins, Luther and Lance, who have been recently fired from the Tyrell Corporation. They reveal that every organ in the body of a replicant is designed and manufactured by different groups, so the key to longevity is distributed between each manufacturer. It is the eyes that contain a high number of retrograde viruses, which implies that they are the source of the body's decay. This information expands the signification of the eyes as the curse of the replicants, since it allows humans to identify them and trigger their death.

Ontological Ambiguity

One of the themes that deserves its own section is the ambiguity that pervades the fictional world, which derives from the key question posed by Warrick cited above—how do we tell the authentic human from that which only masquerades as a human? The answer is characteristically ambiguous, as is most of Dick's work. In fact, ontological instability is a defining feature of his work; novels such as *Ubik* (1969) or *The Man in the High Castle* (1963) present worlds where reality and dreams, actuality and imagination are in constant friction, and the reader is never sure of the authenticity of the events. *Do Androids Dream of Electric Sheep?* plays with this ambiguity in some sections, although in the end it is always resolved. For example, Deckard is arrested for harassing Luba Luft, one of the androids he is chasing. Although he works for the police, he is taken to a station he did not know existed. Another blade runner, Phil Resch, accuses him of being a replicant, while the Lieutenant in the station tells Deckard that

Resch is really a replicant. Every character doubts their own humanity as well as their antagonist's for several pages until the conundrum is resolved—the lieutenant and the policemen in this new station are all replicants, while Resch is a human blade runner they had deceived and controlled for their own uses, such as protecting their own when they were in danger. What is unclear is whether Resch was retiring replicants under their command, or whether he was killing humans for them.

The movie also partakes in this ambiguity, as the previous sections already discussed. Rachael reminds us of how difficult it can be to spot a replicant, and asks Deckard whether he has ever retired a human by mistake. Although the player can make assumptions as to whether Deckard is a replicant or not, the game thrives on leaving the ambiguous identity of the detective open. The *Blade Runner* game takes advantage of this inconclusiveness to make it part of the game mechanics and to determine the end of its story.

As mentioned above, the player's actions determine their level of empathy toward other characters. The player can select different attitudes to speak with other characters in a menu if she wants the dialogue to be selected automatically; these options include being polite or curt, choose a random attitude or letting the player choose an option whenever there is dialogue. Along with the Voight-Kampff test and who the player chooses to shoot or let go, dialogue options are another factor that determines the player character's empathy. These empathy levels dictate whether McCoy is acting like a human or replicant, which changes the events and the game's ending.

The game manual explains that every character has a different agenda whenever the player starts the game. The characters move around the world and exchange information about what they have seen and who they consider friend or foe. They behave according to a set of rules, based on the procedural properties of the medium. At times they may pick up a clue that the player missed, or they appear in different places at different times. The game also randomly determines who is a replicant or human when the game starts (Bates, 1997), so it is difficult to complete the game the same way twice. Only two of the characters, Clovis and his henchman Zuben, are always replicants; the rest of the cast can go one way or another, which will determine their attitude toward humans. Although the game was advertised on the variability of its gameplay, the key events and the backstory do not really change. What varies is the way in which the player can solve the case; each game walkthrough consulted offers slightly different ways to traverse the game.

The game deals with the difficulty of differentiating androids from humans with a story that is constantly transforming, which depends on a series of player decisions as well as the computer running the game. Thus, it tackles this key theme of the novel and the book by thriving on two of the properties of digital environments – procedurality and user participation – to create a narrative that is unstable and dependent on player's input. What video games do best is reinforce the transformative nature of the story itself.

CONCLUSION

The *Blade Runner* game thrives on its relationship with its source texts, where Philip K. Dick's novel established the world and the themes, and Ridley Scott's film provided a vision of that world and a link to noir film and detective stories. Intertextuality not only provides additional layers of meaning, but is necessary and inescapable in order to create an interactive environment. The game needs a rich, deep world that the player can explore and do detective work in; it also demonstrates how the adaptation from traditional narrative media into video games cannot always rely on reproducing a series of events, but on creating a world that the player participates in, explores and interprets, where the systems of the world translate the rules established in the source materials.

The intersection between the novel, the film and the game shows that intertextuality goes beyond mere references between each text—they allow the reader / viewer / player to access the texts that make up the world from different entry points, and each medium contributes what it does best to create a rich and complex world to explore. Thus the relationship between these three texts is an example of transmedia storytelling before the term itself was defined, showing us how looking back at older works can teach us pre-existing strategies and understand transmedia in a new way.

REFERENCES

Anderson, M. (1976). *Logan's run*. Action, Adventure, Sci-Fi.

Bates, J. (1997, September). Westwood's *Blade Runner*. *PC Gamer, 4*(9). Retrieved from http://media. bladezone.com/contents/game/

Boonstra, J. (1982, June). Philip K. Dick's final interview. *Rod Serling's The Twilight Zone Magazine, 2*(3), 47–52.

Bukatman, S. (1997). *Blade runner*. London, UK: British Film Institute.

Chung, P., Jones, A. R., Kawajiri, Y., Koike, T., Maeda, M., Morimoto, K., & Watanabe, S. (2003). *The animatrix*. Animation, Action, Adventure.

de Lauzirika, C. (2007). *Dangerous days: Making Blade Runner*. Documentary.

Dick, P. K. (1981, October 11). *Letter to The Ladd Company*. Retrieved from http://dangerousminds.net/comments/nothing_matches_blade_runner_philip_k._dick_gets_excited_about_ridley_scott

Dick, P. K. (2008). *Do androids dream of electric sheep?* New York, NY: Ballantine Books.

Dick, P. K. (2012a). *The man in the high castle*. New York, NY: Penguin Books Limited.

Dick, P. K. (2012b). *Ubik*. Boston, MA: Houghton Mifflin Harcourt.

Fancher, H., & Peoples, D. (1981). *Blade runner screenplay*. Retrieved from http://www.dailyscript. com/scripthttp://www.dailyscript.com/scripts/blade-runner_shooting.htmls/blade-runner_shooting.html

Genette, G. (1997). *Paratexts: Thresholds of interpretation*. Cambridge, MA: Cambridge University Press. doi:10.1017/CBO9780511549373

Greenwald, T. (2007, September 26). *Q&A: Ridley Scott has finally created the Blade Runner he always imagined*. Retrieved January 14, 2015, from http://archive.wired.com/entertainment/hollywood/magazine/15-10/ff_bladerunner?currentPage=all

Hendrickson, N., Wachowski, A., Wachowski, L., Boren, B., Caponi, E. J., Chadwick, P., (2005). *The matrix online* [Windows].

Jenkins, H. (2004). Game design as narrative architecture. In N. Wardrip-Fruin & P. Harrigan (Eds.), *First person: New media as story, performance, and game* (pp. 118–130). Cambridge, MA: The MIT Press.

Jenkins, H. (2006). *Convergence culture: Where old and new media collide*. New York, NY; London, UK: NYU Press.

Juul, J. (2001). Games telling stories? A brief note on games and narratives. *Game Studies, 1*(1). Retrieved from http://www.gamestudies.org/0101/juul-gts/

Kojima, H. (1998). *Metal gear solid*. Action, Drama, Sci-Fi. [Playstation]

Kristeva, J. (1980). *Desire in language: A semiotic approach to literature and art*. New York, NY: Columbia University Press.

Kucan, J. D., Dick, P. K. (novel), Fancher, H., Kucan, J. D., Leary, D., Peoples, D. W., & Yorkin, D. (1997). *Blade runner* [Windows].

Mikami, S., & Hosoki, M. (1996). *Resident evil*. Action, Horror. [Playstation]

Murray, J. H. (2001). *Hamlet on the holodeck: The future of narrative in cyberspace*. Cambridge, MA: The MIT Press.

Nourse, A. E. (2013). *The bladerunner*. Prologue Books.

On the tail of replidroids in CRL's Blade Runner. (1986, March). *CRASH*, (26).

Polanski, R. (1974). *Chinatown*. Drama, Mystery, Thriller.

Redmond, S. (2008). *Studying Blade Runner*. Auteur Publishing.

Robb, B. J. (2006). *Counterfeit worlds: Philip K. Dick on film*. London, UK: Titan.

Saler, M. (2011). *As if: Modern enchantment and the literary prehistory of virtual reality*. Oxford University Press.

Sammon, P. M. (1996). *Future noir: The making of Blade Runner*. New York, NY: It Books.

Scott, R. (1982). *Blade runner*. Sci-Fi, Thriller.

Scroggy, D. (1982). *Blade runner sketchbook*. San Diego, CA: Blue Dolphin Enterprises.

Silver, A., & Ursini, J. (2005). *L.A. noir: The city as character*. Santa Monica, CA: Santa Monica Press.

Star Trek. (1966). Action, Adventure, Sci-Fi.

Suits, B. (1985). The detective story: A case study of games in literature. *Canadian Review of Comparative Literature, 12*(2), 200–219.

Tosca, S. P. (2005). Implanted memories, or the illusion of free action. In W. Brooker (Ed.), *The Blade runner experience: The legacy of a science fiction classic*. New York, NY: Columbia University Press.

Wachowski, A., & Wachowski, L. (1999). *The matrix*. Action, Sci-Fi.

Wachowski, A., & Wachowski, L. (2003). *Enter the matrix* [Playstation 2].

Wachowski, A., & Wachowski, L. (2005). *The matrix: Path of Neo* [Playstation 2].

Walton, K. L. (1990). *Mimesis as make-believe: On the foundations of the representational arts*. Cambridge, MA: Harvard University Press.

Warrick, P. S. (1987). *Mind in motion: The fiction of Philip K. Dick*. Carbondale, IL: Southern Illinois University Press.

Weise, M. (2009). The rules of horror: Procedural adaptation in *Clock Tower, Resident Evil* and *Dead Rising*. In B. Perron (Ed.), *Horror video games: Essays on the fusion of fear and play* (pp. 238–266). Jefferson, NC: Macfarland.

Wolf, M. J. P. (2012). *Building imaginary worlds: The theory and history of subcreation* (1st ed.). New York, NY: Routledge.

KEY TERMS AND DEFINITIONS

Adaptation: The process of translating a narrative from one medium to another, e.g. theatre to film; comics to television; novels to video games.

Fictional World: An imaginary construct which comprises locations, characters, items and events, which are interrelated through a set of rules, from social and economic systems to physics.

Intertextuality: The intersection between texts, usually within the realm of fiction. These intersections allow to expand and transform the meaning of the connected texts.

Procedural: One of the properties of digital media, which refers to their capacity to follow procedures and systems as part of their content.

Transmedia Storytelling: A storytelling strategy by which a unified narrative is told across different media platforms.

ENDNOTES

[1]   In order to prepare for this article, the author played the original version of the game in CD-ROM. The game needs a special installer for it to run in a current Windows operating system, which was downloaded from this site: http://sierrahelp.com/download.php?file=Files/NonSierra/BladeRunnerSetup.exe

[2]   The first screenplay by Hampton Fancher tried to turn the novel into an action film, which is what initially alienated Philip K. Dick. In the end, thanks to the intervention of screenwriter David Peoples, it became a noir story (Robb, 2006).

[3]   The shop owner's name is a reference to one of the protagonists of another of Dick's novels, *Ubik* (1969).

[4]   The game uses the wrong term to refer to this device. In *The Blade Runner Sketchbook*, this technology is referred to as a *Holoprint Viewer* (Scroggy, 1982, p. 83), whereas *Esper* is the name of the computer system that provides information about the city in real time, from the status of every building to traffic information.

Chapter 3
A Different Kind of Monster:
Uncanny Media and *Alan Wake*'s Textual Monstrosity

Michael Fuchs
University of Graz, Austria

ABSTRACT

In many respects, Alan Wake *reminds of a typical postmodernist text: it draws on various sources, integrates other texts into its textual body, and is highly self-conscious both about its construction and the recipient's role in generating meaning. However,* Alan Wake *is not a postmodernist novel, but a video game. This chapter explores the ways in which this video game incorporates other cultural artifacts and argues that its cannibalistic incorporation of other media transforms* Alan Wake*'s textual body into the game text's true, Gothic monster.*

INTRODUCTION

After its release in the spring of 2010, *Alan Wake*'s story was nearly unanimously celebrated for its innovativeness and complexity. This story centers on the eponymous popular crime fiction, thriller, and horror author suffering from writer's block, who soon discovers that the events unfolding in front of his very eyes are lifted from his yet-to-be-finished (or so he thinks) novel *Departure*. However, Alan and the player soon come to understand that the majority of *Departure* has, in fact, been written. The only problem is that Alan cannot remember composing it, for he suffers from a week-long memory gap following his wife's abduction by what at first seems to be a kidnapper but soon turns out to be a dark force that needs a writer in order to be created. In the course of the game, Alan and the player learn that the events in the Pacific Northwestern town of Bright Falls are, in fact, predetermined by Alan's writing. However, this narrative layer is framed by another one, for the game text suggests that Alan-the-writer is nothing but a character in a story authored by Thomas Zane, who repeatedly appears as a God-like narrator figure in the gameworld and maleptically transgresses diegetic levels. The confusion between and conflation of different storyworlds (and storyworlds-within-storyworlds) extends to a confusion

DOI: 10.4018/978-1-5225-0477-1.ch003

between and conflation of temporal levels, as the past constantly interrupts the present, which, at the end of the day, has already been written.[1] In short, *Alan Wake* presents a very intricate story for any medium, and not just for a video game.

Whereas numerous critics commended *Alan Wake*'s narrative, others considered its evident emphasis on telling a story exemplary of narrative-based video games' neglect of gameplay, which turned out to be rather simplistic and repetitive. While there is some truth to the criticism, I would argue that this assessment reveals a misunderstanding between the developers and critics (and, possibly, players). To be sure, the critique of *Alan Wake*'s apparent prioritization of narrative over gameplay draws on video games' primacy of "participatory interactivity" (Schulzke, 2013), on which scholars such as Markku Eskelinen have elaborated, arguing that "the dominant user function in literature, theatre and film is interpretative, but in games it is the configurative one" (Eskelinen, 2001). In contradistinction, *Alan Wake* emphasizes what Marcus Schulzke (2013) has called "interpretive interactivity," for the game's linear gameplay, which is constantly interrupted by non-linear narrative sequences, assumes a key role in the intertextual games that *Alan Wake* plays, as the repetitive gameplay taps into a central convention of the Gothic, while its linear design metaludically highlights the role agency plays in the game.

In the course of this essay, I will thus suggest that *Alan Wake*'s monotonous gameplay supports the game text's meaning, as it is merely one element in the video game's self-reflexive engagement with its role in the Gothic tradition and its meta-reflections on the medium of the video game in view of other media. Indeed, *Alan Wake*'s metatextual incorporation of other media repeatedly produces uncanny effects, thus reinforcing its position within the Gothic tradition. Yet beyond remediating "haunted media" (Sconce, 2000) for their Gothic effects, *Alan Wake*'s apparently limitless text, I will argue, eventually emerges as the game text's defining monster.

MONSTROSITY, LIMINALITY, AND GOTHIC INTERTEXTUALITY

While traditionally regarded as a historical phenomenon or a genre in its own right, more recent approaches consider the Gothic a "discursive site" (Miles, 2002, p. 4) that may be employed in various genres, from slave narratives and romances to horror. Despite Gothic tales' heterogeneity, these stories generally "represent[] the subject in a state of deracination, [...] rupture, disjunction, fragmentation" (Miles, 2002, p. 3). As a result, Gothic characters are prone to "[c]ompulsive, repetitive, superficially meaningless behaviour" (Miles, 2002, p. 2) that circles around deeper wounds, such as traumatic experiences, which the characters are unable to address properly. The seemingly pointless behavior of compulsive repetition, some scholars have claimed, concerns not only characters in Gothic tales, but also the Gothic mode as such, for it "seems to define itself by constantly recapitulating everything it has been" (O'Brien, 1993, p. 63). Thus, Roger B. Salomon (2002) has ascribed meaninglessness to this repetitive pattern, for "rather than encouraging [meaning] generation," Gothic tales "can only dramatize one paradigmatic experience" (pp. 98–99). However, some self-aware Gothic texts, including *Alan Wake*, turn redundancy and repetition (and, thus, contemporary Gothic's derivativeness) into semantically loaded stylistic devices by emphasizing that a "text does not" simply "belong to a genre," but rather *participates in one or more genres*" (Derrida, 1980, p. 57; italics in original). Indeed, *Alan Wake*'s gameworld is not only replete with quite literal doubles, but also with scenes and moments that function as doubles of past Gothic texts. In this way, the game text constantly summons up the ghost of the Gothic (Figure 1).

Figure 1. Alan Wake *is permeated by Gothic doubles. Here, Alan meets his doppelganger, Mr. Scratch.*
Source: Remedy Entertainment, 2010.

The video game's opening cinematic proves exemplary in this context: Against the backdrop of a lighthouse, Alan drives along a deserted coastal road and narrates, "Following a typical nightmare pattern, I was late, desperately trying to reach my destination, a lighthouse, for some urgent reason I couldn't remember. I've been driving too fast down a coastal road to get there" (Remedy, 2010). Suddenly, Alan hits a hitchhiker. He gets out of his car, but the man, who appeared to be seriously injured (if not dead), has disappeared. Apparently relieved (albeit also somewhat confused by the fact) that the "body was gone" (Remedy, 2010), Alan ventures into the woods in an attempt to reach the lighthouse, where he encounters the hitchhiker again.

Gothic doubles occur in myriad form in this brief, not even four-minute-long, sequence: First, when Alan mentions that the unfolding narrative mirrors a "typical nightmare pattern," the voiceover draws attention to how early psychoanalytic horror criticism established analogies between nightmares and the experience of horror. When Alan then hits the hitchhiker, this moment evokes both iconic hitchhikers and accidents on lonely, coastal roads in the history of horror. The intertextual network does not end there, though, for the apparently dead hitchhiker's 'resurrection' only seconds later references American legends featuring ghosts haunting highways and other Gothic motifs, such as the walking dead. In addition, Wake's crossing from the relatively safe, civilized space of the road into the dangerous woods draws on the early days of the American experience, which were characterized by "the battle between civilization and nature, between the mental landscape of European consciousness and the physical and psychical landscape of the New World" (Mogen, Sanders, and Karpinski, 1993, p. 15). Jeffrey Weinstock has elaborated on this idea, noting that in "the American Gothic tradition the wilderness and the frontier" function "as spaces of danger, savagery, and violence—and as uncanny contact zones with racialized and exoticized Others" (2014, p. 28). In the case of *Alan Wake*, this uncanny Other is the hitchhiker, whom Alan meets on the Pacific coast (i.e., the West) and who tellingly carries an axe, placing the character squarely in the tradition of the frontiersman whose "traits [...] had been productive and heroic" (Slotkin, 1998, p. 126) during the early days of the conquest of the North American continent, yet turned "antisocial and dangerous" (Slotkin, 1998, p. 126) once the frontier was closed. Finally, the entire scene is permeated by intradiegetic doubles of a metaleptic kind: In his dream, Alan does not pass an "Entering Bright Falls" road sign, but rather an "Entering *Night Springs*" sign, indicating that he, in fact, crosses over into the hypodiegetic world of an in-gameworld television show (called *Night Springs*). This transgression of diegetic layers is echoed some moments later when Alan comes to understand that the hitchhiker "was a character from a story [Alan had] been working on" (Remedy, 2010).[2]

While all of these aspects are of narrative and cultural relevance, the linear and repetitive gameplay, likewise, stems from *Alan Wake*'s conscious invocation of the American Gothic. When the game was first announced at the 2005 Electronic Entertainment Expo, *Alan Wake* was conceived as an open-world game. Yet the developers "soon discovered that the open-world format [...] was not well suited to the topography of Gothic horror" (Krzywinska, 2014, p. 510). Indeed, a decade ago, a piece in *Edge* stressed that "the interactivity of games can undermine their scariness" (2005, p. 70). Instead of emphasizing participatory interactivity, the developers reduced player agency to a minimum and opted for a "temporally critical series of cause and effect chains" in order "to recreate the type of pace, suspense, and dramatic tension found in the American Gothic" (Krzywinska, 2014, p. 510). Thus, *Alan Wake*'s repetitive structure and monotonous gameplay serves to performatively situate the game in the tradition of the (American) Gothic, for not only do the constant repetitions emphasize the centrality of repetition to the Gothic mode, but the repetitions and the game's monotony also lull players into feelings of security and control. In this way, the video game creates "suspense," which becomes "interwoven with the interactive and repetitive nature of the game" (Grodal, 2000, p. 206).[3]

The playful invocation of the Gothic on the textual and ludic levels relies on the players' awareness of the Gothic modus operandi. In line with Harold Bloom's argument that intertextuality should not be mistaken for the relatively simple tasks of "source hunting" and "allusion counting" (1973, p. 31), the game text does not require players to track down the spectral present absences of the sources alluded to. Rather, *Alan Wake*'s embedment (or maybe even 'entrapment') in the Gothic tradition indicates how the video game, as an individual text, is practically impotent when exposed to the power of the genre's history and conventions. In this respect, the game text's drawing on the Gothic tradition mirrors the experiences of both Alan and the players, who are similarly exposed to the whims of overpowering forces.

This interconnection between avatar, player, and (game) text leads to another idea that *Alan Wake*'s indebtedness to the Gothic tradition emphasizes: liminality. Similar to the ways in which the player's embodied experience of gaming is located in the liminal space between the physical reality occupied by the player and the simulated reality occupied by the avatar, *Alan Wake*'s text (and its meaning) also emerges from the spaces in-between; the spaces between its constitutive elements (words, images, etc.), but also between the text and its surrounding (con)texts, for the fabric of any (inter)text is as much defined by its interwoven knots as by the spaces between the knots. In other words, intertextuality is inherently liminal, for the phenomenon is located in-between texts, as the prefix 'inter' indicates.[4] This liminal position always promises disruption, for liminality offers ample opportunity for crossing boundaries. After all, liminality, as originally conceived in anthropology, "is associated with a transgressive middle stage of a ritual: it is [...] a threshold, or margin, at which activities and conditions are most uncertain" (Hetherington, 1997, p. 32).

But as much as liminality is connected with intertextuality, in the context of the Gothic, the concept is first and foremost linked to the monster. Considering that the monster is usually "the most complex and interesting character" (Punter, 1996, p. 9) in a Gothic text and thus "becomes a primary focus of interpretation" (Halberstam, 1995, p. 2), one may wonder who *Alan Wake*'s monster truly is. The Dark Force? The taken (i.e., the people possessed by the Dark Force)? Either answer raises a problem, for "[v]ideo game monstrosity is conquerable," as Jaroslav Švelch has illustratively demonstrated (2013, p. 199). Whereas in old media, "[t]he monster always escapes because it refuses easy categorization"

(Cohen, 1996, p. 6), "[t]he logic of informatic control has [...] colonized even the things we fear" (Švelch, 2013, p. 195). This is to say that video game monsters adhere to a (medium-)specific logic, for their primary purpose is to be defeated. Indeed, the relative ease with which players can dispose of the 'monsters' faced in the course of *Alan Wake* (other than the 'Nightmare' mode, in which running away often seems the best option) draws players' attention to the true monster encountered in the course of the game: the media.

Gothic Intermediality and Uncanny Media

Media practitioners, critics, and scholars have long been aware of the uncanny effects produced by media and media technologies. For example, upon first seeing the Lumières' cinematograph in action, a reporter concluded that "death will no longer be absolute" (as cited in Stratton, 1996, p. 83), as the device would allow human beings to exist—to continue 'living'—in spectral form, captured in moving images. Similarly, Roland Barthes famously remarked that photographs "emanat[e a] past reality" (1981, p. 89) and thus make possible the "return of the dead" (1981, p. 9). And Siegbert Soloman Prawer observed that the cinematic "image [...] is a kind of spectral double, the simulacrum of landscapes and townscapes filled with human beings that seem to live, to breathe, to talk, and yet are present only through their absence" (1980, p. 50). Indeed, there is no denying that "[e]very new medium is a machine for the production of ghosts" (Peters, 1999, p. 139). While *Alan Wake*—as a video game—could easily produce ghosts and other monsters (and, in fact, it does), it cleverly employs older media in order to generate uncanny effects.

In fact, *Alan Wake* remediates a number of 'old' media for various purposes, but my journey through the game text's intermedial landscape will begin with the medium that is usually the first point of reference when discussing the intermedial relationships between video games and other media: film. The game's visual style (and its soundscape) is strongly indebted to horror cinema. Indeed, the extent to which *Alan Wake* remediates movies is underlined by the fact that "successful dodges are sometimes highlighted with a cinematic moment" (Remedy, 2010), as the tutorial in the video game's opening minutes stresses. In addition, one of the game's achievements on the Xbox 360 is obtained by "perform[ing] a cinematic dodge 20 times" (Remedy, 2010). While these extradiegetic textual markers stress the remediation of cinematic conventions and effects, one element among the cinematic tools and strategies *Alan Wake* employs deserves special attention: the game's cutscenes.

Like many narrative-based video games, *Alan Wake* tells much of its story through pre-rendered movies. The constant alternation between gameplay and cinematics on the video game's discursive dimension effects a near endless oscillation between moments in which players are in control and moments in which they are not in control on the game's interactive dimension. These changes in the gameplay situation "creat[e] a dynamic rhythm between self-determination and pre-determination" (Krzywinska, 2002, p. 207). By taking control away from players, the cutscenes "reinforc[e] the sense that a metaphysical 'authorial' force is at work, shaping the logic of the game" (Krzywinska, 2002, p. 211). In this way, the cinematics underscore the difference between the (purportedly) non-participatory nature of cinema spectatorship, in which the audience is traditionally thought to be "chained, captured, or captivated" (Baudry, 1974, p. 352) by the cinematic apparatus, and video games' participatory interactivity. However, this feeling of losing control not only operates on the level of interaction (as players no longer control their avatar during the cutscenes), but also on the narrative level. After all, Alan gradually realizes that he is merely a character in a story. Thus, this lack of control (and, by extension, player agency) becomes one of the main sources of horror in the game. Indeed, while the elusive Dark Force, which haunts Bright

Falls and which has kidnapped Alan's wife, assumes the role of the game text's main antagonist, the central problem faced by players (and Alan) is a feeling of helplessness, a feeling that is reinforced by the video game's remediation of cinematic storytelling in order to quite literally rob the players of control. Effectively, the medium of film, incorporated into the video game, turns players into patients who are acted upon rather than agents who act.

Beyond highlighting the players' (and Alan's) lack of agency, cutscenes also introduce and elaborate on the important role writing assumes in the game text. The significance of writing is established as early as the opening cinematic, in which Alan narrates:

Stephen King once said that nightmares exist outside of logic and there's little fun to be had in explanations; they're antithetical to the poetry of fear. In a horror story, the victim keeps asking "why," but there can be no explanation, and there shouldn't be one. The unanswered mystery is what stays with us the longest and is what we'll remember in the end. My name is Alan Wake. I'm a writer. (Remedy, 2010)

Alan's voiceover not only openly acknowledges Stephen King's influences from the get-go, but, moreover, the minimal information players obtain about the character they control is that Alan is a writer. Of course, the fact that this is the only piece of information communicated about the character underlines its significance. Unsurprisingly, Alan's role as a writer takes center stage in the narrative, for the events unfolding in *Alan Wake*'s gameworld follow the blueprint provided by Alan's novel *Departure*.

In order to highlight the diegetic doubling of *Departure* in the 'real' world of Bright Falls, numerous pages of the novel's manuscript are scattered throughout the gameworld. Following Thomas Vogler, these simulated manuscripts may be referred to as 'book objects.' As Vogler explains, 'book objects' are "not books, even though their whole being exists in relation to the book," for these "figurative constructs [...] represent[], imitat[e], or violat[e]" the concept of 'the book' and its functions in culture (2000, p. 459). Johanna Drucker has elaborated on Vogler's ideas and suggested that one of the primary functions of representing books in electronic media is what she calls the "book-as-repository-of-secret-knowledge cliché[]" (2008, p. 220). This notion of books containing secret knowledge assumes two key functions in *Alan Wake*. First, the manuscript pages communicate background information that will remain unbeknownst to players not reading them. More importantly, however, reading the pages often foreshadows things to come, for *Departure* already 'knows' the future. A little over halfway through episode two, for example, Alan finds the following manuscript page:

The night had been one desperate situation after another. I was exhausted and my body felt as though it had been chewed up and spat out.

The flashlight was heavy in my hand, and each pull of the trigger sent a painful shock up my arm. But I was finally out of the woods and things were looking up.

That's when I heard the chainsaw. (Remedy, 2010)

It comes to no surprise that only seconds later, Alan (and the player) hears the sound of a chainsaw and is attacked. Not only does the past narration create an uncanny effect here, as past, present, and future eerily become one, but, moreover, the conflation of temporal levels goes hand in hand with a conflation of diegetic levels, as the embedded narrative embodied by the manuscript page (which is, in fact, not only embedded in the game, but at the same time embeds the story of the game) not simply foreshadows, but, indeed, performs the diegetic action.

This confusion of diegetic layers culminates toward the end of the game (and is continued in the two 'extras'), as objects in the gameworld are represented as words that are performatively written into existence (to the sound of a typewriter) when Alan points his flashlight at the words, which float around in his reality. Whereas the narrative generally stresses that Alan is merely an element in a finished story, here, Alan is writing the story in the very moment he is experiencing it—without the ability to significantly alter it, though. In this way, the game metaludically reflects on the experience of the player, who, like Alan, may perform certain actions, which were, however, hard-coded into the software. Much like the player can only (re-)perform the actions intended by the programmers, Alan can only take the steps he had laid out in his manuscript. *Alan Wake*'s incorporation of the medium of the book thus buttresses both Alan's feeling of helplessness in view of the supernatural forces he encounters and the players' powerlessness vis-à-vis the game's underlying code, as they come to understand that "all playing is a being-played. The attraction of a game, the fascination it exerts, consists precisely in the fact that the game masters the players" (Gadamer, 2004, p. 104). In view of Hans-Georg Gadamer's words, it seems noteworthy that Isabel Cristina Pinedo described the experience of watching horror movies "as an exercise in mastery, in which controlled loss substitutes for loss of control" (1996, p. 26). In *Alan Wake*, this 'exercise in mastery' is reinforced by the participatory interaction characteristic of video games.

However, *Alan Wake*'s quarreling with control does not end there. After all, Alan finds his double from another spatio-temporal dimension caught on images displayed on various screens. This alter-Alan is apparently locked up in a small room (or, possibly, *in* the screens), where he is walking around or working on his manuscript. In either case, the second Alan provides insights into Alan's inner life. More importantly, however, the game text draws on "analogue media's propensity for being corrupted" in order "to communicate a sense of […] mental disintegration" (Kirkland, 2007, p. 410) in these scenes. When Alan sees his double on a screen for the first time, he comments (not coincidentally), "An old portable TV on the shelf had come alive by itself. Impossibly, I could see myself on the screen, talking like a madman" (Remedy, 2010). A little later, he adds, "It'd been me on the TV, talking crazy. Was I losing my mind?" (Remedy, 2010). Indeed, the existence of multiple Alans in different media within the diegetic world appears to provide a relatively straightforward answer to this question, which transforms the issue of control into a question of control of both one's body and mind.

On the other hand, offering glimpses into Alan's thoughts and feelings through the intermediary of film draws on the "institutionalized authority in which cinema […] is historically implicated," especially cinema's use "as a tool of scientific rationality" (Kirkland, 2009, p. 119). By looking at the filmic representations of alter-Alan, Alan and the player effectively assume the role of an analyst whose "medical gaze" (Foucault, 2003) allows him to create distance between himself and the patient and thus to uncover the heart of the problem. In *Alan Wake*, however, both Alan and the player can only hazard a guess as to what is 'really' going on. This ambiguity is the game text's point, though, for not only can there be no (or, for that matter, too many possible) explanation(s) for the mystery surrounding the connection between alter-Alan and Alan, but also the true source of horror remains elusive. In this way, the 'straightforward' answer mentioned toward the end of the previous paragraph, in fact, only raises further questions (Figure 2).

In addition to seeing his Gothic doubles on various screens in the gameworld, Alan watches a recording of his performance on *The Harry Garret Show* (a late-night show) in a flashback that opens the video

Figure 2. Alan sees his double on an old tube screen in a cabin in the woods.
Source: Remedy Entertainment, 2010.

game's sixth episode. In the show, Alan is interviewed about his then-most recent book, *The Sudden Stop*. Tellingly, Sam Lake, the game's writer, is sitting next to Alan on the interviewee couch. While, on one level, *The Harry Garret Show* serves to flesh out Alan's character and points toward aspects in the *Alan Wake* universe that could have been picked up in transmedia expansions, the inclusion of the game's writer Sam Lake on the television-show-within-the-video-game functions as an authorial self-insertion that leaves behind a trace, a "sign […] left in the text by the author" (Gaines, 2002, p. 94). Yet beyond underlining the writer's spectral traces (which raises the question of authorship in the context of a massively collaborative medium), the television show suddenly confronts players with actor Ilkka Villi, who plays Alan in a television show watched by the animated Alan. This situation creates an uncanny Gothic double of a different kind, for Villi's presence on the intradiegetic flat screen not only draws the player's attention to the video game's production process, but also highlights the continuous presence of Villi's specter in the video game, as he served as the model for the animated Alan (motion capturing and capturing of facial expressions included) (Figure 3).

The Harry Garret Show is, however, not the only intradiegetic television show, for the gameworld has its own mystery show called *Night Springs*, which players can watch on television screens scattered across the gameworld. As the game's narrative unfolds, the television show's plots become increasingly interconnected with the game's story, blurring the borderlines between the fiction of the TV show and the 'reality' of the events in Bright Falls in the process. *Night Springs'* aesthetics, however, undermine this ontological nebulosity, for the show-within-the-game is live-action material, which provides a stark contrast to the animated reality of Bright Falls. The crisp images of Alan's reality are thus juxtaposed with the bad image quality of *Night Springs*, which is broadcast in black and white and features blurry images that suffer from various forms of noise. Implicitly, these disadvantages of (especially analog) television are explained by the fact that *Night Springs* is implicated in analog broadcasting (most probably also production) technologies, which highlights that the medium of television "constitute[s] the arcane, the chaotic, the corruptible" (Kirkland, 2009, p. 123). But beyond highlighting differences between the

Figure 3. Alan watches The Harry Garret Show *on his flatscreen TV in his New York apartment.*
Source: Remedy Entertainment, 2010.

medium of video games and the medium of television, the final word in the quotation taken from Ewan Kirkland proves central to another function of the in-gameworld television show, for the antiquated technology opens the door to a different dimension and allows the fiction of the television show to segue into the diegetic reality (and/or vice-versa). In this way, television becomes directly responsible for causing "an uncanny effect" by erasing "the distinction between imagination and reality" (Figure 4) (Freud, 2001, p. 244).

In the world of *Alan Wake*, *Night Springs* is, however, not simply a TV show, but rather part of an in-universe transmedia franchise featuring board games, video games, and—possibly—other media texts. In this context, *Alan Wake*'s engagement with its surrounding mediascape comes full circle, for at one

Figure 4. Alan watches a Night Springs *episode on an old tube screen.*
Source: Remedy Entertainment, 2010.

point, Alan stumbles upon an Xbox 360 console. Wake is thus confronted with the material object that effectively constructs his reality.[5] At this moment, the different media technologies remediated in the video game become symbolically re-integrated into the material object of the video gaming console, and *Alan Wake* suggests that twenty-first-century Westerners' existence is intricately tied to virtual identities performed in various media. In effect, the game text thus highlights that Westerners' subjectivity has become extremely "fragmented, decentered, and schizophrenic" (Figure 5) (Sconce, 2000, p. 171).

CONCLUSION: *ALAN WAKE* AS A MONSTROUS TEXT

Alan Wake's invocation of the Gothic's past, the relative insignificance of the monsters players have to defeat in the course of the game, and the game text's permeation by spectral traces of other media—none of these features alone would turn *Alan Wake* into a particularly innovative (or interesting, for that matter) example of the early-twenty-first-century Gothic, for all of these strategies had been well established prior to *Alan Wake*'s release in 2010. Indeed, when faced with *Alan Wake*'s textual playfulness and derivativeness, which combine to overshadow the "staple emotional responses" (Botting, 2013, p. 6) expected of Gothic texts, some scholars might feel tempted to dismiss the video game as characteristic of the "candygothic" (Botting, 2001) trend they see running rampant in contemporary culture, which epitomizes the Gothic's loss of "its older intensity" (Botting, 2002, p. 287).

However, I detect a peculiarity which characterizes *Alan Wake*: Since the uncanny, monstrous media are part and parcel of *Alan Wake*, the video game is just as much—if not more—monstrous; the true monster of *Alan Wake* is, indeed, *Alan Wake*. Granted, narratologists have employed terms such as "monstrous" (Gibson, 1996) and "savage" (Currie, 1998) when trying to define postmodernist narratives. These scholars primarily connected postmodernism's 'monstrosity' to its deviation from earlier narrative conventions. However, as Tamer Thabet has observed, the "textual anarchy" typical of postmodernism

Figure 5. Alan comes face to face with the material object that constructs his reality.
Source: Remedy Entertainment, 2010.

"does not apply to game fictions" (2011, p. 102), for "the text in a computer game does have a very strict structure" (2011, p. 103). But Andrew Gibson hinted at a different dimension of narrative monstrosity when he wrote, "The narrative itself keeps on developing curious and peculiar growths" (1996, p. 266). Here, Gibson's notion of monstrosity approaches the type of monstrosity I have in mind when terming *Alan Wake* 'monstrous', for *Alan Wake*'s monstrosity is linked to the video game's Gothic roots.

Judith Halberstam suggested that one of the Gothic's defining characteristics is that "[o]ne space […] feeds upon another" (1995, p. 35). The imagery employed by Halberstam implies that "the Gothic is best defined […] by subversion or transgression of boundaries" with the aim of "question[ing], defin[ing], and redefin[ing] them" (Taylor, 2009, p. 49). Since the Gothic "produce[s] a symbol for [its] interpretive mayhem in the body of the monster" (Halberstam, 1995, p. 2), the monster, unsurprisingly, emerges as a "mixed category," which "resists any classification" and instead "demand[s …] a 'system' allowing polyphony" (Cohen, 1996, p. 7). Thus, Jeffrey Jerome Cohen continues, the monster "offers an […] invitation to explore […] new and interconnected methods of perceiving the world" (1996, p. 7).

Of course, some of the quotations in the previous paragraph echo discussions surrounding the concept of intertextuality (especially when it emerged in the 1960s).[6] However, my point here is that *Alan Wake*'s text is exactly such a 'mixed category' that 'resists classification'. Like a cannibal (or vampire, for that matter), *Alan Wake* incorporates other media, as its ludo-narrative existence emerges not only from the interplay between *Alan Wake*, the Gothic tradition it draws on, and the surrounding mediascape, but also from the—both participatory and interpretive—interaction between text and user. In this way, the affordances of the medium of the video game highlight that any text "is experienced only in an activity of production" (Barthes, 1977, p. 157; original in italics).

But if *Alan Wake* is monstrous, the game text raises another question: Since *Alan Wake* requires the player's "practical collaboration" (Barthes, 1977, p. 163) for its coming-into-(virtual-)being, who is the monster here? *Alan Wake*? Or the humanoid creature sitting in front of the screen, which not only assumes a monstrous existence by occupying a liminal zone between physical and virtual reality, but also creates the monstrous text? In other words, who is the 'true' monster: Frankenstein or Frankenstein's creature?

REFERENCES

Barthes, R. (1977). From work to text. In S. Heath (Ed.), *Image—music—text* (S. Heath, Trans.). (pp. 155–164). London, UK: Fontana Press.

Barthes, R. (1981). *Camera lucida: Reflections on photography* (R. Howard, Trans.). New York, NY: Farrar, Straus & Giroux.

Baudry, J.-L. (1974). Ideological effects of the basic cinematographic apparatus (trans. A. Williams). *Film Quarterly*, 28(2), 39–47. doi:10.2307/1211632

Bloom, H. (1973). *The anxiety of influence: A theory of poetry*. New York, NY: Oxford University Press.

Botting, F. (2001). Candygothic. In F. Botting (Ed.), *The Gothic* (pp. 133–151). Cambridge, UK: D. S. Brewer.

Botting, F. (2002). Aftergothic: Consumption, machines, and black holes. In J. Hogle (Ed.), *The Cambridge companion to Gothic fiction* (pp. 277–300). Cambridge, UK: Cambridge University Press. doi:10.1017/CCOL0521791243.014

Botting, F. (2013). *Gothic* (2nd ed.). London, UK: Routledge.

Cohen, J. J. (1996). Monster culture (seven theses). In J. J. Cohen (Ed.), *Monster theory: Reading culture* (pp. 3–25). Minneapolis, MN: University of Minnesota Press.

Currie, M. (1998). *Postmodern narrative theory*. New York, NY: St. Martin's Press. doi:10.1007/978-1-349-26620-3

Denson, S., & Jahn-Sudmann, A. (2013). Digital seriality: On the serial aesthetics and practice of digital games. *Eludamos (Göttingen), 7*(1), 1–32.

Derrida, J., & Ronell, A. (1980). The law of genre (trans. A. Ronell). *Critical Inquiry, 7*(1), 55–81. doi:10.1086/448088

Drucker, J. (2008). The digital codex from page space to e-space. In R. Siemens & S. Schreibman (Eds.), *A companion to digital literary studies* (pp. 216–232). Malden, MA: Wiley-Blackwell.

Edge editors. (2005). Scare tactics: Exploring the bloody battleground between fear and frustration. *Edge, 149,* 69–73.

Remedy Entertainment. (2010). *Alan Wake* [Video game]. Redmond, WA: Microsoft Game Studios.

Eskelinen, M. (2001). The gaming situation. *Game Studies, 1*(1). Retrieved April 17, 2008, from http://www.gamestudies.org/0101/eskelinen/

Foucault, M. (2003). *The birth of the clinic: An archaeology of medical perception* (A. M. Sheridan, Trans.). London, UK: Routledge.

Freud, S. (2001). The "uncanny" (J. Strachey, A. Strachey, & A. Tyson, Trans.). In J. Strachey (Ed.), The standard edition of the complete psychological works of Sigmund Freud, vol. 17: An infantile neurosis and other works (pp. 217–256). London, UK: Vintage.

Fuchs, M. (2012). Hauntings: Uncanny doubling in *Alan Wake* and *Supernatural. Textus: English Studies in Italy, 25*(3), 63–74.

Fuchs, M. (2013). "A horror story that came true": Metalepsis and the horrors of ontological uncertainty in *Alan Wake. Monsters & the Monstrous, 3*(1), 95–107.

Gadamer, H.-G. (2004). *Truth and method* (J. Weinsheimer & D. G. Marshall, Trans.). London, UK: Continuum.

Gaines, J. M. (2002). Of cabbages and authors. In J. M. Bean & D. Negra (Eds.), *Feminist reader in early cinema* (pp. 88–118). Durham, NC: Duke University Press. doi:10.1215/9780822383840-004

Gibson, A. (1996). *Towards a postmodern theory of narrative*. Edinburgh, UK: Edinburgh University Press.

Grodal, T. (2000). Video games and the pleasure of control. In D. Zillmann & P. Vorderer (Eds.), *Media entertainment: The psychology of its appeal* (pp. 197–213). Mahwah, NJ: Lawrence Erlbaum.

Halberstam, J. (1995). *Skin shows: Gothic horror and the technology of monsters*. Durham, NC: Duke University Press.

Hetherington, K. (1997). *The badlands of modernity: Heterotopia and social ordering*. London, UK: Routledge. doi:10.4324/9780203428870

Kirkland, E. (2007). The self-reflexive funhouse of *Silent Hill*. *Convergence (London)*, *13*(4), 403–415. doi:10.1177/1354856507081964

Kirkland, E. (2009). *Resident Evil*'s typewriter: Horror videogames and their media. *Games and Culture*, *4*(2), 115–126. doi:10.1177/1555412008325483

Kristeva, J. (1984). *Revolution in poetic language* (M. Waller, Trans.). New York, NY: Columbia University Press.

Krzywinska, T. (2002). Hand-on horror. In G. King & T. Krzywinskia (Eds.), *ScreenPlay: Cinema/videogames/interfaces* (pp. 206–223). London, UK: Wallflower.

Krzywinska, T. (2014). Digital games and the American Gothic: Investigating Gothic game grammar. In C. L. Crow (Ed.), *A companion to the American gothic* (pp. 503–515). Malden, MA: Wiley–Blackwell.

Miles, R. (2002). *Gothic writing, 1750–1820: A genealogy* (2nd ed.). Manchester, UK: Manchester University Press.

Mogen, D., Sanders, S. P., & Karpinski, J. B. (1993). Introduction. In D. Mogen, S. P. Sanders, & J. B. Karpinski (Eds.), *Frontier gothic: Terror and wonder at the frontier in American literature* (pp. 13–27). Rutherford, NJ: Fairleigh Dickinson University Press.

O'Brien, G. (1993, April22). Horror for pleasure. *The New York Review of Books*, 63–68.

Peters, J. D. (1999). *Speaking into the air: A history of the idea of communication*. Chicago, IL: University of Chicago Press. doi:10.7208/chicago/9780226922638.001.0001

Pinedo, I. C. (1996). Recreational terror: Postmodern elements of the contemporary horror film. *Journal of Film & Video*, *48*(1/2), 17–31.

Prawer, S. S. (1980). *Caligari's children: The film as tale of terror*. Oxford, UK: Clarendon Press.

Punter, D. (1996). *The Literature of Terror* (Vol. I). Essex, UK: Longman.

Salomon, R. B. (2002). *Mazes of the serpent: An anatomy of horror narrative*. Ithaca, NY: Cornell University Press.

Schulzke, M. (2013). Translation between forms of interactivity: How to build the better adaptation. In G. Papazian & J. M. Sommers (Eds.), *Game on, Hollywood: Essays on the intersection between video games and cinema* (pp. 70–81). Jefferson, NC: McFarland.

Sconce, J. (2000). *Haunted media: Electronic presence from telegraphy to television*. Durham, NC: Duke University Press.

Slotkin, R. (1998). *The fatal environment: The myth of the frontier in the age of industrialization, 1800–1890*. Norman, OK: University of Oklahoma Press.

Stratton, J. (1996). *The desirable body: Cultural fascination and the erotics of consumption*. Manchester: Manchester University Press.

Švelch, J. (2013). Monsters by the numbers: Controlling monstrosity in video games. In M. Levina & D.-M. T. Bui (Eds.), *Monster culture in the 21ˢᵗ century: A reader* (pp. 193–208). New York: Bloomsbury.

Taylor, L. N. (2009). Gothic bloodlines in survival horror gaming. In B. Perron (Ed.), *Horror video games: Essays on the fusion of fear and play* (pp. 46–61). Jefferson, NC: McFarland.

Thabet, T. (2011). Monstrous textuality: Game fiction between postmodernism and structuralism. *Loading…: The Journal of the Canadian Game Studies Association, 5*(8), 101–109.

Vogler, T. A. (2000). When a book is not a book. In J. Rothenberg & S. Clay (Eds.), *A book of the book: Some works and projections about the book and writing* (pp. 448–466). New York: Granary Books.

Weinstock, J. A. (2014). Gothic and the new American republic, 1770–1800. In G. Byron & D. Townshend (Eds.), *Gothic world* (pp. 27–36). Abingdon: Routledge.

KEY TERMS AND DEFINITIONS

Diegesis: The term derives from the Greek term for 'narration' and is used to describe the world of the (fictional) story (i.e., the gameworld in the case discussed in this chapter).

Extradiegetic: Whereas the diegesis is the fictional world occupied by characters and other existents, the extradiegetic level is the level of narration.

Hypodiegetic: Within a given storyworld, there may be different diegetic levels (as Gérard Genette originally argued) or (sub-)worlds (as narratologists have argued more recently). While the diegesis is the fictional world, the hypodiegesis (also referred to as 'metadiegesis' by some scholars) is an embedded storyworld; the world of a story-within-the-story.

Metalepsis: The somewhat paradoxical situation in which parts of one (sub-)world within a fictional world cross over into another, embedding or embedded, storyworld.

Metatextual: A textual feature that calls attention to the text's own textuality; its creation, distribution, and/or reception.

Uncanny: This psychological concept derives from the German word 'unheimlich', which conveys an idea of being 'homely' and its exact opposite at the same time. Thus, 'uncanny' is a process by which something known and familiar suddenly takes on strange, unknown qualities.

ENDNOTES

[1]   For a more detailed discussion of metalepses in *Alan Wake*, see Fuchs (2013).

[2]   For a more detailed discussion of doubles in *Alan Wake*, see Fuchs (2012).

[3]   Note, however, that Shane Denson and Andreas Jahn-Sudmann have stressed that "through their familiar segmentation into distinct levels or worlds," video games "establish[] a serial schema of repetition and variation at the very heart of gameplay" (2013, p. 2). From this perspective, repetition is not only characteristic of video games that draw on the Gothic, but video games at large.

4   According to Julia Kristeva, intertextuality may, tellingly, be considered a "*passage* from one signifying system to another" (1984, p. 60, my emphasis). Barthes, likewise, suggested that a text is "a passage, an overcrossing" (1977, p. 159).

5   Arguably, the effect is not the same when playing the PC version of the game. Here, the inclusion of an Xbox 360 in the gameworld may even suggest the PC's ability to incorporate (or simulate) video game consoles.

6   Roland Barthes noted that the re-focus on the text rather than the work was "obtained by the [...] overturning of former categories" (1977, p. 156).

Chapter 4
Intermediality and Video Games:
Analysis of *Silent Hill 2*

Mehdi Debbabi Zourgani
Paris 5 Descartes, France

Julien Lalu
UFR SHA Poitiers, France

Matthieu Weisser
UFR SHA Poitiers, France

ABSTRACT

This chapter proposes to study intermediality in video games in order to highlight media interactions. The purpose is to analyze some intermedia processes to illustrate how intermediality can create significa-tion. The chapter is focused on the survival horror game Silent Hill 2 *(Konami, 2001). More specifically, it is about, but not only, two protagonists: James Sunderland and Eddie Dombrowski. Analyses follow three different intermediality levels that can be applied in video games to get a better comprehension of it. The co-presence shows what is played between the media included in the game. The transfer has an interest to the links between video games and other objects in order to find how its language is created.* Silent Hill 2, *as a Japanese production, includes many Japanese symbols. The emergence reveals what creates the specific identity of the video game as a medium by observing the interactions between the different media composing it.*

INTRODUCTION

Kristeva (1974) defines intertextuality as "the transposition from a system of signs to another" (p. 59). It means showing influences found in a text and its relations with other texts. The notion of intertextuality allows the development of a different approach in text analysis. Following this emerging path, in the late 90s, this new kind of perspective needed a new term, a word referring not exclusively to a "text".

DOI: 10.4018/978-1-5225-0477-1.ch004

So academics chose the words *intermedia* (Higgins, 1967) and then *intermediality*. As Vos (2005) explains, Higgins uses *intermedia* to refer to: "[works] in which the materials of various more established art forms are conceptually fused rather than merely juxtaposed." (p. 325)

Intermediality is generally theorized through concepts of intertextuality. However the term "intermediality" led academics to consider cultural objects in a different way. Thus it was, at the time, acknowledged to segment art works into different media phenomena in order to analyze them separately (Müller, 2000). Intermedial references suggest a crossing of media borders and medial *inter*-actions. Another difference is that intermediality sets itself apart from intertextuality by insisting on technological, media, and social elements, as well as the historical context associated with the object studied. It is important to consider the content of the analyzed artifact, its meaning, and how this content is used (Gumbrecht, 2003). Intermediality, in some way, takes place between media and can't be confused with interartiality. The latter is being limited to the reconstruction of artistic links:

The sustained success and growing international recognition of the concept of intermediality, therefore, point less to new types of problems per se than (at least potentially) to new ways of solving problems, new possibilities for presenting and thinking about them, and to new, or at least to different views on medial border-crossing and hybridization ; in particular, they point to a heightened awareness of the materiality of artistic and of cultural practices in general. (Rajewski, 2005, pp. 43-44)

Rajewski (2005) explains that intermediality is "more widely applicable than previous used concepts, opening up for relating the most varied of disciplines" (p. 44). Intermedial analyses allow to understand how aesthetic experiences are used to connect different media together. Each medium uses a specific language and interacts with others in order to reach a consistent and understandable result. Each medium does not exist "beside" but "with" other different media discourses. Krämer (2003) considers that "[i]ntermediality is an epistemological condition of media-recognition [Medienerkenntnis]" (p. 82) while Müller (2000) explains about the conditions to become an intermedia:

A media product becomes intermedia when it transposes the multimedia side by side, the media quotations system in a conceptual complicity whose aesthetic ruptures and stratifications open other ways to experience. Then rebuilding intermedia relations is one of the interests of science and the media and semiotics history. (Müller, 2000, p. 113)

The purpose of this paper is to analyze the relationship of two characters through the scope of intermediality. Knowing that media discourses interactions can allow the player to live powerful and sensitive narrative experiences, we will try to observe how game designers choose to put all of these intermedial interactions together.

James Sunderland and Eddie Dombrowski, protagonists from the survival horror *Silent Hill 2* (Konami, 2001) want, at first, to help each other in a dark world where their most hidden secrets will be exposed and oppose them. So how can two characters show us emotions, narrative situations that make them change throughout their journey? All of this is being represented by the experience of the player. In addition to these two characters, we will also take a look at other characters in order to compare their representation. According to Gaudreault and Marion (2002), "a good understanding of a medium [...] entails understanding its relationship to other media: it is through intermediality, through a concern with the intermedial, that a medium is understood" (pp. 15-16).

The intermediality can be defined as a communicative-semiotic concept based on the combination of (at least) two media. There is no clear definition of the intermediality phenomenon among academics. However, it is still useful as an axis of relevance and often means the use of different points of view (Besson, 2014) in order to perform intermedial analysis. In this paper, we will refer to:

- **The "Co-Presence":** We will be looking for elements occurring during the cutscenes introducing James and Eddie. Synergy of all the media (video game as well as images, music and text composing it) through intermediality is essential.
- **The "Transfer":** We will identify some cultural references that move from one medium to another. The analysis is about some "prior or contemporaneous elements that could be used (consciously or not) when creating" (Besson, 2014) the cultural object.
- **The "Emergence":** We will try to notice the medium specificities and how they are used. In our case: how video games develop narratives?

INTERDISCIPLINARY ANALYSIS OF *SILENT HILL 2*

James and Eddie's Background, the Co-Presence at Work

As James Sunderland explores Silent Hill, we discover many monsters and some human people. All these human characters are sharing their doubts about the ghost town of Silent Hill. James will meet Pyramid Head, a creature with what seems to be a human body and a huge iron mask (shaped like a pyramid). It looks like this Pyramid head is chasing after the people entering or living in the city. Not long after that James meets Eddie Dombrowski for the first time. When the player enters the apartment 101, we can hear some vomiting noises that guide us to the bathroom where Eddie is standing over the toilet. The first cutscene shows Eddie's back as if we were looking at him through James' eyes. We see a young man untidy and sweaty. Eddie quickly notices that someone is here. At that moment, Eddie looks briefly at James then avoids his stare, as if he was ashamed or wanted to hide a secret. James' flashlight lights up Eddie in the unsanitary bathroom, revealing an unpleasant situation but also a new character.

While Eddie starts feeling sick again, he starts to proclaim his innocence without introducing himself. James does not understand what he is talking about and cannot get a clear explanation at this point of the game. James introduces himself and calmly interrogates Eddie. We learn that Eddie previously denied being behind killing the man that James found in the kitchen of the apartment. Eddie also answers that he does not know about Pyramid Head. However he says that he saw strange monsters that frightened him and are the reason why he has been hiding since.

Even if James asks for more (the player can do it with the action command), Eddie seems unable to answer any more about the mysteries of Silent Hill. During this conversation, James tries to reassure the young Eddie. James is always standing in the shadows; Eddie sits on the ground to vomit.

James can be seen as a "protector" for Eddie by giving him advice. James gives the impression that he "dominates" Eddie, being in a better shape than him but also because of his posture. Eddie is on his knees while James is standing. However, James does not try to take advantage of this situation.

During the discussion between them, we can notice that the camera first stands behind James' shoulder and later next to Eddie to do a reverse shot (the player is thus a mere spectator, having no control over it). So they always share the frame which shows that they face the same troubles in Silent Hill. Furthermore, in agreement with the dirty and strange aesthetics of the city, camera angles are used in a particular way so the players can experience some kind of uneasiness: backwards shots with slow twisting motion and static shots where James is not shown vertically but still leaning (while standing).

We hardly see the characters' faces. We first look at James' back and Eddie has his face buried in the toilet or too far from the camera to be clearly seen. Yet in the final shot of the scene, we can see James' face thanks to his flashlight while Eddies head remains in the shadows. This is the end of the conversation where James gives advice to Eddie and asks him to be careful.

The sound atmosphere is very quiet throughout the scene. The initial meeting is silent in order to highlight Eddie's vomiting sounds. Once the discussion starts, we hear a mysterious melodic phrase. Thus, the listener does not perceive the logic of the musical discourse, which gives the scene a sense of instability. This kind of dizziness is confirmed by the intrusion of distant industrial percussions.

After this scene, and several hours wandering in Silent Hill, James finds Eddie in an abandoned cafeteria. James uses his flashlight and reveals, once again, Eddie sitting against a wall, carrying a revolver in his right hand. It is finally the opportunity to distinctly see his face. A close-up shows Eddie with a disturbing smile on his face when he says: "Killing a person is not big deal. Just put the gun to the head ... pow!"

The only sound heard, very low, is some kind of siren sound: two notes on a minor third interval, which is close to French firemen (second major) or Japanese ambulances (major third). This is probably a hint to warn the player of dangers and injuries to come.

Shocked by Eddies speech, James asks him for explanations. Eddie justifies his murder (supposedly the corpse near him in the cutscene) claiming he was forced to do it. However, he immediately contradicts himself when saying "I did not do anything!"

The next scenes are the beginning of the split between James and Eddie. Eddie is getting more incoherent and aggressive towards James. The young man continues to shock James when he states "He was making fun of me with his eyes". James refutes his argument and Eddie decides to confront James. James only uses words but the player can feel the tension growing between the two characters.

Eddie lets his hate explode against those who mocked him in the past. Seeing James speechless, the young man laughs and invokes a joke claiming he killed nobody. The conversation ends with Eddie leaving in a rush pretending he has something to do with an enigmatic smile on his face. Eddie's face right after that shows his desire for revenge against his bullies and to forget the naive and innocent character that the player was used to seeing. Not able to deal like he wanted with James yet, but not far from using something other than words.

Finally, the player manages to meet Eddie in some kind of a cold room with green lights as a final stage for Eddie, and many corpses on the ground. James immediately requests explanations and can only face an angry Eddie who unleashes his fury in a long monologue punctuated by many different camera shots. The process is also used to put emphasis on specific words and feelings.

Eddie explains that no matter if some people are "smart", "dumb", "ugly", or "pretty", death removes all differences. These four words are punctuated by four different camera angles. The rhythmic structure of this sentence also provides support to some statements, including the last two sentences: "It's all the same once you're dead," and "a corpse cannot laugh". We can suppose that the musical ambience was composed to fit as a "punctuation" for Eddies sentences and macabre thoughts.

The place is an allegory of Eddie's personality; a cold room symbolizing his lack of empathy. On the other hand, pieces of meat represent Eddie's past and his true inner self, a memento of the suffering he has been through and also caused since he came to Silent Hill. Eddie finally assumes his urges; he wants to punish those who made fun of him.

After Eddies statement James asks him if he'd lost his mind. From this point, the musical atmosphere follows the evolution of Eddie's madness. We can hear a single sound resonating, played at the same time as crescendo-decrescendo loops of other sounds. This pattern repeats itself until Eddie says: "From now on, if anyone makes fun of me, I'll kill him. Just like that." Metallic sounds are added to the previous loop and leaves no doubt to the player: a fight can't be avoided. This is the first time, besides the cutscenes, where the player is going to "interact" with Eddie. The situation gives another hint to the player. Eddie is leaving the room down a one way path after his warning. Following will mean that, as a player, you have no choice but to kill him to continue the game.

At the end of the battle, James regrets what he had to do. He killed a human being and he is shocked. But is it really the first time? Eddie is perhaps like "a photo negative". He reveals and triggers something. Finally, through the music, the narration and this specific game mechanic (a "boss" fight), Eddie proves to be an "incarnated" element of intermediality. His character makes James (the player) experiences emotions such as doubt, surprise and even regret. Eddie is a way for the players (and the people analyzing the game) to realize the coherence of Silent Hill as a whole, a plot, a city, a place that can invade characters and even a game system.

We saw that intermediality in itself can lead to multiple effects on a game and, by extension, on players. We will now see what can happen when intermediality crosses the path of social and cultural references.

Intermediality and Socio-Cultural Transfers

The term "representation" refers to the construction of meaning through symbols and images. As a form of media widely distributed in our society, video games have an impact on our conscience and how the modern world can be shaped by these representations, how they are shared by players. Since the early 2000s, transdisciplinary studies dealing with the topic of representations are trying to put video games in their wider social context as do Alexander R. Galloway, Gonzalo Frasca, Jeffrey H. Goldstein, Jesper Juul, Manthos Santorineos, and Nefeli Dimitriadi.

Thus socio-cultural transfers also act from the society to the game. Developers create a game based on their own experience and culture. By doing so, despite the increasing globalization of the growing gaming market, some works retain a socio-cultural "touch" specific to the country where they were made. In this "global culture climate" socio-cultural transfer can be considered as a significant element in intermediality, and of course in video games.

The developers from the Silent Team (the staff behind the game) created Silent Hill as a North American rural town. Its toponymy and topography are inspired by cities from the United States. With the first sequence of the game happening in abandoned public restrooms on the outskirts of the city, pictures from American road movies can immediately come to mind.

The game takes place in a US kind of city but Japanese socio-cultural codes remain in the psychological treatment of the characters, especially Eddie Dombrowski. Usually gentle and shy, he becomes uncontrollable when he is angry. This character is enigmatic and the player asks himself the same question endlessly throughout the game: what is he doing in Silent Hill?

Eddie is the result of exclusion and revenge, mocked for his ugliness and awkwardness, and rejected by most of the people. As a characteristic of anti-hero (but can also be found in heroes as well), exclusion is recurrent in the Japanese popular culture such as manga just like Masashi Kishimoto's *Naruto*. In Japanese manga, characters overcome the criticisms and try to prove they can find a way through or submit to the temptation of vengeance.

This topic implicitly refers to the *ijime* phenomenon in Japan. This word refers to the victims of bullying in their daily lives, mostly in school and work (Daste, 2013). According to Etienne Barral (1999), this phenomenon is an adolescent rite of initiation necessary for psychic structuring of the individual. This daily persecution is used to test the potential of the adolescent. Overcoming these tests prove he can be part of the group (Miyamoto, 2001).

This "ritual" is related to the Japanese society and is a marker of its culture. It does not only exist in Japan, however it seems to be exacerbated in the assimilative society. Moreover, Barral (1999) believes that *ijime*, in Japan, is a mirror of the relationships governing the adult world in the childhood social context.

Eddie embodies this phenomenon because he is going through this kind of transition; a ritual from childhood to adulthood (he is twenty years old). Eddie is insulted and harassed by his entourage (represented in the game by Laura) and goes from submission to revenge.

We saw previously that Eddie first reveals his "true inner self" when the player can see his face. In Japanese culture, eyes are the mirror of the soul. Used in manga, the emphasis on the eyes helps to represent many emotions (anger, sadness, joy) and is not only inspired by occidental fictions:

This is a mistake: faces in manga do not aspire to look "occidental", no more than Japanese. Their function was perfectly explained by Roland Barthes when he was referring to white made-up faces of the Japanese theater: The face is only: "the thing to write" ["la chose à écrire" in French]. Minimalist faces from shônen and shojo manga were designed to facilitate, as much as possible, the graphical expression of feelings and emotions put into their huge round eyes. (Bouissou, 2014)

So if we consider popular culture in Japan and the way to share emotions through it, the topic of the face is the common ground to consider. Historically, the manga, although taken itself in a cultural legacy, is the best media to illustrate this point. Readers of manga outside of Japan often ask why characters look like occidental people (the same goes with video games). This is what we tried to show with the previous quote of Bouissou.

This inspiration, coming from manga and animes, that Japanese video games originally borrowed from its origins in the concept of "Media Mix" is also close to another one developed by Henry Jenkins (2008) in *Convergence Culture*. However, the media mix has its own cultural particularities:

Electronic gaming in Japan needs to be understood as one component of a broader media ecology that includes anime, manga, trading card games, toys, and character merchandise. I borrow the native industry term, "media mix," to describe this linked character-based media. (Ito, 2006, p.2)

Even if we try to compare it to huge success using Media Mix such as the *Pokemon* or *.Hack* series, we are not on the same level of "convergence" described previously (Ito, 2006) ; nevertheless it can explain how manga, animes, and video games are working together, even in survival horror games.

Now that *Silent Hill 2* cultural references from animes, manga and Japanese culture in general have been discussed, we will try to provide the context in which the game was released regarding the chronology of the survival horror genre. Not only to put it on a timeline but to demonstrate that there are social cultural transfers at play in the story of survival horror games itself.

A complete list will be too long and incomplete so we will focus on the games that met critical acclaim, public support and mentioned in scholarly articles. We will describe the main feature that characterized each of these games and what was their addition to the survival horror genre.

- *Alone in the Dark* **(1992) :** Puzzles to solve, weapon breaking after some time, using light source, character selection (one man, one woman with minor changes in the game), dynamic camera changes.
- *D* **(1995) :** Main (and only playable) character is a woman, first person exploration, use of FMV (full motion video) and multiple endings.
- *Resident Evil / Bio Hazard* **(1996) :** Choice of the character with an important impact on the difficulty, ability to mix items together, minor changes in the story depending on your choices and actions, and limited saves. First time the category "Survival Horror" (created by Capcom) is mentioned.
- *Silent Hill 1***:** Released three years later, in 1999, and *Silent Hill 2* in 2001. At this time, *Resident Evil* became the symbol of survival horror. However, what made the difference with *Silent Hill* was how the players experienced fear.

Resident Evil, with its cinematographic approach, was closer to "the jump scare" kind of fear. *Silent Hill* wanted to lose the players, to make them feel disoriented, with or without a weapon.

But all of the aforementioned games, besides *Alone in the Dark*, share one common point. They were all created in Japan, by Japanese teams. It was a hegemony that lasted until the end of the 2000s with games such as the *Fatal Frame* series (beginning in 2001) or the *Forbidden Siren* series (beginning in 2003). This situation won't change before new major games such as *Dead Space* (2008) or *Alan Wake* (2010) and a "rebalancing" between survival horror games coming from Japan and the rest of the world.

In fact, even when Japanese horror games were dominating, the games could be identified both as Japanese due to element coming from Japanese folklore (*Siren, Fatal Frame*) and as western productions (*Resident Evil, Silent Hill*).

These games still share the fact that they are "cultural mirrors" (Pruett, 2010) of both "occidental" and "oriental" horror. However Japanese survival horror games are maybe more appealing to players because people outside of Japan are less familiar with the references coming from this country.

So this is proving that, as players, we tend to need some keys and references to not be lost, which is, paradoxically, a key to some players' pleasure. All of this being possible, in general, thanks to intermediality and sociocultural transfers. A loss of bearings that we can also find in cinema:

We find ourselves strangers in a strange land, unable to guess at where the narrative might be heading, unfamiliar with the conventions that the author is employing. Without the comfort of our usual cultural signals we feel out of control, and in that state the narrative can wield much power over us. The most effective Western horror films achieve the same sense of unease with innovative cinematography and surprising stories, but foreign horror films benefit from it almost automatically. (Pruett, 2010, p.12)

In this part, we saw that it was worth noting that in the dynamics of intermediality and how they are connected to the roots of Japanese culture (via media mix) and to the survival horror genre itself, especially in socio-cultural transfers. Being totally aware of them or not, the player can experience fear or even some kind of dizziness, close to the *ilinx* (Caillois, 1992), another kind of playful experience and pleasure.

For now, let's come back to the analysis of characters in *Silent Hill 2*. At this point, we think that it is important to also pay attention to the female characters in the game. There are four of them so they are a (numerical) majority. Before we go any further, lets introduce them:

- Mary Sheperd-Sunderland is the late wife of the main protagonist James Suderland. She is the reason why James came to Silent Hill after he received a letter from beyond the grave, signed by her.
- Angela Oroso meets James in Silent Hill cemetery right after the beginning of the game. She is looking for her mother. She looks very confused and scared. Her lack of self-esteem can be related to her family's background.
- Maria is described as the opposite of Mary according to the game manual. She alternates between moments of cheering and others where she strongly blames James for not taking care of her.
- Laura is an 8 years old girl who met Mary at the hospital during her last days. Laura dislikes James because he rarely visited Mary during her illness. Laura seems to be the strongest link between the "outside world" and Silent Hill.

Even if this article is focused on intermediality through two male characters, it is interesting to remind the lack of women (and minorities) in video games, a fact known by people from the industry and by the players as well.

This reality is not without effect on games in the making and discourses about them. Basically, representations of characters, other than dominant norms, continue to be an issue. But they are more discussed these last years (Shaw, 2015). Some games now include less stereotyped female characters: Lara Croft in the last *Tomb Raider* reboot, *Bayonetta*, and Nilin, from *Remember Me*, to name a few in AAA productions. These characters can be main or secondary characters, including *Silent Hill 3* whose heroine is a 17 year old girl.

However, after our analysis of James in the light of intermediality, we discovered a male character with various facets, Brave at times but also afraid, caring but also, in a clumsy way, able to fight and to deal with weapons, James is the opposite of the classical video game male hero. A cliché often theorized as "militarized masculinity" (Williams, 1994), referring to a white, heterosexual, cisgendered male in his 30s, a cliché that can, of course, also be found with characters in blockbuster movies and some TV shows. If James shows that some male characters in video games can be something else, can we say the same about women characters with the same intermedial analysis we did for him and Eddie?

We stressed that manga, animations and video games produced in Japan share common roots especially when it comes to the depiction of faces and eyes of a character. Even if *Silent Hill 2* protagonists are closer to reality (with photorealistic graphics) the dedication to faces has the same importance. For example, every 3D model (for the human characters) in *Silent Hill 2* were done thanks to motion capture, except for the faces. Sato Takayoshi (character designer and designer for the cutscenes) wanted the animation to be hand animated (sketches and 3D models) because the motion capture, at that time, couldn't allow some expressions and emotions. Sato Takayoshi (2001) even said he "couldn't trust the motion capture system for the faces". The Japanese crew, Team Silent, seems to stick to the old saying "the face is the mirror of the soul". A philosophy that can be found in Japanese history and its cultural legacy.

Faces in Japan are often related to emotions and emotions to sexual pleasure (Daste, 2015). However, this pleasure is essentially male-orientated in *Silent Hill 2* and in Japanese history. It is called the *honne* (本音). It refers to the pleasure, for some Japanese men, when they surprise a woman during suffering. During the Heian era, in Japan, it was like seeing a woman's "naked face". This emotion on the face must remain private as opposed to *tatamae* (建前), which represents the adequate behavior (in society).

Maybe the best illustration is the cutscene between James and Maria in jail. She talks to James and makes him more confused than ever. He wonders if he is talking to Maria or his late wife Mary. The change of tone and expression on the face of Maria/Mary is probably the reason why this is the most cherished scene for gamers and staff members. Suguru Murakoshi (2001), drama director in charge of the dramatic sections and movies of *Silent Hill 2*, explains how he perceived it:

My favorite scene within the game is where James and Maria talk in jail. […] you can feel the tension there and the unique strangeness we implemented since the facial expression and mannerism are unique and quite succinct from each other.

His description is close to the concept of *onnagata*, where male actors try to capture the essence of "femininity" and incarnate women on stage (Giard, 2006).

Ultimately, we can see the concept of *honne* in *Silent Hill 2* as a reflection of transfer in intermediality; it makes cultural allusions converge in the same game. Nonetheless it emphasizes how key creatives in the industry are mostly men. We can ask ourselves if their discourses, when creating female characters, are not only gender stereotypes reducing the potentialities of intermediality. We will come back to this later in this chapter and to how it articulates with the notion of emergence in game mechanics. But for now, to explain the "emergence", lets focus on James and Eddies relationship one last time.

Intermediality and Video Games: What Specificities Can Emerge through Game Mechanics and Rules?

Dominic Arsenault (2006) considers two kinds of stories in video games. The embedded narrative is provided by designers and the video game narrative differs because it depends on the player's actions and choices. The cutscenes within the game are part of the embedded narrative because they are designed by the developers and start at specific moments. However, what makes the particularity of video games is interactivity; what the player can do with the virtual universe. The player acts with the world through an avatar: James Sunderland in *Silent Hill 2*. The player is the hero and the hero is the game. The narrative development is easier and allows the player to focus on the basics of the scenario. This interactivity helps to create a narrativity.

During *gameplay* sequences, some puzzles allow us to understand Eddie and to learn more about him. Each time we meet him we can notice some elements related to food and death:

• There is a corpse in the apartment's fridge at the first meeting.
• Eddie eats a pizza in the bowling alley when Laura says he is a murderer.
• When he reveals his true nature in the cafeteria of the prison, there is a corpse on a table.
• Finally, he dies in a room full of pieces of meat shaped like human bodies.

These two topics, food and death close to the character's nature, are revealed during cutscenes. But the game also gives information about Eddie in some interactive phases.

During his trip to downtown, James has to explore Silent Hills prison. In the execution chamber, the player can discover three hanging ropes. This is a reference to the three souls tortured by their crimes (James, Eddie and Angela) and a riddle to solve. The player can do it by inserting three plates representing each character. Each plate is composed of an Aztec icon and a clue about the crime. There is the "oppressor", the "seductress" and the "gluttonous pig":

- The "oppressor" shows Tlazolteotl, the Aztec goddess of lust associated with sexuality. It represents a man, refering to James and his frustration because of Mary's disease.
- The "seductress" represents Mayahuel, goddess of fertility, abundance and the Agave (a plant used for alcohol production). This is about Angela, her father's alcoholism and the reasons of his murder.
- The "gluttonous pig" looks like Tlahuizcalpantecuhtli, evil and dangerous deity trying to put down the sun. Representing the Aztec god with a pig's head is an explicit reference to the relationship that Eddie has with food and his violence triggered by his past as a bully.

This example has two levels of narration because of information perceived by the player (extradiegetic) and the avatar (diegetic). The riddle sends James to his own mistakes that he tries to hide. Therefore, it kind of explains - metaphorically - the causes of Angela and Eddies torments. The player can also find information about these two characters but the puzzle gives another indication. It extends the protagonist's story and also helps to know better James Sunderland. On one hand, the diegetic message is used in James' memory. On the other hand, the extradiegetic message is useful for the player to get better insight about James' amnesia.

Characters in video games are evolving, like in other fictions, into architectures. In video games, these models are 3D rendered but we must also consider their impact on gamers. Especially in games with a strong artistic direction such as *Silent Hill 2*, Masahi Tsuboyama, art director, said in a making-of video dedicated to *Silent Hill 2*, in 2001: "I wanted to create something that would really disturb the game players whilst attracting them". This quote is very close to the notion of "painful architecture" mentioned by Mario Gerosa (2008):

Our architect friend Cezary Fish, long resident of Second Life, which true identity is the polish composer Cezary Ostrowski, told us one day, speaking of creations from Second Life, about painful architecture. [...] These videoludical architectures are similar to the images of the Gestalt psychology: they give landmarks to complete with your own sensitivity and they dont show the architecture in its wholeness. So it turns out that the idea of a necessary achievement, an incomplete architecture where an absence, must be filled by the gamer. It is also an interactive architecture because it implies the need to solve the puzzle permanently. (Gerosa, 2008, p. 47)

Gerosa also mentions a special "genre" where these architectures can be found:

Interaction goes with theatricalization, another fundamental element for the videoludical architecture where you can find the best examples in video games tainted with mystery or a feeling of fear. Theatricalization that generates claustrophobia, where the architectural walks [...] and fear helps to draw spaces. Interaction between architecture and the visitor is quite common. It happens in the games S.T.A.L.K.E.R.Shadow of Chernobyl, Farenheit, and Silent Hill 4, where landscapes and rooms are an architectural projection of the gamers fears. (Gerosa, 2008, p. 49, own translation)

So with *Silent Hill*, the player faces both the main characters amnesia and a perturbing place where he must find his way through. Regarding this "painful architecture", another essential element in *Silent Hill 2* – and the whole series – is the Otherworld:

One of the most distinctive traits of the Silent Hill series is its use of the Otherworld, a bleak industrial version of reality where night persists indefinitely and rusted metal and barbed wire are core components of most architecture. [...]

The Otherworld is one of the many original ideas that sets the Silent Hill series apart from its competitors. The concept has everything you could want in a game mechanic: it fits the aesthetic and narrative goals of the series, it provides a method for pacing the player and steadily increasing the tension invoked by the plot, and it is mutable enough to serve very different purposes across a number of games. (Pruett, 2007)

The Otherworld is also a way to experience the "limits" of the game. Instead of using well known game and level design tricks such as "invisible walls" to limits player movement to a specific area, some parts of the city disappear and others just come ex nihilo forcing the player to cope with his/her fear:

At the plot level, the hero/heroine investigates a hostile environment where he/she will be trapped (a building or a town) in order either to uncover the causes of strange and horrible events (Alone in the Dark, Resident Evil, Siren) or to find and rescue a loved one from an evil force [...]. At the action level, in a third-person perspective, the gamer has to find clues, gather objects (you cannot do without keys) and solve puzzles. (Perron, 2004, p. 2)

The assertion of Perron is right, which leads to another game mechanic: *ransacking*. But first of all let's define it:

Ransacking encourages the player to think about his environment as a puzzle rather than as a real place. We're checking mental checklists as we clean rooms out, taking note of rooms we'll need to return to, maintaining a ledger of completing and outstanding tasks. (Pruett, 2015)

Ransacking isn't a game mechanic specific to survival horror. For instance, in point and click games, you have to check where all the items that you will need to solve puzzles later are. In survival you keep the same attitude but the behavior of the player can be different. Cautious player will stock a maximum of ammunitions and spend more time doing it than daredevils, and maybe later on the cautious one will have the upper hand. However, this isn't guaranteed because it depends on the skills of the players. Even with a lot of weapons, a player with poor dexterity can still have a hard time (and vice versa).

Whatever the players choose, they need to be careful about their progression, and to do so they will have to check their inventory. Pause the game and take a breath for instance. Or to be curious about items found with no apparent immediate use.

So in some way, the inventory in the pause menu of *Silent Hill 2* can be seen as an architecture, like we saw with Gerosa, not to be considered as a level design *per se*, but more like a link the player creates while playing the game. The inventory is the place you go to equip yourself with weapons, heal yourself, check and use items for puzzles and read their description.

Basically, it is a "special place". These are the exact same words introducing the game: the letter that James late wife leaves is telling him that his goal is "our special place". The inventory is a place with its own codes, the same way survival horror games have their own codes. You have to come back to the inventory, in general, when you play these kinds of games in order to survive. It even goes beyond these features because the time spent by the player in the inventory can modify the ending of the game. So the inventory, gameplay-wise, is central.

But the inventory can also be considered as a real "painful and emotional architecture", in an intermedial way, because the player is interacting with it in numerous ways. First the inventory gives visual feedback about what kind of items you are carrying and the documents and letters you picked up. When you enter the inventory, a paused and miniaturized representation of the actual game screen (like a photograph) remains in a corner. This photography is colored. If your health status is very good the picture will get a green filter. On the contrary, it becomes red in the opposite status (close to the death of your avatar).

About sound, we can observe that switching between items, using and combining them, produces sounds. The musical ambiance and sounds you hear just before entering in the inventory is still in the background but less loud. A final interaction, musical-wise, is the way you can use your radio by turning it on or off. The radio is given at the beginning of the game and is a signature item of the *Silent Hill* series. It allows the player to know if enemies are close: the radio sound gets louder as the enemy approaches. By default, the radio is turned on but you can choose to turn it off. By doing so, enemies will not spot you because of the sound but the same goes for the player.

A last parallel we can draw between the inventory and our intermedial analysis in the game could be how the player creates a special link with this "place". The gamer is almost creating a second game in this "inventory-place" with its own rules and strong feelings he or she agrees to participate. In his observation about cybererotic spaces, Johann Chateau-Canguilhem (2013) compares the game space with another codified space:

It is no accident that the expression "game space", in the BDSM (Bondage Discipline Sado Masochism) culture, refers to a place breaking with the daily routine, "well limited and regulated". The game space focuses, above all, on the body of the dominated person. The body becomes the place of the action since the dominant uses him/her as an object and exercise an action on him/her. [...] In other words, taking possession of the slave is taking possession of its territories and especially his/her most intimate territories: the body and soul. (p. 119)

The inventory in *Silent Hill 2* can even be seen as a contract between the player and the game: "I agree to play this game and I know (both consciously and subconsciously) that the inventory will be a place I will have to deal with".

This is what each player has to deal with when playing *Silent Hill 2*. Interacting with objects and playing with the limits of the Otherworld. But let's come back to the point we introduced previously: protagonists and especially female characters.

Inventory and Characters: How Game Mechanics and Narration Reunite via Intermediality

We previously mentioned the importance of women characters in *Silent Hill 2* via the notion of transfer in intermediality. We will now observe how intermediality makes the best of these characters but without being reciprocal or even by maintaining stereotypes such as gender roles.

Women in *Silent Hill 2* have subtle roles but most of them are not as consistent as male characters. When men are suffering but following a goal leading them to scenes with both speech and/or action, women are reduced to passive archetypes: a shadow (Angela), a mirror (Maria) or just etheral voices (Mary). Qualities such as innocence (Laura), sensitivity (Marie/Maria) and discretion (Angela) seem to define these characters specifically. They are also devoted to James but in a way that makes them depend on him. But the characters are not the only way to verify this hypothesis. The symbolism and the gameplay are also supporting this argument in *Silent Hill 2*.

For instance, the light is one of the most iconic item in the *Silent Hill* series and even in the survival horror genre. With the radio, the lamp is an essential item in the game, especially during a first run. Both are symbols of helpful items for the player in his experience. While you get the radio when you meet your first opponent, with no clue regarding its "sex" or "gender", the lamp is less equivocal. James picks the lamp on a dress that seems to be the one his late wife was wearing before her death (it can be seen during the game's introduction). So if we try a first interpretation we can see it as "a light in the darkness", a supporting item in the nightmare of Silent Hill, a way for James "to cope with" the death of his wife with a memento, an icon representing "care," to sum it up. However, this analysis seems flawed if we consider that all the women in *Silent Hill 2* are depicted as victims.

Even Laura, as a child, suffers because of the adults (the scene where James remembers and reveals that he killed his wife is heartbreaking for her). It can relate to the *honne* we saw earlier and also the idea of painful and emotional architecture we mentioned beforehand. This hypothesis also includes the way the archetype of each woman is represented, during cutscenes in particular, so as passive characters, not playable and with no action scenes.

Angela is maybe the most obvious example of *honne* even if she loses her mannerism at the end of the game when she accepts her condition. We can suppose that her condition is to be (and stay) a victim in the social order, switching from *honne* to *tatamae*, an adequate face in harmony with (Japanese) society. The social order being incarnated by a man: James.

Angela disappears right after this scene in an ambiguous way, accepting her fate and also asking James if he can save her. Musical-wise, the scene starts with metallic sounds like clinging metal bars and fades out as soon as James enters the room where the cutscene is triggered. Then the *Laura theme – reprise* is played during the whole scene. Angela is one avatar of James dealing with the death of his wife, a shadow, accepting her fate.

Mary and Maria can of course be considered as the two sides of the same medal, the first being reality and how James denied it, the second looking more like the fantasy realm and how James copes with it. Many interpretations, written by players discussing the game (some of them can be found on topics related to the game on forums at gamefaqs.com), are speaking of Maria as an avatar of James' sexual frustration regarding his late wife. We can see Maria as a succubus figure because every time she dies or disappears, James is getting closer to the truth: the fact that he killed his wife. Other people analyze it based on a phallic symbolism: Maria being transpierced by the spear of a Pyramid Head each time she gets killed. When she is alive, Maria's first and most important scenes deal with her body. At the first encounter with James she states that she is alive and lets him check by grabbing his hand and putting it, we can suppose, near her chest. The camera angle plays with this ambiguity so we cannot be sure but James obviously feels uncomfortable as he steps back. Maria is symbolically a "mirror" for James. At the end of the game, what happens to Maria can only be perceived as a reflection of James' behavior and, by extension, of the player's behavior.

Mary is more a lighthouse to James. She helps James - the player – to find his way as much as she confuses him. The first time James gets the radio, we can hear her voice during the cutscene. A way to give hope, even when we know (James and the player) that she is dead.

The emblematic scene of the lighthouse is also the best metaphor for James. The player must get in a rowboat and access James and Mary's secret place. The only landmark is a blurry view of a lighthouse in the horizon. The last song before James finds Mary and confronts the last boss is the same as Laura: *Theme of Laura – reprise*.

Finally, Laura is the avatar of James innocence as we said before, the link between the nightmarish Silent Hill and the "outside". Like all the other women characters, Laura has a binary behavior alternating between aggressive and a more caring behavior regarding James.

We tried, with this last part, to show that intermediality is also at work with the female characters in *Silent Hill 2*. Musically, visually and gameplay-wise, the characters add to the tension and the quality of the whole game. However, we also saw how intermediality is limited to the sole scope of a heterosexual binarism in *Silent Hill 2* and in other productions. Will a broader use of other genders and minorities in video games improve, or at least change, the potentialities of intermediality?

CONCLUSION

Through these short analyses, we tried to expose some significant processes to create emotions and meanings in *Silent Hill 2*. That video game shows some interesting results; maybe because the Silent Team worked a lot to create a powerful and horrific experience.

The horror stands in the pictures, the situations, the city itself and in the *gameplay*. It seems that every detail is thought to be a part of the whole experience. It seems difficult to play the game with one element missing. If you shut the sound off, you miss important information like your enemies' situation. If you do not read the texts, you cannot solve the many riddles and if you simply do not look at the screen... *Silent Hill 2* is a game where each media is important. Many games allow players to shut off the music, for example, but the Silent Team made a good use of what the video game's specificities could offer them when putting it together.

Even if the creators talk about their work, we wonder how much they understand the final product. How much do they understand the intermediality phenomenon? Do they even know and consider it, with another name perhaps? In the previous part, we were asking if developers are aware of the cultural models and use them in their productions.

But intermediality pushes further this work by considering, for example, why the Silent Hill's fog is so important. This is not just a way to scare players by reducing their view; it was also a way to hide the console limitations. The game could not show the whole town, in that way some parts of the city just appeared suddenly when the player was approaching. The creators added a fog to hide this, but it was not, in the first place, designed to scare.

Intermediality can gather many research fields allowing taking a more accurate look upon cultural objects. Video games, as a medium, are a very interesting subject due to their association with pop culture and interactivity. Because of their place in the society, video games can be considered as a way to look into the souls of their users and creators.

REFERENCES

Arsenault, D. (2006). *Jeux et enjeux du récit vidéoludique: La narration dans le jeu video*. (Master thesis). Université de Montréal, Montréal, Canada.

Baral, E. (1999). *Otaku: Les enfants du virtuel*. Paris, France: Denoël.

Besson, R. (2014). Prolégomènes pour une définition de lintermédialité. *Cinémadoc*. Retrieved June 13, 2015, from http://culturevisuelle.org/cinemadoc/2014/04/29/prolegomenes/

Bouissou, J. M. (2014). *Manga. History and universe of Japanese comic books*. Paris, France: Picquier poche.

Caillois, R. (1992). *Les jeux et les hommes: Le masque et le vertige*. Paris, France: Gallimard.

Chateau-Canguilhem, J. (2013). Corps et espaces cybereérotiques. *Hermès, La Revue*, (69), 116-120.

Daste, S. (2013). Introduction à létude de la culture otaku. *Omnsh*. Retrieved June 9, 2015, from http://www.omnsh.org/ressources/441/introduction-letude-de-la-culture-otaku

Daste, S. (2015). *Espaces de fictions générés par les nouveaux médias issus des cultures générationnelles otaku et geek: influences notées dans lart contemporain et ma pratique*. (Unpublished doctoral dissertation). Université Paris-8, Paris, France.

Gaudreault, A., & Marion, P. (2002). The cinema as a model for the genealogy of media. *Convergence*, *8*(4), 12–18.

Gerosa, M. (2008). Architectures émotionnelles et douloureuses. *Médiamorphoses*, (22), 47-54.

Giard, A. (2006). *Limaginaire érotique japonais*. Paris, France: Albin Michel.

Gumbrecht, H. U. (2003). Why intermediality – if at all?, *Intermédialités*, (2), 173-178.

Higgins, D. (1967). Statement on intermedia. In W. Vostell (Ed.), *Dé-coll/age (décollage)*, 6. Frankfurt, Germany: Typos Verlag/Something Else Press.

Ito, M. (2006). *A draft of a position paper for the Girls n games workshop and conference*. University of California, Los Angeles. Retrieved December 12, 2015 from http://www.itofisher.com/mito/ito.girlsgames.pdf

Jenkins, H. (2008). *Convergence culture: Where old and new media collide*. New York, NY: NYU Press.

Krämer, S. (2003). Erfüllen medien eine konstitutionsleistung? Thesen über die rolle medientheoretischer erwägungen beim philosophieren. In S. Münker, A. Roesler, & M. Sandbothe (Eds.), *Medienphilosophie. Beiträge zur klärung eines begriffs* (pp. 78–90). Frankfurt am Main, Germany: Fischer.

Kristeva, J. (1974). *La révolution du langage poétique: Lavant-garde à la fin du XIXe siècle, Lautréamont et Mallarmé*. Paris, France: Seuil.

Miyamoto, M. (2001). *Japon, société camisole de force*. Paris, France: Philippe Picquier.

Müller, J. E. (2000). Lintermédialité, une nouvelle approche interdisciplinaire: Perspectives théoriques et pratiques à lexemple de la vision de la télévision. *Cinémas: revue détudes cinématographiques, 10*(2-3).

Perron, B. (2004). *Sign of a threat: The effects of warning systems in survival horror games, first published at COSIGN 2004 14–16 September 2004*. Croatia: University of Split.

Pruett, C. (2007, December 2). *The changing utility of the Otherworld in the Silent Hill series*. Retrieved December 14, 2015, from http://horror.dreamdawn.com/?p=29211

Pruett, C. (2015, August 9). *Ransacking*. Retrieved December 14, 2015, from http://horror.dreamdawn.com/?p=14800034

Rajewsky, I. O. (2005). Intermediality, intertextuality and remediation: A literary perspective on intermediality. *Intermédialités, 6*(1), 43-64.

Vos, E. (1997). The eternal network. Mail art, intermedia semiotics, interarts studies. In U. Lagerroth, H. Lund, & E. Hedling (Eds.), *Interart poetics. Essays on the interrelations of the arts and media* (pp. 325–336). Amsterdam: Rodopi.

Williams, C. L. (1994). Militarized masculinity. *Qualitative Sociology, 17*(4), 415–422. doi:10.1007/BF02393339

KEY TERMS AND DEFINITIONS

Co-Presence (About Intermedial Analysis): The synergy of all the media.

Embedded Narrative: A narration provided by designers that players cannot interfere with.

Emergence (About Intermedial Analysis): The medium specificities and how they are used.

Honne: It refers to the pleasure experienced by some Japanese men when they surprise a woman during suffering. This facial expression must remain private.

Ijime: This word refers, in Japan, to the victims of bullying in their daily lives, mostly in school and work.

Intermediality: A communicative-semiotic concept based on the combination of (at least) two media. It can be considered as an epistemological condition of media-recognition.

Painful Architecture: Video game architectures that give landmarks to complete with your own sensitivity and don't show the architecture in its wholeness. It is also an interactive architecture because it implies the need to solve the puzzle permanently.

Transfer (About Intermedial Analysis): Cultural references that move from one medium to another.

Video Game Narrative: Narration that depends on the player's actions and choices.

Section 2
Intertextuality

Chapter 5
Gamers (Don't) Fear the Reaper:
Musical Intertextuality and Interference in Video Games

Andréane Morin-Simard
Université de Montréal, Canada

ABSTRACT

Given the pervasiveness of popular music in the contemporary media landscape, it is not unusual to find the same song in multiple soundtracks. Based on theories of intertextuality and communication, this chapter seeks to define the relationship which develops between two or more narrative and/or interactive works that share the same song, and to understand the effects of such recontextualizations on the gamer's experience. The media trajectory of Blue Öyster Cult's "Don't Fear the Reaper" is mapped as a network to categorize the many complex intersections between video games, films and television series which feature the song. Three video games are analyzed to propose that the song's previous associations with other works may positively or negatively interfere with the music's narrative and ludic functions within the game.

INTRODUCTION

As licensed popular music soundtracks have become increasingly present in video games, films and television series, it is not uncommon to find the same song featured in multiple audiovisual works. Hits from the 1960s and 1970s like "Born to Be Wild" (Steppenwolf, 1968), "In-a-gadda-da-vida" (Iron Butterfly, 1968), "Sweet Home Alabama" (Lynyrd Skynyrd, 1974), and "One Way or Another" (Blondie, 1979), among many others, live on in popular culture thanks in part to their integration in a multitude of compiled scores over the past six decades. Yet, as cases such as these abound in the contemporary media landscape, very few scholars have manifested interest in the questions this phenomenon brings to light. Is there a link to be drawn between narrative and ludic works which feature the same song? If so, is it intentional on the part of the creative instances? How can the relationship between works which "borrow" a musical piece from the vast sea of popular music be defined? And, more importantly, how can the recognition of a song in a game and the recall of its previous appearances impact the gamer's experience?

DOI: 10.4018/978-1-5225-0477-1.ch005

This chapter will propose an answer to these questions through a case study of Blue Öyster Cult's "Don't Fear the Reaper" (1976). The original recording, as well as numerous covers of the song, have appeared in more than 40 audiovisual works since 1978, including five video games. Besides the obvious music games (*Rock Band* [Harmonix Music Systems /MTV Games/Electronic Arts, 2007] and *SingStar Amped* [SCEE Studio London/Sony Computer Entertainment Europe, 2007]), "Don't Fear the Reaper" can be heard in an adventure game or "interactive movie" (*Ripper* [Take-Two Interactive Software/GameTek UK, 1996]), a driving game (*Roadkill* [Terminal Reality/Midway, 2003]), and a first-person shooter (*Prey* [Human Head Studios/2K Games, 2006]). The objective of the inquiry is twofold. First, since musical intertextuality has rarely been addressed in the context of video games, this chapter will need to adapt existing models of intertextuality in film and television and develop a theoretical framework which can account for multiple recontextualizations of popular songs in media. Second, the analysis will seek to uncover intersections between the different uses of the song and reflect on their consequences for the functioning of music in video games. Focusing mainly on the three games with a strong narrative component, this chapter will argue that the song's association with previous works may interfere with its functions for gameplay, either by preventing its intended affective "message" from getting across, or by adding on to its intended effect on the player.

POPULAR MUSIC IN VIDEO GAMES

The interactive movie *Ripper*, the first video game to feature Blue Öyster Cult's 1976 hit "Don't Fear the Reaper", was among the first generation of games to integrate original recordings of popular songs. Indeed, up until technological advancements permitted CD audio to be added to game soundtracks in the 1990s (see Collins, 2005), 8-bit and MIDI cover versions were the only way to integrate well-known popular music to the medium. It was only through melody that the player could recognize songs like Journey's "Don't Stop Believin'" (*Escape*,1981) in the Atari 2600 action game *Journey Escape* (Data Age, 1982), or Michael Jackson's "Thriller" (*Thriller*, 1983) in the beat 'em up game *Michael Jackson's Moonwalker* (Sega, 1990). MIDI versions the likes of Steppenwolf's "Born to be Wild" (*Steppenwolf*, 1968) in the racing game *Rock 'n' Roll Racing* (Silicon & Synapse/Interplay, 1993) added more instrumental texture, but they were still instrumental versions.

From 1994 onwards, integral versions of well-known songs the likes of White Zombie's "Thunder Kiss '65" (*La Sexorcisto: Devil Music, Vol. 1*, 1992), Aerosmith's "Dude (Looks Like a Lady)" (*Permanent Vacation*, 1987) and Iron Butterfly's "In-a-gadda-da-vida" (*In-a-gadda-da-vida*, 1968) could be found in games like *Way of the Warrior* (Naughty Dog/Universal Interactive Studio, 1994), *Revolution X* (Midway, 1994) and *Leisure Suit Larry: Love for Sail!* (Sierra On-Line, 1996), respectively. By the time "Don't Fear the Reaper" was used in *Roadkill* in 2003, and then in *Prey* in 2006, popular songs in game soundtracks had become common ground.

As is evident with the time span covered by these examples, songs from different periods coexist in game soundtracks. The development of the "classic rock" radio format in the 1990s ensured that songs from the 1960s-1980s got as much air play as newer songs, thus rendering oldies contemporary despite their "pastness". So too with the medium of video games: although classics like the Rolling Stones' "Paint it Black" (*Aftermath,* 1966) and Creedence Clearwater Revival's "Fortunate Son" (*Willy and the Poor Boys*, 1969) are sometimes used to authenticate the narrative setting of Vietnam era war games the likes of *Conflict: Vietnam* (Pivotal Games/Global Star Software, 2004), and *Call of Duty: Black Ops*

(Treyarch/Activision, 2010), many older songs appear in contemporary set games, detached from their original context of production. Such is the case with "Don't Fear the Reaper"'s multiple videoludic appearances; *Ripper* is even set in the distant future (the year 2040).

Popular songs are used in a multitude of game genres set in various time periods and putting the player in loads of different gameplay situations, but the aforementioned examples all share one characteristic: the high number of times the songs have appeared in media prior to or after their inclusion in a given game[1]. With forty occurrences, "Don't Fear the Reaper" is one of the classic rock songs that have been used the most by contemporary producers and game developers. Not only does this high number of appearances ensure that it has had enough cultural visibility to be recognized by most gamers of *Ripper*, *Roadkill* and *Prey*, but it also gives enough grounds to reflect on the complexity of the song's intertextual network and its potential effects on the gamer's experience in three different genres of games: the interactive movie, the open-world action-adventure game and the first-person shooter.

Many more instances of multiple recontextualizations of songs in games and other media can be found, and it is thus surprising that the consequences of such practices have not garnered more attention from scholars studying video game music. Karen Collins' seminal book *Game Sound* briefly discusses musical intertextuality on the broader levels of genre and theme, stating that when a well-known popular song is inserted in a soundtrack, "the intertextual references in the music (or game) likely help to connect the game or music connotatively to specific types of films, books, or social groups" (2008, p. 117), and hinting at the "interference or intertextual referencing between the games and the paramusical phenomena associated with [...] artists (videos, concerts, album covers, and so on)" (Collins, 2008, p. 129). Besides an absence of definitions for the notions of "interference" and "intertextual referencing", her brief comment about the artists featured in the game *Need for Speed: Carbon* (EA Black Box, 2006) stops at the mention of the connection of "urban, illicit aspects of certain games to hip-hop music" (*ibid.*), and eschews specific associations between a given song and other images or sequences of gameplay belonging to other works[2].

Such inquiries have been undertaken in other areas of media studies. Various television and film appearances of Phil Collins' "In the Air Tonight" (*Face Value*, 1981), Bob Dylan's "All Along the Watchtower" (*John Wesley Harding*, 1967), and the Johann Strauss waltz "The Blue Danube" (1866), have been the objects of textual analyzes by Robynn Stilwell (1995), Russel Reising (2010) and Michaël Andrieu (2011), respectively. These case studies offer detailed descriptions of the fluctuations of meaning of their respective songs as they are integrated in fictional and commercial texts, but their semantic analyzes somewhat minimize the effects of the repetition of the song on the viewer's experience. Moreover, video games are completely excluded from the equation[3].

What is needed, at this point, is a clear model of intertextuality that can account for the numerous intersections created by "Don't Fear the Reaper" which can eventually be applied to other cases that swarm the cultural landscape. Although intertextual theory has its roots in literary studies, the following discussion will focus mainly on the concept as it has been imported in television and film studies, for the resulting categorizations and definitions offer the most potential for the development of musical intertextuality in video games.

Intertextuality

In his seminal book *Television Culture*, John Fiske offers the following definition of intertextuality:

The theory of intertextuality proposes that any one text is necessarily read in relationship to others and that a range of textual knowledges is brought to bear upon it. These relationships do not take the form of specific allusions from one text to another and there is no need for readers to be familiar with specific or the same texts to read intertextually. Intertextuality exists rather in the space between texts. (Fiske, 2011, p. 109)

Fiske uses Madonna's music video for "Material Girl" (*Like a Virgin*, 1984) as an example. The video's parody of Marilyn Monroe's "Diamonds Are a Girl's Best Friend" musical number in *Gentlemen Prefer Blondes* (Howard Hawkes, 1953) is not, according to Fiske, an example of intertextuality, because:

... its effectiveness depends upon specific, not generalized, textual knowledge – a knowledge that, incidentally, many of Madonna's young girl fans in 1985 were unlikely to possess. The video's intertextuality refers rather to our culture's image bank of the sexy blonde star who plays with men's desire for her and turns it to her advantage. It is an elusive image, similar to Barthes's notion of myth, to which Madonna and Marilyn Monroe contribute equally and from which they draw equally. The meanings of Material Girl depend upon its allusion to Gentlemen Prefer Blondes and upon its intertextuality with all texts that contribute to and draw upon the meaning of "the blonde" in our culture. (Fiske, 2011, p. 109)

Fiske's distinction between allusion and intertextuality is symptomatic of what Sébastien Babeux calls "the two solitudes characterizing the majority of work on intertextuality" (2007, p. 80, author's translation):

... on one side, theorists studying intertextuality as a typology of concrete textual relationships, leaning on specific examples while conveniently leaving aside abstract relations; on the other side, those concerned with the intertext as indeterminate and unidentifiable multiplication of intersections while reducing works leaning on concrete relations to the embarrassing study of sources. (ibid.)

What Babeux calls "concrete relations" are the intersections created between the text and other easily identifiable works which the "creative instance" (*instance autoriale*) deliberately points to through the means of quotation, allusion or parody. Musical quotations and allusions in film have been briefly discussed by Anahid Kassabian (2001) as part of a "music history continuum", which corresponds to the degree to which a viewer knows the soundtrack prior to its inclusion in a film. In Kassabian's continuum, quotations correspond to the inclusion of pre-existent popular songs in a film's soundtrack. Allusion is also a type of quotation, in which "the works quoted belong to an entire narrative, such as opera or ballet; in a few seconds of film time, an allusion can evoke another whole narrative for the perceiver familiar with the excerpt" (Kassabian, 2001, p. 50). Pre-existent popular songs are excluded from Kassabian's definition of allusion "unless they belong to a larger narrative work" (2001, p. 50).

It could be tempting to discard Kassabian's allusion, and Babeux's concrete relations altogether, on account of a popular song's lack of a "legitimate" ownership in its media appearances. Released in 1976 as a single off the album *Agents of Fortune*, "Don't Fear the Reaper" had a life of its own two years prior to its first inclusion in a soundtrack, John Carpenter's *Halloween* (1978). The song does not rightfully "belong" to *Halloween*, no more than it does any of the subsequent works that have used it ever since. A concrete relation could therefore hardly be established between two works using "Don't Fear the Reaper".

However, it is useful to challenge such a definition of ownership by considering the following two audiovisual sequences of events. As a soldier is guarding the entrance of a military base, an alarm goes off: an experiment has gone wrong and a virus has accidentally been released out of a research lab. Prior to closing the base's gates, the soldier runs to his nearby house and grabs his wife and baby and they make a run for it in the soldier's car. As the car speeds away, the camera lingers on a crow examining a doll lying on the ground, and continues its way into the soldier's empty guarding post, where it zooms in on surveillance monitors. "Don't Fear the Reaper" plays non-diegetically on the soundtrack as a series of tracking shots shows the dead bodies of the base's residents scattered through the installations. Cut to the soldier's car, speeding on the road as the song's chaotic guitar solo slowly fades out of the soundtrack.

In the second sequence, the sun is burning in the sky. "Don't Fear the Reaper" starts to play as the camera pans down to a desert and cuts to the front of a driving car. The camera lingers on a pitchfork decorated with human skulls and zooms into one of the skulls' eye as the car drives away. The car passes by a human skeleton lying on the side of the road, its head falling off as the car drives away. The volume of the song lowers as an amalgam of non-diegetic echoing broadcast journalists' voices announce an epidemic outbreak. A shot of a scientist conducting tests in a hazmat suit is followed by superimposed images of alarming newspaper headlines "floating" behind the driver's head. He stops the car abruptly as "Don't Fear the Reaper"'s solo starts, and listens to a radio broadcast inviting survivors to Paradise City for protection in this now lawless world. The character drives off and, as the solo reaches its full power, it fades out and the camera lingers on a skeleton hanging from a street light, while the voices announce their last broadcast and the image switches to black and white.

While far from identical, the two sequences described above bare some striking resemblances which go beyond the inclusion of "Don't Fear the Reaper" on their respective soundtracks: the apocalyptic setting, the virus outbreak, tracking shots of dead bodies in various stages of decay, and the raging guitar solo accompanying a character's speeding car. As stated above, Blue Öyster Cult's song does not legitimately belong to any of the works in which it has appeared, however it would not be unreasonable to assume that the first sequence – the opening of the television miniseries *Stephen King's The Stand* (Mick Garris, 1994) – served as the inspiration for the second sequence – the introductory cutscene of the vehicular combat game *Roadkill*. The latter could very well be an allusion to the former's way of using the song. The consequences of that allusion will be examined in a further section. For now, it seems essential to expand the understanding of "ownership" of a musical piece as being constantly negotiated and culturally or individually determined, whether by the author or the reader.

Although other concrete relations can be found among the various uses of "Don't Fear the Reaper"[4], all intersections between works featuring the song cannot be so neatly classified: not only has it been used in over forty different works belonging to a diversity of genres (horror films, dramatic series, comedies, teen films, adventure and action games), it has also appeared in conjunction with contrasting imagery and competing narrative themes (which will be discussed shortly). It is therefore useful to consider the other side of intertextual studies, which Babeux classifies as abstract relations (*relations non concrètes*). Just like in John Fiske's example of "the blonde" as partially constructed by Madonna's video and Marilyn Monroe's musical number, texts belonging to the abstract relations category work together to help produce meaning, but not one of them acts as a specific intended reference on the part of the author. Clichés and recurring objects or places:

… do not pose a concrete reference to an identified work also using the same figure, but rather use the latter's significant thickness, accumulated throughout its appearances in different systems. These vague

and undetectable intersections remind one of other signifying systems and recall experiences or stored knowledge, therefore arousing various inferences from the reader-viewer and promoting the (unlimited) extension of his/her interpretations. (Babeux, 2007, p. 91; author's translation)

Such abstract relations can also be found on the level of genre (see Gray, 2006; Fiske, 2011; Bussolini, 2013), recurring characters, actors, directors or crew members (see Reader, 1990; Fiske, 2011; Bussolini, 2013) or overall theme (see Gray, 2006). In all these cases, one does not need to link the text to other, specific texts in order to make meaning out of the presented images and sounds.

Abstract relations are quite useful to study the multiple appearances of popular songs in media. Clichés can certainly be identified in relation to the use of popular songs in film and television narratives, like the association of Survivor's "Eye of the Tiger" (*Eye of the Tiger*, 1982) with a training montage or competition sequence[5]. "Don't Fear the Reaper" could also be found guilty of such a figure, as noted by a YouTube user in what Fiske (2011) would call a "tertiary text" – a commentary below a video walkthrough of *Prey*: "don't fear the reaper being the harbinger of the shit hitting the fan is such a cliché...... But an effective cliché nonetheless" (domkex, 2012). In light of the extension of its dissemination in the cultural landscape, specific occurrences of the song may not be remembered, but the essence of its usual role in this type of text – in *Prey*'s case, the game is linked with other first-person shooter games through its gameplay mechanics, but it is also linked with science fiction and horror narratives through its setting – is attached to the song and contributes to its creation of meaning.

The relationships created between films and games by a popular song cannot so easily be dismissed as abstract relations. Although a given listener cannot possibly remember every contact they have had with a specific song, it is part of their condition that they are "predictable, singable, rememberable, and physically involving" (Altman, 2001, p. 118), thereby attracting much more attention to themselves than would other elements susceptible to create abstract relations, such as a school or library. Although a viewer/gamer's contact with every film and game featuring a song is not likely to be comprehensive, certain occurrences of a song in games or films will likely be remembered with more accuracy than others. Babeux's concept of interference is the first step towards understanding the consequences of such memories for the gamer's experience.

Interference

As many scholars have pointed out, it is part of the condition of intertextual reading that each reader or viewer will decode or interpret a given text differently. What Roland Barthes has termed "the writerly function" entails that "Readers bring their own language and style to the text, and they recognize particular references and influences, including ones never intended or foreseen by the author" (Bussolini, 2013). Such projections of intersections by readers and viewers are rarely given much attention and are usually drowned in a global understanding of abstract relations. Far from ignoring such connections, Babeux seeks them out in contemporary film productions and gives them a name, that of interference.

In the context of a specific film viewing, interference can be understood under the scope of communication theory, as illustrated by Babeux's reformulation of Claude Shannon and Warren Weaver's (1969) transmission model (Figure 1). In the process of transmission of meaning, the author ("instance autoriale") sends a message to the viewer in the form of a signifying system ("système signifiant"): the film as a finished product. Every single textual or cultural element the viewer may draw from to understand the message sent by the author forms the signifying system's intertext, which contains both

Figure 1. Sébastien Babeux's model of intertextuality and interference
Source: Babeux, 2007, p. 96.

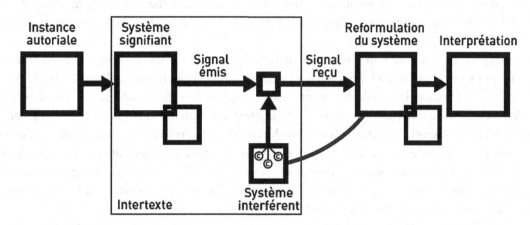

concrete and abstract relations. As concrete relations point to identifiable works which act as legitimate references, they are part of the author's message, as illustrated by the small square appended to the "système signifiant". Among the intertext's abstract relations, the specific connections produced by the viewer outside of the author's control are part of the message *as reconstructed by the viewer*: any film the viewer has seen may be interpreted as a reference and prompt a projection of supplementary meaning on the part of the receiver. Since the author didn't plan for this added meaning when conceiving the message, the projected reference acts as a source of "noise" which disturbs the signal and transforms its nature at the time of interpretation (see the "système interférent" which hits the signal as it is being passed from the transmitter to the receiver). While in the concrete relation the film which is being referenced contributes semantically to the other film's meaning, in the interferential relation any semantic contribution constitutes an over-interpretation on the part of the viewer.

The concept of interference can account for instances in which a specific occurrence of a given song occupies a more prominent position in a user's cultural baggage and contributes more strongly to the meaning he/she attributes to the song. The song may preserve traces of this occurrence in the viewer's memory and prompt an addition of meaning upon viewing or playing any other text featuring the song. Babeux's conception of interference also proposes a figure which presents a lot of potential for thinking about the way all the narrative and ludic works featuring the same song relate to one another, that of the network. Drawing on French philosopher Michel Serres's (1972) conception of the encyclopedia, Babeux imagines every film the viewer has been in contact with as part of a network, where each film acts as a crossroads potentially leading to any other film featuring similarities in setting, *mise en scène* and narrative. Inside the network, relations are non-hierarchical: no film acts as a legitimate reference for another film. Like in an interchange, texts in the network don't actually cross each other; they merely give the illusion of being connected though the viewer's interpretation.

Babeux's notion of hierarchy of textual relations is based on the idea of an author's deliberate reference to another text and, as such, it does not exclude the fact that certain texts may occupy a more important position in the mind of a specific viewer. Therefore, the interferential network is quite a relevant figure to illustrate the connection between all works featuring the same song. However, Babeux's model was constructed with regard to general properties of narrative film, and his typology is based on visual and narrative similarities between two or more works. It is not intended to comprehend intertextual relationships created by music, and cannot, by itself, account for its effects in video games. Philip Tagg's (2013) circular model of musical communication can help shed some light on the way music produces meaning across multiple texts and proposes another level of interference which offers an interesting complement to Babeux's concept.

According to Tagg, music's meaning is constructed through a store of signs – the association of sounds, instruments, rhythms and other musical features with certain moods or "feels" (Tagg, 2013, p. 122) – and a set of sociocultural norms – intentions and motivations for using music as well as acceptable behavior with regard to the social and cultural context in which the music is produced or listened to (Figure 2). These associations and norms are developed through repetition of musical features in social and cultural contexts, whether in the listener's everyday life, in live performances or in media. If the transmitter – a composer, performer, producer or game developer – conceives their musical message in accordance with a shared store of signs and sociocultural norms, the receiver – a listener, viewer or gamer – will most likely respond "adequately" to the music.

Just like in Babeux's intertextual model, however, there are many instances in which the transmitter's intentions and the received message are not the same. What Tagg calls "codal incompetence" hap-

Figure 2. Philip Tagg's model of musical communication
Source: Tagg, 2013, p. 121.

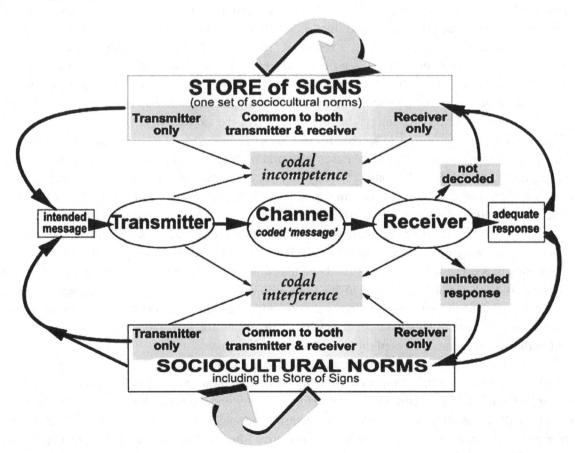

pens when certain layers of meaning are not decoded because of a lack of knowledge on the part of the listener. This is often attributable to generational or cultural differences. Young gamers playing *Call of Duty: Black Ops* or *Battlefield: Vietnam* (Digital Illusions CE/Electronic Arts, 2004) may not know that Creedence Clearwater Revival's *Fortunate Son* was composed in reaction to social inequities in the drafting process during the Vietnam War. The (unintentional) irony of the fact that it is used for its raw energy to structure cutscenes and gameplay sequences which glorify stereotypical aspects of the Vietnam War might be lost on a whole generation who has not been in contact with the relevant information concerning the song's context of production.

What Tagg calls "codal interference" happens when the transmitter's message is understood, but personal tastes or sociocultural norms prevent the listener from responding "adequately" to or appreciating the music. In her thesis on industrial music, Karen Collins has referred to this kind of interference as "supplementary connotations". In her case study, both fans and non-fans of industrial music perceive the same connotations of darkness and dystopia, but the latter do not appreciate the music in the same way as the former because "the meaning is enriched by the connotations of those connotations" (Collins, 2002, p. 356). Tagg's definition of codal interference also includes situations of "connotative highjacking" (Tagg, 2013, p. 131): instances where media producers deliberately subvert connotations related to a song's production context (i.e., identity and social status of the performer). It could be argued that "anempathetic" (Chion, 1995) uses of songs in narrative media are also forms of voluntary codal interference, since they aim to augment the impact of an event by producing an affective or cognitive contrast.

The idea of an "adequate" or "inadequate" response may seem to suggest that there is only one correct way to interpret the music or audio-visual sequence. This is not the case. Tagg's model should be understood in the context of commercial and mass communication in which a hired composer or media producer tries to offer a specific type of experience to a listener, viewer or gamer. Indeed, music that is used in video games is meant to fulfill a number of purposes. Its narrative functions include communicating emotions (Collins, 2008; Zehnder & Lipscomb, 2006), establishing mood (Bessell, 2002; Nitsche, 2008; Whalen, 2004; Zehnder & Lipscomb, 2006), characterizing the environment with cultural, historical and social connotations (Collins, 2005, 2008; Gibbons, 2011; Nitsche, 2008; Zehnder & Lipscomb, 2006), maintaining continuity between levels and marking beginnings and ends of sections of the game (Bessell, 2002; Collins, 2005, 2008; Zehnder & Lipscomb, 2006). Most importantly, music fulfills purposes for gameplay, like informing the player of the state of the surrounding environment and alerting of approaching enemies (Collins, 2005, 2008; Egenfeldt-Nielsen, Smith & Tosca, 2008; Nitsche, 2008; Whalen, 2004; Zehnder & Lipscomb, 2006), motivating the player to move forward (Whalen, 2004), and focusing the player's emotional response during combat sequences (Bessell, 2002; Collins, 2008). Even though the gamer has the last word in this communication process, it is therefore relevant to take the transmitter's intentions into account when studying specific occurrences of music in games.

Far from being understood as negative, situations of codal incompetence and interference are essential to the evolution of musical meaning in a given culture (Tagg, 2013, p. 124). Each act of musical communication produces a reaction which in turn confirms or modifies the signs and sociocultural norms at play in the production of a song's meaning (see the arrows going from "not decoded" to "store of signs", and from "unintended response" to "sociocultural norms" on the right side of the model). It may be argued that if a song is frequently used in a given narrative or ludic context, this same context could become part of the song's signification for a great number of listeners, just like the effective subversion of its "original" meaning may contribute to the modification of its meaning for a given culture. Supplementary connotations may have been inscribed on "Don't Fear the Reaper" by force of its repeated appearance in a threatening or fatal context: as will be discussed in the next section, many creative instances have seized the opportunity to represent the song's Reaper into human or supernatural form.

Even though Tagg and Babeux develop their models in different disciplines (respectively, musicology and film studies) and draw on different traditions (linguistics and philosophy of science), both are applying the same principle: there is a superimposition of estranged elements on or in the same object. This superimposition simply occurs at different levels of reception. When there is codal interference, the meaning a song takes on through its appearance in a given work interferes cognitively or affectively with the idea the listener previously had of the song's meaning, or vice versa. It is when the viewer or gamer establishes a specific relationship with one or more of the forty non-hierarchical uses of "Don't Fear the Reaper" that interference as conceived by Babeux manifests itself. To avoid confusion between both levels of interference, and because Babeux's interference relates to the viewer or gamer's interpretation and anticipation of narrative events, this second level will hereby be referred to as narrative interference.

Both levels of interference may have an impact on the functions of the song within a video game. It seems fair to assume that voluntary codal interference directly participates in determining the function of the music: it may contribute to an ironic commentary or heighten the emotional impact of a troubling event. That may not be the case when codal interference is involuntary or when it comes to narrative interference. Supplementary connotations or the over-interpretation of the relationship a given work has with another work featuring the same song may prevent the transmitter's message from getting across. On a semantic level, referential functions like the portraying of a character or the identification of a place and time period may be blurred. On an affective level, both levels of interference may provoke conflicting emotions in the player. A closer examination of "Don't Fear the Reaper"'s presence in *Ripper*, *Roadkill* and *Prey* can help shed some light on the interferential process in different types of game segments.

Musical Interference in Games: *Ripper*, *Roadkill*, and *Prey*

The point-and-click horror adventure game *Ripper* was released on the DOS and Macintosh platforms in February of 1996. Technological advances had permitted full motion video to be introduced to the world of video games in the early 1990s, thus allowing the creation of a genre which sought to bridge the gap between video games and films: the interactive movie. As a hybrid object situated at the crossroads between two media, "the interactive movie was more concerned with questions of nonlinear storytelling and photorealistic imagery than the development of innovative gameplay" (Perron, 2008, p. 127). As such, gameplay mechanics were often based on the player "determining the order in which already-generated elements are accessed" (Lev Manovich, as cited in Perron, 2003, p. 239). It is no surprise, then, that most of the player's contact with "Don't Fear the Reaper" would happen through cutscenes: indeed, the song both opens and closes *Ripper*.

The game opens with a low-angle shot of an animated house against a dark sky. "Don't Fear the Reaper" plays non-diegetically, sharing the soundtrack with diegetic sounds of wind and thunder crashes. Cut to a woman – a live action actress on an animated background – walking alone in deserted city streets, the sound of her footsteps resonating against the backdrop of "Don't Fear the Reaper"'s chorus. The song's "chilling […] echoing Byrds-like La la la, la la/La la la, la la" (Marsh, 1999, p. 629) fill the soundtrack as the woman keeps looking over her shoulder, with lightning flashes illuminating the expression of fear on her face. The woman enters her house, and close-ups and low-angle shots follow her as she walks up the stairs. A shot from outside the house shows a shadowy figure passing in one of the windows. Back inside the house, close-ups of the woman screaming and spattered blood in the camera's "lens" are accompanied by the overdubbed voice of Dharma Roeser. The volume of the song lowers to make room for the player-character's voice-over intervention. An image of the house at dawn with "Manhattan, 2040 A.D., Dawn: A Ripper has struck" in red letters is shown as reporter Jake Quinlan explains that his editor is sending him – e.g., the player – to investigate this most recent murder. The music's volume comes back up, and a second set of "las" is heard before the music fades out. The player will have to unmask The Ripper by interviewing various characters and solving puzzles. The choice of suspects comes down to four characters: Detective Vince Magnotta (Christopher Walken), Doctor Clare Burton (Karen Allen), computer hacker Joey Falconetti (David Patrick Kelly), or journalist Catherine Powell (Tahnee Welch).

Like *Ripper*, *Roadkill* opens and closes with "Don't Fear the Reaper". However, it belongs to a completely different genre: the open-world action-adventure game, released on PlayStation 2, GameCube and Xbox in 2003, has been described as "the result of a shotgun wedding between *Twisted Metal Black* [Incognito Entertainment/Sony Computer Entertainment, 2001] and the next-gen *Grand Theft Auto* series [Rockstar Games/Capcom, 1997-2015]" (Carle, 2003). Set in a post-apocalyptic world taken over by gangs, *Roadkill*'s missions have the player fighting rivals aboard various types of vehicles with a variety of firearms. *Roadkill*'s opening cutscene has already been described in a previous section: the player-character, Mason, drives a car through a desert riddled with human skeletons as echoing voices and superimposed newspaper headlines explain the virus outbreak backstory.

Neither *Ripper*'s or *Roadkill*'s player is physically engaged in gameplay during the presentation of "Don't Fear the Reaper". This does not mean that he/she is not otherwise involved or engaged in the game. Katie Salen and Eric Zimmerman stress that cutscenes play a big role in "narrative play", and fulfill such functions as "establish[ing] mood, or reinforce[ing] the emotional arc of game events" (2004, p. 410). The music heard in the opening cutscene, then, can be seen as fulfilling similar functions as television opening themes, which, according to Philip Tagg, serve "to prepare listeners or viewers emotionally with an affective musical description of the general mood found in the subsequent presentation" (2000, p. 93). In the case of video games, however, subsequent events are not merely presented to the viewer; they are, in various degrees, submitted to his/her control.

In both *Ripper*'s and *Roadkill*'s cases, the developers have chosen to play on "Don't Fear the Reaper"'s darker connotations. The ambiguous lyrics, the relentless guitar riff and, in the second case, the chaotic guitar solo, combine with the images of death and decay to create an ominous mood. The effectiveness of this intended message then depends, among other individual factors, on the player's prior knowledge of the song, which is shaped by their previous contacts with it in personal and cultural contexts. "Don't Fear the Reaper"'s other media uses offer plenty of occasions for intertextual and interferential readings.

The plausible allusion to *Stephen King's The Stand* in *Roadkill*'s opening cutscene has already been mentioned in a previous section. Now that the inner workings of music's meaning have been laid out, a distinction must be made between the allusive process as conceived by intertextual theory and the musical allusion as it is produced through the "borrowing" of a song featured in another work. According to Sébastien Babeux's definition of the filmic allusion, the original text contains a key to the interpretation of the narrative. *Roadkill*'s allusion to *The Stand*, however, must be understood on the affective, rather than semantic, level. By coupling "Don't Fear the Reaper" with images of corpses and disease, *Roadkill*'s developers seek to recreate a familiar effect, rather than point to an element that will guide the player's interpretive activity. *Ripper*, *Roadkill* and *The Stand* are however part of a much larger network of texts related through "Don't Fear the Reaper" (see Figure 3). Thematic affiliations can be observed between the video games under study and other works which, like the developers of *Ripper*, have seized the opportunity to represent the song's Reaper into human or supernatural form. John Carpenter's and

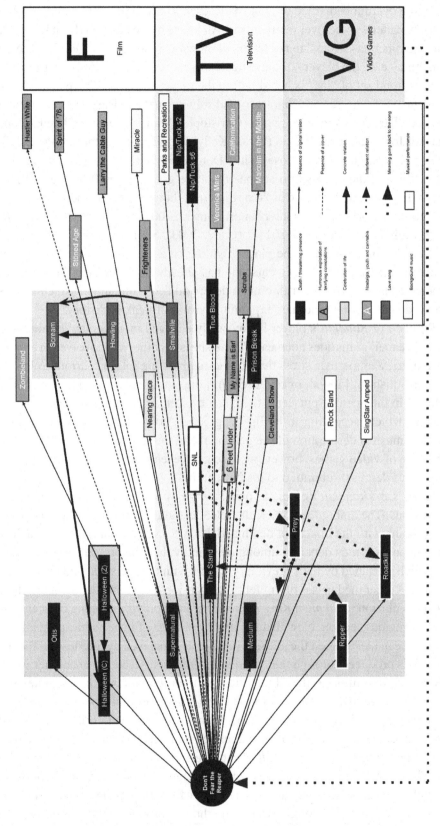

Figure 3. "Don't Fear the Reaper"'s interferential and intertextual network
Source: The Author.

Rob Zombie's *Halloween* (1978 and 2007, respectively), *Otis* (Tony Krantz, 2008), *Medium* ("There Will Be Blood… Type A", Arlene Sanford, 2005), *Supernatural* ("Faith", Allan Kroeker, 2005), and the other video game which will be analyzed shortly, *Prey*, either couple BÖC's song with a serial killer, an actual reaper or an alien spaceship threatening the lives of the characters (see the black tabs in Figure 3). Along with *Roadkill* and *The Stand*'s representations of the apocalypse, those uses of the song all seek to communicate, or even to induce, a similar affect: uneasiness, anxiety, or even terror. Even those who use Gus Black's cover[6] of "Don't Fear the Reaper" as a love song (*Scream* [Wes Craven, 1996], *Smallville* ["Precipice", Thomas J. Wright, 2003] and *The Howling: Reborn* [Joe Nimziki, 2011]), maintain a certain darkness and (more or less) veiled threat to their message (see the darker gray tabs in Figure 3).

The first question to ask when considering the potential interferential relations between the games and other points in the network is that of chronology. At the time of *Ripper*'s release, "Don't Fear the Reaper" hadn't circulated in popular media as much as it has today. *Halloween, The Stand* and *Scream* were the only thematically affiliated works a player might have seen. Given the fact the song is significantly transformed and hidden behind dialogue in the latter, it might not have even been noticed by many viewers.

Although it should be noted that the lifespan of video games is somewhat limited by the conditions of an ever-changing technological market, the interferential network should not be viewed under the scope of chronological considerations. As new genres and platforms are being released on the market, older games can rapidly become obsolete, and *Ripper* and *Roadkill* are no longer at the peak of their popularity, but this does not render them completely irrelevant, even by today's standards. Numerous video walkthroughs of both games can still be found on social media platforms like YouTube, and user reviews have been posted on websites like *MobyGames.com, Gamespot.com* and *Metacritic.com* as recently as 2013. Consequently, many players may have played *Ripper* or *Roadkill* years after their initial release dates, and their perception of "Don't Fear the Reaper" may have been shaped by further growths of the network.

With this in mind, the aforementioned thematically affiliated "Don't Fear the Reaper" uses may beneficially affect the communication or inducement of mood in the player by way of narrative interference. The threatening entities associated with the song – *Halloween*'s Michael Myers, *Supernatural*'s cadaverous reaper, *Otis*' serial kidnapper, and *Medium*'s and *Ripper*'s serial killers – may all potentially substitute for Blue Öyster Cult's Reaper, and their shared characteristics may superimpose during subsequent contacts with the song. As such, the gamer's anticipation of what is to come in the subsequent gameplay sequence can be shaped by the memory of any of those threatening entities. *Ripper*'s player, for example, might even use what they know about one or many of the other killers in their search for the Ripper.

But even as the music mentally and affectively prepares the player for gameplay and interference from other dark uses of "Don't Fear the Reaper" can contribute to further shape the player's mood as they enter the game, the gamer's posture during the presentation of the song is mainly that of a viewer. The situation is otherwise in the third game to feature the BÖC song: the first-person shooter *Prey* features the song in a gameplay sequence involving the player character Tommy's and non-player characters' fate.

As the gamer gets in their first combat sequence – a bar fight with two drunken patrons – the lights start flickering and the entire building starts shaking. "Don't Fear the Reaper" comes on the jukebox as the character's girlfriend Jen and grandfather Enisi get pulled up toward the open ceiling by a ray of light. The player remains in control of the character while the NPCs are abducted, and only loses it when Tommy himself is taken.

According to Bernard Perron:

To play a video game is not merely to understand a story, but rather to solve problems, to overcome obstacles, to take on opponents, to explore a virtual world, etc. The gamer's actions and this world's reactions will indeed arouse emotions "of a different nature", gameplay emotions. (Perron, 2006, p. 358; author's translation)

While the player cannot do a single thing to prevent the abduction, the song's rousing rhythm can nevertheless stimulate his/her activity and let them believe they have their share of responsibility in the outcome of this encounter of the third kind. Moreover, the abduction's consequences can be troubling for the player who will have to face whichever creatures are responsible for it. It is precisely because of this feeling of responsibility, and because the player must eventually come face to face with the entity which has triggered the appearance of the song on the soundtrack, that their anxiety may be increased by narrative interference with the multiple gruesome occurrences of "Don't Fear the Reaper". The impact of the gameplay emotions may further contribute to the inscription of dark supplementary connotations on "Don't Fear the Reaper", and allow *Prey* to occupy a privileged position in the network.

The fact that *Ripper* and *Roadkill* don't allow the player to physically interact with the game during the presentation of "Don't Fear the Reaper" does not preclude them from occupying a similarly privileged position in the interferential network. As mentioned before, not only is "Don't Fear the Reaper" the first piece of music the player hears, it is also the last.

After *Roadkill*'s player has defeated the final boss, a cutscene is triggered in which "Don't Fear the Reaper" plays on a car radio. The enemy creeps up behind Mason for what the player expects to be one last confrontation, therefore reinforcing the song's menacing connotations once again, but the threatening character is quickly swept away by a speeding bus. The song plays on as Mason straightens up his car and leaves to answer another destroyed city's call for help, and the credits roll, allowing the song to play until the end. In addition to their emotional purposes, cutscenes, as noted by Rune Klevjer, also act as rewards for the player's efforts (2014, p. 301). The ending cutscene, then, is the ultimate reward: after spending many hours trying to achieve the objectives set by the game, the player has reached the final goal and the narrative comes to a close. The feelings conveyed by the representation combine with the player's sense of accomplishment and feeling of triumph. The affective impact of such a sequence can thus be quite powerful and leave a lasting impression on the player.

In the case of *Ripper*, it is not in the final cutscene that the song is heard, but over the closing credits. It is first heard as pictures of the characters in action are presented in conjunction with the names of the actors. The song fades out during the second verse, plays again from the start to accompany the credit roll, and once again fades out after the second verse. When the music is over, *Ripper* leaves the player with one last image: when the player selects the "exit" option, a final threat by the Ripper is followed by shots of computers monitoring a person's vitals (or lack thereof). A zoom in on one of the computer screens shows the lead character, Jake Quinlan, dead on the floor. Once again, the ending of *Ripper* serves to reinforce "Don't Fear the Reaper"'s dark connotations. Even though the last image is not shown in direct conjunction with the song, it has just played twice, and the association between the Reaper and the Ripper is still as valid as it was when the game started.

The fact that using "Don't Fear the Reaper" as an indicator for an immediate threat has become somewhat of a cliché, as mentioned above, does not necessarily diminish its effectiveness, but the situation is otherwise if competing occurrences create narrative or codal interference. Indeed, all media occurrences of the song are not as grim, and works coupling "Don't Fear the Reaper" with death or a threatening presence as well as works using Gus Black's acoustic cover as a threatening love song coexist with other, more "harmless" contexts. There are those who have recontextualized the song's terrifying connotations to create a humorous effect, as is the case with *Scrubs'* JD (Zach Braff, ("My Lawyer's in Love", Mark Stegemann, 2009) and the titular character of *Larry the Cable Guy: Health Inspector* (Trent Cooper, 2006) fearing the wrath of an angry boss (see the medium gray tabs with black writing in Figure 3). It has notably been used to communicate spontaneity and a celebration of life (*Six Feet Under* ["It's the Most Wonderful Time of the Year", Alan Taylor, 2002] and *Nearing Grace* [Rick Rosenthal, 2005]) (see the light gray tabs in Figure 3). Others move away from the sense transmitted by the lyrics and play on connotations related to the song's era of production: the 1970s. It is sometimes used to authenticate the narrative setting (*The Stöned Age* [James Melkonian, 1994]; *The Spirit of '76* [Lucas Reiner, 1990]), to communicate a character's nostalgia (*Veronica Mars*; *Malcolm in the Middle* ["Hal's Friend", Jeff Melman, 2003]), or to accompany an activity which is heavily associated with the decade's youth, smoking cannabis (*The Spirit of '76*; *Zombieland* [Reuben Fleischer, 2009]) (see the medium gray tabs with white writing in Figure 3). Some works use "Don't Fear the Reaper" as mere ambiance music in the background of bar scenes (*Miracle* [Gavin O'Connor, 2004] and *Parks and Recreation* ["Ron & Tammy: Part Two", Tucker Gates, 2011]) (see the lighter gray tabs in Figure 3). Finally, "Don't Fear the Reaper" is sometimes the focus of a musical performance, by a video game player (*Rock Band*, *SingStar Amped*) or otherwise (*Saturday Night Live*) (see the white tabs on the chart). Such occurrences contribute to shape the meaning of the song in ways which sometimes dramatically differ from the darker media uses that have been discussed so far. Either one of such specific occurrences, or an accumulation of them, can work against *Ripper*'s, *Roadkill*'s or *Prey*'s intended message and undermine the uneasy feeling the developers are trying to convey.

An April 2000 *Saturday Night Live* sketch, for instance, seems to represent a privileged source of interference. It features Christopher Walken as producer "*The* Bruce Dickinson", who overlooks the recording of "Don't Fear the Reaper" by BÖC (Chris Kattan, Jimmy Fallon, Chris Parnell and Horatio Sanz). He demands with ever increasing insistence that fictional cowbell player Gene Frenkle (Will Ferrell) play louder and cure his "fever" with "more cowbell", to which the cowbell player reacts with a more and more enthusiastic – and exaggerated – performance. Since its first airing in April of 2000, the sketch has gone viral on the Internet[7], and many references to it can be found in YouTube user comments relating to video walkthroughs of *Ripper, Roadkill* and *Prey*, which suggests that the "More Cowbell" segment occupies an important position in "Don't Fear the Reaper"'s intertextual network. Such a humorous occurrence of the song may therefore act as a source of "noise" interfering with the developers' intended message of uneasiness or anxiety – especially in the case of *Ripper* which, incidentally, also features Christopher Walken – thereby completely transforming the player's experience of the game segment.

THE NETWORK OF "DON'T FEAR THE REAPER": PLACEMENT AND (RE)CONFIGURATION

The previous discussion has focused mainly on thematic affiliations and effects of interference on the gaming experience, but it is also essential to discuss the placement of the different works inside the network, for their position determines the power they have over the song's production of meaning. Although Sébastien Babeux's concept of the interferential network served as the inspiration for the present illustration, "Don't Fear the Reaper"'s network as it has been outlined here departs from Babeux's network in two respects. First, while Babeux's network has no center, the present graph has been "centered" around the song itself. Not only is it the element which ties all these works together, but it is also the object from which creators and developers draw to produce meaning based on affective or rhythmic value (illustrated by the arrows going from the song on the left to every work featured on the chart). Second, while Babeux's network has no hierarchical relations, "Don't Fear the Reaper"'s network contains both concrete (illustrated by the bold arrows linking certain tabs) and interferential relations. In order to avoid an overabundance of arrows, all potential interferential relations have not been illustrated. Since all the works represented contain the song, they are all related inside the network. In order to fully illustrate the complexity of "Don't Fear the Reaper"'s network, the ideal representation would be three dimensional and would deploy around the center, intertwining films, television series and video games. However, since all three media propose different reception postures, they have been separated, and the network spreads horizontally.

As Tagg's model of musical communication stipulates, every contact with the song produces a response which feeds back into the music's store of signs and sociocultural norms. Therefore, every audiovisual work featuring "Don't Fear the Reaper" has the potential to give a portion of its meaning back to the song. Once again, in order to relieve the chart from an overabundance of lines, this potential connotative return has been illustrated globally instead of individually (see the arrow leaving the "F/TV/ VG" rectangle on the bottom right and leading to the circle on the left).

Since all occurrences of "Don't Fear the Reaper" can't possibly contribute to its meaning with the same weight, occurrences which are most likely to inscribe supplementary connotations on the song have been positioned closer to the "core" of the network, and the works which seem less significant have been positioned in its "periphery".

The previous analysis has shown that *Ripper*, *Roadkill* and *Prey* occupy a privileged position in the network because of their prominent use of "Don't Fear the Reaper" and the strong emotional impact the song may produce on the player. As the soundtrack of cutscenes and closing credits, it is the first and the last piece of music the player hears in relation to *Ripper* and *Roadkill*, and as the musical accompaniment to the player's abduction, it is the element that foreshadows the game's threat in *Prey*. Moreover, since all three games seek to create a similar affective impact as other works associating the song with death, they simultaneously benefit from and participate in an accumulation effect. *Ripper* has been positioned in a vertical lineage with other works linking "Don't Fear the Reaper" with a specific entity, thus illustrating the potential superimposition of character traits on the song's Reaper. *Roadkill* has also been positioned in a vertical line with its influencing text, *The Stand*.

The predominance of black tabs in the chart illustrates that dark uses of "Don't Fear the Reaper" form a significant part of its network, and the sinister images and threatening gameplay situations are susceptible to guide the gamer's reception toward such an intertextual reading of the song. However, as the analysis has shown, neither game is impervious to interference from competing views of the song. All the works in the network may prompt a differential reading from the one intended by the game developers, but a special emphasis has been put on the *SNL* "More Cowbell" sketch because of its privileged position in the cultural landscape, as illustrated by the dotted line arrow leaving the *SNL* tab toward *Ripper*, *Roadkill* and *Prey*.

The network contains a multitude of other connections which have not been explored, and a discussion of the specific positioning of every other text is beyond the scope of this paper[8]. Works using a cover version have been positioned further from the core because of the possibility that the song may not be recognized. As have works which use "Don't Fear the Reaper" as hardly audible background music: its presence may go unnoticed by the viewer, and such works may then hardly steer one's reading of the song in a specific direction.

It is important to note that the present illustration is a fixed representation of a dynamic process, momentarily crystallized to illustrate the specificities of the theoretical framework, the potential effects of the wealth of musical intertextual connections on video games, and the potential power of video games in the evolution of a song's meaning. The model was designed from the perspective of an ideal listener, viewer and gamer, who enters the network through the song's original recording and thereafter comes in contact with every one of its audiovisual appearances. It goes without saying that such a wealth of knowledge is reserved to a very small number of users (i.e., the scholar doing research on multiple re-contextualizations of a particular song), and that the size and configuration of the network varies from one individual to another.

Among the factors that may contribute to the model's restructuration, the point of entry of a given user is crucial. Age and generational belonging greatly determine the visibility of certain works: young gamers may not have sought to access older films like *Halloween*, just like older adults may never come into contact with video games or teen comedies featuring "Don't Fear the Reaper". The concept of competence has been touched on with respect to the decoding of a musical message, but it also applies to the perception of intersections created by a popular song. Some parts of the illustrated network may disappear completely on account of a given user's failure to notice some potential connections. On the other hand, the attribution of the song's origin to a specific film or game, whether stemming from misinformation or from an increased attachment, may contribute to re-center the network around a singular audiovisual work instead of around the song's original recording. The song is at the core of the illustrated network because creative instances selecting the music for a soundtrack must reflect on its lyrical or rhythmic contribution to the story or gameplay sequence, but the user who projects a relation between two works does not necessarily embark on the same interpretive path. The network's structure is also prone to temporal fluctuations, and each new appearance of the song, by strengthening or subverting its connotations, calls for a restructuring of the relations within the network.

CONCLUSION

As the investigation of "Don't Fear the Reaper"'s complex media trajectory has shown, popular songs inserted in video game soundtracks are filled with extratextual associations emerging from their previous appearances in popular culture. They may therefore act as a crossroads to all other texts featuring the same song, and video game soundtracks should not be studied in isolation. While this case study has permitted to touch on the range of consequences emerging from the placement of licensed music in games, it also opened up the discussion surrounding games' role in shaping the way music from another era continues to be received by younger generations. Emotions felt during gameplay can be quite powerful, and the impact of the juxtaposition of the music with the player's active engagement in an intense gameplay sequence is likely to leave a lasting impression, thereafter allowing video games to act on a song's cultural meaning in a significant way.

Each case of multiple occurrences of the same popular song convenes different relationships and brings its own sets of issues. Mapping "Don't Fear the Reaper"'s network of media occurrences has nevertheless allowed foundations to be laid which may eventually be applied to hundreds of other cases swarming in the current media landscape.

REFERENCES

Altman, R. (2001). Cinema and popular song: The lost tradition. In A. Knight & P. R. Wojcik (Eds.), *Soundtrack available: Essays on film and popular music* (pp. 19–30). Durham, NC: Duke University Press. doi:10.1215/9780822380986-001

Andrieu, M. (2011). *Réinvestir la musique: Autour de la reprise et de ses effets au cinéma.* Paris, France: L'Harmattan.

Babeux, S. (2007). Le spectateur hors jeu: Investigation ludique du réseau interférentiel. *Intermédialités,* (9), 79-98.

Bessell, D. (2002). What's that funny noise? An examination of the role of music in *Cool Boarders 2, Alien Trilogy* and *Medievil 2.* In G. King & T. Krzywinska (Eds.), *Screenplay: Cinema/videogames/ interfaces* (pp. 136–143). New York, NY: Wallflower Press.

Bussolini, J. (2013). Television intertextuality after *Buffy*: Intertextuality of casting and constitutive intertextuality. *Slayage: The Journal of the Whedon Studies Association, 10*(1). Retrieved March 19, 2013, from http://slayageonline.com/essays/slayage35/Bussolini.pdf

Butler, M. (2003). Taking it seriously: Intertextuality and authenticity in two covers by the Pet Shop Boys. *Popular Music, 22*(1), 1–19. doi:10.1017/S0261143003003015

Carle, C. (2003). Roadkill. *IGN.* Retrieved November 2015, from http://ca.ign.com/articles/2003/11/04/ roadkill

Chion, M. (1995). *La musique au cinéma.* Paris, France: Fayard.

Collins, K. (2002). *The future is happening already: Industrial music, dystopia, and the aesthetic of the machine.* (Doctoral dissertation). University of Liverpool, Liverpool, UK. Available from EThOS Dissertations and Theses database. (http://ethos.bl.uk/OrderDetails.do?uin=uk.bl.ethos.272629)

Collins, K. (2005). From bits to hits: Video games music changes its tune. *Film International,* (12), 4-19.

Collins, K. (2008). *Game sound: An introduction to the history, theory, and practice of video game music.* Cambridge, MA: MIT Press.

domkex. (2012). *Prey the game full movie.* Retrieved November 2015, from https://www.youtube.com/ watch?v=4IP7DthcSBM

Egenfeldt-Nielsen, S., Smith, J. H., & Tosca, S. P. (2008). *Understanding video games: The essential introduction.* New York, NY: Routledge.

Fiske, J. (2011). *Television culture* (2nd ed.). London, UK: Routledge.

Gibbons, W. (2011). Wrap your troubles in dreams: Popular music, narrative, and dystopia in *Bioshock. Game Studies, 11*(3). Retrieved October 10, 2012, from http://gamestudies.org/1103/articles/gibbons

Gray, J. (2006). *Watching with The Simpsons: Television, parody, and intertextuality.* New York, NY: Routledge.

Klevjer, R. (2014). Cut-scenes. In M. J. P. Wolf & B. Perron (Eds.), *The Routledge companion to video game studies* (pp. 301–309). New York, NY: Routledge.

Marsh, D. (1999). *The heart of rock & soul: The 1001 greatest singles ever made.* New York, NY: Da Capo Press.

Morin-Simard, A. (2014). *L'interférence musicale au cinéma, à la télévision et dans le jeu vidéo.* (Master's thesis). Université de Montréal, Montréal, Canada. Available from Papyrus: Dépôt institutionnel. (https://papyrus.bib.umontreal.ca/xmlui/handle/1866/11628)

Newton, D. (Director). (2013). Great American rock anthems: Turn it up to 11. In BBC (Producer).

Nitsche, M. (2008). *Video game spaces: Image, play, and structure in 3D worlds.* Cambridge, MA: MIT Press. doi:10.7551/mitpress/9780262141017.001.0001

Perron, B. (2003). From gamers to players and gameplayers: The example of interactive movies. In M. J. P. Wolf & B. Perron (Eds.), *The video game theory reader* (pp. 237–258). New York, NY: Routledge.

Perron, B. (2006). Jeu vidéo et émotions. In S. Genvo (Ed.), Le game design de jeux vidéo. Approches de l'expression vidéoludique (pp. 347-366). Paris, France: L'Harmattan.

Perron, B. (2008). Genre profile: Interactive movies. In M. J. P. Wolf (Ed.), *The video game explosion: A history from Pong to Playstation and beyond* (pp. 127–134). Westport, CT: Greenwood Press.

Reader, K. (1991). Literature/cinema/television: Intertextuality in Jean Renoir's Le testament du docteur Cordelier. In M. Worton & J. Still (Eds.), *Intertextuality: Theories and practice* (pp. 176–189). Manchester, UK: Manchester University Press.

Reising, R. (2010). Covering and un(covering) the truth with "All along the watchtower": From Dylan to Hendrix and beyond. In G. Plasketes (Ed.), *Play it again: Cover songs in popular music* (pp. 153–175). Farnham, Surrey, UK; Burlington, VT: Ashgate.

Salen, K., & Zimmerman, E. (2004). *Rules of play: Game design fundamentals.* Cambridge, MA: MIT Press.

Serres, M. (1972). *L'interférence.* Paris, France: Editions de Minuit.

Shannon, C. E., & Weaver, W. (1969). *The mathematical theory of communication.* Urbana, IL; Chicago, IL: The University of Illinois Press.

Stilwell, R. (1995). In the air tonight: Text, intertextuality, and the construction of meaning. *Popular Music and Society, 19*(4), 67–103. doi:10.1080/03007769508591607

Tagg, P. (2000). *Kojak: 50 seconds of television music. Toward the analysis of affect in popular music.* New York, NY: Mass Media Music Scholar's Press.

Tagg, P. (2013). *Music's meanings: A modern musicology for non-musos.* New York, NY: Mass Media Music Scholar's Press.

Whalen, Z. (2004). Play along: An approach to videogame music. *Game Studies, 4*(1). Retrieved September 23, 2012, from http://www.gamestudies.org/0401/whalen/

Zehnder, S. M., & Lipscomb, S. D. (2006). The role of music in video games. In P. Vorderer & J. Bryant (Eds.), *Playing video games: Motives, responses, and consequences* (pp. 241–258). Mahwah, NJ: Lawrence Erlbaum Associates.

KEY TERMS AND DEFINITIONS

Abstract Relation: A relationship between texts where all texts work together toward the production of meaning in a non-hierarchical manner. The resulting effect may take the form of cliché, genre, theme, or contribute to the semantic construction of a recurring object, place, or character (see Babeux, 2007).

Concrete Relation: A relationship between two or more texts in which one acts as a reference for the other and contributes to its narrative meaning. The resulting intersection is intended by the author, as in quotations, allusions or parodies (see Babeux, 2007).

Interferential Network: An accumulation of films, television series and video games which are inter-related by the presence of the same popular song on their respective soundtrack. Each text contributes to the song's meaning in a more or less prominent manner according to individual and cultural variables.

Intertext: The store of artistic, literary or cultural texts which a viewer or gamer may refer to in order to decode a given work.

Intertextuality: An all-encompassing term which describes all types of intersections between texts.

Musical Allusion: A relationship between texts in which one refers to the other through an excerpt of its soundtrack. The evocation of the other narrative is intended to contribute to the viewer or gamer's emotional experience by recreating a familiar effect.

Musical Interference: The projection, by a viewer or gamer, of a relationship between two or more texts on account of the presence of the same song on their respective soundtracks. The intersection is not intended by the author and may lead to an over-interpretation of narrative meaning or to an addition of emotional meaning.

Quotation: The inclusion, in an audiovisual work, of images or sounds belonging to another work.

ENDNOTES

[1]   For example, "Born to Be Wild" was featured in over 35 works between 1969 and 2015; "In-a-gadda-da-vida" made more than 25 appearances between 1970 and 2013, and "Fortunate Son" was featured in over 37 works between 1980 and 2015.

[2]   It is interesting to note that in addition to being featured in *Need for Speed: Carbon*, Goldfrapp's "Ride a White Horse" (*Supernature*, 2005) has also appeared in the television drama series *The Sopranos* ("Members Only", 2006) and *The L Word* ("Literacy License to Kill", 2007) and the simulation game *The Sims 3* (The Sims Studio/Electronic Arts, 2009), and Lady Sovereign's "Love Me or Hate Me" (*Public Warning*, 2006) has appeared in *Ugly Betty* ("The Box and the Bunny", 2006), *The OC* ("The Metamorphosis", 2006), *CSI: Crime Scene Investigation* ("Meet Market", 2007), and has been used as the theme song for reality-TV show *Bad Girls Club* (2006-).

[3]   This can be explained by the status of each song at the time of publication: "In the Air Tonight"'s first video game appearance was in 2006, in *Grand Theft Auto: Vice City Stories* (Rockstar Games).

"All Along the Watchtower" can be performed in *Guitar Hero* 5 (Activision/Red Octane, 2009), which must have been published during the writing or publication process of Reising's text. "The Blue Danube", however, has made appearances in numerous video games, namely *Elite* (Acornsoft Limited, 1984), *Captain Comic* (Color Dreams, 1988), and *Alone in the Dark* (Infograme, 1992).

4   Other concrete relations include *Halloween* (John Carpenter, 1978) and its remake by Rob Zombie (2007), *Scream*'s (Wes Craven, 1996) allusion to Carpenter's *Halloween*, and *Scream*'s relationship with the television series *Smallville* ("Precipice", Thomas Jay Wright, 2003) and the horror film *The Howling: Reborn* (Joe Nimziki, 2011). Even though these series of relations have been graphically represented in figure 3, they will not be discussed in the present chapter, as they don't contain video games. See the author's unpublished master's thesis for a more detailed discussion (Morin-Simard, 2014).

5   Although "Eye of the Tiger" was composed for the soundtrack of *Rocky III* (Sylvester Stallone, 1982), the song has been used so many times (over forty five) that it has since lost its connection to its "parent" film. Viewers who discovered the song through *Rocky III* may still entertain the connection, but it is less likely for younger viewers who have not been in contact with the film.

6   Insofar as "covers provide an intertextual commentary on another musical work or style" (Butler, 2003, p. 1), the original version is always present in the listener's mind as soon as the new version is recognized. As such, cover versions are as much a part of "Don't Fear the Reaper"'s network of media appearances as are uses of its master recording.

7   The popularity of *SNL*'s sketch is such that the catchphrase now has its own *Wikipedia* page (https://en.wikipedia.org/wiki/More_cowbell).

8   For a more detailed discussion of other connections, see the author's unpublished master's thesis (Morin-Simard, 2014).

Chapter 6
BioShock and the Ghost of Ayn Rand:
Universal Learning and Tacit Knowledge in Contemporary Video Games

Chris Richardson
Young Harris College, USA

Mike Elrod
Young Harris College, USA

ABSTRACT

This chapter examines the popular 2007 video game BioShock *and its relation to the work of Objectivist author Ayn Rand. Using Jacques Rancière's model of emancipatory learning and Polanyi's concept of tacit knowledge, the authors explore how video games can instill transferable skills and knowledge by forming intertextual connections to other media. Including an interview with* BioShock *creator Ken Levine, the authors discuss how players may learn about works such as Rand's* Atlas Shrugged, *forming opinions, criticisms, and applications of her philosophy, without ever receiving explanations of it in the game. They conclude the chapter by demonstrating the potential for such forms of learning to become more prominent in video games, while also acknowledging the inherent limitations of the medium.*

A being who does not know automatically what is true or false, cannot know automatically what is right or wrong, what is good for him or evil. Yet he needs that knowledge in order to live. He is not exempt from the laws of reality (Ayn Rand, 1964, p. 18)

A man chooses. A slave obeys. (Andrew Ryan, as cited in BioShock, 2007)

DOI: 10.4018/978-1-5225-0477-1.ch006

INTRODUCTION

A specter is haunting Rapture—the specter of Ayn Rand. As players move through this horrific underwater city, shooting deranged citizens and saving genetically modified girls from certain death, Rand's name will never be uttered, her books will never be mentioned, and her theories will never be discussed. Yet, Rand's ghost floats through every scene of *BioShock*.

Numerous scholars have considered this lingering ghost in the machine.[1]Packer (2010) argues the game is a forceful critique of Rand because success "depends upon the player universalizing the idea that Objectivists are dangerous" (p. 216). Rose (2015), on the other hand, argues that *BioShock* "isn't an anti-Randian statement so much as a cautionary tale about being blinded by one's ideology" (p. 22). Meanwhile, Lizardi (2014) suggests the game "represents an encouragement of complex historical interpretations as opposed to simplistic accepted histories" (para 2). Tavinor (2009a) explores the artistic nature of the game, suggesting it could be read as "a parody of Ayn Rand's objectivist novel *Atlas Shrugged*" (p. 91). Drawing attention to the use of music in the game, Gibbons (2011) argues that the soundtrack creates "both a palpable sense of irony in its atmosphere—one of the game's most-praised aspects—and a complex web of intertextual references, involving musical 'puns' based on song titles and lyrics" (Conclusions, para 2). But one important aspect of this relationship remains unclear: What knowledge can players be said to have of Rand after experiencing *BioShock*? Is it, in fact, possible to learn about works such as *Atlas Shrugged* through the allusions that permeate the game?

In this chapter, we begin by outlining the major attributes of both *BioShock* and Rand's oeuvre, demonstrating the myriad connections the landmark video game shares with the writer's work. We then introduce two theories of learning that allow us to negotiate the questions we have posed. We argue that Rancière's model of intellectual emancipation and Polanyi's tacit knowing provide valuable conceptual tools through which to form our answers. We include excerpts from our interview with Ken Levine, who wrote the story for *BioShock* and oversaw the production of the game as its creative director to explore how many of his intentions align with these theories and support our claim that video games can help players develop what Rancière introduces as "universal learning" strategies. Ultimately, we argue that *BioShock* demonstrates the potential for video games to create intertextual environments that push players to explore and build their tacit knowledge and intellectual positions without resorting to the stultifying learning conditions that perpetuate the dichotomy of master and student. We make no claims that video games ought to replace professors or textbooks. We do, however, embrace the aspects of video games that encourage exploration rather than explanation because of their potential to foster understanding in ways that extend far beyond the immediate content of the game.

BACKGROUND

The Objectivist Dystopia of *BioShock*

BioShock is a first-person shooter that takes place in the underwater city of Rapture. Set in 1960, the game introduces players to a society composed of artists, businessmen, scientists, and other cultural elites who sought solace from overbearing governmental structures. Now, however, that dream has disintegrated and deranged citizens scavenge buildings looking for ADAM, a currency that allows them to buy genetic modifications. Similarly altered "Little Sisters" wander the decomposing neighborhoods under the protection of men in steroidal diving gear named "Big Daddies." Those who haven't gone mad seem to have disappeared. And no one knows just what happened to the city's founder.

Playing as Jack, you survive a plane crash at the beginning of the game and are plunged into the middle of the Atlantic Ocean. You swim to a mysterious lighthouse, the interior of which features a large statue of Rapture founder Andrew Ryan (a nod to Ayn Rand). This scene is the first of many allusions to Rand and her Objectivist ideas within the game. Under the statue, a banner reads "No Gods or Kings. Only Man," further linking Rapture's foundational paradigms to Rand's ideals of individualism and self-reliance. Descending in a diving pod, you watch a pre-recorded message from Ryan that explains how Rapture was built. It was to be a utopia of unfettered creativity, where the imagination and skill of citizens would be unrestricted by law or morality. In Rapture, no government would control the inhabitants. The economy alone would drive innovation and social interactions.

The pod docks in an underground terminal where you enter the city. Before the pod doors open, you see a deformed human with two scythes eviscerate his victim. The monstrous figure then turns his attention to you and begins cutting away at the metal hull but, unable to break through, he moves on. You later learn that this person is one of many genetically modified humans known as Splicers, who crawl on ceilings and hunt survivors in Rapture. The scene in the station is dark, the only light coming through a large window that filters in the ocean water from outside, signaling *BioShock's* use of horror and noir conventions. Through a handheld radio, you receive guidance from a man named Atlas, who introduces himself as a citizen of Rapture who has become part of a rebellion against Ryan (a storyline that parallels the Bolshevik revolution Rand experienced as a child and alludes to one of her most well-known books, *Atlas Shrugged*).[2] Through further gameplay, you learn that on New Year's Eve 1958, Rapture's class war came to a head. This was the second war over the city, the first being the battle against Ryan led by Frank Fontaine (an allusion to Rand's novel *The Fountainhead*).

BioShock plays with gamers' expectations to create a compelling narrative unlike previous first-person shooters. It uses the plot points of genetic modification and memory manipulation to fold into the story the mechanics of the game, challenging players to think about why they are doing certain tasks and who is really making the decisions. This self-reflexive technique becomes dramatically evident in the climax, when you, as Jack, are revealed to have been manipulated by Atlas throughout your adventure. You discover that Atlas is in fact Fontaine, who faked his own death in order to escape Ryan's clutches. You are actually Ryan's illegitimate child but have no memory of this because you were smuggled out of the city to be used as Fontaine's sleeper agent. It is further revealed that you were subconsciously implanted with the key phrase "would you kindly" to prime you to do Fontaine's bidding throughout the game. With the help of Little Sisters and other characters, you overcome this brainwashing and Ryan and Fountain meet their doom. In the end, if you have chosen to save the little sisters during the narrative, you return to the surface and grow old watching the young women live fulfilling lives. If you harvested a little sister for their ADAM, however, splicers return to the surface alongside you to wreak havoc on the world.

THE GHOST IN THE MACHINE

BioShock explores Rand's philosophy of Objectivism, focusing on the two basic tenets of selfishness and unregulated competition. To begin, the character Andrew Ryan, already a partial anagram of the author of *Anthem* (1938/2014), *The Fountainhead* (1943/1994), *Atlas Shrugged* (1957/2005), and *The Virtue of*

Selfishness (1964), represents both an embodiment of Rand as well as her ideal man (as personified by John Galt and Howard Roark in her own work). Through her fictional narratives, Rand describes interactions between modern-day supermen and the clueless middlemen who stall their achievements with regulations, red tape, and taxation. Painting her philosophy with these bold strokes, Rand generated strong emotional reactions from readers, both for and against her ideas. As Daniels (2010) argues, Rand's use of such representative fiction, regardless of her intentions, made her synonymous with her protagonists.

Much of Rand's work focuses on institutional requirements to help others. She argues that taking care of one's self produces an ideal, where needs and desires are fulfilled by our own actions rather than the helping hand of the state. Instead of an unfavorable definition of selfishness, Rand develops the term in opposition to the more popular ideal of altruism. For Rand, a society that enforces altruism creates dependency on the state and restricts progress and innovation. During a 1959 interview with Mike Wallace, she offered an example of her definition of selfishness by explaining her love for her husband (PBS, 2015). When asked if she would financially support him as he embarked on a career in art, she admitted that she would help him if necessary, not because it would be a kind thing to do but because she loved him with selfish pleasure and would therefore receive something of value from the exchange.

Rand develops her ideals in *Atlas Shrugged,* particularly through the contrast between John Galt, a self-reliant entrepreneur and the throngs of citizens who rely on the ideas and hard work of others. Ironically, her description of an American dystopia brought about by mediocrity, conformity, and collectivist politics in the novel reads very similarly to the collapse of Rapture due to its selfish and sinister population:

The newspapers did not mention the outbreaks of violence that had begun to burst across the country—but she watched them through the reports of train conductors about bullet-riddled cars, dismantled tracks, attacked trains, besieged stations, in Nebraska, in Oregon, in Texas, in Montana—the futile, doomed outbreaks, prompted by nothing but despair, ending in nothing but destruction. Some were the explosions of local gangs; some spread wider. There were districts that rose in blind rebellion, arrested the local officials, expelled the agents of Washington, killed the tax collectors—then, announcing their secession from the country, went on to the final extreme of the very evil that had destroyed them, as if fighting murder with suicide: went on to seize all property within their reach, to declare community bondage all to all, and to perish within a week, their meager loot consumed, in the bloody hatred of all for all, in the chaos of no rule save that of the gun, to perish under the lethargic thrust of a few worn soldiers sent out from Washington to bring order to the ruins. (Rand, 2005, p. 1003)

Atlas Shrugged relies heavily on Rand's personal experiences as a child during the Bolshevik Revolution. For her, revolutionary action without a plan to change the core of the problem, namely government-mandated collectivist ideals, will never bring about a better society. The irony of revolutions (exemplified in *Atlas Shrugged*) is that they require large amounts of people to unify under a shared idea much like the governments against which revolutionaries fight. This requirement of group thought dooms it to failure. It is the fulfillment of one's ability to care for one's own needs (i.e., selfishness) that allows people living alongside one another to flourish. Rand's Objectivist world is the basis for the character of Andrew Ryan, his followers, and their underwater city. Theirs was an experiment in individual human greatness rather than in group mediocrity. The difference between *BioShock* and works such as *Atlas Shrugged,* however, is that Rand describes dystopian cities that became so by *not* following her Objectivist principles, while Levine creates Rapture as an image of what a city would look like if it *did* follow them.

Rand and Ryan can easily be seen as devils who corrupt the souls of others, but closer observation of both the person and fictional character reveal a hopefulness about what society can become. Rand's belief that the economy would be best served by keeping government out of the picture has become a selling point to many economists, politicians, and political activists since the publication of *Atlas Shrugged* (Burns, 2009; Peikoff, 1993; Weiss, 2012). Her ideal selfish society is built on laissez-faire capitalism, which evolves on its own to form a better civilization. And she was not alone; many entrepreneurs, politicians and artists continue to sight her as influential in their own worldviews. One of her many admirers included Alan Greenspan, Chairman of the Federal Reserve from1987 to 2006. While Greenspan (2007) no longer wholeheartedly agrees with her philosophy, he writes that "Ayn Rand and I remained close until she died in 1982, and I'm grateful for the influence she had on my life. I was intellectually limited until I met her…Rand persuaded me to look at human beings, their values, how they work, what they do and why they do it, and how they think and why they think. This broadened my horizons far beyond the models of economics I'd learned" (p. 53). Rand believed that we would never create the ultimate version of the world without this open market model. She argued that the American economic system that profited by taxing hardworking people and regulating the ideas of entrepreneurs that she argued kept humanity from achieving its full potential. Through regulation by uncreative middle-men, creators and producers became convinced that they could not survive without those who took their profits. A true utopia, for Rand, was one where such practices were abolished and those who created were the ones who profited. This is only a piece of Rand's work and philosophy, but is the crux of the world in which *BioShock*'s events occur.

Ultimately, Rand argued that an economic system should stand separate from ethics, which frees it to grow through human innovation rather than intervention. Economics, like art, could not thrive if hampered by concerns of what should or shouldn't be created, bought, or sold. Allusions to this ideal are scattered throughout Rapture in the form of advertisements for the genetic modifications called Plasmids. These displays embody the aesthetics of the post-war appliance commercials reminiscent of The Jetsons or Disney's Tomorrowland. *BioShock's* advertisements for telekinesis, incineration, and invisibility harken back to a time when no vision of the future seemed too outlandish and Rand's popularity was at its peak. The irony is that players encounter the displays already broken and crumbling, alluding to our knowledge that many of the dreams of this period never came to be.

LEARNING FROM VIDEO GAMES

Intertextuality and the Ignorant Schoolmaster

Having identified the intertextual connections between *BioShock* and Rand, the question we seek to answer remains open: what knowledge can one be said to possess about Objectivism after having played the game? Furthermore, is it possible to learn something from a source that makes no claim to teach it? Many scholars consider intertextuality in relation to works that assume some previous knowledge on the part of the reader. But what happens when the texts are linked through allusions the reader may not know? When *BioShock* players, for instance, encounter Randian ideas for the first time, can we say they have encountered *Atlas Shrugged* on a meaningful level? To explore this relationship, we turn to an often-overlooked text by French philosopher Jacques Rancière, *Le Maître Ignorant*, originally published in French in 1987 and translated into English in 1991 as *The Ignorant Schoolmaster: Five Lessons in*

Intellectual Emancipation. The book, based on the records of Joseph Jacotot, examines how a French exile developed a method to teach law to his Flemish-speaking students without knowing the language. Through his experience, Jacotot introduced the concept of universal teaching in the early nineteenth century, an idea Rancière revived in the 1980s under the moniker of intellectual emancipation.

Jacotot argued that anyone could learn anything. He went so far as to assert that one could be ignorant of the subject and still teach it. What mattered was not previous knowledge or educational status but simply the will to know and the motivation to make connections that move from the known to the unknown. In this way, students could develop proficiencies in literacy, languages, mathematics, and virtually anything else. They merely needed to begin at the first word of a book or prayer or math formula and build connections outwards from there.

Presented with scholars who could not speak French and knowing no Flemish himself, Jacotot had his students read a French-Flemish version of Fénelon's utopian novel *Télémaque*. Through the help of a translator, Jacotot asked students to recite, memorize, translate, question, and reflect upon the work. He found that students were not only capable of replacing words with their equivalents, they also arrived at new understandings of language, grammar, ethics and political thought. They learned without didactic lectures, without acknowledged experts, and without any explicit instructions beyond the initial imperatives that had them read and reflect.

Jacotot's students achieved nuanced understandings without any of the taken-for-granted elements of traditional education, a feat that most pedagogues, even today, would likely have thought impossible. [3] Yet the method succeeded. Through Jacotot's "universal teaching," translation becomes a path to knowledge. Jacotot's students, much like gamers left to fend for themselves in a mysterious new environment, reflected upon what they already knew, expanding the horizon of that knowledge as they made their way through the pages. "Understanding is never more than translation," writes Rancière (1991), "that is, giving the equivalent of a text, but in no way its reason" (p. 9). Removing the assumption of a deeper, master's knowledge, Rancière insists that students can know a text as much as anyone else simply by translating, substituting, and drawing conclusions. In doing so, his work provides an interesting possibility for the intertextual powers of games like *BioShock*, which can create new understandings through their translations of concepts such as Objectivism.

BioShock transforms Rand's work, describing her ideas in new ways and through new examples that call for further reflection and interpretation. This technique is akin to Rand's own method of communicating her philosophy by putting it into narratives that see its consequences unfold. And if readers of *Atlas Shrugged* can develop an understanding of Objectivist philosophy by reading the dialogues between Dagny Taggart and Francisco D'Anconia, it stands to reason that interactions between Jack and Fontaine will also provoke contemplation of Rand's philosophy. Furthermore, both works assume participants are capable of connecting the narratives with their economic, political, and social insights. In essence, then, *BioShock* translates *Atlas Shrugged*, which is already a translation of Rand's philosophy, further illustrating Rancière's maxim that understanding is never more than translation.

Rancière (1991) begins with the assumption that everyone has an innate capacity to learn. As Ross suggests in her introduction to the English translation of *The Ignorant Schoolmaster*, Rancière "places equality-virtually-in the present" (xxiii). Traditional pedagogy begins with the assumption that people cannot learn on their own—if they could, there would be no need for teachers. Rancière, however, flips this assumption. He argues that the teacher impedes learning. "It is the explicator who needs the incapable and not the other way around," posits Rancière (p. 6). By forcing students into positions of inferiority, they do not see themselves as capable learners but as passive receivers of wisdom. Rancière refers to this situation as "the myth of pedagogy." And while we take a somewhat less extreme position in this chapter—we do not seek to expose pedagogy as a myth—we nevertheless believe that *BioShock* demonstrates the potential for video games to teach players and allow them to acquire knowledge and skills in a way that closely resembles this emancipatory learning paradigm.

In many respects, video games align closely with Rancière's vision of emancipatory learning by assuming players can achieve success on their own. As anyone who has tried to explain to new players, step-by-step, how to succeed in a video game knows, telling players what buttons to press and what doors to enter will only make them grow impatient and annoyed. But put a controller into their hands and they will figure out how to maneuver within the virtual world, finding keys, slaying monsters, winning races, etc. And they will continue to refine their skills with each new move. Video games would look very different if players relied on experts to explain the techniques of winning, perhaps by attending lectures, completing weekly quizzes, and sitting a final exam.[4] The gamers' self-confidence to learn without seeking a master's explanation is crucial to their success.

If we are to argue, however, that players can understand a text like Rand's simply by playing a first-person shooter, we must question what it means to "understand" her work in the first place. Rancière (1991) writes that "unfortunately, it is just this little word, this slogan of the enlightened—understand—that causes all the trouble" (p. 8). The word, he argues, divides knowledge between those "learned little men" who possess understanding and the "groping animal" who cannot understand without the intervention of a master. This way of knowing a text divides it between those with the social and cultural competencies to understand it (e.g., the English scholar's knowledge of Shakespeare, the Physicist's knowledge of Einstein, or the Political Scientist's knowledge of Rand) and those who must acknowledge their lack of understanding and have the text explained to them. In this way, the traditional model of education, or "stultification" in Rancière's terms, forms an impassible chasm between master and student. And for such practitioners, there is little doubt as to whether one could understand Rand and Objectivism through *BioShock*. The answer would clearly be "no." But under the emancipatory model of intellectual development, which challenges this separation as a false dichotomy, it seems quite possible that one could attain knowledge of her text through playing the game.

Not only do video games seem to promote Rancière's concept of emancipatory learning, Levine's intentions when creating the game closely reflect this model. "I'm not really that interested in teaching a lesson," Levine told us (personal communication, June 17, 2015). "I've read *The Fountainhead* and *Atlas Shrugged*…well *most* of *Atlas Shrugged*. I think I got the idea." Rather than set out to explain it or criticize its premises, however, Levine considered the game a "thought experiment," in which players move through a city that puts the selfish, laissez-faire society expounded by Rand into practice. Levine took on *BioShock* already having a reputation for narrative-driven games that explore "thought experiments." Working at Looking Glass Studios, he produced games such as *Thief: The Dark Project*, a genre-defining stealth game that garnered a cult following and saw multiple sequels, community modifications, and a 2014 reboot. Soon after its release, Levine started his own production company, *Irrational Games,* which released *BioShock* in 2007. Much like Rand created works of fiction such as *Atlas Shrugged*, *The Fountainhead*, and *Anthem* to translate her ideas into compelling narratives, Levine designed characters who were left disfigured after the collapse of their unregulated society to illustrate the possible repercussions of Rand's ideas. Levine compares his narrative to George Orwell's *Animal Farm*, a work that greatly influenced him. As in *Animal Farm*, the allegory of the Russian revolution in which livestock take over the farmer's barn, Levine's *BioShock* uses the dystopian city of Rapture, with its Big Daddies and Little Sisters, to think through some of Rand's concepts. "I hope somebody got an *Animal Farm* experience out of *BioShock*. I don't know if anybody did," he says.

This style of learning differs significantly from more traditional explanations or academic critiques by relying almost completely on allusions and intertextual connections rather than explicit argumentation. "I don't really know if I'm someone capable of teaching lessons because I'm so confused myself," said Levine jokingly. Rather than a master passing down knowledge about the work, or systematically appraising its quality, Levine, like Orwell and Rand before him, translates ideas into poignant stories through a popular medium and puts them before readers (or players) whose role it becomes to think through them. "What I took away from the book was not necessarily a critique of extreme left ideologies. It was something larger about how society works," states Levine. "I don't know Orwell. Potentially, the authorial intent had nothing to do with what I took away from *Animal Farm*." Thus, rather than explain or critique Rand's work, Levine creates a situation through which players encounter and respond to her ideas.

As Bruno Latour (2004) famously pointed out, explanation and critique, particularly in contemporary social sciences and humanities departments, often fail to achieve the wisdom they seem to promise. "What's the real difference between conspiracists and a popularized, that is a teachable version of social critique inspired by a too quick reading of, let's say, a sociologist as eminent as Pierre Bourdieu?" asks Latour (pp. 228-9). "In both cases, you have to learn to become suspicious of everything people say because of course we all know that they live in the thralls of a complete illusion of their real motives." In essence, Latour, and those who have taken up his ideas (Andrejevic, 2013; Ang, 2011; Diken, 2009; Felski, 2011; Mallavarapu & Prasad, 2006; Sterne & Leach, 2005; White, 2013), demonstrate convincingly that contemporary critique may not be as useful or enlightening as traditional scholars once presumed. "I find something troublingly similar in the structure of the explanation," writes Latour (2004, p. 229). "What if explanations resorting automatically to power, society, discourse had outlived their usefulness and deteriorated to the point of now feeding the most gullible sort of critique?" (pp. 229-230).[5] Furthermore, these practices require experts who must explain things to those who have failed to understand them. Universal learning, on the other hand, dissolves the distinction. It opens the possibility of learning without seeking explanations or critiques from authorities. This recognition is particularly useful because, as many *BioShock* players and Rand readers will argue, there is a less tangible, almost inexplicable quality that often eludes the critiques and explanations of these works. Thus, we suggest in the next section an alternative way of understanding (inter)texts to more fully assess how players connect to these narratives and ideas.

Tacit Knowledge

Michael Polanyi's famous talks on tacit knowledge, first given as Terry Lectures at Yale University in 1962 and later published as *The Tacit Dimension*, provide a valuable tool for better understanding the relationship between *BioShock* and *Atlas Shrugged*. According to Polanyi, we use tacit knowledge regularly to negotiate the world around us. But we generally cannot explain it. In other words, tacit knowledge is what we know without really knowing that we know it. And it goes without saying that these skills and understandings are difficult to teach to others.

In certain respects, tacit knowledge *is* intertextual knowledge. Referring to the functional relation between the object of knowledge and the knower, Polanyi argues that "we know the first term only by relying on our awareness of it for attending to the second" (p. 10). He uses examples from psychological experiments in which participants were given a shock after hearing a certain sound within a random assortment of nonsense syllables. They soon began to anticipate the shock, connecting it with the specific syllable without being able to consciously explain the connection they were making. Similarly, in a study that punished people for uttering things associated with certain "shock words," participants began avoiding punishable statements without being able to explain how they knew what phrases to avoid. Following from these examples, *BioShock* players may not be able to name the characters in Rand's novels or the academic debates that have taken place around them, but they will likely recognize many of her Objectivist views through tacit knowledge. In short, they will be able to assess many of the tenets of Objectivism without necessarily possessing its vocabulary.

Polanyi argues that tacit knowledge comprises four essential aspects: function, phenomena, semantics, and ontology. Identifying these aspects can help us better investigate the process at work in video games like *BioShock*. The functional aspect relates to the way in which one thing, such as the movements of facial muscles, work to trigger the recognition of a second thing, the acknowledgement of anger for example. This connection between muscles and emotion is not explicit. Tacit knowers may not be able to identify the alterations of the procerus and mentalis muscles when they identify an angry person. The knowledge nevertheless *functions* when the knower sees anger on the person's face. The phenomenal aspect, Polanyi writes, refers to our focus on a first object to anticipate the presence of a second. Again, we may not know how we are looking for the appearance of emotion but we know when it's there. Furthermore, the semantic aspect deals with the way we recognize meaning. We know, for example, that the dropped eyebrows, narrowing lips, and glaring eyes indicate anger without necessarily being able to identify these signifiers beforehand. Nevertheless, the signifiers take on meaning through the recognition of what it is they signify—anger. Thus, we can say *that* means he is angry without being able to identify specifically what "that" is. Finally, the ontological aspect appears when we recognize the existence of the thing itself. By recognizing anger in someone's face, we acknowledge the possibility of an angry person. Despite our inability to lay out its features and explain our interpretations, we do not doubt that an emotional being exists before us.

When presented with the idea of tacit knowledge, Levine told us that he relied heavily on that kind of awareness as he constructed the game (personal communication, June 17, 2015). On a simple level, for instance, cameras, turrets, and Big Daddies have lights that subtly indicate how much of a threat they represent for players. "Why you would create a security system that would warn you it's going to shoot you…well that's us cheating a little bit, leveraging the existing knowledge players have about stop lights, etc." On a more subtle level, the body language between the Big Daddies and the Little Sisters demonstrates to players that the large, submariners care deeply for their younger charges, whom they will protect with their lives. "I was watching a nature show, watching how predators interact with their prey and how some animals protect other animals, such as mothers and their cubs, and I was like, 'wow, without words, there's so much we can parse from this. What if we tried to do a world where there are clear predators and prey and protectors?'" asks Levine. "Without a word, we were leveraging, as you would say, the 'tacit knowledge' that people have from other experiences of seeing children and parents, nature shows, and stuff like that. The first design element we came up with for the game, I guess, was really that tacit relationship."

Polanyi's concept of tacit knowledge, which continues to influence scholars' views of video games (e.g., Ash, 2013; Jansz, 2005; Thomas & Brown, 2009; Wagner, 2008; Zackariasson, Styhre, & Wilson, 2006), helps us unpack some of the learning that we suggest transpires through *BioShock*. As players use previous skills from negotiating busy intersections to having watched wildlife documentaries, they will look to see how such knowledge can be translated into the context of a crumbling underwater world that requires stealth, curiosity, and quick decision making. These translations of earlier intertextual knowledge allow players to continue building a repertoire as they apply the knowledge acquired through *BioShock* to other contexts. Tacit knowledge explains how many players navigate easily through the world of Rapture with little or no formal guidance, harnessing previous experience and forming implicit connections. But it does not fully reveal how players interpret and assess the ghost of Rand that permeates the game. For this final exploration, we return to Rancière's work on emancipatory learning.

The Challenges of Emancipatory Game Design

While Rancière's (1991) emancipatory learning method does not refer specifically to video games, it does propose that students learn best by exploring and assessing phenomena without explanations that perpetuate distinctions between teachers and students. He argues that "The student must see everything for himself, compare and compare, and always respond to a three-part question: what do you see? what do you think about it? what do you make of it?" He adds that this infinite process "is no longer the master's secret; it is the student's journey" (p. 23). Such a method is clearly suited to video games, in which players traverse new environments, assessing what they see, what they think, and what they make of such worlds, with no more explication than perhaps a naming of the controller's functions. Such environments encourage—but do not guarantee—that players embody the principles of universal learning.

As Levine maintains, "I think you can learn a lot about Objectivism from playing *BioShock*." His reworking of Rand's ideas in an attempt to better understand her philosophy closely resembles the process of translation Rancière argues lies at the heart of knowledge. "I didn't have seventy-five pages to line it up. So I came up with things like "No Gods or Kings. Only Man" for when you first come in there [to the lighthouse in the opening scene]." Since the game's release, myriad posters, animations, and other artistic creations, both official and unofficial, translate this line and others into alternative contexts and situations. One particularly poignant example of this intertextual translation is a meme that features Walt Disney as Ryan speaking the lines in relation to his family-oriented entertainment company.[6] Thus, *BioShock* becomes a source of knowledge among a complex genealogy that includes Rand's works as well as that of Walt Disney, George Orwell, Jacques Cousteau, John Ford, Orson Wells, J. J. Abrams, and the biblical stories of Adam and Eve to name just a few.

The concept of emancipatory learning, however, raises some difficult questions. For example, Rancière (1991) argues that covert or elliptical ways of presenting information are just as problematic as a master's explicit explanation—perhaps more so. "The Socratic method of interrogation that pretends to lead the student to his own knowledge is in fact the method of a riding school master," argues Rancière (p. 59). Here, video games enter a murky area. Jacotot urged students to pursue any line of enquiry to attain knowledge. But video games necessarily constrict the possibilities of exploration through the size of the digital environment, the movements of the character, and the twists and turns of the storyline that allows players to progress. While the level of detail and the expanses of space have increased exponentially, particularly with breakthrough sandbox games such as the *GTA* series and with the continuously updating massively multiplayer online role-playing games such as *EverQuest* and *World of Warcraft*, the possibilities within video games remain bounded by the capacities of consoles, graphics cards, and production budgets. This lack of possibility has led authors such as Travis (2010) to compare the constrictions of *BioShock* and other games to Plato's cave, arguing that "every game's ethical choices work within a framework reducible to the prisoners' interaction with the shadow-puppet play, wherein they are made to feel themselves invested in the cave-culture-game because of their capacity to obtain rewards for their interaction with the play" (p. 94). Furthermore, as Packer (2010) argues, players cannot choose to be pacifists in a shooting game. In fact, the most successful technique in FPS games is often the most violent, which is not likely a message anyone would want players to apply in real-world situations. Such limits, no matter how self-reflective games like *BioShock* may be, represent a difference between the ideal universal learning structure and contemporary video games.

Furthermore, the reliance on conventions found in previous games could be argued to perpetuate the kind of regulation Rancière criticizes, which he argues sets a dangerous expectation for guidance. Having gamers seek to increase their purses, maintain their life-bars, seek out treasures and upgrade their weapons all become second nature and thus stand to become regimented elements of the culture rather than objects of reflection. Rancière writes that "each one of us describes our parabola around the truth. No two orbits are alike. And this is why the explicators endanger our revolution" (p. 59). He also states that "what is essential is to avoid lying, not to say that we have seen something when we've kept our eyes closed, not to believe that something has been explained to us when it has only been named." Here, we urge a reading of game design as akin to "naming" but not "explaining," by which we mean that designers like Levine challenge players by presenting Ryan as a foe to battle and ADAM as a substance to acquire, but do not provide explicit lessons or explanations, leaving open the meaning of these events.

Finally, there is implicit learning to consider, which we argue is best explored through Polanyi's concept of tacit knowledge. Players transfer skills and knowledge that may be difficult to explain, yet allows them to attend to dangers, solve problems, and overcome challenges. But they often must venture outside of the game itself to gain the ability to explicitly make sense of their knowledge. *BioShock* players, for instance, may intuit many of Rand's ideas and recognize them when they see *Atlas Shrugged* on a book shelf. But only in reading it will they be able to draw explicit connections to the characters and plotlines of the two texts. Such intertextual linkages, we argue, can develop into emancipatory learning experiences for motivated players but such outcomes are not guaranteed. If good video games teach anything, however, it is that challenges can be faced without masters' explanations and answers can be found through seeking them out rather than having them handed to us. In games, there are no masters and slaves, no teachers and students, only players.

CONCLUSION

Almost a decade after its release, *BioShock* remains one of the most well respected series of all time. Its attention to detail, innovation in storytelling, and inventive blending of mystery, horror, science fiction, and tragedy have cemented its place in video game history. Similarly, Rand's *Atlas Shrugged* remains a top-selling novel many decades after its initial publication. Its success lies not in its explanation of Objectivism, but in its compelling translation of her philosophy into a narrative that challenges readers to reflect on and interpret its messages. At first, the relationship between the two works may seem superficial, the game having taken inspiration from the novel. But if we take seriously Rancière's exploration of universal learning, we can see that the two are intricately linked both in content and delivery method. Without explaining Rand and her work, *BioShock* allows players to walk away with a deeper appreciation of novels such as *Atlas Shrugged*. Levine's translation does not seek to replace the book or reveal its true nature. It simply assumes that players are capable of moving through the dangerous emerald city, much like a reader will navigate through Rand's dystopian American landscape, answering questions such as: what do I see? what do I think about it? and what do I make of it? With each iteration of these questions, players become more knowledgeable.

The number of video game scholars exploring the new medium and its potential for teaching seems to grow daily (Bogost, 2007, 2011; Griffiths, 2002; Gee, 2003, 2004, 2007; Gros, 2007; Kafai, 2006; Prensky, 2006). It is no secret, as these scholars discuss in more detail, that informal learning in such forms of popular entertainment can be very effective. Video games may not be perfect tools for universal learning. Their landscapes are bounded, the players' choices limited, and many games do not offer the kind of depth that *BioShock's* narrative delivers. But, through these kinds of thought experiments, players tacitly learn to shed their dependence on masters' explanations and journey through scenarios that inspire self-reliance, curiosity, and skills that can translate to new situations, both actual and virtual. Using games as vehicles for teaching is becoming a common strategy. With this popular notion, however, comes the potential pitfall of structuring video games in a way that replicates the master/student distinction. If video games are to truly offer more than the stultifying learning experiences of the past, designers must draw on the medium's potential to create open worlds where players seek out and surpass previous understandings on their own, building skills, knowledge, and confidence as they move from one challenge to the next. By necessity, game designers must limit the possibilities of what can and cannot occur in their virtual environments. But, when done well, the intertextual connections they create allow the narratives to move far beyond the limits of the platform to become part of a larger, potentially infinite, conversation.

REFERENCES

Andrejevic, M. (2013). Whither-ing critique. *Communication and Critical. Cultural Studies*, *10*(2-3), 222–228.

Ang, I. (2011). Navigating complexity: From cultural critique to cultural intelligence. *Continuum*, *25*(6), 779–794. doi:10.1080/10304312.2011.617873

Ash, J. (2013). Technologies of captivation videogames and the attunement of affect. *Body & Society*, *19*(1), 27–51. doi:10.1177/1357034X11411737

Bogost, I. (2007). *Persuasive games: The expressive power of videogames*. Cambridge, MA: MIT Press.

Bogost, I. (2011). *How to do things with videogames*. Minneapolis, MN: University of Minnesota Press. doi:10.5749/minnesota/9780816676460.001.0001

Breaking the mold: The art of BioShock . (2007). 2K Games.

Burns, J. (2009). *Goddess of the market: Ayn Rand and the American right*. Oxford, UK: Oxford University Press.

Cuddey, L. (Ed.). (2015). *BioShock and philosophy: Irrational game, rational book*. Malden, MA: Wiley Blackwell. doi:10.1002/9781118915899

Daniels, A. (2010). Ayn Rand: Engineer of souls. *New Criterion, 28*(6), 4-9. Retrieved from http://www.newcriterion.com/articles.cfm/Ayn-Rand--engineer-of-souls-4385

Deco devolution: The art of BioShock 2 . (2010). 2K Games.

Diken, B. (2009). Radical critique as the paradox of post-political society. *Third Text*, *23*(5), 579–586. doi:10.1080/09528820903184815

Felski, R. (2011). Critique and the hermeneutics of suspicion. *M/C Journal, 15*(1). Retrieved from http://journal.media-culture.org.au/index.php/mcjournal/article/viewArticle/431

Freire, P. (2000). *Pedagogy of the oppressed*. London, UK: Bloomsbury Publishing.

Gee, J. P. (2003). *What video games have to teach us about learning and literacy*. New York, NY: Palgrave MacMillan.

Gee, J. P. (2004). Learning by design: Games as learning machines. *Interactive Educational Multimedia*, (8), 15-23.

Gee, J. P. (2007). *Good video games+ good learning: Collected essays on video games, learning, and literacy*. New York, NY: P. Lang.

Gibbons, W. (2011). *Wrap your troubles in dreams: Popular music, narrative, and dystopia in BioShock. Games studies: The International Journal of Computer Game Research, 11(3)*.

Goldberg, H. (2011). *All your base are belong to us: How fifty years of videogames conquered pop culture*. New York, NY: Three Rivers Press.

Greenspan, A. (2007). *Age of turbulence*. New York, NY: Penguin.

Griffiths, M. (2002). The educational benefits of videogames. *Education for Health*, *20*(3), 47–51.

Gros, B. (2007). Digital games in education: The design of games-based learning environments. *Journal of Research on Technology in Education*, *40*(1), 23–38. doi:10.1080/15391523.2007.10782494

Gross, M., & McGoey, L. (Eds.). (2015). *Routledge international handbook of ignorance studies*. New York, NY: Routledge.

Heller, A. (2009). *Ayn Rand and the world she made*. New York, NY: Doubleday.

Jansz, J. (2005). The emotional appeal of violent video games for adolescent males. *Communication Theory*, *15*(3), 219–241. doi:10.1111/j.1468-2885.2005.tb00334.x

Kafai, Y. B. (2006). Playing and making games for learning instructionist and constructionist perspectives for game studies. *Games and Culture*, *1*(1), 36–40. doi:10.1177/1555412005281767

Khine, M. S. (Ed.). (2011). *Learning to play: Exploring the future of education with video games*. New York, NY: Peter Lang.

Latour, B. (2004). Why has critique run out of steam? From matters of fact to matters of concern. *Critical Inquiry*, *30*(Winter), 225–248. doi:10.1086/421123

Lizardi, R. (2014). *BioShock*: Complex and alternate histories. *Games studies*: *The International Journal of Computer Game Research, 14*(1). Retrieved from http://gamestudies.org/1401/articles/lizardi

Mallavarapu, S., & Prasad, A. (2006). Facts, fetishes, and the parliament of things: Is there any space for critique? *Social Epistemology, 20*(2), 185–199. doi:10.1080/02691720600784782

Packer, J. (2010). The battle for Galt's gulch: *BioShock* as critique of Objectivism. *Journal of Gaming and Virtual Worlds, 2*(3), 209–224. doi:10.1386/jgvw.2.3.209_1

PBS Digital Studios. (2015, June 9). *Ayn Rand on love and happiness* [Video file]. Retrieved from https://youtu.be/mQVrMzWtqgU

Peikoff, L., & Ward, J. (1993). *Objectivism: The philosophy of Ayn Rand*. New York, NY: Meridian.

Polanyi, M. (2009). *The tacit dimension*. Chicago, IL: University of Chicago Press.

Prensky, M. (2006). *Don't bother me, mom, I'm learning!: How computer and video games are preparing your kids for 21st century success and how you can help!* New York, NY: Paragon.

Rancière, J. (1991). *The ignorant schoolmaster: Five lessons in intellectual emancipation* (K. Ross, Trans.). Stanford, CA: Stanford University Press.

Rand, A. (1964). *The virtue of selfishness*. New York, NY: New American Library.

Rand, A. (1994). *The fountainhead*. New York, NY: Penguin. (Original work published 1943)

Rand, A. (2005). *Atlas shrugged*. New York, NY: Penguin. (Original work published 1957)

Rand, A. (2014). *Anthem. Mineola, New York*. NY: Dover. (Original work published 1938)

Rose, J. (2015). The value of art in BioShock: Ayn Rand, emotion, and choice. In L. Cuddy (Ed.), *BioShock and philosophy: Irrational game, rational book* (pp. 15–26). Malden, MA: Wiley Blackwell.

Ryle, G. (2002). *The concept of mind*. Chicago, IL: University of Chicago Press. (Original work published 1949)

Schneider, J. L. (2014). Unculting Ayn Rand. *Boulevard, 30*(1), 175–189.

Simental, M. (2013). The Gospel according to Ayn Rand: *Anthem* as an atheistic theodicy. *The Journal of Ayn Rand Studies, 13*(2), 96–106. doi:10.5325/jaynrandstud.13.2.0096

Sterne, J., & Leach, J. (2005). The point of social construction and the purpose of social critique. *Social Epistemology, 19*(2-3), 189–198. doi:10.1080/02691720500224657

Tavinor, G. (2009a). *BioShock* and the art of Rapture. *Philosophy and Literature, 33*(1), 91–106. doi:10.1353/phl.0.0046

Tavinor, G. (2009b). *The art of videogames*. London, UK: Wiley-Blackwell. doi:10.1002/9781444310177

Thomas, D., & Brown, J. S. (2009). Why virtual worlds can matter. *International Journal of Learning and Media, 1*(1), 37–49. doi:10.1162/ijlm.2009.0008

Travis, R. (2010). *BioShock* in the cave: Ethical education in Plato and in video games. In K. Schrier & D. Gibson (Eds.), *Ethics and game design: Teaching values through play* (pp. 86–101). Hershey, PA: Information Science Reference. doi:10.4018/978-1-61520-845-6.ch006

Wagner, C. (2008). Learning experience with virtual worlds. *Journal of Information Systems Education*, *19*(3), 263–266.

Weise, M. J. (2008). *BioShock*: A critical historical perspective. *Eludamos (Göttingen), 2*. Retrieved from http://www.eludamos.org/index.php/eludamos/article/viewArticle/vol2no1-12/65

Weiss, G. (2012). Ayn Rand nation: The hidden struggle for America's soul. New York, NY: St. Martin's Press.

White, H. (2013). Materiality, form, and context: Marx contra Latour. *Victorian Studies, 55*(4), 667–682. doi:10.2979/victorianstudies.55.4.667

Younkins, E. W. (Ed.). (2007). *Ayn Rand's Atlas Shrugged: A philosophical and literary companion.* Burlington, VT: Ashgate Publishing, Ltd.

Younkins, E. W. (2014). Philosophical and literary integration in Ayn Rand's *Atlas Shrugged. The Journal of Ayn Rand Studies, 14*(2), 124–147. doi:10.5325/jaynrandstud.14.2.0124

Zackariasson, P., Styhre, A., & Wilson, T. L. (2006). Phronesis and creativity: Knowledge work in video game development. *Creativity and Innovation Management, 15*(4), 419–429.

KEY TERMS AND DEFINITIONS

ADAM: A fictional type of stem-cell harvested from sea-slugs that allows for the genetic manipulation of EVE. Also, a form of gameplay currency for buying genetic modifications in *BioShock*.

Big Daddy: The name given to characters in *BioShock* who live co-dependently with Little Sisters, harvesting ADAM for survival. Physically, they are humans who have been surgically grafted to diving suits.

EVE: The product of unregulated scientific advances that allows for genetic manipulation of the human body in Rapture.

First-Person Shooter: A type of video game in which the player assumes the field of vision of the protagonist, often presenting the character's weapon in the foreground, which moves with the players point of view.

Ignorant Schoolmaster: Based on the work of Joseph Jacotot, a French professor who taught his Flemish-speaking students law without knowing the language himself, the concept of the ignorant schoolmaster refers to the argument that illiterate parents could begin to teach their children literacy and other topics they did not know themselves.

Intellectual Emancipation: Becoming a learner who is free from the need to seek masters to explain material.

Little Sisters: Young girls who were genetically modified during the peak of Rapture to harvest ADAM from corpses around the city.

Objectivism: The belief associated with Ayn Rand that certain things, especially moral truths, exist independently of human knowledge or perception of them. This approach is closely linked to laissez-faire capitalism, which opposes government intervention and favors free markets where selfishness, or the concern with one's own interests, is understood to best lead societies to develop and prosper.

Rapture: A failed underwater utopia based implicitly on the philosophy of Objectivism and the location of the events in *BioShock*.

Splicers: Genetically modified and mutated humans with the ability to crawl on ceilings and perform murderous acrobatic maneuvers.

Tacit Knowledge: Skills and familiarity that may not be consciously explained by the knower, yet nevertheless present themselves through their functionality.

Understanding: Unlike traditional definitions, Rancière argues that understanding represents the construction of a gulf between a knower and the ignorant.

ENDNOTES

1   In naming Rand as a "ghost in the machine," we refer both to Ryle's (1949/2002) famous description of the mind and Tavinor's (2009b) concept of the video game as a "fiction machine."

2   Atlas's name, as in Rand's novel, draws upon the myth of the primordial Titan who holds the heavens on his shoulders to separate them from the Earth (Younkins, 2007). But while Rand's Atlas bears the weight of a collectivist society, Levine's Atlas seems to bear the weight of Rapture and its citizens as he attempts to save them from tyranny.

3   There are, of course, exceptions to this rule, among which Paulo Friere's *The Pedagogy of the Oppressed* is likely the most celebrated. In fact, there has even been significant growth in "ignorance studies," of which Jacotot could easily be seen as a founding father. As Gross and McGoey (2015) write, "over the last decade or so, the terrain of ignorance studies has developed into a dynamic field that has forged links across many disciplines" (p. 1).

4   It is thus interesting to see the recent prevalence of online tutorials and walk-throughs that have sprung up, particularly with the advent of YouTube and other online databases, where players can receive explicit instruction on how to succeed in the game world. This development, of course, stands to hinder the potential for emancipatory learning that could take place if players choose to rely on such instructions rather than struggle to come to their own conclusions.

5   While Latour writes of a specific form of explanation, we believe his insights can profitably be extended in broader directions.

6   For more information about the intertextual influences and allusion in *BioShock* in addition to Rand, such as the aesthetic influences of art deco and the belle epoch and the mysterious plane-crash motif that parallels the *Lost* television series, see Goldberg, 2011; *Breaking the Mold: The Art of BioShock* (2007), and *Deco Devolution: The Art of BioShock 2* (2010).

Chapter 7
Exploring Complex Intertextual Interactions in Video Games:
Connecting Informal and Formal Education for Youth

Kathy Sanford
University of Victoria, Canada

Timothy Frank Hopper
University of Victoria, Canada

Jamie Burren
University of Victoria, Canada

ABSTRACT

This chapter explores the intertextual nature of video games. Video games are inherently intertextual and have utilized intertextuality in profound ways to engage players and make meaning. Youth who play video games demonstrate complex intertextual literacies that enable them to construct and share understandings across game genres. However, video game literacy is noticeably absent from formal education. This chapter draws from bi-monthly meetings with a group of youth video gamers. Video game sessions focused on exploring aspect of video game play such as learning and civic engagements. Each session was video recorded and coded using You Tube annotation tools. Focusing on intertextuality as an organizing construct, the chapter reports on five themes that emerged that were then used to help explore the use of video games as teaching tool in a grade 11 Language Arts class. A critical concept that emerged was the idea of complex intertextual literacy that frames and enables adolescents' engagement with video games.

INTRODUCTION

Video games have increasingly become part of the lives of today's youth (McGonigal, 2010); they seamlessly connect to the myriad of other texts youth engage with on a regular basis. Although video games have often been dismissed and disparaged by adults through media, schooling, and parental concerns

DOI: 10.4018/978-1-5225-0477-1.ch007

(Sabella, 2010), despite no empirical evidence other than excessive engagement (Subrahmanyam et al., 2001; Carnagey & Anderson, 2010), there is evidence to the contrary indicating the benefits of video games (Boot 2007; Gee 2005). However, we rarely see teachers embracing this modern phenomena as part of the school curriculum, leaving their students to navigate these new media realms without guidance (Squire, 2005). In this paper we consider the potential of video games to form a critical space to engage students in meaning making, enabling them to engage in thoughtful dialogue on the ideas that flood into their digital spaces through the intertextual constructs used in video games. These intertextual constructs enable gamers to share complex meanings and sophisticated insights on human interactions. To interpret how intertextuality operates between game players and between players and the game we have used a complexity theory framework to explain how our gamers, as agents of an eco-system of gamers, learn how to play and adapt to the challenges of video games. In this study we tap into the complex collective consciousness of youth video gamers who self-organize around the challenges and narratives of popular video games like *Halo*, *World of Warcraft* and *Fallout* that are taken up by the youth video gaming culture.

In agreement with others we note that adolescents are provided incentives through video games to make connections to a wide array of diverse print, visual, and multimodal texts found online, on television and film, and in school (Jenkins, 2010; Kahne, Middaugh, & Evans, 2009; Spence & Feng, 2010). We feel that considerable time and resources are expended in developing and playing video games, and it is vital that educational researchers pay more attention to the knowledge and understandings of the world that gamers are acquiring and using to create their own texts.

Sources of Data in the Paper

This paper explores the highly intertextual world of six youth as they help three researchers/teachers understand the complexity of the world they live through video games. These six youth have been classified as serious gamers as they have regularly played video games as teenagers, each reporting that they have committed well over the 10,000 hours to be considered experts (Gladwell, 2008). Drawing on a post-structural sensibility and complexity theory, we demonstrate how the intertextual richness of video games enable these gamers to make sense of the world in ways not generally understood by adults (parents, educators, policy-makers). We suggest, and offer examples, that this intertextual richness can be used as a critical catalyst to engage more youth in school curriculum through game connections and the participatory pedagogies nurtured in video gaming environments.

These youth met with the researchers bi-monthly to explore their insights on video games they played. The intent of the research was to explore how engagement with video games influenced the youths with respect to their potential for democratic/civic engagement as future citizens. Data came from interactive sessions with the youth that involved sharing the video games they were playing as well as engaging with the youth through different genres of video games followed by focus group debriefing their experiences in the games in relation to learning process and democratic/civic engagement. This study served as the impetus for one of the authors to use video games in a high school language arts curriculum in class of 23 grade 10 students. Insights from the initial study will be presented first in relation to intertextuality. This is then followed by narrative accounts from the teacher researcher as he reflects on his experience using video games as a curriculum tool in a high school. We conclude with the potential of using video game intertextuality as part of modern day high school curriculum.

Framing Intertextuality

Within video gaming intertextuality refers to the way different texts "relate to and reference other texts, through devices such as allusion, quotation, pastiche, and parody" (Plothe, 2014). Plothe describes video games as "rich, intertextual environments that pull references and techniques from a myriad of different media sources", and as texts are read, they are filtered by cultural codes developed from other texts. In video games, text often appears onscreen as narration and description but using a broadened conception of 'text': scenery, character appearance, and diegetic sound could also be considered text. All these texts are referential in nature, referring to other cultural texts (Meinhof & Smith, 2000). In this way intertextuality in video games is a process of multi-media interpretation where the viewer identifies references within a text to other media texts creating meaning and expectations of things to come in the game. The rules of a single video game are therefore part of a larger complex social system of knowing developed from participatory activity within the genre of interactive video games.

It is not possible to have a conversation with a gamer without intertextual references; these are interwoven within the gameplay, character development, out-of-game interactions between gamers, and game critiques. Gamers make connections as they play, and create their own connections through chat, blogs, and other forms of ongoing communication. Building on Kristeva's (1966) definition of intertextuality, video game texts are constellations of textual relations, continuously linking to a vast array of other texts. This paper argues that intertextuality defines video games and that it contributes significantly to the pleasure of video game play that can largely be derived from connections made by the gamers using their vast insider knowledge and references. These texts are interwoven within the gameplay, character development, out-of-game interactions between gamers, and game critiques. Gamers make connections as they play, and create their own connections through chat room discussion blogs, and other forms of ongoing communication available through the internet (Perron & Wolf, 2008; Barron, 2006; Gee, 2005).

Exploring Intertextuality with Complexity Theory

A text, as Barthes points out, is an assemblage of knowledge and understanding of pre-existing texts. Video games are rich intertextual spaces that create meaning via a powerful network of other texts. Such networks speak to a self-organizing system of gamers who, attracted to a common purpose through the narratives of the games, learn to communicate using multiple short-range relationships both in person and on-line, through the intertextual nature of the genre based games. Kaveney (2005) comments that "specific genre-based texts are consciously intertextual in order to encourage fans of the genre to engage with the text on a deeper more personal level" (p.6). Corneliussen and Walker (2008) suggest that "intertextuality informs genre-based games at different levels and in different registers", enabling connections to be made in diverse ways. In massively multi-player online games such as *World of Warcraft,* intertextuality operates at numerous registers that allow for multifaceted interpretation and creates a unique player experience based on the users' meaning making through the genre (Schrader, Lawless, & McCreery, 2009). Additionally, many video game developers have created connected interdependent relationships between film and video games so as to construct a game-based experience around an already popular story. Gamers develop a greater awareness of mythological narratives and fantasy that heightens their engagement in games. Intertextual references through humour are regularly identified in video games that connect gamers to other games and forms of text.

We believe that the intertextual nature of video games that operates between players creates a complex emergent learning system. Complexity theory has been used to describe the organizational structures that emerge in both nature and social spaces (Capra & Luigi Luisi, 2014; Waldrop, 1992). Though difficult to define, complexity theory seeks to understand how order and stability arise from the interactions of many components according to a few simple rules (Mason, 2008). Complexity theory offers a way of studying complex phenomena through order-creation that seeks to describe how order can emerge within complex systems (Richardson & Cilliers, 2001), offering a way of researching collective behaviour where

… emergence implies that, given a significant degree of complexity in a particular environment, or critical mass, new properties and behaviours emerge that are not contained in the essence of the constituent elements, or able to be predicted from a knowledge of initial conditions. (Mason, 2008, p. 3)

This means that complex systems cannot be reduced to parts to be studied, but have to be interpreted based on emergent phenomena. Complex systems are made of separate agents who self-organize together around certain attractors based on simple rules and optimum conditions. These complex systems allow the agents to adapt together into self-sustaining collectives often in unpredictable but coherent ways (Cilliers, 2000; Mason, 2008).

Complexity theory offers a way to explore the vast array of networked intertextual connections afforded by video games and their related texts (i.e. blogs, YouTube videos, twitter, Reddit, graphic novels, feature films, etc.). From a complexity theoretical framework a form of complexity thinking can be used to interpret phenomena (Hopper & Sanford, 2010; Davis & Sumara, 2006). This form of thinking refers to identifying certain features needed to be present for a complex system (collection of interconnected agents) to form and to be considered a learning system. As noted by Mason (2008), a complex learning system develops within non-linear processes (not predictable from knowledge of constituent elements) and is based on the dynamic interactions between multiple variables that are nested within other indeterminate and transient systems that in turn contribute to the environment of a system. In relation to video games we believe a complex learning system develops around players of games both within their close social group playing the same game but also to a global group engaged in the same game or related genre of games. These learning systems form around multilayered complex systems that self-organize around a common commitment to master a particular game.

Intertextuality in video games creates a playfulness (continuous sense of instability within a sense of control) that characterizes a dynamic system and enables systems thinking in players as they learn to navigate the digital world of the video game (Gee, 2003). Systems thinking encourages gamers to become aware of relationships, in this case between texts, where meaning emerges as the player or group of players self-organize their collection of related texts to make sense of the video game, and ultimately through adaptation to challenges, trial and correction, to achieve a level of mastery and the opportunity to complete the game or achieve a quest. We suggest that intertextuality plays a critical role in the gamers' complex learning system that allows the players to learn to play the sophisticated array of games generated in society. In particular, we have clustered the following six features into two areas that we feel need to be present for a complex learning system to form around video games: inter-connections between diverse agents through neighbourly interactions and redundancy and adaptive emergence through decentralized control, ambiguously bounded structures and recursive elaboration.

1. **Inter-Connections Between Diverse Agents:** In relation to video game playing, interconnections among diverse agents provide generative possibilities within a system where different agents of a system bring an array of different interpretative possibilities and skills to a situation. The neighbourly interactions refer to the capacity for each agent to have multiple short range relationships associated with the game they are playing, these serving as a source of information and a place to share insights, and long range or weak relationships to sources of information outside their community where insights from a global community can offer insights on game challenges. The redundancy between agents, or a degree of commonality, is essential for communication of shared understandings between gamers. This common understanding helps to constitute the play that is afforded through the intertextuality of video games.

2. **Adaptive Emergence:** The adaptive emergence cluster refers to a decentralized system of control with no person as authority but rather a network of information systems. Games allow for understandings and interpretations to be generated in context from the bottom-up, by each agent of a system, without the need to connect to a central organizing authority. Texts that emerge in games or are referred to in games are ambiguously bounded, they are continuously exchanging meanings with their surroundings, adapting to feedback loops in the game, avoiding any strict boundaries as they are constantly in a state of flux with their surroundings and their cultural context. The process of playing games immerses players in texts through narratives, video, images and cultural artefacts that are constantly invoking and elaborating established associations in a cyclical dynamic process. At the individual level an iterative process rather than linear is always present; "one's history both enables (and constrains) one's perceptions of new experiences" (Davis et al., 2008, p. 201). The intertextuality contributes meanings that are shared through a common culture of texts that interact and frame the meaning of new texts that in turn emerge in gameplay, which are then shared to develop in future gameplay.

Youths' Intertextual Knowing

Individuals who self identify as gamers demonstrate a comprehensive understanding – both explicitly and implicitly – of the intertextual nature of video games and video gaming. Video games are interactive media, enabling gamers to actively create meaning as they engage in the game. Gamers actively 'read' the games and this active reading facilitates construction of new texts (i.e. YouTube video, Machinima[1], game walkthroughs) that demonstrate their knowledge of intertextual relationships between various media forms (Consalvo, 2003). This participatory culture (Jenkins, 1992) stimulates players curiosity and motivation to make further intertextual connections as they engage in online chat, read blog posts, browse the Internet, chat over a coffee and choose further games to play. Intertextuality in video games is so important that large media corporations work with other businesses to produce these 'synergies' for their products through common character images, movie and television deals (Consalvo, 2003). The intertextual elements of games shift the video game text from one coherent story to much more complex storylines, in part shaped by the players themselves, drawing on multiple sources, experiences, and other texts. And by virtue of the fact that video games cross game/ludic and story/narrative boundaries, they draw on diverse (inter)textual elements of gameplay/rules and storylines. Gamers create their own rich stories with intertextual elements continually interwoven throughout as they draw on their own diverse backgrounds to create the narrative text. One of the reasons our participant gamers return to particular games is their love of the story and the characters they have shaped, which have the potential to change and adapt, seeing characters and plot in more depth and complexity.

Video games often *rely* on gamers' intertextual understanding, crediting game players with the necessary knowledge to understand the mechanisms and allusions with which the games make use. In interviewing, observing, and working with individuals who identify as video game players, we have observed that they are able to understand both the literary elements of a game – such as theme, plot, tone, genre – and the mechanics of a game through an extensive intertextual knowledge base. In this case study of six youths we draw on passages from research interviews and gameplay sessions in order to highlight how the gamers make use of intertextuality *or intertextual understanding* in video games.

Context and Participants

Our research draws from one of many bi-monthly meetings with a group of youth video gamers with an age range of 18 to 21 years. The six gamers, recruited by one gamer from an earlier study, volunteered to participate, signing an ethics consent form giving them an understanding that the research project was interested in exploring how engagement with video games influences youth with respect to their potential for democratic/civic engagement as future citizens. The study has been supported by a four-year research grant from the Social Science Humanities Research Council in Canada[2]. Working closely with this particular group of youth gamers over a three-year period, we have seen that not only are youth aware of and articulate about their learning, but they have developed connections between the video game texts they know so well with other texts that interest them, in both intentional and unintentional ways. Our research sessions with the group were video recorded and then continuously coded using the annotation tool in a private YouTube account. These annotations were then cross-referenced and categorized using hyper-links to Google-docs for recurring insights on how the adolescents understood and drew on their experiences of playing video games. Working with the youth, in particular two gamers Marcus and Nic, we arranged the sessions to focus on an aspect of video gaming the group wanted to explore such as the learning process in video games, the transfer of meanings between games, and how the different genres of games engage the players. The sessions were conducted in a relaxed atmosphere, with snacks and refreshments supplied; we asked questions and discuss ideas about video games as the youth participants played video games sharing their insights on how they knew what they knew. Throughout our sessions with these youth gamers we have found that the meetings allowed us to continually share connections between video gaming, learning, civic engagement and society in many different ways that were previously unknown to us as researchers.

Of the three researchers two are tenured faculty members, while one is currently writing his graduate studies thesis. Two of the researchers teach English language arts at high school or university. The youngest researcher would be considered a gamer and has served as a mediator of meaning between the research team and the youth participants. The six youth who regularly attended the video game club and whose insights are shared here are:

1. **Sid:** Works for an IT company that provides in-home computer support, primarily for the elderly in the Greater Victoria Area. Sid enjoys games that are often extraordinarily complex and have a steep learning curve. Sid has a deep knowledge of programming and is intrigued by the systems that games use to operate. He is currently working towards a certificate in Computer programming.

2. **Marcus:** Plays a wide variety of video games and has a large appreciation for the history of video games. Primarily interested in PC games, Marcus has always shown an interest in games that rely on community or cooperation in order to play. Marcus has been involved in the research project Video Games Youth and Civic Engagement for the past 5 years, and has grown into an engaging speaker, often co-presenting at conferences and classrooms around British Columbia.

3. **Nic:** Regularly engages in role-playing games. He is a player who likes to consider the character development in the games he plays. He often refers to ways that existing games extend their narrative-building in new extensions. He started a university degree in psychology but withdrew because he did not find the degree engaging. He often found classes too slow and boring. He shares a house with other gamers.

4. **Joe:** Has a computer science degree and works in the IT department of a granite countertop company. Joe is drawn to character-driven narrative based games. He is often able to recall specific qualities of characters; especially obscure ones, from a variety of significant gaming titles. Joe's knowledge about games, characters, and gaming history is vast, and he is able to make connections between seemingly disparate titles very quickly.

5. **Dina:** Enjoys numerous role-playing games, and will often play all of the games within a specific series. She is drawn to games that allow for player character creation and divergent narrative paths. Dina works as a Page at various branches of the local public library and often links the narrative arcs in the novels she reads to arcs in the games she plays.

6. **John:** Currently works as a sale associate and lives in a house with other gamers. John is interested in games that are quirky and unique. He often searches out and plays games that are considered rare or unusual. He also enjoys the social aspects of gaming, playing in what is known as couch co-op sessions where gamers play games together in the same room rather than over an Internet connection.

Using an intrinsic case study design (Merriam, 1991; Yin, 1984) we focused on how intertextuality influences youth video game playing and how our youth participants can guide us in developing school-based curriculum to draw on the intertextual nature of video games.

Insights on Video Games: Connecting Series, Texts, and Creators

Intertextuality manifests itself through gamers' connections of new iterations to earlier games, e.g., the *Mass Effect* series. Prior to the release of *Mass Effect 3*, one of the gamers Nic replayed each of the two previous games in order to revisit the connections as a lead-up to playing the new game. In this instance he was actively seeking the intertextual connections between the three games in the trilogy to enhance his understanding and enjoyment of the game. Additionally, the group described the comic series *Descender*[3] that makes explicit thematic connections to *Mass Effect*, exploring the classic set-up of human vs robot. Further, they made references to blog posts on Reddit.com that discuss/anticipate the upcoming release of *Mass Effect 4*, enabling gamers to relive their earlier gaming experiences with the trilogy, read about the upcoming game, and to engage in discussion comparing character development, plot, and dialogue between the existing and new games.

Intertextuality also is demonstrated through recognition of the same creator of different games, seeing riffs of earlier games. An example we observed was a discussion of *Uncharted* and *The Last of Us*, both developed by Naughty Dog. The gamers see humour/in-jokes in game creators' embedded references to other texts/games. Their skills and knowledge are immediately and unconsciously transferred. The youth were able to quickly recognize the developer's style in these third-person games, allowing them to easily transfer their knowledge from one game to another. Additionally, they were able to share their views on the film adaptation, had insights about the prequel and sequel, comic book adaptation, novel, and behind-the scenes book. Backstory, for these youth, is a critical element of their favourite games (Sanford & Bonsor-Kurki, 2014) providing explanations, further stories, and history connected to the game stories. For example, they had all read *Halo* books and graphic novels, again connecting to historical information, elaboration of characters, and alternative representations. They were able to discuss *Tomb Raider* (as both game and film) and the textual references and connections to the *Indiana Jones* films. Additionally, these youth were able to articulate the differences and similarities between RPGs and Japanese role playing games (JRPGs), knowing the history, strengths, and problems of games in this genre. For example,

Nic: *Umm... so a Western JRPG, a JRPG, and an RPG are very similar but have defining, distinct characteristics for certain people. So, I might go -- Final Fantasy is a JRPG, and then everyone will go, 'Okay, yeah, no that generally makes sense. It's a Japanese publishers, Japanese developers, Japanese uh style -- in terms of mechanics and stuff like that.' And, then someone might go, ' Cthulhu Saves The World, it's a JRPG', but, like John said it's made by western developers, in a JRPG style. So, someone might go, 'No it's a western (J)RPG.', or someone might even leave out the J, or...*

Complex Intertextual Mechanics (Ludology) and Story (Narrative)

There are essentially two ways in which our data shows that gamers possess a complex intertextual understanding of video games. The first way they demonstrate this is through the act of playing video games, navigating the mechanics of the game (ludology). The second is the narratives that the games create and draw on. In relation to game mechanics it was especially evident when we had the participants playing a game that they have never played before. For example, in one situation Sid says:

Sid: *No, uh.. generally in first-person games uhh...the W A S D controls are pretty standard.* (Jamie [researcher]: *Yep) And then looking around is just with the mouse* (Jamie: *Yeah) Uhmm engaging with items is usually the E key. Uhmm, and you know doing actions like uhh you know like attacking or something like that is usually a left click, and then secondary fire, or alternate actions are usually the like the right click.*

Here we can see evidence of what we are going to call complex intertextual literacy where a player reads multiple, seemingly complex textual prompts to quickly interpret how to play and engage with the game. Sid uses his intertextual knowledge to understand the mechanics of the game. He easily identifies the game as a "first-person" game. Although this may appear to refer simply to a perspective shared between different games, it actually denotes a particular style and genre of game. Sid uses his intertextual understanding of first-person games in order to learn how to control the game. In fact the game is reliant on the player's ability to understand the intertextual reference provided by the perspective in order to understand how to play the game. The game provides no further instruction for control other than perspective. Sid articulates the entire control scheme for the game – from player movement to interactions with the game world – within a matter of seconds. The game relies on the player having played previous first-person games, in order to interact with it. In fact many games rely on intertextuality in order for the players to be successful.

The second example of complex intertextuality involves Nic playing a *Guild Wars 2* expansion, responding to a question about why he likes the expansion. Drawing on the narratology of the game Nic provides a detailed comment, as he was playing:

I'd really need to show you the trailer and you just, like, watch my face (laughter). Ummm....like.... They announced a new profession so like they had eight professions that were available for the five playable races, now they have nine, uh, total classes.... that one, it goes into the lore. So it's, it's called the Revenant and you channel heroes of the world's history – to use your skills. Soo... Uh... you'd have to have played it in the first game, but they reference a character that you were fighting along side in the first game, which takes place 250 years ago.

[...] So he's called King Jalice Iron Hammer. He's a dwarf, and he's Russian, and he's wonderful. (Laughter) But, in the first game he was, you know, he was like 'okay, you have to help us, and we'll maybe help you'. And, then you do, and then he helps you kill an undead Prince, and stops Olage from starting a cataclysm in the world and bringing the Titans out. And, so he, like, he's someone that you can use the skills of.

In this segment Nic, while playing the *Guild Wars 2* expansion, references an earlier iteration of the game, connecting to the lore described in the game, describes the characters, tropes, and makes historical references. In this instance we can begin to understand that games are reliant upon gamers' intertextual knowledge in order to be understood and appreciated. Nic's familiarity with the character "King Jalice Iron Hammer" from an earlier *Guild Wars* game allows him to recognize that he will be of use in the expansion of the game. Nic's connection to the character – "He's a dwarf, and he's Russian, and he's wonderful" – is a potent example of how video games create narrative that presupposes the gamers' intertextual understanding of the game world. Nic is able to construct an understanding of, and relationship to, a particular character based on the events of a previous game.

'I Research the Games They're Based On'

In a conversation, Joe introduces *Elite Dangerous*, the fourth in a series of *Elite* space adventure video games. He asks Nic, "Did you play the first one?" to which Nic responds:

No. (Shakes head) I did not play a lot of the older games that like... So, Civilization Beyond Earth came out, and that's based off of Alpha Centauri. A lot of people haven't played Alpha Centauri 'cause it's like, it's a really hard to play game, but a lot of the time I'll like research the games they're based off of. So I know a lot, or a bit about Alpha Centauri, and in this case Elite, but I don't actually play them. I don't put myself through, going through all that.

Nic's response provides a significant insight into the ways in which gamers develop a further understanding of the games they play. Researching games, and understanding gaming history is a key aspect of video gaming. Much in the same way as an English major may 'research' the earlier works of a particular author in order to better understand a piece of literature, Nic (and other gamers) will often "research the games they're based on", in order to more fully appreciate a current release. Although Nic may not have played a lot of the "older games", he still understands that a level of familiarity with older games allows for a greater appreciation of current titles. Nic voluntarily researches games, as a substitute for playing through entire titles, and although here he does not directly specify what his 'research' involves, we can suppose that it provides him with enough information that he can read/interpret the current titles intertextual references to the games which came before.

Assigning a Game to a Genre

A final example during gameplay refers to the group's conversation about JRPGs. Dina describes a key characteristic of JRPGs (with specific reference to *Dragon Quest*) as a turn-based game and Sid adds a description of JRPGs:

It's a Japanese RPG. But it's, well not all of them are made in Japan. Sometimes, it's just the style of the..., You have a variety of characters that each have stats, and different abilities and things, and usually there's stuff that involves, you know, going to different, uh, you know very vividly coloured places err very, err, very interesting places. You have to fight monsters and people, usually in some sort of battle system, or something like that, and you know there's, there's story and stuff that develops along as well.

Further conversation elaborates the genre/trope:

Nic: *Yeah, so... so like a few things that like define it are the art style, the general story telling and a few of the game mechanics like...*
Sid: *Gameplay structure is...*
John: *I mean, I mean there's games like Undead and Cthulhu Saves the World where it's like...*
Marcus: *Cthulhu Saves the World is great.*
John: *They're JRPG's but they're American made.*
Nic: *Yeah.*
Marcus: *It's a western JRPG.*
John: *Yeah it's... (Laughter) It's an actual term for them.*
Marcus: *Yeah it is, Western JRPG.*
Dina: *WJRPG.*

In this example we see the group negotiating the elements that will define a game's genre. A further discussion of game mechanics, as defining genres, ensued; Nic had suggested that there is no clear categorization of game genres, but rather they are broadly categorized. Kim (researcher)'s question about the subjectivity of the categories of these games categories elicited an elaborate response from Nic:
Kim asks, "Then how can it be negotiable?"

Nic: *When it comes down to like a Shooter it's 'are you firing guns?', check, Shooter. 'Are you first-person, or third person?', 'first-person', it's now an FPS, check, done.*
John: *Is there RPG progression though? Cause then it could be an FPS RPG.*

Jamie (Researcher): Yeah, look at something like Fallout.
Sid: *Then you get into the whole, like, genre mashing.*

The discussion of genre above illustrates a complex intertextual literacy. Participants identify series of criteria as belonging to specific genres, and then question as to whether or not genre in gaming can ever be truly fixed so it is ambiguously bounded, coherent but always adapting. Genre, while present, is a fluid concept in gaming, the minutiae of details allowing a game to be classified in various genres at once, while at the same time belonging completely to a specific genre. Further, the participants demonstrate that while certain characteristics can be indicative of a certain genre, assigning a particular game to a genre is ultimately in the hands of the individual gamer who uses his or her interpretations to his or her actions in the game.

Throughout the gamers' descriptions of their gameplay and their connections, they are showing obvious delight at insider connections/jokes that are activated within the group through short references and commentaries Humour amongst individuals who identify as gamers is, as is most humour, inherently intertextual. Here the participants are literally 'in on the joke', via their understandings of game genres. Comments are taken up by the group as humorous, which 'outside' individuals may not recognize as being funny as implied by the idea of Western (J)RPG discussed earlier.

Genealogy and Transfer between Games

Another way we see intertextual understanding being demonstrated by the participants is through our focus-group discussions following game-play. The recorded conversations we have with the participants at the beginning and the end of our meetings are rife with evidence of this. In particular we are reminded of the conversation we had at the end of the session in which the group played *Unturned*[4] in which everyone was explaining the different types of role playing genres, and the characteristics which are beholden to each.

For example, Kim asked, "So what kind of game did this remind you of, when you were playing?" Sid immediately responded,

"Day Z" and John simultaneously chimed in,

Day Z. Uhh, I played a lot of Day Z.

Marcus added, "Me too!" They continued to add the following exchange:

Sid: *That was one of the first ahhh... one of the first Zombie survival games. It was based off a military shooter (pause) game.*
Marcus: *Hyper realistic military shooter.*
Sid: *Yeah, hyper realistic military shooter... that takes place in like absolutely massive areas, like the equivalent of like four square kilometers of space, or something like that.*
Marcus: *It takes a good half an hour to run across the map.*
Sid: *And...Day Z was based off of its' Zombie survival mode. You have to do essentially the exact same thing here -- go around salvaging trying to find stuff. If you run into other people, there's a good chance you're going to get shot and die, because people.. they don't take chances. If you see another person they're probably going to shoot you so a lot of people...*

In this exchange Sid and Marcus trace the influences of the game *Unturned* that they had just finished playing, to a previously released game *Day Z*. However, both Sid and Marcus go further by specifying that *Day Z* itself was based on a "Zombie survival mode", from an even earlier released game, which they do not specifically name, but classify as a "hyper-realistic military shooter". Here, we witness a comprehensive understanding on the part of Marcus and Sid of the game influences that informed the development of the game *Unturned*.

The conversation continued as Jamie then asked,

"What other games, you said, mentioned Day Z, does this game borrow from, that you recognized?" Instantaneously, Sid, Dina, Marcus, and Joe said, "Minecraft!" Sid continued,

It's got the same sort of visual aspect to it as Minecraft. The same sort of concepts or.... (John: Boxel based) Like as soon as I clicked I was like ughh (makes punching motion with right arm) I was like... yeah, that's Minecraft.

Jamie: *So you knew...like as soon as you pushed the first button, you were like this is the same mechanics as Minecraft?*
Nic: *It's got like the same control scheme that Minecraft uses...*

At which point Marcus, Dina, Jamie, and Sid all added, "Yeah!"

The *Day Z* game linked to games that are over five years old; youth gamers still draw on these games as they play more sophisticated games, yet still find *Minecraft*-like games to be cool and useful. Further in this exchange was an opportunity to learn intertextually from one another. John had introduced the term "boxel game" and Jamie cycled back in the conversation to ask, "What did you call it? (pointing to John), like the boxel?"

John: *Boxel based game.*
Marcus: *Bunch of cubes or squares.*
John: *Yeah where the, where the graphics are the where the game world is cube based.*
Jamie: *Oh, okay.*

And they continued.

John: *Yeah, yeah it's a boxel game.*
Marcus: *Yeah, cause the cubes, the cubes are called Boxels, they make up the world.*
Jamie: *Oh, okay.*
Marcus: *Yeah. It ...it allows for like interesting item materials...*
John: *Well it wasn't really so much, cause there was like flat plains and things...*
Marcus: *There was but it was still like Minecraft and stuff. Like all the squares and stuff... it allows for also, also like terrain alteration and like in games like Cube World or whatever. Boxel based RPG. Like you can throw a bomb and things will explode and go flying that's because the boxels are not technically all connected.*
Jamie: *Ohh...*
Marcus: *They're just kind of all sitting on top of each other.*

Joe: *They're 3D pixels.*

John: *Yeah, and also it's way easier on processing and stuff like that.*

Marcus: *Yeah... once you play Minecraft. Cause that game, that game takes like a super computer to run properly.*

At one point in the conversation, Marcus takes the opportunity to introduce a joke that he has heard through online conversation and takes great pleasure in explaining it to the others.

Sid: *Who, which does?*

Marcus: *Minecraft.*

Sid: *What?*

Marcus: *You don't know about that joke? The fact that Minecraft can be so intensive on your PC that you need like a Super Computer to...*

John: *Well yeah, if you literally like, make the best.*

Marcus: *Yeah, Yeah. But I love, I love, it's a joke. There's this one guy and he has like this huge 6000 dollar computer, and He's like '6000 dollar computer, but it only runs Minecraft.' And, it's like, it's like, 'and, it runs it perfectly. It's fantastic, and all this stuff, but it runs Minecraft.' (laughs).*

In the above conversation, and Marcus's subsequent joke we see the extent to which the participants are able to recognize the intertextual connections that are inherent in even seemingly insignificant details. In this case the visual style of the game *Unturned* is instantly recognized by the group as having been borrowed from the massive hit *Minecraft*. The *boxel* style is recognized as being desirable as it allows for the game world to be manipulated by the player with relatively little strain on the processing power of the computer. However, Marcus is reminded of a joke which operates on the basic contradiction that exist in the game of *Minecraft* -- this being that despite the game's seemingly simple visual style, it can still require an enormous amount of processing power due to the nearly infinite possibilities available to the player. The joke requires that the other members of the group are familiar with the game *Minecraft* and the many ways in which the users/players of *Minecraft* have interacted with the game.

Complexity Thinking and Complex Intertextual Literacies in Video Games

The insights from our gamers highlight the interconnections of their sophisticated intertextual knowledge about video games. Though all six gamers have a vast repertoire of games they have played, there are common understandings that emerge as critical to enabling their current and future gameplay. Gamers can interpret games based on diverse intertextual elements such as genealogy of the game in a series, the creator's style of game design, and the genre that locates the game in a certain way of playing and evolving narrative. When playing a game for the first time it became clear how rapidly the gamers learned to adapt to a new game structure, quickly mastering the controls and then interpreting the situation based on graphics, story and characters. Their learning has developed from the ground up through a complex mix of game mechanics, story and playing preference in how to address the challenges set by the game. Learning for the game players is a continuous process of recursive elaboration, connecting to peers, drawing from texts that transfer from other games, and is developed from the ground-up through trial, adjustment and sharing. In all the video gaming sessions it was notable how quickly players shared new discoveries with other players. At times players would be calling out what they had discovered whilst simultaneously working on another task, meanwhile other players would process the new insights, confirm or offer alternatives. This networked communication also led to discoveries of how game structures shifted and reformed based on player choices so that they made one gameplay like another, using this ambiguously bounded reality to create much amusement as players tried to determine the best choices to lead to the new experiences in the games. Playing involved constantly seeking new insights, a participatory form of pedagogy that implies infinite possible rewards for taking risks, exploring and then sharing discoveries with interested gamers, a powerful metaphor for what schooling *could* be, as noted by Jane McGonigal (2010). In all cases the gamers' complex intertextual literacy skills set them up to decipher, note patterns and then engage with an ever-increasing chance of success. Drawing on these intertextual literacy skills as part of the modern day Language Arts class takes us to the last section in this paper.

Intertextuality in Video Games Informing School-Based Learning

We believe that attention to the intertextual nature of video games holds great potential to inform high school English teachers as they help youth navigate the interconnected communities of the 21st century and to engage their students in a wide array of multimodal texts. Video games are an obvious medium/text for demonstrating connections across texts. An intertextual view of texts, via video games, supports the concept that the meaning of a text is produced by the viewer/reader/player in relation not only to the text being explored, but the choices they make and the complex network of texts involved in selecting options, and then producing and understanding emergent texts.

Teachers in schools often either avoid or show disdain towards video games as they are seen as frivolous pursuits that often promote violent and misogynist values. However, as considerable time and resources are expended by youth in elucidating and playing video games, it makes sense that educators become more knowledgeable about the intertextual elements of games and how they connect to their school-based texts. This understanding has the potential to engage students in more meaningful learning, interweaving different elements of texts. It is critically important for educators to recognize what youth today know and how they learn if formal learning (schooling) is going to be useful to our future citizens. And although we are aware of the negative aspects of video games associated with overuse, teachers in schools have little conception of any benefits derived from working/playing with video games. In this last section we describe pedagogical strategies we have started to explore in high school classes that draw on elements of intertextuality as identified in video games. Our initial experiences show how such pedagogical framing of game-based learning can inspire and enrich school-based curriculum.

Video Games in the Classroom

In a high school class of 23 grade 10 students one of us ran a class called *Video Games in the Classroom*. The following account is drawn from this researcher's reflections, shared with his colleagues in a written form and in discussions, on the teaching experience in light of the study with the youth previously reported. Students in the secondary school English class were given the opportunity to use video games in the place of more traditional texts such as Shakespeare's Macbeth or George Orwell's 1984. The course took place over a one-month period equivalent to that of a traditional unit of study within a secondary school setting. The class consisted of students of varying abilities and cultural backgrounds. Eleven of the students were male, and twelve of the students were female. Approximately half of the students in the class reported themselves as being regular video game players, while the other half of the students reported themselves as being occasional players or never having really played video games.

For the first four days of the unit, students were put into five groups selected by the teacher. The students were grouped to ensure a relatively even mix of students who considered themselves gamers and those who did not. Students then played through four 30-minute sessions of four different game titles, including *BioShock Infinite, Gone Home, L.A. Noire,* and *The Stanley Parable.* After each gaming session each group would discuss the experience using a set of discussion questions provided by the teacher. The teacher would check in on both the play sessions and the discussions, ensuring that there was an equal level of participation by all group members.

The games chosen for the first part of the course were deliberately chosen by the teacher in order to represent both a wide variety of game genres and significant narrative depth. The games chosen for the first section of the study were:

1. *BioShock Infinite*: First person Shooter.
2. *Gone Home*: Independent Release. First person exploration.
3. *L.A. Noire*: Third Person Action Adventure.
4. *The Stanley Parable*: Independent release, Experimental Parody.

After the first four days and debriefing of the experience of playing the games, the students were invited to form their own small groups and choose a game to play through. After playing through the game each group was expected to produce an artefact that would represent their understanding of a particular theme, character, and social issue explored by the game. The class organized itself into seven groups of students. The games that the groups elected to play were *BioShock* (1 group of 5 members), *BioShock Infinite* (1 group of 3 members and 1 group of 5 members), *Gone Home* (1 group of 3 members and 1 group of 2 members), *The Legend Of Zelda Majora's Mask* (1 group of 3 members), *Mass Effect 2* (1 group of 2 members).

The following is a brief description of two of the group's game choice and proposal:

1. *BioShock* (**1 Group of 5 Members**): A first-person shooter that takes place in an underwater city called Rapture. The group proposed the game as appropriate they felt the story was "very deep", and they were interested in exploring the relationship between the main character, and the enigmatic villain "Andrew Ryan" who had created the city of Rapture
2. *Gone Home* (**1 Group of 3 Members and 1 Group of 2 Members**): (*Gone Home*: Gone Home is an independent game (not produced by a major gaming studio) which was created by an openly transgendered game developer. The game puts players in the role of Kaitlynn Greenbriar, who upon returning home discovers here family is missing. Using only clues left behind by her family, it is up to the player to sort out what has become of her family. The game was chosen as it directly explores issues of sexuality, family relationships, and teenage angst. Neither group had played the game before and had little idea of what to expect. They both proposed that the idea for their final project would come out of the discussions and play sessions. As the researcher was familiar with the game there was confidence that this would result in a suitable outcome for the students.

Over the next week and a half, students were given 40 minutes of class time to play their chosen games, and were required to spend 30 minutes in small discussions. The teacher sat in on both the group discussions and play sessions.

The final week of the unit involved the students creating the artefact to represent their findings. This required that some of the groups replay certain sections of the games in order to more fully explore the game, while other groups began using supplemental materials to explore major themes or ideas that their play sessions and discussions brought forward. Group projects varied from more traditional choices such as essays, to more creative representations such as artworks and journals. Throughout the unit the teacher made observations, and a journal was kept of the students discussions and play sessions. As the unit progressed many students made significant intertextual connections between the games they were playing, and various films, novels, historical events, political ideologies, and life events. Below are brief accounts of the ways in which students throughout the course made intertextual connections.

BioShock Group

One group of students, who elected to play *BioShock,* found that during their play sessions in-game references to Objectivism, a philosophy that was largely created by the author Ayn Rand, continually appeared. Objectivism posits the notion that each individual is responsible for his or her own happiness through rational self-interest, and that a capitalist system free from any government interference is the only acceptable social system. The game *BioShock* invites players into an underwater world that was created based on the foundational idea of this system, and has experienced a series of terrible tragedies due to the insistence of the absolute adherence to this system by the founder Andrew Ryan. This spurred the group to explore the origins of Objectivism and led them to Ayn Rand. While only some members of the group elected to read her works, each student came away with an understanding of Objectivism, and was able to identify where and how the game made use of it as a major thematic arc. In this instance the students discovered an intertextual connection between the *BioShock* and a major American literary work. This connection emerged throughout the unit of study as each student began to research the game online for class. As they did so they found online discussion threads, which connected the game to the literary works of Ayn Rand. The students then played through the game, paying careful attention to the ways in which the game referenced the literary work on which it was based.

Gone Home Groups

Another group of students who played *Gone Home* found connections between the story of a young girl hiding her sexuality from her parents and a number of current events in the news. They specifically made a connection to stories that detailed gay youth being sent by their parents to Christian Conversion camps. They explored the way those stories linked to the in-game story of Kaitlynn's sister and her parents' difficulty in accepting her sexuality. The project involved the students making connections between the game, current events, and their own lives. Although none of the students reported having parents who would not support them if they were to come out as gay, they all reported that they would feel uncomfortable discussing matters of sexuality with their parents.

Additionally, another student who played the game *Gone Home* made connections between the isolation of the game's main protagonist and her own life. The student then elected to create a series of drawings, and journal entries, which explored some of the personal issues she was working through at the time. She created three abstract drawings that were said to represent the confusion and unrest she was feeling at the time, and one collage that represented her changing interests and philosophies from her childhood to her current age.

The Role of the Teacher

Many of the connections that the students made throughout the unit were discovered on their own, without the direct support of the teacher. However, students reported that discussions with the teacher were valuable as the students were sometimes unaware that the connections they were making were of value in the context of an English Language Arts class. Further, discussions with each other and with the teacher enabled the recognition, confirmation, and development of their intertextual connections.

What became evident, based on the discussions and the work produced by the students, was that students, even those who did not report as gamers, were able to negotiate the medium of video games and make significant intertextual connections using games as a source text. The majority of the students reported the unit of instruction as a great learning experience that connected to them meaningfully. As with all high school classes, some students who struggled to engage in the traditional curriculum did not necessarily respond immediately to this use of video games. Though it was noted that attendance increased and several students, not known for keenness in language arts, came to the lesson early and eager to start. Although these examples only represent some of the insights from a Language Arts course taught using video games, it became obvious that using video games as a text in the classroom enabled students to explore various issues and make significant intertextual connections without having them pointed out by the teacher.

CONCLUSION

In this paper we offer examples of emerging categories from focus group meetings with the participant youth that reflect the types of intertextuality they reported from the video games they routinely play. The complex intertextual literacy that the youth demonstrated when playing new games and unpacking games they had previous played implied a rich vein of knowledge and deep thinking. The participatory pedagogy implied in video games offers a process to engage youth in challenging and sustained learning that has been advocated by a variety of education scholars (Dewey, 1963; Osberg, Biesta, & Cilliers, 2008; Siemens & Matheos, 2012). Indeed, as described in this paper, the attempt to use a more participatory pedagogy approach where students selected a video game, researched its intertextual references and then represented their learning in relation to core human issues offers insight on how to expand the notion of literary devices that can be used within the classroom. We believe that youth are able to negotiate the medium of video games in meaningful ways and can recognize complex intertextual connections if given the space to do so. Therefore video games can be a useful pedagogical tool for educators -- especially those willing to allow students to explore connections, both personal and otherwise, allowing learning to emerge without excessive interference.

Since the coining of 'intertextuality' by Kristeva in 1966, the term has been used in many different ways to describe the ways that texts relate to and reference other texts. Since the growth of video games, intertextuality has become an important concept to explain their referential nature. Orr (2003) suggests that the transformative nature of intertextuality alters the work that came before it, which has been seen in the examples provided by the youth referenced in this paper. Orr also comments that the interactivity of media such as video games add a further layer, or complexity, to the understanding and sharing of the text's meaning. The complex intertextual nature of video games expands the definition of intertextuality to broaden it from reference to literary texts to encompass a wider array of multi-modal and popular texts as well as literary texts. Complexity thinking, focused on emergent, adaptive and self-organizing systems, helps to understanding the fundamental nature of intertextuality through the bifurcation process of one game to another forming genres in all popular video game. Understanding this process of development provides useful insights for teachers, who are often not gamers, into the burgeoning set of possible referential texts drawn on by a significant number of their students.

This paper offers examples of emerging categories from focus group meetings with the participant youth that reflect the types of intertextuality they reported from the video games they routinely play. We conclude that teachers need to explore the capacity of these 21st century 'digital' learners of our informational processing society, and to recognize the skills and understandings that can inform our post-industrial age thinking. A focus on the intertextual richness of video games can provide new ways to engage youth in their learning and recognize the connections across diverse genres to enhance their learning and make meaningful connections between school-based texts, societal issues texts and video game texts.

REFERENCES

Anderson, C. A., Shibuya, A., Ihori, N., Swing, E. L., Bushman, B. J., Sakamoto, A., & Saleem, M. et al. (2010). Violent video game effects on aggression, empathy, and prosocial behavior in Eastern and Western countries: A meta-analytic review. *Psychological Bulletin, 136*(2), 151–173. doi:10.1037/a0018251 PMID:20192553

Barron, B. (2006). Interest and self-sustained learning as catalysts of development: A learning ecology perspective. *Human Development, 49*(4), 193–224. doi:10.1159/000094368

Boot, W. R., Kramer, A. F., Fabiani, M., Gratton, G., Simons, D. J., & Low, K. et al. (2006). The effects of video game playing on perceptual and cognitive abilities. *Journal of Vision (Charlottesville, Va.), 6*(6), 942–968. doi:10.1167/6.6.942

Capra, F., & Luigi Luisi, P. (2014). *The systems view of life: A unifying vision.* New York, NY: Cambridge University Press. doi:10.1017/CBO9780511895555

Cilliers, P. (2000). What can we learn from a theory of complexity? *Emergence, 2*(1), 23–33. doi:10.1207/S15327000EM0201_03

Consalvo, M. (2003). Zelda 64 and video game fans: A walkthrough of games, intertextuality, and narrative. *Television & New Media, 4*(3), 321–333. doi:10.1177/1527476403253993

Corliss, J. (2011). Introduction: The social science study of videogames. *Games and Culture, 6*(1), 3–16. doi:10.1177/1555412010377323

Corneliussen, H., & Walker Rettberg, J. (Eds.). (2008). *Digital culture, play, and identity: A World of Warcraft reader.* Cambridge, MA: The MIT Press.

Davis, B., & Sumara, D. (2006). *Complexity and education: Inquires into learning, teaching and research.* London, UK: Lawrence Erlbaum.

Dewey, J. (1963). *Experience and education.* New York, NY: Macmillan.

Fiske, J. (1987). *Television culture.* London, UK: Routledge.

Gee, J. (2003). *What videogames have to teach us about learning and literacy.* New York, NY: Palgrave Macmillan.

Gee, J. (2005). Why videogames are good for your soul: Pleasure and learning. *E-learning, 2*(1), 5–16. doi:10.2304/elea.2005.2.1.5

Gladwell, M. (2008). *Outliers.* London, UK: Penguin Books.

Hopper, T., & Sanford, K. (2010). Occasioning moments in the game-as-teacher concept: Complexity thinking applied to TGfU and video gaming. In J. Bulter & L. Griffin (Eds.), More teaching games for understanding: Moving globally (pp. 121–138). Champaign, IL: Human Kinetics.

Ivory, J. D., & Kalyanaraman, S. (2009). Videogames make people violent—Well, maybe not that game: Effects of content and person abstraction on perceptions of violent videogames' effects and support of censorship. *Communication Reports, 22*(1), 1–12. doi:10.1080/08934210902798536

Jenkins, H. (1992). *Textual poachers: Television fans and participatory culture.* New York, NY: Routledge.

Jenkins, H. (2010). *Reality bytes: Eight myths about videogames debunked.* Retrieved 14th September, 2010, from http://www.pbs.org/kcts/videogamerevolution/impact/myths.html

Kahne, J., Middaugh, E., & Evans, C. (2009). *The civic potential of videogames, Digital Mediapp.* Available from http://www.macfound.org/atf/cf/%7Bb0386ce3-8b29-4162-8098-e466fb856794%7D/CIVIC_POTENTIAL_VIDEO_GAMES.PDF

Kapp, K. M. (2012). *The gamification of learning and instruction: Game-based methods and strategies for training and education.* San Francisco, CA: Pfeiffer.

Kaveney, R. (2005). *From Alien to The Matrix: Reading science fiction film.* London, UK: I.B. Tauris & Company, Limited.

Mason, M. (2008). What is complexity theory and what are its implications for educational change? In M. Masson (Ed.), *Complexity theory and the philosophy of education* (pp. 32–45). Hong Kong, China: Wiley-Blackwell. doi:10.1002/9781444307351.ch3

Mason, M. (2008). Complexity theory and the philosophy of education. In M. Masson (Ed.), *Complexity theory and the philosophy of education* (pp. 1–15). Hong Kong, China: Wiley-Blackwell. doi:10.1002/9781444307351.ch1

McGonigal, J. (2010). Gaming can make a better world. *Tedcom: TED: Ideas Worth Spreading.*

Meinhof, U. H., & Smith, J. (2000). The media and their audience: Intertextuality as paradigm. In U. H. Meinhof & J. M. Smith (Eds.), *Intertextuality and the media: From genre to everyday life* (pp. 1–17). Manchester, UK: Manchester University Press.

Merriam, S. B. (1991). *Case study research in education: A qualitative approach*. Oxford, UK: Jossey-Bass Publishers.

Möller, I., & Krahé, B. (2009). Exposure to violent videogames and aggression in German adolescents: A longitudinal analysis. *Aggressive Behavior*, *35*(1), 75–89. doi:10.1002/ab.20290 PMID:19016226

Orr, M. (2003). *Intertextuality: Debates and contexts*. Cambridge, UK: Blackwell Pub.

Osberg, D., Biesta, G., & Cilliers, P. (2008). From representation to emergence: Complexity's challenge to the epistemology of schooling. *Educational Philosophy and Theory*, *40*(1), 213–227. doi:10.1111/j.1469-5812.2007.00407.x

Perron, B., & Wolf, M. J. P. (Eds.). (2008). *The video game theory reader 2*. New York, NY: Routledge.

Plothe, T. (2014). *Intertextuality and the virtual world on celluloid*. Retrieved from https://blogs.commons.georgetown.edu/cctp-725-fall2014/author/tp443/

Richardson, K., & Cilliers, P. (2001). What is complexity science? A view from different directions. *Emergence*, *3*(1), 5–22. doi:10.1207/S15327000EM0301_02

Sabella, R. A. (2010). Negative potential of video games. *Education.com*. Retrieved June 30, 2015, from http://www.education.com/reference/article/negative-potential-video-games/

Sanford, K., & Bonsor Kurki, S. (2014). Videogame literacies: Purposeful civic engagement for 21st century youth learning. In K. Sanford, T. Rogers, & M. Kendrick (Eds.), *Everyday youth literacies: Critical perspectives for new times* (pp. 29–46). Singapore: Springer. doi:10.1007/978-981-4451-03-1_3

Schrader, P. G., Lawless, K. A., & McCreery, M. (2009). Intertextuality in Massively Multiplayer Online Games. Handbook of Research on Effective Electronic Gaming in Education, 3, 791–807.

Siemens, G., & Matheos, K. (2012). Systemic changes in higher education. *Education*, *18*(1), 3–18.

Spence, I., & Feng, J. (2010). Videogames and spatial cognition. *Review of General Psychology*, *14*(2), 92–104. doi:10.1037/a0019491

Squire, K. (2005). Changing the game: What happens when video games enter the classroom. *Innovate Journal of Online Education*, *1*(6), 25–49.

Subrahmanyam, K., Greenfield, P., Kraut, R., & Gross, E. (2001). The impact of computer use on children's and adolescents' development. *Journal of Applied Developmental Psychology*, *22*(1), 7–30. doi:10.1016/S0193-3973(00)00063-0

Waldrop, M. M. (1992). *Complexity: The emerging science at the edge of chaos and order*. New York, NY: Simon and Schuster.

Yin, K. (1984). *Case study research: Design and methods*. Newbury Park, CA: Sage.

KEY TERMS AND DEFINITIONS

Complex Learning Systems: A complex learning system develops within non-linear process (not predictable from knowledge of constituent elements) and is based on the dynamic interactions between multiple variables that are nested within other indeterminate and transient systems.

Complexity Thinking: Complexity thinking refers to being aware of certain features needed to be present for a complex system (collection of inter-connected agents) to form and become a learning system. Complexity thinking is not a meta-theory—that is, an explanatory system that exceeds or subsumes all others. Rather, complexity thinking is an inter-theory—that is, a notion that arises when other frames are brought into conversation with one another.

Emergence: Emergence refers to how collective properties arise from the properties of parts, leading to "unforeseen occurrence" from the interactive of related parts. Emergence refers to how behavior at a larger scale arises from the detailed structure, behavior and relationships at a finer scale.

Intertextual Literacies: With intertextual literacies the teacher asks students to find ways in which the stories are similar and ways they are different. Intertextual literacies confirm for the reader, on the basis of prior experience, what the combination of internal elements in a text does together in order to create meaning.

Intrinsic Case Study: An intrinsic case study focuses on the particulars of one specific phenomenon rather seeking generalizations. The focus in an intrinsic case study arises from the particulars and potentially specific or unique aspects of the case. In contrast instrumental case studies usually describe a specific case of a more general phenomenon.

Literary Devices: Literary devices are linguistic techniques that produce a specific effect, such as a figure of speech, narrative style, or plot mechanism. In particular writers use literary devices to create text that is clear, interesting, and memorable.

Participatory Pedagogy: Participatory pedagogy focuses on the dynamic interplay of events and personal experience in the process of teaching students. This approach advocates a theory of learning in which space is provided to learners to actively create their own meaning through participation.

ENDNOTES

[1] *Machinima* is the use of real-time computer graphics engines to create a cinematic production.
[2] Federally funded research council http://www.sshrc-crsh.gc.ca/home-accueil-eng.aspx
[3] See http://kotako.com/
[4] *Unturned* is a free-to-play, zombie-themed survival comic horror game designed by Nelson Sexton (http://store.steampowered.com/app/304930/)

Chapter 8

"You Can't Mess with the Program, Ralph":
Intertextuality of Player–Agency in Filmic Virtual Worlds

Theo Plothe
Walsh University, USA

ABSTRACT

This essay posits two crucial elements for the representation of digital games in film: intertextuality and player control. Cinematically, the notion of player-agency control is influenced greatly by this intertextuality, and player control has been represented in a number of films involving video games and digital worlds. This essay looks at the use and representation of player-agency control in films that focus on action within digital games. There are three elements that are essential to this representation: 1) there is a separation between the virtual and the real; 2) the virtual world is written in code, and this code is impossible for player-agents to change, though they can manipulate it; 3) the relative position of the player to the player-agent, is one of subservience or conflict. I argue that the notion of player-agency control is essential to the cinematic representation of video games' virtual worlds.

INTRODUCTION

The digital game industry is now the largest, most popular, and profitable form of media on the planet. The worldwide video game marketplace is expected to grow to $111 billion by 2015. According to the Entertainment Software Association, digital games are being played by more a diverse population than ever, finding that 59% of American adults play some kind of digital games and that the average U.S. household owns at least one dedicated game console, pc, or smartphone (ESA, 2014). Digital games, then, represent a large aspect of popular culture, and elements of games, from their narratives, characters, game worlds, and particularly game mechanics (discussed here as ludological features), are the object of representation and exploration in other popular media, particularly film.

DOI: 10.4018/978-1-5225-0477-1.ch008

Brookey (2010) discussed at length the convergence of the film and digital game industries, where films are adapted into digital games and vice versa. This is a rich area of scholarship in considering the effects of media convergence on both of these industries, as well as the similarity of digital games and film elements. In this essay I instead examine the representation of game experiences in narrative films. Cultural products such as these are important to study in order to consider the place of digital games in culture at large, the elements of digital games represented, and the ways in which elements of these games are considered. Burrill (2008) also noted the importance of studying digital games and their influence through the ideologies they impart to culture at large: "In a world where 'play' has become an operant word and war looks like a video game, it is essential to avoid categorizing the games as simply dangerous or trivial" (p. 83). As game elements become part of larger cultural narratives like films, it is important to consider their greater impact in examining how elements of games are taken up in other media.

This chapter examines notions of player agency, a tenant of digital games' position as an interactive medium. How do films remediate these notions of player agency in their cinematic representation, especially in films that take place in the "virtual world" of digital games or systems? Often, player agency control becomes a central point of conflict within these film's narratives, and this chapter seeks answers within the rule-bound system of films that represent digital game worlds. This study focuses not on films that are adaptations of digital games, but on films that represent digital game and virtual worlds. While some of these films are not explicit games, like *The Matrix*, they contain game-like elements in virtual worlds. These films include *Tron* (1982), *Tron: Legacy* (2010), *The Matrix* (1999), *The Matrix Reloaded* (2003), *The Matrix Revolutions* (2003), *The Lawnmower Man* (1992), *eXistenZ* (1999), *Avalon* (2001), *Spy Kids 3-D: Game Over* (2003), and *Wreck-it Ralph* (2012). While not exhaustive, this list is comprehensive in presenting a range of representative films that take place in a virtual world. Through a consideration of the gaming elements represented in these films, this essay suggests important criteria for the representation of games in cinema: There are three elements essential to this representation: 1) there is a separation between the virtual and the real; 2) the virtual world is written in code, and this code is impossible for player-agents to rewrite, though they can manipulate it; 3) the relative position of the player to the player-agent, is one of subservience or conflict. The chapter argues that not only is the notion of player-agency control elemental, it is essential to the cinematic representation of digital games' virtual worlds.

BACKGROUND

Intertextuality

As discussed by Wolf (2001), digital games draw upon divergent texts and provide an interactive environment for users to read these texts. They are rich, intertextual environments that pull references and techniques from a myriad of different media sources, particularly films. Orr (2003) emphasized the transformative nature of intertextuality in the ability of textual references to alter the work that came before it (p. 10). While Orr's definition was concerned with text, she noted that electronic hypertext and interactive media have added "a further layer" to text, a "virtual text" (p. 170), and that intertextuality as a term can be applied to any medium conceived of after print, including film. Orr acknowledged that Kristeva's grounding of the term intertextuality within French postmodernism separated her concept from other similar modes of cultural borrowing "as specifically highbrow" (p. 20). In unifying these ideas, I would argue that Orr's concept of the transformative nature of intertextuality anticipated later definitions of remix; interactive media, then, are not simply added layers of intertexuality, but are instead fundamental to the process itself.

Orr (2003) noted that the interactive nature of hypertext brings writers and readers together (p. 51). This was a key aspect Meinhof & Smith's (2000) definition of intertextuality, as "the process of viewers and readers interpreting texts which exhibit the dynamic interactivity of several semiotic modes, and interpreting them in ways that are partially controlled by this multimodality" (p. 11). These scholars saw intertextuality as a process of interpretation, and through this process, the audience identifies references within a text to other media texts. A film that references a novel draws attention to the ways that different media forms trade ideas and concepts, yet these concepts are represented in a way specific to that particular medium. Ideas traverse media, but their representations are media specific. Conversations of intertextuality in television in particular emphasize genre conventions and the role of the audience, especially their role in shaping audience expectations for a particular media text. As Meinhof and van Leeuwen (2000) described, a TV commercial will inspire different expectations and reception than a music video or news report. These authors, then, see intertextuality as also the blending of multiple genre forms.

Schumaker (2011) argued that analyses of intertextuality in film often lean too heavily on literary criticism or study the features of particular directors rather than the function of intertextuality within the genre itself. Schumaker used the term "super-intertexuality" to describe an exaggerated version of intertextuality present in contemporary film, defining it as "a self-reflexive theoretical model evolving from the unique text-to-text relationships that start the intertextual discourse" (p. 129). Schumaker's analysis of the superhero film *Kick-Ass* noted its connections both to digital game culture and contemporary music. The author described a sequence filmed from a first-person point of view that "quickly evolves into a shootout reminiscent of first-person shooters, like *Halo* and *Doom*. In this sequence, the camera oscillates between the first-person perspective of Hit-Girl and the third-person, suggesting a shift from digital game storytelling to stereotypical film storytelling, and shows how the two mediums can coexist" (pp. 141-142). The sequence is accompanied by a cover of the theme song to *The Banana Splits Adventure*, a 1969 children's television program performed by The Dickies, an American punk band. This short scene, then, references popular culture texts in television and music through a digital game-like action sequence, demonstrating the complex function of intertextuality in today's contemporary culture:

The intertextual path which leads from television shows to generically related games indicates that it is the games which activate the everyday environment of play. There the game show stands in a familiar circle of activity. Crossword puzzles are not solved by individuals, but form the center of social activities. (Mikos & Wulff, 2000, p. 106)

Digital games take individual, specific elements of other media and place them within larger contexts and situations. The rules of a simple game, then, become part of a larger social system of activity within an interactive digital game.

The *Kick-Ass* example demonstrates the ways that films also utilize digital games elements and situations. Because of the importance of intertextuality within digital games, it is also an important element of films that represent digital games, as Schumaker's analysis of *Kick-Ass* demonstrates. The primary mechanism for this intertextuality explored in this paper is the representation of player agency in films.

Player Agency

Player agency is the process through which gamers make decisions and intervene within digital gamespaces; player agency is often represented within a digital game through an avatar. Juul (2005) described digital games as "rules and fiction," containing narrative stories within specific ludic frameworks (p. 12). Digital games allow users to manipulate objects within digital worlds, providing them with the means to direct the narrative and action of the game in ways different from those afforded by other media. While digital games have structure and particular rules (just like any other structured system) there are an infinite number of ways through which the goals of a game can be achieved, and gamers are able to use creative invention and their own agency within the gameworld, usually through an avatar. The notion of player-agency has long been an area of inquiry in games studies (Behrenshausen, 2012). Morris (2002) described the ways that gamers take an active role in the digital games they play, calling them "producers of fiction" within gameplay (p. 90).

Navarro (2012) called controllable objects within the game "an extension of player agency" and described the ways in which avatars allow gamers to interact within the space of the digital game. While many studies of avatars discuss player embodiment, player agency is interested more in the gamer imposing his/her will within the gamespace, which may or may not include a body, but is integrated through what Ensslin (2012) called a "cybernetic feedback loop," linking hardware, software, and the gamer. Brice & Rutter (2002) noted that many digital games expand the parameters in which gamers can interact, even building levels, changing narratives, and adding characters (pp. 76-77).

In cinematic representations of gaming, the notion of player-agency control is influenced greatly by this intertextuality. In order to represent the agency of players within a game, films rely on intertextual references: connections to digital games and other media. I posit that there are three elements essential to this representation of player agency within films about digital games:

1. There is a separation between the virtual and the real.
2. The virtual world is written in code, and this code is impossible for player-agents to change, though they can manipulate it.
3. The relative position of the player to the player-agent is one of subservience or conflict.

Not only is the notion of player-agency control representative, it is essential to the cinematic representation of video games' virtual worlds. The rest of the essay will explore specific examples of intertextuality that utilize these elements to consider the ways that player agency is understood and represented in films.

DIGITAL GAMES IN FILM

Burrill (2008) argued that the original *Tron* film, released in 1982, represents one of the first of many peaks for digital games within popular culture, tying it to the success of Pong and other game genres still popular today (p. 94). Burrill also noted that the narrative of the film "functions as a series of games, or competitive segments performed by the avatars sucked into cyberspace and the preexisting programs populating the competitions" (p. 92). All of these films represent virtual worlds in film through these intertextual elements.

Intertextuality works throughout *Tron* and *Tron: Legacy* in that way, by representing digital game elements as small competitions within the virtual space of the game. *Tron* stars Jeff Bridges as computer programmer Kevin Flynn, who is trapped inside a virtual world by nemisis Ed Dillenger, and the film chronicles his fight within the virtual world against the Master Control Program (MCP), an artificial intelligence written by Dillinger. *Tron Legacy* (2010) returns two decades later, when Flynn's son, Sam (Garrett Hedlund) is transported to the Grid, the virtual world created by his father in the first film now ruled by CLU, Kevin Flynn's original hacking program, which has been now corrupted by jealousy and twisted desire for revenge.

The Lawnmower Man (1992) also represents an early film dealing with digital games and their societal impact. In this film, Dr. Lawrence Angelo (Pierce Brosnan) conducts experiments on Jobe Smith (Jeff Fahey), a gardener with an intellectual disability. Angelo uses virtual reality experiments to increase Smith's intelligence, which gives him telekinetic and pyrokinetic powers. Smith then attempts to evolve into "pure energy" within the virtual world, and to distribute his consciousness throughout the Internet.

The Matrix (1999) and its sequels *The Matrix Reloaded* (2003) and *The Matrix Revolutions* (2003), are set in a futuristic world where machines rule and the reality that humans experience is a simulation created by a machine that uses humans for an energy source. Neo (Keanu Reeves), a computer programmer, learns the truth about the Matrix from Morpheus (Lawrence Fishburne), the leader of a human resistance force that fights against the machines. The three films chronicle Neo and Morpheus' war against the machines, inside and outside of the virtual world they create.

David Cronenberg's film *eXistenZ* (1999) features a virtual game world, but one that uses biological material, and players connect to the gameworld through bioports installed in their own bodies. This film plays with multiple levels of reality; in the first level, a group of gamers is testing a new game by creator Allegra Geller (Jennifer Jason Leigh) when they are interrupted by an assassination attempt on her life that damages her game pod, on which the only copy of this game exists. Geller convinces her bodyguard, Ted Pikul (Jude Law), to enter the game *eXistenZ* with her, where they play a game involving conflict between a game pods company and the Realist Underground of anti-gamers. After Geller makes Pikul as a double agent, the film backs out to another level, revealing that *eXistenZ* is actually a game within another game, *transCendenZ*, the game actually undergoing focus group testing. The end of the film, however, questions that level of reality as well, and the audience is left with questions about separating the virtual from reality.

Spy Kids 3-D: Game Over (2003) the third film in the Spy Kids franchise, focuses on Juni Cortez (Daryl Sabara), who must save his sister and fellow spy Carmen (Alexa Vega) from a villain named the Toymaker (Sylvester Stallone), imprisoned in cyberspace. The Toymaker created a virtual reality game called Game Over, and Cortez must be digitized to enter the game.

Avalon (2001), a Polish language film directed by Mamoru Oshii, features a virtual reality role-playing game of the same name, and in the film, the protagonist Ash, goes on a quest within the game as both redemption and to reach a new stage of consciousness. Like *eXistenZ*, the film blurs the boundaries between the real and virtual worlds.

Wreck-It Ralph (2012) is a Disney animated film about a video game character Ralph (John C. Reilly) who tires of his role as the villain in his arcade game *Fix It Felix, Jr.*, and leaves his game to earn a medal and become a hero in another game in the arcade. The film's conflict involves Vanellope von Schweetz (Sarah Silverman), a glitchy character who is trying to take her place within the main object of her game, a race against other characters.

Virtually, a Real Separation

MacTavish (2002) argued that part of the appeal of digital games is that they "draw attention to the game's virtual world as *virtual* [...] For many gamers, the pleasure of computer gameplay is substantially composed of admiration for, and participation within, the game's exhibition of advanced visual and auditory technology" (p. 34). Many of these films were praised for their own special effects in presenting virtual spaces, and marking the separation or the transition between physical and virtual worlds is a common trope.

Burrill (2008) described the original *Tron* film as "an attempt to narrativize the space of a video game through a plot that joins the 'real' and the cyber" (p. 88), yet the film also creates a boundary between these two spaces. The first scene of Tron clearly demarcates the separation of virtual and the real as it opens in Flynn's arcade and we hear a player and others talk about the *Lightcycle* game. We see the player start the game with a quarter and grab the joystick. The notion of a user in player-agency is very prominent from the start as the action shifts to the playing field inside the game. The virtual world's antagonist Sark (also played by Warner) is shown in action defeating the player in a lightcycle battle. The MCP talks to Sark after the match mentioning that they have kidnapped some military programs" (via his intrusion into the Pentagon and the Kremlin) and asks if Sark would like to take them on next in more "lethal matches." Sark bemoans the "cream puff accounting programs" he's been sent to combat recently and readily agrees to engage these new virtual combatants.

A prominent way to distinguish between the virtual and the real is show the character(s) entering the virtual from the real via some digital or technological process. *Tron* shows the artificial intelligence of the game digitizing the protagonist, Flynn, into the ENCOM mainframe cyberspace using an experimental laser. After the laser finishes digitizing Flynn's corporeal self, the viewer is then sent on a first-person ride through the electronic kaleidoscope from the *real* to the *virtual*, as if Flynn is shooting through the network cable into the ENCOM mainframe. The CGI-lightshow visually represents this journey so the viewer knows she isn't in the *real* world anymore, but the stark barren grid of *virtual* cyberspace.

In the *Matrix*, this process happens in reverse. When Neo takes the now infamous "red pill," he is thrust out of the Matrix, a virtual world he has always thought to be though real, a bit askew. As he awakens, he sees the world not as the machines wish him to, but as it is: humans are farmed for their energy compositing stacks of batteries that stretch as far as the eye can see. Interestingly, these films follow a similar trope of "jacking in," where the physical embodiment in the virtual world is achieved through a physical connection via the technology, whether it's a coaxial cable to the skull, or much less intrusive helmets or visors.

Cronenberg's oeuvre is filled with explorations of embodiment in relation to technology, be the vagaries of television in *Videodrome*, the scientists against nature of *The Fly*, or even to talking insect-like typewriter of *Naked Lunch*. In *eXistenZ*, gamers connect to fleshy organic gamepods through "umby cords" wired into a "bioport" at the base of their spine. Unlike the previous examples, the transition from real to virtual isn't shown to the viewer. Allegra Geller and Ted Pikul wake up inside the game, which looks and feels just as the real world. Pikul, played by Jude Law, turns to Geller, the designer of this particular game, and states, "I feel just like me. Is that kind of transition normal? That kinda... smooth, interlacing from place to place?" Geller replies, "It depends on the style of game. you can get jagged, brutal cuts, slow fades, shimmering little morphs." Even in a world where the transition is seamless, there are no flashing lights like there are in the Matrix and Tron, there is still a notion of the real v. the virtual. The game still has to make a distinction between the two worlds through language, setting, and action.

In the course of the game, Pikul expresses his discomfort within the world of the game and the influence of the virtual gameworld. Pikul says, "I'm feeling a little… disconnected from my real life. Kinda losing touch with the texture of it, you know what I mean? I mean, I actually think there's an element of psychosis involved here." Geller is excited that her game has caused him to react so viscerally "It means your nervous system is fully engaging with the game architecture." Pikul jumps out of his chair, screams "existent is passed" and collapses, face pressed to the table. He wakes up back in the lodge discombobulated, feeling unsure of what's real and what's in the game.

Unlike the previous films, *Wreck-It Ralph* is purely digital in that the protagonists originate in the virtual realm; no one enters it and no one leaves, yet the digital is fully aware of its position relative to the real. To its digital denizens, Wreck-It Ralph's characters see the real world from a very Cartesian perspective: within the old video game arcades, such as Litwack's Arcade from *Wreck-It Ralph*, the real looks in on their virtual worlds as if through a window in space.

In all of these films, the boundary between the physical and virtual worlds is clearly marked, and this separation is often dramatized by transition sequences in which the player enters the virtual space. This demarcation, however, does not mean that the virtual world has no effect on the actual world, and all of these films in actuality show how deeply connected these two worlds are. Ensslin (2012) noted that the word "real" applies to both the "actual" world and the "virtual" or second world (p. 25).

Rewriting the Code

In comparing films and digital games, Brice and Rutter (2002) argued that gamers are able to "actively engage in the modification of the game narrative and environments" (p. 76). In films depicting digital games, then, these modifications play a central role within the films. There is a limit, however, to the type of changes that player agents can make within these virtual game worlds. Through training and his mystical abilities as "the One," Neo is able to actually visualize the binary code of the game and through this, how to manipulate it in a remarkably tactile way. Within these films, there is a great deal of slippage in the ways in which the material code of the game is represented, moving between the data and the algorithms of the game. In *The Matrix*, for example, though he cannot rewrite the code as a modder can do with a digital game or as a hacker or cheat code can do, Neo is able to change the algorithms of the physical virtual environment, i.e. slowing bullets.

A well-known scene in *The Matrix* involves the main character Neo manipulating the code of the virtual world enough to stop a hail of bullets as they are flying toward him. Suspended in space before him, Neo plucks one out of the air, cocks his head in amusement at his now God-like command, and causes the other projectiles to fall harmlessly to the floor. This scene is an example of the ways that player agents can interact with the code of the game; he cannot destroy the data, but he can manipulate how it behaves. While Neo cannot destroy the bullets, he grinds their progress through the air to a halt.

Earlier in the film, Neo tries to dodge Agent Jones' bullets managing to avoid nearly an entire clip while standing in space. After Trinity makes the save, she queries, "How did you do that? You moved like they do. I've never seen anyone move that fast." In the *Matrix Reloaded*, as he did with the bullets at the conclusion of the first film, Neo reaches into the code with a tactile approach, plucking the bullets from inside Trinity's green shimmering body. He cannot simply destroy the projectiles, removing them from the virtual world, but he can manipulate what is present.

Similarly, in *Tron*, Flynn hijacks a broken down regulator, a flying war machine used to suppress enemies of the MCP. On the lam, Flynn and a mortally wounded Ram find a decrepit regulator among the cavernous outskirts of gamespace. Here, Flynn is able to revive the machine simply by concentrating on its repair and manipulating the code to fix the engine and the structural integrity of the ship. Ram's eyes widen with awe and reverence as he questions whether Flynn is a user. Yet within the virtual world of the game, Flynn cannot create a new vehicle, though he can manipulate ones already present.

One of the major in-jokes of *Wreck-It Ralph*'s digital world is the normalcy of the characters lives. They wake up at the start of each day as Mr. Litwak opens the arcade, and work a 9-5 just as any working stiff might. But the digital worlds still behave according to algorithms. The character King Candy, for example, is seen using a common cheat code that has significance within gamer culture to manipulate the code of the game in which he exists: up-up-down-down-left-right-left-right-B-A start. This sequence is commonly referred to as the "Konami code," in reference to the digital game company Konami, which will give a player infinite lives within a game. A remnant of the game creation and testing process, it is an artifact that was then used to players' advantage. This scene in *Wreck-it Ralph* not only pays homage to this aspect of digital game culture, it is the only means through which a character can adjust the behavior of the game. One has to use the constraints provided in the code.

As algorithms, games are rule-bound constructs. In *Avalon*, when Ash meets with Murphy inside the game seeking information on the nine sisters, she expects he'll want something in return. Murphy snarls that he'll just take her gear. "People would pay good cash for the data that's stored on that equipment." Ash retorts that "selling a player's data is against the rules." Murphy feigns concern, "Yeah, well a guy's got to earn and living, even in Avalon."

Secondly, there exists an idea that characters cannot delete these algorithms completely, though they can be manipulated. When her betrayal becomes apparent, Demetra tells the hero Juni in *Spy Kids 3D*, "Sorry Juni, it's in my programming." Though, even though as a digital construct, she's somehow she's fallen in love with Juni, but cannot violate the code which demands she must lead our heroes into a trap.

The parameters of this algorithm manipulation can be best parsed in *Wreck-it Ralph's* initial foray into *Hero's Duty*, a first-person-shooter (FPS) where a team of space marines mount an offensive against the evil alien swarm, the Cy-Bugs. During the resultant chaos, we see Calhoun repeatedly turning to the FPS instructing the player on what to do. The player's face appears on the flat screen as she does this; intertextually, this is action is common in gaming as a playable tutorial during which the game instructs the player on game rules and mechanics within the game's narratives. When Ralph steps out of line, Calhoun pushes him to the side and nervously looks back to the FPS, proceeding with her instructions. After the beacon is turned on resulting in all the bugs flying to their death, Calhoun reads the riot act to Ralph (as Markowski), reminding him of the player-character's subservience to the player. "What's the first rule of Hero's duty? Never interfere with the first-person-shooter. Our job is to get the gamers to the top of that building so they can get a medal, and that's it! So stick to the program, soldier!"

Films that represent games focus on these two elements of games' materiality – the nature of the virtual world and the code through which it operates. While these elements are sometimes understood reductively in these films, these are two elements that identify games as distinct. Representing a digital game means exploring the distinction between the real and the virtual, a common element in all of these films. Games are also bound by specific worlds, and like the boundary between the game and the real world, the limits of that game are also explored through its code.

Who's Playing Whom?

Each of these films also represents the complex relationship between the avatar in the game and the player agent outside of it. Jorgensen (2009) noted that the avatar is an extension of the player into the gameworld and "there must be a real-time and continuous relationship between the player and the avatar" (p. 2). The relationship between these two entities is often one of conflict within these films. Ensslin (2012) argued that players' bodies are "doubly situated" while playing a digital game. Players both interact with the hardware and software of the game (the controllers and the game interface), while at the same time they are "re-embodied" within the virtual world of the game through their avatars. Each of these films portrays this relationship between player and the player agent within the game differently, but for each it is a site of conflict.

In *Tron* users are worshiped as gods; they are the unseen overlords who control programs' movements in the field and with an awareness that the programmers wrote the programs. Tron himself declares, "I fight for Alan," a bold statement of loyalty to his creator. In another scene, a program, later revealed as "Crom," is led down a hallway and can be heard complaining to his captors that he's "Just a compound interest program. I work at a savings and loan. I can't play these video games." As his captors back him against a door he continues, "Hey, look. You guys are gonna make my User, Mr. Henderson, very angry. He's a full branch manager!" The guard replies, "Great. Another religious nut!" From the guards' perspective, Crom's adherence to the user is repulsive. As with the MCP, the digital game rebels against its maker, seeking autonomy and independence from the user. Once in the cell, Crom's neighbor introduces himself as Ram, welcoming him to their punishment and asking if Crom truly believes in the higher power known as the user. Crom replies that of course he does, "If I don't have a User, then who wrote me?"

In the sequel nearly 30 years later, belief in the user has changed dramatically. Sam is quickly captured despite his protests of "I'm not a program" when he first arrives in the grid. Eventually, he is captured and sent to fight in "the Games", but is rescued by his father's "apprentice" Quorra, an isomorphic algorithm created by the game, a spontaneous program if you will. CLU sees these "ISOs" as imperfect aberrations and purges the system of them via mass extermination. CLU seeks to capture Flynn's "identity disc," unlocking its master key so that he can escape the system through the "I/O portal" and impose his idea of perfection on the real world.

The user (player) acts as an independent agent within the system. In this example, he retains control of his individual actions, and can affect certain spheres of influence directly around him, but the program has grown beyond his control, as witnessed by the ISOs. In this sense, player-agency is only cursory; the player's ability to play the game is defined by the boundaries constructed and enforced by the game. Contrasted with the first film, where Flynn was exploring the game and discovers his power as the player and exerts some sense of control, in the sequel he sees that the player is just another cog in the machine. At one point, Flynn bemoans Clu's betrayal and dominance: "It's his game now. The only way to win is not to play."

The final film of the *Matrix* trilogy, *The Matrix Revolutions*, culminates with a final battle between Neo and Agent Smith with the matrix. In this example, the relative position of the player to the player-agent is one of subservience or conflict. In that battle, Neo is tied to the Source, and his agency is tethered to that as well. Neo within the matrix is being played by the program as much as he is playing, while Agent Smith, a rogue program at this point battles for sentience outside the game against his computer overlords.

Rather than remaining subservient to the physical world, *The Lawnmower Man* presents the premise that virtual reality epitomizes the "evolution" of man, and the player agent becomes superior to the human outside of the game. As Jobe grows intellectually during his forays into the virtual world, he begins to show examples of telekinetic power in the real world. Eager to demonstrate his growing sophistication, he sneaks Marnie, the woman he is dating, into Angelo's lab for a tryst in virtual reality. Jobe's avatar begins to act in a violent and horrific manner, attacking Marnie's avatar and taking a monstrous form snarling and spitting at a now terrified Marnie. Jobe protests that it's simply what her subconscious wants even as his avatar begins assaulting her mind directly. The result leaves Marnie in a near catatonic state, driven insane and softly laughing to herself. In this case, Jobe's subconscious took control through his avatar. Jobe remarks in the film, "This whole universe is mine. I am God here." He sees his player agent within the game as stronger than the individual outside of it.

In *eXistenZ*, however, gamers are put in contrary positions as they negotiate their identity within the player-agents they play as. Early in the film, Pikul is horrified after he snaps viciously at a rather innocent question from the proprietor at a video games store in the game. Ashamed, Pikul turns to Geller and says he didn't mean to be so rude, that he couldn't believe he reacted with such incivility. This becomes a running theme of the film, Pikul's discomfort at reckoning the desires and needs of his player-agent and that of his own within the virtual world of *eXistenZ*. Back at the restaurant mentioned earlier in this chapter, the special turns out to be a plate full of two-headed lizards seen earlier in the film. Despite being thoroughly disgusted at the sight of the grotesque dish before him, Pikul feels an overwhelming craving to eat the butchered lizards in a rather slimy duck sauce. Geller reassures him, "It's a genuine game urge. It's something your game character was born to do. Don't fight it." Here we can see not only Cronenberg investigating notions of free will, but also the relative position of the player to the player-agent, in this case, one of conflict. Geller, the game designer and experienced gamer herself, chooses to submit to the code; she's obviously been in this position before. But Pikul, as the gaming neophyte, is troubled by his lack of agency in the virtual world.

For these films, the player-agent becomes a central point of conflict as the characters in each film negotiate their role in both real and virtual environments. In exploring the distinctions between the real and the virtual, these films also represent the position of the player-agent as the individual's representative in the virtual world. This relationship, however, remains one of subservience. In each of these examples, the player outside of the game is seen as the authentic self, while the player agent is a derivative or reductive version of that self. Even in *The Lawnmower Man*, Jobe's desire to live in the virtual world and obtain ultimate power within it is seen as delusional. This goal is achieved only with the reduction of his physical self.

CONCLUSION

The intertextual nature of films that feature digital games points to the central elements that preoccupy filmmakers and audiences. The films are deeply layered, complex texts that represent specific aspects of digital game play and culture. From visual representations of interfaces and references to gamer culture, these films are profoundly influenced by the digital games and technologies of the times in which they were created. This paper has argued that in addressing player agency, these films comment how game scholars can make sense of video game experiences and their growing place within mainstream culture.

King and Krzywinska (2006) noted that analysis of the meanings of films includes an analysis of the kinds of "personal characteristics" endorsed (p. 126). What does that mean for games? Each of these films explore one's ability for agency within a system, which means a digital game. While in most cases, a player cannot change the underlying structure of the program (any more than an individual can change an economic or political system) one has agency to work within it.

The power to manipulate a virtual world is seen in each of these films as required to enact change, yet the effect of these changes on the physical world are always seen as more important. In *Tron* and the *Matrix* triology, for example, mastering the virtual world enacts change in the physical one. The representation of games is ultimately a conservative and reductive one. The emphasis on the virtual world and its separation from the physical world, as well as the role of the player-agent within the film, establishes games as a distant second to the activities that occur in the "real world."

The films discussed here ultimately reflect an anxiety about the power of digital games and their influence on society as a whole. In reducing the experiences of digital games to three tropes, these works remain deeply concerned about the relationship between virtual worlds and physical ones, the ability to manipulate what is often described as the mythical algorithms, or "programs" of digital games, and the role of the player-agent within virtual spaces. In this list, it is notable that the most recent film *Wreck-It Ralph*, is that which takes place almost entirely within the digital world. Yet in this case as well, the digital world of each of the arcade games requires their physical existence within the arcade. In the examples, then, digital games are seen as somewhat less than real. For games researchers, the ongoing representation of digital games within films is an important reflection of overall anxieties about the perceptions of virtual worlds. While playing digital games is an increasingly common activity within the public at large, these films demonstrate that it is an activity still fraught with misunderstanding and anxiety.

REFERENCES

Allen, G. (2000). *Intertextuality*. London, UK: Routledge.

Avellan, E., & Rodriguez, R. (Producers), & Rodriguez, R. (Director). (2003). *Spykids 3-D: Game over* [Motion Picture]. United States: Buena Vista Pictures.

Bailey, S., Silver, J., & Lisberger, S. (Producers), & Kosinski, J. (Director). (2010). *Tron: Legacy* [Motion picture]. United States: Walt Disney Studios.

Brookey, R. A. (2010). *Hollywood gamers: Digital convergence in the film and video game industries*. Bloomington, IN: Indiana University Press.

Bryce, J., & Rutter, J. (2002). Spectacle of the deathmatch: Character and narrative in first-person shooters. In G. King & T. Krzywinska (Eds.), *ScreenPlay: Cinema/videogames/interfaces* (pp. 66–80). New York, NY: Wallflower Press.

Burrill, D. A. (2002). "Oh, grow up 007": The performance of Bond and boyhood in film and videogames. In G. King & T. Krzywinska (Eds.), *ScreenPlay: Cinema/videogames/interfaces* (pp. 181–193). New York, NY: Wallflower Press.

Cronenberg, D., Hámori, A., & Lantos, R. (Producers), & Cronenberg, D. (Director). (1999). *eXistenZ* [Motion picture]. Canada. Alliance Atlantic.

Deterding, S. (2010). Living room wars : remediation, boardgames, and the early history of video wargaming. In N. B. Huntemann & M. T. Payne (Eds.), *Joystick soldiers: The politics of play in military video games* (pp. 21–38). New York, NY: Routledge.

Ensslin, A. (2012). *The language of gaming*. Houndmills, UK: Palgrave Macmillan.

Entertainment Software Association. (2014). *Game player data*. Retrieved June 23, 2014, from http://www.theesa.com/wp-content/uploads/2014/10/ESA_EF_2014.pdf

Everett, G. (Producer), & Leonard, B. (Director). (1992). *The lawnmower man* [Motion Picture]. United States. New Line Cinema.

Gee, J. P. (2007). *What video games have to teach us about learning and literacy*. New York, NY: Palgrave Macmillan.

Giddings, S., & Kennedy, H. W. (2006). Digital games as new media. In J. Bryce & J. Rutter (Eds.), *Understanding digital games* (pp. 129–147). London, UK: SAGE Publications. doi:10.4135/9781446211397.n8

Hjorth, L. (2009). Playing the gender game: The performance of Japan, gender and gaming via Melbourne female cosplayers. In L. Hjorth & D. Chan (Eds.), *Gaming cultures and place in the Asia-Pacific region* (pp. 273–288). London, UK: Routledge.

Jenkins, H. (2006). *Convergence culture: Where old and new media collide*. New York, NY: New York University Press.

Kijima, Y. (2007). The fighting gamer otaku community : What are they "fighting" about? In M. Ito, D. Okabe, & T. Tsuji (Eds.), *Fandom unbound: Otaku culture in a connected world* (pp. 249–274). New Haven, CT: Yale University Press.

Kress, G. (2000). Text as the punctuation of semiosis: Pulling at some of the threads. In U. H. Meinhof & J. M. Smith (Eds.), *Intertextuality and the media: From genre to everyday life* (pp. 132–154). Manchester, UK: Manchester University Press.

Kristeva, J. (1980). *Desire in language: A semiotic approach to literature and art*. New York, NY: Columbia University Press.

Kubo, A. (Producer) & Oshii, M. (Director). (2001). *Avalon* [Motion picture]. Poland: Miramax.

Kushner, D. (Producer), & Lisberger, S. (Director). (1982). *Tron* [Motion picture]. United States: Buena Vista Pictures.

Lessig, L. (2009). *Remix: Making art and commerce thrive in the hybrid economy*. New York, NY: Penguin Books.

Lugo, J., Sampson, T., & Lossada, M. (2002). Latin America's new cultural industries still play old games: From the banana republic to *Donkey Kong*. *Game Studies, 2*(2). Retrieved from http://www.gamestudies.org/0202/lugo/

Mactavish, A. (2002). Technological pleasure: The performance and narrative of technology in *Half-Life* and other high-tech computer games. In G. King & T. Krzywinska (Eds.), *ScreenPlay : cinema/videogames/interfaces* (pp. 33–49). London: Wallflower Press.

Meinhof, U. H., & Smith, J. M. (2000). The media and their audience: Intertextuality as paradigm. In U. H. Meinhof & J. M. Smith (Eds.), *Intertextuality and the media: From genre to everyday life* (pp. 1–170). Manchester, UK: Manchester University Press.

Meinhof, U. H., & Van Leeuwen, T. (2000). Viewers' worlds: image, music, text and the Rock "n" roll years. In U. H. Meinhof & J. M. Smith (Eds.), *Intertextuality and the media: From genre to everyday life* (pp. 61–75). Manchester, UK: Manchester University Press.

Mikos, L., & Wulff, H. J. (2000). Intertextuality and situative contexts in game shows: the case of *Wheel of fortune*. In U. H. Meinhof & J. M. Smith (Eds.), *Intertextuality and the media: From genre to everyday life* (pp. 98–114). Manchester: Manchester University Press.

Miller, K. (2008). The accidental carjack: Ethnography, gameworld tourism, and *Grand Theft Auto*. Retrieved from http://gamestudies.org/0801/articles/miller

Morris, S. (2002). First-person shooters - A game apparatus. In G. King & T. Krzywinska (Eds.), *ScreenPlay: Cinema/videogames/interfaces* (pp. 81–97). New York, NY: Wallflower Press.

Navarro, V. (2012). I am a gun: The avatar and avatarness in FPS. In G. A. Voorhees, J. Call, & K. Whitlock (Eds.), *Guns, grenades, and grunts: First-person shooter games* (pp. 63–88). New York, NY: Continuum.

Orr, M. (2003). *Intertextuality: Debates and contexts*. Cambridge, UK: Blackwell Pub.

Rutter, J., & Bryce, J. (Eds.). (2006). *Understanding digital games*. London, UK: SAGE Publications.

Schumaker, J. S. (c2011.). Super-intertextuality and 21st century individualized social advocacy in Spider-Man and Kick-Ass. In R. J. Gray & B. Kaklamanidou (Eds.), The 21st century superhero: Essays on gender, genre and globalization in film (pp. 129–143). Jefferson, NC: McFarland.

Silver, J. (Producer), & The Wachowski Brothers (Director). (1999). *The matrix* [Motion picture]. United States: Warner Bros.

Silver, J. (Producer), The Wachowski Brothers (Director). (2003). *The matrix reloaded* [Motion picture]. United States: Warner Bros.

Silver, J. (Producer), The Wachowski Brothers (Director). (2003). *The matrix revolutions* [Motion picture]. United States: Warner Bros.

Spencer, C. (Producer), & Moore, R. (Director). (2012). *Wreck-it Ralph* [Motion picture]. United States: Walt Disney Studios.

Suchenski, R. (2004, July). Mamoru Oshii. *Senses of Cinema*, (32).

Wolf, M., & Perron, B. (2003). *The video game theory reader*. New York, NY: Routledge.

Wolf, M. J. P. (2001). *The medium of the video game*. Austin, TX: University of Texas Press.

Worton, M., & Still, J. (1990). *Intertextuality: Theories and practice*. Manchester, UK: Manchester University Press.

KEY TERMS AND DEFINITIONS

Digital Game: Also defined as "video game" or "computer game," the term digital game is the current scholarly term used to describe multimedia games played on digital devices, which does not presuppose a specific type of media used. Digital games can be played on a computer, gaming console, mobile phone, or other portable electronic device.

Player Agency: The will of the player within the game and its ability to act within the gamespace.

Player Agent: Also called an avatar, the player agent is the representation of the game player within the game.

Virtual World: The world or space of a digital game, usually seen as separate or distinct from the physical world and determined by the cod of the digital game.

Chapter 9
Cultural Transduction and Intertextuality in Video Games:
An Analysis of Three International Case Studies

Enrique Uribe-Jongbloed
Universidad del Norte, Colombia

Hernán David Espinosa-Medina
Universidad de La Sabana, Colombia

James Biddle
University of Georgia, USA

ABSTRACT

This chapter addresses the relationship that exists between intertextuality and cultural transduction in video game localization. Whereas the former refers to the dual relationship established between texts and previous texts available to the potential readers and the bridges that are consciously or unconsciously established between them, cultural transduction refers to the conscious process of transforming audio-visual content to suit the interests of a given cultural market. Three case studies are presented to explore the relationship that exists between the place of production, the internal cultural references to other texts within the games and the intended market where the video game is distributed: Finally, the importance of intertextuality as part of the cultural transduction process is highlighted.

INTRODUCTION: THE LOCALIZATION OF VIDEO GAMES

Video games have quickly become the 'new' media of interest in terms of their economic worth and impact upon users/players. Economic prospects for video games at large are very high. They are one of the fastest growing areas in the creative industries discourse, and as part of the new media concept, they have shown an international growth of 60% in exports world-wide between 2002 and 2008, largely thanks to developing economies such as China and Mexico (UNCTAD & UNDP, 2010, p. 160).

DOI: 10.4018/978-1-5225-0477-1.ch009

This growth applies two pressures directly onto video game creators from the whole globe. On the one hand, they have to generate products that can be easily consumed in the growing market, sometimes including localization processes aimed at making a product understandable within specific markets to ensure that cultural barriers are overcome (Consalvo, 2006). On the other hand, there is internal pressure for video games to develop from local successful media products and cultural capital to ensure internal consumption, or to draw from seemingly universal tropes or successful transnational products, to insert themselves within larger global markets (Yoon & Cheon, 2013).

Though it is not difficult to understand why localization is carried out by all media production companies, we are still unclear of how this localization takes place (Waisbord & Jalfin, 2009). The analysis of the *Kingdom Rush* series, *El Chavo Kart* and *South Park: The Stick of Truth* presented here tries to address this question by engaging with both the ludic and the narrative elements of the products, their relationship with previous media texts and infer the particular cultural capital required by those on the receiving end of the communication process – the players. Furthermore, this chapter endeavors to work towards understanding the decision-making process that is evidenced by the specific uses of intertextual references within these products, following Consalvo's (2006, p. 134) advice that "only by examining both culture and its production can we better understand the world of culture and its ever-shifting configurations". Through this analysis we hope to exemplify some of the lessons that can be inferred through close examination of current examples of video games flow and counter flows between various audiovisual markets. The idea is that in the future the conclusions of this analysis added to those of further explorations may yield a set of tools, based on empirical experiences that can be used to better comprehend and develop the industrial practices surrounding the insertion and exchange of audiovisual products. These tools might prove useful to content producers and other professionals involved in content trade, adaptation and production, as well as academics that wish to explore these areas.

LOCALIZATION AND CULTURAL TRANSDUCTION

The concept of localization is used here in its "broader sense, which encapsulates any of a wide range of activities designed to adapt products to the perceived differences between local markets" (Carlson & Corliss, 2011, p. 65). Localization goes beyond translation (Bernal Merino, 2006) and aims at making a media product accepted and understood within specific cultural markets. From this perspective, localization is almost coterminous to *cultural transduction*.

Uribe-Jongbloed and Espinosa-Medina (2014) developed the concept of cultural transduction to provide a framework to the flow of cultural products that transcend national borders. The framework looks at a variety of elements that interplay in the design and distribution of a product from the onset in a methodical procedure with four aspects:

- **Markets:** Looking at the cultural proximity or distance between the market of the original product –or where it was created – and the insertion markets (see Bicket, 2005);
- **Product:** Analyzing conditions of the product, which may explain its appeal, or lack thereof, when crossing over cultural borders;
- **People:** Studying the people involved in the process of recognizing, trading and modifying a product to suit specific cultural markets;
- **Process:** Classifying the mechanism through which the transduction is carried out.

Constructing further on the process aspect, they present three types, drawing from concepts commonly used in recent debates, and they repurpose them for clarity: *Hybridity* (García Canclini, 2000; Kraidy, 2010), redefined as the process of altering cultural products under the decision-making of already established media companies (e.g. dubbing or format adaptations), which they contrast with *Convergence* (Deuze, 2007; Jenkins, 2006), using it to define user-generated content modifications, reconstructions and adaptations (e.g. fandubs). Through this separation between hybridity and convergence, they seem to have addressed the problem of thinking that video game production is, in itself, a convergent process, a critique levied by O'Donnell (2011). Finally, they introduce the possibility of a *Transduction Laboratory*, a space created specifically for the purpose of developing a culturally transductable product.

Even though the framework was developed to address issues of adaptation and translation of television products from one cultural market to another, it can be extended to the case of video games. Carlson and Corliss (2011) have shown the importance of video game localization, which may be as simple as the translation of basic instructions in the manuals or words displayed on buttons in a casual game, but more often than not includes the modification of internal elements.

Because of high quality concerns in this market, "the video game industry is a rare example of the way translation is not seen just as something to be carried out once production has been completed as a sort of unrelated and unimportant appendage" (Chiaro, 2008, p. 153), but as an integral part of the localizing process. This brings our attention to the idea of transduction from the initial stages of the development of the product.

This situation is different from the more traditional case of dubbing films or television series. For instance, *The Simpsons* (Brooks, Groening, & Simon, 1989) is a finished product produced for the American market and then sold all over the world, dubbed or subtitled. There is quite a challenge when dubbing the show, since "[it] is a complex audiovisual product with multiple layers of meaning and its translation into other languages certainly involves a high degree of complexity" (Muñoz Gil, 2009, p. 143). Conceptualizing the potential users or audience at the source diminishes the difficulty to understand the product based on cultural or content expectations. Recent films, including Pixar's *Inside Out* (Docter & Del Carmen, 2015), evidence a more nuanced interest in localization; not only do they dub the film, they also include modification of all texts that appear inside the film into Spanish in the Latin American version, *Intensamente*.

Our capacity to give meaning, and therefore to enjoy, a text, whatever it's form –visual, written, audiovisual, and interactive–, is contingent upon the relationships that can be established in the minds of the audience between the text and other units of meaning (Sakellariou, 2014). As explained by Sander (2006) using James Joyce's *Ulysses* as an example, "an intertextual reading of Ulysses draws readers' imaginations into the realms of Homer, Dante and Shakespeare, stretching far beyond its self-proclaimed horizons and cultural geography. The signifying field appears vast as a result"(p. 7). Inter-relatable elements between texts create meaning in the mind of the audience in diverse ways and it varies according to the context, because meaning is, at the end, a social construction (Allen, 2011, Chapter 1; 2014, pp. 36–37).

Since one of the basic interests when inserting a cultural product into a new market is that it becomes understandable to the target audience, it helps to see how intertextuality plays a role in attempts to define whether and how the insertion is viable. For example, trying to predict the success of a product in a new market, *cultural proximity* states that if a product's original market has cultural similarities to the target market, it is more likely to be understood there. These similarities might help people in the targeted market feel a close relation to the product and therefore might be more inclined to consume it (see La

Pastina, Rego, & Straubhaar, 2003; Straubhaar, 1991; Uribe-Jongbloed & Espinosa-Medina, 2014). Culturally specific elements, such as language, tradition, and religion may appeal to users of some cultural markets while ostracizing others. When cultural proximity is low, *cultural distance* is used to describe that dissimilarity in cultural traits.

However, cultural distance is not the only element that hampers access to other cultural markets. There may be other barriers articulated within the legislation or working procedures of the destination market. In video games localization practices a variety of – at times unacknowledged – forces and pressures that frequently have little to do with how cultural divides (Carlson & Corliss, 2011, p. 70) account for these barriers. In other words, to access a market, there are cultural barriers, and political or economic ones. Even when those are related to one another – as in the case of quotas that are aimed at protecting local cultural products, or censorship of content considered culturally offensive – sometimes they are not necessarily cultural in their reasoning.

CULTURAL LACUNAE AND INTERTEXTUALITY AS BEDFELOWS

Cultural proximity tells us about the similarity between cultural markets, and serves as proxy when thinking of a potential market for a product created in a different one. However, the specific product, rather than the relationship between markets, may engender other types of acceptance or rejection beyond those expected from the cultural distance or market barriers.

The impossibility to understand a cultural media product because of the elements that are integral part of it has been conceptualized by Rohn (2011) as cultural lacunae. She defines lacuna as

… gaps or mismatches between the cultural baggage of the media producers, which influences the topics and the style of the content, and the cultural baggage of the audiences, which influences the kind of media content they select, how they understand it and to what extent they enjoy it. (p. 633)

Rohn offers three separate categories for the cultural lacuna:

- **Content Lacuna:** Refers to the impossibility of an audience to come to terms with the elements present in the product, because they may find them offensive or because they fail to make a connection between themselves and the product.
- **Capital Lacuna:** Addresses the fact that despite acknowledging the content, the cultural elements embedded in the product make it difficult or impossible to access; language is a clear example of capital lacuna.
- **Production Lacuna:** Refers to specificities in terms of the style of the culturally foreign product. In this case it is not that they do not accept it, as in the case of content lacuna, or that they do not understand it, lacking the cultural capital, but rather that they do not like the way the product is made in formal terms.

The general definition for lacuna matches the two perspectives of *intertextuality* presented by Ott and Walter (2000) in their description of the concept: "intertextuality has been used to describe both an interpretive practice unconsciously exercised by audiences living in a postmodern landscape and a textual strategy consciously incorporated by media producers that invites audiences to make specific lateral associations between texts". (p. 430)

The unconscious interpretive practice on the part of the reader/audience/user may render a product irrelevant, since it may fail to match the ideological practice of the audience, the great scheme of unconscious expectations of what that cultural product should be, based on the myriad of previously interconnected texts, including genre predisposition, that have been experienced before. In that sense, Rohn's (2011) content lacuna is similar to an intertextual barrier to the acceptance of a given text. Content lacuna means an inability to come to terms with the whole product, implying there are unconscious processes of rejection.

On the other hand, the textual strategy mentioned by Ott and Walter (2000) refers to the inclusion of particular references as part of the text. Similarly, capital lacuna describes the impossibility to understand the specificity of the content presented, because of its references to unknown texts. The struggle presented above in regards to dubbing *The Simpsons* provides a case in point. Linguistic and cultural capital differences may make it difficult to understand a product, not in the sense that it cannot be recognized, but that it is not possible to make sense of the texts with which it builds connections.

The third category introduced by Rohn (2011) deals with the enjoyment in terms of style and its possible reception. It is linked to the concept of taste, and whether a product manages to appeal to its audience regarding its aesthetic qualities. Although this may also be based on previously received products that create trends, it inherently deals with one of the two options mentioned above.

Cultural capital lacuna goes hand in hand with the inherent intertextual choices of the text creators. Camarero (2008) draws on Genette to elaborate a typology of this type of intertextuality. He describes two types of relationships:

1. Co-presence:
    a. Explicit:
        i. Citations.
        ii. References.
    b. Implicit:
        i. Plagiarism.
        ii. Allusion.
2. Derivation:
    a. Transformation – parody.
    b. Imitation – pastiche (Camarero, 2008, p. 34).

In the case of co-presence, he defines citations in comparison to plagiarism, because the former evidence in some way the precedence of the inserted text, whereas the latter obscures it, as an "undeclared borrowing yet absolutely literal, thus rendering heterogeneity or textual differentiation void" (Camarero, 2008, p. 37). The reference does not reproduce the original text, but rather provides a way to reach it and leaves the reader to insert the content of the reference into the text. Allusion is vaguer in the case of the link between the texts, "because it refers to an enunciate whose full intelligibility assumes the perception of a relationship between this statement and the other … it is a sort of citation, but it is neither literal nor explicit" (Camarero, 2008, p. 38). Derivation refers to the imitation of the style of a usually canonical text. Transformation is the use of the main recognizable elements of the classical text, subverted by ridicule, whereas imitation is the use of the stylistic elements of a given author or authors but in the production of a completely different text.

Along similar lines but focusing on media other than literature, Ott and Walter (2000) identify three intertextual devices applied in media texts:

1. Parodic allusion.
2. Creative appropriation or inclusion.
3. Self-reflexive reference.

The parodic allusion is the use, albeit in a slightly humorous way, of elements of renowned texts. It merely "seeks to amuse through juxtaposition – a goal that is enhanced by the reader's recognition of the parodic gesture" (p. 436). Parodic allusions are allusions in Camarero's model, because they apply to textual connections that are not clearly marked, but that imply a reference or homage rather than poaching or plagiarism.

Creative appropriation or inclusion involves the incorporation of a part of the original text with its stylistic conditions, modifying some aspect through either visual or audio editing. It may be closely related to plagiarism, because it implies the conscious use of material from another text, and sometimes it risks treading over copyright ownership, leading to complex lawsuits. Thus, inclusion seems more common in the case of franchise products, derived from previously existing texts, yet commissioned directly or under licenses. However, the distance between parodic allusion and creative appropriation is more difficult to draw in the case of audiovisual media than it is for the written texts of literature.

Finally, self-reflexive references overcome the barrier of the text, by appealing to or evidencing the text itself. It may be through description of the conditions of the work as part of the narrative strategy or by bringing to the text information that relates to the producers or their role in the creation of the product.

Because Ott and Walter's (2000) classification applies more uniformly to media other than literature as is the case here, it has been privileged in the case studies presented. Since intertextual demands may increase or diminish the pleasure an end user experiences with a text, intertextuality as textual strategy plays a considerable role in the success of an audiovisual product. In other words, a lack of recognition of parodic allusions, inclusions and self-reflexivity, may turn people away from the product, due to cultural lacunae.

VIDEO GAMES AND CULTURAL UNIVERSALS

Video games are a growing area of economic exchange, and they are the media that is overtaking all others as international export and revenue source. New media, the category under which UNCTAD (2010) collects information about video games imports and exports, tripled from $8 billion to $27 billion dollars between 2002 and 2008. PricewaterhouseCoopers (PwC, 2015a) estimates the international video games business to reach over US$93 billion by 2019. Social and casual games are increasing their revenue generation and countries with a traditionally low consumption of video game consoles are a growing market for them (PwC, 2015b). In the specific case of mobile games, Latin America accounts for only a small fraction, below 5%, of the global revenue, yet they house more video gamers than the US and Canada combined (GMGC, 2015, p. 4). Thus, the potential for Latin American video game products within its geo-linguistic boundaries and beyond makes for a good scenario to study.

The question then would move towards the likelihood that games developed elsewhere would encounter an appeal in Latin America, or whether those developed in Latin America would be able to take advantage of the geo-linguistic market, or overcome cultural barriers and reach larger cultural markets. The strategy would be for those products to address the flip side of the cultural lacunae, namely cultural universals.

Rohn (2011) presents three types of cultural universals in media products: *content universals*, *audience-created universals* and *company-created universals*. She defines content universal as the concept used

... to refer to content attributes which can be enjoyed by audiences across cultures. The term is not limited to those attributes that are appreciated by all cultures around the world, but may also apply to attributes that make particular media content successful in a particular culture outside the culture of its production. (p. 635)

This notion can be exploited to ensure the success of the product in the target market in various ways. The first of these alternatives is to try to generate the relations directly in the text, which in terms of cultural transduction could be seen from two perspectives: the content generator might try to make the content transparent, which means that the content can be read in many cultural markets, although the meaning of the text is going to vary from context to context (Olson, 1999); or the same content generator might opt to create the product including elements that point out to specific texts of a particular culture to try and appeal directly to it, making it more shareable within their target market (Singhal & Udornpim, 1997). In either case the people trying to insert the content appeal to a particular cultural flavor in an effort to make it familiar to the target audience (La Pastina & Straubhaar, 2005; Yoon & Cheon, 2013); to exploit its attractiveness because of it's exotic flavor (Iwabuchi, 2002; Yoon & Cheon, 2013); or even to try to make the product *culturally odorless* (Iwabuchi, 2002) by avoiding or removing potential cultural lacunae. These different strategies of transduction are all based on trying to define what the target audience identifies as familiar, exotic or non-culturally-specific, which are notions defined intertextually.

Expanding intertextuality beyond the text itself we can see how it becomes part of the cultural transduction framework. This may require delving deeper into the two other types of cultural universals named by Rohn (2011), *audience-created universal* and *company-created universal*. Simply put audience-created universals "refer to the phenomenon where audiences enjoy foreign-produced media because of the particular way in which they read it" (p. 636) and company-created universals refer to the elements that constitute a situation in which "foreign-produced media is successful because companies have managed to create a competitive advantage for it relative to other media in the market" (p.637). These universals can be connected to *Intertextual Pleasure* and to *Paratextual Constructions*.

Intertextual pleasure can be defined as "[the appeal] to the 'intellectual and aesthetic pleasure'[...] of understanding the interplay between works, of opening up a text's possible meanings to intertextual echoing" (Hutcheon, 2012, p. 117) or, in other words, "the simultaneously pleasurable aspects of reading into such texts in their intertextual and allusive relationship with other texts, tracing and activating the networks of association" (Sanders, 2006, p. 7). Some particular audiences seek these allusions and even generate some of their own. A great example of this dynamic is the case of the television-show *Lost* and the "closed box" concept developed by J. J. Abrams as explained by Rose (2012):

In his first TV series, the teen drama Felicity, the title character's Wiccan roommate had a mysterious wooden box that kept viewers guessing for years. Nearly a decade later, in a 2007 talk at TED, the Technology-Entertainment-Design conference in California, Abrams described his lifelong infatuation *with Tannen's Magic Mystery Box, a $15 cardboard box he had bought at a New York magic shop as a kid. He has never opened it, though it sits even now on a shelf in his office.*

'I realized I haven't opened it because it represents something important to me,' he explained at TED. 'It represents infinite potential. It represents hope. It represents possibility. And what I love about this box, and what I realize I sort of do in whatever it is that I do, is I find myself drawn to infinite possibility and that sense of potential.'

Mystery, he went on to say, is the catalyst for imagination. What are stories if not mystery boxes? What is Lost if not a mystery box? (p. 143)

As it turns out, the hatch in season 1 of the series is presented as a *closed box* and it ended up being the catalyst for the creation of Lostpedia, a Wiki-type page in which users can generate articles explaining their findings and, we can say, readings of the series (Rose, 2012). At the end, understanding intertextual pleasure is a key to unlocking audience-created universals. This is deeply related to the sort of strategies that Steinberg (2012, p. 167) identifies as *Exocolonisation* or *extensive expansion* in terms of audience consumption. In this sort of strategy the media company aims to surround and saturate the audience with content thus seeking to reach a larger public that will expand the consumer base.

But the rabbit hole doesn't end there. Companies also take advantage of intertextual readings as a strategy to help audiences come close to cultural products directly as well. This strategy is identified as *Endocolonization* or *intensive expansion*, through which the content generator tries to intensify consumption in every aspect of the audience's life through ancillary products (Steinberg, 2012). This sort of strategy is related to the notions of intertextuality and to company-created universals if you take into account the way in which the text expands and develops not just as a self-containing unit of meaning, but as a web that encompasses all the material elements that a company can develop around it. These elements, such as trailers, posters, cover art, and merchandising, known as paratexts or paratextual elements, effectively condition the meaning of the text in many different ways (Gray, 2010) –e.g. trailers might generate expectations in the audience through the actors they show, and by establishing the genre of the film. In general terms, the appropriate use of paratextual elements leads to company-created universal.

Video games can be analyzed according to the universals/lacunae present in their intertextual elements. These elements would serve as predictors of the marketing strategy, and evidence its strengths and weaknesses when inserted into a given market. Furthermore, those universals/lacunae may also help us understand how the producers themselves conceive the market for their products and how they position them, as well as the challenges that arise from their particular choices.

THREE VIDEO GAMES AND THEIR INTERTEXTUAL STRATEGIES

The following pages present and discuss three recent video games developed for different platforms. They are analyzed both through the lens of cultural transduction, from its cultural universals/lacunae, and that of the intertextuality both as a textual strategy, including the intertextual pleasure that may be derived from them. These games have been selected because they seem to address the question above, having been developed in either Latin America or the US, with the interest of distribution within or beyond Latin America.

Kingdom Rush Series

The *Kingdom Rush* series comprises three separate games, *Kingdom Rush – KR* (2011), *Kingdom Rush Frontiers - KRF* (2013), and *Kingdom Rush Origins – KRO* (2014) developed by Ironhide Game Studio, a small independent game design company located in Montevideo, Uruguay. *KR* was first developed for Flash and sponsored by Armor Games. It was soon developed for iOS and a couple of years later for Android devices. It is a strategy game under the tower defense subgenre. It is sold at a reduced price on the Apple, Google Play or Amazon App stores. It includes in-app purchase options, but the game does not require them to be played, including the extra levels that come as updates. The first game of the series received favorable reviews, earning the game a gold medal for game of the year (Jayisgames, 2011) and over a million downloads from the Google Play store (Google Play, 2015). The two latter versions did not receive such praise, but have remained staple games in their subgenre.

Visually, the game series is very cartoonish in style and it presents graphics in HD quality for both small and large hand-held devices. The game follows genre conventions with a variety of four towers that can be upgraded on four levels, the last of which allows for a selection of two options per tower type. Most instructions are provided in the way of comic book word balloons. Music and sound effects are epic and comedic at once – including grunts, sighs, clashing swords and fanfare. The game is based on decision-making from building with limited resources and using your fingers in a timely manner to deploy troops or execute actions appropriately when required. Whenever prompted, most towers or characters pronounce certain phrases that give the game a particular feel. These phrases add to the appeal of the game, as most of them have a familiar ring to them.

During the gameplay, there are short periods when the player can look at the background and enjoy it while the enemy troops advance to meet the tower defenses. There are short cameos by characters from other media products and achievement awards to be earned throughout the game. The achievements are mainly cumulative effectiveness of specific towers (e.g. Change soldiers' rally point 200 times in *KR*) but also include some that have nothing to do with the game itself, and require finding some of the Easter Eggs hidden at plain sight (e.g. Scrat's meal – Find the elusive acorn in *KR*).

Intertextual references, mostly in the form of parodic allusions, abound in the series. There are phrases from the characters or towers that relate directly to various sources. Here are some examples: The hero Malik Hammerfury (*KR*) says either 'It's hammer time', 'Can't touch this', or 'I pity the fool!' whenever prodded, with the former two phrases related to performer M.C. Hammer's song, and the latter, a famous quote by Mr. T. in his role as Clubber Lang in *Rocky III* (Stallone, 1982). The Dwarf Hall in *KRF* has many quotes from Gimli, the dwarf in *The Lord of the Rings: The Return of the King* (Jackson, 2003), including the battle shout "Let them come!". In *KRF* the Circle of Life power, at the Forest Keepers level of the Barracks tower when selected, is heard as shouting "Live long and prosper!" the famous farewell of Mr. Spock, the renowned character from the *Star Trek* franchise. Some of the levels include visual references to films (e.g. Anakin with his shadow in the shape of Darth Vader's, as in the famous promotional poster of *Star Wars Episode I: The Phantom Menace* in the Hammerhold Campaign in *KRF*), comics (e.g. Obélix from the French comic series *Astérix* by Goscinny and Uderzo in the Rockhenge Campaign of *KRO*), and cartoons (e.g. the Roadrunner from *Warner Bros Looney Tunes* animations in the Beheader's Seat campaign in *KRO*). They also make references in the achievement section to other video games (e.g. Supermario in *KR* and *KRF*), television shows (e.g. Legen [wait for it]… from *How I met your mother?* Series in *KRF*), songs (e.g. "We are the champions", including an image resembling Freddy Mercury at Wembley stadium in 1986 in *KRO*), films (e.g. "Never tell me the odds", the famous quote by Han Solo, alongside a picture of the Millennium Falcon, from *Star Wars Episode V: The Empire Strikes Back* in *KRO*) and even table-top games (e.g. *D&D* in *KRO*).

This large amount of parodic allusions serves the double purpose of complementing the game with the Easter Eggs hunt, and allowing for players to rejoice at capturing the various bits of references. It increases intertextual pleasure without affecting gameplay. This happens because "successful identification of parodic references allows readers to mark themselves as [in this case, culturally] literate and to identify themselves as part of a selective community" (Ott & Walter, 2000, p. 436). Thus, players of the *KR* series derive pleasure, not only in solving the game puzzles, and overcoming the strategy requirements of the interactive game challenges within the game, they also interact beyond the game, by discovering, sharing and debating the Easter Eggs found in the game with other players, via the forums on the Ironhide game Studio website or socially among friends.

There is another aspect that we have not looked at yet. The product was developed by Uruguayans living and working in Uruguay. The Easter Eggs, however, do not relate to any form of Latin American, or – least so – Uruguayan cultural references. Spanish is not the language of the game, which is the majority language in Uruguay and most of Latin America, nor are there traceable references to Latin American pop culture. Most of the parodic allusions include films or television shows that travelled beyond the Anglo-American or English-only sphere, yet it would be daring to consider them Latin American pop culture. Intertextuality here is not only an aesthetic element, but also a strategic one that positions the game in a certain way for a larger market. By using fantasy elements, mostly from the Western tradition as presented in Hollywood films, the game reaches a certain transparency, using Olson's (1999) definition, by bringing together the tropes of fantasy realms, and taking enough visual and audio cues from *The Lord of the Rings* franchise, a series of books, films and games that have been consumed world-wide. Regarding the film franchise Kuipers and De Kloet (2008) state that

LotR [Lord of the Rings] is a profoundly cosmopolitan media text that is increasingly detached from its assumed origin – the United Kingdom – also because of the particular production circumstances in which the United Kingdom, Hollywood, and New Zealand are involved. The text is deliberately detached from national and local contexts, which explains its transnational appeal. (p. 147)

However, Poor (2012) takes a different stance and criticizes the supposedly transnational appeal of fantasy as something that is not culturally bound. He states that

Fantasy games are based on earlier fantasy tropes, which, for English speakers in the United States and the United Kingdom, are based on European history and historical fantasy. It is predominantly a world of White people. Although that may be historically accurate to some extent, today's world and the gaming industry are much more multicultural and international. (p. 390)

It is precisely the case in point. There is no doubt about the general intertextuality of the *KR* series, and particularly *KRO*, to a mythology of Celtic origin, European fairytales and to the works of Tolkien, including their adaptations. Ironhide seeks to clasp onto that market as a conscious strategy of its intertextual references both in the narrative level of the characters and gameplay, and in the parodic allusions within the text. Bearing in mind that the mobile game market is considerably larger in Europe and the English speaking world – often conceptualized as the West –, and that English is the most widely learnt second language, it does not seem to be a bad strategy to give the game a more universal appeal.

El Chavo Kart

From 1971 to 1980 Roberto Gómez Bolaños, or as many Latin Americans would come to know him 'Chespirito', directed and produced the successful television comedy *El Chavo del 8* (Gómez Bolaños, 1972) that has been broadcast in over 20 different countries and dubbed into various languages –including Portuguese, English, Japanese and Russian– (Díaz Moreno, 2011). The show told the stories of El Chavo, an orphan, that lived in *La Vecindad,* a small urban Mexican neighborhood, and the people who lived in it. El Chavo is still broadcast to date in some Latin American countries. Due to its success, in 2006 Televisa and Gómez Bolaños created the animated version of the show, *El Chavo Animado* (Gómez Bolaños, 2006), that has run ever since and has been broadcasted in multiple markets as well –including Brazil, Mexico, Chile, Colombia and the US.

In 2014 the game publisher *Slang* launched the game *El Chavo Kart,* produced by the Colombian game studio *Efekto Studios*. The game is a kart racing game that mimics many conventions of the genre that encompasses games as *Crash Nitro Kart, Didi Kong Racing, Sonic and Sega: All-star Racing* and *Mario Kart* (Masser, 2012). This game was launched in the context of Gómez Bolaños' 85th birthday (AP, 2014) and is based upon the characters, locations and plots of the animated series. The game was launched in Spanish and Portuguese, and has optional subtitles in those languages and in English. Originally the game was available for PS3 and Xbox 360 consoles, but a light version has been launched for Samsung mobile devices as well.

The interest on studying this game comes from the fact that the game has been distributed across Latin America as well as in parts of the US. Since the game is a direct adaptation of an animated series, itself an adaptation of the original TV show, it is useful to identify its elements of intertextuality and hypothesize how those elements may affect the international distribution of the Kart game.

First of all, it is interesting to see what the potential audience for *El Chavo Kart* might be, based on the choices of distribution, genre, ESRB ratings and narrative elements made by the developers.

From the original series to the animated series there was a clear change in the way the show addressed the audience – the original show reached children and adults alike, criticizing the Mexican society of the time with puns that were aimed at adults and a language, expressions and characters developed for children. The animated series on the other hand has not included any adult references and has included dreaming sequences that show the active imagination of El Chavo and the other children from La Vecindad, even in episodes based on story lines from the original comedy series. The similarity between the two shows is based upon keeping most of the original characters and settings, particularly during the first season of *El Chavo Animado*. It could be ventured that, even though the series exploits the nostalgia of the original show's audience, its target audience is not as wide and it is more children-oriented, making the animated series a perfect show for the former audience to share with their children. Following this line of reasoning and since the game is based on the animated series it would seem to be appealing to its audience, hoping that they will play the game looking to identify the elements shared with the series.

In this sense, it is useful to identify those elements that relate to both products and that ultimately translate into content lacunae or universals, capital and production lacunae, or that are expected to result in company-created universals through intensive and extensive expansion.

The most noticeable of these elements is the characters. Each character rides a car that evokes his or her personality traits, style and place in the animated show. The characters use some of the catch phrases or expressions that they have used since the original show, such as *Quiko*'s 'Chusma, chusma',

Profesor Jirafales' angry 'Ta, ta, ta…' and many others that have also been adopted as running gags in the animated series. However, many of the sound bites that accompany gameplay are brand new and have very little relationship with the shows that came before it other than keeping the voice talents that accompany the animated show in Spanish and Portuguese.

Moreover, other elements point to a targeting of the original show's audience or even to a complete new segment. Firstly, PS3 and Xbox 360 are two high-priced game consoles that aim for a teenage, young adult and adult demographic. This demographic is in part established by the game titles related to these consoles and even with the ergonomic design of the device. In the case of PS3 from the ten top grossing games that have been produced for this console, six are rated M (for mature audiences) and none were targeted at children ("10 best selling PS3 games of all time," 2014) and in the case of Xbox 360 the list of top selling titles includes at least six titles rated M, including two of the *Grand Theft Auto* franchise and three *Call of Duty* titles (Thorne, n.d.).

Second, in terms of the console design even though both Microsoft and Sony have done great efforts to approach alternative control mechanisms –Microsoft's Kinect works with Xbox 360 and Move Controllers– that aim to compete with the successful Nintendo Wii motion controls,, their main controls are still designed with a teenagers size hand in mind, which makes playing children's games in those consoles harder. In general terms, it can be stated that, despite that the game and most other games in this genre are rated E, for everyone, the console itself generates a distinction of the audience to, at best, tweens.

Other elements that point to an older demographic than that of *El Chavo Animado* are the reinterpretation of some of the classic themes from the original series by *La Gusana Ciega*, a Mexican rock band that created rock adaptations of the music for every track in the game, and the use of direct references to the 2014 Brasil World Cup. In this respect, it is interesting to note that intertextuality generates meaning with the context in which the text is being inserted as well as through the relationship with other texts. Although the world cup is not adult content in itself, references to the Maracana stadium through which one of the tracks of the game passes while Mexican and Brazilian flags are waved in the tribunes can be seen as a reference that is not particularly children-related. However, it is a reference to an episode of the animated series in which Profesor Jirafales manages to get tickets for the whole cast to go and watch a soccer match between Mexico and Argentina. These are examples of attempts to produce company-created universals through the use of intertextual references that might have inadvertently ended up as capital lacunae.

This latter point brings us to the last element of the analysis. The track scenarios are references for former and newer audiences of *El Chavo*, because they point to elements of both the classic show and the animated one. For example, the track Chavopulco refers to the episodes filmed in Acapulco which were particularly renowned since they were the only episodes where El Chavo and his gang left the studio set. This same plot was developed in the animated series. For the audience of the classic show there is a track in Tangamandapio the home town of Jaimito, el Cartero, that was always referenced by the character of the same name in the original show, and that the whole cast visits in the animated series. Finally, the space track is a reference to one of El Chavo's dream sequences in the animated series. The tracks are a good example of a content universal generated through the use of elements recognizable by the target audience that help construct the meaning of the text, as well as a company-created universal given that the relation is planted and exploited by the content producers to appeal to the target audience.

All of the elements above point to the intricate relations between audience, contexts, text and other texts that finally help build meaning and hence make the content understandable and ultimately enjoyable. This is a clear example in which the developers try to get close to the audience through the cultural capital that they themselves have helped establish and thus could be seen as an example of company-created universals.

South Park: The Stick of Truth

Based on a concept proposed by the writing team of Trey Parker and Matt Stone in 2009, Ubisoft released the game *South Park: The Stick of Truth – TSoT–*for XBOX 360 and Playstation 4 in March 2014 in the United States. The introduction to the game came after a three-episode-run on the Comedy Central series *South Park* in November-December 2013 in which the main characters participate in a war over obtaining a Playstation Four with the theme of the episodes based on the Red Wedding of the HBO series *Game Of Thrones* (Benioff & Weiss, 2011).

While many gamers were aware of the problems behind the release of the game, the introduction to it at the end of the three episode run (Parker, 2013) identifies the theme of the game, and the potential for its gameplay. What seems to be the most telling of the experience of the game is the monologue delivered by Eric Cartman at the end of the episode. Still dressed as the wizard character, Cartman laments that the war to determine which game system is better had been a pointless war, and he states that

The last few weeks we've been too busy to play video games, and look at what we did. There's been drama, action, romance…I mean, honestly, you guys, do we need video games to play? Maybe we started to rely on Microsoft and Sony so much that we forgot all we need to play are the simplest things. Like… like this [grabs stick from the ground]. We can just play with this. Screw video games, dude. Who fucking need them. Fuck 'em! (Parker, 2013)

As he holds up the stick, the announcement and graphic present, 'Coming soon, *South Park: The Stick of Truth*', a moment that viewers of the program expect from *South Park* and the writing team of Parker and Stone: an almost nihilistic approach to stating that the series has been used to promote the game, which could result in the label of selling out. It is an evident instance of self-reflexivity connecting the new franchise product, while at once seeming to complain about the strategy.

The characters and the viewer collide in the town of South Park. Before the design of the game, an actual map of South Park did not exist. The geographical location of common places such as South Park Elementary, City Wok and Cartman's house had never been defined. Until the map of South Park appeared in season 17, we could only assume the characters experienced the town as a location while the audience had to experience the town of South Park only through the actions of the characters. In this way, Cartman's speech could be reflexive of the reality that in order to have a video game experience for XBOX and Sony, the imagination the audience had of South Park had to be redefined into an interactive experience.

TSoT interface is built upon a turn-based, fantasy roleplaying game. When the *South Park* characters played the game *Lord Of The Rings* (Parker, 2002), this was fantasy play using the town of South Park as the location, unlike re-envisioning their world (Parker, 2004) or having their world re-envisioned for them (Parker, 2006). To participate in the game world, a player must play the role of 'new kid', a reference to many characters from South Park that includes Damien and Tweek. As with the series, the new kid is expected to prove him or herself to be one of the team. The series and the game interconnect with the playable character constantly being challenged with 'Who's side are you on, kid?' and 'You wanna be part of the group, right kid?'

The gameplay delves deep into the intertextual knowledge the player has about video games and *South Park*. Nothing is off-limits to challenge and, often, offend. This bit of company-created universal is maintained and promoted throughout the game. For instance, players of *TSoT* will notice the familiar 'Name Your Character' event at the start of the game - an intertextual reference to the RPG genre. Within a few moments, the player realizes that despite going through the procedure to name the character, the only name allowed is 'Douchebag' – a common term used by the characters in South Park. This practical insult and destruction of the genre convention is the ultimate company-created universal by making the player subject to the character's lack of political correctness.

Furthermore, mini-games familiar to video game players also exist in *TSoT*, but based on situations relevant to *South Park* watchers. For instance, in a version of the game Simon can be played to remove an anal probe from Randy Marsh, Stan's father (based on Episode 1 of Season 1), and similar mini-games involve giving abortions –an obsession of the character Eric Cartman – to Randy Marsh and Mr. Slave, and bosses such as Al Gore. These instances provide the player with a familiar gaming experience, but with what could be called a crude and offensive theme, similar to the *South Park* series being a familiar (perhaps classic) cartoon with crude and offensive themes. This is clearly their company-created universal that comes from franchising the show as a video game.

Finally, *TSoT* and the series interconnect in an endocolonization aspect only understood by those who regularly or casually watch *South Park*. With too many references to list that connect the game to the series, the writers and designer seem to appeal to intertextual pleasure by fostering a need for viewers to start conversations with, 'I love that episode where....' followed by describing the episode and repeating its lines. *South Park*, as a franchise, brings out this need to discuss what has been seen and simply 're-tell the tale'. It can be rationalized that the writers know this is how viewers relate to *South Park*: an ownership of the adventure through re-telling it to others and finding those who listen and re-tell as well. It paves the way to audience-created universals.

An interesting caveat is that the game distribution beyond the US and other English speaking countries does not seem to keep up with the same desire of grooming the audience. In Mexico and Spain, two countries with an ample following of the dubbed version of the series, there was an understandable disappointment when they noticed the game did not include it. The company-created universal, so fondly treasured in the game among the English-language viewers of the series, was broken when the game transcended the linguistic boundaries. This fact had an impact on sales, and evidences a lack of localization which could have proven successful in a relatively simple way.

FUTURE RESEARCH DIRECTIONS

As the three cases above demonstrate, intertextual references are part and parcel of the game localization strategy and, as such, are a fundamental part of the design and development of video games. They are key elements to ensure impact and access for products as they enter particular cultural markets. Latin America, both as market for video games and as creative grounds, has still a long road ahead in the localization and cultural transduction processes, but it is certainly suited for it.

Paying more attention to the cultural transduction process tells us about both the expected cultural capital of the consumers, about the trade-offs of video game producers, and their respective idea of their target audience. Certainly, intertextuality helps bring audiences to specific products, by the intertextual pleasure that they can provide, particularly in the case of endocolonization strategies. Gameplay is also intertextual in the same way as narrative genres, and hardware also defines targeted markets. But intertextuality may serve to appeal beyond the group targeted originally by the hardware or gameplay genre. This possibility opens up a game, such as *Chavo Kart*, to two different audiences (children and parents alike) who have the reference to either version of the *Chavo* shows. On the other hand, *Kingdom Rush* not only reaches the younger generations with a tablet-based tower defense game, but also appeals to a broader audience who understand and enjoy the intertextual pleasure of the Easter Egg hunt.

More research into other cases of localization strategies, whether successful or not, would help us understand the process even further, and lead us to design guidelines for growing markets, such as the Latin American video game market. If we consider that these growing markets are the new space for exocolonization strategies, then the appeal of cultural transduction becomes more evident.

CONCLUSION

The three cases presented show different ways in which video games have made use of intertextual references to appeal to specific markets. *El Chavo Kart* and *South Park: The Stick of Truth* connect with the originating works, following company-created universals and creating a strategy that grows out from previously existing audiences that can enjoy intertextual references. It is a clear endocolonization process, based on creative appropriation as the main intertextual strategy. This is different in the case of the *Kingdom Rush* series which does not draw from a franchise, but uses many pop culture references to suit an Americanized market in an exocolonization strategy.

El Chavo Kart fits within the already large markets of the geo-linguistic region of Latin America, yet is so concerned to be faithful to the series as part of the franchise, that it limits the scenarios to those that may be related to the show. Similarly, *TSoT* remains faithful to the series to such an extent it almost considers usual viewers as their only target, but at the same time loses on a market opportunity by neglecting the dubbed version for the game sold overseas. Both prefer cultural proximity and company-created universals, basing their strategy on the continuous franchise. For the Latin American market this strategy proved positive for *El Chavo Kart*, and detrimental for *TSoT*.

In that same vein, the *Kingdom Rush* series forgoes cultural proximity to its similar markets and embraces plenty of cultural lacunae, with the aim of reaching a larger market, dominated by Western media and their references. The intertextual strategy includes parodic allusions to those elements that are culturally universal to that market, erasing all traces of Latin American media influence, and diminishing Latin American appeal. This trade-off seems to be accepted by the opportunity value of placing a game in a larger market, dominated by US media and, mainly, US pop culture references.

Intertextual pleasure, thus, is at the core of localization strategies, because it helps determine the groups targeted by a given product.

REFERENCES

Allen, G. (2011). *Intertextuality* (2nd ed.). London, UK: Routledge.

AP. (2014). Chespirito celebrará cumpleaños con lanzamiento de "El chavo kart". *eluniverso.com*. Retrieved June 28, 2015, from http://www.eluniverso.com/vida-estilo/2014/02/19/nota/2209091/chespirito-celebrara-cumpleanos-lanzamiento-chavo-kart

Benioff, D., & Weiss, D. B. (2011). *Game of thrones*. USA: HBO.

Bernal Merino, M. (2006). On the translation of video games. *The Journal of Specialised Translation*, (6). Retrieved from http://www.jostrans.org/issue06/art_bernal.php

10 . best selling PS3 games of all time. (2014). *whatisplaystation4.com*. Retrieved June 28, 2015, from http://whatisplaystation4.com/10-best-selling-ps3-games-of-all-time/

Bicket, D. (2005). Reconsidering geocultural contraflow: Intercultural information flows through trends in global audiovisual trade. *Global Media Journal*, *4*(6), 1–16.

Brooks, J. L., Groening, M., & Simon, S. (1989). *The Simpsons*. USA: Fox.

Camarero, J. (2008). *Intertextualidad*. Barcelona: Anthropos.

Carlson, R., & Corliss, J. (2011). Imagined commodities: Video game localization and mythologies of cultural difference. *Games and Culture*, *6*(1), 61–82. doi:10.1177/1555412010377322

Chapoy, P. (2012). *La historia detrás del mito - La vecindad del chavo*. Mexico: Azteca, TV. Retrieved from https://www.youtube.com/watch?v=gv1LNU8hWcM&spfreload=1

Chiaro, D. (2008). Issues in audiovisual translation. In J. Munday (Ed.), *The Routledge companion to translation studies* (pp. 141–165). Oxon, UK: Routledge.

Consalvo, M. (2006). Console video games and global corporations: Creating a hybrid culture. *New Media & Society*, *8*(1), 117–137. doi:10.1177/1461444806059921

Deuze, M. (2007). Convergence culture in the creative industries. *International Journal of Cultural Studies*, *10*(2), 243–263. doi:10.1177/1367877907076793

Díaz Moreno, E. (2011). Hoy cumple cuarenta años el chavo del 8. *Excelsior*. Retrieved June 26, 2015, from http://www.excelsior.com.mx/node/745890

Docter, P., & Del Carmen, R. (2015). *Inside out*. USA: Pixar Animation Studio and Walt Disney Pictures.

García Canclini, N. (2000). *Culturas híbridas: Estrategias para entrar y salir de la modernidad*. Bogotá, D.C., Colombia: Grijalbo.

GMGC. (2015). *Global mobile game industry white book*. Shanghai, China: NewZoo.

Gómez Bolaños, R. (1972). *El chavo del ocho*. Mexico: Televisa S.A. de C.V.

Gómez Bolaños, R. (2006). *El chavo animado*. Mexico: Televisa S.A. de C.V.

Google Play. (2015). Kingdom rush. *Google Play*. Retrieved June 26, 2015, from https://play.google.com/store/apps/details?id=com.ironhidegames.android.kingdomrush&hl=es_419

Gray, J. (2010). *Show sold separately: Promos, spoilers, and other media paratexts*. New York, NY; London, UK: New York University Press.

Hutcheon, L. (2012). *A theory of adaptation*. London, UK: Routledge.

Iwabuchi, K. (2002). *Recentering globalization: Popular culture and Japanese transnationalism*. Durham, DC: Duke University Press. doi:10.1215/9780822384083

Jackson, P. (2003). *The lord of the rings: The return of the king*. USA and New Zealand/Aotearoa: New Line Cinema.

Jayisgames. (2011). Game of the year. *Jayisgames*. Retrieved June 26, 2015, from http://jayisgames.com/best-of/2011/game-of-the-year/

Jenkins, H. (2006). *Convergence culture: Where old and new media collide*. New York, NY; London, UK: New York University Press.

Kraidy, M. M. (2010). Hybridity in cultural globalization. In D. K. Thussu (Ed.), *International communication: A reader* (pp. 434–451). London, UK: Routledge.

Kuipers, G., & De Kloet, J. (2008). Global flows and local identifications? *The Lord of the Rings* and the cross-national reception of characters and genres. In M. Barker & E. Mathijs (Eds.), *Watching The Lord of the Rings. Tolkien's world audiences* (pp. 131–148). New York, NY: Peter Lang.

La Pastina, A. C., Rego, C. M., & Straubhaar, J. D. (2003). The centrality of telenovelas in Latin America's everyday life: Past tendencies, current knowledge, and future research. *Global Media Journal, 2*(2), 1–15. Retrieved from http://www2.fiu.edu/~surisc/centrality of telenovelas.pdf

La Pastina, A. C., & Straubhaar, J. D. (2005). Multiple proximities between television genres and audiences: The schism between telenovelas' global distribution and local consumption. *International Communication Gazette, 67*(3), 271–288. doi:10.1177/0016549205052231

Masser, J. (2012). A brief history of kart racing games. *modojo*. Retrieved June 28, 2015, from http://www.modojo.com/features/a_brief_history_of_kart_racing_games

Muñoz Gil, M. (2009). Dubbing *The Simpsons* in Spain: A case study. In J. Díaz-Cintas (Ed.), *New Trends in Audiovisual Translation* (pp. 142–157). Bristol, UK: Multilingual Matters.

O'Donnell, C. (2011). Games are not convergence: The lost promise of digital production and convergence. *Convergence (London), 17*(3), 271–286. doi:10.1177/1354856511405766

Olson, S. R. (1999). *Hollywood planet: Global media and the competitive advantage of narrative transparency*. Mahwah, NJ: Lawrence Erlbaum Associates, Inc.

Ott, B., & Walter, C. (2000). Intertextuality: Interpretive practice and textual strategy. *Critical Studies in Media Communication, 17*(4), 429–446. doi:10.1080/15295030009388412

Parker, T. (2002). *The return of the fellowship of the rings to the two towers*. USA: Braniff Productions.

Parker, T. (2004). *Good times with weapons*. USA: Braniff Productions.

Parker, T. (2006). *Make love, not warcraft*. USA: South Park Digital Studios.

Parker, T. (2013). *Titties and dragons*. USA: South Park Digital Studios.

Poor, N. (2012). Digital elves as a racial other in video games: Acknowledgment and avoidance. *Games and Culture*, *7*(5), 375–396. doi:10.1177/1555412012454224

PwC. (2015a). Video games: Global revenue. *Global entertainment and media outlook 2015-2019*. Retrieved April 6, 2015, from http://www.pwc.com/gx/en/global-entertainment-media-outlook/assets/2015/video-games-key-insights-1-global-revenue.pdf

PwC. (2015b). Video games: Rate of growth. *Global entertainment and media outlook 2015-2019*. Retrieved June 4, 2015, from http://www.pwc.com/gx/en/global-entertainment-media-outlook/assets/2015/video-games-by-growth-and-scale.pdf

Rohn, U. (2011). Lacuna or Universal? Introducing a new model for understanding crosscultural audience demand. *Media Culture & Society*, *33*(4), 631–641. doi:10.1177/0163443711399223

Rose, F. (2012). *The art of immersion: How the digital generation is remaking Hollywood, Madison Avenue, and the way we tell stories*. New York, NY: WW Norton & Company.

Sakellariou, P. (2014). The appropriation of the concept of intertextuality for translation-theoretic purposes. *Translation Studies*, *8*(1), 35–47. doi:10.1080/14781700.2014.943677

Sanders, J. (2006). *Adaptation and appropriation*. New York, NY: Routledge.

Singhal, A., & Udornpim, K. (1997). Cultural shareability, archetypes and television soaps. *Gazette*, *59*(3), 171–188. doi:10.1177/0016549297059003001

Stallone, S. (1982). *Rocky III*. USA.

Steinberg, M. (2012). *Anime's media mix: Franchising toys and characters in Japan*. Minneapolis, MN: University of Minnesota Press. doi:10.5749/minnesota/9780816675494.001.0001

Straubhaar, J. D. (1991). Beyond media imperialism: Asymmetrical interdependence and cultural proximity.pdf. *Critical Studies in Mass Communication*, *8*(1), 39–59. doi:10.1080/15295039109366779

Thorne, S. (n.d.). *10 best-selling Xbox 360 games ever*. Retrieved June 28, 2015, from http://whatculture.com/gaming/10-best-selling-xbox-360-games-ever.php

UNCTAD, & UNDP. (2010). *Creative economy report 2010*. Retrieved from http://www.unctad.org/Templates/WebFlyer.asp?intItemID=5763&lang=1

Uribe-Jongbloed, E., & Espinosa-Medina, H. D. (2014). A clearer picture: Towards a new framework for the study of cultural transduction in audiovisual market trades. *OBSERVATORIO (OBS*)*, *8*(1), 23–48. Retrieved from http://obs.obercom.pt/index.php/obs/article/view/707/642

Waisbord, S., & Jalfin, S. (2009). Imagining the national: Gatekeepers and the adaptation of global franchises in Argentina. In A. Moran (Ed.), *TV formats worldwide. Localizing global programs* (pp. 55–74). Bristol, UK; Chicago, IL.

Yoon, T.-J., & Cheon, H. (2013). Game playing as transnational cultural practice: A case study of Chinese gamers and Korean MMORPGs. *International Journal of Cultural Studies*, *17*(5), 469–483. doi:10.1177/1367877913505172

KEY TERMS AND DEFINITIONS

Creative Appropriation: The conscious and evident use of discernable elements, including characters, from other texts as part of the narrative in a way that may or may not suit the aspects of the original text.

Cultural Lacuna: Culturally specific references that would not be easily understood in other cultural markets.

Cultural Proximity: The similitude in terms of cultural traits (e.g. religion, language, history) between different cultural markets.

Cultural Transduction: The processes through which a given text goes when being altered to suit a different cultural or national market from the one where it was originally conceived.

Cultural Transparency: A quality of a product that implies there is very little to no cultural references within the text, thus easy to understand despite cultural differences.

Endocolonization: A strategy for promoting consumption through the generation and distribution of ancillary products.

Exocolonization: A strategy for promoting consumption by expanding the consumer base through saturation of the product.

Intertextual Pleasure: Enjoyment derived from recognizing elements that refer to other texts.

Localization: The process of altering an audiovisual product to make it more appealing to a given local audience.

Parodic Allusion: Hints to references, citations or quotes from well-known texts, with a good deal of humor, that seek to amuse through juxtaposition. They are not usually verbatim or identical renditions, but their relationship to the source text is easily spotted.

Chapter 10
Moving Forward by Looking Back:
Using Art and Architectural History to Make and Understand Games

Christopher Totten
American University, USA

ABSTRACT

This chapter explores art history to establish parallels between the current state of the game art field and historical art and architectural periods. In doing so, it proposes methods for both making and studying games that subvert the popular analysis trends of game art that are typically based on the history of game graphics and technology. The chapter will then demonstrate the use of art and design history in game development by discussing the Atelier Games project, which utilizes the styles and techniques of established artists and art movements to explore the viability of classic methods for the production of game art and game mechanics.

INTRODUCTION

Art assets that reference historic art and architectural pieces are not new in games. Throughout the history of the medium, visual intertextuality has been a selling point for games with "epic" themes such as Greek Mythology, Medieval battles, or sci-fi and fantasy settings. Games such as *Defender of the Crown* (Cinemaware, 1986) or *God of War* (SCE Santa Monica, 2005) directly represent the artwork and architecture of historic cultures as a way to build wish fulfillment. By utilizing elements of a culture's aesthetics, that culture becomes a context in which players may embed themselves (Zimmerman & Salen, 2003) as well as a novelty for attracting traditional gaming audiences (Peterson, 2014.) However, these uses of intertextuality in games only scratch the surface of what professional artists, art historians, and architects would argue is the real potential of utilizing games as a cultural junction (Sollers, 1968) for art and architectural work.

DOI: 10.4018/978-1-5225-0477-1.ch010

Critical examinations of game art have historically focused on how art production techniques for games reflect the technical evolution of gaming platforms in both state-of-the-art and retro aesthetics. However, games such as *Dys4ia* (Anthropy, 2012) and *Dominique Pamplemousse* (Squinkifer, 2013) show potential new paradigms in art production. Rather than facing inwards towards established game art styles or themes, they look outward towards analog techniques established in fields such as the visual arts, graphic design, animation, and film. Likewise, studies such as Goodbrey's Hypercomics (2000 – 2014) and Totten's analyses of game levels through architectural theory (Totten, 2014) show that understanding these fields beyond their visual components can bring new insights for understanding games.

This chapter's goal is to give working game developers, artists, and academics a frame with which to understand their work in the context of art and traditional media. It also seeks to explore the practicality of utilizing techniques – traditional in fine art and design but non-traditional in game art – for the production of digital games. To accomplish this, the chapter first analyzes the current state of game art, particularly concerning the types of art employed by large and small studios, and how game art culture has been affected by popular industry trends. The chapter then explores developments in art history to demonstrate how games may be understood through the lens of these fields for purposes of study and design. Finally, it describes how game artists may explore historic art styles, materials, and methods for the production of art assets and new game mechanics. In these ways, artistic intertextuality and architextuality become tools for researchers, students, instructors, and developers to understand and make new game types.

BACKGROUND: THE STATE OF GAME ART

Like in many industries, trends in game art dictate how artists earn jobs. Commonly, these trends are tied to the state of computer graphics technology in home computers and video game consoles. They can, however, also vary based on the size and structure of art teams for games. Large studios more closely mirror technological advancement, as they possess the resources to create "state of the art" graphics for games. Small studios, especially those identifying as "independent"– studios who create games without the backing of large publishers and often within a community of other independent studios (Crecente, 2013) – are more agile in adopting new styles, but are still subject to follow what is "in vogue" to meet consumer demand.

This section will establish art trends within the game industry and offer insight into how these trends are affected by studio sizes, technological trends, and accessible digital art software.

Large Game Studio Job Listings

As the studios most capable of creating high-fidelity graphics, large studios, often referred to as AAA, have historically set art trends in games. These studios employ several hundred developers, artists, musicians, marketing professionals, and others to create a game with budgets rivaling many Hollywood movies (Superannuation, 2014; Weber, 2013). Games produced by these studios tend to be among the best-selling and most well-known among game players and as such, jobs at these studios are in high demand. This demand allows AAA studios to set highly selective standards for art when considering applicants.

A survey of job postings in visual art and design for AAA game jobs at the time of this writing from game industry site Gamasutra reveals two things: the first is an increasing need for specialization, where one artist works on a very specific task, and the second is that these jobs require expertise with a very limited set of complex computer art software. Job titles are defined by which part in the overall art "pipeline" – the assembly-line-like process of creating art – a person will play. Posting titles surveyed for this chapter include UI/UX (user interface/user experience) artist, 2D environmental artist, FX (special effects) artist, lighting artist, and senior character texture/look artist ("Visual Art Jobs," 2015).

Among the jobs surveyed for this chapter from the Gamasutra Visual Arts job page – totaling 41 postings - those that specifically named the studio's preferred software highly favored a limited selection of programs. The most popular were the 3D art and animation package Maya (contained within 16 postings), 2D art program Adobe Photoshop (14 postings), 3D Studio Max (another 3D program - 11 postings), and 3D digital sculpting program ZBrush (eight postings.) Among the most popular game engines – the programs utilized to create the games themselves - included in these listings, the Unreal Engine and the Unity 3D engine tied, each being mentioned in nine postings. Despite a wealth of alternative software with many of the same functions, applicants seeking jobs in the industry are encouraged to focus on these specific pieces of software. Combined with the previously mentioned culture of task specialization, this specificity in tools creates a culture of high specialization where applicants identify strongly with one or two job titles and methods for creating art.

Understanding AAA Style through Popular Portfolio Criteria

Beyond the job titles and tool requirements for jobs in AAA game studios, it is worth identifying the subject matter of art produced by these studios and the stylistic standards for this art. These elements of the "big studio style" will be derived by exploring portfolio requirements for job postings and the contents of studios' own portfolios.

For studios, portfolios are a useful tool for understanding the skillset of the job seeker and seeing whether they are a good fit for a studio. For a job seeker, a portfolio of previously completed work and an art test – a set of art pieces, often relevant to the work the studio is currently doing, that the applicant must complete within a set period of time – are vital communication tools for introducing oneself to a potential employer. When evaluating these pieces, studio members look for not only care and competency, but also artwork that aligns with the style of games that the studio creates.

Of the surveyed job postings, those for 2D-focused artists – concept artists, UI/UX artists, texture artists, etc. – highly favored a process known as "digital painting", where an artist "paints" digital artwork with software that simulates paint and a pen that allows users to "draw" on the computer. This technique is commonly used to create concepts of what the game might look like and illustrations to promote the game. As of this writing, the predominant style of digital painting that major studios use is an idealist style that attempts to depict subjects in situations meant to elicit an excited response from consumers (Figure 1). These pieces commonly show sweeping vistas, scenes of idealized conflict, or skillful characters with powerful weapons. Indeed, these pieces help create the looks for games that feed modern gamers' taste for "epic" escapist settings and power fantasies – a term often used in the pejorative - but useful for describing players' participation and agency in larger-than-life situations through gameplay.

Figure 1. A piece of digitally painted concept artwork
Source: Totten, 2012.

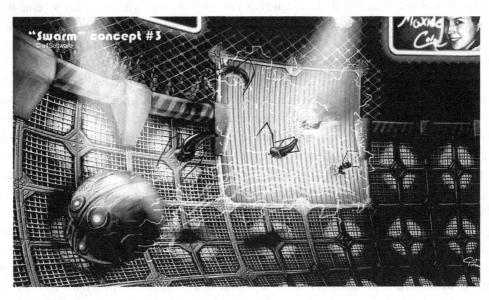

The Evolution of "Indie Style" Game Art

While the art of mass market AAA games woo consumers with increasingly photorealistic art, the low-resolution trends of independent, or "indie" games offer a stark contrast to the idealist big studio look. While many critics of indie games cite a perceived lack of talent or budget as a primary reason that indie games do not look like "high res" AAA games (Grace, 2013), proponents of indie games argue that the "indie game style" has evolved according to a number of other varying factors.

In a paper from the 2014 Foundations of Digital Games (FDG) Conference titled "High-tech Low-tech Authenticity: The Creation of Independent Style at the Independent Games Festival", game scholar Jesper Juul (2014) examines both the factors that contribute to a studio being "indie" and how these factors contribute to art style decisions made by these developers. Among these factors are the limitations of small teams with few artists, the cost of high-end art tools, and whether team members have the skill to create high-resolution art. Of the skill needed to create high-end game art, Terry Cavanagh, the indie developer behind *VVVVVV* (Cavanagh, 2010b), *Don't Look Back* (Cavanagh, 2009), *Super Hexagon* (Cavanagh, 2012), and a myriad of other games, once said:

I don't have the technical ability to make my games look good, so I do what I can to at least make them look interesting. I find it easier to do this when I work within narrow limits - in VVVVVV, for example, I limited the background tiles for each room to just 5 shades of one colour, and then changed colours and patterns as I went along. (as cited in Rose, 2010)

The goal of "making them look interesting" is notable, as what a developer finds visually appealing can vary differently from studio to studio. Cavanaugh's games often employ limited neon color palettes on black backgrounds with lots of quickly flashing objects set to techno music. As such, this could be considered the "Cavanagh style", as it is present in many of his games such as *VVVVVV, Super Hexagon,* and *N.O.T.T.U.B* (Cavanagh, 2010). If one extends this through the entire indie game movement, it might be assumed that little homogeneity exists between individual developers and the styles of art they create for their games. However, Juul (2014) also contends that cultural factors and the ways that indie games are distributed may have also played a part in the evolution of indie game art.

By examining the Seumas McNally Grand Prize winners at the Independent Games Festival (IGF) from 2000-2014 and comparing them to contemporary industry conditions, Juul proposes that "indie style" game art has evolved through a series of clear trends and movements. For example, early winners of the award such as *Tread Marks, Shattered Galaxy,* and *Savage: The Battle for Newerth,* utilized art styles that closely resembled AAA art styles and art subjects of the time. Juul notes that these games were created before the popularization of digital distribution, where players can download a game from the internet rather than buying them from a brick-and-mortar store, and were likely designed to attract major publishers to distribute their game.

A major contributing factor to the uniqueness of indie games was the launch of Valve Corporation's Steam platform in 2004 (Swirsky & Pajot, 2012), the first platform for digitally distributing games. This alternative to buying games at real-world stores eliminated the need of developers to have their games printed on real-world media, so indies did not have to convince publishers to distribute their game. Based on Juul's survey, this quickly affected the styles of games that indies were creating. From 2005 onward, IGF winners featured predominantly 2D and non-AAA styled graphics and caught significant consumer attention. Jonathan Blow's *Braid* (Blow, 2008) sold over 450,000 units over its lifetime – extremely high for an indie game, and The Behemoth's *Castle Crashers* (The Behemoth, 2008) registered over 3 million users on Xbox Live Arcade (Conditt, 2012). Likewise bucking trends in subject matter, some of these games featured characters with "regular person" styled design (Tim from *Braid*), or even weak characters (the boy from *Limbo*) (Playdead, 2010).

After 2010, the trend shifted from 2D games with drawn art games with pixel art. Two factors contributed to this trend: an "indie game explosion" thanks to more accessible development tools and nostalgia for games of previous eras. Engines such as Game Maker and Unity, which became viable development solutions during this era, offered more accessible tools for designers that did not have much previous experience, such as time spent in AAA studios before going indie. For these developers, pixel art became a viable option as it is faster to create than other types of art and requires less effort to reach a pleasing result. Likewise, the accessibility of game making increased the number of games about real life or increasingly personal works, such as Anna Anthropy's *Dys4ia* (Anthropy, 2012) or Richard Hofmeier's *Cart Life* (Hofmeier, 2011).

Juul, however, offers an alternative reason for pixel art appealing to indies seeking to buck large industry trends. Beyond nostalgia, Juul compares pixel art to the Arts and Crafts Movement of the nineteenth century, which sought to create more authentic art by rejecting industrialization for hand-crafted products. Juul's argument is that pixel art offers a "more authentic" style of game art, as it mimics the visuals that older computers and game consoles showed due to their lower-resolution graphics capabilities. Juul's juxtaposition of a typically technical art field with a movement from the history of fine art begs the question of whether finding intertextuality between game art and art movements of the past might yield insight into trends to come.

ESTABLISHING INTERTEXTUALITY BETWEEN GAME ART AND ART HISTORY

Despite efforts to frame it otherwise, the history of digital games is intrinsically tied to the history of computers and computer graphics. Early computer games were technical demos or aids for the development of artificial intelligence (Donovan, 2010). Likewise, the development of more intricate graphics were seen as a challenge for some developers, such as David Crane's representation of a running human on the Atari 2600 in *Pitfall* (Activision, 1982) or John Carmack's creation of pseudo-3D effects for *Wolfenstein 3D* (Kushner, 2004; Id Software, 1992).

Despite the push for greater graphic fidelity in games, the subject matter of digital games pulls heavily from cultural works surrounding the games themselves – popular books, films, television, comic books, and other media. Even games that do not license the rights to utilize copyrighted properties are heavily influenced to use the themes and settings of other popular media, or even look into history for inspiration, utilizing settings that will make them marketable to consumers. This intertextuality, the relationship between two or more texts or works (Genette, 1987), between games and the world around them allows games to mark their place among other expressive media rather than simply being interactive computer software. By establishing parallels between the state of game art and the history of, the inherent intertextuality of games may also be used to establish new art-based methods for game analysis and development. This section establishes parallels between AAA game art, indie game art, and the development of style in art history; particularly in the nineteenth and twentieth centuries when the number and diversity of art styles increased dramatically (Ormiston, 2014).

Academy Art, History Painting, and the Game Industry

To explore the development of art styles that may inform game art, it is important to find a time period where artistic culture resembled that in today's game industry. It has already been established that the AAA portion of the game industry favors an idealist art style that is rendered in either realistic digital paint or in high-fidelity 3D. As this style is rigidly enforced through portfolio reviews and job postings, it can be said to have "rules" by which upcoming artists must adhere in order to create art for the professional game art industry. Typical criteria for creating AAA-style artworks is a high level of detail rendered on a large-sized image, often with dimensions of several thousand pixels on each side. It has also been established that these games favor "epic" escapist settings and larger-than-life situations.

To find an analog for the state of game art in the AAA game industry, we can look for these elements in historic art styles and the ways in which they were addressed by art culture of the time. One promising comparison is between the hiring practices and art styles of large studios and the standards applied to art in the Academy Art style. This style refers to an art movement especially prominent in nineteenth century Western Europe where art academies such as Paris's Ecole des Beaux Arts were the primary venues for aspiring artists to have their work viewed. (Denis & Trodd, 2000)

In the academies, students underwent rigorous training over the course of several years in all elements of the academic style, particularly the drawing and painting of nudes and principles of contour, shape, and lighting. These students began their education by copying other artists' drawings of sculptures, then eventually work their way to drawing and painting live subjects (Figure 2.) Each step was evaluated by a review with the faculty of the academy. After completing their education, students could exhibit at the Salon, which marked their recognition as an artist. Likewise, students could enter art contests such as

Figure 2. An Atelier-style life-painting class at the Ecole des Beaux Arts, late 1800's
Source: Wikimedia Commons, 2012a.

the Prix de Rome, a competition of several stages in which finalists were sequestered to their studios for 72 days so they could complete large format paintings of historic or mythological scenes called history paintings.

History paintings were the highest in a hierarchy of painting styles, or genres, enforced by the Academic Art movement. Genres were distinguished from one another by size of a work and the subject matter. The lowest genre was the still life, a painting of one or more inanimate objects, as it included the copying of non-living objects while history painting included human figures composed from the artist's imagination (Bass, 2008). History paintings could utilize the largest canvas sizes and feature historic or mythological scenes. All other styles were similarly controlled by the size of canvas that could be utilized and the subject matter that could be depicted.

The subjects of history paintings were painted in with subjects shown in an idealist fashion, showing them as poetic or symbolic elements rendered in physically perfect forms rather than as they might actually appear in real life (Ruckstuhl, 1917). Idealism in history paintings focuses on the use of the subject as a method of communicating allegory through the work and expressing the essence of a dramatic scene or idea (Figure 3.) A quote by André Félibien, an important figure in the founding of French academy art and the establishment of the genre system, demonstrates how history painting was seen as analogous to other respected arts:

A painter who paints only portraits has not achieved the highest perfection and cannot pretend to those honours that the most erudite receive. For that one must move from one figure to the representation of several together; one must depict history and fable and represent great deeds like historians, or charming subjects like poets; and climbing even higher, one must in allegorical compositions know how to cover

Figure 3. The Death of Socrates by Jacques-Louis David, oil on canvas, 1787, 4'4" x 6'5"; David was himself an artist in the French Royal Academy, located in what is now the Louvre. Each character is meticulously and theatrically posed and presented in peak physical condition.
Source: Wikimedia Commons, 2014.

under the veil of fable the virtues of great men, and the most exalted mysteries. We call a painter great who can perform such tasks well. (Duro, 2007)

There are a great many similarities between the state of AAA game art and the guidelines imposed upon history paintings in Academy Art. While subject matter can vary according to the production needs of the art – concept art and illustrations often depict landscapes without action – common subject matter includes powerful or skillful characters battling enemies or looking out over picturesque vistas. As stated previously, game art often works to embody escapist or wish-fulfilling action both on screen and in concept. These scenes depict important characters or narrative events in the same way that history paintings depict important historic or mythological scenes. More philosophically, these works fit the definition of idealism by art utilizing subjects not for realistic depictions, but rather as symbols. In the case of promotional art, these art pieces showcase gameplay features or allow players to imagine the unique settings they will encounter, building excitement without forcing players to confront technical issues of screen resolution or rendering. In the case of in-game art, characters and settings are idealized towards their most larger-than-life depictions to create an exhilarating product.

The way in which upcoming artists enter the AAA game industry also resembles the strict system of the academy in the criteria put in place for artworks and portfolios. In industry competitions such as the Entertainment Software Association (ESA) and Academy of Interactive Arts & Sciences' (AIAS) into the Pixel exhibition, shown every year at the Electronic Entertainment Expo (E3), winners predominantly demonstrate idealist digital painted style in epic, action-heavy scenes (ESA & AIAS, 2015). In the surveyed Gamasutra job postings, descriptions of the work to be done and portfolio needs favored a small number of production methods and styles. To earn gainful employment in the industry or enter competitions, artists must conform their work to the styles dictated by these arbiters of game art. The competitive nature of game art jobs have also created a market for learning how to create AAA-friendly art, allowing college programs for game art to flourish. These ingredients have created a culture in which, like in academy art culture, students must develop skills catered towards specific styles to show at a small number of venues, the acceptance at which will mark them as true artists to others in the field.

Indies and the Beginnings of Game Art Avant-Garde

Frustrations with the academic style of art caused open rebellion in the art world in the mid-nineteenth century. Among these detractors was Gustave Courbet (1819-1877), an artist who left an apprenticeship in a prestigious art studio to develop his own style by mimicking Spanish, Flemish, and French paintings in the Louvre (Murray, 2013). His painting, *A Burial at Ornans* (1849-1850) has been cited as an important milestone in the development of the Realist movement, where subjects are rendered as they appear in real life rather than in an idealist fashion (Figure 4.)

Atypical of the genre guidelines of the time, Courbet painted the funeral of his uncle, a commoner, on a canvas of 10'4" x 21'8", a size typically reserved for history paintings. Courbet's breaking of the established style was seen as an outrage, but is among other breaks with tradition that spawned the deluge of art movements from the late nineteenth through the twentieth centuries (Ormiston, 2014).

As Courbet rebelled by remixing elements of dominant painting styles – methods of composing figures, the size of canvases, etc. – indie game developers remix the styles and methods of historic game styles by remixing elements of pixel art, digital painting, and vector art. Some of these decisions are

Figure 4. A Burial at Ornans by Gustave Courbet, oil on canvas, 1849-1850, 10'4" x 21'8"; in its time, this painting was seen as outrageous for utilizing stylistic elements of history paintings, such as a monumental canvas size, to depict a scene of everyday life (in this case, the funeral of Courbet's commoner uncle).
Source: Wikimedia Commons, 2012b.

made because of production needs: it is easier for smaller teams to create lower resolution art – but these styles are themselves developing standards by which they can be judged as artful processes.

Juul's contextualization of pixel art as the Arts and Crafts Movement of game development, thanks to its referencing a time when the pixelization of images was very apparent on screens, highlights indie art as being very process-focused rather than system-focused. The original Arts and Crafts Movement, which sought to rebel against the pervasive industrialization of the nineteenth century by making hand-crafted items, utilized processes that took certain art forms to their roots. A notable example is William Morris' Kelmscott Press, which produced books through medieval printing and illustration techniques such as woodcutting (Meggs, 2011).

The desire for the retro in indie games fit's Juul's narrative of indie art as being an "Arts and Crafts Movement" of game art, often not only in visuals but also in the style of games created by indies. Many popular indie games mimic the styles of games that those developers grew up with such as *Super Mario Bros.* (Nintendo, 1985) with run-and-jump action-based mechanics and pixelated art styles (Swirsky & Pajot, 2012). Beyond pixel art, however, independent games have achieved great success with varied styles of art that reference other bygone eras of games. Playtonic's *Yooka-Laylee* (Playtronic, 2016), Frontier Developments' *Elite: Dangerous* (Frontier Developments, 2015), and countless other games that revive or reference retro game properties have performed well on crowdfunding sites such as Kickstarter. By reclaiming styles that have been put aside by the AAA sector of the industry and creating art as part of a process of creation, indies are establishing an avant-garde based on remixing and imitation similar to Courbet's own remixing of elements that he observed during his explorations of the Louvre.

Is Game-Centric the Best Way for Game Art?

While these elements of the indie movement provide promising diversity of art styles in the game industry, a common thread of the history of both AAA and indie art styles is a connection to the history of computer graphics. Despite even the best efforts to do otherwise, the history of game art has always been in service to the history of graphic technology in computer and video games. Much of AAA's push towards high fidelity idealism is due to large studios' ability to reach state-of-the-art graphics in their games. As styles come and go in AAA, some are revived by indie developers as they seek to create games with fondly remembered retro graphics. One wonders, however, if there are potentially lost opportunities by staying game-centric and not exploring the art and design knowledge of other fields.

Critics of the AAA development system have called it an "arms race" of technology and have raised doubts about the connections between technical sophistication and whether a game is enjoyable (Papathanasis, 2015). The accessibility of highly specialized digital art jobs have been criticized as less obtainable to non-white and non-male applicants from cultures were computers were not accessible due to computers being either too expensive or "for boys." (Campbell, 2013; Henn, 2014) Indie games face similar criticisms related to having a culture of exclusivity (Caldwell, 2012) with accusations of large festivals such as the IGF celebrating a few artists within an established clique or not properly evaluating games (IG, 2012). Likewise, the art styles employed in many indie games have become established to the degree that they now have enforceable criteria similar to the AAA or academic styles. While local scenes remain open and allow developers to form their own identities it is common for makers in small communities to mimic the popular styles of IGF winners or best-selling games to make names for themselves. As with AAA games, following established styles tends to limit the ability of new developers to enter the field.

Developers who use alternative styles may still gain recognition for their work in games, albeit from alternative sources not considered by many mainstream game developers and consumers. In many ways, game developers looking to more greatly tap into the intertextuality of games in such a way that looks beyond the technological history of game art have more options for recognition of their work than those who only utilize consumer game-related news sites, game festivals, and game arcades. Websites such as Kill Screen, an online art and games criticism publication, specialize in game journalism that greatly resembles what one would find in an art magazine (Priestman, 2015). Likewise, art-focused publications are reporting on games that adapt the style or themes of famous artists' works into interactive multimedia projects (Dimopoulos, 2015; Mallonee, 2015; Meier, 2015). Museums like the Smithsonian American Art Museum and art festivals such as Baltimore's Artscape are also honoring such games with inclusion in exhibits and events.

Beyond how early games in the "indie revolution" adapted gaming's low-fidelity past to address game art as a process, games with alternative styles based on elements of real-world art are addressing game art as a process among the entire landscape of art processes. By identifying game-based art styles then addressing them through the context of art history – both as the result of technological trends and as having parallels in the development of art – intertextuality becomes a process for planning games. The next section will more closely explore ideas and processes of art and how they are applied in games.

USING INTERTEXTUALITY TO BREAK AWAY FROM TECHNOLOGICAL TRENDS

As previous sections have focused on parallels between the systems for highlighting works in the AAA and indie sectors of the game industry, this section will look at elements of art movements that came after the academy system. This overview will identify areas where considering the intertextuality between art history and the game industry might offer opportunities for creating exciting new work. While this section highlights games that already feature these parallels, identifying them through historical patterns will help developers incorporate them into their design processes.

Realism

Theme, considered here as the narrative descriptors supplied by art and story elements of a game, is a powerful tool for developers wanting to create works that buck common industry trends. As highlighted previously, games popularly utilize "larger-than-life" or "epic" imagery to create fantastic gameplay scenarios – killing monsters, saving the world, battling enemy hordes, and others – rendered in idealist imagery. As Courbet rebelled against idealist history painting conventions by depicting scenes of everyday life, game developers are juxtaposing video game conventions with everyday themes. Several significant indie developers have already entered the genre of realist video games with autobiographical works such as Richard Hofmeier's *Cart Life,* Anna Anthropy's *Dys4ia*, and *That Dragon, Cancer*, which depicts the developers' experiences having a sick child (Green & Green, 2014). Themes that depict events from real life – either from the lives of the authors or of fictional everyday experiences, are a hallmark of realist video games.

Cart Life, noteworthy as the 2013 Seumas McNally Grand Prize in the IGF (Conditt, 2013), depicts the lives of retail vendors through animated scenes and gameplay scenarios. These scenarios include calculating correct change within a time limit, unpacking newspapers quickly without tearing them, and managing time spent at work and maintaining personal relationships. Gameplay mechanics embody each task that occurs during a character's day: unpacking papers, for example, is rendered in gameplay as a single-try typing test where making a mistake means that the paper being unpacked is slashed by your scissors, rendering it unsellable. The game's pixel art visuals, Hofmeier argues, provides abstraction that "encourages empathy" and allows players to fill in gaps of the characters' emotional states (Lee, 2013).

Similarly to *Cart Life*, *Dys4ia* depicts events from the developers' own life, in this case Anna Anthropy's experiences with gender dysphoria – the dissatisfaction of a person with their birth gender – and subsequent hormone replacement therapy. The gameplay is a series of micro-games akin to Nintendo's *WarioWare* series where players must identify and enact the mechanic of each game quickly to proceed. Anthropy has stated that the game allows players to feel her frustration during her therapy by telegraphing each game's goal to the player, then denying victory through the layout of levels (Kuchera, 2012). Like Hofmeier's game, *Dys4ia* is constructed to build empathy through interactions and abstracted visuals. Pixel art depicts the game's thematic scenarios: characters uncomfortable with their body are *Tetris* blocks that cannot fit through gaps, players are pelted with word balloons filled with male and female symbols, and a disembodied mouth must catch falling hormone pills.

Unlike the two previous games, *That Dragon, Cancer* utilizes 3D polygonal graphics. The game is a series of scenes where players must deal with different experiences of having a terminally ill child such as learning the diagnosis to modifying their lifestyle to accommodate their son's needs. Like the previous two games, however, empathy was a primary goal of the developer. Ryan Green has said that emotions that they hoped to instill in players included love (Robertson, 2013) and experiences of faith and grace (Green, 2013) that they examined through their son's illness. Notably, the characters in *That Dragon, Cancer* have only implied facial features similar to the abstracted features of characters in *Cart Life* and *Dys4ia*.

From this small cross-section, common elements – themes, mechanics, and aesthetics – can be identified as contributing to a game's identification with the realist style. Gameplay often features real-world activities abstracted into short scenes of interaction. Victory and win conditions are either difficult to achieve or identify as a way to communicate the emotion of a scene. Likewise, the aesthetic features abstraction that allows players to inject their own perspective into the game world rather than playing purely make-believe. All of this supports the creation of real-world scenarios that players can empathize with through their cognitive and haptic interactions with the game itself.

As realism was an important step for the development of Western art, it is also an important step for game art. Rendering the experiences of real life through the medium of games, typically reserved for idealist imagery, allows developers to guide players through their own experiences or the experiences of people the developer wishes to highlight. That realism is a style and process in the world of fine art allows game developers to use it as a guide for how they might plan their own empathetic works. Likewise, the analyses of games such as *Cart Life, Dys4ia,* and *That Dragon, Cancer* identify how the language of games can be modified to create these experiences that honor real-life events in the same way that Courbet honored his uncle's funeral through modified elements of genre painting.

Art Movements in the 20th Century: Experimentations with Tools and Materials

Beyond realism, artists through the late nineteenth and into the twentieth century experimented with additional processes for creating increasingly bold styles of art. These experiments moved forward from remixing the language of the previous art establishment to studying the capabilities of artists' tools themselves. Movements and graphic design schools such as the Bauhaus in Weimar, Germany offer a look into how experimentation yielded new art paradigms.

In the early 20th century, graphic designers, particularly in Eastern Europe, experimented with fields of flat color and simple graphics to depict an idea as minimalistically as possible. For some, text became an important pictoral element and was incorporated into the imagery of a work. The process of creating such works was an important topic of research for designers such as Bauhaus faculty member El Lissitzky, who utilized geometric shapes in a series of experiments of painting and arranging different forms that he called *Prouns*. These forms were created through drafting techniques Lissitzky learned in his architectural education and resulted in very precise shapes.

Another member of the Bauhaus faculty, Laszlo Moholy-Nagy, performed both experiments with Constructivist forms and with photography, which at the time had not been fully utilized as a tool for artists. Moholy-Nagy took photos whose framing and composition had symbolic meaning and have been said to transform experience of the photographed objects or places (Prager, 2015). He also created photomontages that utilized the compositional experimentation of Constructivism with photographed elements that he called "photoplastics" (Meggs, 2011).

Moholy-Nagy and Lissitzky, both contemporaries of one another and colleagues at the Bauhaus, could work with their own methods while co-developing the Bauhaus's aesthetic. Each, as implementers of different technological processes in their art works, showed much of the same spirit that indies do by remixing retro art styles, albiet with a more varied palette of tools and influences. By expanding influences to other fields besides games, developers might find new possibilities as early 20th century artists had.

An underutilized tool for game artists is the ability to digitize real-world media or objects in high resolutions through scanning or digital photography. This technology allows for non-digital pieces to be utilized within game development environments, opening a wide possibility of craft-made styles. Three games that break game art trends with craft-made art are Dietrich Squinkifier's *Dominique Pamplemousse* (Squinkifer, 2013), *Sissy's Magical Ponycorn Adventure* (Creighton & Creighton, 2011), and *Ever Yours, Vincent* (Orlati, 2015).

Dominique Pamplemousse utilizes photographed Claymation figurines (Squinkifer, 2012a) and cardboard for its art (Squinkifer, 2012b). Each character is animated though stop-motion photography that is imported into the game engine. Squinkifier experimented with the properties of the materials used to create the game's environments to achieve different effects, such as tearing the surface off of corrugated cardboard to simulate deteriorating walls in a run-down detective's office.

Sissy's Magical Ponycorn Adventure was created at a game jam, an event where developers produce a game in a limited amount of time, by Ryan Creighton and his five-year-old daughter Cassie. Cassie was the writer and artist for the game and utilized crayons to create the art for the game. The crayon art was scanned and imported into Flash and implemented as part of the game (Creighton & Creighton, 2013). This implementation shows how experimenting with real-world techniques for game art can allow previously unable creators, in this case a five-year-old child, to create publishable video games.

Dominique Pamplemousse and *Sissy's Magical Ponycorn Adventure* show that experiments with real-world art for digital games can produce some noteworthy products. *Dominique Pamplemousse* and *Sissy's Magical Ponycorn Adventure* has been honored in industry award competitions such as the IGF. *Sissy's Magical Ponycorn Adventure* was likewise recognized by IndieCade and the Canadian Videogame Awards. Each developer experimented with alternative art generation methods: Squinky wanted to create a musical game on a budget (Squinkifer, 2011), and Ryan Creighton wanted to involve his young daughter in the software development process.

These games also utilized tools from other fields, notably the film technique of stop-motion-animation, to create their art styles. Experimentation with media techniques for games was an important part of how the development of each of these games was planned. While intertextuality with art history did not play a role, one can see how knowledge of the experiments of artists such as those at the Bauhaus might further inform a developer seeking to create unique art for a game. Intertextualities with art history, such as those identified earlier in the chapter between academy art and AAA games, allows developers to experiment with their processes according to previously developed patterns without having to "reinvent the wheel."

The third game, Federica Orlati's *Ever Yours, Vincent* (Orlati, 2015), utilizes experiments in the craft of game assets in the same way that the previous two games did. However, it also utilizes intertextuality with art history as an important element of its design to create an adventure game biographical study of Vincent Van Gogh and an exploration of the artist's thoughts on his work. Created for Orlati's Master's thesis, the game is based on letters Van Gogh sent to his brother after released from a mental institution (Dimopoulos, 2015). The game recreates several of Van Gogh's works as environments in the game and utilizes similar media to that which created the original works. Likewise, puzzles in the game shift and transform the works that form the game environments, reflecting Van Gogh's mental state and his thoughts on the works. With all of these elements, the game plays like an interactive character portrait of the artist and survey of the work that lets players explore it in an interactive fashion. Video games have been utilized as interactive explorations of artists' work such as the Beatles's musical catalog (Schiesel, 2009) or as systems for exploring inaccessible or difficult-to-access places (Adams, 2007). Having been made with several types of media, *Ever Yours, Vincent* can be considered a "mixed media video game." This game, and the previously mentioned games that utilize real-world media for their art, show the potential of experimenting with the ways in which game art is made: methods for producing games cheaply, creating novelty, introducing new developers to game making, and utilizing interactivity as part of a larger art project. *Ever Yours, Vincent* also addresses ideas beyond merely utilizing materials: utilizing the ideas and logic of a medium to generate game mechanics and aid in a game's design itself.

Intertextuality as a Concept for Game Design and Analysis

As *Ever Yours, Vincent* moves beyond generative experiments into finding new things to say about design by exploring an artist's thought processes, intertextuality between games and fine art disciplines allows game makers to find new theories by which to design and analyze games. As early twentieth century artists were finding new implementations of materials, they were also experimenting with the ways that viewers interacted with their art and how meaning could be created with basic graphic elements. As with material experimentations, understanding how historic artists developed the intangible elements of their work gives game makers access to utilizing theories of other fields in their own work.

Two investigations of other disciplines that have yielded game design and game studies results are Daniel Merlin Goodbrey's comic-game hybrids, called *Hypercomics*, and the survey of architectural design theory that resulted in the book *An Architectural Approach to Level Design* (Totten, 2014). Goodbrey's work with comics integrates Juul's characteristics of games (Juul, 2005) to identify how comics work as a medium through the formation of characteristics for comics. The characteristics of both fields are compared to find where the characteristics might be blended to form game/comic hybrids (Goodbrey, 2014a) as seen in Figure 5.

Two Hypercomic games, *A Duck Has an Adventure* (Goodbrey, 2012) and *The Empty Kingdom* (Goodbrey, 2014b) provide insight into the type of work that might be produced when characteristics of

Figure 5. Goodbrey's game/comic hybrids, referred to as Hypercomics, blend characteristics of games and characteristics of comics to create works that utilize the visual language of comics to create interactive experiences with goals and challenges.
Source: Image created by the author after a diagram by Goodbrey.

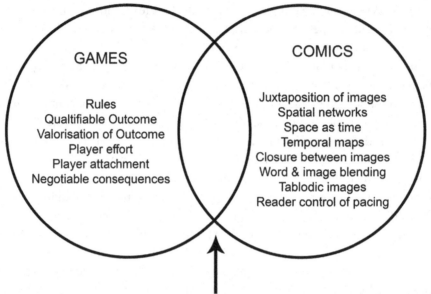

Game comics exist in the middle ground between comics and games

comics and games combine. *A Duck Has an Adventure* has players direct the life of a duck as he makes choices along branching narrative pathways. The game utilizes the comic characteristics of "space as time", "reader control of pacing", and "tablodic images" and the interaction model of choose-your-own-adventure books, where players progress the story by choosing one of several narrative options at specific narrative points. The game is game-like in that it asks players to make choices, but comic-like in its visual delivery and how by playing the game, a strip of frames is produced based on the pathways that players choose.

The Empty Kingdom improves upon the methods prototyped in *A Duck Has an Adventure* through two important methods: a less linear structure and the inclusion of contextual story frames. Players are a king who must gather items and solve puzzles to progress through the world. The game is presented as a series of comic pages that players navigate with the arrow keys on their keyboards. The king only appears in certain frames of each page that represent the pathways through the game world, while other frames on the page contain images of the world around the king's location. As many of the puzzles require items found elsewhere in the world, the game requires backtracking and exploration, similar to dungeon-crawling games like *Zork!* (Infocom, 1981), that lends a non-linear element to the gameplay. The game's contextual story frames develop the world parallel to the player's own movements by featuring images of things that happen around the king walking through an area: a deer being spooked, a bird taking off, or a flowing river.

An Architectural Approach to Level Design likewise recontextualizes elements of games according to spatial theories utilized by architects. In many ways, games and architecture are alike: both are experiential mediums, both can be manipulated by user input, and both utilize functional user-driven design processes. (Totten, 2014) To pull game analysis away from purely technological terms, the author treats elements of games that result from technological limitations in user-based design terms. Thus, elements such as 2D or 3D graphics are discussed as the point of view through which players engage environments and games with limited space for art assets are analyzed as having systems of discreet communicative symbols. This user-based approach generalizes level design as a series of spatial principles that can be used in multiple genres and introduces design-based approaches to level construction.

Once the user-centric outlook is established, game levels are analyzed as one would discuss a piece of architecture. Architectural theories such as types – symbolic building forms utilized in a design to identify what a building is for – or prospect/refuge spatial theory – a principle of moving users through a series of safe and unsafe-feeling spaces – are then described and used as criteria for judging levels in different types of games. The analysis is accompanied by architecturally-based sketching principles that aid game players and developers in their own analysis and design. Sketching for architecture is distinct from sketching for concept art or illustration in that it utilizes highly measured approaches to accurately depict the scale of a space while abstract diagrammatic elements show the user-experience based elements of a space (Figure 6) (Totten, 2014). This type of sketching can be a useful tool for level designers designing spaces with specific user-experiences in mind or for establishing proper measurements for use in game engines.

Beyond creating games with novel art styles, intertextuality through the study of other art and design fields can yield entirely new forms of games and gameplay analysis. Goodbrey's studies of comics and the resultant games show that the exploratory and narrative elements of games can be transformed through the use of another medium's presentational language. Likewise, architectural theories of user-based experience and analysis give game developers tools to conceptualize their own work beyond concept art. The final section of this chapter will demonstrate how intertextuality with historic art and design is applied through the development of games where art style and theme determines game mechanics.

INTERTEXTUALITY AS CORE MECHANICS: PLAYABLE ART HISTORY IN THE ATELIER GAMES PROJECT

A major theme of this chapter has been the utilization of building games' intertextuality with previously underconsidered elements of art and art history. While utilizing influences from other fields in games is nothing new, doing so is often an outlying effort rather than industry-standard. To explore how intertextuality can become an integrated part of a game design process, this section will explore the *Atelier Games* project – a series of games based on the work of 20th century artists and art movements.

Atelier Games is created at the American University Game Lab in Washington, DC and through the indie game studio, Pie for Breakfast Studios. It is named after *atelier,* an instruction method where an apprentice studies under an established master artist to learn the fine or decorative arts. The project's website describes the goals of the projects thusly:

The gameplay of these games is based on themes apparent in each artist's work. Likewise, the methods for creating the art for each game will be derived from the artist's own method. The purpose of this project is to explore new art production techniques using real-world artist materials to determine the viability of such methods in common game production. (Pie for Breakfast Studios, 2015)

Figure 6. Architectural sketching is a tool that can be utilized by level designers for both analysis of existing game levels or planning of new ones. This image from An Architectural Approach to Level Design shows a multiplayer capture-the-flag map analyzed with architectural proximity diagrams.
Source: The Author.

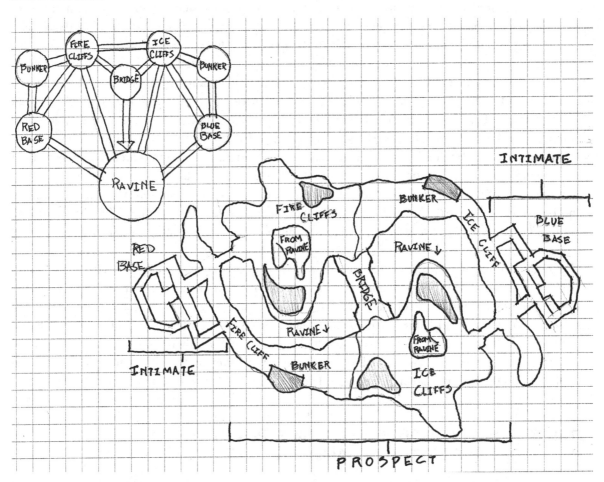

The first game produced for the project was *Lissitzky's Revenge* (Totten, 2015), a game that reinterprets works by El Lissitzky as video game levels. The game utilizes n-digital art production to test the speed and viability for real-world media as production methods for game art. Likewise, the designers derived the game's mechanics from Lissitzky's original work: the violence of Soviet propaganda and the juxtaposition of geographic elements. Likewise, the game allows players to create new artwork through their interactions with the game – transforming each work with their play.

In terms of gameplay, *Lissitzky's Revenge* is an action game based on the poster *Beat the Whites with the Red Wedge* (1919) (Figure 7). Designers utilized paper cutouts to create the game's Constructivist aesthetic, as doing so was a common method for Lissitzky's contemporaries whose work would then be mass produced via lithographic process (Meggs, 2011). The game's mechanics are derived from the "narrative" of Lissitzky's poster: players are a red wedge and must destroy the white circle in each scene by solving puzzles based on other posters and designs by Lissizky.

Figure 7. Beat the Whites with the Red Wedge by El Lissitzky, 1919, poster; this Constructivist piece utilizes symbolic forms to bolster Bolshevik supporters against Czarist rule. Its implied "characters" and the use of figure-ground as a method for creating the action of the poster inspired the mechanics of Lissitzky's Revenge.
Source: Totten, 2015.

Lissitzky's Revenge was a logical beginning to the *Atelier Games* project, as the work it derived from featured the most "video game-like" scenario: an overt conflict between two opposing forces. In this way, the game addresses the Suprematist design elements of Lissitzky's original work. Suprematism was an art movement in the early 20th century that argued for "art for art's sake" (Meggs, 2011), free of political or ideological associations. Works in this movement typically utilized plain geometric shapes and large fields of one color. In having typical conflict-based mechanics, *Lissitzky's Revenge* could be a "game for game's sake" and be an action-oriented title in the *Atelier Games* series (Figure 8.)

Lissitzky's original poster utilizes simple forms: a red wedge superimposed upon a white circle, black and white fields, and various other shapes to signify a critical impact; to denote the Bolshevik "wedge" that could invade and drive into the heart of Russia's ruling class. Likewise, the black and white background creates a *figure-ground* composition where black and white fields are utilized to describe positive and negative space. The overlapping of the white circle into both the black and white fields also gives the impression that the red wedge is breaking into the white circle. This reading is bolstered by graphics around the area where the wedge and circle meet. These graphics seem to burst from the two shapes' collision as though the wedge were bursting through a barrier into the circle. In this way, the black field might be read as a barrier that the red wedge is pushing through to reach the white circle.

Figure 8. Lissitzky's Revenge by Christopher Totten, 2015
Source: Totten, 2015.

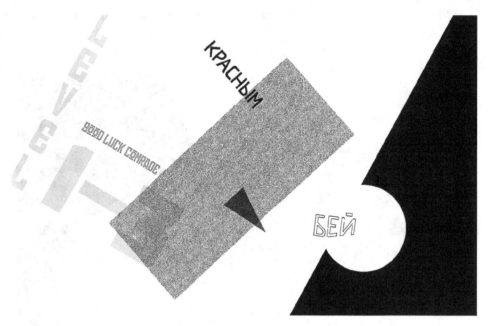

These mechanics: the wedge ramming, the black field protecting the white circle, the wedge breaking the black field to reveal the white circle; give an outline for developers to plan the game. Cyrillic text that in the original poster appear to be flying around the conflict were repurposed as enemy missiles shot by the white circle to stop the player's progress. As planning progressed, developers realized that the mechanic of ramming through a barrier to destroy an enemy that is actively firing upon the player greatly resembled the Atari 2600 game *Yar's Revenge* (Atari, 1981). This led the developers to include the gray squares in the original work as safe zones that players could hide in from enemy attack and charge the wedge's attack so the white circle could be destroyed.

Creating game art assets from the symbols in *Beat the Whites with the Red Wedge* and implementing them in arcade-game style levels was a very quick process – under a weekend's worth of work. As such, more levels were created in the likeness of other Lissitzky posters and utilizing mechanics and art derived from them (Figures 9, 10, and 11). This agility is a result of the short time required to create the game's paper cutout art. Other benefits of this method included the ability to utilize the paper texture to create other custom assets for the game in Photoshop and the building of a simple language of symbols and colors akin to those created by Lissitzky in his own work.

Lissitzky's Revenge is an example of how developers can utilize the visual style and design of an artwork and create a game with it. Beyond merely utilizing intertextuality for reference, this game utilizes it as a basis for deep study into how gameplay might be created to allow players to experience art movements interactively. The speed of the development – three months for the entire game – is also noteworthy and speaks favorably of paper cutouts as a production tool for game artists. Beyond benefits during development, the game has also received significant attention from both games press (Priestman, 2015) and art press (Meier, 2015), as well as being featured in events at the Smithsonian American Art Museum.

Figure 9. A screenshot from Lissitzky's Revenge, created in the style of Proun G7 (1923), which featured a wheel-like object. The in-game wheels rotate to block the player's path and can be moved to form gear systems.
Source: Totten, 2015.

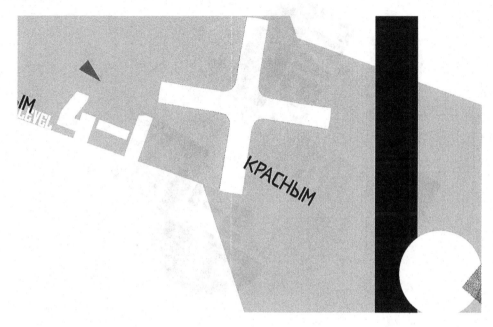

Figure 10. A screenshot from Lissitzky's Revenge, based on Lissitzky's story book, A Suprematist Tale of Two Squares (1920). Players must move squares into place to reveal the white circle. The bright red square is destroyed if the player touches the gray safe zones while holding it, changing these otherwise beneficial pieces into hazards.
Source: Totten, 2015.

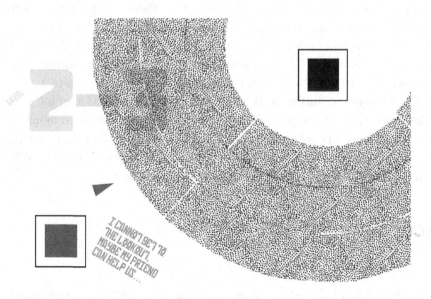

Figure 11. A screenshot from Lissitzky's Revenge, based on Lissitzky's poster for a Bauhaus exhibition (1923). Players manipulate switches in this world to open barriers and reveal the white circle.
Source: Totten, 2015.

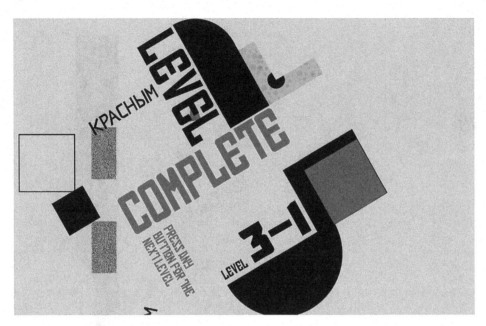

CONCLUSION

While current game industry trends utilize intertextuality to draw connections between games and other popular media or games and other games, finding intertextual connections between games and other forms of art may yield other exciting results. By understanding the current state of the industry in the context of art history, developers may find parallels that help guide them towards new opportunities for game production. Likewise, avant-garde methods such as utilizing non-digital art for games may be recontextualized to bolster their impact by also introducing design logic and theories from historic art styles.

Promising trends at the time of this writing are games made with non-digital materials derived from the work of famous artists (*Ever Yours, Vincent* and *The Atelier Games Project*) and the inclusion of games in museum exhibitions. Further work in these areas might include aligning game designs with a museum's collection or their upcoming exhibits or holding game jam events to complement game exhibitions at cultural institutions. Not only can events like these increase the presence of games in our cultural consciousness, but they can also invite new and more diverse game makers into the fold by increasing the accessibility of game making through traditional art techniques.

REFERENCES

Activision. (1982). *Pitfall*. Activision.

Adams, E. W. (2007). S.T.A.L.K.E.R.: Shadow of Chernobyl: Ludic space as memorial. In F. Von Borres, S. P. Walz, & M. Böttger (Eds.), *Space time play*. Basel: Birkhäuser Verlag AG.

Anthropy, A. (2012). *Dys4ia*. Newgrounds.

Atari. (1981). *Yar's revenge*. Atari.

Bass, L. R. (2008). *The drama of the portrait: Theater and visual culture in early modern Spain*. University Park, PA: Penn State University Press.

Behemoth, T. (2008). *Castle crashers*. San Diego, CA: Microsoft Game Studios.

Blow, J. (2008). Braid. San Francisco.

Caldwell, B. (2012, March 7). The competition: The story behind the IGF's critics. *Rock Paper Shotgun*. Retrieved from http://www.rockpapershotgun.com/2012/03/07/the-competition-the-story-behind-the-igfs-critics/

Campbell, C. (2013). *How to tackle gaming's lack of racial diversity*. Retrieved June 4, 2015, from http://www.polygon.com/2013/9/16/4728320/how-to-tackle-gamings-lack-of-racial-diversity

Cavanagh, T. (2009). *Don't look back*. London, England.

Cavanagh, T. (2010a). N.O.T.T.U.B. London, England.

Cavanagh, T. (2010b). VVVVVV. London, England.

Cavanagh, T. (2012). *Super hexagon*. London, England.

Cinemaware. (1986). *Defender of the crown*. Author.

Conditt, J. (2012). *Castle Crashers clocks in over 3 million "knights in the making"*. Retrieved June 11, 2015, from http://www.engadget.com/2012/09/13/castle-crashers-clocks-in-over-3-million-knights-in-the-making/

Conditt, J. (2013). IGF 2013: And the awards go to... *Cart Life*! Retrieved June 24, 2015, from http://www.engadget.com/2013/03/27/igf-2013-and-the-awards-go-to-cart-life/

Crecente, B. (2013). *What makes a developer indie?* Retrieved June 4, 2015, from Game Studio Job Listings

Creighton, R., & Creighton, C. (2011). *Sissy's magical ponycorn adventure*.

Creighton, R., & Creighton, C. (2013). *Ponycorns and programming kids: Ryan Henson Creighton and Cassandra Creighton at TEDxToronto*. Retrieved June 26, 2015, from https://www.youtube.com/watch?v=hE0K5W7_omI

Denis, R. C., & Trodd, C. (Eds.). (2000). *Art and the academy in the nineteenth century*. Manchester, UK: Manchester University Press.

Developments, F. (2015). *Elite dangerous*. Author.

Dimopoulos, K. (2015). *Freeware garden: Ever yours, Vincent*. Retrieved June 20, 2015, from http://www.rockpapershotgun.com/tag/ever-yours-vincent/

Donovan, T. (2010). *Replay: The history of video games*. East Sussex, UK: Yellow Ant.

Duro, P. (2007). Imitation and authority: The creation of the academic canon in French art, 1648-1870. In A. Brzyski (Ed.), *Partisan canons* (pp. 95–113). Durham, NC: Duke University Press. doi:10.1215/9780822390374-005

ESA, & AIAS. (2015). *Into the pixel*. Retrieved June 4, 2015, from www.intothepixel.com

Genette, G. (1987). *Seuils*. Paris, France: Editions du Seuil.

Goodbrey, D. M. (2012). *A duck has an adventure*. Retrieved June 4, 2015, from http://www.kongregate.com/games/Stillmerlin/a-duck-has-an-adventure

Goodbrey, D. M. (2014a). Game comics: An analysis of an emergent hybrid form. *Journal of Graphic Novels & Comics*, 6(1), 3–14. doi:10.1080/21504857.2014.943411

Goodbrey, D. M. (2014b). *The empty kingdom*. Retrieved June 4, 2015, from http://www.kongregate.com/games/Stillmerlin/the-empty-kingdom

Grace, O. (2013). *Should we give indie games a break?* Retrieved June 10, 2015, from http://www.gamebreaker.tv/video/chat-bubble/should-we-give-indie-games-a-break/

Green, R. (2013). *Why games need grace*. Retrieved June 24, 2015, from http://gamechurch.com/why-games-need-grace/

Green, R., & Green, A. (2014). *That dragon, cancer*.

Henn, S. (2014). *When women stopped coding*. Retrieved June 4, 2015, from http://www.npr.org/sections/money/2014/10/21/357629765/when-women-stopped-coding

Hofmeier, R. (2011). *Cart life*.

IG. (2012). *What's wrong with the IGF*. Retrieved June 4, 2015, from https://therottingcartridge.wordpress.com/2012/02/22/whats-wrong-with-the-igf/

Juul, J. (2014). High-tech low-tech authenticity: The creation of independent style at the independent games festival. In *Proceedings of the 9th International Conference on the Foundations of Digital Games*. Retrieved from http://www.jesperjuul.net/text/independentstyle/

Juul, J. (2005). *Half-real*. Cambridge, MA: The MIT Press.

Kuchera, B. (2012). *Dys4ia tackles gender politics, sense of self, and personal growth... on Newgrounds*. Retrieved June 24, 2015, from http://penny-arcade.com/report/article/dys4ia-tackles-gender-politics-sense-of-self-and-personal-growth-on-newg

Kushner, D. (2004). *Masters of doom*. New York: Random House.

Lee, B. (2013). *"Cart life": How Richard Hofmeier game became a success story*. Retrieved June 4, 2015, from http://www.digitalspy.com/gaming/news/a472874/cart-life-how-richard-hofmeier-game-became-a-success-story.html#~pgAxbf8UaVxI33

Mallonee, L. C. (2015). *A video game lets you navigate Giorgio de Chirico's surreal cityscapes*. Retrieved June 20, 2015, from http://hyperallergic.com/195863/a-video-game-lets-you-navigate-giorgio-de-chiricos-surreal-cityscapes/

Meggs, P. B. (2011). *Meggs' history of graphic design* (5th ed.). San Francisco, CA: Wiley.

Meier, A. (2015). *Be the Bolshevik wedge in a game inspired by El Lissitzky's 1919 propaganda art.* Retrieved June 20, 2015, from http://hyperallergic.com/198635/be-the-bolshevik-wedge-in-a-game-inspired-by-el-lissitzkys-1919-propaganda-art/

Murray, C. J. (Ed.). (2013). Encyclopedia of the romantic era, 1760–1850. New York, NY: Fitzroy Dearborn.

Nintendo. (1985). *Super mario bros.* Author.

Orlati, F. (2015). *Ever yours.* Vincent.

Ormiston, R. (2014). *50 art styles you should know.* New York, NY: Prestel.

Papathanasis, A. (2015). *The tech arms race in AAA - and why I'm abandoning it.* Retrieved June 3, 2015, from http://gamasutra.com/blogs/AndreasPapathanasis/20150601/244768/The_tech_arms_race_in_AAA__and_why_Im_abandoning_it.php

Pie for Breakfast Studios. (2015). *Atelier games - about.* Retrieved June 4, 2015, from http://ateliergames.tumblr.com/about

Playdead. (2010). *Limbo.* Copenhagen, Denmark.

Playtronic. (2016). *Yooka-Laylee.*

Prager, P. (2015). *Making sense of the modernist muse: Creative cognition and play at the Bauhaus.* Author.

Priestman, C. (2015). *Iconic 20th century art is being turned into a series of experimental videogames.* Retrieved June 20, 2015, from http://killscreendaily.com/articles/lissitzkys-revenge/

Robertson, A. (2013). *That dragon, cancer: The video game helping a father face his son's disease.* Retrieved June 24, 2015, from http://www.telegraph.co.uk/technology/video-games/10170337/That-Dragon-Cancer-the-video-game-helping-a-father-face-his-sons-disease.html

Rose, M. (2010). *Intervvvvview: Terry Cavanagh.* Retrieved June 4, 2015, from http://www.indiegames.com/2010/01/intervvvvview_terry_cavanagh.html

Ruckstuhl, F. W. (1917). Idealism and realism in art. *The Art World, 1*(4), 252–256. Retrieved from http://www.jstor.org/stable/25587740?seq=2#page_scan_tab_contents

SCE Santa Monica. (2005). *God of war.*

Schiesel, S. (2009, September 1). All together now: Play the game, mom. *The New York Times.*

Software, I. (1992). *Wolfenstein 3D.*

Sollers, P. (1968). *Theorie d'ensemble.* Paris, France: Éditions du Seuil.

Squinkifer, D. (2011). *A musical adventure game … in stop motion?* Retrieved June 4, 2015, from http://squinky.me/2011/10/27/a-musical-adventure-game-in-stop-motion/

Squinkifer, D. (2012a). *How to pamplemousse : Puppets!* Retrieved from http://squinky.me/2012/08/07/how-to-pamplemousse-puppets/

Squinkifer, D. (2012b). *How to pamplemousse : Sets!* Retrieved from http://squinky.me/2012/09/19/how-to-pamplemousse-sets/

Squinkifer, D. (2013). *Dominique pamplemousse.*

Superannuation. (2014). *How much does it cost to make a big video game?* Retrieved June 4, 2015, from http://kotaku.com/how-much-does-it-cost-to-make-a-big-video-game-1501413649

Swirsky, J., & Pajot, L. (2012). *Indie game: The movie.* Canada: Blinkworks.

Totten, C. W. (2012). *File: swarmdeathsportconcept-small.* Retrieved January 26, 2016, from http://www.christotten3d.com/wp-content/gallery/concept-art/swarmdeathsportconcept-small.png

Totten, C. W. (2014). *An architectural approach to level design.* Boca Raton, FL: CRC Press. doi:10.1201/b17113

Totten, C. W. (2015). *Lissitzky's revenge.*

Visual Art Jobs. (2015). Retrieved June 4, 2015, from http://jobs.gamasutra.com/jobtype/visual-arts/country/+

Weber, R. (2013). *On reflections: First interview with the Ubisoft studio's new MD.* Retrieved June 4, 2015, from http://www.gamesindustry.biz/articles/2014-02-26-on-reflections-first-interview-with-the-ubisoft-studios-new-md

Wikimedia Commons. (2012a). *File: École des beaux-arts (from the live).jpg.* Retrieved January 26, 2016, from https://commons.wikimedia.org/wiki/File:%C3%89cole_des_beaux-arts_(from_the_live).jpg

Wikimedia Commons. (2012b). *File:Gustave Courbet - A Burial at Ornans - Google Art Project 2.jpg.* Retrieved January 25, 2016, from https://commons.wikimedia.org/wiki/File:Gustave_Courbet_-_A_Burial_at_Ornans_-_Google_Art_Project_2.jpg – image in the public domain

Wikimedia Commons. (2014). *File: David - The Death of Socrates.jpg.* Retrieved January 26, 2016, from https://commons.wikimedia.org/wiki/File:David_-_The_Death_of_Socrates.jpg

Zimmerman, E., & Salen, K. (2003). *Rules of play: Game design fundamentals.* Cambridge, MA: The MIT Press.

KEY TERMS AND DEFINITIONS

AAA Game: A game developed by a large studio with financial support from a major video game publisher.

Academic Art: An art movement of the 15th to 19th centuries where entry into art culture required specific education and acceptance from an academy.

Digital Painting: A digital art technique that utilizes computer software that simulates paint and a digital input device that simulates hand-drawing on the computer.

Game Engine: A piece of software that allows a user to create interactive works such as video games or applications without the need to create back-end software needed to display the work.

Game Mechanic: An action that a player takes repeatedly as they interact with a game.

Hypercomic: A work that blends the visual language of comics with the interactive language of games.

Idealism: The philosophy of representing something in its most perfect form rather than as it appears in real life. Utilizing subjects in art as symbolic imagery.

Indie Game: A game created without substantial financial support from publishers or with limited resources. Indie game developers often create games within a social community.

Non-Digital Game Art: Game art generated by utilizing real-world tools and media, then digitizing the work through digital photography or scanning.

Pixel Art: A digital art technique that simulates the low-resolution graphics of early personal computers and game consoles.

Section 3
Hypertextuality

Chapter 11
Artifacts of Empire:
Orientalism and Inner–Texts in *Tomb Raider* (2013)

Kristin M. S. Bezio
University of Richmond, USA

ABSTRACT

This chapter examines Crystal Dynamics' 2013 Tomb Raider *reboot, arguing that the game makes use of intertextual references to the original Core Design* Tomb Raider *(1996) and popular culture archaeology in an effort to revise the original franchise's exploitative depiction of both Lara Croft and archaeological practice. Framed by a theoretical understanding of Orientalism (Said, 1979) and the constraints of symbolic order (Kristeva, 1986a) and the recognition that video games in general and the* Tomb Raider *franchise in specific are "games of empire" (Dyer-Witheford & de Peuter, 2009), it becomes clear that the 2013* Tomb Raider *ultimately fails to escape the constraints of imperial procedural semiotics.*

INTRODUCTION

In 1996, Core Design released *Tomb Raider*, a digital exploration-adventure role-playing game (RPG) featuring a treasure-hunting female protagonist named Lara Croft. By the early 2000s, Lara had been featured on more than 200 magazine covers, listed as one of the "Sexiest Women of the Year," and nominated as British Ambassador for Technology (Lancaster, 2004, p. 87). She had also been repeatedly lambasted as a digital sex object and as representative of the exploitation of native peoples in the name of archaeological discovery. In 2013, Crystal Dynamics "rebooted" the *Tomb Raider* franchise, redesigning the appearance, origins, and ideology of Lara Croft in order to reflect a more inclusive ethos. At its core, the franchise relies upon a set of Western cultural assumptions of superiority which manifest in ways categorized by cultural theorist Edward Said (1979) as "Orientalist." These practices—which appear in *Tomb Raider* games as exploration, combat, and collection mechanics—situate the franchise within a framework of "games of empire" (Dyer-Witheford &de Peuter, 2009), games which manifest in theme, gameplay, and marketing certain sociological codes explicitly associated with capitalist imperialism and conquest.

DOI: 10.4018/978-1-5225-0477-1.ch011

In order to adequately understand how a video game can be both supportive of and subversive toward an imperialist paradigm, it is important to first understand how paradigms come to have cultural meaning, how imperialism functions as a cultural force, how that force causes harm to those it oppresses, how games participate in an imperial paradigm, and, most importantly, how that paradigm makes resistance to its oppression all but impossible. Crystal Dynamics' 2013 reboot enters into this paradox of resistant complicity both consciously and—to an extent—critically through intertextual reference to its direct predecessors, as well as to objects and practices of colonial imperialism. The 2013 *Tomb Raider* deliberately engages with colonial (and post-colonial) criticism of hegemonic masculine imperialism in an attempt to refigure the series, and Lara herself, as a different kind of exploratory agent, more concerned with knowledge acquisition than exploitation or conquest. Yet despite significant revisions to Lara's backstory, the 2013 *Tomb Raider* remains trapped in an imperialist framework; in spite of its desire to escape its own intertextual past of oppressive colonial violence by producing a narrative centered around female-coded space and a capable female protagonist, the 2013 *Tomb Raider* is ultimately constrained by its own procedural imperialism, unable to fully escape its cultural past.

DEFINING GAMES AS ARTIFACTS OF EMPIRE

Games as Semiotic and Symbolic

In the twenty-first century, the globalization of cultural and material markets has produced a planet-wide lexicon of imperialism, an institutionalized system of signifiers, both linguistic and extra-linguistic, that articulates a hierarchical value-system based on an implicit presumption of Western superiority. Described by cultural theorist Julia Kristeva (1986b) as the "symbolic order," such a system "is determined by a set of signifying rules...a general social law" of social and institutional forces which establish and negotiate specific paradigms of authority and identity (p. 25). Put more simply, language both determines and is determined by social mores and conventions, ultimately coming to depict the hierarchical authority of the dominant social paradigm. For Kristeva (1986a), this symbolic order may be resisted by means of the semiotic chora, "a non-expressive totality formed by the drives and their stases in a motility that is as full of movement as it is regulated" (p. 93); the constraints of the imperial symbolic order (the rigidity of lexical communication) can only be subverted by means of the extra-linguistic. Yet games—composed of both lexical and mechanical components—reveal that extra-linguistic elements are just as subject to institutional oppressors as symbolic language.

By virtue of their complexity, games (analog and digital) both rely upon existing linguistic constructs and create new lexica of mechanical signifiers in the process of interacting with players. Games thus produce what Ian Bogost (2007) terms "procedural rhetoric": "the art of persuasion through rule-based representations and interactions rather than the spoken word, writing, images, or moving pictures" (p. ix). Procedural rhetoric structures both rules and gameplay, inhibiting players from transgressing boundaries while also providing the mechanics available to them, and is as functionally rigid as Kristeva's symbolic order.[1] Procedural rhetoric works by means of implicit rather than explicit persuasion; players interact with the design components of a game and are given feedback for those interactions which tell them how the game situates those actions relative to the rest of the gameworld. These rhetorics are inherently intertextual in the sense that they draw on established conventions of gaming, as well as linguistic and symbolic structures. Primary among these is the procedural economy of rewards in terms of experience points and avatar gear, which Edward Castronova (2005) explains "are incredibly powerful tools for shaping behavior" (p. 110), since, he continues, such procedural "mechanisms turn the synthetic world into a place where value can be assigned to anything, and behavior directed accordingly" (p. 111).

Play, as it appears in this study, has multiple meanings. First, and most obviously, is that "play" is the verb assigned to games. Second, following Johan Huizinga (1950) and Roger Caillois (2001), play is "a free and voluntary activity, a source of joy and amusement" (p. 6) which may be augmented by secondary purposes, such as income, social status, or education. Brian Sutton-Smith (2001) recognizes that "major forms of play are introduced and manipulated for their own benefit by the rulers of society," and that these forms of play can be manipulated by "the subordinate classes…to express their own hidden rhetorics of resistance or subversion" (p. 74). Play is thus voluntary activity undertaken for the purpose of deriving joy (qua entertainment) or satisfaction, and which may also seek to engage with, interrogate, or even undermine some component of the dominant socio-political paradigm. Kristeva uses the term "play" in a Derridean sense, in which "play" is "permitted by the lack or absence" of restrictions or boundaries (Derrida, 1978, p. 289), and "is the disruption of presence" (p. 292). In gaming, Caillois (2001) suggests, "The game consists of the need to find or continue at once a response *which is free within the limits set by the rules*. This latitude of the player, this margin accorded to his action is essential to the game and partly explains the pleasure which it excites" (p. 8). Caillois (2001) terms this free-form play within rules *paidia*. During digital gameplay, players are constrained by rules, but are still permitted to take actions which are not necessarily intended by the developer. This desire to enter non-useful areas is an example of choric *paidia* in which the player makes use of the game's procedural mechanics (jumping, mantling, etc.) in order to transgress the prescribed path. Lusory (or ludic) play— gameplay—includes both procedural play which takes place within the bounds of the game's presumed mechanics and *paidia* which takes place outside them. Highly linear games—like *Tomb Raider*—allow less space for this type of play, while open-world or "sandbox" games—like *Grand Theft Auto* (Rockstar, 2002) or *Skyrim* (Bethesda, 2011)—have more. This type of play, described by Huizinga (1950), is "irrational," "the direct opposite of seriousness," "a voluntary activity," and, most importantly, "it is free, is in fact freedom" (pp. 4, 5, 7, 8). *Paidia*, Kristevan/Derridian play, is thus a voluntary activity of freedom which also reacts against the procedural limitations of a paradigmatic system of oppression; games which permit or even encourage this type of play thus simultaneously embody and allow for the undermining of imperial ideology.

From a creator's perspective, "play" in the Kristevan/Derridean sense is more complex. In language, explains María Alfaro (1996), this play manifests as a "writer's efforts to detach him/herself from the work of previous authors as well as to proclaim his/her own creative space" (p. 270). In gaming, such creative play would thus be an attempt to simultaneously engage with and "detach from" the preexisting narrative and procedural rhetorics of extant games. In the case of Crystal Dynamics' 2013 *Tomb Raider*, such "play" forms a central part of the game's attempt to re-envision the central character of Lara Croft as a more intellectual and less exploitative (and less exploited) figure as the developers redesigned Lara's physique, her origins, and her motives for interacting with the artifacts in the gameworld. However, even given this "play" with the original franchise, the rebooted *Tomb Raider* series nevertheless remains constrained—as must any attempt at Kristevan/Derridean play—by the very narrative and procedural systems it is attempting to escape.

Games as Imperial Agents

As artifacts which are simultaneously both lusory and procedural, games (video or analog) possess the capacity to linguistically and mechanically reflect and/or critique imperial symbolic order, both as material objects purchased in a capitalist market and as cultural artifacts which perpetuate an imperial ethos through narrative, artistic, and procedural content.[2] In their 2009 study, *Games of Empire*, Nick Dyer-Witheford and Greig de Peuter state that "video games are paradigmatic media of Empire—planetary, militarized hypercapitalism—and of some of the forces presently challenging it" (p. xv, emphasis in original). But what does it mean to say that video games (primarily mass market or AAA games, like those in the *Tomb Raider* franchise) are "media of Empire"? Dyer-Witheford and de Peuter (2009) define "empire" as "governance by global capitalism" which incorporates specific "conditions of work, forms of subjectivity, and types of struggle" (p. xx); specifically, "the global capitalist ascendancy of the early twenty-first century, a system administered and policed by a consortium of competitively collaborative neoliberal states" which "occupies a strategic position because of its role in intellectually and affectively shaping subjectivities throughout other parts of the system" (p. xxiii). In short, "empire," in the twenty-first century, is a set of paradigmatic systems of intellectual and material (capitalistic) properties which structure a hierarchy of Western privilege and institutionalized oppression. Because they are constructed within this paradigm, most AAA games are necessarily inscribed by imperial discourse—whether they choose to embrace, reject, or remain ambivalent to it.

In terms of AAA titles like *Tomb Raider*, capitalist enterprise coerces games into an imperial framework, which Pierre Bourdieu (1991) suggests is an essential part of cultural production. The "global capitalism" to which Dyer-Witheford and de Peuter (2009) refer ensures that the markets with the highest purchase capacity—predominantly Western markets in Europe and the Americas—are those to which most video games cater. This Western market essentially demands to see itself in the heroic role; this provides an essential structure to the procedural components of most AAA titles in terms of the inclusion of combat, collection, exploration, and survival, all mechanics which are inherently imperial. These expectations become coded into the video game industry as natural components of gameplay, and preordain much of the imperialism inherent in most AAA games. In the case of *Tomb Raider*, the expansive franchise—including video games, graphic novels, action figures, living models, and films—is especially tied to the capitalist markets and the imperial framework which structures them.

To say, then, that games are agents of empire is to suggest that games participate in the dissemination and enforcement of these intellectual and material systems, whether intentionally or incidentally. Such participation, it must be recognized, is not unique to games; all media, whether popular, critical, artistic, political, or otherwise, are necessarily part of either promoting or resisting the discourse and functions of empire. In fact, it would be impossible for any such media not to participate—as either proponent or antagonist, or both—in imperial discourse. Yet at the same time that games participate in an imperial symbolic order, they also necessarily—because they are games—create space for play in both the lusory and paidian senses. In short, being part of the imperial symbolic order is the very thing which enables games to question that order; however, even though a game might attempt to escape its own oppressive hierarchy, the semiotic nature of games is permanently inextricable from imperial order.

Archaeology, Intertextuality, and Orientalism

Having established that games are artifacts of the imperial order bound to that order by procedural semiotics, it is important to consider the ramifications of this ludic imperialism. The procedural rhetoric of the *Tomb Raider* franchise (from 1996 to the present) contains a dominant strain of Western imperial order: the practice of archaeological exploration and exploitation. For Derrida (1978), archaeology—the practice of cataloguing historical events and artifacts—sits in direct opposition to play. Archaeology, he explains, "is an accomplice of this reduction of the structurality of structure and always attempts to conceive of structure on the basis of a full presence which is beyond play" (Derrida, 1978, p. 279). In other words, the purpose of archaeology is to reduce a thing (object, event, person, or belief) to a static totality in which and beyond which there is no uncertainty or flexibility. The work of archaeology is thus to take the unknown, mythic, or mysterious and delineate it, defining and bounding it into certainty. The process of collection and identification eliminates that which is playful by inscribing a use-value or purpose to an artifact, precluding it from the realm of lusory freedom.

For the majority of history from the fifteenth to the twenty-first centuries, archaeology has been predominantly practiced by Western civilizations, producing an ideological paradigm referred to by Said (1979) as "Orientalism." In essence, Orientalism defines 'Oriental' culture by means of the collection, cataloguing, and intertextual cross-referencing of physical and intellectual artifacts in order to create a sterile and static conception of what it meant (or means) to be 'Oriental.' This process of identification is also necessarily relational; the objects, practices, and people of the Orient come to be defined based on what they are not (which is to say, Western) rather than in their own terms, often tending toward dismissal; in a comparison to the West, the Orient appears inferior, lesser than, and therefore deserving of subjugation. Orientalism, continues Said (1979), results in the formation of a "corporate institution for dealing with the Orient—dealing with it by making statements about it, authorizing views of it, describing it, by teaching it, settling it, ruling over it" (p. 3). It is both the producer and product of Western archaeological imperialism in that it dictates not only the intertextual methodology by which the West approaches the East—cataloguing and collecting—but also the justification of these actions by presuming Oriental inferiority. In specific, the eighteenth and nineteenth century practice of archaeology produced highly problematic understandings of Asian and African cultures under the ostensible guise of "rescuing the Orient from the obscurity, alienation, and strangeness" of the East (Said, 1979, p. 121).

Although it is now the twenty-first century, Orientalism persists, surfacing in modern acts of cultural appropriation and misrepresentation, practices which continue to place "the Westerner in a whole series of possible relationships with the Orient without ever losing him the relative upper hand" (Said, 1979, p. 7), often as an unintended byproduct of the oppressive "autonomy of language" (Bourdieu, 1991, p. 41). The consequence of such an interaction reduces the complexity of the 'inferior' position, justifying archaeological imperialist practice:

In the system of knowledge about the Orient, the Orient is less a place than a topos, a set of references, a congeries of characteristics, that seems to have its origin in a quotation, or a fragment of a text, or a citation from someone's work on the Orient, or some bit of previous imagining, or an amalgam of all these. (Said, 1979, p. 177)

This archaeological process makes heavy use of the Kristevan symbolic order, eliminating the choric elements—the non-linguistic and non-representative—which open up space for play and resistance. Said's characterization focuses on the fact that Orientalism relies on *intertextuality*, in which an object specifically recalls a text: a quotation, a citation, a reference to a previous body of specifically Western texts which already claim to circumscribe the Orient. As such, Orientalism itself is inherently intertextual, relying on already extant understandings of what is "Other" or "Oriental" based on historical or fictionalized accounts which may or may not be based in fact.

Orientalism and archaeology as imperial practices rely specifically on the existence of "a space in which a potentially vast number of [such] relations coalesce" (Allen, 2000, p. 12), a framework of often undetermined "texts" which define the "East" as exotic, often tropical, uneducated, barbaric, and technologically un-advanced. These "texts" are presumptions and stereotypes easily recognizable to the Western general public and which form the basis for their contextualization of artifacts, cultures, and peoples of non-Western origin. Codified in popular culture works of fiction (literary and cinematic in particular), this intertextual system forms the basis for the imperial symbolic order's understanding of the "Orient," thus reducing it to a series of intertexts to be analyzed and circumscribed, to be understood, known, and thereby dominated. In essence, the practice of reducing a culture and society to the sum of its collectable artifacts minimizes its human complexity and eliminating its capacity for resistance and play. By entering into this discourse, works of popular culture may seek to perpetuate or undermine these existing paradigms by engaging with, replicating, or seeking to explode extant stereotypes. Modern revisionist works—such as J.M. Coetzee's *Foe* (1986), a retelling of Daniel Defoe's (1719)*Robinson Crusoe*—often attempt to undermine imperial authority by recontextualizing dominant narratives from native perspectives. These works, like Crystal Dynamics' 2013 reboot of the *Tomb Raider* franchise, often encounter the problem of falling into the same imperialist patterns as their predecessors, being (unintentionally) reshaped by the very paradigms they seek to question.

Feminized Colonial Space

One significant and frequent consequence of the Orientalist practice of categorization is a tendency to affiliate the East with various marginalized positions, as Said (1979) explains: "The Oriental was linked thus to elements in Western society (delinquents, the insane, women, the poor) having in common an identity best described as lamentably alien," a tendency which "also encouraged a peculiarly (not to say invidiously) male conception of the world" (p. 207). This penchant for feminization was produced in part because, particularly prior to the twentieth century, exploration and intellectual Orientalism (archaeology) were "an exclusively male province" (Said, 1979, p. 207). This 'natural' feminization of the Orient reproduced a Western-centric paradigm which enforced belief in the supremacy of the Christian, European, male intellect, thereby enabling imperial powers to justify the disparagement, exploitation, and even destruction of the cultures encountered during imperialist expansion as a part of their patriarchal duty.

By extension, explains Ella Shohat (1991), Orientalist practice led to a tradition of Western depictions in text and media that specifically characterized "the (non-European) land as a virgin coyly awaiting the touch of the colonizer," which also "implied that whole continents—Africa, the Americas, Asia and Australia—could only benefit from the emanation of colonial praxis" (p. 52). However, when the land or peoples were unable to be controlled, Shohat (1991) continues, the virginal image was inverted into "that of libidinous, wild femininity. The wilderness, 'no man's land,' is characterized as resistant, harsh and violent" (p. 55). Thus, colonial texts and images frequently "oscillate[] between these two master tropes, alternatively positing the colonized 'other' as blissfully ignorant, pure and welcoming as well as an uncontrollable savage, wild native whose chaotic hysteric presence requires the imposition of the law" (Shohat, 1991, p. 55). The trope of nature as female and therefore dangerous predates the expansionism of the seventeenth and eighteenth centuries, but was reinforced by imperial Orientalist practice and textual accounts (Domosh &Seager, 2001). The gendering of colonial space thus served to reinforce both Orientalist and sexist stereotypes, enabling and justifying the continued oppression of both female and non-European (and North American) perspectives.

The Colonization of Digital Worlds

The praxis of empire appears in the twenty-first century in digital gamespaces, with players frequently assuming the role of colonizer or conqueror. The vast majority of procedural mechanics focus on actions of empire and archaeology: exploring unknown space, claiming territory, collecting loot and resources, killing enemies (usually alien or Otherized). Often, gamespaces are explicitly colonial, unsettled territory (tropical islands, unpopulated medieval or fantasy landscapes, deep space), and the challenges faced by players are directly related to taming the gamespace's 'wildness.' Adele Bealer (2012) explains that "Successful gameplay demands that players read the gamescape" for procedural cues which dictate behavior (p. 28): a red reticule indicates an enemy; loot-glint identifies an object with which to interact. These procedural clues tell players how they should behave in the gamescape: reticules suggest the need for combat; loot glint indicates a collection mechanic; button prompts over non-player characters (NPCs) demand interaction. In many games, survival for the player-character through combat, evasion, collection, and/or puzzle-solving is a core component of gameplay; in these games, observes James Newman (2013), "What is really important to the player is staying alive… long enough to explore, conquer and colonize the space of the gameworld" (p. 110). The most basic player actions in many games are therefore inherently imperialist, whether or not the game's narrative context is overtly imperial. In a game of exploration-and-conquest, the rewards which a player earns for taking these actions—in terms of resources, narrative praise, or even ease of victory over enemies—reinforces the 'goodness' of such procedural actions and the player's relative (imperial) power over the subject-position of enemies and friendly NPCs. Even if the player is not explicitly occupying the territory (as in real-time-strategy games), the process of cataloging, collecting, and conquering replicates colonial praxis and thereby participates in imperialism, much as citizens of an imperial nation—like the United States—are complicit in the country's imperialist actions overseas.

In addition to these procedural cues, "the same gamescape deserves to be read critically for its social constructions and cultural assumptions" (Bealer, 2012, p. 28). These "constructions" and "assumptions" may be encoded in gameplay, but appear in the visual and auditory aesthetics of the gamespace, as well; a game's setting (time period, geographic location, etc.), musical score, character/voice acting, and artistic style, as well as overall genre (RPG, adventure, shooter, platformer, etc.) all contribute to the production of a game's "cultural assumptions." Similarly, Castronova (2005) explains that players entering digital space are "carrying their behavioral assumptions and attitudes with them. As a result, the valuation of things in cyberspace becomes enmeshed in the valuation of things outside cyberspace" (p. 147), a permeability of ideological conceptions that moves in both directions. As the medium of video games matures, these cultural assumptions also incorporate increasingly complex intertextual references. For instance, some games "bear arresting similarities to the New World travel narratives of sixteenth- and seventeenth-century voyages and explorers" (Newman, 2013, p. 109), featuring encounters with alien peoples and landscapes. Such intertextual references can be structural, as above; thematic, such as the essential fantasy theme of the *Warcraft* games (Blizzard, 1994); specific, such as when a character quotes Alfred Lord Tennyson's "Ulysses" in *Mass Effect* (BioWare, 2007); or tropic, as in *Halo* (Bungie, 2001), which Dyer-Witheford and de Peuter describe as "virtual cowboys and Indians, or Allies and Nazis, or any of the other us-against-them scenarios boys perennially enjoy" (p. 82). A series or franchise may also make intertextual reference to its predecessors, a frequent occurrence in series such as *Tomb Raider*.

AN ARCHAEOLOGY OF *TOMB RAIDER*

Origins: Core Design's *Tomb Raider* (1996)

The first game in the *Tomb Raider* franchise was released by Core Design in 1996, featuring Lara Croft, a female, British, aristocratic treasure-hunter. At the game's beginning, Lara is hired to track down a piece of an ancient and mysterious talisman, a job which leads her on a global chase through ruins, fighting enemies animal, human, and supernatural before defeating the final enemy—an ancient Atlantean—and saving humanity. Played from a third-person, over-the-shoulder perspective, the player controls Lara's movements during exploration and combat, collecting objects useful as resources or keys (such as a totem or amulet that may be used to open a door or solve a puzzle) and using her iconic dual pistols to shoot enemies. The game's popularity led to the production of twelve additional titles and rereleases prior to Crystal Dynamics' 2013 reboot. In addition, the franchise has spawned two major motion pictures (West, 2001; Bont, 2003) and several graphic novel series. Lara's notoriety as a figure has often been ascribed to her physical proportions and tight clothing, but much of the game's success relies on the popular culture image of archaeology from the 1980s and 1990s, famously captured in Steven Spielberg's *Indiana Jones* series (1981-1989). As such, the 2013 reboot of the series always already contains explicit intertextual reference to its own archaeological history as a game.

Tomb Raider's original concept "was for a treasure-hunting adventure set in the ruins of ancient Egypt" (Anderson & Levene, 2012, p. 238), drawing from glamorized popular culture archaeological tropes. According to Core Design's director, Jeremy Heath-Smith, *Tomb Raider*'s protagonist "did look like Indiana Jones, and I said, 'You must be insane, we'll get sued from here to kingdom come!'" (Anderson & Levene, 2012, p. 239). Designer Toby Gard had already considered a female protagonist, but "The rules at the time were: if you're going to make a game, make sure the main character is male and make sure he's American" (Anderson & Levene, 2012, p. 239), a practice which reinforced games' patriarchal imperialism. Instead, Gard decided "the lead character [would be] female and as British as I can make her" (Anderson & Levene, 2012, p. 239). Although Heath-Smith was initially skeptical, he allowed the project to proceed (Deuber-Mankowsky, 2001).

Lara's original biography—contained in the game's manual—reads as follows:

Lara Croft, daughter of Lord Henshingly Croft, was raised to be an aristocrat from birth. After attending finishing school at the age of 21, Lara's marriage into wealth had seemed assured, but on her way home from a skiing trip her chartered plane had crashed deep in the heart of the Himalayas. The only survivor, Lara learned how to depend on her wits to stay alive in hostile conditions a world away from her sheltered upbringing. 2 weeks later when she walked into the village of Tokakeriby her experiences had had a profound effect on her. Unable to stand the claustrophobic suffocating atmosphere of upper-class British society, she realised that she was only truly alive when she was travelling alone. Over the 8 following years she acquired an intimate knowledge of ancient civilisations across the globe. Her family soon disowned their prodigal daughter, and she turned to writing to fund her trips. Famed for discovering several ancient sites of profound archaeological interest she made a name for herself by publishing travel books and detailed journals of her exploits. (Core Design, 1996b, p. 3)

As Clauda Breger (2008) observes, Lara's interest in "archaeology is thus presented as a subversive displacement of the traditional Indian adventures of privileged British travelers" (p. 47), especially since Lara's adventures in the 1996 *Tomb Raider* began in Calcutta (Core Design, 1996a). In essence, Lara's origins rely heavily on an intertextual relationship to historical British Imperialism, as well as the popular American cultural trope of the adventuring archaeologist, both of which firmly situate Lara as the embodiment of empire.

Yet, as Breger (2008) notes, Lara's imperial status is mitigated, specifically by her gender, as well as her refusal, in the game's original fiction, to be constrained by aristocratic heteronormativity. Despite this, Lara's rebellion against social roles—both within the game's fiction and as Gard's against-type creation—is rendered acceptable by her visual appearance of extreme femininity, widely criticized by feminists.[3] Kurt Lancaster (2004) explains that Lara's visual appearance mixed with her pursuit of masculine pastimes, "rather than challenging masculine dominance, feeds it and makes this dominance acceptable through feminine curves, seductive lips, and over-sized eyes" (p. 88). Along similar lines, Diane Carr (2002) suggests that while Lara's "physicality and gender invite objectification, yet she operates as a perpetrating and penetrative subject within the narrative" (p. 175). Thus, Lara has historically been a figure of both sexual objectification and subjective agency, imperialism and defiance, a duality which continues in the 2013 reboot.

A Critical Reboot: Crystal Dynamics' 2013 *Tomb Raider*

In the 2013 reboot of the franchise, Lara has been physically and narratively recrafted in an attempt to reframe her story in a way that is less imperialist, more sympathetic, and more socially critical than her earlier incarnation. Her appearance—in particular, her "feminine curves"—has been normalized, her clothing made less revealing and more practical. While she is still unquestionably British, the narrative of an aristocratic marriage, plane crash in the Himalayas, and disownment has been replaced with a more educated background and long-deceased but beloved parents.[4] Furthermore, the Lara Croft of the 2013 *Tomb Raider* does not have extensive treasure-hunting experience, and at one point even ironically says "I hate tombs" (Crystal Dynamics, 2013). The new Lara has a more intellectual motive for her explorations, as she and archaeologist Dr. James Whitman are leading a research team in search of a lost civilization, the most obvious attempt made by the game to escape the more exploitative imperialism of the original franchise's "treasure hunter" Lara. Although the game does not explicitly give Lara's level of education, it does contain a photograph of Lara and her friend Sam (Samantha Nishimura) in academic regalia from University College London, indicating that Lara is an academically trained archaeologist.[5] These explicit alterations—which are themselves intertextual references to the 'original' Lara Croft—seek to resituate the 2013 *Tomb Raider* as distinct from its predecessors, a new version of the popular culture archaeologist who has respect for and knowledge about the artifacts she collects rather than viewing them solely as sources of financial gain. Yet despite this, the 2013 Lara Croft is necessarily accompanied by her own character history; she is always an allusion to her own former self, an intertext the game can never fully escape (nor does it truly wish to—after all, the success of the original franchise is something upon which Crystal Dynamics undoubtedly wishes to capitalize).

In the 2013 *Tomb Raider*, Lara is a leader of an expedition on the ship *Endurance* to find the lost ancient Japanese kingdom of Yamatai.[6] Early in the game, Whitman turns to Lara and exclaims that finding Yamatai is "like finding Atlantis!" (Crystal Dynamics, 2013), an explicit reference to the 1996 game in which the final villain is an Atlantean (Core Design, 1996a). When the ship is caught in a storm and wrecks on a reef, Lara and her companions are trapped on the island. Over the course of the game, Lara discovers that it is impossible to escape due to the mystical power of Himiko, a supernatural being whose soul has been trapped on the island. Himiko herself alludes to the final boss of the original 1996 game, an ancient Atlantean named Natla, and Lara's quest to destroy her echoes the original game's quest to destroy Natla, whose soul was also trapped (Core Design, 1996a). Throughout the game, Lara must explore various locations around the island, scavenge resources, build and improve tools and weapons, solve puzzles, collect or destroy artifacts, and defeat enemies. As such, the procedural actions available to the 2013 Lara provide intertextual (inter-procedural?) links to those of her 1996 predecessor. However, in the 2013 *Tomb Raider*, Lara is confined to a solitary island rather than roaming the world, a geographic restriction that attempts to reverse the earlier trope of Lara-as-colonizer but ultimately fails to separate her from her imperial origins.

Yamatai itself embodies a geography borrowed from Western popular culture, the type of space to which Gregory Woods (1995) refers as a "fantasy island":

Typically, the island refuge from tempest (or, latterly, from nuclear war) includes the following physical features: a coral reef which, once crossed without mishap, offers shelter from the direct force of the ocean and abundant fishing grounds; a calm and shallow lagoon; a curved, sandy beach (where the castaway first comes round from an exhausted sleep after fighting to survive the shipwreck, and where various useful artefacts are also washed ashore); at either end of the beach, rocks;…thick jungle, well provided with fruit trees; a clearing in which primitive peoples have erected, or carved in rock, an inelegant idol or fetish to which, at certain phases of the moon, they return to sacrifice human beings (this place is usually on 'the other side' of the island, and it is on that 'other' side that the savages/cannibals beach their outriggers);…and, of course, a hill or mountain on which laboriously to build a signal bonfire which, at the crucial moment when a schooner is passing, will have been allowed to die out or will not have been lit at all. (p. 127)

Writing before the release of the original *Tomb Raider*, Woods here describes many of the elements used in Crystal Dynamics' 2013 reboot, which appear in colonial texts from early narrative accounts of voyages to the New World—such as the accounts of the wreckage of the *Sea Venture* in Bermuda (Purchas, 1625), which provided the source for William Shakespeare's *The Tempest* (1611)—to modern films and television series such as *Cast Away* (Zemeckis, 2000) and *Lost* (Abrams et al, 2004-2010), the most influential of which is undoubtedly Defoe's (1719)*Robinson Crusoe*. When Lara first washes ashore in the 2013 *Tomb Raider*, she and her companions are on a sandy beach, a location to which they will return later in the game. The jungle of Yamatai provides fruit trees (a source of health for Lara), as well as game, and the rivers and waterfalls are plentiful. Instead of a hill, Yamatai has a mountain retreat with a radio tower which Lara must repair and which ultimately fails to secure aid. Interestingly, in *Tomb Raider* the "primitives" are Westerners (the Solarii) corrupted by their participation in the cult of the Sun

Queen, to whom they sacrifice other stranded travelers. Although the transposition of Western cultists for "primitive peoples" inverts the standard Orientalist trope, it ultimately cannot assuage the game's inherent imperialism, as Lara—as the game's imperial hero—still must conquer both "primitives" (Solarii) and wild island (Himiko-qua-Yamatai) in order to return to civilization. Crystal Dynamics' Yamatai, while conforming to many of the elements described above, is a previously-settled space, and part of the player's mission (as Lara) is to destroy an earlier imperial power which has corrupted the natural forces of the island. In addition, Lara's motivation—intellectual curiosity and altruism rather than capitalist profit—is designed to separate her from more traditional colonial narratives of conquest and riches.

The 2013 reboot does its best to attempt to escape—or at least undermine—heavy-handed imperialism by juxtaposing Lara against the destructive Solarii, as well as against the earlier version of herself. After she rescues Conrad Roth from wolves, he attempts to comfort Lara by telling her she "can do it," because "After all, you're a Croft" (Crystal Dynamics, 2013), a remark which is immediately recognizable as a reference to the earlier franchise titles and the old Lara's capabilities, including a penchant for encountering and killing wolves (Core Design, 1996a). However, Lara rejects the allusion, saying "I don't think I'm that kind of Croft" (Crystal Dynamics, 2013), revealing a desire on the part of the game's creators to escape at least some of the tropes of the earlier series. Yet it is evident to both creators and players that Lara Croft cannot help but be Lara Croft, as Roth rejoins "Sure you are. You just don't know it yet" (Crystal Dynamics, 2013). Although this exchange, on the surface, is a discussion about how Lara does—or does not—take after her father, the intertextuality of the game as a whole demonstrates that it is equally about to what extent this new Lara will repeat or revise her 1996 predecessor. The new professional-archaeologist-Lara is interested in pursuing goals which are not explicitly capitalist in nature: she explores Yamatai to ensure her own survival, to rescue her friends (another new narrative addition), and to unearth knowledge, aligning her more with the popular culture archaeologist-hero Indiana Jones than her own former incarnation. Yet in spite of these changes, Lara is first and foremost an explorer, a "tomb raider" who invades "wild" spaces and plunders them for objects of interest, use-value, and wealth, removing these artifacts from their native context and cataloguing them in Orientalist praxis.

Procedural Orientalism and Historical Inner-Texts

In the 2013 *Tomb Raider*, Crystal Dynamics has included a new class of collectable objects, called Relics, which provide no mechanical gameplay advantage; instead, they exist as an 'inner-textual' archaeological record of the many cultures which occupied Yamatai over the centuries. In addition, the act of collection serves as an example of procedurality which mechanically situates the player-qua-Lara within an Orientalist framework. When the player collects these objects—herbs, fans, dog-tags, and other miscellany—Lara offers information about them: when they were made, how they were used, what they are made of, to whom they likely belonged. Interestingly, the majority of Relics are based on actual artifacts, many of them modeled after objects currently in Western museums, such as the "Ban Chiang Pottery" vase, whose original model is held in the Krannert Art Museum (McGuire, 2013a). In part, the inclusion of these Relics is an attempt to re-humanize the absent 'natives' and non-native colonizers of the gamescape through the introduction of personal objects, thereby encouraging players to consider the impact of war and colonial occupation.

For example, in the Coastal Forest, Lara can find a Relic labeled "Hannya Mask" (Crystal Dynamics, 2013). When the player picks up the Relic, the game shifts to the Relic menu, and Lara's voice says,

"This traditional Noh mask represents a hateful woman in the guise of a demon" (Crystal Dynamics, 2013). If the player rotates it to examine it further, Lara reveals more information: "There are traces of white paint on the inside. Whoever used this mask was of noble birth" (Crystal Dynamics, 2013). In gameplay terms, the mask serves no purpose; it does not give Lara additional health or act as a weapon or resource. Narratively and culturally, however, the mask is more interesting. Culturally, the mask makes reference to an entire set of intertexts: Noh drama, the cultural demonization of women, Western appropriation of Eastern aesthetic objects, and even Western understandings of demonology. As an 'inner-text,' although it does not directly help Lara to determine the answer to a puzzle or provide information necessary to forward progress, the mask foreshadows the game's narrative conclusion: the female demon alludes—unbeknownst to Lara or a first-time player—to Himiko's nobility and demonic nature.

In addition to Relics, there are other artifacts scattered around the island which provide little gameplay advantage: totems, posters, mines, mushrooms, cairns, and flags which Lara must destroy to accomplish quests; journals and diary entries which provide narrative explanations for the events on the island from ancient Yamatai to the present; video and audio journals from the crew of the *Endurance* which provide backstory; and—of course—ancient tombs which Lara must "raid" in order to find maps that reveal the locations of the collectible items. In addition, Lara collects weapons (a bow and firearms), salvaged scrap in order to upgrade her weapons and pickaxe, food (fruit and game, which she has to kill), and bandaging supplies. As in the 1996 *Tomb Raider*, these latter items are all required for Lara's survival; she must kill wolves and Solarii, heal damage taken from falls or injuries, and gather sustenance. Unlike her 1996 predecessor, however, this Lara is uninterested in wealth; her whole purpose is the survival of herself and her companions, a significant shift in Crystal Dynamics' attempt to reframe the franchise in opposition to—or at least not in support of—imperialism.

Altering Lara: Altruism, Orientalism, and a New Kind of "Raiding"

The addition of fellow explorers is one of the key differences between Crystal Dynamics' 2013 *Tomb Raider* and the earlier franchise. Instead of a 'lone-wolf' treasure-hunter, the 2013 Lara Croft sets out not only to survive, but to rescue those for whom she feels responsible, as she explains to Roth as she prepares to go into the Solarii Fortress:

Lara: *I'm going in.*
Roth: *Are you sure about this, Lara?*
Lara: *I'll get them. I'll come back. I promise.* (Crystal Dynamics, 2013)

This initiates a quest entitled "No One Left Behind," requiring her to rescue the rest of the surviving *Endurance* crew (Crystal Dynamics, 2013).[7] The desire to rescue her companions and escape Yamatai provides the impetus for Lara's actions throughout the game.

In the 2013 *Tomb Raider*, Whitman is the quintessential popular culture archaeologist, white, male, and American—an incompetent version of Indiana Jones. Furthermore, the 2013 *Tomb Raider* repeatedly characterizes Whitman as a capitalistic imperialist with little respect for the cultures he studies beyond their fiscal value. The game situates him as Lara's foil and opposition—the "bad" version of her character type which Lara (and the player) struggles to undermine. Most of the player's information about Whitman comes from Sam's video journals, the first of which introduces him as a celebrity archaeologist when Grim asks him, "When were you last in the field without a tv crew behind you?" (Crystal Dynamics, 2013). Even after Whitman has been captured by the Solarii, he remains staunchly capitalistic, as Lara finds a journal ("Whitman: My Great Discovery") in which Whitman announces that he will be able to make "at least two documentaries" about the Solarii, "Maybe even a series!" and Lara remarks to herself that "His obsession with fame and fortune has consumed him" (Crystal Dynamics, 2013). Whitman's failure to find Yamatai on his own, in addition to his obsession with money and fame, illustrates the inadequacy of the popular culture trope of the treasure-hunter, and his opposition to Lara—who is more intellectual and less mercenary—argues against the kind of imperialist exploitation that formed the central premise of the earlier *Tomb Raider* franchise and which provides the foundation of American popular culture archaeology. Lara's interest, even at the very end of the game, is intellectual, as she says "the line between our myths and truth is fragile and blurry. I need to find answers... I must understand" (Crystal Dynamics, 2013), the developers' attempt to show the player the importance of intellectual over capitalist enterprise. Yet despite Lara's intellectual curiosity and good intentions, she nevertheless remains an agent of imperialism, and the game's depictions of both Lara and Yamatai only reinforce colonial stereotypes.

Remapping Conquest: Yamatai as Orientalized Space

However, it is her more metaphoric relationship to Himiko-qua-Yamatai that reveals the game's failure to separate Lara and the new *Tomb Raider* from systemic imperial oppression. As Said (1979) suggests, Oriental spaces are often affiliated with the feminine and insane, and, as Shohat (1991) explains, this feminized wilderness is characterized in imperial discourse as either virginal or libidinous. The first view the player has of Yamatai—after the shipwreck and Lara's escape from a site of human sacrifice in a cave—is aesthetically designed to produce awe and wonder: a land- and sea-scape dotted with the wreckage of airplanes and ships, covered in lush greenery, circling birds, and sunlight which forms a haloed rainbow, which also invokes the trope of the tropical "fantasy island." In this first view are both elements of Orientalized space: both aesthetic beauty and danger, untouched virginal nature and threatening wilderness.

In addition to its wild spaces, Yamatai is home to ruins from the Neolithic period through the twentieth century, demonstrated by the inter- and inner-textual Relics Lara finds: the oldest is a "Kansu Burial Urn" (Crystal Dynamics, 2013), which, Kelly McGuire (2013b) explains, is based on a Banshan-style earthenware jar dated to 2600-2300 BCE. The historical Yamatai itself dates to early in the third century, ending with Himiko's death circa 248 CE ("Dig in Nara," 2009), although *Tomb Raider* does not explicitly explain this. The inclusion of these artifacts lends more legitimacy to Lara's exploration in intellectual terms, as most icons of popular culture archaeology—such as Indiana Jones—do not take the time to explain the historical significance of their "raids" (beyond, perhaps, the central artifact, such as the Ark of the Covenant or Holy Grail).[8] The inclusion of these intertextual references lends more academic legitimacy to Lara's actions, attempting to remove them from a predominantly capitalist paradigm.

In addition to ancient artifacts, Yamatai also contains archaeological evidence of colonial visitors throughout the early modern and modern eras, including twelfth century Japan, thirteenth and fourteenth century China, Edo Japan, early modern Portugal, nineteenth century Europe and Asia, and twentieth-century soldiers and civilians from Japan, Germany, England, and the United States. The presence of these imperial powers in Yamatai reminds the player of the harmful cycle of oppression and rebellion characteristic of colonized nations, particularly during times of war, while also mitigating Lara's culpability as an imperialist. Aesthetically, the game makes the repeated failure of colonial power visible through the ways in which nature has reclaimed most of these ruins; the ancient villages remain largely in harmony with their surroundings, while bunkers and other modern facilities are beginning to crumble, have flooded, are missing pieces of their floors and roofs, or are otherwise damaged by the effects of storm and sea.

In addition to its history of failed colonization, Yamatai is a site of supernatural power, yet another element ascribed to Oriental space in Western imperial tradition. Before Lara reaches the Coastal Forest, she finds a soldier's diary ("Solder: On Stalkers") which explains that something on the island is killing his companions: he says that Oni, "restless, evil spirits…live in the old places of this island," and that "the entire island is a graveyard. It's only a matter of time, the Oni will come for us" (Crystal Dynamics, 2013). This association of the island's 'natives' with the demonic—Himiko, the Oni, and the Stormguard—perpetuates the (specifically Western Christian) Orientalist perspective that native peoples and cultures are superstitious and even diabolical, deserving of subjugation or destruction. Himiko herself is described early in the game by Sam as "beautiful, but also ruthless and powerful," with "shamanic powers" (Crystal Dynamics, 2013), the embodiment of the dangerous feminine Other which threatens not only the island, but also the civilized world. This viewpoint is reiterated through a later reference to Nazi Germany when Lara finds another journal ("Scientist: Secret Project") which explains that the Axis sent a team to Yamatai to study the storms: "The task of identifying the source of the storms will be long and arduous, but if we succeed in our mission here, our victory in this war will be certain" (Crystal Dynamics, 2013). Associating Himiko and the Stormguard with Nazi Germany explicitly marks the island's 'original' inhabitants as demonic, evil, and worthy of destruction.[9] Associating Himiko with the failure of imperial forces to subjugate Yamatai thus valorizes (whether intentionally or not) colonial occupation.

Instead of being depicted as a virginal paradise, Yamatai is therefore depicted as a prison, enacting a kind of reverse colonialism, trapping and subsuming the colonizers into its own 'native' culture. The Solarii, in particular, are evidence of this reverse-colonization process, acting as both victims and colonizers, a paradoxical occupying force oppressed by the magic of Yamatai. Mathias explains to the Solarii that "Out in the world, we are nothing. But here… here we are the Solarii, the Sun Queen's children" (Crystal Dynamics, 2013), an assertion which echoes those made by colonial authorities in places like Trinidad, South Africa, India, and the Bahamas during the height of imperial Britain (Shaw, 2013). By implication, of course, the Solarii are seen by the player—who, after all, is likely to be a Westerner of enough privilege to be able to afford the gaming system upon which *Tomb Raider* is played—as social, cultural, and psychological inferiors, an image of inadequacy reinforced by the violence of their actions, the crudeness of their language, and the disarray of the spaces they occupy.

Despite its natural aesthetic beauty, then, Yamatai (and Himiko, the Stormguard, and the Solarii) becomes Lara's (and the player's) enemy, and the game's final goal is to destroy Himiko in order to save Sam, stop the storms, and escape the island. During the final confrontation with Himiko, the lightning from Himiko's storm and the giant Stormguard attack both Lara and the Solarii indiscriminately, helping to justify Himiko's destruction and undermining any respect which the player might have had for the 'native' space of Yamatai. Once Lara defeats the Solarii and Stormguard, she rushes to the ritual altar, stealing two pistols which she uses to kill Mathias, assuming the iconic dual-pistol-wielding stance of Lara Croft from the earlier franchise (Core Design, 1996a). Lara then kills Himiko (with a stake to the heart), and the storm clears as Lara helps Sam back to the boat, where Reyes and Jonah (the only other survivors of the *Endurance*) are waiting.[10]

The final cinematic of the game shows the boat leaving the island, the sun setting in the West as they sail toward it and away from the Orientalized space of Yamatai. In the final moments of the game, Lara assumes an identity very similar to that of her 1996 predecessor, a survivalist who has lost most of those close to her in a horrific accident (a shipwreck rather than a plane crash), and whose experiences in the untamed wilderness have made her a hardened explorer who will return to continue her Orientalist explorations (to the lost city of Kitezh in Siberia) in *Rise of the Tomb Raider* (Crystal Dynamics, 2015). Ultimately, neither *Rise of the Tomb Raider* nor the end of *Tomb Raider* address the problematic fate of Yamatai itself.[11] The island went functionally undiscovered for centuries due to the protection afforded it by Himiko's magic; with Himiko destroyed, the island is once more vulnerable to the exploitation of imperial forces, whether mercantile, mercenary, or archaeological. In short, by destroying Himiko, Lara has enabled the destruction of centuries of historical and cultural artifacts, a problem with which she appears entirely (and perhaps justifiably) unconcerned.

CONCLUSION

At its conclusion, then, the 2013 *Tomb Raider*, despite its attempts to mitigate the clear imperialism of its predecessors, has succeeded only in rebuilding the very same Lara Croft which it sought to revise. By the end of the game, Lara has assumed nearly the same imperial identity as her predecessor, having pillaged the ruins of Yamatai for valuables which she then used to destroy the island's 'native' culture. In providing justification for these actions, the game directly undermines its own attempts to humanize the peoples—both native and colonial—who occupied Yamatai, ultimately subsuming a history of colonial struggle beneath Lara's imperialist archaeological conquest. Thus, despite its attempts to alter Lara's original identity as a "tomb raider" in the popular culture archaeological tradition of Indiana Jones by elevating her acquisitive practices to the level of intellectual archaeological pursuit, Crystal Dynamics' 2013 *Tomb Raider* is ultimately constrained by its own inter- and (especially) inner-texts, and can only demonstrate the impossibility of fully escaping the procedural semiotics of empire.

REFERENCES

Abrams, J., Lieber, J., & Lindelof, D. (2004-2010). *Lost*. ABC.

Alfaro, M. J. M. (1996). Intertextuality: Origins and Development of the Concept. *Atlantis*, *18*(1/2), 268–285.

Allen, G. (2000). Intertextuality. London, UK: Routledge. Retrieved from http://search.ebscohost.com/login.aspx?direct=true&db=nlebk&AN=62876&site=ehost-live

Anderson, M., & Levene, R. (2012). *Grand thieves & tomb raiders: How British video games conquered the world*. London, UK: Aurum Press Ltd.

Angus Grimaldi. (n.d.). Retrieved July 21, 2015, from http://tombraider.wikia.com/wiki/Angus_Grimaldi

Bealer, A. H. (2012). Eco-performance in the digital RPG gamescape. In *Dungeons, dragons, and digital denizens: The digital role-playing game* (Vol. 1, pp. 27–47). New York, NY: The Continuum International Publishing Group.

Bethesda Game Studios. (2011). *Skyrim: The elder scrolls V* [Xbox 360]. Bethesda, MD: Bethesda Softworks.

BioWare. (2007). *Mass effect* [Xbox 360]. Edmonton: Electronic Arts.

Blizzard Entertainment. (1994). *Warcraft: Orcs & humans* [PC]. Irvine, CA: Activision Blizzard.

Bogost, I. (2010). *Persuasive games: The expressive power of videogames*. Cambridge, MA: The MIT Press.

Bourdieu, P. (1991). *Language and symbolic power* (J. B. Thompson, Trans.). Cambridge, MA: Harvard University Press.

Breger, C. (2008). Digital digs, or Lara Croft replaying Indiana Jones: Archaeological tropes and "colonial loops" in new media narrative. *Aether: The Journal of Media Geography, II*, 41–60.

Bungie. (2001). *Halo: Combat evolved* [Xbox]. Bellevue, WA: Microsoft Game Studios.

Caillois, R. (2001). Man, play and games. (M. Barash, Trans.) (Reprint, 1961). Urbana, IL: University of Illinois Press.

Carr, D. (2002). Playing with Lara. In G. King & T. Krzywinska (Eds.), *ScreenPlay: Cinema/videogames/interfaces* (pp. 171–180). London, UK: Wallflower Press.

Castronova, E. (2005). *Synthetic worlds: The business and culture of online games*. Chicago, IL: The University of Chicago Press.

Champion, E. (2004). Indiana Jones and the joystick of doom: Understanding the past via computer games. *Traffic (Copenhagen, Denmark), 5*, 47–65.

Coetzee, J. M. (1986). *Foe*. South Africa: Raven Press.

Core Design. (1996a). *Tomb raider* [PC]. London, UK: Eidos Interactive, Square Enix.

Core Design. (1996b). *Tomb raider: PC manual*. London, UK: Eidos Interactive.

Crystal Dynamics. (2013). *Tomb raider* [XBox 360]. San Francisco, CA: Square Enix.

Crystal Dynamics. (2015). *Rise of the tomb raider* [XBox 360/One]. San Francisco, CA: Square Enix.

de Bont, J. (2003). *Lara Croft tomb raider: The cradle of life*. Action, Adventure, Fantasy.

Defoe, D. (1719, modern edition published 2003). Robinson Crusoe (reprint). London, UK: Penguin Classics.

Derrida, J. (1978). Structure, sign, and play in the discourse of the human sciences. In *Writing and difference* (A. Bass, Trans.). (pp. 278–294). Chicago, IL: The University of Chicago Press.

Derrida, J. (1982). Différance. In *Margins of philosophy* (pp. 1–27). Chicago, IL: University of Chicago Press.

Deuber-Mankowsky, A. (2005). Lara Croft: Cyber heroine. (D. J. Bonfiglio, Trans.) (English Translation (German, 2001), Vol. 14). Minneapolis, MN: University of Minnesota Press.

Dig in Nara, not Kyushu, yields palatial ruins possibly of Himiko. (2009, November 12). *The Japan Times Online*. Retrieved July 22, 2015, from http://search.japantimes.co.jp/news/2009/11/12/news/dig-in-nara-not-kyushu-yields-palatial-ruins-possibly-of-himiko/

Domosh, M., & Seager, J. (2001). *Putting women in place: Feminist geographers make sense of the world*. New York, NY: The Guilford Press.

Dyer-Witheford, N., & de Peuter, G. (2009). *Games of empire: Global capitalism and video games*. Minneapolis, MN: University of Minnesota Press.

Homuda-wake (Ojin). (1994). The starting point of Yamato Wa. In *Peakche of Korea and the origin of Yamato Japan* (pp. 45–51). Seoul, South Korea: Kudara International.

Huizinga, J. (1955). *Homo ludens: A study of the play-element in culture*. Boston, MA: Beacon Press.

Jonah Maiava. (n.d.). Retrieved July 21, 2015, from http://tombraider.wikia.com/wiki/Jonah_Maiava

Kristeva, J. (1986a). Revolution in poetic language. In T. Moi (Ed.), *The Kristeva reader* (M. Waller, Trans.). (pp. 89–136). New York, NY: Columbia University Press.

Kristeva, J. (1986b). The system and the speaking subject. In T. Moi (Ed.), *The Kristeva reader* (A. Jardine, T. Gora, & L. S. Roudiez, Trans.). (pp. 24–33). New York, NY: Columbia University Press.

Lancaster, K. (2004). Lara Croft: The ultimate young adventure girl or the unending media desire for models, sex, and fantasy. *Performing Arts Journal, 78*, 87–97.

Lara Croft (Rise Timeline). (n.d.). Retrieved July 18, 2015, from http://tombraider.wikia.com/wiki/Lara_Croft_(Rise_Timeline)

McGuire, K. J. (2013a, April 15). Arte-factual: Ban Chiang pottery (*Tomb raider 2013*). *The Archaeology of Tomb Raider*. Retrieved July 22, 2015, from http://archaeologyoftombraider.com/2013/04/15/arte-factual-tomb-raider-2013-ban-chiang-pottery/

McGuire, K. J. (2013b, July 10). Arte-factual: Kansu burial urn (*Tomb raider 2013*). *The Archaeology of Tomb Raider*. Retrieved July 22, 2015, from http://archaeologyoftombraider.com/2013/07/10/arte-factual-tomb-raider-2013-kansu-burial-urn/

Newman, J. (2013). *Videogames* (2nd ed.). London, UK: Routledge.

Purchas, S. (1625). *Hakluytus posthumus or Purchas his pilgrimes*. Stansby for H. Fetherstone.

Rockstar North, R. G. (2002). *Grand theft auto: Vice city* [Xbox]. Edinburgh, Scotland: Take-Two Interactive.

Said, E. W. (1994). *Orientalism (Reprint 1979)*. New York, NY: Vintage.

Samantha Nishimura. (n.d.). Retrieved July 21, 2015, from http://tombraider.wikia.com/wiki/Samantha_Nishimura

Shakespeare, W. (1611, modern edition published 2003). The tempest. (V. M. Vaughan & A. T. Vaughan, Eds.). London, UK: Thomson Learning.

Shaw, J. (2013). *Everyday life in the early English Caribbean: Irish, Africans, and the construction of difference*. Athens, GA: University of Georgia Press.

Shohat, E. (1991). Imaging terra incognita: The disciplinary gaze of empire. *Public Culture*, *3*(2), 41–70. doi:10.1215/08992363-3-2-41

Spielberg, S. (1981). *Raiders of the lost ark*. Paramount Pictures.

Spielberg, S. (1989). *Indiana Jones and the last crusade*. Paramount Pictures.

Sutton-Smith, B. (2001). *The ambiguity of play* (2nd ed.). Cambridge, MA: Harvard University Press.

West, S. (2001). *Lara Croft: Tomb raider*. Action, Adventure, Fantasy.

Woods, G. (1995). Fantasy islands: Popular topographies of marooned masculinity. In D. Bell & G. Valentine (Eds.), *Mapping desire: Geographies of sexualities* (pp. 126–148). London, UK: Routledge.

Zemeckis, R. (2000). *Cast away*. Action, 20th Century Fox.

KEY TERMS AND DEFINITIONS

Chora: Formulated by Julia Kristeva, the chora is a space of non-linguistic expression which serves as a counterpoint to the ordered language and rules of the symbolic order.

Derridean Play: Formulated by Jacques Derrida, this definition of play is movement outside of prescribed rules and boundaries, typically subversive in nature.

Gamescape: The digital setting, including art, music, sound, narrative, and interactive options, in which a video game takes place and with which the player interacts via the player-character or avatar.

Imperialism: The oppressive use of hierarchical systems of power in order to control and subjugate geographical, cultural, and social spaces and peoples, typically enacted through the manipulation of social mores, economics, religion, and/or military force.

Inner-text: A textual artifact or object contained within a larger text which makes reference or operates allusively within the larger text.

Intertext: A textual artifact or object which makes reference either explicitly or implicitly to another textual artifact or object external to itself, often relying upon specific complex social or cultural codes in order to imbue meaning.

Lusory Play: Free action. This is the conventional type of play (as opposed to "Derridean Play," above) in which adults and children engage when acting within a game or using a toy.

Mechanics: The actions designed into gameplay, such as "shooting," "collecting," or "running."

Orientalism: Formulated by Edward Said, Orientalism describes a set of praxis used by the Occident (Western culture) in its engagement with the Orient (Eastern or 'native' culture) characterized by exploration, exploitation, collection, categorization, and textual cross-referencing, and which produces a hierarchical relationship in which the Occident is defined as superior to the Orient.

Paidia: Free play within the constraints of recorded rules, formulated by Roger Caillois.

Procedural Rhetoric: A set of signifiers which are coded into games (specifically, video games) as rules and gameplay mechanics (see "Mechanics," above) which often have particular social and cultural valences.

Semiotics: A field of study which articulates the relationship between objects and their linguistic signifiers (words, images, pictograms).

Symbolic Order: Used by Julia Kristeva as a term encompassing the systemic rules of language (see "Semiotics," above), and which includes an understanding that the symbolic order is characteristic of a masculine-dominated imperial hierarchy.

ENDNOTES

[1]   Certainly, it is possible to cheat in conventional table-top games and to hack video games in order to violate these rules. More interesting, however, are the ways in which players go against the procedural "recommendations" of the game while remaining within its rules.

[2]   For the sake of this specific study, the types of video games to which this section refers are primarily Western (European and American) AAA single-player titles—those which are heavily influenced by a capitalist market and institutionalized means of production via the AAA industry—because the *Tomb Raider* franchise falls into that category. Games produced for smaller or niche markets—indie games, art games, serious games, educational games—tend to fall outside the predominating discourse of empire. Multiplayer games contain a different set of expectations and are often less rigidly structured than single-player games, and therefore interact with the politics of empire differently (see Castronova, 2005). For the remainder of the discussion, references to "games," "video games," and the games industry may be assumed to correlate to AAA mass market titles and development houses.

In this analysis, I discuss the game as a coherent whole, combining the sum of its narrative, mechanics, and relationship to its franchise, understanding that some (if not all) of the contradictions contained within it may be the result of collaboration rather than individual intentionality. Finally, this study is one conducted from a primarily narratological perspective, with some ludological analysis. For more on the economics of the games industry and the *Tomb Raider* franchise, see Castronova (2005), Deuber-Mankowsky (2005), and Dyer-Witheford and de Peuter (2009).

[3]   Interestingly, Gard objected to the sexualization of Lara's character, so much so that he left Core Design, saying "he disliked the prevailing tone of the marketing for *Tomb Raider*, and of Lara Croft" (Anderson & Levene, 2012, p. 245), "because he felt that she 'had more dignity'" (as cited in Mekula, 2010, p. 82).

[4]   Different changes to the original narrative were already part of earlier reboots in which Lara's parents were deceased rather than having disowned her.

[5]   The *Tomb Raider Wiki* gives Lara's age as 21, suggesting that she has a bachelor's degree in archaeology. The image contained in the game, however, appears to show a masters' hood, so Lara may have a more advanced degree at a young age ("Lara Croft [Rise Timeline]," 2015; Crystal Dynamics, 2013).

[6] It is worth noting that Yamatai is a historical place, known as "Yamatai-taikoku," ruled by Queen Himiko, who died circa 248; its geographical location remains a point of speculation, although a dig in 2009 suggests that it may be found in Nara, Japan ("Dig in Nara," 2009).

[7] The *Endurance* crew: Conrad Roth, Angus "Grim" Grimaldi, and Lara Croft are all Anglo-British; Alex Weiss and Dr. James Whitman are Anglo-American; Joslin Reyes is African American; Samantha Nishimura is American of mixed Japanese and Portuguese descent; and Jonah Maiava is an American of indigenous New Zealander descent ("Angus Grimaldi," 2015; "Samantha Nishimura," 2015; "Jonah Maiava," 2015).

[8] In Indiana Jones and the Raiders of the Lost Ark (1981) and Indiana Jones and the Last Crusade (1989), respectively.

[9] The name "Stormguard" itself may also be a reference to the Nazi Schutzstaffel, sometimes referred to as "stormtroopers." This reference may also be an allusion to the *Indiana Jones* series of films, as Jones is opposed in both *Raiders of the Lost Ark* and *The Last Crusade* by Nazis (Spielberg, 1981, 1989).

[10] This method refers to legends of vampires, undead demonic beings (in most lore) who subsist on the blood of the living, and who can only be killed by driving a stake through the heart. The allusion here serves to emphasize Himiko's demonic nature.

[11] There are references to Yamatai in *Rise of the Tomb Raider*, including one scene in which several soldiers have a conversation about being "called to the island to clean up" after "some Sun cult," expressing amazement that "Croft survived that hell" (Crystal Dynamics, 2015).

Chapter 12
Weaving *Nature Mage*:
Collective Intertextuality in the Design of a Book–to–Game Adaptation

Claudio Pires Franco
University of Bedfordshire, UK

ABSTRACT

This chapter is based on the analysis of previous cross-media game adaptations, on empirical research, and on reflection on practice with the design of a game concept for a fantasy book. Book-to-game adaptations are particularly interesting examples of cross-media adaptation. They not only weave the literary source text with intertexts from the game medium, but also require a modal transposition from the realm of words to a visual, interactive, multimodal medium where narrative and ludic logics intersect. This study proposes to look at different layers of cross-media intertextuality in the process of adaptation - at the level of specific texts, at the level of medium conventions, and at the level of genre conventions. It draws on crowd-sourcing research with readers to demonstrate that collaboration operates through multi-layered processes of collective intertextuality through which the intertextual repertoires of individuals meet to weave a final text.

INTRODUCTION

This chapter is based on empirical research and reflection on practice in the design of a game concept for a fantasy book series, *Nature Mage*. It looks at intertextuality in operation when author, games researcher and readers come together to work on a cross-media adaptation.

I met the author Duncan Pile in 2012, when we started thinking about possible adaptations of his story into digital media formats, namely a game. This collaboration forms the basis of practice-based research contributing towards the UNESCO Chair project Crossing Media Boundaries: Adaptation and New Media Forms of the Book, lead by Professor Alexis Weedon at the University of Bedfordshire[1]. It is an ongoing project, and here I reflect on the path walked thus far, focusing on our thinking and work towards reader involvement and the design of a *Nature Mage* game.

DOI: 10.4018/978-1-5225-0477-1.ch012

Video games that adapt source texts from other media are particularly interesting as objects of study for the analysis of intertextuality. From a contextual perspective of production, they provide a window into practices of cross-media adaptation increasingly significant in contemporary media. And, from a textual perspective, games-as-adaptations present a heightened level of intertextual and intermedial complexity since they not only cross media, but also mix narrative and ludic logics.

Etymologically, the meaning of the word text is "a tissue, a woven fabric" (Barthes, 1977, p. 159). The idea of the text, and thus of intertextuality, depends, as Barthes argues, on the figure of the web, the weave, the garment (text) woven from the threads of the "already written" and the "already read". Every text has its meaning, therefore, in relation to other texts, and this meaning is actualised – effectively established – in multiple ways by authors and readers.

Weaving a new game text based on a book means dealing with distinct resources of a different nature: narrative resources from the source book and ludic conventions of the destination game medium. These constitute different kinds of threads used in the weaving of a new text. The adaptation of a book into a game requires a medium translation, entailing a fit into its specific affordances. It involves the transposition of narrative resources from an established literary genre to a more recent hybrid form, influenced both by literary and gaming genres in a complex web of traditions and conventions.

This chapter discusses the intertextual processes and influences, the numerous *threads* used for the weaving of the *Nature Mage* game concept, with the ultimate aim of proposing a model for the analysis of game adaptations as processes of *collective* intertextuality: the meeting of the media repertoires, intertextual references, opinions and desires of the individuals involved in an adaptation, in turn framed by medium-specific affordances, generic conventions and more widely the very contexts of production.

BACKGROUND

The Story: A Hero is Born

The *Nature Mage* series, written and self-published by Duncan Pile (2011, 2013a, 2014) consists of three volumes (see Figure 1) in print and e-book format: *Nature Mage, Nature's Servant and Nature's Peril*. The author is currently working on *Nature Master*, the fourth title in the series. Below you can read a blurb for the first book.

Gaspi is an ordinary boy, living in the mountain village of Aemon's Reach, but life, for Gaspi, is forever changed the day magic erupts in him. He discovers he has a powerful gift – he is a Nature Mage, able to control natural forces and creatures and bend them to his will. It is a rare gift, and no-one has been born with it in centuries, but Gaspi's powers also have a dark side, and without training they will kill him. He is forced to leave his home and travel to the distant city of Helioport, where the Archmages of the College of Collective Magicks will teach him how to use his powers.

Accompanied by his guardian and his best friends, Gaspi sets off on the long journey to Helioport. The journey is fraught with danger, and Gaspi and his friends discover that there are demonic creatures abroad, intent on finding and killing anyone with magical ability.

Figure 1. The Nature Mage books
© *2012-2014 Duncan Pile. Used with permission. Source: Pile, 2013, 2013a, 2014*

As Gaspi begins his magical studies, a shadow hangs over him and over the city of magicians. Gaspi's story of a demonic attack is not an isolated incident. As these stories multiply, Hephistole, the Chancellor of the college, is growing increasingly certain that someone or something is directing the demonic forces, but who, and to what end? As things unfold, Gaspi finds himself in the middle of dark and terrible times, and can only hope that his powerful gift will develop in time to make a difference when the time comes. (Pile, 2016a)

The author describes the series as an "Epic Teenage Fantasy with a gripping plot and believable, down to earth characters. Perfect for fans of teen fiction and fantasy fiction alike." (Pile, 2016b)

The books are clearly - and in some cases, explicitly - influenced by several intertexts. Drawing on an analogy with existing popular titles, the story is set in a Tolkienesque fantasy world with hints of Harry Potter and other wizard-in-the-making stories. It could also be said that, similarly to the Harry Potter series, *Nature Mage* "echoes numerous so-called public school stories" (Gunder, 2004, p. 15), and is also influenced by a mosaic of other genres and sub-genres such as dark fantasy and horror. Drawing again on analyses of Rowling's work, *Nature Mage* could also described "as a generic mosaic in which there is a constant interplay between influences from [several] genres." (Alton, 2003, p. 159)

The *Nature Mage* books thus involve elements common to the fantasy genre traditions: magical training, battles, tournaments, demonic beasts, an array of magical beings and magical weapons. It also contains hints of horror, with terrifying passages relating to torture, demons and the exploration and abuse of humans by other humans. The story is a mix of both the great traditions and memes of the fantasy genre and the growing up challenges faced by teenagers, and the life tribulations of other characters. Besides all the action and adventure typical of the genre, there is a strong 'human' side to the story: growing up, relationships, motional struggles, and troubling pasts. These elements are crucial for the author, they take considerable space and play an essential role in the books - they are not there simply as add-ons to make a fantasy action story emotionally deeper.

Here's how Duncan explains the human side of his stories, in his own words:

In part, my books are written to teach young people essential life skills. Years of experience as a personal development coach has given me a passion for teaching conflict resolution skills, and my fantasy books are littered with positive examples of this.

The teenage characters go through all the usual trials of youth: jealousy, enmity, and sporting and academic rivalry. The adult conflicts are more complex. For example, Jonn (Gaspi's guardian) is a depressed alcoholic, suffering with long-lived guilt about failing to prevent the death of his wife and of Gaspi's parents. That guilt has marred his adult life, burdening him with emotions he can't understand.

The way I see it, fantasy writing is only powerful if it conveys real life messages, set within the framework of a fictional world. (Pile, 2013b)

The Challenge: How We Approached the Adaptation

Adapting across media involves the use of narrative resources from a source text, and a sort of translation onto a new medium, with a different language, different conventions and techniques, and different pleasures. A few concepts from narrative theory may prove useful at this stage.

Chatman (1978, pp. 12-25) suggests splitting narrative into two components: story (the what), the content of the narrative expression, and discourse (the how), the form of that expression, the means by which the content is communicated. Story is further split into existents (characters, settings) and events (actions, happenings). The way in which the events of a story are arranged constitutes the plot.

Games that are adapted from existing films, books or other media manage their source materials in very different ways. Representational elements from existing stories – especially existents such as settings and characters, and parts of the plot – are the obvious elements to integrate in a game adaptation, but the ways in which this is done varies considerably.

The remediation (Bolter & Grusin, 2003) of the source material is often important. For example, Tanya Krzywinska proposes that the *Buffy* game's reliance on a modern high-tech console platform – which provided high quality image and sound – facilitated a smoother "remediation" of the show by lowering "some of the media-specific distinctions between the game and its television counterpart" (2003, p. 2). This lessening of the gap between the two texts was further supported by the use of "locations, music, characters, voices and themes present in the TV show and by the involvement of its scriptwriters, thereby ensuring that the game carries the type of language and storyline that characterizes the show" (2003, p. 3). This set of measures allowed the game to guard itself "against failing to live up to expectations set by the show" (2003, p. 4) and effectively connect to the Buffyverse (the Buffy metaverse).

In some cases only story existents (such as settings and characters) are used and overlaid to existing gaming genres – this could be called the *re-skinning* approach. It includes games such as *The War of the Ring*, a real-time strategy game based on *The Lord of the Rings*, and whose inspiration is "not the text, as such, but transplanting the associations of character and monster to a preset system" (Wallin, 2007) – the adaptation simply becomes a sort of Warcraft expansion kit.

If there's any other game that War of the Ring would thank on Oscar Night, it would undoubtedly be Warcraft III [...] from the menu interface to the bright colourful world it's clear to whom War of the Rings owes its debt of inspiration. (Cervantes, 2003)

In other words, and to use a term common in game deign circles, the game is seen essentially as a re-skinning of an existing game engine (its invisible skeleton) with representational elements from *The Lord of the Rings*.

Some games integrate events or whole plots from the source narrative. Sometimes, however, the desire to stay close to the source material has drawbacks for the playability of the game due to a lack of surprise and plot disclosure (Wallin, 2007, p. 17). In other cases, it is the game conventions that win at the expense of the source narrative (Wallin, 2007, p. 19).

Some game producers build on the source narrative and try adding to the existing storyworld through telling new stories, drawing on the possibilities of the source text (and genre) and taking into account rules of consistency to produce new material that suits the source. The story elements of a source text – for example events, themes or character traits – can inspire the development of ludic features in a game, such as mechanics, challenges or resources.

Diane Carr (2006) interviewed the producers of *The Thing* game, an adaptation of John Carpenter's film (1982) in order to explore design decisions, and understand the ways the narrative resource of the source text had been applied to a new medium. The production team opted for a 3D hybrid, between a first-person-shooter and a role-playing-game. The first-person perspective, coupled with a limited amount of control of player view and the use of gloomy settings similar to those found in the film, facilitated the creation of suspense effects, an essential characteristic of the horror genre of the source film. The producers opted for the use of scripted cut scenes, which they saw as functional components of the game important for storytelling and to "re-establish continuity, plot and characterisation – features that tend to be lost during the played levels" (Carr, 2006, p. 158). Besides using settings, characters and important kernel moments from the movie (some for game action, others for scripted cut scenes), the developers selected core themes (alien infection, team trust) and contexts (isolation, extreme weather) and turned them into mechanics, challenges and resources within the game.

Games that draw on the source text material in this way seem to make the most of the destination medium without losing sight of the source texts. They manage to integrate representational and ludic aspects in an attempted balance between the presence of source narrative material and the necessary (tailored) ludic factors that actually make a game.

An easy solution for an adaptation of *Nature Mage* would be to pick up an existing game genre, then find in the books a suitable scene or passage, pick its settings, characters and plot, and transpose them into a game logic. In the first book there is an attack to the magicians' city of Helioport by waves of demons; Gaspi and his friends have to spread around the city and use their various powers to combat the invading, ever stronger, waves. It sounds very familiar. *Nature Mage* could easily be adapted into a 'tower defence game'[2].

A more complex game adaptation could be based on the epic tournament, The Measure, to create a battle game, or battle arena, similar to the *League of Legends* game, perhaps with warriors and magicians featuring in character cards (sort of trump cards, like the *Pokemon* cards, or *Magic the Gathering*) revealing their backstory and powers in detailed stats.

Perhaps these would make good games. But principally they'd be little else than copies of existing games, with a re-skinning of settings and characters. They'd probably feel a little like playing a version of *Monopoly* linked to a film franchise, something like *Frozen Monopoly* or *Star Wars Monopoly* – where a story (or rather the existents of a story) is directly transposed into an existing game structure.

We would like to try something a little different, a little more in touch with the 'essence' of the *Nature Mage* stories, with the feelings and thoughts readers may experience when they read the books, and in line with its themes and contexts, not simply deriving from evident fantasy action (which would still play a central role). The more human and emotional elements of the story ought to form an important thread in a *Nature Mage* game.

Our challenge was to sow the seeds for the design of a game that could draw on both a rich heritage of great fantasy video games and a deeply human story where feelings and emotions also take centre stage. It was important to understand the ways in which the story was experienced in order to inform the adaptation. In practice, this meant involving our potential audience, namely readers of the books.

Audience Involvement: Readers' Views of the Story

At the time I met Duncan I was working with game development studios and heavily involved in research-for-design, namely game adaptations for film, TV and book publishers. Being an Anthropologist by trade I understood the value of research to understand cultural groups, media audiences included. Digital software and game development was (and still is) at a stage where many developers see the value in lean iterative approaches that place strong emphasis on user/audience involvement. I was an advocate of user-centred approaches to software development, which in practice meant doing research with players and other media audiences - in the very processes of designing games. In the case of cross-media adaptations, this made even more sense since any game adaptation sought to attract not just game players, but also existing audiences and fans of whatever story (or franchise) was being adapted.

The approach thus drew on current trends for the use of audience involvement and co-creation (crowd-sourcing and the like), and was inspired by other projects such as Star Wars Uncut, a "fan mashup remake of the original Star Wars movies" (Pugh, 2009), and the (sometimes too optimistically exaggerated) potential of collaboration outlined by authors such as Henry Jenkins (2006; 2013).

Because ultimately the reading - the weaving of meaning, the interpretation - of a text is subjective and dependent to a great extent on the individual, it is also important to explore what audiences think, including existing fans, typically the most intense critics of any adaptation (Tosca and Klaustrup, 2011). They will scrutinise an adaptation for consistency, and will also compare the style, the tone, and the effects of the game using the source text (the film or book) as a benchmark. A good game adaptation aims to capture the *essence* of a source text. This essence may not be a realistic target (Stam, 2000) – and here we are talking about a translation into a new medium, not a 'faithful' replica of a story – but nonetheless it is important to work around a notion, the producers' and audiences' notion, of essential elements and effects of a story.

Audience involvement has thus been a key approach from day one, and included the following strategies: the design of an online community for readers and invited artists; an online survey of readers; face-to-face interviews and workshops with readers and non-readers via school visits.

The insight gathered through these reader engagement and research approaches – for example, through exploring their views on the most memorable parts of the plot, their ideas, and opportunities for story expansion – informed our game concept ideas.

Overall we engaged with over 70 readers, two artists, six secondary school classes (including students and two teachers) and obviously the author and the researcher. The process also involved informal discussions with colleagues, game designers and other researchers, working both in industry and academia.

The *Nature Mage* online community, built on the *Ning*[3] platform, constituted the central piece of engagement. It was designed as a digital space for creativity and it ran for one year, between July 2013 and July 2014. Readers and art students were invited to discuss the books, provide feedback on our ideas, propose their very own ideas, and create and upload derivative works - drawings, stories and any other materials based on the books - with the intention of using these as inspiration in the production of digital adaptations, including an enhanced digital book and a video game. English and Arts teachers used it to encourage creative work (writing and/or art) based on excerpts of the books and framed by curriculum needs (Figure 2).

The illustration students created visual representations of settings, characters, weapons and so on, which in turn generated discussions among users, the researcher and the author, for example about whether a certain drawing of a character constituted a suitable representation (Figures 3 and 4).

Figure 2. The Nature Mage community homepage
© 2013 Duncan Pile. Used with permission. Source: Franco, 2013.

Figure 3. Artwork uploaded by artist (settings)
© 2013 Duncan Pile. Used with permission. Source: Ledsham, 2013.

The online survey reached 66 readers. It mixed closed and open-ended questions, and it revolved around the following key areas: reactions to the story (to understand what stood out, what is more significant, what was most enjoyed); book reading and media consumption habits; reader ideas for adaptation; and testing of author and researcher ideas (including ideas for story expansion).

In summary, the key insights were that the key touch points with the story revolved around memes typical of the fantasy genre and the more emotional effects of the story. The fantasy memes included a fascination with the different kinds of mages, weapons, artefacts; the training period undertaken by the hero; his tie with the druid and nature elementals; and more action events such as the battle against demons in Helioport and the epic tournament The Measure. They would also like to know more about the "Arcane Wars" (and lost secrets of the past) frequently mentioned throughout the story, and hear more detailed backstories for key characters.

Readers enjoyed the mix of adventure, horror and romance, and what some called the "touching bits" or "human side", such as Jonn's struggles to forget an awful past; and the death of a fire elemental and one of the young magicians. Readers mentioned they could "relate to the characters" and to what they were going through - they could "connect" with them and reflect on their own lives.

All these insights informed the game design concept ideas discussed here.

Figure 4. Artwork uploaded by artist (weapons)
© 2013 Duncan Pile. Used with permission. Source: Ledsham, 2013

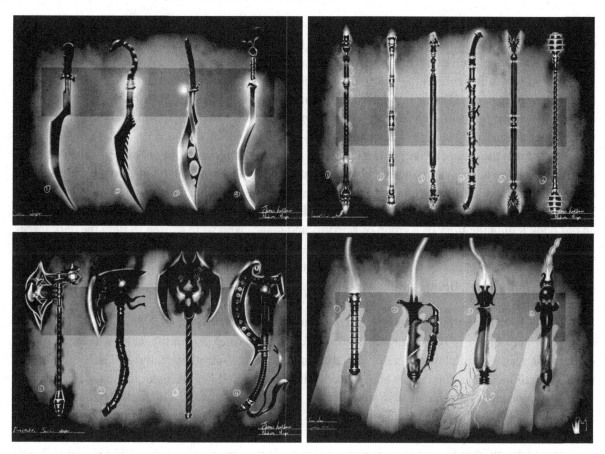

Mapping the Story

Getting immersed in the text that is being adapted is essential, so another strand of work that informed the game design concept consisted of a detailed analysis of the *Nature Mage* books. After re-reading the books in full, whilst bearing in mind the views and ideas from readers and the author, I created maps of the story, which recorded its key elements. In order to focus the mapping I created a framework for the analysis, which provided a rough guide on what to extract from the story, and how to record relevant parts ideas. 1,000 pages and nine A3 papers later we had a map to guide our ideas and conversations.

The maps recorded key existents, kernel events, themes and ideas. The events were split into action events and more human side events and emotions - the "touchy bits" described by readers and the moments of "conflict" described by the author. Themes are elements such as friendship, self-confidence and trust; they are recurring in the story, and condition the behaviours of protagonists and eventually the whole development of the plot.

'Start New Game'

The *Nature Mage* game concept is envisaged as a story-led online role-playing game playable across devices, but designed particularly with laptops and tablet computers in mind. It may include a free-to-play *light version*, as well as a more extensive paid version.

The core target audience is the young reader demographic, aiming to attract a mix of fantasy fans (across literature, film and games) and players of fantasy games and MMORPGs (massively multiplayer online role-playing games) such as *Word of Warcraft* and *RuneScape;* this means that the game design is strongly influenced by *both* the books and (RPG) gaming traditions.

At the start of the *Nature Mage* game players will be shown images of different places in the continent of Antropel, in a trailer-style montage, including a map of the lands, through which the player is taken to the village where the heroes come from, then the ruined city of Elmea, and finally the mage city of Helioport. In Hephistole's library they will be introduced to the story by reading the few pages left from an old book telling the story of a group of warriors and mages who were chosen to fight the dark forces arising throughout the lands.

This use of a book, in fact a remediation of sorts of the source text is present in texts such as *The Lord of the Rings* films. Besides being an aesthetic, stylistic choice, it arguably connects the adaptation with its source text.

All players will start in the College of Collective Magicks or the guards' grounds, in the city of Helioport. The college in particular is a central place in the stories and in the game will act as a kind of headquarters, where players access key characters, quests and other features. The beginning of the game will include a 'tutorial', where players will be explained key navigational and game-playing elements, dependent on their chosen 'class' (type of mage or warrior). This will be a single-player space, but players will be able to visit other classrooms and areas in the warrior training grounds, to practice their skills together in multiplayer areas.

Players will be able to design their own character from a series of options and templates, based on kinds of characters (mages and warriors) found in the books. Players will be able to name their characters, and also optionally create a backstory for them.

It will be possible to see and rate the characters and backstories created by other players in a kind of gallery. Players will also be able to craft (design and make) weapons, magical artefacts and enchanted objects (also present in the story) and swap created artefacts. One of the goals of the overall *Nature Mage* project has been to encourage creativity (both visual and in writing), and these features tie in with that vision; they are based on ideas brought forward by readers, clearly influenced by the offers of a range of existing games, particularly the *RuneScape* MMORPG, where crafting plays an important role).

These kinds of user-generated content are clearly influenced by current practices of digital culture. User-generated content, to different degrees, is growing and evident in a large number of digital spaces used by young adults nowadays. Think, for example, of video uploading on YouTube, the creation of personal profiles across social media, the rating features of numerous recommendations websites, and the flexibility of virtual spaces and large role-playing games to create not just characters but whole worlds.

As players progress through the game they will be shown an expanding map, initially with most lands blurred, but becoming clear (or unlocked) as they progress. The map will be dotted with icons to refer to races, key characters and plot events as the player reaches them; players will be able to click on these to read more about them and see visual representations. Most journeying will be done on foot – or horseback – as in the story, but there will also be some magic transportation objects as those used by the mages in the books. The use of some kind of magical teleportation device is also common to the game genre of fantasy RPGs.

As players meet NPCs (non-player characters) and find new places they will become involved in the main plot of the game, which will be based on the overarching narrative of the books: players must evolve their skills, collaborate with other characters and players, find new allies and overcome obstacles and challenges (such as demon attacks) to face the greatest threat of all, Shirukai Sestin, the once-good healer turned master of the darkest magic.

Single player and multiple (collaborative) player modes will intersect at different stages. Players will be able to switch characters and assume control of other protagonists at kernel events in the (original) story where their actions are key to the success of the group. Multiplayer mode will include pair / group practice, duels and dungeons (special quests where team work is required by bringing together complementary player types, for example warriors, healer, and warrior mages – again typical of fantasy stories and MMORPGs). Single player instances will revolve around training, levelling-up and other activities less related to action and adventure, and more aligned with the emotional elements of the story.

The game narrative will be told essentially through questing, character dialogue, book-like screens and eventually cut scenes. These will mix remediated forms of storytelling (reading and watching) with the more recent practice of story-playing (playing to progress and uncover a story). There will also be aspects of spatial narrative, exploration and objects, symbols and clues that help tell or deepen the story and may form the basis of some puzzle-like challenges.

It is envisaged that the narrative will consist of a pattern of branching and convergence. It will branch at some points, to return to a common point for all players at key points (kernel events in the story). The author – with the input of readers and researcher – will create new strands to the story-world, which will offer new quests and adventures that go beyond the original story. Interestingly, the last book in the series has not been fully written yet, which means the story is in fact very open, and Shirukai Sestin and his minions are still to be defeated. This could be explored in the game, perhaps allowing the author to explore alternative routes.

The author included some 'breadcrumbs' in the story, for example the mention of ancient kinds of magic and the nearly-forgotten Arcane Wars, which he purposely wrote very little about – these seem ideal to be picked up and form the basis for further material for the game and general story-world expansion.

Besides unravelling the story – mainly through quests, dialogue and a few cut scenes (or scenes with images and text, to stay closer to the reading mode of the books) – players will be free to explore some areas of the game world, such as the college library and the magical artefacts chamber. The library will contain several books that tell backstories about key protagonists, about kinds of magic, about demons and beasts, weapons, kinds of magic, other lands and so on, in developing 'glossaries' that grow as the game story unravels. By looking for and reading about these kinds of elements players will unlock new quests to access some of the very objects and weapons they read about. It is worth noting that the idea of creating glossaries was one of the most highly rated by readers in our research.

Player quests will be recorded – as is conventional in RPGs – in the player quest journal. In this game this will look and feel like a book (a remediation of – and homage to – the source text), and will gradually fill in the missing pages of the book shown to players at the start. Players will be able to read *their* very own story so far, the narrative of their path through the game. It will be possible to read on-screen, add to or tweak the text in the quest stories, and also download the *book* as a PDF (and e-book formats) with text and images from the game. From book, we turn to game, and back to book again, encouraging players to read and explore their writing skills if they so wish. All the stories can be shared online via the game community, and players-readers will be able to rate each other's tweaked tales. The community will continue to have creative areas for even more open contributions from the audience, and will strive to consult with users to inform game development on an ongoing basis.

THE CHALLENGES OF GAME ADAPTATION (AND ITS ANALYSIS)

The Obvious Bits? Narrative Existents and the Challenges of Modal Transposition

The adaptation of books into games is an especially interesting case of cross-media adaptation. Books - particularly those with no illustrations (as is the case of *Nature Mage*) – are characterised by "high modality" (Kress, 2009). They use mostly a single mode, text, to make meaning. The challenge is to *translate* them into a visual, multimodal medium such as a game, a medium where players control characters and to a certain extent embody (play as) those characters. The adaptation involves a *modal transposition*, a translation into new modes that has to fill several gaps, using not only the source text (with its more or less defined references) but also a myriad of other texts and experiences as threads to weave the new game text.

A major task to create a game adaptation is therefore to transpose a text based on words (with no visual representation) onto the multimodal space of the game medium. This includes creating settings, creatures, objects, and especially key protagonists (players and important non-player characters). This section relates some of the activities carried out to this effect, and reflects on the challenges posed by such task, linking it to multimodality theory, and reflecting on the ways in which intertextuality effectively takes place in reading and (jointly) producing texts.

The descriptive elements of characters in books include aspects such as the way they look, how they dress, their personality, their behaviours, ethics, and so on and so forth. Some of these descriptive elements are more explicit, factual and more defined than others. Depending on writing style, and also on whether the text tends towards being more *readerly* or more *writerly*[4] (Barthes, 1975), these descriptions leave greater or fewer gaps to be filled, or weaved, by the reader. Less defined elements include, for example, character behaviours, which over a number of pages allow the reader to build an image of personality, of character beliefs, ethical stance and other subjective characteristics. These tend to be more open to a wide range of interpretations than more objective aspects.

The *Nature Mage* books contain both kinds of descriptive elements of characters, especially of key protagonists. Let us take Hephistole, the Chancellor of the college, and overall grand wizard in the story, as an example. Even the more factual, descriptive elements about Hephistole leave a number of gaps, especially in a book like *Nature Mage* where there are no illustrations, no pre-existing visual representation of characters. Some questions thus arise: how old does he look like? How tall is he? What's his face like? The book may provide fewer or greater clues, but readers (including producers looking to make an adaptation) draw on their intertextual repertoire of wizards and wizard-like characters to draw a (more or less defined) mental image of Hephistole. The author does the same when writing, when weaving the text from his own cultural and textual repertoire, when imagining and describing his mental image of the wizard. But his mental image is not equivalent to the words he uses to describe the wizard. They are, at best, an attempt - an attempt to pin down his image of 'wizard' onto a text, in what may be termed a process of textualisation. This process involves concretising an image onto a text, a translation of a mental image or idea, through processes of selection, onto the text, and as I defend here often takes place in a group context of collective intertextuality.

This 'image' or 'idea' of Hephistole - or any other character - draws on several intertexts within the fantasy genre, across media, across the times, and is based on our exposure to different materials. *My image of Hephistole is defined mostly by Gandalf*, the great wizard from Tolkien's Lord of the Rings, and most strongly by its filmic adaptation. But my image of Hephistole is also influenced by the great wizard Professor Albus Dumbledore from the Harry Potter films; and by images of different Merlins I came across; and probably by a series of less conscious intertextual references to characters I have been exposed to... In fact, as intertextuality theory proposes, somehow "the meaning of a text is generated by its relation to literary and cultural systems." (Allen, 2000, p. 127)

Intertextual reading encourages us to resist a passive reading of texts from cover to cover. There is never a single or correct way to read a text, since every reader brings with him or her different expectations, interests, viewpoints and prior reading experiences. (Allen, 2000, p. 7)

My image of 'great wizard' exists outside of the books and any texts in *my* media repertoire or media 'universe'. As I read and weave an image of Hephistole I add it to my repertoire of wizards. Many of these wizards share characteristics, both in terms of the way they look and their ethics, personalities and behaviours. They all have an air of 'wizardness' to them: they are wise, fair, knowledgeable, strong, mentors for younger or weaker characters. They are formed within genres that through time developed certain conventions and shaped archetypal characters, common patterns and themes brought to light in studies such as Campbell's (2008) work on the hero's journey model.

The exercise of multimodal transposition is not limited to character representation. The use of other new modes in the game, such as sound, music and even colour (and dark/light) will be essential to the creation of the right kind of effects. For example, the source books contain several events that are akin to thriller and horror texts. The use of darker environments, alongside adequately gripping sounds and music will be important to achieve the desired effect in the new medium. Again, we will (necessarily) draw to a certain extent on the conventions and devices used to create suspense and horror in games (which in turn draws on the conventions from older media).

For some characters in the *Nature Mage* story I have fewer, or less well defined intertextual references that I can draw on than for 'wizard'. One of these characters is Jonn, the hero's guardian. When the first drawn interpretation of Jonn was uploaded to the online community, a reader revealingly asked "Is that what Jonn looks like?" The author replied "I think it is an appropriate representation of Jonn… he looks like a strong, scarred man who has had his share of trouble!"

This is an example (Figures 5 and 6) of visual canon being established by the author. He is 'stamping' the visual representation as 'suitable', authorised, consistent with the story and perhaps with his more or less defined image of what Jonn could look like.

Another image that triggered an interesting reaction from the author was the image of a demonic beast, a kind of intelligent *warg* (a kind of evil super-sized wolf), commander of lesser wargs. You can see the first visual representation uploaded to the community in Figure 7.

Figure 5. Sketches of character (Jonn)
© *2013 Duncan Pile. Used with permission. Source: Crompton, 2013.*

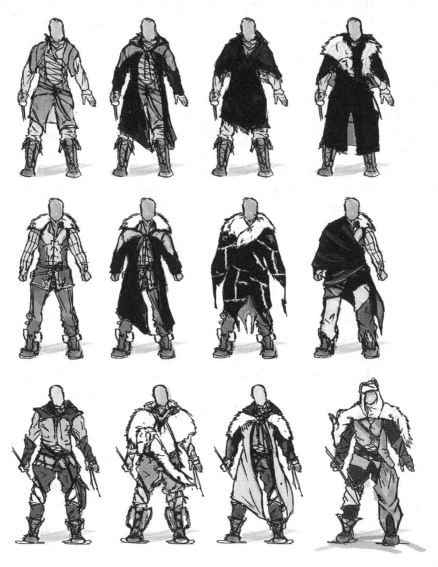

The author commented that it did not look as intelligent and evil as he pictured it; it looked too animal-like. In this case, the author did not use his stamp of approval, but rather tried to bring the sketches closer to his own mental image (and arguably the book's description) of the beast. The final visual representation was thus negotiated between artist and author, who had a final say with regards to the adaptation of his work (Figure 8).

Other drawings were entirely dismissed for breaking the rules of consistency with the story. This was the case of some settings - landscapes and buildings that, according to the author, seemed more suitable to a Victorian age novel than to a fantasy story taking place in an undefined historical period akin to the medieval times of horse and cart, castles and swords.

Figure 6. The 'approved' Jonn
© 2013 Duncan Pile. Used with permission. Source: Crompton, 2013.

Figure 7. The first version of the Warg boss
© 2013 Duncan Pile. Used with permission. Source: Ledsham, 2013.

Figure 8. The revised version of the Warg boss
© 2013 Duncan Pile. Used with permission. Source: Ledsham, 2013.

The Hardest Bit: From Story Events and Themes to Game Features

For the author – and readers – it is important that the game keeps a good level of consistency with the story, not simply at a more superficial level (simpler visual representation of existents), but also at a deeper level, which I may describe perhaps as the level of style, tone and effect. The game-as-adaptation ought to keep a good level of consistency with the very features that make the book series loved by readers. It should let players feel – to a certain extent – the same kind of feelings they had when reading the books. Said perhaps too simplistically, the game needs to draw on the (subjective, I accept) essence of the books.

Translating the effects of a story, feelings, emotions, and other more subjective aspects that form the essence of the story – is not an easy task. "Thanks to the emphasis of games on action, setting and imaginary creatures" some genres (including medieval fantasy, the general theme of *Nature Mage*) are "much more adaptable to the interactive and fundamentally visual nature of games than 'high' literature focused on existential concerns, psychological issues" Ryan (2006, p. 195) and similar themes close to what I am calling 'the human side' of the *Nature Mage* story.

Lebowitz (2011, p. 43) similarly suggests that "there's the simple and undeniable fact that some types of stories just don't work well in games – at least not without a lot of extra planning and effort." Genres that are popular in other media – such as romance – are rarely to be found in games. His argument is that, because games need gameplay they tend to focus on stories that supply "ideal" material, such as fighting, strategy, exploration and puzzle solving. He goes on to claim that "these types of external conflict are far easier to portray in a game than the more internal emotional conflicts that are often the focus of things like romance novels and sitcoms; therefore, a "proper" game story needs to support a large amount of external conflict" (2011, p. 44).

However, Lebowitz then provides examples of games – exceptions, he makes clear – that do tackle such internal themes, or as he puts it "nonideal story types". He resolves the apparent contradiction by saying that using these kinds of stories "is difficult and requires a lot of creativity and careful planning in order to ensure that the story and gameplay make sense and work well together" (2011, p. 45).

Perhaps the explanation is more complex than this. Of course video games are based on games, -analogue games - and as such they are based on their ludic nature (goals, rules, and so on). But the representational elements of games are also shaped - they are historically and culturally situated - by cultures of production and the wider media consumed by players (and producers, who are typically players). The fact that action is more often made into game than romance is not simply, I think, re-lated so obviously to the fact that games equal action, not romance, but that games evolved in that direction – perhaps in tandem with the media and story preferences of players and game makers.

For Lebowitz, the hero's journey is the prime example of an "ideal story" for a game. For him, "fol-lowing tried-and-true narrative structures such as the hero's journey [...] can make writing for games much easier" (2011, p. 68). Indeed. But here I would perhaps add a note of caution and suggest that game producers find it easy to adapt hero's journeys not because it is the perfect story for games, but because this is the way that games have evolved – most often in working environments domi-nated until more recently by young males; this is also significant. The first popular video games were text-based role-playing games in the fantasy genre. Perhaps if we had started with romance-themed games their history would have been very different…

The hero's journey of *Nature Mage* makes it relatively easy to envisage a game where the player levels up through magical training, though acquiring artefacts and magical objects. This happens in the source story, and could be fairly easily adapted. There are many kinds of magic to learn, different classes and professors, different kinds of mages, warriors and tribes (which the player could choose from, in a similar fashion to the options of 'race' and 'class' present in most MMORPGs). It is also fairly straightforward to envisage a tutorial stage, or level, where the player enters the School of Magicks in the city of Heliport, and starts learning spells. Other activities from the book that could be easily translated include learning to enchant objects, practicing fights in an arena, and crafting your own artefacts and weapons. All of these are common features in existing MMORPGs).

Some parts of the *Nature Mage* plot could also serve as inspiration for game features. The sword-and-sorcery tournament The Measure in *Nature's Servant* could suitably be used as inspiration for a game tournament, and for that kind of 'battle arena' with a game mechanic similar to *League of Legends*.

Another essential part of the game - again based on the book - will be the ability to play as a number of characters, as well as being able to play with other characters in teams when the complementary skills and powers of different warriors and mages are required. This is akin to raiding and playing dungeons in MMORPGs. For readers, the ties of friendship were one of the most important components of the story, and this means that in the game it is important to draw on collaboration and co-playing. After all, it is an epic hero's journey where travel companions complement each other.

Harder-to-Gamify Elements

There are other themes of the *Nature Mage* story that would not seem so clearly gamifiable. For me, attempting to incorporate these elements means that we stick as close as possible to the 'essence' of the story, and don't simply use a selection of story existents and more obvious action parts of the plot as the basis for a game that looks, and even more importantly feels, similar to a hundred other fantasy games. These themes relate to the more human side of the story, and include inner (individual) and interpersonal conflicts, such as the relational challenges between boyfriend and girlfriend; the emotional challenges of growing up; several moments where the hero Gaspi loses control; periods of low self-confidence; amongst others.

Current video games place an "emphasis on doing rather than talking, lending themselves to the action format rather than personal interaction" (Krzywinska, 2003, p. 5). However, for readers, these kinds of elements in the story are crucial, and one of its key attractions. *Nature Mage* readers thought the books were different for "the warmth and humanity of the characters", who faced problems that "could happen in real life"[5]. Readers "connect with the real-life challenges that protagonists face" and feel that the human and emotional side of the story is important and a distinguishing factor. Among the ideas suggested by readers for a digital book (another strand of the project) is the introduction of "links to real stories of real people dealing with problems similar to those experienced by the protagonists".

Another idea suggested by readers – the possibility of accessing another character's view on key parts of the story – formed the basis for a game feature. At some stages in the game plot, players will need the help of companions, for example to go on a quest, or to gain more power (perhaps by increasing self-esteem or confidence, as suggested further down). In order to do this they will need to engage in dialogue. Since one of the key issues in the story is that characters do not always say what they are thinking, or indeed know what they *should* say but say something else, the idea is to add an element of uncertainty and variability in dialogues between the player and key characters they have a close relation with, for example boyfriend and girlfriend, or between rivals.

A device that could be used is inspired by the game *Escape from Monkey Island*, whereby selecting a line of dialogue will sometimes result in the player actually saying – or mumbling – something slightly or entirely different to the words shown on screen. This will leave players somewhat out of control, and potentially make them reflect on the differences between thoughts and utterances within relationships and conflict solving. Another idea is to allow players to select what they think the other character is thinking, which in turn will determine different speech options for both the player and that character.

Both features aim to translate the complex nature of relationships, thoughts and real-life dialogue outlined above. Imagine that you, as the player, have spent a long time practicing and battling on your own, and to a certain extent neglected your friends. When you meet them and ask them to go on a quest with you they may be hard to convince. If you select that you think they're a little hurt, your dialogue options will include lines to talk about this; if not, and you keep talking as if nothing is wrong, they may react differently, possibly in a less positive way.

Other themes and contexts could be used as inspiration for game mechanics and resources. A player's level of self-confidence could be a kind of economic resource, similar to energy in other games. The player could lose confidence after defeats or conflict situations with his peers. Then, through dialogue and meditation, perhaps in a setting similar to that from the book (a hidden garden with a running stream, where the player meditates), the player could recover his level of calmness and self-confidence. Another option could be inviting other characters to the local tavern for a meal and a chat, something that occurs recurrently in the books. There could also be a kind of internal dialogue process, whereby the player questions himself on his actions, and tries to come to terms with decisions by selecting from a number of options, leading to resolution (or not) of his emotional dilemmas.

These kinds of game features – partly because they are less game-like, partly because historically they are not present in popular titles in the genre – present a harder challenge. They would certainly bring the *Nature Mage* game closer to the essence of the books, where battles, magic and demons stand shoulder-to-shoulder with growing up, relationships and feelings.

The Nature Mage 'Mix'

The *Nature Mage* game concept intersects story elements with a ludic logic, with game structures. The story elements are mainly drawn from the source text, whilst the ludic components are mainly inspired by existing games. But the two are not separate: the source story intersects with ludic aspects when its elements are used as source of inspiration for new and tailored game mechanics and when game playing unveils narrative.

The *Nature Mage* game concept is clearly framed, more generally, by the current affordances of the game medium, and the conventions and devices used by online RPGs. The game is also, more specifically, influenced by distinct texts, obviously the source *Nature Mage* series, but also games such as *World of Warcraft, RuneScape* and *The Thing*.

The choice of an online RPG seems to a certain extent obvious. It is a game genre that not only fits with – but also shares – a genealogy with the very source text and more widely the fantasy genre. They are part of a wider series, or family tree, of hero's journey texts. More specifically, RPGs are based on, and influenced by: a) more recently, by MUDs (multi-user dungeons, the first text-based role-playing / fantasy video games); dungeons & dragons books and board games and analogue RPGs; b) further back, by hero's journeys in general, fantasy literature, epic stories (like those mentioned by Bakhtin, 1981; and Kristeva, 1980), folk heroes and fairy tales, oral traditions of storytelling and ancient myths of origin present in virtually every human society, as explored in the work of anthropologist Claude Levi-Strauss (1990).

Many of the game concept ideas are inspired by genre conventions, by specific features of specific game titles, which in turn have been greatly influenced by the long heritage of fantasy and hero's journeys across epochs, media and modes. The more challenging, and probably most rewarding features, those linked to the human side of the story, are challenging precisely because they fall outside the affordances (not just technical, but social, linked to the expectations of game players) of the game medium. None-theless, weaving a *Nature Mage* game without this human thread would seem a missed opportunity to do something different, something that would meet the essence and expectations of readers, and create an intertextual 'mashup' that is somehow more original (although never quite so in the strict sense of the word).

Another important aspect in the analysis of intertextuality in the design of the *Nature Mage* game concept is the collective nature of the processes of production. The practice of weaving a new text in a collective manner - through the use of teams with several individuals, and through co-creation and research with readers – implies another form of intersection: the meeting of different intertextual references, of different combinations of intertexts brought forward by all those involved. In the *Nature Mage* case both the author, artists, readers and researcher drew on their own individual media and cultural repertoires, bringing to the mix diverse references and intertexts linked to their own experiences mainly of fantasy and fantasy-related genres across media. The final ideas were the result of this merging of intertexts in what may be termed a process of collective weaving, or collective intertextuality.

SOLUTIONS AND RECOMMENDATIONS

Reflection on Practice

Distinguishing between textual and media influences for analytical purposes seems fruitful. My analysis uses both concepts of intertextuality and intermediality, accepting that in its very widest sense intertextuality encompasses the entire web of texts, intertexts and wider culture (thus making intermediality a kind of subset, or specific layer of intertextuality). A third analytical layer, situated in-between text and medium, involves the consideration of the influences of genre (and themes, or memes) across media.

Game design - and any human creative activity - is never done in a vacuum from a blank canvas. It is influenced by the vast collection of what has been created before, across media, across formats. And besides being influenced by intertexts, the design of a new game is also influenced by the wider forces of genre traditions and medium conventions - crystallisations of ways of doing things in a medium or genre, which then acquire an existence of their own, distinct and independently from any individual text, but of course concretised and observable in individual texts.

The production of games that adapt existing texts (typically films or books) can be metaphorically conceptualised as a multi-layered weaving process that uses several kinds of threads to produce games that draw on a number of resources, conventions and intertextual references both from their source text(s) and from other games. In a more general manner they are also influenced by the wider aesthetics and conventions of both source and destination media (and genres), and are always framed by the affordances of the game medium.

Large numbers of terms in academic discourses have to a certain degree been influenced by the notion of intertextuality and the ideas discussed by its key theorists. One of these terms is intermediality, which I consider useful for the study on intertextuality in games, particularly in a context of cross-media adaptation. I would define intermediality as the complex webs of relations and influences (motifs, genres, aesthetics, conventions, etc.) between *and* across media.

In practice, it is often difficult to distinguish in a text what is an intertextual, an intermedial or a generic influence - except for cases where allegory and explicit references to intertexts are intended, these layers all merge into a consistent whole. Geoff King provides two good examples that illustrate the nuanced differences between intertextual, generic (or motif-based), and intermedial relations between games and, in this case, films.

Many games draw on iconographies that can be linked to particular film titles but that have also become more widely prevalent: the Blade Runner look, for example. Some games draw on more specific and localized cinematic devices. A good recent example is the 'bullet-time' mode used in the action-adventure game Max Payne (2001), based on slow-motion bullet effects used by the Hong Kong action director John Woo and especially its translation into Hollywood in The Matrix. (2002, p. 142)

Intertextuality as a Collective Process of Production

The concept of intertextuality can be understood at different levels. It can mean, in an abstract and unspecific way (without considering any particular text) that all texts are made of intertexts. Defining the intertextuality in, or the intertextual character of, a specific text means the analysis of the several intertexts that can be identified in that text.

Intertextuality can be analysed via textual analysis, but it becomes richer when the production of that very text is also looked at. With the latter we can look not only at the intertexts that made their way or influenced the text under analysis, but also at the dynamic process of creating the text, with its many discussions, debates and considerations about its design, leading to decisions on what influences - what intertexts, what generic conventions, what media devices - actually make their way to the text - and why. Sometimes this may be obvious, purposeful, evident; other times it will be subtle, subconscious, hidden.

Most, if not all, intertextuality is also collective – in more than one way. More generally, it is collective because the "powerful deep currents of culture" described by Bakhtin ((Stam, 2000, p. 65) affect the weaving of all texts - and these can only happen within socio-cultural groups. More specifically, the very weaving of a text is seldom - if anytime - a purely individual endeavour.

In media production intertextuality is witnessed - it emerges - in operation when all those involved in the production of a text bring their repertoires into the table to discuss the design of a new text. This rarely happens to just a single individual in isolation - the romantic vision of the writer in his wooden cabin by the lake, closed from the outside world and with only his own mind to engage with - and is much more often a collective process where groups of individuals, often with different backgrounds and expertise come together to create something new[6].

In all texts we can see hybridization. All texts exhibit polyphony or plurality, they reveal the presence of previous texts, previous forms, language, and a whole raft of other origins. Bakhtin spoke of the "deep generating series" of literature – that is, "the complex and multidimensional dialogism, rooted in social life and history, comprising both primary (oral) and secondary (literary) genres, which reach the text not only through recognisable influences, but also through a subtle process of dissemination" (Stam 2000, pp. 64-65). These explicit "recognisable influences" and the more "subtle influences" on a text become more obvious - they emerge particularly clearly - when producers discuss and negotiate its very weaving.

Having access to the background discussions and processes that lead to the creation of a new text is a privilege for researchers. In some cases the producers of a text are entirely disregarded; in other occasions they are interviewed after the text has been produced; and in rare occasions researchers have the opportunity to follow the design and production of a text, usually as members of the very team creating the text.

CONCLUSION

The adaptation of a book-to-game involves complex processes of intertextuality – or of intertextual weaving – across media, and involving collective discussion, negotiation and decisions. This kind of intertextuality is both cross-medial and collective.

It is cross-medial because it draws on vast webs of intertexts originating from several media. It draws on genre conventions, and on media traditions that again cut across media, not just the source book and the destination game, but a vast array of cultural production, a complex web of intertexts and intertextual 'series', located within a wider society, language and culture. The web of influences, borrowings and analogies is not limited to individual, specific texts. Medium-specific conventions and genre traditions - independently of any specific intertexts, but as a crystallisation of the many texts in a genre or medium - shape the design of new texts.

This kind of intertextuality, seen in operation, is also collective. It recognises the roles of individuals, and looks at the processes of negotiation between them. Individuals – acting in different roles and with different powers – bring to the table their own intertextual universes, their own web of meanings, and the weaving of a new text is made up of a combination of these different threads.

The recognition of the role of the individual, and of collective processes of weaving and deciding what goes into a new text, goes hand-in-hand with the methodology used – not just textual analysis, but ideally researching as part of a production team, or at least having access to production materials and producers as others also defend (Johnson, 1986; Bennett & Woollacott, 1987).

It is when decisions regarding the very weaving of a text from an enormous array of possible intertexts are taken that this emerges. This is very important and often overlooked. Analyses that simply look at the text, a posteriori, and without approaching or hearing from producers, will typically be less rich, less robust – they only look at the final result, and less so at all the processes that lead to specific decisions and to the shaping of the final text.

Intertextuality is a powerful analytical tool to study games, and an irreplaceable tool to engage in research in the current media context of intense convergence, a strong tendency for the production of cross-media adaptations, and the emergence of new hybrid forms.

REFERENCES

Allen, G. (2006). *Intertextuality*. London, UK: Routledge.

Alton, A. H. (2003). Generic fusion and the mosaic of *Harry Potter*. In E. E. Heilman (Ed.), *Harry Potter's world: Multidisciplinary critical perspectives* (pp. 141–162). London, UK: Routledge Falmer.

Bakhtin, M. M. (1981). *The dialogic imagination: Four essays*. Austin, TX: University of Texas Press.

Barthes, R. (1975). *The pleasure of the text*. New York, NY: Hill and Wang.

Barthes, R. (1977). *Image, music, text* (S. Heath, Trans.). London, UK: Fontana.

Bennett, T., & Woollacott, J. (1987). *Bond and beyond: The political career of a popular hero*. London, UK: Routledge Kegan & Paul. doi:10.1007/978-1-349-18610-5

Bolter, J. D., & Grusin, R. (2003). *Remediation: Understanding new media*. Cambridge, MA: The MIT Press.

Buffy the Vampire Slayer. (2002) Developer: EA Games; Publisher: Fox Entertainment.

Campbell, J. (2008). *The hero with a thousand faces*. Novato, CA: New World Library.

Carr, D. (2006). Film, adaptation and computer games. In D. Buckingham, D. Carr, A. Burn, & G. Schott (Eds.), *Computer games: Text, narrative and play* (pp. 149–161). London, UK: Polity Press.

Cervantes, M. (2003). *Review of "Lord of the Rings: War of the Rings"*. Game Chronicles.

Chatman, S. (1978). *Story and discourse: Narrative structure in fiction and film*. Ithaca, NY: Cornell University Press.

Crompton, K. (2013). Drawings based on *Nature Mage* series. Retrieved from http://www.naturemage.com

Escape from Monkey Island . (2000) Developer and Publisher: LucasArts Entertainment Company

Franco, C. P. (2013). *Homepage*. Retrieved from http://www.naturemage.com

Franco, C. P. (2014). The muddle earth journey: Brand consistency and cross-media intertextuality in game adaptation. In R. Pearson & A. N. Smith (Eds.), *Storytelling in the media convergence age: Exploring screen narratives* (pp. 40–53). London, UK: Palgrave Macmillan. doi:10.1057/9781137388155.0008

Gunder, A. (2004). Harry Ludens: *Harry Potter and the Philosopher's Stone* as a novel and computer game. *Human IT*, *7*(2), 1–137.

Jenkins, H. (2006). *Convergence culture: Where old and new media collide*. New York, NY: NYU Press.

Jenkins, H., Ford, S., & Green, J. (2013). *Spreadable media: Creating value and meaning in a networked culture*. New York, NY: NYU Press.

Johnson, R. (1986). What is cultural studies anyway? *Social Text*, (16): 38–80. doi:10.2307/466285

King, G., & Krzywinska, T. (2002). *Screenplay: Cinema/videogames/interfaces*. New York, NY: Wallflower Press.

Kress, G. (2009). *Multimodality: A social semiotic approach to contemporary communication*. London, UK: Routledge.

Kristeva, J. (1980). *Desire in language: A semiotic approach to literature and art*. New York, NY: Columbia University Press.

Krzywinska, T. (2003). Playing Buffy: Remediation, occulted meta-game-physics and the dynamics of agency in the videogame version of *Buffy the Vampire Slayer*. *Slayage: The Online International Journal of Buffy Studies*, (8). Retrieved from http://www.slayage.tv/essays/slayage8/Krzywinska.htm

League of Legends. (2009) Developer and Publisher: Riot Games. Retrieved from: http://na.leagueoflegends.com

Ledsham, J. (2013). *Drawings based on Nature Mage series*. Retrieved from http://www.naturemage.com

Lévi-Strauss, C. (1990). *The raw and the cooked*. Chicago, IL: University of Chicago Press.

Lord of the Rings: The Fellowship of the Ring . (2002) Developer: Black Label Games; Publisher: Vivendi Universal Games.

Lord of the Rings: The Return of the King . (2004). Developer: EA Games; Publisher: Electronic Arts.

Lord of the Rings: The Two Towers . (2004). Developer: EA Games; Publisher: Electronic Arts.

Muddle Earth . (2010). Developer: Dubit Limited; Publisher: BBC [Online]. Retrieved from http://www.muddleearthworld.co.uk

Pile, D. (2013). *Nature mage.* Retrieved from http://www.amazon.co.uk/Nature-Mage-Book-ebook/dp/B00CLOYOKA

Pile, D. (2013a). *Nature's servant.* Retrieved from http://www.amazon.co.uk/Natures-Servant-Nature-Mage-Book-ebook/dp/B00B0F0JKU

Pile, D. (2013b). *The nature mage books.* Paper presented at the Hocklife Conference, University of Bedfordshire.

Pile, D. (2014). *Nature's peril.* Retrieved from http://www.amazon.co.uk/Natures-Peril-Nature-Mage-Book-ebook/dp/B00HTRKGL0

Pile, D. (2016a). *The nature mage series.* Retrieved from http://www.duncanpile.com/the-nature-mage-series

Pile, D. (2016b). *Nature mage (The nature mage series book 1) Kindle Edition.* Retrieved from http://www.amazon.co.uk/Nature-Mage-Book-ebook/dp/B00CLOYOKA

Pugh, C. (2009) *About.* Retrieved from http://www.starwarsuncut.com/about

RuneScape . (2011). Developer and Publisher: Jagex. Retrieved from http://www.runescape.com

Ryan, M. L. (2006). *Avatars of story.* Minneapolis, MN: University of Minnesota Press.

Stam, R. (2000). Beyond fidelity: The dialogics of adaptation. In J. Naremore (Ed.), *Film adaptation* (pp. 54–76). New Brunswick, NJ: Rutgers University Press.

Stam, R., Burgoyne, R., & Flitterman-Lewis, S. (1992). *New vocabularies in film semiotics: Structuralism, post-structuralism and beyond.* London, UK: Routledge.

The Thing . (2002). Developer: Computer Artworks Ltd; Publisher: Black Label Games.

Tosca, S., & Klastrup, L. (2011). When fans become players: LOTRO in a transmedial world. In T. Krzywinska & J. Parsler (Eds.), *Ring bearers: The Lord of the Rings Online as intertextual narrative* (pp. 46–69). Manchester, UK: Manchester University Press.

Van Looy, J. (2010). *Understanding computer game culture: The cultural shaping of a new medium.* Saarbrücken, Germany: Lambert Academic Publishing.

Wallin, M. R. (2007). Myths, monsters and markets: Ethos, identification, and the video game adaptations of *The Lord of the Rings. Game Studies, 7*(1). Retrieved from http://gamestudies.org/0701/articles/wallin

War of the Ring . (2004). Developer: Liquid Entertainment; Publisher: Vivendi Universal Games.

Word of Warcraft . (2004). Developer and Publisher: Blizzard Entertainment.

KEY TERMS AND DEFINITIONS

Collective Intertextuality: The collective process through which individuals jointly weave a new text, bringing into it threads from their very own media repertoires. These are formed by pieces of other texts they have come across, sometimes life experiences (so not necessarily originating from media, from other texts), and make their way into a new text either consciously or unconsciously.

Cross-Media Adaptation: The adaptation of a text (or a series of texts, a story or storyworld) from one medium to another. This involves a transposition of narrative existents and events onto a new way of telling a story, one shaped and framed by the affordances of the destination medium.

Intermediality: The presence of, or rather the influence of one medium on another, patent in the sharing or merging of conventions, devices, stylistic choices, memes and so on.

Intertextuality: A way of looking at texts as only meaningful if seen as part of wider networks of other texts, culture and meaning. Texts only have meaning in relation to what has existed before, to other texts, to language, in specific contexts. If seen in operation, it can also be used to denote the act of analysing the various threads – or constituent intertexts – of a text.

Media Repertoire: The set of media texts consumed by an individual during their lifetime, including: the books they've read, the films they've watched, the games they've played, and so on. Often these become mixed in the individual's perception, and give rise to aggregated or joint elements; for example, my image of a wizard has been shaped by the series of wizards I have come across – but it is more than just the sum of these, it is a hybrid, a mix of images, not quite fully defined.

Remediation: The presence of – or allusion to – other media in a text pertaining to a different medium. The use of conventions, devices or techniques from a (usually older) medium in another (typically more recent) medium.

Textualisation: The process of concretising a mental image onto a text (in any media, so not simply onto words), involving the translation of that image or idea, through processes of selection, onto a media text.

Weaving (of a Text): An analogy that describes the creation of a new text as the result of the weaving together of different threads from previous texts. Weaving can be applied not just to the production of a text, but also to its reading – the meaning of a text is concretised when a reader weaves its symbols, its semiotic systems (images, words, sounds) with his or her own repertoire of meanings.

ENDNOTES

[1]   http://www.unesco.org.uk/unesco-chair-in-new-media-forms-of-the-book-university-of-bedfordshire-2012_

[2]   See examples of this kind of game here: http://www.miniclip.com/games/genre-1145/tower-defense/en.

[3]   http://www.ning.com_.

[4]   Barthes suggested the terms *lisible* ("readerly") and *scriptible* ("writerly") to distinguish between a) texts that are straightforward, closely following convention and with pretty well-defined or closed meaning, from b) texts whose meanings are not as straightforward, more open to interpretation, thus demanding more work from the reader, who is figuratively said to write their meanings.

[5]   Reader survey.

[6]   Authors are clearly influenced by previous authors, and often have editors suggesting tweaks, for example the addition of themes or characters that may resonate with a target market group. We will get back to the ways intertextual influences do not operate in isolation - the design of a text, and the very choice of what intertexts shape a new text - is also shaped by other factors such as budgets or editorial guidelines.

Section 4
Architextuality

Chapter 13
Interprocedurality:
Procedural Intertextuality in Digital Games

Marcelo Simão de Vasconcellos
Oswaldo Cruz Foundation (Fiocruz), Brazil

Flávia Garcia de Carvalho
Oswaldo Cruz Foundation (Fiocruz), Brazil

Inesita Soares de Araujo
Oswaldo Cruz Foundation (Fiocruz), Brazil

ABSTRACT

Intertextuality is present in most digital games since their beginnings. However, despite its importance for understanding games, research about the theme tends to be disproportionally rare and limited to representational aspects (text, images, audio, etc.), leaving out games' most distinctive characteristics, namely, their rules and mechanics. Since the classic concept of intertextuality does not account for this dimension, the authors propose a concept that is to games what intertextuality is for texts, combining principles of intertextuality with the theory of procedural rhetoric, which deals with the construction of meaning in digital games. This concept, interprocedurality, describes the explicit or implicit inclusion of other games' rules and mechanics in a given game. As a way to exemplify its presence in a specific game, this chapter presents a brief analysis of the interprocedurality occurring in the digital game Deus Ex: Human Revolution and the findings it generated.

INTRODUCTION

Digital games seem particularly related to intertextuality. Since their early beginnings, games have been incorporating themes, structures and other elements from previous media like literature, comics and movies. The creator of *Spacewar!* (1962), for example, clearly identifies *Buck Rogers* novels and comics as inspiration for the ship's design in his game, while *Galaxy Game* (1971) and *Computer Space* (1971) were both based on spaceship travel and combat as depicted in many science fiction books (Kent, 2001). Science fiction was not the only influence in digital games, though. Fantasy also was a frequent source

DOI: 10.4018/978-1-5225-0477-1.ch013

of references and inspiration to games. *Colossal Cave Adventure* (1976), Atari 2600's *Adventure* (1979), *Dungeons* (1975), *Telengard* (1976) and *Zork* (1976), had magic, dragons and castles, assumedly taking inspiration from the pen and paper role-playing game *Dungeons & Dragons* (Jerz, 2007).

At first, this probably occurred due their technical limitations, since labeling an enemy as "alien" was an economic way to tap into a rich tradition of science fiction invasion stories, quickly giving players some narrative context about the crude pixels on the screen. Resorting to stereotypes made the apprehension of the new media by the public easier and at the same time, functioned as narrative shortcuts, saving computational resources from the duty of explaining the narrative for the players, in a similar fashion that genre-based authors make conscious use of intertextuality in order to weave complex narratives without having to include long explanations (Kaveney, 2005).

With the advancement of computers, games could store more information, present richer graphics and run complex simulations. *Star Wars*, *Ghostbusters* and other movies became games, even unofficially, as is the case of *Metal Gear Solid* taking many narrative elements from the movie *Escape from New York* (Good, 2015). Now, the links with other texts could be both more frequent and more sophisticated, creating a constant interplay between games and previous media.

However, intertextuality was never a frequent research theme in Game Studies. An inquiry on intertextuality in a number of journals related to Game Studies generates few results, revealing a field of research in need of more attention. Moreover, even the existing studies about intertextuality in digital games usually limit their analysis to games' text, sounds and images (referred in this chapter as representation elements). While this has generated very interesting work, it does not adequately address the peculiarities of digital games. Besides representation elements, games have rules that structure their operations and are codified in procedures processed by a computer. This systemic dimension is also expressive in itself, conveying meaning through processes and algorithms. Moreover, games often copy, change and twist mechanics and rules of previous games. The authors argue that such phenomenon is very similar to intertextuality and, in this sense, looking at such rules and mechanics "migration" could be a useful way to complement intertextual approaches for understanding games.

Therefore, this chapter's objective is to discuss the intertextuality of rules and mechanics in digital games and its relations with the game's representational content. To do this, the authors present a brief overview of intertextuality and combine the concept with procedural rhetoric theory in order to apply it to game rules. Then, a brief analysis of the digital game *Deus Ex: Human Revolution* exemplifies the use of the concept, followed by conclusions. In addition, since the procedural elements of a game underlie the concept, the word intertextuality seems too tied with text. Therefore, for referring to intertextuality detected in the rules and mechanics of a game and not in its representation content, the authors propose the term *interprocedurality*, which will be used hereafter.

This chapter develops some findings cited in previous works. When analyzing the game *Passage*, by indie developer Jason Rohrer, the authors described how the game's creator used visual and thematic references to convey a deeper message through the few rules and assets of the game (Vasconcellos & Araujo, 2013). In another work, the authors described how operational aspects of game interface (like the almost universal use of the W, A, S and D keys to control the avatar) could be understood as an example of intertextuality (Carvalho, Vasconcellos, Ferreira, & Araujo, 2013). In both cases, however, the scope of said texts did not allow for a full description of the concept.

In this chapter, the authors present an initial outline of interprocedurality, but it is important to emphasize that this work focuses on the production domain. Constraints of time and space do not allow for a full account of interprocedurality as perceived by the audiences of a game. The authors' concern here is more modest: broadening the perspective of intertextuality on digital games, dealing with its effect on the most particular characteristic of games, namely, their rules and mechanics. Hopefully, such broadening could further enhance comprehension about how games are conceived, relate among themselves and evolve.

BACKGROUND

Intertextuality

Intertextuality describes the incorporation of a discursive element on another one, the implicit or explicit presence of other texts in a given text. This way, a text always would be formed by other texts' influences, be it in an explicit way (through citations, inclusions or dialogues) or in an implicit way, when it would be possible to see in the text ideas coming from previous sources.

In the early twentieth century, Mikhail Bakhtin developed the concept of dialogism, as a means to acknowledge and study the interchange between authors and their works, portraying a literary text as keeping a continuous dialogue with other texts and authors. In his view, an enunciation, socially and historically situated, could not avoid touching on a number of other enunciations about its object, becoming itself part of this web of dialogism (Bakhtin, 1981).

Combining Bakhtin's dialogism with the semiotics of Saussure, Julia Kristeva coined the word intertextuality, stating that "any text is constructed as a mosaic of quotations; any text is the absorption and transformation of another" (Kristeva, 1986, p. 37). The pieces of such a mosaic could be explicitly defined in the text or subtly merged, but in both situations, they would contribute to the whole. Such parts could be absorbed in a sense of confirmation, but also as contradiction, citation or irony. In all cases, intertextuality allowed to corroborate that a text is historically situated in a network of other texts, taking part in chains of meaning over time (Fairclough, 1993).

Kristeva also identified horizontal and vertical dimensions of intertextuality. The former describes the kind of relations between a chain of texts in time, where a particular text on a specific subject is conditioned by previous ones and at the same time, influences those texts that follow it. The latter is the relationship between a particular text and other texts around it that form its immediate context (Kristeva, 1986).

Working from distinctions made by French discourse analysts (Authier-Revuz, 1982; Maingueneau, 1987), Fairclough (1993) presents two kinds of intertextuality. The first is the manifest intertextuality, which describes explicit inclusions of other texts on one particular text, often depicted with signs like quotations marks and other elements typical of citations. The second kind is the constitutive intertextuality (which Fairclough denominates "interdiscursivity"), describing the relations of a given text with stylistic and discursive conventions from a specific genre. Thus, constitutive intertextuality highlights the discourse conventions collectively surrounding and influencing a particular text.

Many other authors introduced clarifications and modifications to the concept of intertextuality. Despite often using different denominations, their contributions in essence agreed that a text is never isolated, but constructed through many other texts, interlaced in time and space (Authier-Revuz, 1982; Grésillon, 1984; Pêcheux, 1969; Verón, 1980). It is possible to understand intertextuality as a continuous relationship of many texts by a particular author or even several authors, creating a dialogue in a given field, be it language, literature, sciences and even different cultures. For example, there is a clear conscious use of intertextuality when genre-based authors rely on fan's familiarity with the genre to include several layers of references, which allow complex narratives without the necessity of long explanations and digressions (Kaveney, 2005). Moreover, every artist suffers influence from predecessors and models. Thus, even when a creator aims to break with previous traditions, she acts upon a previously constructed context that conditions and enables such disruption.

Milton Pinto (1994) explains intertextuality as an infinite semiosis, a continuous chain of meanings created by the circulation of texts in society. For each text, there is an infinite network of remissive representations in the minds of individuals. Each significant refers to another significant, never reaching a stable or definitive meaning, but always prone to acquire new meanings. This process is socially determined and confirms intertextuality's role as one of the main defining contexts for social production of meaning (Vasconcellos & Araujo, 2014).

In the same way that the concept of dialogism goes beyond literature and appears in many other areas like music, visual arts and film, the relevance of intertextuality goes beyond text. If, in its strict sense, intertextuality only applies to written and spoken texts, in its broadest sense it applies to any kind of symbolic representation, as Verón (1980) confirmed, arguing that analysts should understand text as more than written words. Since the notion of text does not need to limit itself to the written word, but goes far beyond, potentially including any kind of representation, be it image, video, animation or other formats, soon authors started to use the concept of intertextuality when studying other media like visual arts and film. In a similar fashion, it is possible to understand digital games as a new kind of text and, as such, another potential environment for intertextuality: "Digital games are regarded as texts that reflect the cultures from which they emerge, and which potentially contribute to the circulation and naturalization of discourse." (Carr, 2013, p. 32)

The presence of intertextuality in digital games has been visible since the first arcade games, where the processing capabilities of the computer severely limited the use of text and graphics. In order to provide some story, the game developers had to resort to elements like scenarios, characters, devices from previous media that were clearly recognizable by the players. It was an economic way (in technical aspects) to condense complex narratives and tap into players' previous knowledge of similar stories. Despite their simplicity, these first games could draw references from a huge collective of previous texts. Thus, *Space Invaders* (Nishikado, 1978), with its invasion theme, laser cannon and crude aliens, referenced H. G. Wells's novel *The War of the Worlds* and the movie *Star Wars*, exempting itself of lengthy explanations about the game's context (Parkin, 2013). Similarly, Atari's *Adventure* (Robinett, 1979) referenced many elements typical of fantasy stories like magical swords, catacombs, dragons and castles, a strategy that allowed its developer to fit the (at the time) complex game into the strict limits of 4 Kb.

Although not alone as influences on the first digital games, fantasy and science fiction seem frequent sources of inspiration and references. Such sources provided an array of elements that would be inserted, modified and reinterpreted in digital games, working as narrative shortcuts in a still rudimentary media. Such intertextuality also occurred in the parody format, as exemplified by the series of adventure games *Simon, the Sorcerer*, set in a fantasy realm, which constantly mocked and subverted the conventions of fantasy stories, even showing the protagonist breaking the fourth wall and directly addressing the player (Woodroffe, 1993).

With the increasing of computational capabilities, new digital games could store more data, show detailed graphics and run complex simulations. References to other texts became common and more sophisticated, as digital games became more and more inspired by movie franchises. Gamers' desire for more detailed narratives encouraged game developers to continue this trend, including more elements in more nuanced ways, fostering a continuous network of references of games with other media. Soon, such a net of remissions started to form around games themselves, where a particular digital game would refer in an explicit or implicit way to previous games, forging a prolific space for intertextuality. Thus, the study of intertextuality in games can be a powerful way to understand games' history, heritage and evolution, asserting their role as cultural artifacts.

Related Works

Despite the frequency of intertextuality in games, there are few studies that analyze it. The authors searched for the terms "intertextual" and "intertextuality" within a number of Game Studies journals. The journals consulted were: ACM Computers in Entertainment, Digital Creativity, Elsevier Entertainment Computing, Eludamos, Games and Culture, G|A|M|E, Game Studies, Hindawi International Journal of Computer Games Technology, Journal of Gaming and Virtual Worlds, International Journal of Roleplaying, Journal of Virtual Reality and Broadcasting, Journal of Virtual Worlds Research, Loading..., Press Start, SAGE Simulation and Gaming, The Computer Games Journal, ToDiGRA, Television & New Media. The search revealed eight publications along with two others outside of the journals above that explicitly addressed intertextuality in games: an article from a Religion Studies Journal and a conference paper.

A group of texts address intertextuality as part of transmedia occurrences, discussing intertextuality within several installments of a same franchise and its ties with the larger fictional universe (Bonk, 2014) and as the interplay between games and other media like animation, TV and marketing (Kinder, 1991). Other groups addressed intertextuality in digital games' content, discussing the links between horror games and horror movies (Spittle, 2011), representation of analog media in game narrative (Kirkland, 2009), intersections between fictional game narrative and historical elements as opportunities for learning (Iacovides, McAndrew, Scanlon, & Aczel, 2014) and even how religious intertextuality in games fosters player's reflection on his/her own identity (Love, 2010).

Generally, authors understand digital games not as isolated products in a radical new format, but as cultural artifacts that are conceived and received in an intertextual network of references originated from previous media formats (Apperley, 2006). Under the perspective of reception of game media, Consalvo (2003) argues that player's productions like walkthroughs and game guides also work as narratives, intertextually read by other players, which confirm players' sophisticated media apprehension skills and their place as active creators. Carr (2013), analyzing the game *Deus Ex: Human Revolution,* presents intertextuality in games as the several different contexts of different players playing the same game and constructing their particular meaning thanks to each individual's network of references. These intertextual effects also happen the other way around, when, for example, the Gulf War was nicknamed the "Nintendo War" because of its strong emphasis in technology like digitally controlled bombings broadcasted live on television (Scodari, 1993).

As a whole, there were very few results considering the relevance of intertextuality for digital games, suggesting that intertextuality is a marginal theme in Game Studies, to say the least. Furthermore, despite their strengths and insights, the analyzed texts addressed intertextuality in representation terms only, without taking into account its presence in game mechanics and rules — the aforementioned interprocedurality.

Defining Interprocedurality

Despite the importance of representational elements, it is important to underline that the most specific components of games (and digital games in particular) are rules and mechanics. These components distinguish games from other media and as such, have to appear prominently in any analysis of the medium. There is much debate about the differences between game rules and game mechanics, and, for the purposes of this chapter, the authors adopt definitions proposed by Miguel Sicart (2008), briefly presented below.

Game mechanics are methods invoked by agents in games in order to interact with game states (Sicart, 2008). As such, they are actions available to the player and computer-controlled characters in game. Often they map directly to interface controls, like the "jump" mechanic, normally activated by pressing the space key on computer games. Briefly, mechanics are ways in which the player exerts agency in the game world, while game rules define the inner workings of games.

In digital games, the rules also maintain the systems of the game world, so, it is possible to distinguish between game rules, which govern winning and losing conditions (like "collect 5 coins to win this level") and world rules, which define the game world (like "there is a night and day cycle" or "the gravity is inverted"). While the game mechanics are a space for players' actions, game rules structure the game itself. They guide and condition player actions, setting up their consequences (as victory or failure) as well (Sicart, 2008).

Games have rules and mechanics, which, when actuated, start processes, comprised of sets of rules. As digital environments, games embody the procedurality, defined by Murray as "the ability to execute a series of rules" (Murray, 1998).

Based on this understanding, Bogost (2007) presented the concept of procedural rhetoric as the main form of meaning production in video games defining it as "the art of persuasion through rule-based representations and interactions rather than the spoken word, writing, images, or moving pictures" (preface, para. 6). Another author, Gonzalo Frasca (2003), prefers the term "simulation rhetoric", but his take on the concept is essentially the same: a game is a system of ordered procedures conveying some kind of ideology.

Rhetoric refers to the art of persuasion, created by Plato and expanded by Aristotle, which was later expanded to include all forms of expression (and not only those aiming to change the opinion of others), both verbal and in any other symbolic system. Despite acknowledging the role of text, audio and image as expressive elements in games, procedural rhetoric theory states that digital games have the unique ability to express meaning through dynamic processes (Bogost, 2007).

According to this view, while a book expresses meaning to the reader through its words, a game would convey such meaning through player's direct interaction with its rules. Because of their procedural rhetoric, games are capable of depicting real world processes using digital processes that happen inside the game. Instead of precise representations, these game processes work as a dynamic metaphor for real world events, mediations of real-world processes, arranged in an expressive representation (with greater or lesser degree of simulational fidelity) in the game (Bogost, 2007). Such representation is never a perfect simulation, though, but product of interpretations and simplifications of real systems since there are both technological constraints and game designers' ideologies shaping the game (Bogost, 2007; Frasca, 2003).

Procedural rhetoric defines a game as a sequence of actionable arguments, operated by the player. The meaning of a digital game would emerge when the player interacts with its rules and completing the game would be the only way to uncover its message. Such interaction would follow parameters and rules previously defined by the game designer and by reconstructing the meaning embedded in the rules, the player would "solve" or "win" the game. It follows from this approach that any digital game requires careful planning to build a procedural argument in order to convey the correct message to the player (Bogost, 2007).

A direct consequence of the procedural rhetoric is that the potential meaning of a game resides in its rules and mechanics. It presupposes two essential elements: a player who plays the game in a predictable, specific way and a game without room for players' additions or contributions (Sicart, 2012).

However, as the complexity of digital games increase, the more varied ways players interact with their rules, intervening in the flow of procedural rhetoric built by the game designers (Ferrari, 2010). Therefore, an exaggerated emphasis on procedural rhetoric's tenets tend to promote a deterministic or instrumental view of game media, relegating they player to connecting the dots previously laid out by the game designer (Ferrari, 2010). It could imply that there is a "right way" to experience a game, assuming that adequate reception of the game supposedly would result in a perfect transfer of its message (Vasconcellos, 2013). Ultimately, this disregards the creative potential of players, who often ignore rules, play inefficiently on purpose and even subvert the rules for their amusement (Ferrari, 2010).

Despite these limitations of the procedural rhetoric, for the purposes of this chapter, its emphasis on the centrality of rules and mechanics opens a fruitful angle for investigating games. Of course, there is a whole player performance space that operates in conjunction with the rules and mechanics created by game designers. However, relying on procedural rhetoric allows highlighting the constitutive structure of games. By focusing on games' rules and mechanics (i.e. how they build their procedural rhetoric), it is possible to trace connections, inheritances and influences between a vast array of games, which would be not visible considering only their representation elements.

Therefore, as intertextuality describes the implicit or explicit presence of other texts in a given text, its procedural counterpart, called here interprocedurality, is the incorporation of preexistent rules and mechanics in a given game. Interprocedurality adds another layer of interrelations between a given game and other games both in time and in space, which, when combined with other analytical methods, allows a deeper reading of game media.

First, interprocedurality makes easier to identify reskinned games. In game design, reskinning is the use of new graphics and text over a preexistent system of game rules and mechanics (Bogost, 2007). Bogost describes the political advertising game from the Republican Party called *Tax Invaders*, a reskin of classic *Space Invaders* where, instead of fighting aliens, the player fights Democratic Party's John Kerry's tax plans. Despite the huge differences between the settings, representation content and purposes of *Space Invaders* and *Tax Invaders*, both follow the same rules and mechanics, keeping an interprocedural relation.

Another example of interprocedurality comes from Bogost's practice as game designer. As a means of criticizing the increasing use of money grabbing schemes in Facebook social games, Bogost created a small game called *Cow Clicker,* where everything the player can do is to click on a cow periodically, without any effects besides gaining a chance to click again. He used such simple mechanics, typical of games like *Farmville*, while subverting its function in a humorous, satirical way in order to expose games he considered ruses and exploitation (Tanz, 2015). *Cow Clicker* worked both as parody and as criticism of social games. As parodies in literature employ intertextuality, this particular case of parody in game is effective thanks to its interprocedural connections with preexistent Facebook social games.

Game rules and mechanics are continuously migrating between games, suffering mutations in the process. In a way, even the game industry and game stores acknowledge this, organizing games not necessarily in genres like science fiction, western, fantasy, etc., but preferring categories derived from game rules and mechanics like Shooter, RTS (Real Time Strategy), FPS (First Person Shooter) and Roguelike games. Despite such categories being far from standardized, they represent emergent initiatives for a classification based mainly on functional aspects of games.

Hence, as intertextuality is present in the representational elements of games, interprocedurality is present in their rules and mechanics, which reference a net of remissions to rules of other games, both digital and non-digital. This interprocedurality also influences how this network of references affects the way players interact and construct meaning of said game. Moreover, the same way intertextuality presupposes a wider social context where the text exists and circulates, interprocedurality also presupposes a social context where games are constantly emerging and circulating as cultural practices, in a continuous process of production of meaning operated by their players. In this sense, interprocedurality reaffirms the importance of the social domain when analyzing digital games.

On production aspects, there is a very pragmatic reason for game designers' use of interprocedurality. When dealing with complex digital systems (as games often are), a user benefits if such a system keeps similarities of operation with previous systems. This reasoning lead to the birth of modern usability on the 1980s, which grew significantly with dissemination of the World Wide Web, trying to unify the countless styles of interfaces in a coherent and intelligible whole (Sauro, 2013). As this standardization of some basic interaction procedures developed, it spread to digital games as well and slowly, some patterns of functionality emerged. Game developers soon learned that their interfaces and control schemes would benefit from following such patterns, making it easier for players to grasp the basic operation of their games. Hence, the interface operation of games benefits from a sensible use of interprocedurality.

Some games employ manifest interprocedurality as part of its themes, making explicit citations to other games. For example, in *Evoland* (2013) each game level represents a stage of evolution in game history, employing gameplay and aesthetics reminiscent of the time. In *The Stanley Parable* (Wreden & Pugh, 2013), player's choices are contested and contradicted at every moment, by the voice of the narrator, making a parody of the fake choices available in some games. While there are few examples of games with such manifest interprocedurality, as far as the authors could investigate, most games present constitutive interprocedurality, which, like constitutive intertextuality, is implicit and in this case highlights rules and mechanic conventions surrounding and influencing a particular game.

Instead of fixed genres, games tend to be categorized by players through their mechanics and rules, which describe the way they are played. This way, it is possible to describe a game as being a "3D action game with RPG elements", or another as "RTS without base building" or a third one as an "adventure game with quick time events". Interprocedurality accounts for this player practice and, as mentioned, allows the researcher to find connections between games that are not explicit in terms of content. As such, it provides a deeper reading of a game and its relations and connections within the broader context of game media.

Examining *Deus Ex: Human Revolution*

It is important to investigate if the concept of interprocedurality actually helps in analyzing a game. Unfortunately, due to space constraints, it is not feasible to conduct here a full analysis of interprocedurality in a game. However, in order to exemplify some concrete occurrences of the concept, it was applied in an analysis of some aspects of the game *Deus Ex: Human Revolution* (hereafter abbreviated to *DE:HR*).

The procedural nature of games makes a mere artifact reading ineffective, instead demanding such games to be analyzed not only as object, but as a nexus of player practices that construct meaning from it

(Bateman, 2015). In the present case, such analysis took the form of an auto-ethnography, encompassing phases of playing the game in an exploratory way, closely observing the interaction with game's rules and mechanics, taking field notes and screenshots for documentation and posterior analysis. After each game session, there was a self-reflection over the experiences in game and the choices made during play in order to contribute to the analysis (Foith, 2013).

DE:HR is the last chapter of a classic franchise of digital games. It occupies a unique place due to its classic inheritance and its wide range of literary and visual influences, which make it a good example for discussion. *DE:HR* is a science fiction digital game originally released for PC, PlayStation 3 and Xbox 360, in 2011, created by Eidos Montreal. It is the third game in the *Deus Ex* series and a prequel to the original game released in 2000. While the original Deus Ex (released in 2000) is set in a dystopian world during the year 2052, *DE:HR* takes place in 2027, depicting events that would eventually lead to the first game.

As a whole, the *Deus Ex* series present typical elements of the cyberpunk theme, like near future setting, dystopian world, social conflicts, low quality of life, cutting edge, often invasive, technology and the ethical interrogations regarding science (Deus Ex: Human Revolution, 2015). *DE:HR* follows the same style, with a heavier emphasis on the cybernetic implants, artificial replacements for body parts, which are largely used. Such implants are no more called prosthesis but "augmentations", since their objective is rather to improve life than correct disability. On the other side, there is much social prejudice against augmented persons, one of the main points of the game.

The game protagonist is Adam Jensen, security manager at Sarif Industries, a leading biotech company that specializes in human augmentations. Jensen is mortally wounded in a violent terrorist attack and undergoes radical surgeries that replace large areas of his body with advanced prostheses and internal organ systems (Deus Ex: Human Revolution, 2015). The game starts after Jensen's recovery, when he starts an investigation about the attack. During his search, he will become embroiled in a global machination for the control of the human enhancement technology, involving major themes like corporations' role in society, globalization, espionage, health, human survival, poverty, and the ethics of transhumanism (Deus Ex: Human Revolution, 2015).

Regarding the gameplay, DE:HR is a mix between First Person Shooter (FPS) and action Role-Playing Game (RPG), featuring evolution of the character through experience points, unlockable cybernetic abilities, a full combat system with varied firearms and stealth mechanics. Actually, the game allows a remarkable latitude of actions to complete each level's objectives, ranging from open combat featuring weapons and augmentations to radical non-violent approaches, where the player can choose to take out the guards one by one silently or even evade them altogether. There is also a system for using social skills through a conversation system, where the player performs long dialogues with another characters in order to bend them to their will, making them reveal important information, creating different outcomes (Francis, 2015). The storyline also offers many different side-quests that are all optional, but several of them add information to the overall story. All such options reinforce themes explored in the narrative, leading the player to experience the consequences of his previous actions.

Intertextuality in the Game

Regarding constitutive intertextuality, *DE:HR* draws from the large pool of cyberpunk science fiction, mixing themes of cybernetic implants, gene manipulations and corrupt science employed for political or economic gains, making implicit references to movies like *Blade Runner* and *Ghost in the Shell* and to the collective works of authors like William Gibson, Neal Stephenson and Bruce Sterling. Additionally, *DE:HR* shows a complex network of technological breakthroughs and their violent impact in people's lives, interlacing it with the philosophical and political views of transhumanism, which defends the improvement of human body and mind through radical technology (Chislenko, More, Sandberg, Vita-More, & Yudkowsky, 2001). Transhumanism appears constantly in the game, through the idea of augmentations as a new evolutionary step, desirable for all humankind (Foith, 2013).

DE:HR also references the first installment of the franchise, *Deus Ex*. Warren Spector, creator of the original game, declared how he was influenced by the paranoia that surrounded the turn of the millennium, which inspired him to twist the cyberpunk theme, introducing conspiracy elements inspired in the television show *The X-Files* (Spector, 2015). In *DE:HR* the conspiracy elements are also frequent and, since it is a prequel of the original game, they present some veiled references to it, foreshadowing future events. As *Deus Ex* drew inspiration of the current events of its time, *DE:HR* draws inspiration from current events, echoing contemporary society's worries about issues like the right to health, dangers of technology and invasion of privacy.

Supplementing this aspect, there are many examples of manifest intertextuality in the game, mainly in the form of digital books scattered on rooms around the map, which the player can collect and read to gain insight about the game world. In some cases, the information presented in such books is authentic to the point of presenting a complete scientific citation (Foith, 2013).

On the surface, its cyberpunk setting shows all the rich imagery of technology mixed with decadence. However, *DE:HR*'s art direction is distinctive in its use of a visual style reminiscent of the Renaissance, with copious use of warm orange and sepia tones in ambient, lighting and even in the characters' clothes. Dubbed *cyber renaissance* by the game developers, this visual style symbolizes the similarities between the game's period and the Italian Renaissance, both times of rapid technological innovation, cultural turmoil and emphasis on the metaphor of the human body as a machine. Besides setting the atmosphere of the game, the cyber renaissance fashion in characters' clothes and homes help to distinguish those who favor the augmentations, while the objectors of cybernetic advancements use contemporary clothes (Deus Ex: Human Revolution, 2015). These examples of visual intertextuality extend to the graphical user interface, which shows Adam's augmentations appear projected onto his body, allowing the player to see the bones and organs beneath, like da Vinci's anatomy drawings. In addition, icons typical of today's digital systems, like Wi-Fi, battery and speakers symbols appears over less detailed sequences of hexadecimal characters, decorating the interface with a high-tech flair.

On the whole, *DE:HR* is very prolific in many forms of intertextuality, a characteristic that is both intentional and unavoidable, since it is a prequel — and, in a certain way, also a revival — of a historic PC game. For the same reasons, *DE:HR* is also prolific in interprocedurality.

Interprocedurality in *Deus Ex: Human Revolution*

Interprocedurality is more evident in *DE:HR* in three main aspects: its movement and physical space representation, its interface and its progression system.

DE:HR incorporates mechanics from two main categories of digital games: the FPS and the RPG. Despite not dealing (only) with shooting, all the experience is in first person, making the player only see the hands of Adam Jensen for most of the time. In consequence, most of the mechanics for controlling the avatar follows a pattern that is typical of FPSs: the keys WASD (respectively forward, left, backward, right), space for jumping and "E" for executing actions like opening doors and activating computers.

DE:HR follows this pattern so faithfully that its tutorial messages could easily teach the player how to play a number of other contemporary first person games.

One addition that diverges from this pattern, however, is the cover system, a kind of mechanic more common in third person shooters (where the player continuously sees his avatar on the screen). Cover allows players to avoid enemy fire hiding behind barriers. Its use in modern digital games was popularized by *Gears of War*, a console game that influenced many subsequent shooters (Ashcraft, 2010).

Cover was an important addition to *DE:HR*, since it fits perfectly the kind of infiltration missions that are part of the game. But it also implies that *DE:HR* is a more lethal kind of game, where the protagonist cannot withstand a frontal confrontation with armed opponents without serious risk of dying. By referencing other games, the mere presence of cover in *DE:HR* starts signaling the player that it involves subterfuge and requires a tactical instance more careful than typical FPSs. Therefore, interprocedurality acts in this case preparing the player beforehand for the challenges ahead.

However, a cover mechanic on a first person game is not easily implemented, since player's information about the virtual environment is limited to sight and sound, lacking more subtle data like the sense of proprioception. The developers' solution to implement cover in *DE:HR* was almost to the letter of the one present in *Gears of War*: when Adam Jensen takes cover, the game's perspective changes from first person to third person, which allows the player a better sense of his surroundings and more information for tactical decisions. This rotational point of view during a game is very unusual, marking a clear case of interprocedurality: a mechanic from a previous influential game inspired *Deus Ex* to the point of causing an odd — even if effective — game design decision.

Regarding the interface of *DE:HR*, its Head-Up Display (HUD) is an omnipresent overlay of relevant game information (health, ammunition, current objectives, etc.) on the screen. As part of game mechanics, HUDs are an established convention of digital games, to the point of being (ironically) almost invisible to the player. In this sense, the HUD in *DE:HR* references a vast amount of games that came before, particularly the first person games. However, in later years, there has been an effort by many game developers to reduce HUD's visual elements on screen, as a way to increase immersion in the game world. Games like *Metro 2033* employs a diegetic interface, removing most of visual overlay, relying instead on the game world elements (for example, using the watch in the avatar's hand to show the time) to convey to the player the necessary information (Stonehouse, 2014).

In *DE:HR*, the game developers employed an opposite approach in order to reach the same objective of increasing immersion: since Adam Jensen is a cyborg, the game presents the HUD as part of his optical augmentations, incorporating the mechanic in the game's narrative. This is also highlighted in the later part of the game, when a HUD malfunction renders Jensen (and the player by extension) helpless in a combat scene. Such interlacing between HUD mechanic and story appears also in the event of player's failure. When Adam dies in the game, the screen shows a red, broken HUD. In this sense, *DE:HR*'s HUD is an example of interprocedurality in two aspects. First, it inherits and reinterprets the tradition of game HUDs, particularly from FPSs and RPGs. In second place, it reinforces the contemporary trend for immersion, in this particular case not so much as removing HUD's elements, but reimagining them with the support of the game's fictional content. In this example, it is possible to see the fruitful interplay between the game's rules and mechanics and the narrative content.

Regarding the progression system of the game, like previously mentioned, *DE:HR* is a hybrid game, incorporating elements from different types of games, particularly FPS and RPG genres. If on one hand the player's point of view comes from FPS domain, on the other hand the progression of protagonist's abilities in game is based on those typical of RPGs. In fact, one of the most typical mechanics of RPGs is the gaining of experience as a way to improve the avatar's abilities.

Experience, numerically measured in "experience points", is so ingrained in the mind of players of the RPG genre that it becomes naturalized. For example, one could ask: Why not consider only the experience of the player as in the majority of other games? After all, time spent playing a game naturally grants a gradual boost in player's skill. Instead, in RPGs the experience of the protagonist is the focus, its importance often surpassing the influence of player talent in the game. Therefore, the experience mechanic appears in an RPG game as an uncontested convention. Most players simply accept that the game's protagonist gradually will improve with time and, most importantly, each activity in game, particularly optional quests, will represent a way to increase such experience. It is a defining characteristic of *DE:HR* as an action RPG.

Of course, the point of increasing experience is improving the protagonist's abilities, another solid convention of RPGs. In most games in this genre, experience points grow and, in specific thresholds, the protagonist earns one or more "points" to "buy" skills, abilities or powers. *DE:HR* follows these same rules with a twist. Adam Jensen's skills do not refer to knowledge or practical skills like investigation, shooting and other abilities "naturally" gained. Instead, they come only from his mechanical augmentations.

In the beginning of the game, Adam Jensen is informed that some of his augmentations are not yet active, but in due time he will be able to use them. During the course of game, as the player performs missions and gains experience, he receives *Praxis* points, used for activating augmentation's functions. Such a name suggests the idea that Adam has to "practice" in order to achieve full use of his augmentations and in this limited sense *Praxis*, regardless of name and place in narrative, procedurally functions as a typical skill system of RPGs. However, there is a kind of augmentation canister scattered in the game world, called *Praxis kit*, which, when activated inside a clinic, gives a *Praxis* point regardless of Adam's current experience. This mechanic is at odds with the narrative, making the player wonder why could not Sarif Industries give Adam many *Praxis kits* from the start, instead of letting him to find them for himself. Here, the influence of interprocedurality seems to have made the game developers rely on a standard RPG set of rules for player progression, without considering the specificities of the game narrative of *DE:HR*.

In addition, save for augmentations, Adam's natural abilities do not improve with his experience and his human skills do not even appear in game. The skill of the player, however, obviously improves as she progresses in the game and in this sense, *DE:HR* deviates from standard RPGs where the protagonist's progression mimics player's experience. In this case, the focus on augmentations and the disregard for Adam Jensen's human skills reinforce the theme of the game: cybernetic implants are becoming more important than inborn abilities.

Finally, by employing, adapting and twisting mechanics from other games, like hacking, uncovering documents, multiple routes for the objectives and RPG mechanics like experience points, *DE:HR* presents itself to the player as an exploratory game in at least three aspects.

First, it fosters an exploratory instance due to the careful construction of the game world, showing detailed scenarios, full of elements that can be examined closely. Personal computers in offices have e-mail messages with varied conversations, medical reports show clues about Adam's origin and opponents and civilians' conversations can be overheard, enriching the world and the story. Worth mentioning are the many books scattered around the game's levels, with excerpts detailing technological advancements and political struggles. They contribute greatly to construct a living world and give the narrative more credibility as a potential future. Such affordances echo previous games (including the original *Deus Ex*) where exploring is vital to the player.

Second, *DE:HR* encourages the player to explore different routes and strategies for accomplishing the game's goals. There is always more than one way to solve a problem or reach a particular place, something that the game designers declared as one of their main objectives when developing *DE:HR*. Such freedom to pursue different solutions for challenges in game reinforces the link with the first game in the franchise, praised for successfully accommodating many styles of play.

Lastly, the mere fact that *DE:HR* carries RPG elements helps fostering this exploratory instance in players, since in most RPGs exploration of space is a ubiquitous feature. In *DE:HR*, exploration seems part of its RPG inheritance and it is often rewarded. The player does not run through each level. Instead, she will take her time to explore carefully each nook and cranny in order to find relevant clues, additional background information, items like ammunition and consumables and the occasional secret area, typically containing a better reward like a new weapon or a *praxis kit*. This is another example how the references to mechanics from previous games — in this case, RPGs — decisively change player's experience of the game. Thanks to interprocedurality, as soon as the player sees the experience, skill and inventory mechanics in place, she tacitly understands that the game follows RPG conventions and the game space is not so much to be conquered quickly as to be explored in detail. Revealing hidden items in each level is as important as taking out all the enemies and sometimes even more rewarding. These first signals fundamentally influence the player's approach to play the game.

CONCLUSION

Thanks to this brief analysis of *DE:HR*, it is possible to highlight three main considerations about interprocedurality.

First, if in many cases referring to rules from previous games is involuntary, in other cases is a strategy for broadening the player base of a new game, both for commercial and artistic reasons. *DE:HR* brings these two occurrences. There is an unconscious interprocedurality, employed by the game designers as a natural consequence of them living in a context full of references and echoes coming from different games. This confirms its role as an important aspect of meaning production, since the game developers expressed their creative ideas reiterating and reimagining rules and mechanics from other games.

There is also intentional interprocedurality. It is possible to perceive a concern about making *DE:HR* accessible to contemporary players, employing mechanics widely known and approved as a way to reduce any struggle that players could have in trying to learn the game. In addition, the designers aimed to create a game whose rules and mechanics would place it in a specific position in the game market (rich history, immersive, challenging, not necessarily violent, but with multiple ways of acting, etc.). Adapting the words of Kristeva (1986), there is a vertical interprocedurality around *DE:HR*, where the game dialogues with other games similar or near its place in the broader context of games. Although this allows to infer a worry about marketing issues (making the game accessible to the majority of consumers), as a whole, it also shows that game developers, as artists in general, wish to communicate their ideas with as many people as possible. In both cases, it is clear the strong social component of interprocedurality in games. If intertextuality is often a case of authors employing "narrative shortcuts" for conveying a deeper meaning to their text (Kaveney, 2005), interprocedurality is often the use of "cognitive shortcuts" by developers in order to smooth players' apprehension of game rules and mechanics, facilitating their enjoyment of the game.

Second, interprocedurality works along time. Of course, there were obvious commercial reasons to keep ideas from the original *Deus Ex* game in *DE:HR*, preserving distinctive traces of a successful franchise. This inheritance worked as way to call back old fans to the new installment and, in a sense, tried to continue a tradition. It also highlights an ideology behind the game design principle that came from the first game, of giving players the maximum freedom possible for dealing with the games' challenges. Thus, the mechanical aspects which appear in *DE:HR* are a tangible consequence of a philosophy of game design embraced by the game developers, inspired by the team who created the original game. With this, *DE:HR* acknowledges its ancestry and becomes part of such legacy. Again, adapting Kristeva (1986), it is a dialogue between games occurring through time, exemplifying a horizontal dimension of interprocedurality, where rules and mechanics respond, reinterpret and assimilate those of previous games. Also in this aspect, interprocedurality brings a clear sense of social production of meaning, which happens not only in the present, but extends itself through history.

Third, despite usually forgotten, this procedural layer is very relevant to understanding digital games. Game rules and mechanics are frequently inspired, adapted or even simply copied from previous digital games. The repetition and refinement of game mechanics in the game industry led to the development of game categories around such mechanics, leading to the emergence of terms like "First-person-shooters" (or FPS), "sandbox" and "roguelike". On one hand, players become fond of certain game mechanics over another and many tend to restrict themselves to games with that particular feel. On the other hand, the game industry, in order to cater to the needs of these groups, creates games that precisely fit such categorizations, sometimes making hard the emergence of new mechanics.

Finally, the authors wish to highlight that this chapter is a first approach to exploring the concept of interprocedurality. As such, it focused on the production aspects and did not delve into the reception side, namely, how players receive and construct meaning through the interprocedurality perceived in the game. This is a far more complex endeavor, nonetheless, an important direction for future research. For now, this initial proposal of the concept of interprocedurality tried to acknowledge that rules and mechanics are the most distinctive characteristic of games, emphasizing the importance of knowing how they migrate, change and evolve from game to game. This makes interprocedurality relevant to digital games and deserving further study along its more traditional counterpart.

REFERENCES

Apperley, T. H. (2006). Genre and game studies: Toward a critical approach to video game genres.[abstract]. *Simulation & Gaming, 37*(1), 6–23. http://sag.sagepub.com/content/37/1/6 doi:10.1177/1046878105282278

Ashcraft, B. (2010). How cover shaped gaming's last decade. *Kotaku.* Retrieved July 10, 2015, from http://kotaku.com/5452654/how-cover-shaped-gamings-last-decade

Authier-Revuz, J. (1982). Hétérogénéité montrée et hétérogénéité constitutive: Éléments pour une approche de l'autre dans le discours. *DRLAV. Revue de Linguistique, 26*, 91–151.

Bakhtin, M. (1981). *The dialogic imagination.* Austin, TX: University of Texas Press.

Bateman, C. (2015). The essence of RPGs (1): Children of TSR. *ihobo*. Retrieved June 17, 2015, from http://blog.ihobo.com/2015/04/the-essence-of-rpgs-1-children-of-tsr.html

Bogost, I. (2007). Persuasive games: The expressive power of videogames (Kindle ed.). Cambridge, MA: The MIT Press.

Bonk, J. (2014). Finishing the fight, one step at a time: Seriality in Bungie's *Halo. Eludamos (Göttingen), 8*(1), 65–81. Retrieved from http://www.eludamos.org/index.php/eludamos/article/view/vol8no1-5

Carr, D. (2013). Bodies, augmentation and disability in *Dead Space* and *Deus Ex: Human Revolutions.* In *Context Matters! — Proceedings of the Vienna Games Conference 2013: Exploring and Reframing Games and Play in Context*. Vienna, Austria: New Academic Press.

Carvalho, F. G., Vasconcellos, M. S., Ferreira, P. C., & Araujo, I. S. (2013). Jogos digitais como cultura participatória: O modelo do mercado simbólico aplicado à concepção de um jogo digital sobre a prevenção de DST e Aids. In Proceedings do XII Simpósio Brasileiro de Jogos e Entretenimento Digital (SBGames 2013).

Chislenko, A., More, M., Sandberg, A., Vita-More, N., & Yudkowsky, E. (2001). Transhumanist FAQ. *Humanity+*. Retrieved July 7, 2015, from http://humanityplus.org/philosophy/transhumanist-faq/#top

Consalvo, M. (2003). *Zelda 64* and video game fans: A walkthrough of games, intertextuality, and narrative.[abstract]. *Television & New Media, 4*(3), 321–334. doi:10.1177/1527476403253993

Deus Ex. (2015). *Human Revolution*. Tokyo: Square Enix. [Digital Game]

Evoland. (2013). Bordeaux: Shiro Games. [Digital game]

Fairclough, N. (1993). *Discourse and social change*. Cambridge, MA: Polity Press.

Ferrari, S. (2010). *The judgement of procedural rhetoric*. (Doctoral Dissertation). Retrieved from Georgia Tech SMARTech database. Retrieved from http://hdl.handle.net/1853/33915

Foith, M. (2013). Virtually witness augmentation now: Video games and the future of human enhancement. *M/C Journal, 16*(6). Retrieved from http://journal.media-culture.org.au/index.php/mcjournal/article/viewArticle/729

Francis, T. (2015). *Deus Ex: Human Revolution* review. *PC Gamer*. Retrieved June 15, 2015, from http://www.pcgamer.com//deus-ex-human-revolution-review/

Frasca, G. (2003). Simulation versus narrative: Introduction to Ludology. In M. J. P. Wolf & B. Perron (Eds.), *The video game theory reader* (pp. 221–235). New York, NY: Routledge.

Good, O. S. (2015). *Metal Gear Solid* wasn't sued over *Escape from New York* ties because Kojima's 'a nice guy'. *Polygon, 2015*. Retrieved from http://www.polygon.com/2015/10/28/9625556/metal-gear-solid-escape-from-new-york-lawsuit-kojima-john-carpenter

Grésillon, A. M. D., & Maingueneau, D. (1984). Polyphonie, proverbe et détournement, ou un proverbe peut en cacher un autre. *Langages, 19*(73), 112–125. doi:10.3406/lgge.1984.1168

Iacovides, I., McAndrew, P., Scanlon, E., & Aczel, J. (2014). The gaming involvement and informal learning framework.[abstract]. *Simulation & Gaming, 45*(4-5), 611–626. doi:10.1177/1046878114554191

Jerz, D. G. (2007). Somewhere nearby is *Colossal Cave*: Examining Will Crowther's original adventure in code and in Kentucky. *Digital Humanities Quarterly, 1*(2). Retrieved from http://www.digitalhumanities.org/dhq/vol/001/2/000009/000009.html

Kaveney, R. (2005). *From Alien to The Matrix: Reading science fiction film*. New York, NY: I. B. Tauris.

Kent, S. L. (2001). *The ultimate history of video games: From Pong to Pokémon and beyond - the story behind the craze that touched our lives and changed the world*. New York, NY: Three Rivers Press.

Kinder, M. (1991). *Playing with power in movies, television, and video games: From Muppet Babies to Teenage Mutant Ninja Turtles*. Berkeley, CA: University of California Press.

Kirkland, E. (2009). *Resident Evil*'s typewriter: Survival horror and its remediations.[abstract]. *Games and Culture, 4*(2), 115–126. doi:10.1177/1555412008325483

Kristeva, J. (1986). *The Kristeva reader*. New York, NY: Columbia University Press.

Love, M. C. (2010). Not-so-sacred quests: Religion, intertextuality and ethics in video games. *Religious Studies and Theology, 29*(2), 191–213.

Maingueneau, D. (1987). *Nouvelles tendances en analyse du discours*. Paris, France: Hachette.

Murray, J. H. (1998). *Hamlet on the holodeck: The future of narrative in cyberspace*. Cambridge, MA: The MIT Press.

Nishikado, T. (1978). *Space invaders* [Digital Game]. Tokyo, Japan: Taito.

Parkin, S. (2013). The space invader. *The New Yorker, 2015*. Retrieved from http://www.newyorker.com/tech/elements/the-space-invader

Pêcheux, M. (1969). *Analyse automatique du discours*. Paris, France: Dunod.

Pinto, M. J. (1994). *As marcas lingüísticas da enunciação: Esboço de uma gramática enunciativa do português*. Rio de Janeiro, Brazil: Numen.

Robinett, W. (1979). *Adventure* [Digital game]. Sunnyvale: Atari.

Sauro, J. (2013). A history of usability. *UXmas*. Retrieved July 2, 2015, from http://uxmas.com/2013/history-of-usability

Scodari, C. (1993). Operation Desert Storm as "wargames": Sport, war, and media intertextuality. *Journal of American Culture, 16*(1), 1–5. doi:10.1111/j.1542-734X.1993.1601_1.x

Sicart, M. (2008). Defining game mechanics. *Game Studies, 8*(2). Retrieved from http://gamestudies.org/0802/articles/sicart

Sicart, M. (2012). Against procedurality. *Game Studies, 11*(3). Retrieved from gamestudies.org/1103/articles/sicart_ap

Spector, W. (2015). DX15: The legacy of *Deus Ex*. *IGN*. Retrieved July 2, 2015, from http://www.ign. com/videos/2015/06/26/dx15-the-legacy-of-deus-ex

Spittle, S. (2011). "Did this game scare you? Because it sure as hell scared me!" *F.E.A.R.*, the abject and the uncanny.[abstract]. *Games and Culture*, *6*(4), 312–326. doi:10.1177/1555412010391091

Stonehouse, A. (2014). User interface design in video games. *Gamasutra*. Retrieved July 5, 2015, from http://gamasutra.com/blogs/AnthonyStonehouse/20140227/211823/User_interface_design_in_video_games.php?print=1

Tanz, J. (2015). The curse of *Cow Clicker*: How a cheeky satire became a videogame hit. *Wired Magazine*. Retrieved June 12, 2015, from http://archive.wired.com/magazine/2011/12/ff_cowclicker/

Vasconcellos, M. S. (2013). *Comunicação e saúde em jogo: Os video games como estratégia de promoção da saúde*. (Doctoral Dissertation). Retrieved from Fiocruz ARCA database. (http://www.arca.fiocruz.br/handle/icict/8547)

Vasconcellos, M. S., & Araujo, I. S. (2013). Os discursos de *Passage*: A análise do discurso aplicada a um jogo digital independente. In *Proceedings do XII Simpósio Brasileiro de Jogos e Entretenimento Digital (SBGames 2013)*. São Paulo, Brazil: SBPC.

Vasconcellos, M. S., & Araujo, I. S. (2014). *Video games and participation in health: How online games can foster population's participation in public health policies*. Paper presented at the 3rd International Conference on Serious Games and Applications for Health, SeGAH 2014, Niterói. doi:10.1109/SeGAH.2014.7067095

Verón, E. (1980). *A produção do sentido*. São Paulo, Brazil: Cultrix / USP.

Woodroffe, S. (1993). *Simon the sorcerer* [Digital game]. Sutton Coldfield, UK: Adventure Soft.

Wreden, D., & Pugh, W. (2013). *The Stanley parable* [Digital game]. Galactic Cafe.

KEY TERMS AND DEFINITIONS

Avatar: Digital customizable agent operated by a player to act in a virtual environment.

Cyberpunk: Subgenre of science fiction, generally set in near, dystopic future, focusing on high technology, advanced information technology and cybernetic body modifications, against a nihilistic, decayed social context.

First Person Shooter (FPS): Digital game genre featuring combat in a 3D (or simulated 3D) environment where the player perspective is in first-person, i.e., the player sees what the game's character is seeing. In most FPSs, a player never sees the avatar, with exception of his hands. In the last years, some have preferred "first person perspective", as a way to describe games not centered on combat.

Level: The space a player traverse in order to complete objectives in a digital game. In some cases, levels take the form of rooms, in other take the form of maps or zone, but in either way there is an element of game progress in completing a level.

Real Time Strategy: Digital game genre where the player controls many units (soldiers, vehicles and buildings) and battles the computer or other players. The game flows continually, in opposition to Turn-Based Games, where each participant has a specific turn to take actions.

Roguelike: Subgenre of RPGs featuring turn-based gameplay, random generation of levels (or maps) and tile-based graphics.

Third Person Shooter: A digital game genre featuring combat in a 3D (or simulated 3D) environment where the player perspective is behind the game's protagonist. This perspective tends to give the player more information about the space surrounding the avatar. In the last years, some have preferred "third person perspective", as a way to describe games not centered on combat.

Walkthrough: A game strategy guide, featuring step-by-step instructions for all the actions one must perform in order to successfully complete a digital game.

Chapter 14
Architextuality and Video Games:
A Semiotic Approach

Maria Katsaridou
Aristotle University of Thessaloniki, Greece

Mattia Thibault
University of Turin, Italy

ABSTRACT

Even though literary genres are instrumental for the study and analysis of video games, we should also take into consideration that, nowadays, the boundaries of literature have been crossed and we have to deal with a broader transmedia reality. Approaching it can be quite challenging and, in addition to the already existing genre theory, it requires the implementation of appropriate analytic tools, both adaptable to different languages and media and able to reconstruct and motivate the isotopies woven into the net. In the authors' opinion, semiotics is particularly suitable for this task, for many reasons. The aim of this chapter, then, is to propose a semiotic methodology, oriented toward the analysis of the architextual aspects of video games. Two case studies will be taken into consideration, in order to shed some light on the inner working of architexts featuring video games, as one of their most relevant components: the horror genre and the high fantasy genre.

INTRODUCTION

In a world where communication is more and more shaped by intermediality and where transmedia storytelling has emerged as a powerful trend, the need of studies on transtextuality is stronger than ever. Notably, three of the categories proposed by French narratologist Gérard Genette (1997, 2004) are of particular relevance: intertextuality, hypertextuality and architextuality. Intertextuality, according to Genette (1997), means the presence of a text or part of a text in another one. Quotes are a common example of intertextuality, but more complex relationships are possible – for example when it is a *structural* part of a text that is retrieved (e.g. an entire character).

DOI: 10.4018/978-1-5225-0477-1.ch014

Hypertextuality, on the other hand, is defined as an imitation of the original text, able to generate new meaning without overshadowing its hypotext. Again, there are more straightforward examples of hypertextuality, such as *parodies*, and more complex ones, like remediations or intersemiotic translations (commonly called "adaptations").

Finally, Gérard Genette, in his *Palimpsests* (1997), also describes *architextuality*, which comprehends "all general or transcendent categories – types of discourse, enunciation modes, literary genres, etc. – governing every single text" (p.1). The notion of architext is therefore similar to the idea of "literary genre". As Daniel Chandler (1997) notes,

Conventional definitions of genres tend to be based on the notion that they constitute particular conventions of content (such as themes or settings) and/or form (including structure and style) which are shared by the texts which are regarded as belonging to them. (p. 2)

Nowadays, however, many genre scholars such as David Duff (2000), Rick Altman (1999) and David Buckingham (1993) agree that new approaches to genres are needed in order to face a complex and heterogeneous multi-media reality.

Moreover, games (and especially the digital ones) apart from the "literary" genre that they belong to are subject to a sophisticated classification in "genres" based on the gameplay (first person shooter, RPG's, adventure etc. see Baer & Wolf [2001]) and on many other characteristics:

A game can simultaneously be classified according to the platform on which it is played (PC, mobile phone, Xbox), the style of play it affords (multiplayer, networked, or single user, for instance), the manner in which it positions the player in relation to the game world (first person, third person, 'god'), the kind of rules and goals that make up its gameplay (racing game, action adventure), or its representational aspects (science-fiction, high fantasy, urban realism). All these possibilities for classification coexist in games, and none are irrelevant, but we would argue that the style of gameplay on offer is of fundamental significance. (Carr et al., 2006, p. 16)

This classification of game genres, obviously, can't be applied to non-digital and non-playful texts, as films or fiction books, and therefore is limited to games themselves. However, this article aims at investigating the relations that incur also between different media and this can be achieved only by focusing on architexts that include texts belonging to each of them. This brings us back to Genette's theories.

However, the three concepts mentioned above (architextuality, intertextuality and hypertextuality), if considered separately, are unable to adequately explain complex phenomena as transmedia storytelling (Scolari, 2013), which appear to pertain to all three categories. The authors, therefore, propose to use the term "architextuality" in a broader sense. The word "architext", thus, will be used to refer to a *set* of text pertaining to different media which, thanks to a series of isotopies (the intertextual and hypertextual relationships that they share), are commonly identified as pertaining to the same genre. These architexts are multi-media sets of textualities that include many different cultural products, such as: games, movies, comics, novels, gadgets, short stories, but also practices, such as cosplay, conventions, LARPs etc. These relations are structured in an intricate architextual net, which is often impossible to reconstruct completely.

An analytic approach to an architext can't simply consist in pinpointing commonalities between different texts, but it must investigate both the structural and semantic features that the texts of a same architext share. Achieving this goal, however, is quite challenging. It requires appropriate analytic tools, both adaptable (in order to investigate phenomena that use different languages and codes) and able to reconstruct and motivate the isotopies woven into the net. In the authors' opinion, semiotics is particularly suited to this task, for many reasons.

First of all, semiotics is very often used in intertextual studies, due to its ability to go under the surface, to the deep structure of the text, in order to map and analyze the plan of the content. The idea of "intersemiotic translation" (see Torop, 2000) was firstly described by Roman Jakobson (1959), and now has become part of the wider theories of Translation Studies (Baker & Saldanha, 1997). It indicates the translation of content between two different substances of the expression, or in other words, how meaning can – and cannot – be translated from one medium to another. The key idea is that each text has its own content (i.e. its semantic value: what the text is about) which is selected, organized and articulated in its substance of expression (what the text is made of) (Jakobson, 1959). The latter, therefore, has a strong influence on the meaning that will be expressed from the text hence the importance – and difficulties – of intersemiotic translations.

Secondly, semiotics' analytic point of view can fruitfully investigate both wide cultural phenomena (cultural semiotics) and focus on single textualities or groups of texts that form a semiotic system (text semiotics), emphasizing fractal recurrences as well as underlining emerging differences.

Finally, semiotics has a very useful heuristic tool that is the concept of *text*. The notion of "text" in semiotics has evolved in time and shouldn't be taken literally. The idea of text rather refers to a cultural, somewhat separate, cluster of meaning, expressed with a code and recorded in a media. "A text is an assemblage of signs (such as words, images, sounds and/or gestures) constructed (and interpreted) with reference to the conventions associated with a genre and in a particular medium of communication" (Chandler, 2007). Semioticians, approaching very different phenomena, are thus able to find the common structures, without overlooking their peculiarities. This is particularly useful in the study of differences in texts, which belong to the same genre: "genres are instances of repetition and difference […] difference is absolutely essential to the economy of genre" (Neale, 1980, p. 43).

The semiotic methodology, in addition, is particularly suited to the study of games. It is a discipline able to approach a wide range of texts, belonging to different media, finding their recursive structure, but without forgetting their specificity. Play practices involve an incredible number of parameters to research on: artifacts, digital constructs, mindsets, sets of rules, ways of communication and so on. In order to approach this wide ensemble, a versatile discipline is needed – and the authors believe semiotics is up to the task. Furthermore, semiotics has a well-defined metalanguage, in which it is possible to translate many useful concepts borrowed from other disciplines. In this way, it is possible to approach playfulness and games from a compact, yet interdisciplinary theoretical framework.

However, one could argue if video games – the focus of this essay – can be truly considered as texts. Unlike regular texts, (movies, novels, comic books etc.), games are interactive, they can be endless, and sometimes it is difficult to tell if they are narratives or not (let's think of the dreaded *Tetris* case). "Concerning game studies, ever since the establishment of the field, there has been a debate between scholars who analyzed games as narratives and others that opposed to the narrative nature of video games in favor of their ludological character. Between the two extremes, Gonzalo Frasca (1999, 2003) proposed a reconciling position in which he acknowledges the importance of narrative in game analysis. More recently, Espen Aarseth (2012) in his article *A Narrative Theory of Games* presented a narrative theory of games, 'building on standard narratology, as a solution to the conundrum that has haunted computer game studies from the start'. Aarseth points out that, if we want to have storygames, which are games that are interesting on the storytelling level, we should have compelling, rich, deep characters" (Katsaridou, forthcoming).

Moreover, some scholars actually do consider video games as a peculiar kind of text (Ferri, 2007). The authors' position is that we can safely claim that all games have a repertory of texts, which are employed while playing. There are virtual worlds, with their aesthetics and scenarios. There are characters with their own features. There are music, loading screens, cinematic, recorded dialogues or phrases etc. All these components of the game can be considered as texts, or sub-texts that can safely go under a semiotic analysis. In addition, many of the games under discussion in this chapter do have narratives, hence they are what Aarseth (2012, p. 131) calls: storygames.

The aim of this chapter, then, is to propose a semiotic methodology oriented towards the analysis of the architextual aspects of video games and to test it on two case studies: the horror genre and the high fantasy genre.

THEORETICAL FRAMEWORK

Semiotics is a wide discipline, featuring many theories that aren't always possible to integrate. The authors, hence, have chosen two semiotic "schools", that are particularly suited to this purpose and that, despite their differences, can be easily integrated: generative semiotics, from the French school of semiotics of Ferdinand de Saussure and Algirdas J. Greimas, and cultural semiotics from the Tartu–Moscow Semiotic School of Yuri Lotman. These two theories, though very different, have been proven to be compatible and to be able to work fruitfully together (see Migliore, 2010; Sedda, 2015).

Generative Semiotics

Algirdas Greimas – building on Ferdinand de Saussure's theory and on Vladimir Propp's *Morphology of the Folk Tale* (Propp, 1928/1968) and his syntagmatic analysis of the Russian folk tales – delineate a canonical narrative structure and a schema of actantial and thematic roles, both of which are very useful in this study. Greimas (1966/1983) replaced the thirty-one functions of Propp's folk tales, with six *actants*, which are abstract elements of the deep structure of the narrative. Greimas distinguishes the actants into three pairs of oppositional values: subject – object, giver – receiver and helper – opponent. For Greimas, actors are abstract elements too, but in antithesis to actants, which are structures of the general narrative syntax, actors are the manifestations of the actants in a specific narrative. In other words, Greimas proposed a methodology towards a paradigmatic analysis of narrative structure. Moreover, Greimas adapted one of the fundamental principles of Ferdinand de Saussure's theory in his analysis, namely that in a semiotic system, meaning is produced by the relationships and the antithesis between the signs that consist it. (Saussure, 1916/1983)

On one hand, reconstructing narrative mechanics will help the authors focus on the common traits of related texts, going beyond their different languages. On the other hand, the mapping and analysis of isotopies and their relations, which are forming *themes* (that, in this chapter, can be associated with the thematic roles in Greimas' theory) is a powerful tool to analyze the deep structure of the text. Thematic roles (such as the *zombie*, or the *wizard*) and their related signs (e.g., respectively, the "bloodstained jaw" and the "wand") are often the most common traits that can be detected in an architext. Hence, identifying and analyzing them is strongly desirable in order to properly address the phenomenon of transmedia architextuality.

Semiotics of Culture

In addition to Greimas' theory and in order to describe such a various and polymorphous phenomenon, the authors will integrate some concepts from the works of Yuri Lotman (in particular 1974, 2004, and 2011) in their analysis. The *Tartu-Moskow semiotic school* founder elaborated a very powerful heuristic tool: the theory of the *Semiosphere*. A semiosphere (Lotman, 1994), is the semiotic space of a culture, a modeling system or a single text. It is the space where the rise of meaning (semiosis) can happen. Each culture has its semiosphere (e.g. 19th century Russian culture's semiosphere), as well as each social phenomenon (e.g. Christmas semiosphere) or genre (the horror genre semiosphere). Lotman describes very well the synchronic organization[1] and diachronic dynamics of semiospheres, underlining the importance of their boundaries – which are porous spaces of translation – and of the movement from their more unregulated peripheries to their static but influential centers.

The idea of semiosphere as a dynamic, seething ensemble of meaningful cultural artifacts is very well suited for the analysis of the intertextual net of texts that forms an architext. It will provide the authors the tools to describe its inner movements (for example how games are rapidly heading toward the center) as well as its relationships with elements outside it. The modeling ability of semiotic systems (i.e. their ability to mirror the world and to be prototypes for other semiotic systems) has also been studied in detail by Yuri Lotman, who thus builds, once again, a useful theoretical framework to work within.

Finally, when dealing with intersemiotic translations, it is important to remember Lotman's claims of untranslatability (Lotman, 1974). According to him, in every intersemiotic translation (as well as in every form of translation) there are areas of untranslatability: on the one hand, the range of instances that different media are capable to express do not completely overlap and, on the other hand, the influence of the substance and form of the expression on the content cannot always be faithfully recreated in another medium.

ANALYZING TWO ARCHITEXTS: THE HIGH FANTASY AND HORROR GENRES

In order to test the methodology and, most of all, to shed some light on the inner working of architexts, two quite relevant architexts will be analyzed here: high fantasy[2] and horror[3]. The choice of this double focus, although sometimes problematic, follows a precise heuristic strategy: the authors aim at giving a stereoscopic dimension to their analysis (highlighting commonalities and differences between the two architexts) that should be reinforced by the synergy of the two different semiotic methodologies.

These two genres, in addition, share a close relation, as they both belong within the fantastic, as described in Todorov (1973). They are also both well-established in contemporary culture and deeply rooted in literature (Timmerman, 1983). Despite their longevity (or maybe thanks to it) both genres are heavily represented in many video games of all eras. In the next paragraphs, the authors will investigate what these video games, that are part of these genres, have taken from previous texts, and how they have implemented it into their game mechanics.

The High Fantasy Genre

The high fantasy genre (among whose founders we can mention J. R. R. Tolkien, Michael Moorcock and Robert E. Howard) – is a very broad and successful transmedia genre that covers, as mentioned above, a wide amount of different kinds of texts. The fantasy genre pertains to novels, comics, board games, toys, performances (as cosplay and LARPs), digital games and various forms of merchandising. Today games, however, have a central importance in this semiotic ecosystem. With hundreds of board-games and video games such as *The Elder Scrolls* series, *The Witcher* series, the *Dragon Age* series and many others, the presence of games in the fantasy genre is extremely relevant, and they could be safely considered as one of its major parts.

To approach such a wide and heterogeneous corpus, the authors decided to focus on a case study: the architextual relations among a limited set of texts, pertaining to three different media: novels, role-playing games and MMORPGs[4]. For the novels the choice has been J.R.R. Tolkien's books, especially *The Hobbit* and *The Lord of The Rings*. The authors chose Tolkien among the founders of the high fantasy genre because of his decisive influence on all the following texts and on the definition of the architext itself. For the RPGs the choice wasn't hard: *Dungeons & Dragons* is at the same time the first and most famous role-playing game in the world and, as we will see, it played a very important part in the gram-maticalization of the common traits of the architext. Also the first and most famous MMORPG, *World of Warcraft*, belongs to the high fantasy genre and so it will be included in our corpus. The fact that its predecessors, the fortunate series of RTS *Warcraft*, share the same setting, will be a useful added value, as it will allow us to reconstruct the evolution in time of the elements of the genre present in the games.

Looking for common traits between these texts can be, at first glance, quite complicated, particularly when we take into consideration *Dungeons and Dragons* (*D&D* from now on). The role-playing game, according to its nature, does not propose any specific narrative (it is not a *storygame*), any precise setting or even any defined character – it is up to the players and the Dungeon Master to create them. However, *D&D* is still is an undeniably important part of the high fantasy genre. It will be useful, thus, for our investigation, to wonder what this text has in common with the others, as it lacks some of the more common traits of narration.

The System of Thematic Roles of the Fantasy Genre

What RPGs are based on – as their name clearly states – is "roles", a word, however, somewhat vague and of many meanings. In particular, *D&D* proposes two different sets of roles that can be combined: classes (wizard, warrior, rogue...) and races (human, dwarf, elf...). These roles consist in a series of traits (both physical and psychological), abilities and features that are presented as common to all the characters pertaining to that role. In semiotic terms, we can say that they are rich thematic roles: coher-ent ensembles of figures, competences and virtual narrative programs, that give birth to an actor (i.e. a character) when accompanied by an actantial role – the narrative role that the actor will play in the story. In other words, while playing an RPG, the player chooses two thematic roles that are dependent on the choices he made in game (the actantial role) and participate in the creation of the "hero" of the game. Thematic roles, hence, are a core part of RPGs and the list of thematic roles and their composition would appear to determine the architextual aspect of the game: in a fantasy RPG players will expect to meet wizards and warriors, elves and dwarves[5].

If identifying the thematic role is pretty straightforward for Role-Playing Games, thanks to the explicitness of the medium, it can be more complicated when we approach a novel. In Tolkien's book, for example, even if many different races do exist (humans, hobbits, orcs, goblins, dwarves and elves) they lack a clear, unique definition. As for the classes, it can be even more problematic: there are, indeed, wizards, rangers and warriors (and even a "burglar": Bilbo himself), but their role is neither definite nor universally recognized. To reconstruct these thematic roles is necessary to look in the text for all their single traits.

Thibault (2012), after listing all the quotes from Tolkien's books that took part in the construction of thematic roles, claims that before him, *D&D* developers did the same. Every single quote found, in effect, has a reflection in the rules of the 3.5 edition of *D&D*, even in the cases of traits typical of a single character. Hence, the fact that Bilbo is good at throwing stones becomes a bonus to all Halflings who do the same, or the fact that Tolkien mentions that dwarves do not suffer from any heavy load, is transformed in a bonus for Dwarves wearing heavy armors. As for the classes, even if some have completely different ancestors (as the Barbarian, who is obviously an heir of *Conan,* see Bertetti 2011), many of their traits are taken from the novels as well (the *Rangers* from the homonym role, the *Rogue* from the *Burglar,* the *Paladin* from the *White Rider*). The author, additionally, shows how some of the novel's characters (Tom Bombadill and Beorn) were stripped of their personality and given a "Celtic" name in order to create new thematic roles (the *Bard* and the *Druid*). *D&D*, then, bases its effect of architextuality on an attentive retrieval of Tolkien's thematic roles, which had to be, of course, the object of an intersemiotic translation and hence adapted to the new medium in which they have been employed.

Interestingly enough, Warcraft also uses a similar approach. In the first chapter of the saga, *Orcs and Humans*, the system of thematic roles is very simple, but the influences of *D&D* are already visible, particularly with the units "Cleric" and "Necrolite", which are extremely similar to the good and evil Clerics of the RPG. In the second Warcraft game, *Tides of Darkness*, things start to get more complicated, with the introduction of new races. A deeper look, however, shows that the new traits are very few, and that the new races are often the result of some "thematic roles alchemy". Trolls, for example, are the *elvish version of Orcs*, as they are thinner, paler, long eared and haired and prefer long distance weapons. The same can be said for Goblins, the green version of Gnomes. Even if some roles remain untouched (Paladins are exactly the same as their *D&D* versions), one can see an evident desire to innovate, without risking losing the effect of architextuality that allows the game to be perceived as part of the fantasy genre. This desire for innovation reaches its azimuth in *Warcraft III* and continues, with the same techniques, in *World of Warcraft*. Again, the new traits are quite few (some aspects of the Greek mythology and of Native American culture and a couple of roles from the horror genre), but the organization of the traits in thematic roles, especially for the races, presents many innovations. In particular Thibault (2012) underlines four main strategies of innovation:

- **Intensification:** A trait of a thematic role is exaggerated in order to renew the role (the love of Dwarves for metallurgy becomes the ability to create Steampunk machines);
- **Reversal:** A trait of a thematic role is changed with its opposite (Orcs are smart, Undead are freedom fighters, Dranei are blue and good devils, etc.);
- **Dissociation:** The traits of a thematic role are divided in two groups and used to create two new roles (Elf's *nature* and *magic* traits are divided between Night Elves and Blood Elves);
- **Hybridization:** Several traits from different roles and characters are mixed to create a new role (the Warlock features powers form the Dreadlords, Mannoroth etc.).

The thematic roles, then, appear to be a way to organize and gramaticalize a semantic repertory – a deposit of meaning – that stays the same in all the texts analyzed. This repertory has its own economy: traits can be added, or ignored, only if a sort of balance is kept and the innovative changes do not exceed a certain amount. Innovation is possible, then, but nonetheless this semantic and thematic economy must be respected.

Additionally, the thematic roles are organized in a system: they entertain axiological relations (of love/hate, more/less ability to cooperate, proximity/distance etc.). Thus, if a role changes, also the other roles will have to adapt and reflect that change (Ibid.). The interaction between roles in their system, is also part of what gives them meaning – which, hence, is not limited to the amount of semantic material they own.

In conclusion, the creation of an effect of architextuality will require from a text to build such a system, mainly based on the traits already existing in the architext (i.e. in the existing texts), with some innovation, but respecting the semantic economy.

Spatial Organization in the Fantasy Genre

In addition to the system of thematic roles, the other element required for a text to be part of the high fantasy genre appears to be the presence of a *striated space*, a space in which different places will bear different meanings, according to the characteristic features of the genre.

D&D, of course, doesn't have a specific setting. However, it gives the player (or, better, the *Dungeon Master* or DM) an important set of tools for the creation of three different kinds of places: the civilized world (in which the heroes recover and gear up), the dungeon (an underground place full of monsters and treasures) and the wilderness (savage and wild territories, still uncivilized, populated by brutal races and monsters). Interestingly enough, these three different kinds of places are also present in Tolkien's books (e.g. The Shire, Moria and Mirkwood) and in the *Warcraft* series (e.g. Stormwind, the Barrens, old Scholomance). In the games, the civilized world allows the players to rest and/or buy provisions and items while the dungeon and the wilderness offer different amounts of experience points (and, therefore, new competencies) and treasures. In Tolkien's book the situation isn't very different: Galadriel's gifts (provisions, jewelry and magic items) are given in the civilized Lorien, while in the dungeons many treasures are found (the Ring, Glamdrang and Orcrist, Smaug's treasure...) and in the wilderness some characters learn how to survive and fight (especially Bilbo at Mirkwood and Sam in Mordor).

Also the system of thematic roles influences the spatial organization of the setting. In addition to these three kinds of places mentioned, fantasy texts quite often feature areas that are devoted to a single race (Tolkien's Elves live in Lorien, *Warcraft* Dwarves in Ironforge and so on) or to a class (wizard schools, druid woods etc.). This feature appears as a projection of the system of thematic roles presented in the text and can be extremely explicit (as in World of Warcraft, in which every race has its own capital and lands) or more implicit (in Tolkien's books and in *D&D* race descriptions there can be several places devoted to each race, but also races that only live with others).

These geographical features of the setting have an active role on the hero's narrative program: crossing the space is generally synonymous with advancing the story. It is interesting to mention that this striated space is very often represented by a map, which is a rather important element in the high fantasy genre. Tolkien drew himself the maps of the Middle Earth, which were presented in all of his books. In Warcraft games there is always a mini-map (which, however, is featured in many games regardless of the genre), but often there are also more "narrative" maps, not directly linked to the game play, but important to create an atmosphere – as, for example, in the loading screens of Warcraft III. Finally, many *D&D* published settings and adventures feature many maps and, as any *D&D* player will know, all DMs like to draw a detailed map of the world that they have invented. These maps – being the result of the projections aforesaid – become then a representation of the narratological program of the text, which will follow the paths and roads drawn in the map and stop in each meaningful area encountered to expand in a broader story-line, before being off on the road again.

The Horror Genre

The video games that will be examined under the framework of horror genre will be the *Resident Evil* (Capcom, 1996-2015) and the *Silent Hill* (Konami, 1999-2012) video game series, which are considered to be the most emblematic games in the Survival horror[6] genre. Furthermore, even though the games follow the structure and the stereotypes of the horror genre that are based on pre-existing literary sources such as Edgar Allan Poe's (1809–1849) and Howard Phillips Lovecraft's (1890–1937) texts (while the specific thematic role of the zombies owes much to Mary Shelley's *Frankenstein* [1818], Bram Stoker's *Dracula* [1897] and more recently to George Andrew Romero's films like *Night of the Living Dead* [1968]), they are not a mere revival of existing narratives. They all feature original narratives which have led to many adaptations available through various other media such as films, books and comics, expanding further the architext. It is important for our analysis that, while the two game series belong to the same genre, they are negotiating completely different themes and are incorporating different thematic roles. While the *Resident Evil* game series has as its central theme a "zombie apocalypse", the *Silent Hill* games focus on the eponymous, nightmarish, little town and a religious cult that worships a demonic creature. These differences give us the opportunity to address and examine broader manifestations of the elements deriving from the horror genre's repertory.

Resident Evil Video Game Series: The Zombie Apocalypse

The first *Resident Evil* video game was released by the Japanese company Capcom (1996), establishing the *survival horror* genre in games and implementing, for the first time, the zombie apocalypse narrative. After the first release and its huge commercial success, more than fifteen *Resident Evil* installments were produced and until today, five live action and two animation film adaptations were based upon the video game series. As mentioned above, the *Resident Evil* games draw their material from the horror genre, and thus, they can be approached as part of a broader – and very diverse – architext, whose main theme is that of the "zombie apocalypse". Zombies' thematic role has its literary roots in Romero's films and it appears in many other texts, as, for example, in the recent films *Zombieland* (Fleischer, 2009) and *World War Z* (Forster, 2013) and of course, the *Resident Evil* movie series. While *Resident Evil* games are different from all these texts, both as media and as narratives, they share with them many similarities, due to the role of zombies in their narrative.

The basic storyline of the games involves the creation and spread of artificially created lethal viruses or ancient parasites – mainly by the evil *Umbrella Corporation*, but also by other groups of bioterrorists – that turn humans into zombies, and in parallel, the effort of the heroes to survive and to stop the bioterrorists from destroying the world. In their effort, the heroes have to confront various monstrous creatures, like zombie dogs and humans infected by the virus who have become bloodthirsty zombies.

In most of the games there is a regular pattern: most of the citizens of the infected area have become zombies, while the uninfected survivors/heroes fight for their lives in their effort to escape.

In *Resident Evil 4* and *Resident Evil: Code Veronica* there is a differentiation from the norm, and the heroes have to encounter a religious cult that uses a breed of ancient parasites to turn humans into mind-controlled victims. The use of religious cults is another very common theme in survival horror games and, as it will be discussed below, it consists as a key motif in the *Silent Hill* video games.

In the entire "zombie apocalypse" narratives the heroes are humans. Their *object* is to survive, save others and eliminate the zombies. The main opponents, in almost all the narratives, are the zombies. The differentiation of *Resident Evil 4* and *Resident Evil: Code Veronica* will be discussed more analytically below.

The fundamental antithesis which governs both games and movies, hence, is "zombies versus humans", namely the antithesis between the undead and the living, the *unnatural* versus the natural. While the unnatural has the negative connotations of evil, monstrous and sinister, the natural on the other hand, connotes the good, human and familiar. This antithesis is present in most texts belonging to the horror genre. So, what are the particular characteristics that define a "zombie apocalypse" text?

Most of all, the presence of the thematic role of the *zombie*, which comprehends a series of traits like putrefaction, bloody jaws, veiled eyes, inability to communicate, filthiness, unnatural movements and actions, mainly walking in large groups, killing and biting/eating. These traits are applicable not only to humans, but as in the case of "zombie" dogs, can be exaggerated or inverted in order to create different kinds of monsters, like those that reside in *Resident Evil*.

In addition, unlike other undead creatures - for example, vampires - zombies don't have personality, feelings, or any other characteristics suggesting the existence of self-awareness. The lack of individuality and personality is the reason why zombies are limited only to the role of the opponent, and never that of the hero or of the assistant. They make the perfect enemy for the player: "…they are strong, relentless, and already dead; they look spectacularly horrific; and they invite the player to blow them away without guilt or a second thought" (Krzywinska 2008:153). Zombies don't think, don't have feelings, don't form relations, and they cannot take decisions. The only thing they have is an instinct for killing and eating. In *World War Z* zombies have a preference for eating healthy people, but this relates more to a self-preservation instinct, rather than to any expression of personal choice. Zombies are plain monstrous and they look monstrous. In all the games and the films they look filthy, they have blood on their face, mouth and clothes and they move unnaturally. But unlike other monstrous creatures, as it stressed in Backe & Aarseth's *Ludic zombies: An examination of zombieism in games* (2013) "their appearance is not coded in a few artificial signifiers (like the vampire's pointed teeth, pale skin, and possibly black cape), but has a more complex semantics: 'the zombie directly manifests the visual horrors of death: unlike most ghosts and vampires, zombies are in an active state of decay' (Bishop, as cited in Backe & Aarseth, 2013, p. 5). The moving, yet decaying bodies 'are devoid of personality, yet they continue to allude to personal identity. [...] They are empty shells of life that scandalously continue to function in the absence of any rationale and of any interiority'" (Shaviro, as cited in Backe & Aarseth, 2013, p. 5). The players and the film heroes cannot interact with them, in any other way than killing them or becoming their pray. Usually they move together, in droves, putting the heroes in an even more difficult position. In addition, it's very difficult to "kill" a zombie. While the way zombies can be killed is not the same in all texts, it's never easy. For example, in *Resident Evil* games, if the zombies are not decapitated or burned, they will become "red head zombies", something even more monstrous.

Despite what caused their situation, being a zombie is an irreversible state of being, because zombies are fundamentally dead. There are, in fact, some texts in which a cure for zombies is possible. In these cases, however, we will have only "zombie-like creatures" and not "real" zombies. The proof can also be found in the fact that such texts are never pertaining to the horror architext. A good example can be found in the romantic comedy film *Warm Bodies* (2013) based upon Isaac Marion (2011)'s novel *Warm Bodies* (2011), where the "zombie" hero has feelings and in the end of the film he and all the other zombies are cured and they become human again.

Taking the above into account, we should stress that *Resident Evil 4* and *Resident Evil: Code Veronica* fail to give a sense of architextuality. They don't belong to the "zombie apocalypse" game canon that apply to the other *Resident Evil* games, as the mind-controlled victims that the player has to confront are humans and pretty much alive! Even though there is an aesthetic of "zombieness" that is proposed in these games, their deep structure is different from the other games. This alteration, which provoked the lack of architextuality, also provoked some negative reactions among the Resident Evil's players.

Moreover, in the games, like in the films, the environment, once familiar, has become alienated, hostile and frightening, due to the existence of zombies that are violating the natural laws, turning the world into something 'other' and terrifying. This "lost" familiarity makes the zombie worlds even more frightening, because there is no escape; there is nowhere to go. The heroes didn't move to some distant, unknown "evil" place like in the case of *Silent Hill*. In this case, their known world became evil and everybody in this world, even the dearest persons to them, can become monsters. But where *Resident Evil* environment is a setting, *Silent Hill*'s nightmarish town plays an active role in the narrative.

Silent Hill: The "Evil" Place

The *Silent Hill* video game series, produced by the Japanese company Konami, belongs to the survival horror genre and is considered as one of the most important and typical paradigms. Cris Pruett (2010) and Grant Tavinor (2007) use it to define the genre. Tavinor writes that a survival horror game is "A game such as Silent Hill with horror and mystery elements and often where the player is placed in a weakened state relative to adversaries, encouraging a pervasive feeling of threat, and cautious gameplay." (2007, p. 207)

A very important aspect of the game series is the creation of a very solid *storyworld*, based on the codes and conventions of the horror genre and especially those addressing the "evil" place thematology. The success of the series has led to the expansion of the franchise, which now includes two feature films and several spin-off video games.

The series consists of eight main games. Their narratives are not all connected to each other and their common feature is that they all take place in the small, abandoned and nightmarish town of Silent Hill. Many horrible things have happened in this town, which have resulted in the transformation of Silent Hill into a hellish place. The town has become a place where two dimensions coexist: that of the natural world, and that of the supernatural, which is called the "Otherworld", a dark place full of monsters, supernatural creatures, religious cults and grotesque imagery. The borders between these two worlds are vague and the heroes pass the threshold without noticing it until it is too late. The heroes of the games go to Silent Hill for personal reasons, and they get trapped in the town. Their objective is, again, to survive, achieve their goals and get out of the town. The Silent Hill town, apart from being a very solid storyworld, has the role of the opponent in the narratives. Unlike other opponents, which serve only as actants to the hero's narrative, the town has its own fully developed narrative program. It has a past, a goal and a personality. Its object is to entrap and finally kill the heroes that have come in the city: if the player fails to successfully finish the game, the town achieves its objective. In other words, Silent Hill is an "evil" place and also the main opponent.

"Evil" places are a very common theme in the horror genre; it is also a very broad topic, with many variants. A place can be considered as "evil" for many reasons: it can be the inhabitance of supernatural or monstrous creatures like ghosts and spirits, as for example in the films *The Others* (Amenábar, 2001) and *Poltergeist* (Hooper, 1982), or horrible things could have happened there leaving their "echo" in the place, like in *The Orphanage* (Bayona, 2007), or, as in the film *1408* (Håfström, 2007), a place can be evil for no specific reason, it can be "just an evil … room" as the director of the hotel, played by the actor Samuel L. Jackson, explains in the film.

The *Silent Hill* games are built upon a combination of themes belonging to the horror genre, such as the religious cult, the evil place and the monstrous creatures, that are broadly met in literature texts such as in Edgar Alan Poe's short story *The Fall of the House of Usher* (Poe, 1839/2009). In the story, the house plays a significant role, both in the development of the narrative as well as in the creation of the feeling of fear and weakness to the reader, which is very similar to the feelings that *Silent Hill* provokes in the player. In all the texts mentioned above, the "evil" place traps the visitors in a *liminal space* between the *natural* world and the *supernatural* one, triggering questions about what is real and what is a construction of the hero's own mind. The antithesis *out* versus *in* the frightful place, and the constant feeling that there is "no way out", intensifies the feelings of claustrophobia to the player/reader/viewer.

All these feelings are magnified in *Silent Hill* games due to the fog[7] and the darkness that surrounds it. The players can only see pieces of the environment, while they are in a situation of constant danger, as monsters lurk in almost every corner, ready to attack. Fog is a very common element in horror genre and especially in "evil" places. It appears in Poe's short story and in many other texts; for example, more recently it is used in the film *The Shrine* (Knautz, 2010) in order to 'hide' a demonic cult[8].

This lack of knowledge and control over the environment accompanied by insufficient ammunition in order to confront the monsters, that is, the manifestations of the evil town, puts the players in a weak position, in antithesis with the town, which is powerful, almost unbeatable. The players can confront and kill the monsters, achieve their objectives and win the game, but they can never permanently destroy the evil town per se. What they have to beat, in order to survive and finish the game, are the various monstrous expressions of the town. Even when the players win and finish a game, it is always a temporary victory over the evil: the town of Silent Hill is always there, waiting for the next game to be produced and the next "visitors" to arrive in town.

Roles and Space in the Horror Genre

The importance of thematic roles and spatial organization, therefore, is of central importance also for the horror genre. The narrative follows a simple structure: a group of "normal" people are trapped in an area that they do not completely understand, either because of physical obstacles such as fog, or because of their insufficient knowledge (for example of the history of Silent Hill). In this "dangerous place" they are weak and constantly under menace, so they try their best to leave it and reach a "safe place". This situation, with only small changes, is present in all the games, novels and films that have been taken into consideration.

The "dangerous" place is also the place in which the opponents might be encountered. While in the "zombie apocalypse" themed texts the main opponent is the eponymous thematic role – declined in many different ways – in the Silent Hill series and in similar texts, on the other hand, the opponent is the non-anthropomorphic actant that is the "evil" place itself: a *locus horridus* that, due to various reasons, is not inanimate anymore, but it hosts a *genius loci* that will actively try to kill the main characters. In this case the place itself becomes the real antagonist (and the basic thematic role) and all the monsters, cultists etc. are only his helpers.

In both cases there is a thematic and spatial opposition between what is natural and what is unnatural or supernatural. In the games under consideration, the only possible victory is to escape towards the natural order again.

CONCLUSION

The Semiotic Space of an Architext

An architext is a very rich object of study, full of meaning, tropes, figures and themes. However, looking deeper, all this semiotic material can be seen as organized and structured. Many stereotypes – roles and situations – are found in a very broad set of texts: there are recurrences, similarities, analogies.

In particular, the fantasy genre's system of thematic roles is central: the lack of such a system is enough to endanger the participation to the architext. The high fantasy system of thematic roles is extremely rich and complex, often subject to innovation and changes and to a rigid economy. The structure of spatial organization, on the other hand, is the product of a reflection of this system, but also a representation of the text's narrative mechanisms. Hence the importance of maps, are arguably a pictorial representation of the narrative (or of the possible narratives) of the text they belong to.

On the contrary, in the horror genre, the system of thematic roles is mainly based on the opposition between natural and un/super-natural, and is generally limited to two or three basic roles (the survivor, the zombie, the "evil place"…). However, it appears that the spatial isotopies are central, so important in fact, that the place itself can become an actant, can be the main villain, unbeatable and all-mighty.

Both levels, namely the thematic roles and the storyworlds, however, are susceptible to modification and innovation, but not all modifications can be easily accepted. Above we used the expression "semantic economy", but in order to understand better why architexts tend to be semantically conservative and how new traits can be implemented in an existing genre, the concept of semiosphere could be more useful. Each architext has its own semiosphere, that is, its own semiotic space. Terms as "cult" or "thief" have very different meanings if taken outside the genres we have analyzed in this chapter. This semiotic space, hence, forms a rich ensemble of meaningful traits that can be employed with great liberties in the creation of texts that, regardless of their quality, will be perceived as part of the architext. As in every semiosphere, there is a center, in which the most important traits reside (as "magic" or "zombieness") and a periphery, where, contrarily, we can find the less common traits (like "Pandarens" or "Lickers[9]").

The semiosphere also has a boundary, which, although delineating an inside and an outside, is a porous space of translation. In order to insert a new trait in an architext, then, a translation is needed into the "language" of the genre. The trait will have to be included in a system – it will need connections and variants in order to become an integral part of the semiosphere. When Blizzard developers decided to include Native American cultural traits in *Warcraft III*, they had to insert them in several thematic roles and figures, and to mix them with other traits: hence, the Minotaur carrying a totem on his back won't be perceived as weird, but as perfectly fitting in the setting and in the genre. On the other hand, "mind controlled victims" failed to pass the boundary and become part of the "zombie apocalypse" semiosphere, exactly because they fail to incorporate the fundamental traits of the semiosphere in their thematic role.

In conclusion, we can say that in order to create a video game perceived as part of an architext, one must operate inside the semiosphere of the genre, build a solid system of thematic roles, and respect the organization between spatial isotopies. Depending on the type of game, the importance of any of these parameters can vary, but despite the degree, they are all present in the games under consideration. Following these three principles can lead to the creation of a sense of architextuality, which is a key component, though not the only one, towards the creation of a successful game.

REFERENCES

1408. (2007). Dir. Mikael Håfström, Prod. Dimension Films. USA.

Aarseth, E. (2012). *A narrative theory of games*. ACM Digital library. Retrieved November 18, 2015, from http://dl.acm.org/citation.cfm?id=2282365

Altman, R. (1999). *Film/genre*. London, UK: British Film Institute.

Backe, H.-J., & Aarseth, E. (2013). Ludic zombies: An examination of zombieism in games. *Proceedings of the 2013 DiGRA International Conference*. Retrieved November 18, 2015, from http://www.digra.org/wp-content/uploads/digital-library/paper_405.pdf

Baker, M., & Saldanha, G. (Eds.). (1997). *Routledge encyclopedia of translation studies*. London, UK: Routlege.

Bertetti, P. (2011). *Conan il mito*. Pisa, Italy: ETS.

Bethesda Game Studios. (2008). *Fallout 3* [Videogame]. Bethesda Softworks. [Disc]

Bethesda Game Studios. (2011). *The elder scolls V: Skyrim* [Videogame]. Bethesda Softworks. [Download]

Blizzard Entertainment. (1994). *Warcraft: Orcs and humans* [Videogame]. Blizzard Entertainment. [Disc]

Blizzard Entertainment. (1996). *Warcraft II: Beyond the dark portal* [Videogame]. Blizzard Entertainment. [Disc]

Blizzard Entertainment. (1996). *Warcraft III: Reign of chaos* [Videogame]. Blizzard Entertainment. [Disc]

Blizzard Entertainment. (2007). *World of warcraft* [Videogame]. Blizzard Entertainment. [Disc]

Brown, D., & Krzywinska, T. (2009). Movie-games and game-movies: Towards an aesthetics of transmediality. In W. Buckland (Ed.), *Film theory and contemporary Hollywood movies* (pp. 86–102). New York, NY: Routledge.

Buckingham, D. (1993). *Children talking television: Making of television literacy*. London, UK: Routledge Falmer.

Capcom. (1996). *Resident evil*, [Videogame] [Disc] [Microsoft Windows] Virgin Interactive Entertainment.

Capcom. (1998). *Resident evil 2*, [Videogame] [Disc] [Microsoft Windows] Capcom Entertainment Inc.

Capcom. (1999). *Resident evil 3: Nemesis,* [Videogame] [Disc] [Microsoft Windows] Eidos.

Capcom. (2001). *Resident evil code: Veronica,* [Videogame] [Disc] [PlayStation 2] Capcom.

Capcom. (2002). *Resident evil outbreak,* [Videogame] [Disc] [PlayStation 2] Capcom Entertainment Inc.

Capcom. (2005). *Resident evil 4,* [Videogame] [Disc] [PlayStation 2] Capcom Entertainment Inc.

Capcom. (2007). *Resident evil: The umbrella chronicles,* [Videogame] [Disc] [PlayStation 3] Capcom Entertainment Inc.

Capcom. (2009). *Resident evil 5,* [Videogame] [Disc] [PlayStation 3] Capcom.

Capcom. (2012). *Resident evil 6,* [Videogame] [Disc] [PlayStation 3] Capcom.

Carr, D., Buckingham, D, Burn, A., & Schott, G. (2006). *Computer games: Text, narrative and play.* Cambridge, MA: Polity Press.

Chandler, D. (1997). *An introduction to genre theory.* Retrieved November 18, 2015, from http://visual-memory.co.uk/daniel/Documents/intgenre/chandler_genre_theory.pdf

Cook, M., Tweet J., & Williams, S. (2003). *Dungeons and dragons: Player's handbook* (3.5 edition) [Role-playing game rulebook] Wizards of the Coast.

Cook, M., Tweet J. and S. Williams (2003). *Dungeons and dragons: Master's guide* (3.5 edition) [Role-playing game rulebook] Wizards of the Coast. (Original work published 1974).

Cook, M., Tweet J. and S. Williams (2003). *Dungeons and dragons: Monster manual* (3.5 edition) [Role-playing game rulebook] Wizards of the Coast. (Original work published 1974).

Duff, D. (2000). *Modern genre theory.* Essex, UK: Longman.

Dungeons and dragons . (2000). Dir. C. Solomon, New Line Cinema, USA and Czech Republic.

Ferri, G. (2007). Narrating machines and interactive matrices, a semiotic common ground for game studies. In *Proceedings of DiGRA 2007.* Retrieved February 18, 2015, from http://www.digra.org/wp-content/uploads/digital-library/07311.02554.pdf

Frasca, G. (2003). *Ludologists love stories, too: Notes from a debate that never took place.* DIGRA Conference 2003. Retrieved April 2, 2015, from http://www.ludology.org/articles/frasca_levelUP2003.pdf

Frasca, G. (n.d.). *Ludology meets narratology: Similitude and differences between (video)games and narrative.* Retrieved November 18, 2015, from http://web.cfa.arizona.edu/art435a/readings/frasca_ludology.pdf

Genette, G. (1997). *Palimpsests: Literature in the second degree.* Lincoln, NE: University of Nebraska Press.

Genette, G. (2004). *Métalepses, de la figure à la fiction.* Paris, France: Seuil.

Greimas, A. J. (1983). *Structural semantics: An attempt at a method.* Lincoln, NE; London, UK: University of Nebraska Press. (Original work published 1966)

Jakobson, R. (1987). On linguistic aspects of translation. In R. Jakobson (Ed.), *Language in literature*. The Jakobson Trust.

Havířová, T. (2007). *Fantasy as a popular genre in the works of J. R. R. Tolkien and J. K. Rowling.* (Master Thesis). Masaryk University. Retrieved November 20, 2015 from https://is.muni.cz/th/74471/ff_m/m.a.pdf

Irrational Games. (2007). *BioShock*, [Videogame] [Disc] [Microsoft Windows] 2K Games and Feral Interactive.

Kaklamanidou, B., & Katsaridou, M. (2013). Silent Hill: Adapting a video game. Literature. *Film Quarterly, 41*(1), 266–277.

Katsaridou, M. (forthcoming). From literature texts to video games: Recent adaptations of *Sherlock Holmes. Animation Journal.*

Katsaridou, M. (forthcoming). Adaptation of video games into films: The adventures of the narrative. In *12th World Congress of Semiotics proceedings*. Berlin, Germany: De Gruyter Mouton.

Kirkland, E. (2006). Alessa unbound: The monstrous daughter of *Silent Hill* (2006). In S. Ni Fhlainn (Ed.), *Dark reflections, monstrous reflections: Essays on the monster in culture.* Inter-Disciplinary Press. Ebook. Retrieved January 18, 2016 from http://www.inter-disciplinary.net/publishing/?s=Dark+Reflec tions%2C+Monstrous+Reflections%3A+Essays+on+the+Monster+in+Culture

Krzywinska, T. (2008). Zombies in gamespace: Form, context, and meaning in zombie-based videogames. In S. McIntosh & M. Leverette (Eds.), *Zombie culture: Autopsies of the living dead* (pp. 153–168). Lanham, MD: Scarecrow Press.

Lotman, Y. (1974). Primary and secondary communication-modeling systems. In Materials of the all union symposium on secondary modeling systems, 1(5), 224-228.

Lotman, Y. (1992). *La semiosfera. L'asimmetria e il dialogo nelle strutture pensanti.* Venezia, Italy: Marsilio.

Lotman, Y. (2004). *Culture and explosion.* Berlin, Germany: Mouton de Gruyter. (Original work published 1992)

Lotman, Y. (2011). The place of art among other modelling systems. *Sing System Studies, 39*(2/4), 251–270.

Marion, I. (2011). *Warm bodies.* New York, NY: ATRIA.

Migliore, T. (Ed.). (2010). Incidenti ed esplosioni. A. J. Greimas e J. M. Lotman Per una semiotica delle culture. Rome, Italy: Aracne Editrice.

Monson, M. J. (2012). Race-based fantasy realm essentialism in the *World of warcraft. Games and Culture, 7*(1), 48–71. doi:10.1177/1555412012440308

Neale, S. (1980). *Genre.* London, UK: British Film Institute.

Night of the living dead. (1968). Dir. George A. Romero, Prod. Image Ten, Laurel Group, Market Square Productions, Off Color Films. USA.

Perron, B. (2005). *Coming to play at frightening yourself: Welcome to the world of horror video games.* Retrieved September 10, 2015 from http://www.aestheticsofplay.org/perron.php

Perron, B. (Ed.). (2009). *Horror video games: Essays on the fusion of fear and play.* Jefferson, NC: McFarland.

Perron, B. (2011). *Silent hill: The terror engine.* Michigan, MI: U of Michigan P. doi:10.3998/lvg.11053908.0001.001

Perron, B., & Wolf, M. J. P. (Eds.). (2009). *The video game theory reader 2.* London, UK: Routledge.

Poe, E. A. (2009). *Fall of the house of Usher and other tales.* New York, NY: New American Library. (Original work published 1839)

Poltergeist. (1982). Dir. Tobe Hooper, Prod. Metro-Goldwyn-Mayer (MGM), SLM Production Group. USA.

Prohászková, V. (2012). The genre of horror. *American International Journal of Contemporary Research,* *2*(4), 132–142.

Propp, V. (1968). *Morphology of the folk tale.* Austin, TX: University of Texas Press. (Original work published 1928)

Pruett, C. (2010). The anthropology of fear: Learning about Japan through horror games. *Interface,* *4*(6). Retrieved June 29, 2015 from http://journals.sfu.ca/loading/index.php/loading/article/view/90/87

Saussure, F. (1983). *Course in general linguistics.* Illinois, IL: Open Court Publishing Company. (Original work published 1916)

Scolari, C. (2013). *Narraivas transmedia, cuando todos los medios cuentan.* Barcelona, Spain: Deusto.

Sedda, F. (2015). Semiotics of culture(s): Basic questions and concepts. In P. P. Trifonas (Ed.), *International Handbook of Semiotics* (pp. 675–696). New York, NY; London, UK: Springer. doi:10.1007/978-94-017-9404-6_31

Tavinor, G. (2007). *The art of videogames.* West Sussex, UK: Wiley-Blackwell.

Team Silent. (1999). *Silent hill,* [Videogame] [Disc] [PlayStation] Konami (Europe).

Team Silent. (2001). *Silent hill 2* [Videogame]. Konami. [Disc]

Team Silent. (2003). *Silent hill 3,* [Videogame] [Disc] [PlayStation 2] Konami (Europe).

Team Silent. (2004). *Silent hill 4: The Room,* [Videogame] [Disc] [PlayStation 2] Konami (Europe).

The orphanage. (2007). Dir. J.A. Bayona, Prod. Esta Vivo! Laboratorio de Nuevos Talentos, Grupo Rodar, Rodar y Rodar Cine y Televisión, Telecinco Cinema, Televisió de Catalunya (TV3), Warner Bros. Pictures de España, Wild Bunch. Spain.

The others. (2001). Dir. Alejandro Amenábar, Prod. Cruise/Wagner Productions, Sogecine, Las Producciones del Escorpión, Dimension Films, Canal+, Lucky Red, Miramax. USA, Spain, France, Italy.

The shrine . (2010). Dir. Jon Knautz, Prod. Wesley Clover Media, Brookstreet Pictures. Canada.

Thibault, M. (2012). *Trasmissione, innovazione e recupero dei ruoli: Un'analisi comparativa di gioco di ruolo, videogiochi e letteratura (transmission, innovation and retrieving of roles: a comparative analysis of role-playing games, video games and literature).* (Master thesis). University of Turin, Turin, Italy.

Timmerman, J. H. (1983). *Other worlds: The fantasy genre.* Bowling Green, OH: Popular Press.

Todorov, T. (1973). *The fantastic: A structural approach to a literary genre.* Cleveland, OH: Case Western Reserve University.

Tolkien, J. R. R. (1937). *The hobbit, or, here and back again.* Crows Nest, Australia: Allen & Unwin.

Tolkien, J. R. R. (1954). *The lord of the rings.* Crows Nest, Australia: Allen & Unwin.

Torop, P. (2000). Intersemiosis and intersemiotic translation. *European Journal for Semiotic Studies,* *12*(1), 71–100.

Warm bodies. (2013). Dir. Jonathan Levine, Prod. Summit Entertainment, Make Movies, Mandeville Films, Quebec Film and Television Tax Credit. USA and Canada.

Warnes, C. (2005). *Baldur's Gate and history: Race and alignment in digital role playing games, Proceedings of the 2005 DiGRA.* Retrieved June 29, 2015 from http://www.digra.org/digital-library/publications/baldurs-gate-and-history-race-and-alignment-in-digital-role-playing-games/

Waskul, D., & Lust, M. (2004). Role-playing and playing roles: The person, player, and persona in fantasy role-playing.Symbolic Interaction, (27), 333–356. doi:10.1525/si.2004.27.3.333

Wolf, M. J. P. (2001). *Genre and the video game in the medium of the video game.* Austin, TX: University of Texas Press.

World War Z. (2013). Dir. Marc Forster, Prod. Paramount Pictures, Skydance Productions, Hemisphere Media Capital, GK Films, Plan B Entertainment, 2DUX^2, Apparatus Productions, Latina Pictures. USA.

Zombieland. (2009). Dir. Ruben Fleischer, Prod. Columbia Pictures, Relativity Media, Pariah. USA.

KEY TERMS AND DEFINITIONS

Actantial Model: A method to analyze narratives, developed by Algirdas Julien Greimas.

Architext: According to Genette (1997) it means all general or transcendent categories pertaining to a text. The authors use the term in a broader way, including all the intertextual and hypertextual relationships that link together all the texts pertaining to the said category

Semiosphere: The semiotic space of a culture, a modeling system or a single text. It is the space inside which the rise of meaning (semiosis) can happen.

Semiotics: A discipline that studies signs, meaning, and meaning generating mechanisms. It consists in various approaches, mainly focusing on *texts* or on *cultures*.

Storyworld: A term that is used in transmedia storytelling. A storyworld refers to the shared (common) universe, used by several different media, within which one or more narratives exist.

Texts: According to semiotics it is not simply a written text, but any cultural, somewhat separate, cluster of meaning, expressed with a code and recorded on a media.

Thematic Roles: They consist in the semantic value of a single role, constituted as a small, coherent, ensemble of *figures* and virtual actions.

Transmedia (or Transmedia Storytelling): The technique of telling one or many stories that share the same storyworld, across multiple platforms and formats including - but not limited to - books, games, cinema and television.

ENDNOTES

[1]   The terms *synchrony – diachrony* derives from Saussure's theory. Synchrony is the study of a semiotic system at a given point of time, while diachrony is the study of the evolution of a semiotic system on a historical axis.

[2]   The fantasy genre is described as "imaginative fiction dependent for effect on strangeness of setting (such as other worlds or times) and characters (such as supernatural beings)" (Merriam-Webster's Encyclopedia of Literature) and it's rooted in fairy tales, ancient myths, and legends. The high fantasy, on the other hand is a subgenre of Fantasy fiction, born in the 1950s when its major works by C. S. Lewis and J. R. R. Tolkien were published. High fantasy narratives are "generally serious in tone and often epic in scope, dealing with themes of grand struggle against supernatural, evil forces. It is one of the most popular subgenres of fantasy fiction. Some typical characteristics of high fantasy include fantastical elements such as elves and dwarfs, magic, wizards, invented languages, quests, coming-of-age theme, and multi-volume narratives." (Havířová, 2007, p. 27)

[3]   "Based on the historic tradition and the frequent occurrence of supernatural elements, the genre of horror is considered as one 'apex of the popular fantasy triangle' together with fantasy and science fiction. It is so despite the fact that fantastic horror is only one of the two flows of this genre that exist together with the so-called realistic horror. Unlike science fiction and fantasy, the definitions of the genre of horror do not stand on the structure of various works; they rather focus on the aesthetic aspect and emotions, which are evoked in the readers (fear, horror, anxiety etc.) [....] One of the attributes of horror are some typical archetypal characters: vampire, werewolf, zombie, monster, mad scientist, demon, ghost, eternal wanderer, serial killer, psychopath, bad child, possessed person, and antichrist. The genre is characterized by dynamism, and therefore it is necessary to note that these are only just a few of the archetypes, because they keep evolving along with the genre and new archetypal characters are created perpetually. Another of the genre's dominants is the environment in which the story is revolving: places out of the modern world, such as cemeteries, abandoned castles, gloomy forests, castle ruins, old houses etc. Most of all, these are places intensively charged with mystery and that have 'their own lives'. This is also true for the modern environment that cuts its way into the modern horror" (Prohászková, 2012, p. 134).

[4]   As many readers will have noticed, the authors have decided to avoid fantasy films in their analysis. This is both due to a matter of cohesion and to the fact that most fantasy films are adaptations, and so do not properly pertain to architextuality, but rather to a (simpler) form of hypertextuality. One could also argue that the lack of success of films inspired by fantasy videogames like *Dungeons and Dragons* (2000) is due to their inability to translate an RPG in a narrative: exploiting an effect of architextuality does not guarantee success.

[5]   For an in depth analysis of the concept of "race" in fantasy videogames see Monson (2012), Warnes (2005) and Waskul and Lust (2004).

[6]   Survival horror games are either a first or a third person shooter. Players usually have to find their way through unknown and hostile places, confront monsters, solve puzzles, discover clues and combine them in order to survive. The narrative of survival horror games is usually very well constructed and has limitations per se: there is a limited number of characters that the players can choose to play with, and they have to make very specific choices in order to end the game.

[7]   It should be noted that the fog was also a way to overcome rendering issues, in times that a PC or console wasn't able to process too much information.

[8]   Cults are a common theme in video games. It is part of *Silent Hill* games storyline. Also, a cult appears in *Resident Evil 4*.

[9]   The Licker is a mutation experienced by zombies in *Resident Evil* game series, which transforms them into deadlier hunters.

Section 5
Paratextuality

Chapter 15
Paratext:
The In-Between of Structure and Play

Daniel Dunne
Swinburne University of Technology, Australia

ABSTRACT

This chapter examines paratext as an active element within video games. Paratext, as taken from Gérard Genette's works has often been cited within the context of video games, but not examined in detail. Current scholarship focuses on epitext, but not peritext, which is Genette's primary focus. Mia Consalvo and Peter Lunenfeld's work discuss the epitextual importance of paratext within video games, with only a hint towards the importance of peritext. Through a brief exploration of paratext's history in both literature and games, this chapter will reveal a need for deeper analysis within video game studies. Focusing on in-game, in-system and in-world types of paratexts this paper will attempt to formalise the unaddressed issue of paratext in video games.

INTRODUCTION

Paratext in video games has been, more or less, a succinct byword for the extension of narrative beyond the players' experience of games. Paratext is broadly considered to be the elements which surround a text[1], but are not part of it. In a book this might be the composition of chapters, or paragraphs, or something as unique as the typeface. This is only one part of paratext. Paratext can also be expanded to include efforts to advertise a text, in interviews, posters, trailers, and word of mouth. All of these examples are a form of paratext, but video game scholarship has tended to focus on the later, the epitextual (external influences to the text), rather than the former, peritextual (internal influences to the text), in their use of the term. This development of paratext, while it can be understood historically as a development out of media studies, is not an accurate representation of "what paratext is" within literature. As such, the current representation of paratext only displays one possibility out of many for the use of paratext within video games. As paratext can be applied to texts, video games can also be considered as a form of text. The text being the notion of gameplay or narrative, not just purely the idea of a narrative. This chapter highlights what paratext can do to further video game studies, specifically in relation to a textual analysis.

DOI: 10.4018/978-1-5225-0477-1.ch015

Paratext, in regards to its earlier form in literature, can provide game scholars with a wider scope to analyze and present elements that target reader and game character; its structure and diegesis (within the story); and its system mechanics that directly and indirectly affect the playing of a game. While these elements are present within games (saving, loading, cut-scenes, menus, etc.), they are rarely discussed in a manner that deals with both their importance and their overall effect on the appreciation of the game. Paratext fills this in-between status looking at elements that both help structure the game, but also provide a better enjoyment of the game. Games scholarship occasionally delves into discussion related to paratext, but rarely intentionally – as often good paratext achieves its goals without drawing attention to itself. As such, there is an inherent need to look at these elements to better analyze and design video games.

This chapter is divided into two sections. The first section discusses the history of paratext within the context of literature, media and video game studies. The second section provides a re-definition of paratext which will be introduced through applying Genette's theory to video games.

Through providing a history of the term paratext an overview of the concept can be developed. This focuses on Gérard Genette's definition of the term in literature, in relation to his notion of paratext as being made up of two parts: peritext and epitext. From there, the chapter explores the differences in the term's use from literature to media and video game studies, focusing on theorists such as Mia Consalvo and Peter Lunenfeld. To counter these prominent viewpoints within the field, there will be a comparison with the word's use through David Jara's work, who argues for a return to Genette's original notion of paratext.

The re-definition of paratext applies these prior works, with an emphasis on peritextual analysis, to video games. This model focuses on three distinct areas within video games where paratext can be discovered: in-game, in-system, and in-world. These areas, while not all encompassing, provide some direction as to how to view games with a paratextual analysis. This re-definition is not just concerned to what Genette's work suggests, but also addresses a need within game studies for a tool which deals with this in-between area of structure and text.

The last section of this chapter will discuss the uses of this peritextual approach, and how it situates itself with the already prominent epitextual use of paratext that currently dominates the field. It is the hope of this chapter to clearly show the need for a peritextual focused paratext within the pre-existing literature.

HISTORY OF PARATEXT

Literary Paratext

The term, paratext originally came from Gérard Genette in his early text *Introduction à l'architexte* (1979)[2] and then elaborated upon in *Paratexts. Thresholds of Interpretation* (1997).[3] In both, Genette demarcates the types of textual relationships that books and other types of media have in relation with each other. Originally slated as a further explanation of transtextuality with intertextual, hypertextual, and hypotextual relationships, Genette quickly focuses upon the individual text as a topic worth discussing. In particular Genette's discussion focuses on the relationships at work within the individual text itself, leading to the development of paratext. This concept deals with the relationship of the structuring or physical elements that make up the text, and the text itself. An idea that "make[s] present, to ensure the text's presence in the world" (Genette & Maclean, 1991, p. 261). This focus, entitled paratext, was Genette's holistic look into the techniques that an author (or publisher) draws upon to influence an audience. "[T]his fringe [paratext] […] of transition but also of transaction [is] a privileged place of a pragmatic and strategy, of an influence of the public" (Genette, 1997, p. 2). In doing so Genette drew attention to the product of the novel and the process of its development to create a new understanding of what books could do beyond a strictly textual analysis.

Genette separated his notion of Paratext into two separate focuses, Epitext and Peritext.

- **Epitext:** Paratext that is externally based on events or elements. An example would be advertisements, and interviews with the author and/or publisher. This type of paratext directs readers towards the text foremost and informs the reader about the text.
- **Peritext:** Paratext that is based internally. These peritext elements are present in the physical book itself. For example font, paragraph location, spacing and front covers would be some, but not all elements of the peritexts evident in the novel. Primarily this paratext pushes the reader towards the text and helps to shape their interpretation of the text.

Through Genette's explanation of paratext in *Paratexts. Thresholds of Interpretation*, his focus is mainly upon the peritextual elements.[4] The focus of Genette's analysis of peritext over epitext could be due to the complexity involved in trying to go systematically through the types of epitext that exist – there is simply too much to possibly analyze.[5] Genette sought to investigate an unexplored part of literary analysis, as Genette (1997) identifies clearly:

Whereas on many occasions we have noted the relative neglect accorded the peritext by the literary world (including specialists), the situation of the epitext is obviously very different. Critics and literary historians have long made extensive use of the epitext in commenting on works. (p. 346)

The focus of Genette's work is to look at "the beaten track" of peritext to examine the extent to which elements that are situated within a text but are not 'part' of it can affect the reading of the text. Unfortunately for Genette the notion of paratext has been attributed towards epitext, going against the "relative neglect," which Genette sought to correct.

Both types of paratext provide types of structure that are necessary for the text to exist, but also influences the audiences' reception of the text. These influences can occur in a diegetic function, from having the structure relate directly to the narrative or through having the narrative (the diegesis) make note of its structure (e.g. Italo Calvino's *If On A Winter's Night a Traveler*[6]). Alternatively these paratexts can exist in a non-diegetic space (e.g. the rough texture of a novel's paper), or between the diegetic and non-diegetic (e.g. the inclusion of a map within a book). These paratexts have no direct effect on the story yet add to the reader's interpretation of the text. This appreciation can be purely aesthetical, or if the reader interprets these paratexts as relating to the story adding to the narrative. Although the diegetic interaction of the paratext will be more explicit than the non-diegetic, both do affect the audiences' interpretation of the text on some level.

Though these are not all of the specific qualities present in the epitext and peritext, they are the main points of difference and similarity. Genette goes on to express the differences within these paratexts. They can be summarized within the concept of spatiality, officiousness, and temporality.[7]

Spatiality

The primary difference between the two subsets of paratext revolves around the notion of spatiality as highlighted by Genette (1997), "The criterion distinguishing the epitext from the peritext [...] is in theory purely spatial. The epitext is any paratextual element not materially appended" (p. 344). Peritext is limited to the physical constraints of the book in question, whereas epitext can exist independently of the novel. Although it seems that epitext has no bounds to its existence, within its own makeup there still has to be some link to the source text (whether a connection of the author's name, the publishing house, or more directly citing the novel's title).

Spatiality not only occupies the physical presence of media texts, as is the case with peritext, but also occupies the ideological space where the epitext does have some bearing on the book. Although the two occupations of space are somewhat different, they still do relate to the text.

Temporality

Temporality defines how relevant and how successful these paratextual elements are on the reception of the text. Obviously the closer that these paratexts are to the critical reception of the novel, the more effective they will be on the audiences' interpretation of the text. By this, the more contemporary the paratext, the more relevant it will be seen by audiences.

Temporality primarily affects epitexts due to their status as advertising or reviews – these are much more related to the period in which the text is promoted (Genette, 1997, p. 12). Epitexts due to their external nature, are related much more to their time of publication, presenting the text as something which can be accessed by the culture at that point in time. This allows for a good insight into who the text is being directed towards, but as time progresses is not as relevant.

Peritext being spatially close to the text and much more integral to its production means that temporality is less of a concern. The inclusion of paragraphs, types of font, or the presentation of chapters, while potentially dated are presented alongside the text as is and are rarely questioned. It is mostly in the scope of introductions, which contextualize the piece to temporary audiences, that temporality becomes relevant for peritext. A new introduction to an old text, will hold a higher value than one written five years after a text.

Officiousness

Officiousness, or authorial significance, is a method of discerning the authenticity of commentary around or within a text. This officiousness, is primarily dictated by an author's considerations, but can also include publishers or advertisers. As such officiousness is usually a contentious consideration in relation to the epitext, rather than the peritext.

Genette (1997) highlights this in "pragmatic status of a paratext," (p. 8), in the idea of the senders (p. 73), and also in the use of the word authorial (pp. 196-293). In each section Genette gives credence to those who produce, send, or control the text, as being the officiator of the text. Authors, as Genette asserts, usually have control over how their work is published, and with peritextual elements dictate strongly what occurs in the presentation of the text. It is often in later editions of novels where the author is not available that publishers have greater sway in the scheme of the text's peritexts.

Within advertising, reviews, and other epitexts such authorial control is not as singular and instead is negotiated with other parties who will interpret the text. Due to this negotiated presentation, the officiousness is no longer as clear cut to author and publisher, but further to advertisers, reviewers and interviewers who contribute to the epitext.

Paratext Overview

Peritext and epitext, in conjunction with these three qualities of spatiality, officiousness, and temporality are included in the concept of paratext. Genette, in separating this notion of paratext from previous definitions made sure that its focus is primarily upon the work and intentions of the author (peritext), with some discussion given to external forces (epitext). In this Genette was concerned with the in-between nature of paratext, separating, but yet including, the text and structure, which in turn would provide meaning to readers. Genette (1997) summarizes this in his conclusion:

The paratext provides an airlock that helps the reader pass without too much respiratory difficulty from one world to the other, a sometimes delicate operation, especially when the second world is a fictional world. (p. 408)

It is with regard to the process of guiding readers (or players) to their text, and the effect of peritextual influences on a reader, that current scholarship within video games should be developed. As current scholarship has explored the epitextual aspects of paratext, to make full use of paratext, peritext too needs to be explored.

Paratext, Video Games, and Media

The examination of paratext in video games, while loosely based upon Genette's work, tends to focus on the epitextual paratext resulting in an interpretation of elements external to the text. This interpretation tends to overlook the internal peritext elements within video games. This preference can be seen notably in the works of Mia Consalvo and Peter Lunenfeld, who both use the term to highlight the direction of produces and publishers in how they present videogames to players. The implementation of paratext can be seen below:

Genette generated his theories from a study of literature and considers the paratext in terms of the publishing industry: cover design, book packaging, publicity materials, and so on. (Lunenfeld, 2000, p. 14)

Although for Genette paratext is mainly textual [...] his arguments [...] can also be adapted to signify and explain [a] larger set of paratexts. (Consalvo, 2007, p. 21)

Both scholars are primarily interested in viewing paratext as advertisements (Lunenfeld) or as a metatextual readings (Consalvo, who makes use of the surrounding infrastructure of community groups and their discussion as a 'commentary,' to the main text of games). Both of these interpretations are brief in the scheme of each academic's work,[8] and while they offer some interesting thoughts, they do not engage with Genette's full definition of paratext. Consalvo does mention that Genette's approach is mainly textually based, which somewhat highlights the peritextual focus of Genette's work. However, as Consalvo is concerned with the external elements of paratext she does not extend this discussion further.

Other game scholars have used paratext in a similar fashion to examine an audience's relationship with a text. Discussion revolving around epitextual analysis of paratext (*Using gaming paratexts in the literacy classroom* [Walsh & Apperley, 2012]) has resulted in thinking about the effect of trailers, marketing, and community groups. This reflects much of Consalvo and Lunenfeld's approaches and as such discussions of paratext can be seen as epitextually focused.

This focus on epitextual paratexts has provided interesting results in the scope of presenting community groups and publishers as influencing an interpretation of video game texts in a non-traditional manner. Yet due to this success paratext has been equated as solely epitext instead of a combination of both epitext and peritext. Through this development, paratext has increasingly become associated as the external elements that shape the experience and reception of video games. In this regard, the use of the term in video game studies aligns with its use by media and film studies, which also focuses on the epitextual approach. This can be seen primarily through the works of Robert Stam and Jonathan Gray.

Robert Stam provides a brief look into paratext, in the chapter "Beyond Fidelity: The Dialogics of Adaptation". Stam (2000) thinks of paratext as an external focus: "In the case of film, the paratext might include widely quoted prefatory remarks by a director at a film's first screening, reported remarks by a director about a film" (p. 65). This echoes Lunenfeld's focus, but ties it closely to the idea of officiousness with the director being the spokesperson for the film. This follows Genette's concept of epitext; however it does not take the peritext approach into consideration. This can possibly be through the convention of media studies to incorporate a number of different techniques in the analysis of film or television (examining the camera techniques, the use of sound effects, orchestral scores, costume design, and so on). The analysis provided by media studies allows for many of these paratextual elements, the in-between, to be present. Other media scholars have nevertheless applied the term within media studies to provide a further distinction within the analysis of film.

Media scholar, Jonathan Gray (2010), continues this trend of an outward focus of paratext in *Show Sold Separately*. Paratext in Gray's analysis has been significantly remodeled to suit film's temporal qualities, rather than Genette's spatial focus. Paratexts for Gray (2010) exist as a temporal occurrence prior to, while and after texts are viewed (p. 6, pp. 25-26, pp. 35-38). Gray further separates paratext as "entry way paratexts" (p. 35, p. 79) which introduce audiences to the text, and as "in media res paratext" (p. 40) which occurs around the film's inception. Although this can be situated with Genette's notion of epitext and peritext, the transition from a spatial foundation to a temporal one is not fully negotiated. As the application of paratext by Gray mirrors some of Genette's intended uses, it loses the versatility of Genette's terminology. Gray's "in media res" paratext does not provide an analysis of what structures and influences occur within the text but rather introduces a transmedia argument[9] of how meaning is conveyed across a range of texts. Indeed many of the "in media res" paratext examples given refer more to a number of transmedia developments (webisodes, comics, websites[10]) rather than content that is located within a singular media form. Although this development can be analyzed through some aspects of paratext, this discussion is better suited within transmedia discussions. Gray's work provides a good indication of external elements that need to be considered, if a holistic view of a franchise is sought. However in the consideration of structures and influences that occur within a text Gray's approach is too expansive.

This scholarship develops methods for analyzing community involvement and explaining how a variety of texts can interact with each other. However this use of paratext primarily focuses on epitextual qualities. The current definition of paratext has limited the exploration of video game analysis as it largely ignores the internal structure of video games that affect the reception of the game's text. It would be remiss of media and video game scholars to ignore the internal aspects that peritext offers. In this a peritextual analysis of video games would explore the elements that prefaced the playing of the text, and the elements that, while not strictly part of the text (like user interfaces or menu screens) still affect the reception of and access to the game.

Finding Peritext

Unfortunately discussion around the internal structure of video games has been minimal, or lacking the necessary language to effectively analyze what is occurring. Peritext can be seen as hinted towards through case studies, or introduced generally as contextualizing the video game in within a certain convention.

This case study analysis is seen in the discussion of game objectives in *Bioshock* (Tulloch, 2010), or Jordan Mechner discussing the meta-narrative of *Prince of Persia: Sands of Time* (Harrigan & Wardrip-Fruin, 2010, p. 109). Mechner and Tulloch's analysis focuses on the importance of gameplay elements and agency, and furthermore its constraints by the narrative of the game. Certainly while these elements do add to an illusion of agency and greater narrative success there is no deep analysis into the general use of these paratextual qualities. Instead, both papers only hint to the in-between nature of these mechanics as being structural important to these specific case studies and not to a larger range of video games. Other examples do exist, but they focus on paratexts as being the unique features of the chosen case study rather than a prevalent feature of video games. Nevertheless these papers do provide an indication that there is an awareness for such paratexts to have a great impact upon the interpretation of video game texts.

The notion of paratext as being present as a convention of videogames can be seen in David Jara's work, *A Closer Look at the (Rule-) Books: Framing and Paratexts in Tabletop Role-playing Game*s (2003). As Jara (2003) directly interacts with Genette's notion of paratext, and address Consalvo's definition directly:

Not only is Wolf's re-definition of the term 'paratext' necessary, but it is also an important one [...] considering the fact that the latter has been broadly used in game theory since its introduction to the field by Mia Consalvo in her influential book Cheating (2007). (p. 40)

Jara reintroduces paratext as a term that is more peritextually focused by comparing paratext with Werner Wolf's framing techniques. Framing techniques for Wolf (1999) are techniques which explain to readers how to read a text, though this does not need to be explicit: "literary texts, more than non-literary ones, are usually accompanied by framings referring to the specificity of the text and giving hints as to how to read it." (p. 102). Wolf makes specific reference to the style of prose, the presentation and the effects of those features in the audiences' appreciation of the text, because they are told to read, and hence structure (frame) their readings in a certain way. Jara's comparison between Wolf's framing paratext and Consalvo's external paratext is especially valuable in determining its use within videogames.

An overview of peritext and epitext in video games and media can be found in the discussion by Steven E. Jones (2008) in *The meaning of video games: Gaming and textual strategies*. Jones provides an analysis of both peritext and epitext in the beginning of the text, however as Jones explores case studies he ceases to distinguish between the types of paratexts. Within the game, peritext, and the content external to it, epitext. From this Jones asserts, as Lunenfeld did, that due to the complex nature of publishing and producing content, paratext can no longer be separated into mutually exclusive boundaries. Jones through this argument is focusing on an outward perspective on paratext.

Peritextual methodologies and analysis are limited within video game scholarship, even when the scope is widened to explore where case studies presented where peritext is not explicitly mentioned. When paratext is discussed the majority of scholarship makes use of Consalvo or Lunenfeld's interpretation of paratext, which overlooks the peritextual possibilities that can occur within video game studies. Further implementation of peritext can provide another tool for the analysis of game structures, and in how audiences interpret a text. As such, a redefinition of paratext in relation to video game studies needs to occur.

The remainder of this chapter provides a framework for a peritextual analysis of video games. This involves both the framework, but also a series of case studies where peritext applications can be seen within video games. Epitext will not be focused upon due to the saturation of such scholarship as has been observed through the works of Genette, Jara and Wolf. Slight reference to epitext will inevitably occur in the discussion of paratext.

RE-DEFINITION OF PARATEXT

A New System

Returning to the notion that Genette presents for paratext, with peritext in particular, this chapter has shifted the focus towards the in-between elements of text. In this context paratext can be seen at once as a structure, transition, and an amorphous element of texts.

Indeed this fringe always the conveyor of a commentary that is authorial or more or less legitimated by the author, constitutes a zone between text and off-text a zone not only of transition but also of transaction a privileged place of a pragmatics and a strategy of an influence on the public, an influence that —whether well or poorly understood and achieved is at the service of a better reception for the text and a more pertinent reading of it (more pertinent of course in the eyes of the author and his allies). (Genette, 1997, p. 2)

Paratext should not be dismissed as simply the setting up for the text or the system of a video game, but rather should be broadened to be both the system, as well as part of the video game text (encompassing the notion of gameplay and narrative). This is analogous to a framing perspective (as Wolf & Bernhardt [2006] would argue). However, this severely limits the ability of paratext. It is important to stress that paratext not only provides a method in which the reader can access the text (i.e. preparation), but paratext is also part of the text, in actively telling and constraining what the reader can and cannot do. At the same time it informs the reader of narrative and gameplay segments within the video game.

This division of paratext is from the perspective of making an effective analysis. It is not a method in which paratext is restricted to being one thing or another. Rather it can be thought effectively as a progressive spectrum that with each iteration either is closer to or further from the text. As with the original title of Genette's writings on paratext (1987) it is the *Seuils,* or threshold, of interpretation.

Structure

Using the concept of spatiality as the foundation for identifying peritexts; paratext within video games is divided into three forms: in-game, in-system, and in-world paratexts. These will be discussed in more detail within the case studies of each section. These can broadly be defined as:

- **In-Game Paratext:** In-game paratext is internal to the text. This would encapsulate any event that structures or informs the player's game. In-game paratext occurs within the text while playing the game from the moment that the executable file runs.
- **In-System Paratext:** In-system paratext is internal to the system. This encapsulates any event that structures or informs the player's game that occurs within the system. In-system paratext is required to play the game, and so a necessary part of accessing the text. The access process may include navigation through system files, the application of different files and installation methods, searching the internet, or the alteration of drivers to the system's hardware. In short in-system paratext encompasses a variety of system related steps that allow a player to access the text.
- **In-World Paratext:** In-world paratext is a physical presence that accompanies the text. This encapsulates any event that structures or informs the player's game that occurs within the world that is physically tangible. This is in thinking of the video game as a physical object, as a tangible product. This can be further divided up into subsections of the game disk, manual, packaging box, paraphernalia and figurines. In short in-world paratext is anything physically tangible that comes with the video game.

Analysis of Conditions

These paratextual divisions primarily adhere to the notions of spatiality and follow Genette's discussion of differences between peritext and epitext (Genette, 1997, p. 344). However other elements of temporality and officiousness, are included in this division but are not focused upon. As with literature this division occurs within video games. This focus on spatiality is due to the close ties that spatiality inevitably has with peritextual elements. Focusing on temporality or officiousness, while certainly interesting would inevitably lead the discussion to an epitextual paratext, which is unneeded based on the pre-existing literature. Nevertheless, below is an overview of how temporality, officiousness, and spatiality can be used in relation to video games.

Temporality in Games

The idea of temporality has been avoided as a precondition for these peritext focused paratexts. Primarily because temporality is harder to define than spatiality, within video games. The complexity involved with this idea of temporality is that with each iteration of 'new' elements added by the publishers or developers of a game, while improving the game through gameplay or bug fixing, leads to an entirely different game text being present.

Taking this argument further, the entire presentation of the game in respect to temporality might be considered as a completely new text instead of an extension of the original text (consider *Mass Effect 3*, or the enhanced *Witcher* editions). Although such developments have been discussed in relation to texts, the constantly changing nature of video games – especially when taking into account the presence of patches and mods – makes this a complex issue to address succinctly. For the most part differences often are tied into playability, rather than game function – though obviously exceptions do exist within video games. Temporality, while an interesting aspect of paratext, is currently outside the scope of this investigation.

Officiousness in Games

Officiousness has been limited in this analysis to those that have worked on the game – the developers and publisher. Since the focus of this discussion is upon authors of the text and not epitexts, such as advertisements or reviews, officiousness is not contested. If the scope were increased to the entire video game product (the franchise) officiousness could be explored within the scope of an epitextual analysis.

Officiousness adds to this peritextual approach. It identifies which elements of a game are implemented by publishers or developers, and which should be given more credence. This is reliant on these elements being spatially close to the game. As such, alternative authors of officiousness will most likely be found in the game files or in the manual, rather than found in the in-game sections.

Spatiality in Games

Spatiality is central to this discussion as the differences between each of the paratextual levels. While physically these divisions occur around the text, their effect and influences change depending on their theoretical closeness to the text. As such the divide between in-game, in-system, and in-world, is important to understand the relationship of the paratext to the reader (player), but also where these paratexts are in relationship to the text.

Within video games, the notion of spatiality can readily identify the locations of these paratexts. This approach especially makes the surrounding "interlocking gates" of paratext easier to find when the text is considered to be the focal point. From this focal point the in-game paratext surrounds the text, the in-system surrounds the in-game, and the in-world surrounds the in-system. Each allows the player to be closer to the reading of the game text. This series of paratextual gates can be seen in Figure 1.

Figure 1. Diagram of video game paratext
Source: The Author.

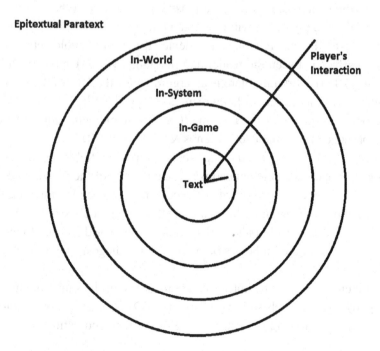

Players may not directly interact with the in-system, or in-world paratext elements as much as the in-game elements, it is still necessary "to pass through them," to access the text. How much notice the player gives to these sections may vary, but the fact that they have to work through each section is undeniable. This identification of where paratext occurs can also document their effect on the player. This is an effective method in which to determine possible influences on a player that echoes strongly of Genette's methodology.

It should be noted that while these paratexts can be diegetic influences within a video game,[11] they can also be used in a non-diegetic manner for structuring purposes and influence the relationship a reader has with the text to a smaller degree. Some structural paratexts have been noted in the resulting analysis, but there is an acknowledged tendency to focus upon the paratext that shapes the reader's interpretation of the text to a large extent with by virtue of both its structure and its effect on the narrative.

The following analysis is by no means comprehensive, but is meant to highlight prominent paratexts, and directions for further study.

Video Game Paratexts

In-Game Paratext

With in-game paratext the focus is on the internal support for a game (menus, system mechanics, company promotional videos, commentaries, loading bars), which are not direct elements of gameplay or narrative, but are mainly the supporting structures that help the overall feel, and actual performance of the game. This is the most expansive area for paratext in games in that it has a lot of content that is easily identifiable and accessible to players. Its impact is also likely stronger since it actively frames the game or text existing consistently through the play of games. Primarily this aspect of in-game paratexts can be seen within the notion of user interfaces and heads up displays.

Heads up displays (HUDS) or user interfaces (UI) are the primary identifiable in-game paratexts, with game menus, loading screens, non-diegetic music, and a host of other paratext features. The inclusion of UIs and HUDs are presented within the game itself, and aid the player in the playing of the game (see Figure 3). Both UIs and HUDS act as a device that is applicable between the player and the game, acting as an interface between the reader and the game world (Clarke & Duimering, 2006, pp. 6-8; Johnson & Wiles, 2003). Certainly there is an argument for the UI or HUD to be considered to be part of the gameplay (as would cutscenes [Newman, 2013, pp. 16-17; Rouse, 2010, pp. 17-18]), but it seems that in relation to the purity of the in-game 'text,' these elements adorn the central element of play and narrative, or indeed the game itself (Llanos & Jørgensen, 2011).

With *Fallout 3* and *Fallout: New Vegas* the implementation of the Pipboy can be seen as both a diegetic and structural element. The diegetic element adds to the narrative of the game, while the structural element allows for many of the mechanical processes necessary to a role playing game. These mechanical processes include inventory management (a requirement of the game's structure) to be portrayed in a fashion that not only was interesting but also reflected the game world (adding to the game's narrative). Figure 2 and Figure 3 highlight the Pipboy as being part of the diegesis, yet also essentially structuring the text.

In Figure 2 and Figure 3 it should be noted that the presence of the same font and coloured (yellow) text of in-game Pipboy and HUD also offers a further link that situates both paratexts as part of the same game world. Both are allowing for a structuring of the text (indicating an amount of health, am-

Figure 2. The presence of the Pipboy as an in-world paratext is made particularly evident in this screen-shots, as the device is attached to the player-character's arm and so is viewed when selected. The Pipboy menu can be seen highlighting the different status of body parts.
Source: Obsidian Entertainment, 2010.

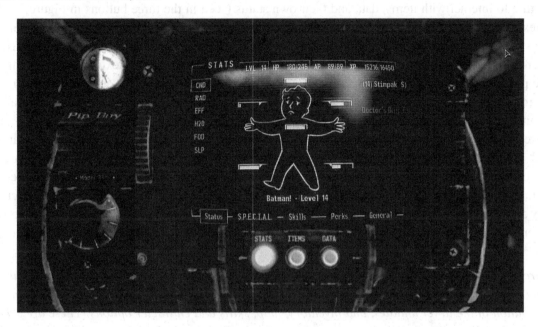

Figure 3. A progression screenshot highlighting the diegetic nature of the Pipboy. Further the HUD for the game can also be seen in the form of the bars and writing on the lower left and right of the screen.
Source: Obsidian Entertainment, 2010.

munition on the right, and in Figure 2 showing the condition of various limbs) both are situated within the context of the video game. This can be seen as an implementation of peritext that contributes to the notion of structure affecting a player's reading of the text – through the Pipboy players are given a further structure to interact with items, data and their own status (seen in the three buttons in Figure 2). This peritext is a progression of Genette's notion of interlocking gates which afford access for the reader, as it allows for various pieces of information to be presented in a diegetic fashion. In other words because the player-character is within the *Fallout* world they would interact with these paratextual aspects. Although these paratext features are essentially structuring the text (in order to do some actions the player must go through and manage their condition, or inventory), through the presence of the Pipboy, the player is effectively sees this structure as part of the diegetic.

Previously such peritext can be seen in the earlier *Fallout* games by Interplay (both *Fallout 1* and *2*), which is presented in an isometric fashion and with a less complex UI. The similar paratext element is there of situating the player within the text, as can be seen in Figure 4. This implementation of peritext is primarily done through the UI's aesthetic match to the *Fallout* world in that the display reflects the gritty and post-apocalyptic scenery and machinery that is seen during gameplay. The peritext is actively influencing the player's perception of the text to further strengthen the notion that the diegetic world exists.

Figure 4. A scene from the original Fallout which displays the characters and the scene as well as providing information as to dialogue occurring in the game (text in the lower left; the player weapons (the large button in the lower middle); and inventory, map, skills and character options (These are seen as the buttons surrounding the middle section).Of note is the Pipboy which in these earlier games is regulated to an abstract menu which reveals objective information, as well as some of the in-game fiction. The fact that the Pipboy is an electronic device on the player's wrist is only revealed in the dialogue. Source: Interplay Entertainment, 1997.

In this original release of *Fallout* the paratext structures present are much more obvious, in that each of the onscreen elements can be interacted with like any interface, whereas in *Fallout: New Vegas* such information is presented as intrinsically present in the Pipboy and also the HUD (Figure 2 and Figure 3). Both *Fallout* games show a similar notion of structuring the game so that it can be played (much like paragraphs or chapters in novels), but furthermore presenting these structures in a manner that suits the diegetic of the game world. The overall effect in *Fallout 1* might not be as diegetic as the later installments of *Fallout*, but there is still this influence upon the player affecting the manner in which they play. This occurs at the same time as the UI is structuring the text allowing the player to access necessary mechanics in an enjoyable manner.

Of course there are many other examples to use from other games, since paratext, especially if thought of as a framing technique, is inherent in all UI and menu screens. As such, the above examples are good case studies into video games that stretch the constraints of paratext.

In-System Paratext

With in-system paratext, the elements are considered to be those restricted to the process of accessing the game on a system (accessing game files, code, or installation). This is one of the hardest divisions to define because it is the literal in-between space between the reader and the text – that is to say the system or machine. To compare this to reading a text, the audience needs to make sure that their system, the console or computer, can read the text, not just themselves. It is not simply a matter of the audience's own comprehension, but also the ability of their various systems. As such, analysis is difficult to come across because paratext in this category is more focused towards helping the reader access the text, and therefore does not draw attention to itself. Nevertheless, there are examples that point to in-system paratext.

Both *Crimson Skies* and *Red Alert 2*, use their installation screens as a platform to create game files on the computer while also providing a prologue to the game's fiction (Figure 5 and Figure 6). Traditionally installations are structural phenomenon, a requirement of video games which are intensive on the video game system. For both *Red Alert 2* and *Crimson Skies* the installation process proves allows time for the game to provide a backstory. This is achieved through a radio play for *Crimson Skies*, and a briefing for *Red Alert 2* that plays during the installation process (placing files from the game disc to the computer's hard drive). Both are accompanied by slides to refer to various key scenes. The interesting element of this paratext is that the 'mise en scene' is kept true to the main text as much as possible – the fact that *Crimson Skies* radio play is presented with the air of pulp adventure novels of the 1920s, on a clipboard with stills of aerial combat, accentuates the game world in which it is set. The same effect is found in *Red Alert 2* within its military style briefing, 1960s futuristic interface, and the *click click* of each slide accentuating that the briefing is being told through the use of a projector. All of these elements contribute to the notion of the game world in which *Red Alert 2* is set. The installation is a necessary structure for these texts to exist, it simultaneous acclimatizing the audience to the text has begun, in much the same way as an introduction may lead itself to the text, so too do these installations provide an entry point into their texts.

The Last Express developed by Jordan Mechner provides another in-system paratext to examine through the game files. Here specific game files were scattered throughout the four CDs on which the game was released. Some game files were given the extension *.egg and others were displayed with the icon of a Faberge egg (Figure 7). These game files provided a notion of what the narrative of the game would revolve around foreshadowing the Faberge egg motif within the game text, and, furthermore, provided

Figure 5. An image depicting the installation of Crimson Skies. The installation provides the player with an introduction to the setting, characters and type of gameplay expected. The player is essentially being introduced to the game text even before they have started playing.
Source: Zipper Interactive, 2000.

Figure 6. An image of the installation screen of Red Alert 2 which displays the installation process as a type of briefing to the player. This presents the installation as a paratext that structures the way that players interact with the text. Of note is the formulation of the display which remains a constant through the game play (in-game), options are always presented within the bar to the right side of the screen.
Source: Westwood Pacific, 2000.

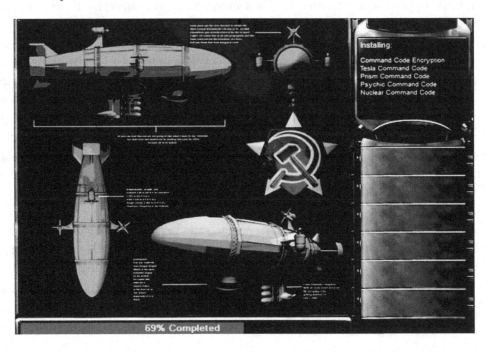

Figure 7. The installation files in the directory of The Last Express can be seen as influencing the player even before they have started the game. The icon of the executable file (*.exe) is that of a Faberge egg while the *.egg file type (here titled blue.egg) provides a hint to one of the game's puzzles which revolves around the Faberge egg.
Source: Smoking Car Productions, 1997.

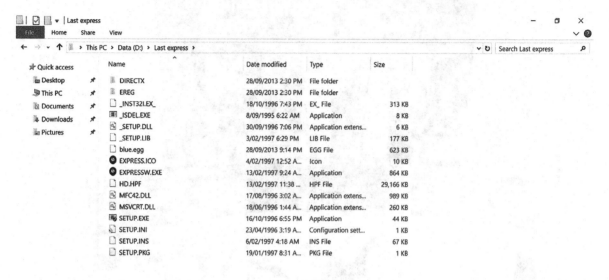

a hint to one of the game's puzzles. These executable and *.egg extension files were primarily intended as a practicality for setting up the game to be played, but with the inclusion of these file extensions and game icons provide a further means in which the text can be interpreted.

Further examples are present within code and can be highlighted via the various supporting documents ("readme" files) and accompanying code of a game.[12] This paratext seems to directly work with Genette's analogy to a canal lock, providing a series of checkpoints in which the reader can gain access to the text. The player's interaction with their game system leads them towards the playing of the game, while in-game paratext further strengthens the mediation of text to player allowing players to interact more easily with game options. Although most in-system paratexts are subtly introduced, these paratexts nonetheless shape and influence a player's interaction with their game, allowing them closer access to the text.

In-World Paratext

With in-world paratext, the physical interaction with the video game in question will be examined (disks, box, manual, etc.). This convention was a lot more prevalent before digital distribution became widespread after 2006, but the practice of providing physical additions to video games is still prevalent.

Blendo Games has subverted the distribution norm through providing digital box art for their collection of games (Figure 8). Originally devised by the developer Brendon Chung to display the range of video games at a convention, Chung later put up his designs for players to print out so as to have a physical presence of these digital releases.[13] Although this in-world paratext is produced after the initial release it still provides some influence to the player's relationship with the game allowing for these game texts to exist physically.

Figure 8. Blendo Games box art which was produced for the sole purpose of providing a display at a conference, as all of these video games are only available through online distribution
Source: Chung, 2012.

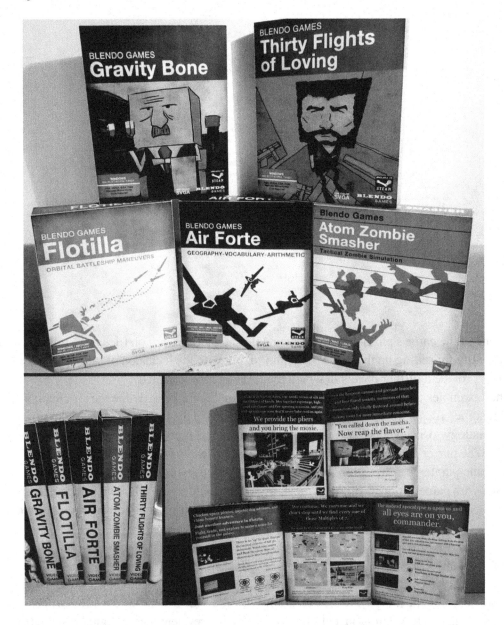

Other more common examples of in-world paratext include collector, pre-order and special editions of games. These physical products usually come with a collection of physical objects. These can include maps, posters, models of 'in-game' objects, art books, concept art, short stories, or manuals. An example of this would be *The Witcher 2: Assassins of Kings* which contained a letter from the in-game king, a map, a coin and a game guide (in-game text) to accompany the game disk, manual and sound track (Figure 9). Although these objects on their own do not convey much of a story, in conjunction with the video game they became influential paratexts. These paratexts are objects that the player can refer to for

Figure 9. The real world items provided with the purchase of a physical copy of the video game. It should be noted that digital copies also had access to digital versions of the same material and so could opt to print out these materials in a similar fashion to Blendo Games.
Source: CD Projekt, 2012.

further comprehension of the narrative, or they could be used to perform in-game functions (finding out different monster weaknesses, and hence improving an understanding of gameplay). Independently of the game these objects also allow players a range of different interactions otherwise not available through the video game: the texture of the map, the weight of the coin or the smell of ink, while not necessary to play the game do allow for the player to be drawn further into the text.

It appears that physical copies, including those of special and collector editions, explicitly add to the paratextual content of video games. Yet due to the increasing value of digital sales these physical manifestations of digital content have been increasingly considered premium content rather than a method of just representing the text. If the in-world paratexts are not available in a majority of texts then the effect that it has on audiences will only be so to those who purchase this content. Although potentially an issue with officiousness - in that the in-world paratext distributed is not one which the developers see as necessary, but for publishers it is of high import – the notion of who has access to these physical in-world paratexts is an interesting one for further study. In particular a discussion of how integral these physical paratexts are on the video game texts.

In-world paratext while providing the player with a diegetic explanation of many of the game features and narrative, is a strongly influencing paratext. Video games that lack a range of physical paratexts can still exert an influence on the audience, yet not to the same degree. A physical manifestation of a video game and its peripheries are what constitute an in-world paratext.

Overlap

There is room for overlap between different sets of paratext. This is encouraged for paratext to work as a system of interlocking gates, yet for the purposes of identification overlapping paratexts make the framework difficult to initially define. For instance the relationship between in-world content and in-game content (seen in the *Witcher 2: Assassins of Kings*), could be argued as an extension of the in-game paratext, as opposed to an in-world paratext. Though this ties in with what paratext encompasses, being at once both the border and barrier to concepts, it is where each gateway exists that first needs to be established before overlaps can be examined. The example of *Metal Gear Solid* will be explored in this section to give an example of how in-world, in-system and in-game paratexts can be seen within a text.

In *Metal Gear Solid*'s infamous Psycho Mantis mindreading battle a noticeable overlap of paratexts can be seen. In this battle the player needs to defeat Psycho Mantis through physically swapping their controller from the Player 1 slot of the Playstation to Player 2. Prior to this action Psycho Mantis can 'read' the actions of the player through the Player 1 slot of the Playstation. Further Psycho Mantis proves his psionic abilities by 'moving' the controller through the rumble feature (after telling the player to place the controller on the ground), and further 'reading' the player's previous game history from the memory card data. The interplay between in-game, in-system and in-world are all merged together into a single scene where the complex interrelation of paratext's many forms is shown to work, influencing the player to think about their play in a very different manner.

This is just one explicit example of paratextual overlaps, as many other examples do exist within video games. For the purposes of analysis these spatial separations of in-game, in-system and in-world provide clarification. The focus when analyzing paratext should not immediately be a holistic experience, but rather how each of these paratexts can contribute to the overall experience. Once these spatial elements have been outlined in relation to a specific video game text then the overall effect of paratext on a text can be observed.

SUMMARY

Each of these three categories, in-game, in-system, in-world, relate to the main game 'text' in different ways. Each category works along the notion of the internal peritext exploring how the text is structured, and through that how the player is influenced to interpret their game. These different categories of in-game, in-system, and in-world do highlight game areas which are not immediately thought of when looking into how video games are received, most notably within in-system paratext. Although many of the examples were focused on improving the diegetic nature of games, there are paratexts which focus on improving the gameplay, or purely the structure of a game. These could be focused on more to elucidate gameplay terminology – the presence of joysticks for flight simulators could be seen as an essential paratext in establishing the 'right' method for interpreting a text.

Granted the examples listed are by no means exhaustive, they are intended to provide preliminary ground for further analysis into video game paratext that exists beyond the current epitextual scholarship. With these definitions in place, the idea of the elements surrounding games' as having an active part in game analysis means that many academics, critics and developers will have a greater toolset in which to discuss video games.

CONCLUSION

Paratext, as discussed in this chapter, is an underutilized concept within video game studies. Game and media scholars have been shown to use paratext as a shorthand for describing external content for texts rather than engaging with Genette's methodology of the term. Through an analysis of paratext's literary history through Genette and comparing that with current game scholarship has shown a need to readdress the application of paratext. Furthermore this chapter has highlighted paratext's ability as an internal peritextual tool for video game scholarship. This was further explored through categorizing peritexts into three spatial divisions of in-game, in-system and in-world paratext.

Paratext provides game scholars with a larger scope to analyze and present specific video game elements that target both the internal 'text' elements of video games and its surrounding structure. These elements are ever-present within games (saving, loading, cut-scenes, and menus) and are rarely discussed in detail, perhaps due to an inadequate methodology. Paratext answers this need for methodology by providing an examination of paratextual that help structure the video game, and help influence players' interpretation of the text. There is an inherent need to look at these elements of structure and of game text to better analyze and create video games. As research into this area grows, the complexity of players' interaction with games will be perceived not solely as playing the game, but the player's entire interaction with the game text.

REFERENCES

Bethesda Game Studios [PC]. (2008). *Fallout 3*. Bethesda Softworks.

Bioware [PC]. (2012). *Mass effect 3*. Electronic Arts.

Black Isle Studios [PC]. (1998). *Fallout 2*. Interplay Entertainment.

Calvino, I. (1983). *If on a winter's night a traveller* (W. Weaver, Trans.). London, UK: Random House.

CD Projekt [PC]. (2012). *The witcher 2: Assassins of kings*. Bandai Namco Games.

Chung, B. (2012, September 10). Blendo big boxes. *Blendo Games*. Retrieved May 10, 2015, from http://blendogames.com/news/?p=374

Clarke, D., & Duimering, P. (2006). How computer gamers experience the game situation: A behavioral study. *Computers in Entertainment (CIE). Theoretical and Practical Computer Applications in Entertainment, 4*(3), 1–12.

Consalvo, M. (2007). *Cheating: Gaining advantage in videogames*. London: The MIT Press.

Foster, A. (2013, June 17). Alternate reality game puzzle design. *Gamasutra*. Retrieved August 20, 2014, from http://gamasutra.com/blogs/AdamFoster/20130617/194321/Alternate_Reality_Game_puzzle_design.php

Genette, G. (1992). The architext: An introduction. Vol. 31. of Quantum books. Berkley, CA: University of California Press.

Genette, G. (1997). *Paratexts: Thresholds of interpretation* (J. Lewin, Trans.). New York, NY: Cambridge University Press. doi:10.1017/CBO9780511549373

Genette, G., & Lewin, J. (1983). *Narrative discourse: An essay in method.* Cornel University Press.

Genette, G., & Maclean, M. (1991). Introduction to the paratext. *New Literary History*, *22*(2), 261–272. doi:10.2307/469037

Gray, J. (2010). *Show sold separately: Promos, spoilers, and other media paratexts.* New York, NY: New York University Press.

Harrigan, P., & Wardrip-Fruin, N. (2010). *Second person: Role-playing and story in games and playable media.* Boston, MA: The MIT Press.

Interplay Entertainment [PC]. (1997). *Fallout.* Interplay Entertainment.

Jara, D. (2013). A closer look at the (rule-)books: Framing and paratexts in tabletop role-playing games. *International Journal of Role-Playing*, *4*, 39–54.

Jenkins, H. (2006). *Convergence Culture: Where old and new media collide.* New York, NY; London, UK: New York University Press.

Johnson, D., & Wiles, J. (2003). Effective affective user interface design in games. *Ergonomics*, *46*(13-14), 1332–1345. doi:10.1080/00140130310001610865 PMID:14612323

Jones, S. E. (2008). *The meaning of video games: Gaming and textual strategies.* London, UK: Routledge.

KCEJ [PS]. (1998). *Metal Gear Solid.* Konami.

Llanos, S., & Jørgensen, K. (2011*). Do players prefer integrated user interfaces? A qualitative study of game UI design issues.* Paper presented at DiGRA 2011 Conference: Think Design Play, University of Utrecht, Netherlands. Retrieved August 24, 2014, from http://www.digra.org/wp-content/uploads/digital-library/11313.34398.pdf

Lunenfeld, P. (Ed.). (2000). *The digital dialectic: New essays on new media.* Boston, MA: The MIT Press.

Newman, J. (2013). *Videogames.* London, UK: Routledge.

Obsidian Entertainment [PC]. (2010). *Fallout: New Vegas.* Bethesda Softworks.

Rouse, R. III. (2010). *Game design: Theory and practice.* Burlington, MA: Jones & Bartlett Learning. doi:10.4324/9780203114261.ch11

Smoking Car Productions [PC]. (1997). *The last express.* Brøderbund.

Stam, R. (2000). Beyond fidelity: The dialogics of adaptation. J. Naremore (Ed.), Film adaptation (pp. 54-78). New Brunswick, NJ: Rutgers University Press.

The Cutting Room Floor . (2009, October 25) Retrieved August 24, 2014, from http://tcrf.net

Tulloch, R. (2010). A man chooses, a slave obeys: Agency, interactivity and freedom in video gaming. *Journal of Gaming & Virtual Worlds*, *2*(1), 27–38. doi:10.1386/jgvw.2.1.27_1

Walsh, C., & Apperley, T. (2012). Using gaming paratexts in the literacy classroom. In C. Martin, A. Ochsner, & K. Squire (eds.), *Proceedings GLS 8.0: Games +Learning +Society Conference* (pp. 323-330). Pittsburg, PA: ETC Press.

Westwood Pacific [PC]. (2000). *Command & conquer: Red alert 2*. EA Games.

Wolf, W. (1999). Framing fiction: Reflections on a narratological concept and an example: Bradbury, "Mensonge. In W. Grünzweig & A. Solbach (Eds.), *Grenzüberschreitungen: Narratologie im kontext/ Transcending boundaries: Narratology in context* (pp. 97–124). Tübingen, Germany: Gunter Narr Verlag.

Wolf, W., & Bernhardt, W. (2006). *Framing borders in literature and other media*. Amsterdam, Netherlands: Rodopi.

Zipper Interactive [PC]. (2000). *Crimson skies*. Microsoft Game Studios.

KEY TERMS AND DEFINITIONS

Epitext: The external structure of a text that alerts a reader towards a text. These can include interviews, reviews, and advertisements. These elements point towards a text, but do so externally from the text.

Officiousness: A term that identifies those with authority of a text, usually the author or the publisher. This is to identify the importance of the paratext involved, depending on who implements the paratext, and their relationship to the text, determines how regarded the paratext will be.

Paratext: The elements that surround a text, but are not part of it. These elements are the structure of the text and provide the reader with help in order to interpret the text.

Peritext: The internal structure of a text that can also shape a reader's experience of a text. These can include font, pictures, table of contents, index, etc. These elements point inwards to promote a text.

Spatiality: A term coined by Genette to identify the main differences between peritext and epitext. Mainly that one paratext is internal to a text (peritext), and the other is external to the text (epitext).

Temporality: A term which identifies the notion of time in conjunction with paratexts. Depending on the period of time between the original publication of the text and when the reader encounters the text determines how relevant the paratext is, and thus its importance to the reader. For example a videotape cassette provided with a novel will be of little use to a reader in the 21st century.

Transmedia: A cross-media development of a text, usually used in relation to the notion of franchises. In this web pages, webisodes, television episodes, videogames, comic books and other media can collaborate to tell a different narrative of the same text.

ENDNOTES

[1]   Text is thought of as an idea expressed through a medium.

[2]   Later translated to English in 1992 under the title of *The Architext: an Introduction*.

[3]   Earlier references to paratext do occur in other translated documents. See Genette & Lewin (1983) and Genette, & Maclean (1991).

4   Genette in *Paratexts. Thresholds of Interpretation* spends ten chapters exploring peritext (chapters 2-12), and only examining epitext (chapters 13 and 14).

5   This difficulty of paratext is highlighted in relation to translations and graphic works (1997, pp. 404-407).

6   In Calvino's work the chapter describes the reader's attempts at reaching, or reading, towards the next chapter – this is done through a second person perspective. This explicit referencing of structure can be seen as a diegetic method of making use of the paratext.

7   These concepts are expressed in Genette's work as spatial, temporal, substantial, pragmatic and functional (Genette, 1997, p. 4 & 12). Both pragmatic and functional concepts are covered under officiousness.

8   This mention of paratext is limited to a single sentence for Lunenfeld (2000, p. 14), whereas Consalvo gives the idea three paragraphs (2007, pp. 21-22).

9   Transmedia here is based primarily from Henry Jenkins' *Convergence Culture Where Old and New Media Collide* (Gray, 2010, p. 41).

10   For a good example of this transmedia development see "Alternate Reality Game puzzle design," by Adam Foster in *Gamasutra*.

11   For further diegetic interactions by structuring elements of the text, see metalepsis in Gérard Genette's *Narrative Discourse: An Essay in Method*.

12   For further examples of mainly code based paratexts, look to *The Cutting Room Floor*.

13   See Brendon Chung's blog "Blendo Big Boxes," (2012) regarding the implementation of this box art.

Chapter 16

"Footage Not Representative":
Redefining Paratextuality for the Analysis of Official Communication in the Video Game Industry

Jan Švelch
Charles University in Prague, Czech Republic

ABSTRACT

This chapter provides a revised framework of paratextuality which deals with some of the limitations of Gérard Genette's (1997b) concept while keeping its focus on the relationship between a text and socio-historical reality. The updated notion of paratextuality draws upon Alexander R. Galloway's (2012) work on the interface effect. The proposed revision is explained in a broader context of intertextuality and textual transcendence. Regarding Genette's terminology, this chapter rejects the constrictive notion of a paratext and stresses that paratextuality is first and foremost a relationship, not a textual category. The new framework is then put to the test using four sample genres of official video game communication – trailers, infographics, official websites of video games and patch notes.

INTRODUCTION

The concepts of paratexts and paratextuality are not new to the area of game studies (Carter, 2015; Consalvo, 2007; Harper, 2014; Jara, 2013; Jones, 2008; Paul, 2010, 2011; Payne, 2012; Rockenberger, 2014). Still, their implementation and use has been rather nonsystematic, taking bits and pieces from Gérard Genette's (1997b) framework and combining it with different approaches to paratextuality (Jara, 2013; Rockenberger, 2014; Wolf, 2006) or intertextuality in general. Considering the vast number of promotional and technical texts circulated by the video game industry and the recent emergence of transmedia storytelling techniques, it seems even more urgent to appropriate the fairly medium-specific framework of paratexts to an ecosystem of a different medium.

Many scholars have already noted the importance of paratexts and ancillary texts in both the traditional media industries, such as film and TV (Gray, 2010), and in new media. Peter Lunenfeld in 1999 already

DOI: 10.4018/978-1-5225-0477-1.ch016

suggested that the new media paratexts were becoming more important than the main texts themselves, arguing that digital media blur the traditional distinction between content and packaging because they effectively consist of the same data: "In addition, the backstory – the information about how a narrative object comes into being is fast becoming almost as important as that object itself. For a vast percentage of new media titles, backstories are probably more interesting, in fact, than the narratives themselves." (Lunenfeld, 1999, p. 14) Regardless of this power relationship between texts and paratexts in general, video game publishers also seem to be crossing the traditional boundaries between the texts and their surrounding promotional activities. The fictional worlds of video games are expanded through various means – from tie-in novels, board games, trailers or by website presentations – while these same means ground the text(s) in the historical condition and establish a conversation between the text, the producers and the audience.

Due to this simplifying division between main texts and paratexts this chapter goes further and provides an updated framework of paratextuality. In addition, the exploratory part of the chapter will then focus on paratextuality of four specific types (or genres) of video game culture: trailers, infographics, official websites and patch notes. This selection does not strive to paint an exhaustive image of video game paratextuality. Its goal is rather to demonstrate the variety of paratextual relationships regarding the specific topics such as representativity or ephemerality, but also to account for different levels of multimodality and different stages of a video game's life cycle.

BACKGROUND: PARATEXTUALITY REVISITED AND REVISED

The term paratext is closely connected to two key topics of literary theory that have since been picked up by many other scholarly fields (game studies included) – intertextuality and reception. In order to update and revise the concept of paratextuality, it is first necessary to understand its role regarding the two aforementioned concepts.

Paratextuality in game studies is most often conceptualized as a system of relationships between the main texts – video games – and surrounding texts. However, the traditional hierarchy between texts and paratexts is often contested by many scholars who argue that paratexts are not peripheral, but central to gameplay experience (Carter, 2015; Consalvo, 2007; Harper, 2014). Still, many applications of Genette's concept overlook its role within the broader context of intertextuality. Before moving on, it is important to note that the Genettian umbrella term transtextuality (or textual transcendence[1]) closely corresponds to broad definitions of intertextuality used by Julia Kristeva (1985), Michael Riffaterre (1984) or Linda Hutcheon (2012). The difference between these notions of textual relationships is mostly terminological. Genette uses a more restrictive version of intertextuality that accounts only for presence of one text within another, albeit not necessarily explicit or declared. Paratextuality, as it is defined by Genette (1997a), is just one of five relationships between texts and cannot be fully understood without the others.

Apart from intertextuality and paratextuality, Genette (1997a) distinguishes three more relationships. It is necessary to understand all of them, to elaborate on the position of paratextuality within the greater debate on intertextuality. The third relationship – metatextuality – is that of a critical commentary. While reviews come first to mind when speaking about metatextuality, Genette acknowledges the existence of less obvious commentaries that do not require citing the main text or even naming it at all[2]. Hypertextuality is another relationship that creates slight terminological confusion because it is in no way connected to Ted Nelson's (1992) notion of textual organization. Instead, Genette uses the prefix to illustrate a palimpsestine quality of layering of texts over each other. In this sense, hypertextuality relates to literary practices of adaptation, parody or pastiche. Lastly, architextuality is the most abstract of these relationships as it connects texts to a greater discursive formation and genre.

The authors deliberately avoid the use of the terms intertext, paratext, metatext, hypertext and architext throughout the introduction of Genette's (1997a) framework in order to stress their questionable nature. These terms should not be taken for granted, because the underlying concepts of five types of textual transcendence do not automatically establish a typology of texts. Such a categorization would obscure the interconnectedness of the five relationships: "First of all, one must not view the five types of transtextuality as separate and absolute categories without any reciprocal contact or overlapping. On the contrary, their relationships to one another are numerous and often crucial." (Genette, 1997a, p. 7)

However, Genette's (1997b) later work on paratexts undermines his remarks on the reciprocity of the transtextual relationship by dealing not only with the typology of intertextuality but also with the typology of texts. This terminological oversimplification gets only more obvious when we try to compare various types of "transtexts". While paratexts and to some extent metatexts are common terms in game studies as well as in other fields that build upon the foundations of literary theory, intertexts, hypertexts and architexts are used only seldom. Hypertexts could be employed as an umbrella term for various kinds of adaptation. Genres and discourses could be respectively called architexts, although such classification would seem contra intuitive to say the least considering that the relationship of a text towards a literary practice lacks a singular material manifestation. Therefore, the categorization further problematizes a possible derivative typology of texts based on transtextual relationships. Lastly, the potential category of intertexts fully reveals the underlying problem of the whole typology: When do texts cease to be texts by themselves and become defined by their relationships to other texts?

Game studies scholars have labeled various phenomena – game guides, trailers, online discussions, developer diaries, demos, previews, patch notes, errata, rulebooks, game statistics, introductory sequences or easter eggs (see Consalvo, 2007; Harper, 2014; Jara, 2013; Jones, 2008; Paul, 2010; Rockenberger, 2014) – as paratexts suggesting that they are dominantly defined by their paratextual relationship towards a video game. Despite their variety, they would still be paratexts first and texts or other types of transtexts second. Genette himself points to the issue of subordination that is implied by his definition of paratextuality when speaking about hypertexts which are in his own words "more frequently considered a 'properly literary' work than is the metatext" (Genette, 1997a, p. 5). However, the authors could as easily add paratexts as an example of "improper" literary work[3].

Paratextuality is often used to describe a text, a paratext in particular, although it is rarely the only transtextual relationship present in a given text. Genette (1997a) is aware of this interplay between transtextualities. For example, he claims that architextuality is often explicated through paratextual clues. Metatexts and paratexts are especially interconnected – prefaces (paratexts in Genette's terms) often contain commentary, while reviews (metatexts par excellence) function effectively as a paratext providing a reader with a threshold of interpretation. Take, for example, a video game trailer that features quotes from reviews: Such a trailer exhibits paratextuality by informing potential players about a video game. It also comments on the game through quoting excerpts from reviews, therefore acting metatextually. The excerpts are also a manifestation of intertextuality, while the designation "trailer", if it is present, marks the architextual relationship to an established industry practice. Nonetheless, anyone can call such trailer a text by itself, effectively putting its relationships towards other texts aside.

Given the aforementioned inconsistencies in terminology, paratexts become a very constrictive term that obscures other qualities and relationships of a text. It is then quite easy to understand why some scholars (Guins, 2014; Johnston, 2008) who study phenomena (or epiphenomena) that could be labeled paratexts completely avoid this framework as it often leads to the oversimplification of media ecologies. However, the authors would argue that while Genette's framework may reduce the social reality around the texts, it still possesses an analytical value that only needs to be rearticulated. As a starting point the authors propose Alexander R. Galloway's (2012) work on interfaces. Here he draws the comparison between paratextuality and diegesis and argues that both dichotomies – textual/paratextual and diegetic/non-diegetic[4] – can be understood as questions of center and periphery (or edge). In this perspective, the definition frame of paratextuality can be changed – it is no longer based primarily on a relationship between texts but on a relationship between a text and the surrounding social and historical reality. Paratextuality thus becomes the connection of a work to the outside world in which it exists, "an arrow pointing to the outside" (Galloway, 2012, p. 42).

This redefinition firstly deals with the rather problematic distinction between paratexts that are spatially bound to the body of work (peritext) and paratexts which are located elsewhere (epitext). These spatial categories of Genette's framework have been already criticized (Carter, 2015; Jones, 2008) for their limited scope that only takes into account texts in the form of traditional codex books. While the classical book industry easily allows for distinction between peritexts and epitexts, current distribution channels blur the line between the two categories. As there is no longer a need to rely on the existence of two or more texts in order to talk about paratextuality, it can thus be situated in the text itself, rendering the category of peritext no longer necessary. Spatially remote texts then can be understood as belonging to a bigger textual ecology. These texts can carry textual, paratextual and other transtextual qualities – they can play a constitutive role on the inside layer of a work (for example, as parts of transmedia storytelling), as well as point to the outside social and historical reality.

This proposed reframing of paratextuality also copes better with another questionable feature of Genette's framework – the so-called factual paratext. This type of paratextuality is in fact any contextual information that influences the reception of a work: "By factual I mean the paratext that consists not of an explicit message (verbal or other) but of a fact whose existence alone, if known to the public, provides some commentary on the text and influences how the text is received." (Genette, 1997b, p. 7) Genette lists gender and age of the author as examples of this particular paratextuality. A factual paratext as it was defined seems to undermine otherwise very materialistic framework. This inconsistency has already been criticized by literary theorist Werner Wolf (2006) whose remarks were later applied to the area of game studies by Annika Rockenberger (2014). Wolf offers a more restrictive definition of paratexts that only accounts for paratexts of textual forms. He calls the broader set of influencing factors, including the contextual information, framings alluding to Goffman's (1986) influential work on cognitive frames. While Wolf's redefinition resolves the issue to some extent, it still keeps the overwhelmingly structuralist approach. In the proposed redefinition the issue of factual paratext is no longer a problem, as the new framework does not require paratextuality to take place only among texts, but generally between the text and the social and historical reality. Gender and age of the author are in fact paratextual clues that point to the socio-historical context of the work and as such fit into the new framework.

Finally, the redefinition also directly connects the paratextual debate to the question of reception as it was established by the Constance school of literary theory, particularly by Hans Georg Jauss (1970, 1982). Jauss explored the relationship between literary history and the study of reception and introduced the concept of the horizon of expectations which functions as historically-determined threshold of interpretation. Quite similarly to Genette (1997a), Jauss also locates the foundations within the text's relationship to other texts and genres: "The new text evokes for the reader (listener) the horizon of expectations and rules familiar from earlier texts, which are then varied, corrected, changed or just reproduced. Variation and correction determine the scope, alteration and reproduction of the borders and structure of the genre." (Jauss, 1970, p. 13) These expectations are set exactly by paratextuality which explicates the place of a work within a given historical moment of social reality. In consequence, reception is influenced by paratextuality.

EXPLORING FOUR SAMPLE SITES OF PARATEXTUALITY

Methodology

The authors approach the proposed revision of a paratextual framework from the perspective of official communication surrounding video games. By official communication the authors mean any text that is through any transtextual relationship related to a video game intellectual property and is produced by the publisher, the developer or any officially authorized third party. While paratextuality is in no way limited to official producers, the pragmatics of steering recipient's expectations are most palpable in this area. Paratextuality in non-officially produced communication (e.g. fan cultures) is much more often paired with metatextuality which makes any analysis much more complex and no longer focusing on paratextuality itself[5]. That does not bar metatextuality from taking place within official communication, but only in dialogue with independent (or at least with pseudo-independent) critique. Paratextuality manifests itself both in the persuasive communication of marketing and promotion as well as in the technical communication[6]. As we'll see in the exploratory part of the chapter these two types of communication are in many cases overlapping.

Before moving further, it is necessary to point out that this chapter considers video games a medium. It uses Jesper Juul's (2005) widely accepted definition of video games as interplay of rules and fiction. However, it is important to say that such a definition in itself influences the forms of observable paratextuality. Communication regarding the "fictional" part of the game will be more often categorized as textual in the sense of transmedia storytelling (Jenkins, 2006) thanks to being part of a greater work that includes not only the seemingly central video game, but other types of media with narrative affordances. On the other hand, communication about rules will be considered more technical and indeed paratextual as it is relating directly to social reality. Galloway rather eloquently describes this aspect of the "rules & fiction" definition of video games even though he speaks about software in general: "software is functional and thereby exacerbates and ridicules the tension within itself between the narrative and mechanic layers – the strictly functional transcodings of software, via a compiler or a script interpreter for example, fly in the face of the common sense fact that software has both an executable layer, which should obey the rules of a purely functional aspect of the code (similar to what Genette calls "paratextual" in literature), and a scriptural layer, which would obey the rules of semantics and subjective expression […]" (Galloway, 2012, p. 76) For example, patch notes or manuals would be then considered "more" paratextual than spin-off comic books due to their functional and technical aspects. Still, this property of the framework can be easily sidestepped by refocusing the analysis from paratexts to paratextuality. Then there is no need to measure the amount of paratextuality to evaluate whether a text is a paratext or not.

The selection of the four analyzed textual forms is driven primarily by their varied roles within promotion and technical communication of video games. Chronologically, the four sample types of texts come into play at different stages of the video game production cycle (Carlson, 2009) – trailers and web presentations primarily promote video games long before their launch, while patch notes become more important after the release, although they communicate video game development in the stages of beta-testing. Infographics can be employed both in the promotion phase and the after-release phase of community building. The four types also possess different modalities: from usually monomodal patch notes to increasingly multimodal infographics, trailers and the web presentations where all these forms converge.

While the selection could be easily expanded to include more types of texts (e.g. demos, game covers, manuals, retailer game listings), due to the lack of actual empirical research of paratextuality it should serve as a sufficient although admittedly arbitrary introduction. So far only few types of texts that exhibit paratextuality were analyzed by game studies scholars: rulebooks for non-digital roleplaying games (Jara, 2013), interviews with game developers and making-of videos (Payne, 2012), patches and patch notes (Paul, 2010; Sherlock, 2014), analog game errata (Švelch, 2014) and video game trailers (Švelch, 2015). In the context of digital literary theory, website presentations of interactive fiction were also analyzed (Stewart, 2010). Although there is a slight overlap between previous research efforts and the aims of the chapter, the authors intend to present a more methodologically oriented approach to the study of paratextuality that will be supported by selected case examples and that could be used as a guide on how to apply the redefined framework as an analytical tool for study of other texts.

The Myth of the Representative Trailer

Since the premiere of the teaser for *Star Wars Episode I: The Phantom Menace* in 1998, trailers have become a popular type of online content (Johnston, 2008). Video game trailers are no exception as they easily reach millions of views on YouTube. The biggest game industry events, for example the Electronic Entertainment Expo (E3), might seem to a spectator at home like merely a grandiose parade of video game trailers – only occasionally we get to see live presentations of gameplay. Video game publishers employ this promotional tool heavily before the lifetime of a video game – the biggest AAA games often get ten or more trailers. Video game journalists also seem to ascribe great importance to video game trailers, as they deem a release of a new trailer newsworthy enough to justify its own story[7]. Still, video game trailers are mostly unexplored phenomena of game culture, especially when compared to film trailers (see Gray, 2010; Johnston, 2009; Kernan, 2004).

Formally, video game trailers are greatly influenced by their cinematic counterparts from which they inherited their means of expression. But unlike movie trailers, video game trailers regularly feature content created specifically for the trailer. Video game trailers are significantly diversified, taking different forms (Švelch, 2015) to accommodate various stages of video game development (Carlson, 2009). In such light and given the fact that video games are non-linear texts while trailers are linear, any notion of a representative video game trailer should be taken with a grain of salt. But video game developers try hard to either establish the idea of representativity or to explicitly distance the trailer from the game. Still, the perceived representativity of video game trailers is very much embedded into video game culture, as recent controversies (Purchese, 2015) around adequateness of trailers for *The Witcher 3: Wild Hunt* (CD Projekt Red, 2015) show[8].

Unfortunately, some scholars reinforce this rather unfounded myth. For example a study of racial and gender stereotypes in video games that was based on a content analysis of trailers, introductory sequences and game covers claimed that "game trailers are representative game playing of skilled players" and that "the trailer and the game cover will be a more typical representation of the game than a particular individual's playing clip." (Mou & Peng, 2008, p. 925) Recent cases[9] show that such statements significantly oversimplify the game industry practice where the visuals alone differ across trailers and the final product. Representativity should be in no way taken for granted. On the contrary, it should be analyzed in regards to paratextuality and its role in establishing the link between the game, the trailer and socio-historical reality.

The trailer for the upcoming *Mass Effect: Andromeda* (EA, 2015) can serve as a case example. Debuted at 2015's E3, a roughly two-minute video starts with the information about the age rating of the game which varies according to a region. ESRB's[10] notice is very upfront about the trailer's paratextual quality and explicitly states that "The content of the following trailer has been approved for a general audience by the Entertainment Software Rating Board. The game is anticipated to be rated mature." PEGI's[11] notice is more subtle and only shows the symbol for rating 18 with the title "provisional", but in effect it establishes a very similar paratextual link to the ESRB's notice. Australian Classification, although seemingly most cryptic – it only shows a symbol of CTC rating –, actually supplies as much paratextual clues as the other ratings, at least for viewers familiar with the system of Australian ratings. CTC stands for "Check the classification" and in this context means that "the content has been assessed and approved for advertising unclassified films and computer games." (Australian Classification, n.d.) Despite minor differences, all three rating notices at the beginning of the trailer exhibit paratextuality in the way that they connect the trailer and the broader set of texts to the social-historical situation. First, both the ESRB and Australian Classification explicitly communicate that the video is in its basic function promotional. Second, the ESRB adds the information that the product advertised is a video game; in the case of the Australian Classification it can be either a video game or a movie. What the spectator learns from the PEGI notice is that the video is somehow connected to a video game that has not yet been released, otherwise there wouldn't be the word "provisional". Viewers can only safely assume that the trailer is part of the advertising.

Just by watching the notice the spectator gets information about the paratextual quality of the video which would influence their expectations and interpretation of the remainder of the video accordingly. Overall, the viewer knows that they are watching a promotional video for a video game or a movie. Going further into the trailer this information connected to the computer visuals makes it more likely that the product advertised is a video game. Here the paratextuality works across the many layers of texts pointing towards the social reality behind the video. If the viewer was not certain whether the product is a movie or a video game, the titles at 1:07 that say "Discover a new galaxy" make it even more probable that the video belongs to a video game franchise. Such personal address is much more typical for video games than for movies that would more likely talk about the hero in a third person. Going back to 1:05, there is a shot showing the insignia "N7" on the hero's armor. For the fans, this detail directly connects the video to the *Mass Effect* franchise where N7 signifies the rank of the elite human soldiers including the hero of the previous installments, Commander Shepard. On its own, the relationship between the trailer and the *Mass Effect* video games established by this insignia can be interpreted as intertextuality, but in conjunction with the aforementioned paratextual aspects it further strengthens the paratextual quality of the trailer. The gameplay scenes that follow further strengthen the connection between the trailer and the *Mass Effect* franchise by showing the (updated) signature Mako vehicle and squad combat featuring the protagonist of the trailer and two more soldiers dressed in the same uniforms. Finally, the connection is fully established by the logo of the new sequel *Mass Effect Andromeda*.

Although the gameplay footage stops here, new paratextual clues continue to connect the video to the socio-historical situation. One of these ties takes the form of the planned released date "Holiday

2016". This information also grounds the trailer in the specific historical context. Other connections are established through logos of the publisher (EA), developer (BioWare) and the game engine (Frostbite 3). Probably the most important paratextual clue is hidden at the end of the video, here the titles in the European and US version of the trailer boast "Captured in engine. Representative of game experience." The Australian trailer leaves out the notion of representativity, but the message is similar: "Footage captured in engine." These final captions reframe all the visual content present in the trailer. What could have easily been an outsourced CGI trailer, is now explicitly revealed to be gameplay footage, or rather footage of the same visual quality as the planned product. This gives viewers more information on the role of the trailer and its connection to the game, further developing the paratextual relationships between the trailer, the game and the socio-historical situation. To sum up, the paratextual aspects of the trailer which are manifested by some of the individual parts of the trailer but also by interplay of many other parts, inform viewers that they are watching a trailer for the new Mass Effect sequel called Andromeda set to be released in the Holiday season of 2016 and that the trailer is built in the game engine which sets the expectations regarding the visuals of the game[12].

The sample analysis of the revised paratextual framework shows the complex relationships that establish the text's paratextuality. Paratextuality is not disconnected from other intertextual or transtextual relationships, on the contrary, it often works in conjunction with them. Any text also exhibits two interconnected and inseparable types of paratextuality – (1) it connects its own text to socio-historical reality and (2) it connects its own text to the greater set of texts and through this relationship it establishes a link to socio-historical reality.

Even though paratextuality is a complex relationship that cannot be easily reduced to its individual parts, some typical constituents of video game trailers are notable for their paratextual quality – age ratings information, release dates, company logos among others. The style of visual content along with the information about its representativity also strongly influences the paratextuality of a trailer. While publishers are most often either claiming the representativity of trailers or they do not address it at all, some trailers contain a warning about the lack of representativity to avoid subsequent criticism and lawsuits[13]. For example, *BioShock Infinite* TV Commercial[14] trailer (2K Games, 2013) explicitly informs that it does not show "actual gameplay footage". Still, the debates about representativity mostly deal with the question of visuals[15].

The Dual Data of Video Game Infographics

While video game infographics to some extent establish paratextual relationships through the same means as video game trailers, they are specific due to the selection of data they visualize. Since infographics are after all usually considered to be a form of data (or information) visualization (Chen, Härdle, & Unwin, 2007), it only makes sense to focus on the type of data that video game infographics present to players.

Unlike trailers, infographics are not as widespread and established as a form of video game culture, and as such, have so far been overlooked by game studies scholars. Historically, infographics can be seen as evolving from the graphical visualization of statistics. Some of the early statistical pictograms can be dated back to the 1920s and to Austrian philosopher Otto Neurath (Chen et al., 2007). But as Galloway (2012) points out, data visualization, and in our case infographics, deal with the underlying philosophical question of the ontological difference between data and information. If we consider that data, contrary to information, do not have any particular form, then the act of data visualization becomes first a question of how to turn data into visual information and only later a question of visualization itself:

"any data visualization is first and foremost a visualization of the conversion rules themselves, and only secondary a visualization of the raw data." (Galloway, 2012, p. 83) The tools of visualization and the aesthetics then become a frame of definition for infographics which are then no longer limited to visualization of (statistical) data but they can also show information and also become instances of linguistic "text rendered as an image" (De Jager-Loftus & Moore, 2013, p. 274). This implies that video game infographics are also not limited to displaying data, but they can visualize various types of information using the same multimodal means of expression. At this stage, the authors propose a working definition that video game infographics visualize data and information connected to a video game. By exploring the relationship of the data or the information and its visualization we can understand and analyze the paratextual quality of video game infographics.

For example, *Evolve*'s (Turtle Rock Studios, 2015) promotional campaign featured various infographics and continues in this trend also in post-launch period. Among the 23 infographics that have been so far released, two basic types of infographics can be identified. The vast majority (20) of *Evolve*'s infographics focuses primarily on playable characters, only three infographics visualize various player metrics and game statistics for specific time periods.

Evolve is an asymmetric multiplayer shooter in which four player-controlled hunters fight against a one player-controlled monster. As of writing this article, 17 different hunters and 4 monsters have been made available. All playable characters, except the recently released hunter Lennox, were featured in a dedicated infographic. While hunter and monster infographics differ in their size and amount of information they provide about characters – monsters have much more sizeable infographics which is understandable considering their smaller number –, they exhibit the same paratextual relationships. Starting with the most obvious paratextual clues, every infographic includes the logo of the publisher (2K Games) and the developer (Turtle Rock Studios), the copyright information and *Evolve*'s game logo. Character infographics then feature the name and the class of the character along with visualized information about skills and weapons. This fictional background information and functional description of character abilities is often compared to real-world phenomena and facts. For example, Caira's acceleration field ability is explained using an example of a plane flight: "If acceleration field was used on an airplane, travel from NYC to London in half the time (4 HRS)." This obvious link to the properties of the real world and real physics clearly establishes a mode of realistic representation that is to be expected from such a game although it is a work of fiction. Such connections are definitely paratextual and were previously explored by Hutcheon (1989) regarding the representation within literary fiction and non-fiction. Character infographics manifest paratextuality by aforementioned ways and also by using the aesthetics of infographics – the final paratextual relationship forms an expectation of a game that allows player agency, primarily by offering roster of playable characters, and uses a realistic representation of a game world. The infographic paratextually interprets itself as a guide that informs the player about the game as if it were both a fictional safari and a rather delicate activity that requires preparations and planning.

The second category of infographics presents three periods of actual live gameplay – Big Alpha, Open Beta, and the first launch week – using various statistics from popularity of classes, ratio of wins between hunters and monsters, or Twitch views. At first glance, these infographics resemble in-game statistics and player metrics that often recap multiplayer matches[16]. However, infographics differ in the scope and their paratextual relationship – they speak for the whole community over a longer period of time and present a rather static snapshot of the "state" of the game, while in-game statistics serve as feedback information for potential individual or team debriefings. The infographics from the second category use very much the same expressive elements as the first category – the aesthetics are identical and real-world comparisons are also present (for example Big Alpha: "2 061 140 hours watched – Long enough to travel more than half way across the Milky Way at the speed of light"). These elements, however, create a different paratextual relationship in conjunction with the content and the focus of these infographics. The infographic is no longer a guide but an evidence of a cultural event of noteworthy impact and dimensions. The unimaginable statistics are converted to real-world phenomena to convey the game's importance and popularity within the socio-historical situation. It does not mean that the whole infographic follows this celebratory mode and that there is no place for fun. For example, the Big Alpha infographic compares the longest game round to an obscure world record: "40 minutes – longest round. Just about the world record for not blinking (41 minutes)." This anecdote, however, does not detract from the overall paratextual relationship between the infographic, the game and the socio-historical reality. The selected game periods are still presented as notable cultural events.

The seemingly simple forms of infographic can establish widely different paratextual relationships. *Evolve*'s case should not be considered an exception; BioWare uses infographics in very similar ways in their official communication of *Dragon Age: Inquisition* (BioWare, 2014). The revised framework allows for an in-depth analysis of particular constituents of a paratextual relationship. If all of *Evolve*'s infographics were labeled just as paratexts, all the insight that comes from the need to trace the sources of paratextuality would be lost. While both categories of infographics inform about a video game, connect itself to social and historical situation, the paratextual relationships are different and focus on different aspects of games as a social practice. A revised framework motivates its users to inspect these differences which could be then used, for example, as a starting point for a rhetorical analysis.

The Ephemerality of Official Websites

Website presentations are usually overlooked as a possible site of paratextuality due to practical and methodological reasons. Apart from Gavin Stewart's (2010) analysis of online paratextual elements of the interactive fiction *Inanimate Alice* (BradField Productions, 2005), there has been no significant empirical work on website presentations. Official websites of video games usually combine different content and genres and in consequence create complex arrays of promotional and technical communication. As such they are often hard to navigate, not only for scholars undertaking their analysis, but also for fans searching for particular information. This chapter does not aim to present a complete case study of a website presentation, but rather to point at specific sources of paratextuality. Still, to keep the following remarks grounded in current industry practice, the authors use the example of the current *Borderlands*[17] official website.

The first thing that a visitor to the website encounters is an age gate. This type of adult verification system blocks a direct access to the website and requires a person to fill in a date of birth. Essentially, it conveys the same message as age ratings systems (ESRB, PEGI), but unlike those it requires some minimal effort to pass through by selecting the right month, day and year. Still, age gates can be much more easily implemented to the overall visual presentation of the website, because they lack a prescribed form. *Borderlands* age gate combines the visual style of the video game series with the formal need of an age gate along with the logos of video game platforms, the developer and the publisher. The paratextual relationship established by this first page informs a visitor about the fact that *Borderlands* is a video game for mature players.

Upon a successful pass through the age gate, the visitor enters the main page which overflows with information. A slideshow of four different products takes the center stage, while the space above and below is reserved for tabs leading to other sections of the website. The ever-shifting visuals create an overwhelming feeling, but a closer look reveals that there is not much information after all. There is a sample of the most recent news posts, examples of merchandise and a Twitter widget. The Games tab evokes a feeling that the website is indeed a hub for all entries in the *Borderlands* franchise, but there is no mention of the spin-off adventure game *Tales from the Borderlands* (Telltale Games, 2014). Even searching for the spin-off using the dedicated search window yields no results. In consequence, the website provides a rather incomplete picture of the franchise as it only features games by the main developer Gearbox Software. However, the official *Borderlands* Facebook fan page includes *Tales from the Borderlands*. The incompleteness of information and paratextual relationships go hand in hand with outdated content and a confusing structure of the website[18].

What does the incomplete and outdated nature of the website mean in regards to paratextuality? Unlike social media profiles and singular texts like trailers or infographics, the official websites consist of relatively large amount of content, which is not structured chronologically. The expectation of a complete overview that an official website should provide, collides with the fact that not all content is updated. The website then presents historically-conditioned paratextual relationships that evoke the idea of non-digital promotional texts that cannot be easily updated, sometimes also called ephemera (Grainge, 2011). This ephemeral quality of some of the parts of the website creates rather inconsistent paratextuality of the website as a whole. But it is exactly the viewpoint of revised paratextual framework that allows for exploration of the complex nature of the official website presentation. While the *Borderlands* website seemingly presents an up-to-date overview of the franchise, a deeper look into its architecture reveals rather dated content whose ephemerality becomes apparent in comparison to the other elements of the page. This points to the fact that while paratextuality ties a text to socio-historical reality, manifestations of paratextuality are also historical and easily become ephemeral.

The Social History inside Patch Notes

Patches, patch notes and video game documentation in general are gradually attracting more and more scholars (Carter, 2015; Consalvo, 2007; Paul, 2010; Sherlock, 2014) and journalists[19]. Although being mostly technical in their nature, patch notes should not be reduced to a mere technical account of changes made by a respective patch. Recent articles (Paul, 2010; Sherlock, 2014) have focused on the rhetorical aspects of patch notes and similar texts like developer notes or developer interviews arguing that these texts are often also persuasive: "Beyond just reporting, organizing, and archiving information, releasing patch notes represents an opportunity to frame specific arguments to specific audiences and is a pivotal moment in ethos construction." (Sherlock, 2014, p. 166) While Sherlock points out that patch notes serve as a historical record of iterative game design, it should be stressed that they can as well map the paratextual relationship between the ecology of video game texts and socio-historical reality, thereby functioning as a record of social history of play behind the game.

Take, for example, notes for Hot Fix 5 from September 25th 2014 for multiplayer shooter *Destiny* (Bungie, 2014), which informs about a fix for the famous Loot Cave exploit[20]. While it is, on the one hand, a historical document of iterative game design as it explicitly states changes in respawn rates of enemies in certain locations, it also records, on the other hand, how the game was played at the given moment. The subtitle alone – "Refinements to rewards" – gives the impression that there was something wrong with reward system before the patch. A closer look at the summary of the patch reveals that "In Hotfix 5, we made a few changes to reduce the effectiveness of a humbling number of economy exploits."

It is therefore implied that players were exploiting design loopholes, at least from the perspective of the developer. The remainder of the patch notes is very technical, but one sentence stands out for its diegetic twist: "The Hive of the holy 'Treasure Cave' have realized the futility of their endless assault on Skywatch and have retired to lick their wounds and plan their next attack." This sentence describes the effect of the Hot Fix 5 from the diegetic perspective and translates technical notes on increased respawn times into the fictional world of *Destiny*. It can also be seen as a light-hearted attempt at reframing the design flaws as an irrational behavior of the fictional enemy faction. The subtitle of the Hot Fix along with these two sentences paint a rather rich paratextual picture of the social and historical context of the patch and of the state of play at that time. The rhetorical aspect of the Hot Fix 5 is further maintained in linked developer notes which frame the player behavior and try to establish an ethos of desirable gameplay. Still, paratextuality should not be overlooked because it serves as a backdrop for the persuasive communication of the developer. Without the paratextual relationship between the patch and the socio-historical reality, framing of the events, gameplay and design choices would not be possible.

CONCLUSION: THE BENEFITS OF REVISED PARATEXTUALITY

This chapter aimed at showing that the idea of paratextuality as it was first formulated in 1982 by Gérard Genette (1997a) is still a valid analytical concept and has a place in game studies. Rather than replicating limitations of Genette's framework and its subsequent interpretations and applications, the authors have proposed a new revised definition of paratextuality inspired by Alexander R. Galloway's (2012) work on interfaces. This redefinition respects the foundations laid by Genette but rejects the oversimplification of the label paratexts. The redefined paratextuality is now based on a relationship between a text and the socio-historical reality. Such a revision, on the one hand, deals with the issue of subordination of paratexts that have been widely criticized but still replicated by the use of the same terminology, which defines a text by one transtextual relationship. On the other hand, the new framework allows for analysis of the very fundamental paratextual issues of the relationship between textual immanence and transcendence as it directly connects paratextuality of a text to a particular social and historical situation while allowing for links between systems of texts or textual ecologies. Paratextuality is understood as interplay between textual and intertextual qualities of a text that cannot be reduced to a single element of a work but rather manifests itself in the conjunction with various aspects of a text.

The revised framework also has noteworthy practical and terminological implications. First, the rejection of paratexts as a category of secondary texts acknowledges the richness of video game culture, as well as of other cultural areas. The whole notion of paratexts as secondary texts even when applied solely to promotional materials overlooks the fact that, for example, trailers are often the first and the last thing the viewer comes into contact with. The realities of media convergence (Jenkins, 2006) even destabilize the notion that a movie has to be the biggest source of income, merchandising (material or virtual in many cases of video games[21]) often takes center stage. Such perspective may seem outdated now when many producers create rich transmedia storytelling worlds, but evidence of systematic cross-media promotion can even be dated as far back as the book publishing industry[22].

Second, the revised paratextuality no longer operates in a vaguely defined space between intertextuality (in Genetteian sense) and metatextuality. Paratextuality is no mere "informing" about video games, it is grounded in its relation to social and historical reality. Therefore, many texts that Genette (1997b) calls paratexts (prefaces, table of contents, notes, even interviews with author) still possess paratextual qualities, but they are no longer reduced to secondary texts – paratextuality is one of the possible qualities that any text can possess.

Third, by redirecting the question of paratexts to paratextuality, scholars are forced to actually look at the specific ways paratextuality works. It is no longer sufficient to apply the label "paratext" just based on an indistinct intertextual relationship. Paratextuality as both a relationship and an effect has to be precisely located in its connection to a socio-historical reality.

Lastly, the most apparent outcome of the revised framework is the shift in terminology. To support the notion that all texts within ecology are equally important in regards to textual and intertextual qualities they can possess, the chapter deliberately avoided using the term paratext. This change was motivated by the aforementioned tendency to consider paratexts as secondary texts, which was already noted by Genette (1997a). Instead of "paratext", the chapter used the term paratextuality (and synonyms paratextual aspects, paratextual clues) to denote the relationship between a text (and possibly a textual ecology) and the socio-historical reality. The textual ecology (Mason, 2013) here stands for a formation of texts that are connected by the social practice of game playing, it roughly corresponds to Consalvo's (2007) notion of the "system" which is closely related to game industry.

The exploratory part of the chapter then focused on four specific sites of paratextuality – video game trailers, infographics, official websites and patch notes. The question of paratextuality's reception has been mostly neglected at this stage in favor of more basic implementations of the revised framework. The case examples of paratextual analysis were partly structured as testing grounds for the revised framework, but they also aspired to connect the rather general question of paratextuality to some specific issues regarding the four types of texts – video game trailers, infographics, official websites and patch notes. The revised paratextuality is not a means to its own end, but rather a tool that allows us to explore how various texts interact with the socio-historical reality and other texts. Paratextuality then sheds light on the questions of representativity of video game trailers, the data behind the video game infographics, the complicated ephemerality of official video game websites or the socio-historical affordances of patch notes. These are but few examples showing that the revised framework is applicable to empirical research and pointing in directions of possible future research. Nonetheless, the chapter presented the new framework in the wider context of video game intertextuality as a very specific relationship that is connected to other types of intertextuality in its broadest sense, but still possesses a unique quality that distinguishes it from them.

ACKNOWLEDGMENT

This research was supported by the Charles University in Prague, project GA UK No. 306414.

REFERENCES

Australian Classification. (n.d.). *Check the classification | Australian classification*. Retrieved June 29, 2015, from http://www.classification.gov.au/Guidelines/Pages/Check-the-Classification.aspx

BioWare. (2014). *Dragon age: Inquisition* [PC, PS3, PS4, Xbox 360, Xbox One]. EA.

BradField Productions. (2005, 2015). *Inanimate Alice*. Retrieved June 29, 2015, from http://www. inanimatealice.com/

Bungie. (2014). *Destiny* [PS3, PS4, Xbox 360, Xbox ONE]. Activision.

Carlson, R. (2009). Too human versus the enthusiast press: Video game journalists as mediators of commodity value. *Transformative Works and Cultures, 2009*(Vol 2).

Carter, M. (2015). Emitexts and paratexts: Propaganda in *EVE Online*. *Games and Culture, 10*(4), 311–342. doi:10.1177/1555412014558089

Chen, C., Härdle, W. K., & Unwin, A. (2007). *Handbook of data visualization*. Berlin, Germany: Springer Science & Business Media.

Consalvo, M. (2007). *Cheating: gaining advantage in videogames*. Cambridge, MA: The MIT Press.

Crecente, B. (2014, August 11). *Sega to tentatively pay out $1.25M in Aliens suit while Gearbox fights on*. Retrieved June 21, 2015, from http://www.polygon.com/2014/8/11/5993509/aliens-colonial-marines-class-action-settlement

De Jager-Loftus, D. P., & Moore, A. (2013). #gathercreateshare: How research libraries use Pinterest. *Internet Reference Services Quarterly, 18*(3-4), 265–279. doi:10.1080/10875301.2013.840714

DeWinter, J., & Moeller, R. M. (Eds.). (2014). *Computer games and technical communication: Critical methods & applications at the intersection*. Burlington, VT: Ashgate Publishing Company.

Dontnod Entertainment. (2015). *Life is strange* [PC, PS4, PS3, Xbox 360, Xbox ONE].

EA. (2015). *MASS EFFECT™: ANDROMEDA official E3 2015 announce trailer*. Retrieved from https://www.youtube.com/watch?v=uG8V9dRqSsw

Freeman, M. (2014). Advertising the yellow brick road: Historicizing the industrial emergence of transmedia storytelling. *International Journal of Communication*, (8): 2362–2381.

Galloway, A. R. (2012). *The interface effect*. Cambridge, UK: Polity.

2K . Games. (2013). *BioShock Infinite TV commercial (full version)*. Retrieved from https://www.youtube.com/watch?v=RvrnUcB8ZJc

2K . Games. (2014). *Evolve — 4v1 interactive trailer* [English PEGI]. Retrieved from https://www.youtube.com/watch?v=51YhRPYQHtY

Gearbox Software. (2009). *Borderlands* [PS3, Xbox 360, PC]. 2K Games.

Gearbox Software. (2012a). *Borderlands 2* [PS3, Xbox 360, PC]. 2K Games.

Gearbox Software. (2012b). *Borderlands Legends* [IOS]. 2K Games.

Gearbox Software. (2013). *Aliens: Colonial marines* [PC, PS3, Xbox 360]. Sega.

Gearbox Software, & 2K Australia. (2014). *Borderlands: The pre-sequel!* [PS3, Xbox 360, PC]. 2K Games.

Genette, G. (1990). *Narrative discourse: an essay in method (1. publ., 4. print)*. Ithaca: Cornell University Press.

Genette, G. (1997a). *Palimpsests: Literature in the second degree* (C. Newman & C. Doubinsky, Trans.). Lincoln, NE: U of Nebraska Press.

Genette, G. (1997b). *Paratexts: Thresholds of interpretation* (J. A. Lewin, Trans.). Cambridge, MA; New York, NY: Cambridge University Press. doi:10.1017/CBO9780511549373

Genette, G. (1997c). *The work of art*. Ithaca, NY: Cornell University Press.

Goffman, E. (1986). Frame analysis: An essay on the organization of experience (Northeastern University Press ed.). Boston, MA: Northeastern University Press.

Grainge, P. (2011). *Ephemeral media: Transitory screen culture from television to YouTube*. Basingstoke, UK: Palgrave Macmillan.

Gray, J. (2010). *Show sold separately: Promos, spoilers, and other media paratexts*. New York, NY: New York University Press.

Guins, R. (2014). *Game after: A cultural study of video game afterlife*. Cambridge, MA: The MIT Press.

Harper, T. (2014). *The culture of digital fighting games: Performance and practice*. New York, NY: Routledge.

Hutcheon, L. (1989). *The politics of postmodernism*. London, UK: Routledge. doi:10.4324/9780203426050

Hutcheon, L. (2012). *A theory of adaptation*. London, UK: Routledge.

Irrational Games. (2013). *BioShock infinite* [PC, PS3, Xbox 360]. 2K Games.

Jara, D. (2013). A closer look at the (rule-) books: Framings and paratexts in tabletop role-playing games. *International Journal of Role-Playing*, (4).

Jauss, H. R. (1982). *Towards an aesthetic of reception*. Minneapolis, MN: University of Minnesota Press.

Jauss, H. R., & Benzinger, E. (1970). Literary history as a challenge to literary theory. *New Literary History*, *2*(1), 7–37. doi:10.2307/468585

Jenkins, H. (2006). *Convergence culture: Where old and new media collide*. New York, NY: New York University Press.

Johnston, K. M. (2008). The coolest way to watch movie trailers in the world: Trailers in the digital age. *Convergence (London)*, *14*(2), 145–160. doi:10.1177/1354856507087946

Johnston, K. M. (2009). *Coming soon: Film trailers and the selling of Hollywood technology*. Jefferson, NC: McFarland.

Jones, S. E. (2008). *The meaning of video games: Gaming and textual strategies*. London, UK: Routledge.

Juul, J. (2005). *Half-real: Video games between real rules and fictional worlds*. Cambridge, MA: The MIT Press.

Kernan, L. (2004). *Coming attractions: Reading American movie trailers* (1st ed.). Austin, TX: University of Texas Press.

Kristeva, J. (1985). *Sēmeiōtikē: Recherches pour une sémanalyse*. Paris, France: Seuil.

Kuchera, B. (2015, November 17). *Dragon Age: Inquisition gets a chill-inducing launch trailer, come watch!* Retrieved June 30, 2015, from http://www.polygon.com/2014/11/17/7236631/dragon-age-inquisition-launch-trailer

Lunenfeld, P. (Ed.). (1999). *The digital dialectic: New essays on new media*. Cambridge, MA: The MIT Press.

Mason, J. (2013). Video games as technical communication ecology. *Technical Communication Quarterly*, *22*(3), 219–236. doi:10.1080/10572252.2013.760062

Milner, R. M. (2013). Contested convergence and the politics of play on GameTrailers.com. *Games and Culture*, *8*(1), 3–25. doi:10.1177/1555412013478684

Mou, Y., & Peng, W. (2008). Gender and racial stereotype in popular videogames. In R. Ferdig (Ed.), *Handbook of research on effective electronic gaming in education* (pp. 922–937). Hershey, PA: IGI Global. doi:10.4018/978-1-59904-808-6.ch053

Naughty Dog. (2013). *The last of us* [PS3]. Author.

Nelson, T. H. (1992). *Literary machines: the report on, and of, project Xanadu concerning word processing, electronic publishing, hypertext, thinkertoys, tomorrow's intellectual revolution, and certain other topics including knowledge, education and freedom*. Sausalito, CA: Mindful Press.

Paul, C. A. (2010). Process, paratexts, and texts: Rhetorical analysis and virtual worlds. *Journal of Virtual Worlds Research*, *3*(1).

Paul, C. A. (2011). Optimizing play: How theorycraft changes gameplay and design. *Game Studies, 11*(2).

Payne, M. T. (2012). Marketing military realism in *Call of Duty 4: Modern Warfare*. *Games and Culture*, *7*(4), 305–327. doi:10.1177/1555412012454220

Projekt Red, C. D. (2015). *The witcher 3: Wild hunt* [PC, PS4, Xbox ONE]. CD Projekt.

Purchese, R. (2015, May 20). *CD Projekt tackles The Witcher 3 downgrade issue head on*. Retrieved June 21, 2015, from http://www.eurogamer.net/articles/2015-05-19-cd-projekt-red-tackles-the-witcher-3-graphics-downgrade-issue-head-on

Riffaterre, M. (1984). Intertextual representation: On mimesis as interpretive discourse. *Critical Inquiry*, *11*(1), 141–162. doi:10.1086/448279

Rockenberger, A. (2014). Video game framings. In D. Nadine & D. Apollon (Eds.), *Examining paratextual theory and its applications in digital culture* (pp. 252–286). Hershey, PA: IGI Global.

Schrier, J. (2013, April 8). *Witness how much BioShock Infinite has changed over the past few years*. Retrieved June 21, 2015, from http://kotaku.com/witness-how-much-bioshock-infinite-has-changed-over-the-471184935

Sherlock, L. M. (2014). Patching as design rhetoric: Tracing the framing and delivery of iterative content documentation in online games. In J. DeWinter & R. M. Moeller (Eds.), *Computer games and technical communication: Critical methods & applications at the intersection* (pp. 157–170). Burlington, VT: Ashgate Publishing Company.

Stewart, G. (2010). The paratexts of inanimate Alice: Thresholds, genre expectations and status. *Convergence (London)*, *16*(1), 57–74. doi:10.1177/1354856509347709

Švelch, J. (2014). Regarding board game errata. *Analog Game Studies, 1*(5). Retrieved from http://analoggamestudies.org/2014/12/regarding-board-game-errata/

Švelch, J. (2015). Towards a typology of video game trailers: Between the ludic and the cinematic. *G\A\M\E, the Italian Journal of Game Studies, 2015*(4).

Telltale Games. (2014). *Tales from Borderlands* [PS4, PS3, Xbox 360, Xbox ONE, PC]. Telltale Games.

Turtle Rock Studios. (2015). *Evolve* [PS4, Xbox One, PC]. 2K Games.

Wolf, W. (2006). Introduction: Frames, framings, and framing borders in literature and other media. In W. Bernhart & W. Wolf (Eds.), *Framing borders in literature and other media* (pp. 1–40). Amsterdam: Rodopi.

Yin-Poole, W. (2015, April 3). *Sega adds disclaimer to Aliens: Colonial Marines trailers after admitting they didn't accurately reflect final game*. Retrieved June 22, 2015, from http://www.eurogamer.net/articles/2013-04-03-sega-adds-disclaimer-to-aliens-colonial-marines-trailers-after-admitting-they-didnt-accurately-reflect-final-game

KEY TERMS AND DEFINITIONS

CGI: Computer generated imagery.

Gameplay: An act of playing a video game or the actual scenes seen on a screen while playing a video game.

Multiplayer: A video game where two or more human players interact and influence each other's gameplay experience. Multiplayer games can impose various relationships upon players (cooperative, competitive, asymmetric, etc.).

Patch: A fix or an update for software.

Representativity: A quality of one text to stand in for another text and truthfully describe it.

Shooter: One of the most popular genres of video games (e.g. Doom, Quake, Call of Duty series).

Trailer: A promotional video for a media product (film, TV series, video game, book, etc.).

ENDNOTES

[1] By using the word textual transcendence Genette (1997c) addresses the question of so-called regimes of art which he later explored in the book *The Work of Art: Immanence and Transcendence*.

Transcendence in this sense means the way in which the work surpasses and obscures the object, material or ideal, of which it consists. All types of intertextuality would be considered transcendence, hence the name transtextuality.

2   Genette (1997a) paradoxically supports his claims with an example that contains a direct link to the object of commentary (Hegel's *Phenomenology of the Spirit* and Diderot's *Rameau's Nephew*). However, we can find evidence of such a relationship, for example, in the *The Last of Us* (Naughty Dog, 2013), where the main character Joel criticizes a fictional movie about werewolves alluding to overall poor critical reception of the *Twilight* saga.

3   Hutcheon (2012) notes that adaptations (subcategory of hypertexts) are also often considered secondary or inferior to original works. Still, the authors would argue that adaptations are nonetheless considered works of art (texts) even if their quality is a priori questioned. However, paratexts and metatexts are rarely seen as more than just promotion, technical communication or journalism.

4   Genette (1990) himself explored the question of diegesis in his narratological work. However, he only draws occasional links between diegesis and paratextuality mostly in the context of fictional prefaces and fictional notes and also regarding the narrative fiction where intertitles are part of the diegesis, e.g. David Copperfield by Charles Dickens (Genette, 1997b). Some possible links between narratology and paratexts in game studies are also explored by Annika Rockenberger (2014).

5   Producers also mix paratextuality with seemingly critical commentary; such evaluations of one's own content would most likely be considered unreliable and part of a communication strategy.

6   The field of technical communication deals with similar questions as paratextuality in context of video games (see DeWinter & Moeller, 2014; Mason, 2013). Connecting these perspectives is one of the possible future research endeavors.

7   For example, launch trailer for *Dragon Age: Inquisition* (BioWare, 2014) had its own news story at gaming news site Polygon (Kuchera, 2015).

8   *The Witcher 3: Wild Hunt* (CD Projekt Red, 2015) trailer controversy was caused by the fact that a different version of the game engine was used for early trailers than the final game. This made the final game look visually downgraded compared to trailers (Purchese, 2015).

9   Apart for aforementioned *The Witcher 3*, we could also list *Aliens: Colonial Marines* (Gearbox Software, 2013) and *BioShock Infinite* (Irrational Games, 2013) as recent examples of misleading trailers (Crecente, 2014; Schrier, 2013).

10   Entertainment Software Rating Board (ESRB) is the US age rating board for video games.

11   Pan European Game Information (PEGI) is the European age rating system for video games.

12   It is important to note that the sample paratextual analysis assumes that the viewer is watching the trailer without knowing its title and its description and also out of the context of E3 but with basic knowledge of video game culture and the previous *Mass Effect* games. For example, the opening frames with the age ratings were missing in the actual E3 premiere of the trailer and were only added to the YouTube versions of the trailer. The paratextual clues lost by the omission of the ratings would be however fully substituted by the context of EA press conference at E3. Viewers in such specific situation would not need the information from ratings; the trailer would communicate its paratextual aspects rather effectively in such context.

13   For example, Sega was sued for false advertising of *Aliens: Colonial Marines*. The company lost and had to add the following disclaimer to their YouTube trailers "The trailer footage shown uses the in-game engine, and represents a work in progress." (Yin-Poole, 2015)

14   TV advertising is, in general, more tightly controlled by laws than online environment. This means that additional paratextual clues about the type of the displayed footage are more likely to appear in trailers and other promotional videos which are also intended for TV broadcasting.

15   Only few trailers tackle the problem of missing interactivity that clearly marks the line between the traditional trailers and video games. Most recently, *Evolve*'s (Turtle Rock Studios, 2015) 4v1 Interactive Trailer (2K Games, 2014) tried to mimic the gameplay of this multiplayer online first-person shooter by allowing the viewer to switch between viewpoints of five different players. Nonetheless, paratextuality of video game trailers is closely connected to the idea of adequate representation and representativity.

16   Recently, in-game statistics have been featured in Telltale's adventure games or in *Life Is Strange* (Dontnod Entertainment, 2015). Here they fulfill a slightly different function by informing a player about game choices he might have missed out.

17   *Borderlands* (borderlandsthegame.com) is a series of co-operative multiplayer first-person shooters. It consists of three main titles: *Borderlands* (Gearbox Software, 2009), *Borderlands 2* (Gearbox Software, 2012a), and *Borderlands: The Pre-Sequel!* (Gearbox Software & 2K Australia, 2014). There are two spin-off games: an episodic adventure game *Tales from Borderlands* (Telltale Games, 2014) and a mobile game *Borderlands Legends* (Gearbox Software, 2012b).

18   For example, interactive skill trees, which allow a player to plan out character progression before buying the game, are one of the few exclusive features of the official website. However, finding them on the website is not an easy task. They are not featured in the game description of the latest entry *Borderlands: The Pre-Sequel!* (Gearbox Software & 2K Australia, 2014), and not even the product pages for the DLC characters contain a link to the interactive skill trees. Searching the page yields one outdated article from September 2014 that lists only four original characters. The actual trees, however, link to all the other characters, including the two additionally released DLC characters.

19   For example, journalist Alice O'Connor runs a blog about mod notes and documentation called Readme.txt (readmedottxt.tumblr.com).

20   The so-called "Loot Cave" exploit received a lot of attention from the gaming press. Functionally, it was a gameplay activity that allowed players to relatively safely farm valuable in-game items by repetitive killing of quickly respawning enemies.

21   Microtransactions serve as an alternative revenue source for the traditional AAA game industry, although they are rather unpopular among players, especially when they are attached to full-price video game titles (Milner, 2013). They are, however, a successful business model for many so-called free-to-play or casual games.

22   For example, Frank L. Baum was using these techniques at the brink of 20th century when he was promoting sequels to his *Wizard of Oz* franchise by comic strips syndicated to US newspapers (Freeman, 2014).

Compilation of References

10 best selling PS3 games of all time. (2014). *whatisplaystation4.com*. Retrieved June 28, 2015, from http://whatisplaystation4.com/10-best-selling-ps3-games-of-all-time/

1408. (2007). Dir. Mikael Håfström, Prod. Dimension Films. USA.

2K Games. (2013). *BioShock Infinite TV commercial (full version)*. Retrieved from https://www.youtube.com/watch?v=RvrnUcB8ZJc

2K Games. (2014). *Evolve — 4v1 interactive trailer* [English PEGI]. Retrieved from https://www.youtube.com/watch?v=51YhRPYQHtY

2K Boston. (2007). *BioShock*. Novato, CA: 2K Games.

A. T. (2011). *Twitter and epic poetry: The first real work of digital literature?* Retrieved June 30, 2015, from http://www.economist.com/blogs/prospero/2011/10/twitter-and-epic-poetry

Aarseth, E. (2012). *A narrative theory of games*. ACM Digital library. Retrieved November 18, 2015, from http://dl.acm.org/citation.cfm?id=2282365

Abrams, J., Lieber, J., & Lindelof, D. (2004-2010). *Lost*. ABC.

Activision. (1982). *Pitfall*. Activision.

Adams, E. W. (2007). S.T.A.L.K.E.R.: Shadow of Chernobyl: Ludic space as memorial. In F. Von Borres, S. P. Walz, & M. Böttger (Eds.), *Space time play*. Basel: Birkhäuser Verlag AG.

Alfaro, M. J. M. (1996). Intertextuality: Origins and Development of the Concept. *Atlantis, 18*(1/2), 268–285.

Allen, G. (2000). Intertextuality. London, UK: Routledge. Retrieved from http://search.ebscohost.com/login.aspx?direct=true&db=nlebk&AN=62876&site=ehost-live

Allen, G. (2011). *Intertextuality* (2nd ed.). London, UK: Routledge.

Althusser, L. (2001). 1971). Ideology and ideological state apparatuses. In *Lenin and philosophy, and other essays* (B. Brewster, Trans.). New York, NY: Monthly Review Press.

Altman, R. (1999). *Film/genre*. London, UK: British Film Institute.

Altman, R. (2001). Cinema and popular song: The lost tradition. In A. Knight & P. R. Wojcik (Eds.), *Soundtrack available: Essays on film and popular music* (pp. 19–30). Durham, NC: Duke University Press. doi:10.1215/9780822380986-001

Alton, A. H. (2003). Generic fusion and the mosaic of *Harry Potter*. In E. E. Heilman (Ed.), *Harry Potter's world: Multidisciplinary critical perspectives* (pp. 141–162). London, UK: Routledge Falmer.

Anderson, C. A., Shibuya, A., Ihori, N., Swing, E. L., Bushman, B. J., Sakamoto, A., & Saleem, M. et al. (2010). Violent video game effects on aggression, empathy, and prosocial behavior in Eastern and Western countries: A meta-analytic review. *Psychological Bulletin, 136*(2), 151–173. doi:10.1037/a0018251 PMID:20192553

Anderson, M. (1976). *Logan's run.* Action, Adventure, Sci-Fi.

Anderson, M., & Levene, R. (2012). *Grand thieves & tomb raiders: How British video games conquered the world.* London, UK: Aurum Press Ltd.

Andrejevic, M. (2013). Whither-ing critique. *Communication and Critical. Cultural Studies, 10*(2-3), 222–228.

Andrieu, M. (2011). *Réinvestir la musique: Autour de la reprise et de ses effets au cinéma.* Paris, France: L'Harmattan.

Angenot, M. (1989). *1889, un état du discours social.* Longueuil, Canada: Le Préambule.

Ang, I. (2011). Navigating complexity: From cultural critique to cultural intelligence. *Continuum, 25*(6), 779–794. doi:10.1080/10304312.2011.617873

Angus Grimaldi. (n.d.). Retrieved July 21, 2015, from http://tombraider.wikia.com/wiki/Angus_Grimaldi

Anthropy, A. (2012). *Dys4ia.* Newgrounds.

AP. (2014). Chespirito celebrará cumpleaños con lanzamiento de "El chavo kart". *eluniverso.com.* Retrieved June 28, 2015, from http://www.eluniverso.com/vida-estilo/2014/02/19/nota/2209091/chespirito-celebrara-cumpleanos-lanzamiento-chavo-kart

Apperley, T. H. (2006). Genre and game studies: Toward a critical approach to video game genres.[abstract]. *Simulation & Gaming, 37*(1), 6–23. http://sag.sagepub.com/content/37/1/6 doi:10.1177/1046878105282278

Aristotle, , Butcher, S. H., & Gassner, J. (1951). *Aristotle's theory of poetry and fine art: With a critical text and translation of the Poetics.* New York, NY: Dover.

Armature Studio. (2013). *Batman: Arkham origins Blackgate.* New York, NY: Warner Bros. Interactive Entertainment.

Arnott, L. (2015). *Narrative epic and new media: The totalizing spaces of postmodernity in The Wire, Batman, and The Legend of Zelda.* (Unpublished doctoral dissertation). The University of Western Ontario, London, Canada.

Arnott, L. (in press). -a). Mapping *Metroid:* Narrative, space, and *Other M. Games and Culture.* doi:10.1177/1555412015580016

Arnott, L. (in press). -b). Epic and genre: Beyond the boundaries of media. *Comparative Literature.*

Arsenault, D. (2006). *Jeux et enjeux du récit vidéoludique: La narration dans le jeu video.* (Master thesis). Université de Montréal, Montréal, Canada.

Arsenault, D. (2009). Video game genre, evolution and innovation. *Eludamos (Göttingen), 3*(2), 149–176.

Ashcraft, B. (2010). How cover shaped gaming's last decade. *Kotaku.* Retrieved July 10, 2015, from http://kotaku.com/5452654/how-cover-shaped-gamings-last-decade

Ash, J. (2013). Technologies of captivation videogames and the attunement of affect. *Body & Society, 19*(1), 27–51. doi:10.1177/1357034X11411737

Atari. (1981). *Yar's revenge.* Atari.

Australian Classification. (n.d.). *Check the classification | Australian classification*. Retrieved June 29, 2015, from http://www.classification.gov.au/Guidelines/Pages/Check-the-Classification.aspx

Authier-Revuz, J. (1982). Hétérogénéité montrée et hétérogénéité constitutive: Éléments pour une approche de l'autre dans le discours. *DRLAV. Revue de Linguistique, 26*, 91–151.

Avellan, E., & Rodriguez, R. (Producers), & Rodriguez, R. (Director). (2003). *Spykids 3-D: Game over* [Motion Picture]. United States: Buena Vista Pictures.

Babeux, S. (2007). Le spectateur hors jeu: Investigation ludique du réseau interférentiel. *Intermédialités, (9)*, 79-98.

Backe, H.-J., & Aarseth, E. (2013). Ludic zombies: An examination of zombieism in games. *Proceedings of the 2013 DiGRA International Conference*. Retrieved November 18, 2015, from http://www.digra.org/wp-content/uploads/digital-library/paper_405.pdf

Bailey, S., Silver, J., & Lisberger, S. (Producers), & Kosinski, J. (Director). (2010). *Tron: Legacy* [Motion picture]. United States: Walt Disney Studios.

Baker, M., & Saldanha, G. (Eds.). (1997). *Routledge encyclopedia of translation studies*. London, UK: Routlege.

Bakhtine, M. (1970). *La poétique de Dostoïevski*. Paris, France: Seuil.

Bakhtine, M. (1978). *Esthétique et théorie du roman*. Paris, France: Gallimard.

Bakhtin, M. (1981). *The dialogic imagination*. Austin, TX: University of Texas Press.

Bakhtin, M. M. (1981). Epic and Novel. In M. Holquist (Ed.), *The dialogic imagination: Four essays* (M. Holquist & C. Emerson, Trans.). Austin, TX: University of Texas Press.

Bakhtin, M. M. (1981). *The dialogic imagination: Four essays*. Austin, TX: University of Texas Press.

Baral, E. (1999). *Otaku: Les enfants du virtuel*. Paris, France: Denoël.

Barron, B. (2006). Interest and self-sustained learning as catalysts of development: A learning ecology perspective. *Human Development, 49*(4), 193–224. doi:10.1159/000094368

Barthes, R. (1974). Texte (théorie du). *Encyclopædia Universalis*. Retrieved from http://www.universalis-edu.com/encyclopedie/theorie-du-texte

Barthes, R. (1973). *Le plaisir du texte*. Paris, France: Seuil.

Barthes, R. (1975). *The pleasure of the text*. New York, NY: Hill and Wang.

Barthes, R. (1977). From work to text. In S. Heath (Ed.), *Image—music—text* (S. Heath, Trans.). (pp. 155–164). London, UK: Fontana Press.

Barthes, R. (1977). *Image, music, text* (S. Heath, Trans.). London, UK: Fontana.

Barthes, R. (1981). *Camera lucida: Reflections on photography* (R. Howard, Trans.). New York, NY: Farrar, Straus & Giroux.

Bass, L. R. (2008). *The drama of the portrait: Theater and visual culture in early modern Spain*. University Park, PA: Penn State University Press.

Bateman, C. (2015). The essence of RPGs (1): Children of TSR. *ihobo*. Retrieved June 17, 2015, from http://blog.ihobo.com/2015/04/the-essence-of-rpgs-1-children-of-tsr.html

Bates, J. (1997, September). Westwood's *Blade Runner. PC Gamer, 4*(9). Retrieved from http://media.bladezone.com/contents/game/

Bates, C. (Ed.). (2010). *The Cambridge companion to the epic.* Cambridge, UK: Cambridge University Press. doi:10.1017/CCOL9780521880947

Baudry, J.-L. (1974). Ideological effects of the basic cinematographic apparatus (trans. A. Williams). *Film Quarterly, 28*(2), 39–47. doi:10.2307/1211632

Bealer, A. H. (2012). Eco-performance in the digital RPG gamescape. In *Dungeons, dragons, and digital denizens: The digital role-playing game* (Vol. 1, pp. 27–47). New York, NY: The Continuum International Publishing Group.

Behemoth, T. (2008). *Castle crashers*. San Diego, CA: Microsoft Game Studios.

Benioff, D., & Weiss, D. B. (2011). *Game of thrones*. USA: HBO.

Bennett, T., & Woollacott, J. (1987). *Bond and beyond: The political career of a popular hero*. London, UK: Routledge Kegan & Paul. doi:10.1007/978-1-349-18610-5

Bernal Merino, M. (2006). On the translation of video games. *The Journal of Specialised Translation*, (6). Retrieved from http://www.jostrans.org/issue06/art_bernal.php

Bernardi, D. (1998). *Star Trek and history: Race-ing toward a white future*. New Brunswick, N.J.: Rutgers University Press.

Bertetti, P. (2011). *Conan il mito*. Pisa, Italy: ETS.

Bessell, D. (2002). What's that funny noise? An examination of the role of music in *Cool Boarders 2, Alien Trilogy* and *Medievil 2*. In G. King & T. Krzywinska (Eds.), *Screenplay: Cinema/videogames/interfaces* (pp. 136–143). New York, NY: Wallflower Press.

Besson, R. (2014). Prolégomènes pour une définition de lintermédialité. *Cinémadoc*. Retrieved June 13, 2015, from http://culturevisuelle.org/cinemadoc/2014/04/29/prolegomenes/

Bethesda Game Studios [PC]. (2008). *Fallout 3*. Bethesda Softworks.

Bethesda Game Studios. (2008). *Fallout 3* [Videogame]. Bethesda Softworks. [Disc]

Bethesda Game Studios. (2011). *Skyrim: The elder scrolls V* [Xbox 360]. Bethesda, MD: Bethesda Softworks.

Bethesda Game Studios. (2011). *The elder scolls V: Skyrim* [Videogame]. Bethesda Softworks. [Download]

Bicket, D. (2005). Reconsidering geocultural contraflow: Intercultural information flows through trends in global audiovisual trade. *Global Media Journal, 4*(6), 1–16.

Bioware [PC]. (2012). *Mass effect 3*. Electronic Arts.

BioWare. (2007). *Mass effect* [Xbox 360]. Edmonton: Electronic Arts.

BioWare. (2014). *Dragon age: Inquisition* [PC, PS3, PS4, Xbox 360, Xbox One]. EA.

Black Isle Studios [PC]. (1998). *Fallout 2*. Interplay Entertainment.

Blizzard Entertainment. (1994). *Warcraft: Orcs & humans* [PC]. Irvine, CA: Activision Blizzard.

Blizzard Entertainment. (1994). *Warcraft: Orcs and humans* [Videogame]. Blizzard Entertainment. [Disc]

Blizzard Entertainment. (1996). *Warcraft II: Beyond the dark portal* [Videogame]. Blizzard Entertainment. [Disc]

Blizzard Entertainment. (1996). *Warcraft III: Reign of chaos* [Videogame]. Blizzard Entertainment. [Disc]

Blizzard Entertainment. (2007). *World of warcraft* [Videogame]. Blizzard Entertainment. [Disc]

Bloom, H. (1973). *The anxiety of influence: A theory of poetry*. New York, NY: Oxford University Press.

Blow, J. (2008). Braid. San Francisco.

Bogost, I. (2007). Persuasive games: The expressive power of videogames (Kindle ed.). Cambridge, MA: The MIT Press.

Bogost, I. (2007). *Persuasive games: The expressive power of videogames*. Cambridge, MA: MIT Press.

Bogost, I. (2011). *How to do things with videogames*. Minneapolis, MN: University of Minnesota Press. doi:10.5749/minnesota/9780816676460.001.0001

Bolter, J. D., & Grusin, R. (1999). *Remediation: Understanding new media*. Cambridge, MA: The MIT Press.

Bonk, J. (2014). Finishing the fight, one step at a time: Seriality in Bungie's *Halo. Eludamos (Göttingen), 8*(1), 65–81. Retrieved from http://www.eludamos.org/index.php/eludamos/article/view/vol8no1-5

Boonstra, J. (1982, June). Philip K. Dick's final interview. *Rod Serling's The Twilight Zone Magazine, 2*(3), 47–52.

Boot, W. R., Kramer, A. F., Fabiani, M., Gratton, G., Simons, D. J., & Low, K. et al. (2006). The effects of video game playing on perceptual and cognitive abilities. *Journal of Vision (Charlottesville, Va.), 6*(6), 942–968. doi:10.1167/6.6.942

Botting, F. (2001). Candygothic. In F. Botting (Ed.), *The Gothic* (pp. 133–151). Cambridge, UK: D. S. Brewer.

Botting, F. (2002). Aftergothic: Consumption, machines, and black holes. In J. Hogle (Ed.), *The Cambridge companion to Gothic fiction* (pp. 277–300). Cambridge, UK: Cambridge University Press. doi:10.1017/CCOL0521791243.014

Botting, F. (2013). *Gothic* (2nd ed.). London, UK: Routledge.

Bouissou, J. M. (2014). *Manga. History and universe of Japanese comic books*. Paris, France: Picquier poche.

Bourdieu, P. (1991). *Language and symbolic power* (J. B. Thompson, Trans.). Cambridge, MA: Harvard University Press.

Bourdieu, P. (1993). *The field of cultural production: Essays on art and literature*. New York, NY: Columbia University Press.

Box Office Mojo. (2015). *The dark knight rises (2012)*. Retrieved June 14, 2015, from http://www.boxofficemojo.com/movies/?id=batman3.htm

BradField Productions. (2005, 2015). *Inanimate Alice*. Retrieved June 29, 2015, from http://www.inanimatealice.com/

Breaking the mold: The art of BioShock. (2007). 2K Games.

Breger, C. (2008). Digital digs, or Lara Croft replaying Indiana Jones: Archaeological tropes and "colonial loops" in new media narrative. *Aether: The Journal of Media Geography, II*, 41–60.

Brooker, W. (2012). *Hunting the dark knight: Twenty-first century Batman*. London, UK: I. B. Tauris.

Brookey, R. A. (2010). *Hollywood gamers: Digital convergence in the film and video game industries*. Bloomington, IN: Indiana University Press.

Brooks, J. L., Groening, M., & Simon, S. (1989). *The Simpsons*. USA: Fox.

Brown, D., & Krzywinska, T. (2009). Movie-games and game-movies: Towards an aesthetics of transmediality. In W. Buckland (Ed.), *Film theory and contemporary Hollywood movies* (pp. 86–102). New York, NY: Routledge.

Brukman, J. (2013). *Inside the Batman: Arkham Origins soundtrack.* Retrieved June 1, 2015, from http://www.rollingstone.com/culture/news/inside-the-batman-arkham-origins-soundtrack-20131018

Bryce, J., & Rutter, J. (2002). Spectacle of the deathmatch: Character and narrative in first-person shooters. In G. King & T. Krzywinska (Eds.), *ScreenPlay: Cinema/videogames/interfaces* (pp. 66–80). New York, NY: Wallflower Press.

Buckingham, D. (1993). *Children talking television: Making of television literacy.* London, UK: Routledge Falmer.

Buffy the Vampire Slayer. (2002) Developer: EA Games; Publisher: Fox Entertainment.

Bukatman, S. (1997). *Blade runner.* London, UK: British Film Institute.

Bungie. (2001). *Halo: Combat evolved* [Xbox]. Bellevue, WA: Microsoft Game Studios.

Bungie. (2014). *Destiny* [PS3, PS4, Xbox 360, Xbox ONE]. Activision.

Burns, J. (2009). *Goddess of the market: Ayn Rand and the American right.* Oxford, UK: Oxford University Press.

Burrill, D. A. (2002). "Oh, grow up 007": The performance of Bond and boyhood in film and videogames. In G. King & T. Krzywinska (Eds.), *ScreenPlay: Cinema/videogames/interfaces* (pp. 181–193). New York, NY: Wallflower Press.

Bussolini, J. (2013). Television intertextuality after *Buffy*: Intertextuality of casting and constitutive intertextuality. *Slayage: The Journal of the Whedon Studies Association, 10*(1). Retrieved March 19, 2013, from http://slayageonline.com/essays/slayage35/Bussolini.pdf

Butler, M. (2003). Taking it seriously: Intertextuality and authenticity in two covers by the Pet Shop Boys. *Popular Music, 22*(1), 1–19. doi:10.1017/S0261143003003015

Caillois, R. (2001). Man, play and games. (M. Barash, Trans.) (Reprint, 1961). Urbana, IL: University of Illinois Press.

Caillois, R. (1992). *Les jeux et les hommes: Le masque et le vertige.* Paris, France: Gallimard.

Caldwell, B. (2012, March 7). The competition: The story behind the IGF's critics. *Rock Paper Shotgun.* Retrieved from http://www.rockpapershotgun.com/2012/03/07/the-competition-the-story-behind-the-igfs-critics/

Calvino, I. (1983). *If on a winter's night a traveller* (W. Weaver, Trans.). London, UK: Random House.

Camarero, J. (2008). *Intertextualidad.* Barcelona: Anthropos.

Campbell, C. (2013). *How to tackle gaming's lack of racial diversity.* Retrieved June 4, 2015, from http://www.polygon.com/2013/9/16/4728320/how-to-tackle-gamings-lack-of-racial-diversity

Campbell, J. (2008). *The hero with a thousand faces.* Novato, CA: New World Library.

Capcom. (1996). *Resident evil,* [Videogame] [Disc] [Microsoft Windows] Virgin Interactive Entertainment.

Capcom. (1998). *Resident evil 2,* [Videogame] [Disc] [Microsoft Windows] Capcom Entertainment Inc.

Capcom. (1999). *Resident evil 3: Nemesis,* [Videogame] [Disc] [Microsoft Windows] Eidos.

Capcom. (2001). *Resident evil code: Veronica,* [Videogame] [Disc] [PlayStation 2] Capcom.

Capcom. (2002). *Resident evil outbreak,* [Videogame] [Disc] [PlayStation 2] Capcom Entertainment Inc.

Capcom. (2005). *Resident evil 4,* [Videogame] [Disc] [PlayStation 2] Capcom Entertainment Inc.

Capcom. (2007). *Resident evil: The umbrella chronicles,* [Videogame] [Disc] [PlayStation 3] Capcom Entertainment Inc.

Capcom. (2009). *Resident evil 5,* [Videogame] [Disc] [PlayStation 3] Capcom.

Capcom. (2012). *Resident evil 6,* [Videogame] [Disc] [PlayStation 3] Capcom.

Capra, F., & Luigi Luisi, P. (2014). *The systems view of life: A unifying vision.* New York, NY: Cambridge University Press. doi:10.1017/CBO9780511895555

Carle, C. (2003). Roadkill. *IGN.* Retrieved November 2015, from http://ca.ign.com/articles/2003/11/04/roadkill

Carlson, R. (2009). Too human versus the enthusiast press: Video game journalists as mediators of commodity value. *Transformative Works and Cultures, 2009*(Vol 2).

Carlson, R., & Corliss, J. (2011). Imagined commodities: Video game localization and mythologies of cultural difference. *Games and Culture, 6*(1), 61–82. doi:10.1177/1555412010377322

Carr, D. (2013). Bodies, augmentation and disability in *Dead Space* and *Deus Ex: Human Revolutions.* In *Context Matters! — Proceedings of the Vienna Games Conference 2013: Exploring and Reframing Games and Play in Context.* Vienna, Austria: New Academic Press.

Carr, D., Buckingham, D, Burn, A., & Schott, G. (2006). *Computer games: Text, narrative and play.* Cambridge, MA: Polity Press.

Carr, D. (2002). Playing with Lara. In G. King & T. Krzywinska (Eds.), *ScreenPlay: Cinema/videogames/interfaces* (pp. 171–180). London, UK: Wallflower Press.

Carr, D. (2006). Film, adaptation and computer games. In D. Buckingham, D. Carr, A. Burn, & G. Schott (Eds.), *Computer games: Text, narrative and play* (pp. 149–161). London, UK: Polity Press.

Carter, M. (2015). Emitexts and paratexts: Propaganda in *EVE Online. Games and Culture, 10*(4), 311–342. doi:10.1177/1555412014558089

Carvalho, F. G., Vasconcellos, M. S., Ferreira, P. C., & Araujo, I. S. (2013). Jogos digitais como cultura participatória: O modelo do mercado simbólico aplicado à concepção de um jogo digital sobre a prevenção de DST e Aids. In Proceedings do XII Simpósio Brasileiro de Jogos e Entretenimento Digital (SBGames 2013).

Castronova, E. (2005). *Synthetic worlds: The business and culture of online games.* Chicago, IL: The University of Chicago Press.

Cavanagh, T. (2010a). N.O.T.T.U.B. London, England.

Cavanagh, T. (2010b). VVVVVV. London, England.

Cavanagh, T. (2009). *Don't look back.* London, England.

Cavanagh, T. (2012). *Super hexagon.* London, England.

CD Projekt [PC]. (2012). *The witcher 2: Assassins of kings.* Bandai Namco Games.

Cervantes, M. (2003). *Review of "Lord of the Rings: War of the Rings".* Game Chronicles.

Champion, E. (2004). Indiana Jones and the joystick of doom: Understanding the past via computer games. *Traffic (Copenhagen, Denmark), 5,* 47–65.

Chandler, D. (1997). *An introduction to genre theory.* Retrieved November 18, 2015, from http://visual-memory.co.uk/daniel/Documents/intgenre/chandler_genre_theory.pdf

Chapoy, P. (2012). *La historia detrás del mito - La vecindad del chavo*. Mexico: Azteca, TV. Retrieved from https://www.youtube.com/watch?v=gv1LNU8hWcM&spfreload=1

Chateau-Canguilhem, J. (2013). Corps et espaces cybereérotiques. *Hermès, La Revue*, (69), 116-120.

Chatman, S. (1978). *Story and discourse: Narrative structure in fiction and film*. Ithaca, NY: Cornell University Press.

Chen, C., Härdle, W. K., & Unwin, A. (2007). *Handbook of data visualization*. Berlin, Germany: Springer Science & Business Media.

Chiaro, D. (2008). Issues in audiovisual translation. In J. Munday (Ed.), *The Routledge companion to translation studies* (pp. 141–165). Oxon, UK: Routledge.

Chion, M. (1995). *La musique au cinéma*. Paris, France: Fayard.

Chislenko, A., More, M., Sandberg, A., Vita-More, N., & Yudkowsky, E. (2001). Transhumanist FAQ. *Humanity+*. Retrieved July 7, 2015, from http://humanityplus.org/philosophy/transhumanist-faq/#top

Chung, B. (2012, September 10). Blendo big boxes. *Blendo Games*. Retrieved May 10, 2015, from http://blendogames.com/news/?p=374

Chung, P., Jones, A. R., Kawajiri, Y., Koike, T., Maeda, M., Morimoto, K., & Watanabe, S. (2003). *The animatrix*. Animation, Action, Adventure.

Cilliers, P. (2000). What can we learn from a theory of complexity? *Emergence*, 2(1), 23–33. doi:10.1207/S15327000EM0201_03

Cinemaware. (1986). *Defender of the crown*. Author.

Clarke, D., & Duimering, P. (2006). How computer gamers experience the game situation: A behavioral study. *Computers in Entertainment (CIE)*. *Theoretical and Practical Computer Applications in Entertainment*, 4(3), 1–12.

Coetzee, J. M. (1986). *Foe*. South Africa: Raven Press.

Cohen, J. J. (1996). Monster culture (seven theses). In J. J. Cohen (Ed.), *Monster theory: Reading culture* (pp. 3–25). Minneapolis, MN: University of Minnesota Press.

Collins, K. (2002). *The future is happening already: Industrial music, dystopia, and the aesthetic of the machine*. (Doctoral dissertation). University of Liverpool, Liverpool, UK. Available from EThOS Dissertations and Theses database. (http://ethos.bl.uk/OrderDetails.do?uin=uk.bl.ethos.272629)

Collins, K. (2005). From bits to hits: Video games music changes its tune. *Film International*, (12), 4-19.

Collins, J. (1991). *Batman: The Movie*, narrative: The hyperconscious. In R. E. Pearson & W. Uricchio (Eds.), *The many lives of the Batman: Critical approaches to a superhero and his media* (pp. 164–181). New York, NY: Routledge.

Collins, K. (2008). *Game sound: An introduction to the history, theory, and practice of video game music*. Cambridge, MA: MIT Press.

Compagnon, A. (1979). *La seconde main ou le travail de la citation*. Paris, France: Seuil.

Conditt, J. (2012). *Castle Crashers clocks in over 3 million "knights in the making"*. Retrieved June 11, 2015, from http://www.engadget.com/2012/09/13/castle-crashers-clocks-in-over-3-million-knights-in-the-making/

Conditt, J. (2013). IGF 2013: And the awards go to... *Cart Life*! Retrieved June 24, 2015, from http://www.engadget.com/2013/03/27/igf-2013-and-the-awards-go-to-cart-life/

Consalvo, M. (2003). Zelda 64 and video game fans: A walkthrough of games, intertextuality, and narrative. *Television & New Media*, *4*(3), 321–333. doi:10.1177/1527476403253993

Consalvo, M. (2006). Console video games and global corporations: Creating a hybrid culture. *New Media & Society*, *8*(1), 117–137. doi:10.1177/1461444806059921

Consalvo, M. (2007). *Cheating: Gaining advantage in video games*. Cambridge, MA: The MIT Press.

Consalvo, M. (2007). *Cheating: gaining advantage in videogames*. Cambridge, MA: The MIT Press.

Consalvo, M. (2007). *Cheating: Gaining advantage in videogames*. London: The MIT Press.

Cook, M., Tweet J. and S. Williams (2003). *Dungeons and dragons: Master's guide* (3.5 edition) [Role-playing game rulebook] Wizards of the Coast. (Original work published 1974).

Cook, M., Tweet J. and S. Williams (2003). *Dungeons and dragons: Monster manual* (3.5 edition) [Role-playing game rulebook] Wizards of the Coast. (Original work published 1974).

Cook, M., Tweet J., & Williams, S. (2003). *Dungeons and dragons: Player's handbook* (3.5 edition) [Role-playing game rulebook] Wizards of the Coast.

Core Design. (1996a). *Tomb raider* [PC]. London, UK: Eidos Interactive, Square Enix.

Core Design. (1996b). *Tomb raider: PC manual*. London, UK: Eidos Interactive.

Corliss, J. (2011). Introduction: The social science study of videogames. *Games and Culture*, *6*(1), 3–16. doi:10.1177/1555412010377323

Corneliussen, H., & Walker Rettberg, J. (Eds.). (2008). *Digital culture, play, and identity: A World of Warcraft reader*. Cambridge, MA: The MIT Press.

Crecente, B. (2013). *What makes a developer indie?* Retrieved June 4, 2015, from Game Studio Job Listings

Crecente, B. (2014, August 11). *Sega to tentatively pay out $1.25M in Aliens suit while Gearbox fights on*. Retrieved June 21, 2015, from http://www.polygon.com/2014/8/11/5993509/aliens-colonial-marines-class-action-settlement

Creighton, R., & Creighton, C. (2011). *Sissy's magical ponycorn adventure*.

Creighton, R., & Creighton, C. (2013). *Ponycorns and programming kids: Ryan Henson Creighton and Cassandra Creighton at TEDxToronto*. Retrieved June 26, 2015, from https://www.youtube.com/watch?v=hE0K5W7_omI

Crompton, K. (2013). Drawings based on *Nature Mage* series. Retrieved from http://www.naturemage.com

Cronenberg, D., Hámori, A., & Lantos, R. (Producers), & Cronenberg, D. (Director). (1999). *eXistenZ* [Motion picture]. Canada. Alliance Atlantic.

Crystal Dynamics. (2015). *Rise of the tomb raider* [XBox 360/One]. San Francisco, CA: Square Enix.

Csikszentmihalyi, M. (1990). *Flow: The psychology of optimal experience*. New York, NY: Harper & Row.

Cuddey, L. (Ed.). (2015). *BioShock and philosophy: Irrational game, rational book*. Malden, MA: Wiley Blackwell. doi:10.1002/9781118915899

Currie, M. (1998). *Postmodern narrative theory*. New York, NY: St. Martin's Press. doi:10.1007/978-1-349-26620-3

Dällenbach, L. (1976). Intertexte et autotexte. *Poétique*, (27), 282-296.

Daniels, A. (2010). Ayn Rand: Engineer of souls. *New Criterion, 28*(6), 4-9. Retrieved from http://www.newcriterion.com/articles.cfm/Ayn-Rand--engineer-of-souls-4385

Daste, S. (2013). Introduction à létude de la culture otaku. *Omnsh*. Retrieved June 9, 2015, from http://www.omnsh.org/ressources/441/introduction-letude-de-la-culture-otaku

Daste, S. (2015). *Espaces de fictions générés par les nouveaux médias issus des cultures générationnelles* otaku *et geek: influences notées dans lart contemporain et ma pratique.* (Unpublished doctoral dissertation). Université Paris-8, Paris, France.

Davis, B., & Sumara, D. (2006). *Complexity and education: Inquires into learning, teaching and research.* London, UK: Lawrence Erlbaum.

de Bont, J. (2003). *Lara Croft tomb raider: The cradle of life.* Action, Adventure, Fantasy.

De Jager-Loftus, D. P., & Moore, A. (2013). #gathercreateshare: How research libraries use Pinterest. *Internet Reference Services Quarterly, 18*(3-4), 265–279. doi:10.1080/10875301.2013.840714

de Lauzirika, C. (2007). *Dangerous days: Making Blade Runner.* Documentary.

Deco devolution: The art of BioShock 2 . (2010). 2K Games.

Defoe, D. (1719, modern edition published 2003). Robinson Crusoe (reprint). London, UK: Penguin Classics.

Dena, C. (2009). *Transmedia fictions: Theorizing the practice of expressing a fictional world across distinct media and environments* (Unpublished doctoral dissertation). University of Sydney, Sydney, Australia.

Denis, R. C., & Trodd, C. (Eds.). (2000). *Art and the academy in the nineteenth century.* Manchester, UK: Manchester University Press.

Denson, S., & Jahn-Sudmann, A. (2013). Digital seriality: On the serial aesthetics and practice of digital games. *Eludamos (Göttingen), 7*(1), 1–32.

Derrida, J. (1978). Structure, sign, and play in the discourse of the human sciences. In *Writing and difference* (A. Bass, Trans.). (pp. 278–294). Chicago, IL: The University of Chicago Press.

Derrida, J. (1982). Différance. In *Margins of philosophy* (pp. 1–27). Chicago, IL: University of Chicago Press.

Derrida, J., & Ronell, A. (1980). The law of genre (trans. A. Ronell). *Critical Inquiry, 7*(1), 55–81. doi:10.1086/448088

Deterding, S. (2010). Living room wars : remediation, boardgames, and the early history of video wargaming. In N. B. Huntemann & M. T. Payne (Eds.), *Joystick soldiers: The politics of play in military video games* (pp. 21–38). New York, NY: Routledge.

Deuber-Mankowsky, A. (2005). Lara Croft: Cyber heroine. (D. J. Bonfiglio, Trans.) (English Translation (German, 2001), Vol. 14). Minneapolis, MN: University of Minnesota Press.

Deus Ex. (2015). *Human Revolution.* Tokyo: Square Enix. [Digital Game]

Deuze, M. (2007). Convergence culture in the creative industries. *International Journal of Cultural Studies, 10*(2), 243–263. doi:10.1177/1367877907076793

Developments, F. (2015). *Elite dangerous.* Author.

Dewey, J. (1963). *Experience and education.* New York, NY: Macmillan.

DeWinter, J., & Moeller, R. M. (Eds.). (2014). *Computer games and technical communication: Critical methods & applications at the intersection*. Burlington, VT: Ashgate Publishing Company.

Díaz Moreno, E. (2011). Hoy cumple cuarenta años el chavo del 8. *Excelsior*. Retrieved June 26, 2015, from http://www.excelsior.com.mx/node/745890

Dick, P. K. (1981, October 11). *Letter to The Ladd Company*. Retrieved from http://dangerousminds.net/comments/nothing_matches_blade_runner_philip_k._dick_gets_excited_about_ridley_scott

Dick, P. K. (2008). *Do androids dream of electric sheep?* New York, NY: Ballantine Books.

Dick, P. K. (2012a). *The man in the high castle*. New York, NY: Penguin Books Limited.

Dick, P. K. (2012b). *Ubik*. Boston, MA: Houghton Mifflin Harcourt.

Dictionary.com. (2012). *The worst words of 2012*. Retrieved June 1, 2015, from http://blog.dictionary.com/worst-words-of-2012/

Dig in Nara, not Kyushu, yields palatial ruins possibly of Himiko. (2009, November 12). *The Japan Times Online*. Retrieved July 22, 2015, from http://search.japantimes.co.jp/news/2009/11/12/news/dig-in-nara-not-kyushu-yields-palatial-ruins-possibly-of-himiko/

Diken, B. (2009). Radical critique as the paradox of post-political society. *Third Text*, *23*(5), 579–586. doi:10.1080/09528820903184815

Dimopoulos, K. (2015). *Freeware garden: Ever yours, Vincent*. Retrieved June 20, 2015, from http://www.rockpaper-shotgun.com/tag/ever-yours-vincent/

Docter, P., & Del Carmen, R. (2015). *Inside out*. USA: Pixar Animation Studio and Walt Disney Pictures.

domkex. (2012). *Prey the game full movie*. Retrieved November 2015, from https://www.youtube.com/watch?v=4IP7DthcSBM

Domosh, M., & Seager, J. (2001). *Putting women in place: Feminist geographers make sense of the world*. New York, NY: The Guilford Press.

Donovan, T. (2010). *Replay: The history of video games*. East Sussex, UK: Yellow Ant.

Dontnod Entertainment. (2015). *Life is strange* [PC, PS4, PS3, Xbox 360, Xbox ONE].

Dormans, J. (2006). The world is yours: Intertextual irony and second level reading strategies in *Grand theft auto*. *Game Research*, [En ligne] http://game-research.com/index.php/articles/the-world-is-yours-intertextual-irony-and-second-level-reading-strategies-in-grand-theft-auto (Page consultée le 20 septembre 2011).

Dozier, W. (Producer), & Martinson, L. H. (Director). (1966). *Batman: The movie*. [Motion Picture] Twentieth Century Fox.

Drucker, J. (2008). The digital codex from page space to e-space. In R. Siemens & S. Schreibman (Eds.), *A companion to digital literary studies* (pp. 216–232). Malden, MA: Wiley-Blackwell.

Duchet, C., & Maurus, P. (2011). *Un cheminement vagabond: Nouveaux entretiens sur la sociocritique*. Paris, France: Honoré Champion.

Duff, D. (2000). *Modern genre theory*. Essex, UK: Longman.

Duffy, J. (1997). Claude Simon, Joan Miro et l'interimage. In E. Le Calvez & M.-C. Canova-Green (Eds.), *Texte(s) et intertexte(s)* (pp. 113–139). Amsterdam, Netherland; Atlanta, GA: Rodopi.

Dungeons and dragons . (2000). Dir. C. Solomon, New Line Cinema, USA and Czech Republic.

Duret, C. (2015). Écosystème transtextuel et jeux de rôle participatifs en environnement virtuel: Le sociogramme de l'ordre naturel dans les jeux de rôle goréens. In F. Barnabé & B.-O. Dozo (Eds.), *Jeu vidéo et livre*. Liège, Belgium: Bebooks.

Duro, P. (2007). Imitation and authority: The creation of the academic canon in French art, 1648-1870. In A. Brzyski (Ed.), *Partisan canons* (pp. 95–113). Durham, NC: Duke University Press. doi:10.1215/9780822390374-005

Dyer-Witheford, N., & de Peuter, G. (2009). *Games of empire: Global capitalism and video games*. Minneapolis, MN: University of Minnesota Press.

EA. (2015). *MASS EFFECT^{TM}: ANDROMEDA official E3 2015 announce trailer*. Retrieved from https://www.youtube.com/watch?v=uG8V9dRqSsw

Eco, U. (2003). Ironie intertextuelle et niveaux de lecture. In *De la littérature* (pp. 269–298). Paris, France: Grasset et Fasquelle.

Edge editors. (2005). Scare tactics: Exploring the bloody battleground between fear and frustration. *Edge, 149*, 69–73.

Egenfeldt-Nielsen, S., Smith, J. H., & Tosca, S. P. (2008). *Understanding video games: The essential introduction*. New York, NY: Routledge.

Egliston, B. (2015). Playing across media: Exploring transtextuality in competitive games and eSports. In *Proceedings of DiGRA 2015: Diversity of play: Games – cultures – identities*. Retrieved from http://www.digra.org/digital-library/publications/playing-across-media-exploring-transtextuality-in-competitive-games-and-esports/

Elliott, A. B. R. (Ed.). (2014). *The return of the epic film: Genre, aesthetics and history in the twenty-first century*. Edinburgh, UK: Edinburgh University Press. doi:10.3366/edinburgh/9780748684021.001.0001

Ensslin, A. (2012). *The language of gaming*. Houndmills, UK: Palgrave Macmillan.

Entertainment Software Association. (2014). *Game player data*. Retrieved June 23, 2014, from http://www.theesa.com/wp-content/uploads/2014/10/ESA_EF_2014.pdf

ESA, & AIAS. (2015). *Into the pixel*. Retrieved June 4, 2015, from www.intothepixel.com

Escape from Monkey Island . (2000) Developer and Publisher: LucasArts Entertainment Company

Eskelinen, M. (2001). The gaming situation. *Game Studies, 1*(1). Retrieved April 17, 2008, from http://www.gamestudies.org/0101/eskelinen/

Everett, G. (Producer), & Leonard, B. (Director). (1992). *The lawnmower man* [Motion Picture]. United States. New Line Cinema.

Evoland. (2013). Bordeaux: Shiro Games. [Digital game]

Fairclough, N. (1993). *Discourse and social change*. Cambridge, MA: Polity Press.

Fairclough, N. (2003). *Analysing discourse: Textual analysis for social research*. London, UK: Routledge.

Fancher, H., & Peoples, D. (1981). *Blade runner screenplay*. Retrieved from http://www.dailyscript.com/scripthttp://www.dailyscript.com/scripts/blade-runner_shooting.htmls/blade-runner_shooting.html

Felski, R. (2011). Critique and the hermeneutics of suspicion. *M/C Journal, 15*(1). Retrieved from http://journal.media-culture.org.au/index.php/mcjournal/article/viewArticle/431

Ferrari, S. (2010). *The judgement of procedural rhetoric.* (Doctoral Dissertation). Retrieved from Georgia Tech SMART-ech database. Retrieved from http://hdl.handle.net/1853/33915

Ferri, G. (2007). Narrating machines and interactive matrices, a semiotic common ground for game studies. In *Proceedings of DiGRA 2007.* Retrieved February 18, 2015, from http://www.digra.org/wp-content/uploads/digital-library/07311.02554.pdf

Fiske, J. (2011). *Television culture* (2nd ed.). London, UK: Routledge.

Foith, M. (2013). Virtually witness augmentation now: Video games and the future of human enhancement. *M/C Journal, 16*(6). Retrieved from http://journal.media-culture.org.au/index.php/mcjournal/article/viewArticle/729

Foster, A. (2013, June 17). Alternate reality game puzzle design. *Gamasutra.* Retrieved August 20, 2014, from http://gamasutra.com/blogs/AdamFoster/20130617/194321/Alternate_Reality_Game_puzzle_design.php

Foucault, M. (2003). *The birth of the clinic: An archaeology of medical perception* (A. M. Sheridan, Trans.). London, UK: Routledge.

Francis, T. (2015). *Deus Ex: Human Revolution* review. *PC Gamer.* Retrieved June 15, 2015, from http://www.pcgamer.com//deus-ex-human-revolution-review/

Franco, C. P. (2013). *Homepage.* Retrieved from http://www.naturemage.com

Franco, C. P. (2014). The muddle earth journey: Brand consistency and cross-media intertextuality in game adaptation. In R. Pearson & A. N. Smith (Eds.), *Storytelling in the media convergence age: Exploring screen narratives* (pp. 40–53). London, UK: Palgrave Macmillan. doi:10.1057/9781137388155.0008

Frasca, G. (2003). *Ludologists love stories, too: Notes from a debate that never took place.* DIGRA Conference 2003. Retrieved April 2, 2015, from http://www.ludology.org/articles/frasca_levelUP2003.pdf

Frasca, G. (n.d.). *Ludology meets narratology: Similitude and differences between (video)games and narrative.* Retrieved November 18, 2015, from http://web.cfa.arizona.edu/art435a/readings/frasca_ludology.pdf

Frasca, G. (2003). Simulation versus narrative: Introduction to Ludology. In M. J. P. Wolf & B. Perron (Eds.), *The video game theory reader* (pp. 221–235). New York, NY: Routledge.

Freeman, M. (2014). Advertising the yellow brick road: Historicizing the industrial emergence of transmedia storytelling. *International Journal of Communication,* (8): 2362–2381.

Freire, P. (2000). *Pedagogy of the oppressed.* London, UK: Bloomsbury Publishing.

Freud, S. (2001). The "uncanny" (J. Strachey, A. Strachey, & A. Tyson, Trans.). In J. Strachey (Ed.), The standard edition of the complete psychological works of Sigmund Freud, vol. 17: An infantile neurosis and other works (pp. 217–256). London, UK: Vintage.

Frye, N. (2000). *Anatomy of criticism: Four essays.* Princeton, NJ: Princeton University Press.

Fuchs, M. (2012). Hauntings: Uncanny doubling in *Alan Wake* and *Supernatural. Textus: English Studies in Italy, 25*(3), 63–74.

Fuchs, M. (2013). "A horror story that came true": Metalepsis and the horrors of ontological uncertainty in *Alan Wake. Monsters & the Monstrous, 3*(1), 95–107.

Gadamer, H.-G. (2004). *Truth and method* (J. Weinsheimer & D. G. Marshall, Trans.). London, UK: Continuum.

Gaines, J. M. (2002). Of cabbages and authors. In J. M. Bean & D. Negra (Eds.), *Feminist reader in early cinema* (pp. 88–118). Durham, NC: Duke University Press. doi:10.1215/9780822383840-004

Galloway, A. R. (2012). *The interface effect*. Cambridge, UK: Polity.

García Canclini, N. (2000). *Culturas híbridas: Estrategias para entrar y salir de la modernidad*. Bogotá, D.C., Colombia: Grijalbo.

Gaudreault, A., & Marion, P. (2002). The cinema as a model for the genealogy of media. *Convergence*, *8*(4), 12–18.

Gearbox Software, & 2K Australia. (2014). *Borderlands: The pre-sequel!* [PS3, Xbox 360, PC]. 2K Games.

Gearbox Software. (2009). *Borderlands* [PS3, Xbox 360, PC]. 2K Games.

Gearbox Software. (2012a). *Borderlands 2* [PS3, Xbox 360, PC]. 2K Games.

Gearbox Software. (2012b). *Borderlands Legends* [IOS]. 2K Games.

Gearbox Software. (2013). *Aliens: Colonial marines* [PC, PS3, Xbox 360]. Sega.

Gee, J. P. (2004). Learning by design: Games as learning machines. *Interactive Educational Multimedia*, (8), 15-23.

Gee, J. (2003). *What videogames have to teach us about learning and literacy*. New York, NY: Palgrave Macmillan.

Gee, J. (2005). Why videogames are good for your soul: Pleasure and learning. *E-learning*, *2*(1), 5–16. doi:10.2304/elea.2005.2.1.5

Gee, J. P. (2003). *What video games have to teach us about learning and literacy*. New York, NY: Palgrave MacMillan.

Gee, J. P. (2007). *Good video games+ good learning: Collected essays on video games, learning, and literacy*. New York, NY: P. Lang.

Genette, G. (1992). The architext: An introduction. Vol. 31. of Quantum books. Berkley, CA: University of California Press.

Genette, G. (1979). *Introduction à l'architexte*. Paris, France: Seuil.

Genette, G. (1982). *Palimpsestes: La littérature au second degré*. Paris, France: Seuil.

Genette, G. (1987). *Seuils*. Paris, France: Editions du Seuil.

Genette, G. (1990). *Narrative discourse: an essay in method (1. publ., 4. print)*. Ithaca: Cornell University Press.

Genette, G. (1997). *Palimpsests: Literature in the second degree*. Lincoln, NE: University of Nebraska Press.

Genette, G. (1997). *Paratexts: Thresholds of interpretation*. Cambridge, MA: Cambridge University Press. doi:10.1017/CBO9780511549373

Genette, G. (1997a). *Palimpsests: Literature in the second degree* (C. Newman & C. Doubinsky, Trans.). Lincoln, NE: U of Nebraska Press.

Genette, G. (1997c). *The work of art*. Ithaca, NY: Cornell University Press.

Genette, G. (2004). *Métalepses, de la figure à la fiction*. Paris, France: Seuil.

Genette, G., & Lewin, J. (1983). *Narrative discourse: An essay in method*. Cornel University Press.

Genette, G., & Maclean, M. (1991). Introduction to the paratext. *New Literary History*, *22*(2), 261–272. doi:10.2307/469037

Gerosa, M. (2008). Architectures émotionnelles et douloureuses. *Médiamorphoses*, (22), 47-54.

Giard, A. (2006). *Limaginaire érotique japonais*. Paris, France: Albin Michel.

Gibbons, W. (2011). Wrap your troubles in dreams: Popular music, narrative, and dystopia in *Bioshock. Game Studies, 11*(3). Retrieved October 10, 2012, from http://gamestudies.org/1103/articles/gibbons

Gibbons, W. (2011). *Wrap your troubles in dreams: Popular music, narrative, and dystopia in BioShock. Games studies: The International Journal of Computer Game Research, 11(3).*

Gibson, A. (1996). *Towards a postmodern theory of narrative.* Edinburgh, UK: Edinburgh University Press.

Giddings, S., & Kennedy, H. W. (2006). Digital games as new media. In J. Bryce & J. Rutter (Eds.), *Understanding digital games* (pp. 129–147). London, UK: SAGE Publications. doi:10.4135/9781446211397.n8

Gladwell, M. (2008). *Outliers.* London, UK: Penguin Books.

GMGC. (2015). *Global mobile game industry white book.* Shanghai, China: NewZoo.

Goffman, E. (1986). Frame analysis: An essay on the organization of experience (Northeastern University Press ed.). Boston, MA: Northeastern University Press.

Goldberg, H. (2011). *All your base are belong to us: How fifty years of videogames conquered pop culture.* New York, NY: Three Rivers Press.

Gómez Bolaños, R. (1972). *El chavo del ocho.* Mexico: Televisa S.A. de C.V.

Gómez Bolaños, R. (2006). *El chavo animado.* Mexico: Televisa S.A. de C.V.

Good, O. S. (2015). *Metal Gear Solid* wasn't sued over *Escape from New York* ties because Kojima's 'a nice guy'. *Polygon, 2015.* Retrieved from http://www.polygon.com/2015/10/28/9625556/metal-gear-solid-escape-from-new-york-lawsuit-kojima-john-carpenter

Goodbrey, D. M. (2012). *A duck has an adventure.* Retrieved June 4, 2015, from http://www.kongregate.com/games/Stillmerlin/a-duck-has-an-adventure

Goodbrey, D. M. (2014b). *The empty kingdom.* Retrieved June 4, 2015, from http://www.kongregate.com/games/Stillmerlin/the-empty-kingdom

Goodbrey, D. M. (2014a). Game comics: An analysis of an emergent hybrid form. *Journal of Graphic Novels & Comics, 6*(1), 3–14. doi:10.1080/21504857.2014.943411

Google Play. (2015). Kingdom rush. *Google Play.* Retrieved June 26, 2015, from https://play.google.com/store/apps/details?id=com.ironhidegames.android.kingdomrush&hl=es_419

Grace, O. (2013). *Should we give indie games a break?* Retrieved June 10, 2015, from http://www.gamebreaker.tv/video/chat-bubble/should-we-give-indie-games-a-break/

Grainge, P. (2011). *Ephemeral media: Transitory screen culture from television to YouTube.* Basingstoke, UK: Palgrave Macmillan.

Gray, J. (2006). *Watching with The Simpsons: Television, parody, and intertextuality.* New York, NY: Routledge.

Gray, J. (2010). *Show sold separately: Promos, spoilers, and other media paratexts.* New York, NY; London, UK: New York University Press.

Green, R. (2013). *Why games need grace.* Retrieved June 24, 2015, from http://gamechurch.com/why-games-need-grace/

Green, R., & Green, A. (2014). *That dragon, cancer.*

Greenspan, A. (2007). *Age of turbulence*. New York, NY: Penguin.

Greenwald, T. (2007, September 26). *Q&A: Ridley Scott has finally created the Blade Runner he always imagined*. Retrieved January 14, 2015, from http://archive.wired.com/entertainment/hollywood/magazine/15-10/ff_bladerunner?currentPage=all

Greimas, A. J. (1983). *Structural semantics: An attempt at a method*. Lincoln, NE; London, UK: University of Nebraska Press. (Original work published 1966)

Grésillon, A. M. D., & Maingueneau, D. (1984). Polyphonie, proverbe et détournement, ou un proverbe peut en cacher un autre. *Langages, 19*(73), 112–125. doi:10.3406/lgge.1984.1168

Griffiths, M. (2002). The educational benefits of videogames. *Education for Health, 20*(3), 47–51.

Grodal, T. (2000). Video games and the pleasure of control. In D. Zillmann & P. Vorderer (Eds.), *Media entertainment: The psychology of its appeal* (pp. 197–213). Mahwah, NJ: Lawrence Erlbaum.

Gros, B. (2007). Digital games in education: The design of games-based learning environments. *Journal of Research on Technology in Education, 40*(1), 23–38. doi:10.1080/15391523.2007.10782494

Gross, M., & McGoey, L. (Eds.). (2015). *Routledge international handbook of ignorance studies*. New York, NY: Routledge.

Guins, R. (2014). *Game after: A cultural study of video game afterlife*. Cambridge, MA: The MIT Press.

Gumbrecht, H. U. (2003). Why intermediality – if at all?, *Intermédialités, (2)*, 173-178.

Gunder, A. (2004). Harry Ludens: *Harry Potter and the Philosopher's Stone* as a novel and computer game. *Human IT, 7*(2), 1–137.

Halberstam, J. (1995). *Skin shows: Gothic horror and the technology of monsters*. Durham, NC: Duke University Press.

Harper, T. (2014). *The culture of digital fighting games: Performance and practice*. New York, NY: Routledge.

Harrigan, P., & Wardrip-Fruin, N. (2010). *Second person: Role-playing and story in games and playable media*. Boston, MA: The MIT Press.

Harrigan, P., & Wardrip-Fruin, N. (Eds.). (2009). *Third person: Authoring and exploring vast narratives*. Cambridge, MA: The MIT Press.

Harvey, D. (1989). *The condition of postmodernity: An enquiry into the origins of cultural change*. Oxford, UK: Blackwell.

Havelock, E. A. (1963). *Preface to Plato*. Oxford, UK: Blackwell.

Havířová, T. (2007). *Fantasy as a popular genre in the works of J. R. R. Tolkien and J. K. Rowling*. (Master Thesis). Masaryk University. Retrieved November 20, 2015 from https://is.muni.cz/th/74471/ff_m/m.a.pdf

Heller, A. (2009). *Ayn Rand and the world she made*. New York, NY: Doubleday.

Hendrickson, N., Wachowski, A., Wachowski, L., Boren, B., Caponi, E. J., Chadwick, P., (2005). *The matrix online* [Windows].

Henn, S. (2014). *When women stopped coding*. Retrieved June 4, 2015, from http://www.npr.org/sections/money/2014/10/21/357629765/when-women-stopped-coding

Hetherington, K. (1997). *The badlands of modernity: Heterotopia and social ordering*. London, UK: Routledge. doi:10.4324/9780203428870

Higgins, D. (1967). Statement on intermedia. In W. Vostell (Ed.), *Dé-coll/age (décollage), 6*. Frankfurt, Germany: Typos Verlag/Something Else Press.

Hjorth, L. (2009). Playing the gender game: The performance of Japan, gender and gaming via Melbourne female cosplayers. In L. Hjorth & D. Chan (Eds.), *Gaming cultures and place in the Asia-Pacific region* (pp. 273–288). London, UK: Routledge.

Hofmeier, R. (2011). *Cart life*.

Homuda-wake (Ojin). (1994). The starting point of Yamato Wa. In *Peakche of Korea and the origin of Yamato Japan* (pp. 45–51). Seoul, South Korea: Kudara International.

Hopper, T., & Sanford, K. (2010). Occasioning moments in the game-as-teacher concept: Complexity thinking applied to TGfU and video gaming. In J. Bulter & L. Griffin (Eds.), *More teaching games for understanding: Moving globally* (pp. 121–138). Champaign, IL: Human Kinetics.

Huizinga, J. (1955). *Homo ludens: A study of the play-element in culture*. Boston, MA: Beacon Press.

Hutcheon, L. (1984). *Narcissistic narrative: The metafictional paradox*. London, UK; New York, NY: Routledge.

Hutcheon, L. (1989). *The politics of postmodernism*. London, UK: Routledge. doi:10.4324/9780203426050

Hutcheon, L. (2006). *A theory of adaptation*. New York: Routledge.

Iacovides, I., McAndrew, P., Scanlon, E., & Aczel, J. (2014). The gaming involvement and informal learning framework. [abstract]. *Simulation & Gaming, 45*(4-5), 611–626. doi:10.1177/1046878114554191

id Software. (1993). *Doom*. New York, NY: GT Interactive.

IG. (2012). *What's wrong with the IGF*. Retrieved June 4, 2015, from https://therottingcartridge.wordpress.com/2012/02/22/whats-wrong-with-the-igf/

Interplay Entertainment [PC]. (1997). *Fallout*. Interplay Entertainment.

Irrational Games. (2007). *BioShock*, [Videogame] [Disc] [Microsoft Windows] 2K Games and Feral Interactive.

Irrational Games. (2013). *BioShock infinite* [PC, PS3, Xbox 360]. 2K Games.

Ito, M. (2006). *A draft of a position paper for the Girls n games workshop and conference*. University of California, Los Angeles. Retrieved December 12, 2015 from http://www.itofisher.com/mito/ito.girlsgames.pdf

Ivory, J. D., & Kalyanaraman, S. (2009). Videogames make people violent—Well, maybe not that game: Effects of content and person abstraction on perceptions of violent videogames' effects and support of censorship. *Communication Reports, 22*(1), 1–12. doi:10.1080/08934210902798536

Iwabuchi, K. (2002). *Recentering globalization: Popular culture and Japanese transnationalism*. Durham, DC: Duke University Press. doi:10.1215/9780822384083

Jackall, R. (2010). Moral mazes: The world of corporate managers (20th anniversary ed.). Oxford, UK: Oxford University Press.

Jackson, P. (2003). *The lord of the rings: The return of the king*. USA and New Zealand/Aotearoa: New Line Cinema.

Jakobson, R. (1987). On linguistic aspects of translation. In R. Jakobson (Ed.), *Language in literature*. The Jakobson Trust.

Jameson, F. (1991). *Postmodernism, or, the cultural logic of late capitalism*. Durham, NC: Duke University Press.

Jameson, F. (2005). *Archaeologies of the future: The desire called utopia and other science fictions.* New York, NY: Verso.

Jansz, J. (2005). The emotional appeal of violent video games for adolescent males. *Communication Theory, 15*(3), 219–241. doi:10.1111/j.1468-2885.2005.tb00334.x

Jara, D. (2013). A closer look at the (rule-) books: Framings and paratexts in tabletop role-playing games. *International Journal of Role-Playing*, (4).

Jara, D. (2013). A closer look at the (rule-)books: Framing and paratexts in tabletop role-playing games. *International Journal of Role-Playing, 4*, 39–54.

Jauss, H. R. (1982). *Towards an aesthetic of reception.* Minneapolis, MN: University of Minnesota Press.

Jauss, H. R., & Benzinger, E. (1970). Literary history as a challenge to literary theory. *New Literary History, 2*(1), 7–37. doi:10.2307/468585

Jayisgames. (2011). Game of the year. *Jayisgames.* Retrieved June 26, 2015, from http://jayisgames.com/best-of/2011/game-of-the-year/

Jenkins, H. (2003). *Transmedia storytelling: Moving characters from books to films to video games can make.* Retrieved June 3, 2015, from http://www.technologyreview.com/news/401760/transmedia-storytelling/

Jenkins, H. (2010). *Reality bytes: Eight myths about videogames debunked.* Retrieved 14th September, 2010, from http://www.pbs.org/kcts/videogamerevolution/impact/myths.html

Jenkins, H. (1992). *Textual poachers: Television fans and participatory culture.* New York, NY: Routledge.

Jenkins, H. (2004). Game design as narrative architecture. In N. Wardrip-Fruin & P. Harrigan (Eds.), *First person: New media as story, performance, and game* (pp. 118–130). Cambridge, MA: The MIT Press.

Jenkins, H. (2006). *Convergence culture: Where old and new media collide.* New York, NY: New York University Press.

Jenkins, H. (2006). *Convergence Culture: Where old and new media collide.* New York, NY; London, UK: New York University Press.

Jenkins, H., Ford, S., & Green, J. (2013). *Spreadable media: Creating value and meaning in a networked culture.* New York, NY: NYU Press.

Jerz, D. G. (2007). Somewhere nearby is *Colossal Cave*: Examining Will Crowther's original adventure in code and in Kentucky. *Digital Humanities Quarterly, 1*(2). Retrieved from http://www.digitalhumanities.org/dhq/vol/001/2/000009/000009.html

Johns, G., Snyder, Z., Snyder, D., & Wilson, C. (Producers), & Ayer, D. (Director). (2016). *Suicide squad.* [Motion Picture] Warner Bros.

Johnson, D., & Wiles, J. (2003). Effective affective user interface design in games. *Ergonomics, 46*(13-14), 1332–1345. doi:10.1080/00140130310001610865 PMID:14612323

Johnson, R. (1986). What is cultural studies anyway? *Social Text*, (16): 38–80. doi:10.2307/466285

Johnston, K. M. (2008). The coolest way to watch movie trailers in the world: Trailers in the digital age. *Convergence (London), 14*(2), 145–160. doi:10.1177/1354856507087946

Johnston, K. M. (2009). *Coming soon: Film trailers and the selling of Hollywood technology.* Jefferson, NC: McFarland.

Jonah Maiava. (n.d.). Retrieved July 21, 2015, from http://tombraider.wikia.com/wiki/Jonah_Maiava

Jones, S. E. (2008). *The meaning of video games: Gaming and textual strategies*. London, UK: Routledge.

Juul, J. (2001). Games telling stories? A brief note on games and narratives. *Game Studies, 1*(1). Retrieved from http://www.gamestudies.org/0101/juul-gts/

Juul, J. (2005). *Half-real*. Cambridge, MA: The MIT Press.

Juul, J. (2014). High-tech low-tech authenticity: The creation of independent style at the independent games festival. In *Proceedings of the 9th International Conference on the Foundations of Digital Games*. Retrieved from http://www.jesperjuul.net/text/independentstyle/

Juul, J. (2005). *Half-real: Video games between real rules and fictional worlds*. Cambridge, MA: The MIT Press.

Kafai, Y. B. (2006). Playing and making games for learning instructionist and constructionist perspectives for game studies. *Games and Culture, 1*(1), 36–40. doi:10.1177/1555412005281767

Kahne, J., Middaugh, E., & Evans, C. (2009). *The civic potential of videogames, Digital Mediapp*. Available from http://www.macfound.org/atf/cf/%7Bb0386ce3-8b29-4162-8098-e466fb856794%7D/CIVIC_POTENTIAL_VIDEO_GAMES.PDF

Kaklamanidou, B., & Katsaridou, M. (2013). Silent Hill: Adapting a video game. Literature. *Film Quarterly, 41*(1), 266–277.

Kapp, K. M. (2012). *The gamification of learning and instruction: Game-based methods and strategies for training and education*. San Francisco, CA: Pfeiffer.

Katsaridou, M. (forthcoming). Adaptation of video games into films: The adventures of the narrative. In *12th World Congress of Semiotics proceedings*. Berlin, Germany: De Gruyter Mouton.

Katsaridou, M. (forthcoming). From literature texts to video games: Recent adaptations of *Sherlock Holmes. Animation Journal*.

Kaveney, R. (2005). *From Alien to The Matrix: Reading science fiction film*. London, UK: I.B. Tauris & Company, Limited.

KCEJ [PS]. (1998). *Metal Gear Solid*. Konami.

Kent, S. L. (2001). *The ultimate history of video games: From Pong to Pokémon and beyond - the story behind the craze that touched our lives and changed the world*. New York, NY: Three Rivers Press.

Kernan, L. (2004). *Coming attractions: Reading American movie trailers* (1st ed.). Austin, TX: University of Texas Press.

Khine, M. S. (Ed.). (2011). *Learning to play: Exploring the future of education with video games*. New York, NY: Peter Lang.

Kijima, Y. (2007). The fighting gamer otaku community : What are they "fighting" about? In M. Ito, D. Okabe, & T. Tsuji (Eds.), *Fandom unbound: Otaku culture in a connected world* (pp. 249–274). New Haven, CT: Yale University Press.

Kinder, M. (1991). *Playing with power in movies, television, and video games: From Muppet Babies to Teenage Mutant Ninja Turtles*. Berkeley, CA: University of California Press.

King, G., & Krzywinska, T. (2002). *Screenplay: Cinema/videogames/interfaces*. New York, NY: Wallflower Press.

Kirkland, E. (2006). Alessa unbound: The monstrous daughter of *Silent Hill* (2006). In S. Ni Fhlainn (Ed.), *Dark reflections, monstrous reflections: Essays on the monster in culture*. Inter-Disciplinary Press. Ebook. Retrieved January 18, 2016 from http://www.inter-disciplinary.net/publishing/?s=Dark+Reflections%2C+Monstrous+Reflections%3A+Essays+on+the+Monster+in+Culture

Kirkland, E. (2007). The self-reflexive funhouse of *Silent Hill*. *Convergence (London)*, *13*(4), 403–415. doi:10.1177/1354856507081964

Kirkland, E. (2009). *Resident Evil*'s typewriter: Horror videogames and their media. *Games and Culture*, *4*(2), 115–126. doi:10.1177/1555412008325483

Klastrup, L., & Tosca, S. (2013). *Transmedial worlds: Rethinking cyberworld design*. Retrieved May 17, 2015, from http://www.itu.dk/people/klastrup/klastruptosca_transworlds.pdf

Klevjer, R. (2014). Cut-scenes. In M. J. P. Wolf & B. Perron (Eds.), *The Routledge companion to video game studies* (pp. 301–309). New York, NY: Routledge.

Kojima, H. (1998). *Metal gear solid*. Action, Drama, Sci-Fi. [Playstation]

Kollar, P. (2013). *Batman: Arkham origins review: Knightfall*. Retrieved June 1, 2015, from http://www.polygon.com/2013/10/25/5026574/batman-arkham-origins-review-knightfall

Kraidy, M. M. (2010). Hybridity in cultural globalization. In D. K. Thussu (Ed.), *International communication: A reader* (pp. 434–451). London, UK: Routledge.

Krämer, S. (2003). Erfüllen medien eine konstitutionsleistung? Thesen über die rolle medientheoretischer erwägungen beim philosophieren. In S. Münker, A. Roesler, & M. Sandbothe (Eds.), *Medienphilosophie. Beiträge zur klärung eines begriffs* (pp. 78–90). Frankfurt am Main, Germany: Fischer.

Kress, G. (2000). Text as the punctuation of semiosis: Pulling at some of the threads. In U. H. Meinhof & J. M. Smith (Eds.), *Intertextuality and the media: From genre to everyday life* (pp. 132–154). Manchester, UK: Manchester University Press.

Kress, G. (2009). *Multimodality: A social semiotic approach to contemporary communication*. London, UK: Routledge.

Kristeva, J. (1974). *La révolution du langage poétique: Lavant-garde à la fin du XIXe siècle, Lautréamont et Mallarmé*. Paris, France: Seuil.

Kristeva, J. (1980). *Desire in language: A semiotic approach to literature and art*. New York, NY: Columbia University Press.

Kristeva, J. (1984). *Revolution in poetic language* (M. Waller, Trans.). New York, NY: Columbia University Press.

Kristeva, J. (1985). *Sēmeiōtikē: Recherches pour une sémanalyse*. Paris, France: Seuil.

Kristeva, J. (1986). *The Kristeva reader*. New York, NY: Columbia University Press.

Kristeva, J. (1986a). Revolution in poetic language. In T. Moi (Ed.), *The Kristeva reader* (M. Waller, Trans.). (pp. 89–136). New York, NY: Columbia University Press.

Kristeva, J. (1986b). The system and the speaking subject. In T. Moi (Ed.), *The Kristeva reader* (A. Jardine, T. Gora, & L. S. Roudiez, Trans.). (pp. 24–33). New York, NY: Columbia University Press.

Krzywinska, T. (2003). Playing Buffy: Remediation, occulted meta-game-physics and the dynamics of agency in the videogame version of *Buffy the Vampire Slayer*. *Slayage: The Online International Journal of Buffy Studies*, (8). Retrieved from http://www.slayage.tv/essays/slayage8/Krzywinska.htm

Krzywinska, T. (2002). Hand-on horror. In G. King & T. Krzywinskia (Eds.), *ScreenPlay: Cinema/videogames/interfaces* (pp. 206–223). London, UK: Wallflower.

Krzywinska, T. (2006). Blood scythes, festivals, quests, and backstories: World creation and rhetorics of myth in *World of warcraft*. *Games and Culture*, *4*(1), 383–396.

Krzywinska, T. (2008). World creation and lore: *World of Warcraft* as rich text. In H. G. Corneliussen & J. W. Rettberg (Eds.), *Digital culture, play, and identity: A World of Warcraft reader* (pp. 123–142). Cambridge, MA: The MIT Press.

Krzywinska, T. (2008). Zombies in gamespace: Form, context, and meaning in zombie-based videogames. In S. McIntosh & M. Leverette (Eds.), *Zombie culture: Autopsies of the living dead* (pp. 153–168). Lanham, MD: Scarecrow Press.

Krzywinska, T. (2014). Digital games and the American Gothic: Investigating Gothic game grammar. In C. L. Crow (Ed.), *A companion to the American gothic* (pp. 503–515). Malden, MA: Wiley–Blackwell.

Krzywinska, T., MacCallum-Stewart, E., & Parsler, J. (2011). *Ringbearers: The Lord of the rings online as intertextual narrative.* Manchester, UK: Manchester University Press.

Kubo, A. (Producer) & Oshii, M. (Director). (2001). *Avalon* [Motion picture]. Poland: Miramax.

Kucan, J. D., Dick, P. K. (novel), Fancher, H., Kucan, J. D., Leary, D., Peoples, D. W., & Yorkin, D. (1997). *Blade runner* [Windows].

Kuchera, B. (2012). *Dys4ia tackles gender politics, sense of self, and personal growth… on Newgrounds.* Retrieved June 24, 2015, from http://penny-arcade.com/report/article/dys4ia-tackles-gender-politics-sense-of-self-and-personal-growth-on-newg

Kuchera, B. (2015, November 17). *Dragon Age: Inquisition gets a chill-inducing launch trailer, come watch!* Retrieved June 30, 2015, from http://www.polygon.com/2014/11/17/7236631/dragon-age-inquisition-launch-trailer

Kuipers, G., & De Kloet, J. (2008). Global flows and local identifications? *The Lord of the Rings* and the cross-national reception of characters and genres. In M. Barker & E. Mathijs (Eds.), *Watching The Lord of the Rings. Tolkien's world audiences* (pp. 131–148). New York, NY: Peter Lang.

Kushner, D. (Producer), & Lisberger, S. (Director). (1982). *Tron* [Motion picture]. United States: Buena Vista Pictures.

Kushner, D. (2004). *Masters of doom.* New York: Random House.

La Pastina, A. C., Rego, C. M., & Straubhaar, J. D. (2003). The centrality of telenovelas in Latin America's everyday life: Past tendencies, current knowledge, and future research. *Global Media Journal, 2*(2), 1–15. Retrieved from http://www2.fiu.edu/~surisc/centrality of telenovelas.pdf

La Pastina, A. C., & Straubhaar, J. D. (2005). Multiple proximities between television genres and audiences: The schism between telenovelas' global distribution and local consumption. *International Communication Gazette, 67*(3), 271–288. doi:10.1177/0016549205052231

Lancaster, K. (2004). Lara Croft: The ultimate young adventure girl or the unending media desire for models, sex, and fantasy. *Performing Arts Journal, 78,* 87–97.

Lang, D. J. (2015). *Review: An epic final flight for Batman in Arkham Knight.* Retrieved July 1, 2015, from http://www.salon.com/2015/06/23/review_an_epic_final_flight_for_batman_in_arkham_knight/

Lara Croft (Rise Timeline). (n.d.). Retrieved July 18, 2015, from http://tombraider.wikia.com/wiki/Lara_Croft_(Rise_Timeline)

Latour, B. (2004). Why has critique run out of steam? From matters of fact to matters of concern. *Critical Inquiry, 30*(Winter), 225–248. doi:10.1086/421123

Le Calvez, E. (1997). La charogne de *Bouvard et Pécuchet*: Génétique du paragramme. In E. Le Calvez & M.-C. Canova-Green (Eds.), *Texte(s) et intertexte(s)* (pp. 233–261). Amsterdam, Netherland; Atlanta, GA: Rodopi.

Le Guin, U. K., & Attebery, B. (Eds.). (1993). *The Norton book of science fiction: North American science fiction, 1960-1990*. New York, NY: W.W. Norton.

League of Legends . (2009) Developer and Publisher: Riot Games. Retrieved from: http://na.leagueoflegends.com

Ledsham, J. (2013). *Drawings based on Nature Mage series*. Retrieved from http://www.naturemage.com

Lee, B. (2013). *"Cart life": How Richard Hofmeier game became a success story*. Retrieved June 4, 2015, from http://www.digitalspy.com/gaming/news/a472874/cart-life-how-richard-hofmeier-game-became-a-success-story.html#~pgAxbf8UaVxI33

Lessig, L. (2009). *Remix: Making art and commerce thrive in the hybrid economy*. New York, NY: Penguin Books.

LeTendre, B. (2009). *Paul Dini talks Batman: Arkham Asylum*. Retrieved June 1, 2015, from http://www.comicbookresources.com/?page=article&id=20931

Lévi-Strauss, C. (1990). *The raw and the cooked*. Chicago, IL: University of Chicago Press.

Lizardi, R. (2014). *BioShock*: Complex and alternate histories. *Games studies: The International Journal of Computer Game Research, 14*(1). Retrieved from http://gamestudies.org/1401/articles/lizardi

Llanos, S., & Jørgensen, K. (2011*). Do players prefer integrated user interfaces? A qualitative study of game UI design issues*. Paper presented at DiGRA 2011 Conference: Think Design Play, University of Utrecht, Netherlands. Retrieved August 24, 2014, from http://www.digra.org/wp-content/uploads/digital-library/11313.34398.pdf

Lord of the Rings: The Fellowship of the Ring . (2002) Developer: Black Label Games; Publisher: Vivendi Universal Games.

Lord of the Rings: The Return of the King . (2004). Developer: EA Games; Publisher: Electronic Arts.

Lord of the Rings: The Two Towers . (2004). Developer: EA Games; Publisher: Electronic Arts.

Lotman, Y. (1974). Primary and secondary communication-modeling systems. In Materials of the all union symposium on secondary modeling systems, 1(5), 224-228.

Lotman, Y. (1992). *La semiosfera. L'asimmetria e il dialogo nelle strutture pensanti*. Venezia, Italy: Marsilio.

Lotman, Y. (2004). *Culture and explosion*. Berlin, Germany: Mouton de Gruyter. (Original work published 1992)

Lotman, Y. (2011). The place of art among other modelling systems. *Sing System Studies, 39*(2/4), 251–270.

Love, M. C. (2010). Not-so-sacred quests: Religion, intertextuality and ethics in video games. *Religious Studies and Theology, 29*(2), 191–213.

Lugo, J., Sampson, T., & Lossada, M. (2002). Latin America's new cultural industries still play old games: From the banana republic to *Donkey Kong. Game Studies, 2*(2). Retrieved from http://www.gamestudies.org/0202/lugo/

Lukács, G. (1971). *The theory of the novel: A historico-philosophical essay on the forms of great epic literature*. Cambridge, MA: The MIT Press.

Lunenfeld, P. (Ed.). (2000). *The digital dialectic: New essays on new media*. Boston, MA: The MIT Press.

MacGregor-Scott, P. (Producer), & Schumacher, J. (Director). (1997). *Batman & Robin.* [Motion picture] Warner Bros.

Mactavish, A. (2002). Technological pleasure: The performance and narrative of technology in *Half-Life* and other high-tech computer games. In G. King & T. Krzywinska (Eds.), *ScreenPlay : cinema/videogames/interfaces* (pp. 33–49). London: Wallflower Press.

Maiberg, E. (2015). *Batman: Arkham Knight review roundup*. Retrieved June 22, 2015, from http://www.gamespot.com/articles/batman-arkham-knight-review-roundup/1100-6428357/

Maingueneau, D. (1987). *Nouvelles tendances en analyse du discours*. Paris, France: Hachette.

Mallavarapu, S., & Prasad, A. (2006). Facts, fetishes, and the parliament of things: Is there any space for critique? *Social Epistemology*, *20*(2), 185–199. doi:10.1080/02691720600784782

Mallonee, L. C. (2015). *A video game lets you navigate Giorgio de Chirico's surreal cityscapes*. Retrieved June 20, 2015, from http://hyperallergic.com/195863/a-video-game-lets-you-navigate-giorgio-de-chiricos-surreal-cityscapes/

Manovich, L. (2001). *The language of new media*. Cambridge, MA: The MIT Press.

Marion, I. (2011). *Warm bodies*. New York, NY: ATRIA.

Marsh, D. (1999). *The heart of rock & soul: The 1001 greatest singles ever made*. New York, NY: Da Capo Press.

Martin, L. (2013). *Batman: Arkham Origins tops charts, sales half those of Arkham City*. Retrieved June 1, 2015, from http://www.digitalspy.co.uk/gaming/news/a526846/batman-arkham-origins-tops-charts-sales-half-those-of-arkham-city.html#~peyO0GRzxv0823

Mason, J. (2013). Video games as technical communication ecology. *Technical Communication Quarterly*, *22*(3), 219–236. doi:10.1080/10572252.2013.760062

Mason, M. (2008). Complexity theory and the philosophy of education. In M. Masson (Ed.), *Complexity theory and the philosophy of education* (pp. 1–15). Hong Kong, China: Wiley-Blackwell. doi:10.1002/9781444307351.ch1

Mason, M. (2008). What is complexity theory and what are its implications for educational change? In M. Masson (Ed.), *Complexity theory and the philosophy of education* (pp. 32–45). Hong Kong, China: Wiley-Blackwell. doi:10.1002/9781444307351.ch3

Masser, J. (2012). A brief history of kart racing games. *modojo*. Retrieved June 28, 2015, from http://www.modojo.com/features/a_brief_history_of_kart_racing_games

McGonigal, J. (2010). Gaming can make a better world. *Tedcom: TED: Ideas Worth Spreading*.

McGonigal, J. (2011). *Reality is broken: Why games make us better and how they can change the world*. London, UK: Jonathan Cape.

McGuire, K. J. (2013a, April 15). Arte-factual: Ban Chiang pottery (*Tomb raider 2013*). *The Archaeology of Tomb Raider*. Retrieved July 22, 2015, from http://archaeologyoftombraider.com/2013/04/15/arte-factual-tomb-raider-2013-ban-chiang-pottery/

McGuire, K. J. (2013b, July 10). Arte-factual: Kansu burial urn (*Tomb raider 2013*). *The Archaeology of Tomb Raider*. Retrieved July 22, 2015, from http://archaeologyoftombraider.com/2013/07/10/arte-factual-tomb-raider-2013-kansu-burial-urn/

Meggs, P. B. (2011). *Meggs' history of graphic design* (5th ed.). San Francisco, CA: Wiley.

Meier, A. (2015). *Be the Bolshevik wedge in a game inspired by El Lissitzky's 1919 propaganda art*. Retrieved June 20, 2015, from http://hyperallergic.com/198635/be-the-bolshevik-wedge-in-a-game-inspired-by-el-lissitzkys-1919-propaganda-art/

Meinhof, U. H., & Smith, J. (2000). The media and their audience: Intertextuality as paradigm. In U. H. Meinhof & J. M. Smith (Eds.), *Intertextuality and the media: From genre to everyday life* (pp. 1–17). Manchester, UK: Manchester University Press.

Meinhof, U. H., & Van Leeuwen, T. (2000). Viewers' worlds: image, music, text and the Rock "n" roll years. In U. H. Meinhof & J. M. Smith (Eds.), *Intertextuality and the media: From genre to everyday life* (pp. 61–75). Manchester, UK: Manchester University Press.

Melniker, B., Register, S., Tucker, J., & Uslan, M. (Producers), & Oliva, J. & Spaulding, E. (Directors). (2014). *Batman: Assault on Arkham*. [DVD] Warner Bros.

Merriam, S. B. (1991). *Case study research in education: A qualitative approach*. Oxford, UK: Jossey-Bass Publishers.

Migliore, T. (Ed.). (2010). Incidenti ed esplosioni. A. J. Greimas e J. M. Lotman Per una semiotica delle culture. Rome, Italy: Aracne Editrice.

Mikami, S., & Hosoki, M. (1996). *Resident evil*. Action, Horror. [Playstation]

Mikos, L., & Wulff, H. J. (2000). Intertextuality and situative contexts in game shows: the case of *Wheel of fortune*. In U. H. Meinhof & J. M. Smith (Eds.), *Intertextuality and the media: From genre to everyday life* (pp. 98–114). Manchester: Manchester University Press.

Miles, R. (2002). *Gothic writing, 1750–1820: A genealogy* (2nd ed.). Manchester, UK: Manchester University Press.

Miller, G. (2010). *Batman: Arkham asylum (game of the year) review*. Retrieved June 1, 2015, from http://ign.com/articles/2010/05/27/batman-arkham-asylum-game-of-the-year-review

Miller, K. (2008). The accidental carjack: Ethnography, gameworld tourism, and *Grand Theft Auto*. Retrieved from http://gamestudies.org/0801/articles/miller

Milner, R. M. (2013). Contested convergence and the politics of play on GameTrailers.com. *Games and Culture*, 8(1), 3–25. doi:10.1177/1555412013478684

Miyamoto, M. (2001). *Japon, société camisole de force*. Paris, France: Philippe Picquier.

Mogen, D., Sanders, S. P., & Karpinski, J. B. (1993). Introduction. In D. Mogen, S. P. Sanders, & J. B. Karpinski (Eds.), *Frontier gothic: Terror and wonder at the frontier in American literature* (pp. 13–27). Rutherford, NJ: Fairleigh Dickinson University Press.

Möller, I., & Krahé, B. (2009). Exposure to violent videogames and aggression in German adolescents: A longitudinal analysis. *Aggressive Behavior*, 35(1), 75–89. doi:10.1002/ab.20290 PMID:19016226

Monson, M. J. (2012). Race-based fantasy realm essentialism in the *World of warcraft*. *Games and Culture*, 7(1), 48–71. doi:10.1177/1555412012440308

Moretti, F. (1996). *Modern epic: The world-system from Goethe to García Márquez*. London, UK; New York, NY: Verso.

Morin-Simard, A. (2014). *L'interférence musicale au cinéma, à la télévision et dans le jeu vidéo*. (Master's thesis). Université de Montréal, Montréal, Canada. Available from Papyrus: Dépôt institutionnel. (https://papyrus.bib.umontreal.ca/xmlui/handle/1866/11628)

Morrison, G., & McKean, D. (1989). *Arkham asylum: A serious house on serious earth*. New York, NY: DC Comics.

Morris, S. (2002). First-person shooters - A game apparatus. In G. King & T. Krzywinska (Eds.), *ScreenPlay: Cinema/videogames/interfaces* (pp. 81–97). New York, NY: Wallflower Press.

Mou, Y., & Peng, W. (2008). Gender and racial stereotype in popular videogames. In R. Ferdig (Ed.), *Handbook of research on effective electronic gaming in education* (pp. 922–937). Hershey, PA: IGI Global. doi:10.4018/978-1-59904-808-6.ch053

Muddle Earth . (2010). Developer: Dubit Limited; Publisher: BBC [Online]. Retrieved from http://www.muddleearth-world.co.uk

Müller, J. E. (2000). Lintermédialité, une nouvelle approche interdisciplinaire: Perspectives théoriques et pratiques à lexemple de la vision de la télévision. *Cinémas: revue détudes cinématographiques, 10*(2-3).

Muñoz Gil, M. (2009). Dubbing *The Simpsons* in Spain: A case study. In J. Díaz-Cintas (Ed.), *New Trends in Audiovisual Translation* (pp. 142–157). Bristol, UK: Multilingual Matters.

Murray, C. J. (Ed.). (2013). Encyclopedia of the romantic era, 1760–1850. New York, NY: Fitzroy Dearborn.

Murray, J. H. (2001). *Hamlet on the holodeck: The future of narrative in cyberspace.* Cambridge, MA: The MIT Press.

Nagy, G. (1999). Epic as genre. In M. H. Beissinger, J. Tylus, & S. L. Wofford (Eds.), *Epic traditions in the contemporary world: The poetics of community* (pp. 21–32). Berkeley, CA: University of California Press.

Narcisse, E. (2013). *Batman: Arkham Origins: The Kotaku review.* Retrieved June 1, 2015, from http://kotaku.com/batman-arkham-origins-the-kotaku-review-1451970358

Naughty Dog. (2013). *The last of us* [PS3]. Author.

Navarro, V. (2012). I am a gun: The avatar and avatarness in FPS. In G. A. Voorhees, J. Call, & K. Whitlock (Eds.), *Guns, grenades, and grunts: First-person shooter games* (pp. 63–88). New York, NY: Continuum.

Neale, S. (1980). *Genre.* London, UK: British Film Institute.

Nelson, T. H. (1992). *Literary machines: the report on, and of, project Xanadu concerning word processing, electronic publishing, hypertext, thinkertoys, tomorrow's intellectual revolution, and certain other topics including knowledge, education and freedom.* Sausalito, CA: Mindful Press.

Newman, J. (2013). *Videogames* (2nd ed.). London, UK: Routledge.

Newton, D. (Director). (2013). Great American rock anthems: Turn it up to 11. In BBC (Producer).

Night of the living dead. (1968). Dir. George A. Romero, Prod. Image Ten, Laurel Group, Market Square Productions, Off Color Films. USA.

Nintendo R&D1 & Intelligent Systems. (1994). *Super metroid.* Kyoto, Japan: Nintendo.

Nintendo. (1985). *Super mario bros.* Author.

Nishikado, T. (1978). *Space invaders* [Digital Game]. Tokyo, Japan: Taito.

Nitsche, M. (2008). *Video game spaces: Image, play, and structure in 3D worlds.* Cambridge, MA: MIT Press. doi:10.7551/mitpress/9780262141017.001.0001

Nourse, A. E. (2013). *The bladerunner.* Prologue Books.

O'Brien, G. (1993, April22). Horror for pleasure. *The New York Review of Books*, 63–68.

O'Donnell, C. (2011). Games are not convergence: The lost promise of digital production and convergence. *Convergence (London), 17*(3), 271–286. doi:10.1177/1354856511405766

Obsidian Entertainment [PC]. (2010). *Fallout: New Vegas.* Bethesda Softworks.

Olson, S. R. (1999). *Hollywood planet: Global media and the competitive advantage of narrative transparency.* Mahwah, NJ: Lawrence Erlbaum Associates, Inc.

On the tail of replidroids in CRL's Blade Runner. (1986, March). *CRASH*, (26).

Orlati, F. (2015). *Ever yours*. Vincent.

Ormiston, R. (2014). *50 art styles you should know*. New York, NY: Prestel.

Orr, M. (2003). *Intertextuality: Debates and contexts*. Cambridge, UK: Blackwell Pub.

Osberg, D., Biesta, G., & Cilliers, P. (2008). From representation to emergence: Complexity's challenge to the epistemology of schooling. *Educational Philosophy and Theory*, *40*(1), 213–227. doi:10.1111/j.1469-5812.2007.00407.x

Ott, B., & Walter, C. (2000). Intertextuality: Interpretive practice and textual strategy. *Critical Studies in Media Communication*, *17*(4), 429–446. doi:10.1080/15295030009388412

Packer, J. (2010). The battle for Galt's gulch: *BioShock* as critique of Objectivism. *Journal of Gaming and Virtual Worlds*, *2*(3), 209–224. doi:10.1386/jgvw.2.3.209_1

Papathanasis, A. (2015). *The tech arms race in AAA - and why I'm abandoning it*. Retrieved June 3, 2015, from http://gamasutra.com/blogs/AndreasPapathanasis/20150601/244768/The_tech_arms_race_in_AAA__and_why_Im_abandoning_it.php

Parker, T. (2002). *The return of the fellowship of the rings to the two towers*. USA: Braniff Productions.

Parker, T. (2004). *Good times with weapons*. USA: Braniff Productions.

Parker, T. (2006). *Make love, not warcraft*. USA: South Park Digital Studios.

Parker, T. (2013). *Titties and dragons*. USA: South Park Digital Studios.

Parkin, S. (2013). The space invader. *The New Yorker, 2015*. Retrieved from http://www.newyorker.com/tech/elements/the-space-invader

Paul, C. A. (2011). Optimizing play: How theorycraft changes gameplay and design. *Game Studies, 11*(2).

Paul, C. A. (2010). Process, paratexts, and texts: Rhetorical analysis and virtual worlds. *Journal of Virtual Worlds Research*, *3*(1).

Payne, M. T. (2012). Marketing military realism in *Call of Duty 4: Modern Warfare*. *Games and Culture*, *7*(4), 305–327. doi:10.1177/1555412012454220

PBS Digital Studios. (2015, June 9). *Ayn Rand on love and happiness* [Video file]. Retrieved from https://youtu.be/mQVrMzWtqgU

Pêcheux, M. (1969). *Analyse automatique du discours*. Paris, France: Dunod.

Peikoff, L., & Ward, J. (1993). *Objectivism: The philosophy of Ayn Rand*. New York, NY: Meridian.

Perron, B. (2005). *Coming to play at frightening yourself: Welcome to the world of horror video games*. Retrieved September 10, 2015 from http://www.aestheticsofplay.org/perron.php

Perron, B. (2006). Jeu vidéo et émotions. In S. Genvo (Ed.), *Le game design de jeux vidéo*. Approches de l'expression vidéoludique (pp. 347-366). Paris, France: L'Harmattan.

Perron, B. (2003). From gamers to players and gameplayers: The example of interactive movies. In M. J. P. Wolf & B. Perron (Eds.), *The video game theory reader* (pp. 237–258). New York, NY: Routledge.

Perron, B. (2004). *Sign of a threat: The effects of warning systems in survival horror games, first published at COSIGN 2004 14–16 September 2004*. Croatia: University of Split.

Perron, B. (2008). Genre profile: Interactive movies. In M. J. P. Wolf (Ed.), *The video game explosion: A history from Pong to Playstation and beyond* (pp. 127–134). Westport, CT: Greenwood Press.

Perron, B. (2011). *Silent hill: The terror engine*. Michigan, MI: U of Michigan P. doi:10.3998/lvg.11053908.0001.001

Perron, B. (Ed.). (2009). *Horror video games: Essays on the fusion of fear and play*. Jefferson, NC: McFarland.

Perron, B., & Wolf, M. J. P. (Eds.). (2008). *The video game theory reader 2*. New York, NY: Routledge.

Peters, J., & Guber, P. (Producers), & Burton, T. (Director). (1989). *Batman*. [Motion Picture] Warner Bros.

Peters, J. D. (1999). *Speaking into the air: A history of the idea of communication*. Chicago, IL: University of Chicago Press. doi:10.7208/chicago/9780226922638.001.0001

Phillips, C. N. (2012). *Epic in American culture: Settlement to reconstruction*. Baltimore, MD: Johns Hopkins University Press.

Pickering, R. (1997). Écriture et intertexte chez Valéry: Portée et limites génétiques. In E. Le Calvez & M.-C. Canova-Green (Eds.), *Texte(s) et intertexte(s)* (pp. 219–232). Amsterdam, Netherland; Atlanta, GA: Rodopi.

Pie for Breakfast Studios. (2015). *Atelier games - about*. Retrieved June 4, 2015, from http://ateliergames.tumblr.com/about

Pile, D. (2013). *Nature mage*. Retrieved from http://www.amazon.co.uk/Nature-Mage-Book-ebook/dp/B00CLOYOKA

Pile, D. (2013a). *Nature's servant*. Retrieved from http://www.amazon.co.uk/Natures-Servant-Nature-Mage-Book-ebook/dp/B00B0F0JKU

Pile, D. (2013b). *The nature mage books*. Paper presented at the Hocklife Conference, University of Bedfordshire.

Pile, D. (2014). *Nature's peril*. Retrieved from http://www.amazon.co.uk/Natures-Peril-Nature-Mage-Book-ebook/dp/B00HTRKGL0

Pile, D. (2016a). *The nature mage series*. Retrieved from http://www.duncanpile.com/the-nature-mage-series

Pile, D. (2016b). *Nature mage (The nature mage series book 1) Kindle Edition*. Retrieved from http://www.amazon.co.uk/Nature-Mage-Book-ebook/dp/B00CLOYOKA

Pinedo, I. C. (1996). Recreational terror: Postmodern elements of the contemporary horror film. *Journal of Film & Video, 48*(1/2), 17–31.

Pinto, M. J. (1994). *As marcas lingüísticas da enunciação: Esboço de uma gramática enunciativa do português*. Rio de Janeiro, Brazil: Numen.

Playdead. (2010). *Limbo*. Copenhagen, Denmark.

Playtronic. (2016). *Yooka-Laylee*.

Plothe, T. (2014). *Intertextuality and the virtual world on celluloid*. Retrieved from https://blogs.commons.georgetown.edu/cctp-725-fall2014/author/tp443/

Poe, E. A. (2009). *Fall of the house of Usher and other tales*. New York, NY: New American Library. (Original work published 1839)

Polanski, R. (1974). *Chinatown*. Drama, Mystery, Thriller.

Polanyi, M. (2009). *The tacit dimension.* Chicago, IL: University of Chicago Press.

Poltergeist. (1982). Dir. Tobe Hooper, Prod. Metro-Goldwyn-Mayer (MGM), SLM Production Group. USA.

Poor, N. (2012). Digital elves as a racial other in video games: Acknowledgment and avoidance. *Games and Culture, 7*(5), 375–396.

Poor, N. (2012). Digital elves as a racial other in video games: Acknowledgment and avoidance. *Games and Culture, 7*(5), 375–396. doi:10.1177/1555412012454224

Prager, P. (2015). *Making sense of the modernist muse: Creative cognition and play at the Bauhaus.* Author.

Prawer, S. S. (1980). *Caligari's children: The film as tale of terror.* Oxford, UK: Clarendon Press.

Prensky, M. (2006). *Don't bother me, mom, I'm learning!: How computer and video games are preparing your kids for 21st century success and how you can help!* New York, NY: Paragon.

Priestman, C. (2015). *Iconic 20th century art is being turned into a series of experimental videogames.* Retrieved June 20, 2015, from http://killscreendaily.com/articles/lissitzkys-revenge/

Prohászková, V. (2012). The genre of horror. *American International Journal of Contemporary Research, 2*(4), 132–142.

Projekt Red, C. D. (2015). *The witcher 3: Wild hunt* [PC, PS4, Xbox ONE]. CD Projekt.

Propp, V. (1968). *Morphology of the folk tale.* Austin, TX: University of Texas Press. (Original work published 1928)

Pruett, C. (2007, December 2). *The changing utility of the Otherworld in the Silent Hill series.* Retrieved December 14, 2015, from http://horror.dreamdawn.com/?p=29211

Pruett, C. (2010). The anthropology of fear: Learning about Japan through horror games. *Interface, 4*(6). Retrieved June 29, 2015 from http://journals.sfu.ca/loading/index.php/loading/article/view/90/87

Pruett, C. (2015, August 9). *Ransacking.* Retrieved December 14, 2015, from http://horror.dreamdawn.com/?p=14800034

Pugh, C. (2009) *About.* Retrieved from http://www.starwarsuncut.com/about

Punter, D. (1996). *The Literature of Terror* (Vol. I). Essex, UK: Longman.

Purchas, S. (1625). *Hakluytus posthumus or Purchas his pilgrimes.* Stansby for H. Fetherstone.

Purchese, R. (2015, May 20). *CD Projekt tackles The Witcher 3 downgrade issue head on.* Retrieved June 21, 2015, from http://www.eurogamer.net/articles/2015-05-19-cd-projekt-red-tackles-the-witcher-3-graphics-downgrade-issue-head-on

PwC. (2015a). Video games: Global revenue. *Global entertainment and media outlook 2015-2019.* Retrieved April 6, 2015, from http://www.pwc.com/gx/en/global-entertainment-media-outlook/assets/2015/video-games-key-insights-1-global-revenue.pdf

PwC. (2015b). Video games: Rate of growth. *Global entertainment and media outlook 2015-2019.* Retrieved June 4, 2015, from http://www.pwc.com/gx/en/global-entertainment-media-outlook/assets/2015/video-games-by-growth-and-scale.pdf

Radomski, E., Timm, B., & Burnett, A. (Producers). (1992). Batman: The animated series. [Television Series] New York, NY: Warner Bros.

Rajewsky, I. O. (2005). Intermediality, intertextuality and remediation: A literary perspective on intermediality. *Inter-médialités, 6*(1), 43-64.

Rancière, J. (1991). *The ignorant schoolmaster: Five lessons in intellectual emancipation* (K. Ross, Trans.). Stanford, CA: Stanford University Press.

Rand, A. (1964). *The virtue of selfishness.* New York, NY: New American Library.

Rand, A. (1994). *The fountainhead.* New York, NY: Penguin. (Original work published 1943)

Rand, A. (2005). *Atlas shrugged.* New York, NY: Penguin. (Original work published 1957)

Rand, A. (2014). *Anthem. Mineola, New York.* NY: Dover. (Original work published 1938)

Rastier, F. (1997). Parcours génétiques et appropriation des sources: L'exemple d'Hérodias. In E. Le Calvez & M.-C. Canova-Green (Eds.), *Texte(s) et intertexte(s)* (pp. 193–218). Amsterdam, Netherland; Atlanta, GA: Rodopi.

Reader, K. (1991). Literature/cinema/television: Intertextuality in Jean Renoir's Le testament du docteur Cordelier. In M. Worton & J. Still (Eds.), *Intertextuality: Theories and practice* (pp. 176–189). Manchester, UK: Manchester University Press.

Redmond, S. (2008). *Studying Blade Runner.* Auteur Publishing.

Reiner, A. (2009). *Batman: Arkham Asylum: The best Batman game ever made.* Retrieved June 1, 2015, from http://www.gameinformer.com/games/batman_arkham_asylum/b/xbox360/archive/2009/09/27/review.aspx

Reising, R. (2010). Covering and un(covering) the truth with "All along the watchtower": From Dylan to Hendrix and beyond. In G. Plasketes (Ed.), *Play it again: Cover songs in popular music* (pp. 153–175). Farnham, Surrey, UK; Burlington, VT: Ashgate.

Remedy Entertainment. (2010). *Alan Wake* [Video game]. Redmond, WA: Microsoft Game Studios.

Retro Studios. (2002). *Metroid prime.* Kyoto, Japan: Nintendo.

Ricardou, J. (1971). *Pour une théorie du nouveau roman.* Paris, France: Seuil.

Ricardou, J. (1974). "Claude Simon", textuellement. In J. Ricardou (Ed.), *Lire Claude Simon* (pp. 7–38). Bruxelles, Belgium: Les Impressions Nouvelles. (Original work published 1986)

Richardson, K., & Cilliers, P. (2001). What is complexity science? A view from different directions. *Emergence, 3*(1), 5–22. doi:10.1207/S15327000EM0301_02

Riesman, A. (2015). *The hidden story of Harley Quinn and how she became the superhero world's most successful woman.* Retrieved June 1, 2015, from http://www.vulture.com/2014/12/harley-quinn-dc-comics-suicide-squad.html

Riffaterre, M. (1982). L'illusion référentielle, In Littérature et réalité (pp. 91-118). Paris, France: Seuil.

Riffaterre, M. (1979). *La production du texte.* Paris, France: Seuil.

Riffaterre, M. (1984). Intertextual representation: On mimesis as interpretive discourse. *Critical Inquiry, 11*(1), 141–162. doi:10.1086/448279

Robb, B. J. (2006). *Counterfeit worlds: Philip K. Dick on film.* London, UK: Titan.

Robertson, A. (2013). *That dragon, cancer: The video game helping a father face his son's disease.* Retrieved June 24, 2015, from http://www.telegraph.co.uk/technology/video-games/10170337/That-Dragon-Cancer-the-video-game-helping-a-father-face-his-sons-disease.html

Robinett, W. (1979). *Adventure* [Digital game]. Sunnyvale: Atari.

Rockenberger, A. (2014). Video game framings. In D. Nadine & D. Apollon (Eds.), *Examining paratextual theory and its applications in digital culture* (pp. 252–286). Hershey, PA: IGI Global.

Rockstar North. (2013). *Grand theft auto V*. New York, NY: Rockstar Games.

Rockstar North, R. G. (2002). *Grand theft auto: Vice city* [Xbox]. Edinburgh, Scotland: Take-Two Interactive.

Rocksteady Studios. (2009). *Arkham asylum. London, UK: Eidos Interactive; Warner Bros*. Batman: Interactive Entertainment.

Rocksteady Studios. (2011). *Batman: Arkham city*. New York, NY: Warner Bros. Interactive Entertainment.

Rohn, U. (2011). Lacuna or Universal? Introducing a new model for understanding crosscultural audience demand. *Media Culture & Society*, *33*(4), 631–641. doi:10.1177/0163443711399223

Rose, M. (2010). *Intervvvvvview: Terry Cavanagh*. Retrieved June 4, 2015, from http://www.indiegames.com/2010/01/intervvvvvview_terry_cavanagh.html

Rose, F. (2012). *The art of immersion: How the digital generation is remaking Hollywood, Madison Avenue, and the way we tell stories*. New York, NY: WW Norton & Company.

Rose, J. (2015). The value of art in BioShock: Ayn Rand, emotion, and choice. In L. Cuddy (Ed.), *BioShock and philosophy: Irrational game, rational book* (pp. 15–26). Malden, MA: Wiley Blackwell.

Rouse, R. III. (2010). *Game design: Theory and practice*. Burlington, MA: Jones & Bartlett Learning. doi:10.4324/9780203114261.ch11

Roven, C., Thomas, E., & Nolan, C. (Producers), & Nolan, C. (Director). (2008). *The dark knight*. [Motion Picture] Warner Bros.

Ruckstuhl, F. W. (1917). Idealism and realism in art. *The Art World*, *1*(4), 252–256. Retrieved from http://www.jstor.org/stable/25587740?seq=2#page_scan_tab_contents

RuneScape . (2011). Developer and Publisher: Jagex. Retrieved from http://www.runescape.com

Rutter, J., & Bryce, J. (Eds.). (2006). *Understanding digital games*. London, UK: SAGE Publications.

Ryan, M.-L. (2008). Transfictionality across media. In J. Pier & J. A. Garcia (Eds.), Theorizing narrativity (pp. 385-417). Berlin, Germany: de Gruyter.

Ryan, M. L. (2006). *Avatars of story*. Minneapolis, MN: University of Minnesota Press.

Ryan, M.-L. (2013). Transmedial storytelling and transfictionality. *Poetics Today*, *34*(3), 361–388.

Ryle, G. (2002). *The concept of mind*. Chicago, IL: University of Chicago Press. (Original work published 1949)

Sabella, R. A. (2010). Negative potential of video games. *Education.com*. Retrieved June 30, 2015, from http://www.education.com/reference/article/negative-potential-video-games/

Said, E. W. (1994). *Orientalism (Reprint 1979)*. New York, NY: Vintage.

Saint-Gelais, R. (2000). *La fiction à travers l'intertexte: Pour une théorie de la transfictionnalité*. Retrieved July 25, 2015, from http://www.fabula.org/forum/colloque99/PDF/Saint-Gelais.pdf

Saint-Gelais, R. (2011). *Fictions transfuges: La transfictionnalité et ses enjeux*. Paris, France: Seuil.

Sakellariou, P. (2014). The appropriation of the concept of intertextuality for translation-theoretic purposes. *Translation Studies*, *8*(1), 35–47. doi:10.1080/14781700.2014.943677

Salen, K., & Zimmerman, E. (2004). *Rules of play: Game design fundamentals*. Cambridge, MA: MIT Press.

Saler, M. (2011). *As if: Modern enchantment and the literary prehistory of virtual reality*. Oxford University Press.

Salomon, R. B. (2002). *Mazes of the serpent: An anatomy of horror narrative*. Ithaca, NY: Cornell University Press.

Samantha Nishimura. (n.d.). Retrieved July 21, 2015, from http://tombraider.wikia.com/wiki/Samantha_Nishimura

Sammon, P. M. (1996). *Future noir: The making of Blade Runner*. New York, NY: It Books.

Sanders, J. (2006). *Adaptation and appropriation*. New York, NY: Routledge.

Sanford, K., & Bonsor Kurki, S. (2014). Videogame literacies: Purposeful civic engagement for 21st century youth learning. In K. Sanford, T. Rogers, & M. Kendrick (Eds.), *Everyday youth literacies: Critical perspectives for new times* (pp. 29–46). Singapore: Springer. doi:10.1007/978-981-4451-03-1_3

Sauro, J. (2013). A history of usability. *UXmas*. Retrieved July 2, 2015, from http://uxmas.com/2013/history-of-usability

Saussure, F. (1983). *Course in general linguistics*. Illinois, IL: Open Court Publishing Company. (Original work published 1916)

SCE Santa Monica. (2005). *God of war*.

Scheidel, W. (2006). Population and demography. Princeton/Stanford Working Papers in Classics.

Schiesel, S. (2009, September 1). All together now: Play the game, mom. *The New York Times*.

Schneider, J. L. (2014). Unculting Ayn Rand. *Boulevard*, *30*(1), 175–189.

Schrader, P. G., & Kimberly, A. Lawless, & McCreery, M. (2009). Intertextuality in massively multiplayer online games. Handbook of Research on Effective Electronic Gaming in Education, (3), 791–807.

Schrader, P. G., Lawless, K. A., & McCreery, M. (2009). Intertextuality in Massively Multiplayer Online Games. Handbook of Research on Effective Electronic Gaming in Education, 3, 791–807.

Schrier, J. (2013, April 8). *Witness how much BioShock Infinite has changed over the past few years*. Retrieved June 21, 2015, from http://kotaku.com/witness-how-much-bioshock-infinite-has-changed-over-the-471184935

Schulzke, M. (2013). Translation between forms of interactivity: How to build the better adaptation. In G. Papazian & J. M. Sommers (Eds.), *Game on, Hollywood: Essays on the intersection between video games and cinema* (pp. 70–81). Jefferson, NC: McFarland.

Schumaker, J. S. (c2011.). Super-intertextuality and 21st century individualized social advocacy in Spider-Man and Kick-Ass. In R. J. Gray & B. Kaklamanidou (Eds.), The 21st century superhero: Essays on gender, genre and globalization in film (pp. 129–143). Jefferson, NC: McFarland.

Scodari, C. (1993). Operation Desert Storm as "wargames": Sport, war, and media intertextuality. *Journal of American Culture*, *16*(1), 1–5. doi:10.1111/j.1542-734X.1993.1601_1.x

Scodari, C. (1993). Operation desert storm as "wargames": Sport, war, and media intertextuality. *Journal of American Culture*, *16*(1), 1–5. Retrieved from http://onlinelibrary.wiley.com/doi/10.1111/j.1542-734X.1993.1601_1.x/pdf

Scolari, C. (2013). *Narraivas transmedia, cuando todos los medios cuentan*. Barcelona, Spain: Deusto.

Scolari, C. A. (2009). Transmedia storytelling: Implicit consumers, narrative worlds, and branding in contemporary media production. *International Journal of Communication*, *3*, 586–606.

Sconce, J. (2000). *Haunted media: Electronic presence from telegraphy to television*. Durham, NC: Duke University Press.

Scroggy, D. (1982). *Blade runner sketchbook*. San Diego, CA: Blue Dolphin Enterprises.

Sedda, F. (2015). Semiotics of culture(s): Basic questions and concepts. In P. P. Trifonas (Ed.), *International Handbook of Semiotics* (pp. 675–696). New York, NY; London, UK: Springer. doi:10.1007/978-94-017-9404-6_31

Serres, M. (1972). *L'interférence*. Paris, France: Editions de Minuit.

Shakespeare, W. (1611, modern edition published 2003). The tempest. (V. M. Vaughan & A. T. Vaughan, Eds.). London, UK: Thomson Learning.

Shannon, C. E., & Weaver, W. (1969). *The mathematical theory of communication*. Urbana, IL; Chicago, IL: The University of Illinois Press.

Shaw, J. (2013). *Everyday life in the early English Caribbean: Irish, Africans, and the construction of difference*. Athens, GA: University of Georgia Press.

Sherlock, L. M. (2014). Patching as design rhetoric: Tracing the framing and delivery of iterative content documentation in online games. In J. DeWinter & R. M. Moeller (Eds.), *Computer games and technical communication: Critical methods & applications at the intersection* (pp. 157–170). Burlington, VT: Ashgate Publishing Company.

Shohat, E. (1991). Imaging terra incognita: The disciplinary gaze of empire. *Public Culture*, *3*(2), 41–70. doi:10.1215/08992363-3-2-41

Sicart, M. (2008). Defining game mechanics. *Game Studies, 8*(2). Retrieved from http://gamestudies.org/0802/articles/sicart

Sicart, M. (2012). Against procedurality. *Game Studies*, *11*(3). Retrieved from gamestudies.org/1103/articles/sicart_ap

Siemens, G., & Matheos, K. (2012). Systemic changes in higher education. *Education*, *18*(1), 3–18.

Silver, J. (Producer), & The Wachowski Brothers (Director). (1999). *The matrix* [Motion picture]. United States: Warner Bros.

Silver, J. (Producer), The Wachowski Brothers (Director). (2003). *The matrix reloaded* [Motion picture]. United States: Warner Bros.

Silver, J. (Producer), The Wachowski Brothers (Director). (2003). *The matrix revolutions* [Motion picture]. United States: Warner Bros.

Silver, A., & Ursini, J. (2005). *L.A. noir: The city as character*. Santa Monica, CA: Santa Monica Press.

Simental, M. (2013). The Gospel according to Ayn Rand: *Anthem* as an atheistic theodicy. *The Journal of Ayn Rand Studies*, *13*(2), 96–106. doi:10.5325/jaynrandstud.13.2.0096

Sinervo, K. A. (2015). *Mapping Gotham*. Retrieved July 1, 2015, from http://www.firstpersonscholar.com/mapping-gotham/

Singhal, A., & Udornpim, K. (1997). Cultural shareability, archetypes and television soaps. *Gazette*, *59*(3), 171–188. doi:10.1177/0016549297059003001

Slotkin, R. (1998). *The fatal environment: The myth of the frontier in the age of industrialization, 1800–1890*. Norman, OK: University of Oklahoma Press.

Smoking Car Productions [PC]. (1997). *The last express*. Brøderbund.

Software, I. (1992). *Wolfenstein 3D*.

Sollers, P. (1968). Écriture et révolution. In *Tel quel: Théorie d'ensemble*. Paris, France: Seuil.

Sollers, P. (1968). *Theorie d'ensemble*. Paris, France: Éditions du Seuil.

Spector, W. (2015). DX15: The legacy of *Deus Ex*. *IGN*. Retrieved July 2, 2015, from http://www.ign.com/videos/2015/06/26/dx15-the-legacy-of-deus-ex

Spence, I., & Feng, J. (2010). Videogames and spatial cognition. *Review of General Psychology*, *14*(2), 92–104. doi:10.1037/a0019491

Spencer, C. (Producer), & Moore, R. (Director). (2012). *Wreck-it Ralph* [Motion picture]. United States: Walt Disney Studios.

Spielberg, S. (1981). *Raiders of the lost ark*. Paramount Pictures.

Spielberg, S. (1989). *Indiana Jones and the last crusade*. Paramount Pictures.

Spittle, S. (2011). "Did this game scare you? Because it sure as hell scared me!" *F.E.A.R.*, the abject and the uncanny. [abstract]. *Games and Culture*, *6*(4), 312–326. doi:10.1177/1555412010391091

Squinkifer, D. (2011). *A musical adventure game ... in stop motion?* Retrieved June 4, 2015, from http://squinky.me/2011/10/27/a-musical-adventure-game-in-stop-motion/

Squinkifer, D. (2012a). *How to pamplemousse : Puppets!* Retrieved from http://squinky.me/2012/08/07/how-to-pamplemousse-puppets/

Squinkifer, D. (2012b). *How to pamplemousse : Sets!* Retrieved from http://squinky.me/2012/09/19/how-to-pamplemousse-sets/

Squinkifer, D. (2013). *Dominique pamplemousse*.

Squire, K. (2005). Changing the game: What happens when video games enter the classroom. *Innovate Journal of Online Education*, *1*(6), 25–49.

Stallone, S. (1982). *Rocky III*. USA.

Stam, R. (2000). Beyond fidelity: The dialogics of adaptation. J. Naremore (Ed.), Film adaptation (pp. 54-78). New Brunswick, NJ: Rutgers University Press.

Stam, R. (2000). Beyond fidelity: The dialogics of adaptation. In J. Naremore (Ed.), *Film adaptation* (pp. 54–76). New Brunswick, NJ: Rutgers University Press.

Stam, R., Burgoyne, R., & Flitterman-Lewis, S. (1992). *New vocabularies in film semiotics: Structuralism, post-structuralism and beyond*. London, UK: Routledge.

Star Trek. (1966). Action, Adventure, Sci-Fi.

Steinberg, M. (2012). *Anime's media mix: Franchising toys and characters in Japan*. Minneapolis, MN: University of Minnesota Press. doi:10.5749/minnesota/9780816675494.001.0001

Sterne, J., & Leach, J. (2005). The point of social construction and the purpose of social critique. *Social Epistemology*, *19*(2-3), 189–198. doi:10.1080/02691720500224657

Stewart, G. (2010). The paratexts of inanimate Alice: Thresholds, genre expectations and status. *Convergence (London)*, *16*(1), 57–74. doi:10.1177/1354856509347709

Stilwell, R. (1995). In the air tonight: Text, intertextuality, and the construction of meaning. *Popular Music and Society*, *19*(4), 67–103. doi:10.1080/03007769508591607

Stonehouse, A. (2014). User interface design in video games. *Gamasutra*. Retrieved July 5, 2015, from http://gamasutra. com/blogs/AnthonyStonehouse/20140227/211823/User_interface_design_in_video_games.php?print=1

Stratton, J. (1996). *The desirable body: Cultural fascination and the erotics of consumption*. Manchester: Manchester University Press.

Straubhaar, J. D. (1991). Beyond media imperialism: Asymmetrical interdependence and cultural proximity.pdf. *Critical Studies in Mass Communication*, *8*(1), 39–59. doi:10.1080/15295039109366779

Subrahmanyam, K., Greenfield, P., Kraut, R., & Gross, E. (2001). The impact of computer use on children's and adolescents' development. *Journal of Applied Developmental Psychology*, *22*(1), 7–30. doi:10.1016/S0193-3973(00)00063-0

Suchenski, R. (2004, July). Mamoru Oshii. *Senses of Cinema*, (32).

Suits, B. (1985). The detective story: A case study of games in literature. *Canadian Review of Comparative Literature*, *12*(2), 200–219.

Suleiman, S. R. (1983). *Le roman à thèse ou l'autorité fictive*. Paris, France: PUF.

Superannuation. (2014). *How much does it cost to make a big video game?* Retrieved June 4, 2015, from http://kotaku. com/how-much-does-it-cost-to-make-a-big-video-game-1501413649

Sutton-Smith, B. (2001). *The ambiguity of play* (2nd ed.). Cambridge, MA: Harvard University Press.

Švelch, J. (2014). Regarding board game errata. *Analog Game Studies*, *1*(5). Retrieved from http://analoggamestudies. org/2014/12/regarding-board-game-errata/

Švelch, J. (2015). Towards a typology of video game trailers: Between the ludic and the cinematic. *G|A|M|E, the Italian Journal of Game Studies*, *2015*(4).

Švelch, J. (2013). Monsters by the numbers: Controlling monstrosity in video games. In M. Levina & D.-M. T. Bui (Eds.), *Monster culture in the 21ˢᵗ century: A reader* (pp. 193–208). New York: Bloomsbury.

Swirsky, J., & Pajot, L. (2012). *Indie game: The movie*. Canada: Blinkworks.

Tagg, P. (2000). *Kojak: 50 seconds of television music. Toward the analysis of affect in popular music*. New York, NY: Mass Media Music Scholar's Press.

Tagg, P. (2013). *Music's meanings: A modern musicology for non-musos*. New York, NY: Mass Media Music Scholar's Press.

Tanz, J. (2015). The curse of *Cow Clicker*: How a cheeky satire became a videogame hit. *Wired Magazine*. Retrieved June 12, 2015, from http://archive.wired.com/magazine/2011/12/ff_cowclicker/

Tavinor, G. (2009a). *BioShock* and the art of Rapture. *Philosophy and Literature*, *33*(1), 91–106. doi:10.1353/phl.0.0046

Tavinor, G. (2009b). *The art of videogames*. London, UK: Wiley-Blackwell. doi:10.1002/9781444310177

Taylor, L. N. (2009). Gothic bloodlines in survival horror gaming. In B. Perron (Ed.), *Horror video games: Essays on the fusion of fear and play* (pp. 46–61). Jefferson, NC: McFarland.

Taylor, P. A. (2010). *Žižek and the media*. Cambridge, UK: Polity.

Team Silent. (1999). *Silent hill,* [Videogame] [Disc] [PlayStation] Konami (Europe).

Team Silent. (2001). *Silent hill 2* [Videogame]. Konami. [Disc]

Team Silent. (2003). *Silent hill 3,* [Videogame] [Disc] [PlayStation 2] Konami (Europe).

Team Silent. (2004). *Silent hill 4: The Room,* [Videogame] [Disc] [PlayStation 2] Konami (Europe).

Telltale Games. (2014). *Tales from Borderlands* [PS4, PS3, Xbox 360, Xbox ONE, PC]. Telltale Games.

Thabet, T. (2011). Monstrous textuality: Game fiction between postmodernism and structuralism. *Loading…: The Journal of the Canadian Game Studies Association, 5*(8), 101–109.

The Creative Assembly. (2014). *Alien: Isolation*. Tokyo, Japan: Sega.

The Cutting Room Floor . (2009, October 25) Retrieved August 24, 2014, from http://tcrf.net

The orphanage. (2007). Dir. J.A. Bayona, Prod. Esta Vivo! Laboratorio de Nuevos Talentos, Grupo Rodar, Rodar y Rodar Cine y Televisión, Telecinco Cinema, Televisió de Catalunya (TV3), Warner Bros. Pictures de España, Wild Bunch. Spain.

The others. (2001). Dir. Alejandro Amenábar, Prod. Cruise/Wagner Productions, Sogecine, Las Producciones del Escorpión, Dimension Films, Canal+, Lucky Red, Miramax. USA, Spain, France, Italy.

The shrine . (2010). Dir. Jon Knautz, Prod. Wesley Clover Media, Brookstreet Pictures. Canada.

The Thing . (2002). Developer: Computer Artworks Ltd; Publisher: Black Label Games.

Thibault, M. (2012). *Trasmissione, innovazione e recupero dei ruoli: Un'analisi comparativa di gioco di ruolo, videogiochi e letteratura (transmission, innovation and retrieving of roles: a comparative analysis of role-playing games, video games and literature). (Master thesis).* University of Turin, Turin, Italy.

Thomas, E., Nolan, C., & Roven, C. (Producers), & Nolan, C. (Director). (2012). *The dark knight rises*. [Motion Picture] Warner Bros.

Thomas, E., Roven, C., & Franco, L. (Producers), & Nolan, C. (Director). (2005). *Batman begins*. [Motion picture] Warner Bros.

Thomas, D., & Brown, J. S. (2009). Why virtual worlds can matter. *International Journal of Learning and Media, 1*(1), 37–49. doi:10.1162/ijlm.2009.0008

Thon, J.-N. (2009). Computer games, fictional worlds, and transmedia storytelling: A narratological perspective. In: J. R. Sageng (Ed.), *Proceedings of the philosophy of computer games conference 2009* (pp. 1-6). University of Oslo, Norway. Retrieved August 18, 2015, from http://www.hf.uio.no/ifikk/english/research/projects/thirdplace/Conferences/proceedings/Thon%20Jan-No%C3%ABl%202009%20-%20Computer%20Games,%20Fictional%20Worlds,%20and%20Transmedia%20Storytelling%20A%20Narratological%20Perspective.pdf

Thorne, S. (n.d.). *10 best-selling Xbox 360 games ever*. Retrieved June 28, 2015, from http://whatculture.com/gaming/10-best-selling-xbox-360-games-ever.php

Timmerman, J. H. (1983). *Other worlds: The fantasy genre*. Bowling Green, OH: Popular Press.

Todorov, T. (1973). *The fantastic: A structural approach to a literary genre*. Cleveland, OH: Case Western Reserve University.

Tolkien, J. R. R. (1937). *The hobbit, or, here and back again.* Crows Nest, Australia: Allen & Unwin.

Tolkien, J. R. R. (1954). *The lord of the rings.* Crows Nest, Australia: Allen & Unwin.

Tolman, E. C. (1948). Cognitive maps in rats and men. *Psychological Review, 55*(4), 189–208. doi:10.1037/h0061626 PMID:18870876

Torop, P. (2000). Intersemiosis and intersemiotic translation. *European Journal for Semiotic Studies, 12*(1), 71–100.

Tosca, S. P. (2005). Implanted memories, or the illusion of free action. In W. Brooker (Ed.), *The Blade runner experience: The legacy of a science fiction classic.* New York, NY: Columbia University Press.

Tosca, S., & Klastrup, L. (2011). When fans become players: LOTRO in a transmedial world. In T. Krzywinska & J. Parsler (Eds.), *Ring bearers: The Lord of the Rings Online as intertextual narrative* (pp. 46–69). Manchester, UK: Manchester University Press.

Totten, C. W. (2012). *File: swarmdeathsportconcept-small.* Retrieved January 26, 2016, from http://www.christotten3d.com/wp-content/gallery/concept-art/swarmdeathsportconcept-small.png

Totten, C. W. (2015). *Lissitzky's revenge.*

Totten, C. W. (2014). *An architectural approach to level design.* Boca Raton, FL: CRC Press. doi:10.1201/b17113

Travis, R. (2010). *BioShock* in the cave: Ethical education in Plato and in video games. In K. Schrier & D. Gibson (Eds.), *Ethics and game design: Teaching values through play* (pp. 86–101). Hershey, PA: Information Science Reference. doi:10.4018/978-1-61520-845-6.ch006

Tulloch, R. (2010). A man chooses, a slave obeys: Agency, interactivity and freedom in video gaming. *Journal of Gaming & Virtual Worlds, 2*(1), 27–38. doi:10.1386/jgvw.2.1.27_1

Turtle Rock Studios. (2015). *Evolve* [PS4, Xbox One, PC]. 2K Games.

UNCTAD, & UNDP. (2010). *Creative economy report 2010.* Retrieved from http://www.unctad.org/Templates/WebFlyer.asp?intItemID=5763&lang=1

Uribe-Jongbloed, E., & Espinosa-Medina, H. D. (2014). A clearer picture: Towards a new framework for the study of cultural transduction in audiovisual market trades. *OBSERVATORIO (OBS*), 8*(1), 23–48. Retrieved from http://obs.obercom.pt/index.php/obs/article/view/707/642

Van Looy, J. (2010). *Understanding computer game culture: The cultural shaping of a new medium.* Saarbrücken, Germany: Lambert Academic Publishing.

Vasconcellos, M. S. (2013). *Comunicação e saúde em jogo: Os video games como estratégia de promoção da saúde.* (Doctoral Dissertation). Retrieved from Fiocruz ARCA database. (http://www.arca.fiocruz.br/handle/icict/8547)

Vasconcellos, M. S., & Araujo, I. S. (2014). *Video games and participation in health: How online games can foster population's participation in public health policies.* Paper presented at the 3rd International Conference on Serious Games and Applications for Health, SeGAH 2014, Niterói. doi:10.1109/SeGAH.2014.7067095

Vasconcellos, M. S., & Araujo, I. S. (2013). Os discursos de *Passage*: A análise do discurso aplicada a um jogo digital independente. In *Proceedings do XII Simpósio Brasileiro de Jogos e Entretenimento Digital (SBGames 2013)*. São Paulo, Brazil: SBPC.

Verón, E. (1980). *A produção do sentido.* São Paulo, Brazil: Cultrix / USP.

Vetters, C. (2011). Quand le Sam Spade de Dashiell Hammett devient celui de John Huston: Hammett revu et corrigé par Hays et Warner. Médiation et Information, n°33, Littérature & communication: la question des intertextes, p. 49-58.

Visual Art Jobs. (2015). Retrieved June 4, 2015, from http://jobs.gamasutra.com/jobtype/visual-arts/country/+

Vogler, T. A. (2000). When a book is not a book. In J. Rothenberg & S. Clay (Eds.), *A book of the book: Some works and projections about the book and writing* (pp. 448–466). New York: Granary Books.

Vos, E. (1997). The eternal network. Mail art, intermedia semiotics, interarts studies. In U. Lagerroth, H. Lund, & E. Hedling (Eds.), *Interart poetics. Essays on the interrelations of the arts and media* (pp. 325–336). Amsterdam: Rodopi.

Wachowski, A., & Wachowski, L. (2003). *Enter the matrix* [Playstation 2].

Wachowski, A., & Wachowski, L. (2005). *The matrix: Path of Neo* [Playstation 2].

Wachowski, A., & Wachowski, L. (1999). *The matrix*. Action, Sci-Fi.

Wagner, C. (2008). Learning experience with virtual worlds. *Journal of Information Systems Education, 19*(3), 263–266.

Waisbord, S., & Jalfin, S. (2009). Imagining the national: Gatekeepers and the adaptation of global franchises in Argentina. In A. Moran (Ed.), *TV formats worldwide. Localizing global programs* (pp. 55–74). Bristol, UK; Chicago, IL.

Waldrop, M. M. (1992). *Complexity: The emerging science at the edge of chaos and order*. New York, NY: Simon and Schuster.

Walker, A. (2015). *Superheroes, cities, and empty streets*. Retrieved July 25, 2015, from http://www.giantbomb.com/articles/superheroes-cities-and-empty-streets/1100-5241/

Wallin, M. R. (2007). Myths, monsters and markets: Ethos, identification, and the video game adaptations of *The Lord of the Rings. Game Studies, 7*(1). Retrieved from http://gamestudies.org/0701/articles/wallin

Walsh, C., & Apperley, T. (2012). Using gaming paratexts in the literacy classroom. In C. Martin, A. Ochsner, & K. Squire (eds.), *Proceedings GLS 8.0: Games +Learning +Society Conference* (pp. 323-330). Pittsburg, PA: ETC Press.

Walton, K. L. (1990). *Mimesis as make-believe: On the foundations of the representational arts*. Cambridge, MA: Harvard University Press.

War of the Ring . (2004). Developer: Liquid Entertainment; Publisher: Vivendi Universal Games.

Warm bodies. (2013). Dir. Jonathan Levine, Prod. Summit Entertainment, Make Movies, Mandeville Films, Quebec Film and Television Tax Credit. USA and Canada.

Warner Bros. Games Montreal. (2013). Batman: Arkham origins. New York, NY: Warner Bros. Interactive Entertainment.

Warnes, C. (2005). *Baldur's Gate and history: Race and alignment in digital role playing games, Proceedings of the 2005 DiGRA*. Retrieved June 29, 2015 from http://www.digra.org/digital-library/publications/baldurs-gate-and-history-race-and-alignment-in-digital-role-playing-games/

Warrick, P. S. (1987). *Mind in motion: The fiction of Philip K. Dick*. Carbondale, IL: Southern Illinois University Press.

Waskul, D., & Lust, M. (2004). Role-playing and playing roles: The person, player, and persona in fantasy role-playing. Symbolic Interaction, (27), 333–356. doi:10.1525/si.2004.27.3.333

Weber, R. (2013). *On reflections: First interview with the Ubisoft studio's new MD*. Retrieved June 4, 2015, from http://www.gamesindustry.biz/articles/2014-02-26-on-reflections-first-interview-with-the-ubisoft-studios-new-md

Weinstock, J. A. (2014). Gothic and the new American republic, 1770–1800. In G. Byron & D. Townshend (Eds.), *Gothic world* (pp. 27–36). Abingdon: Routledge.

Weise, M. (2009). The rules of horror: Procedural adaptation in *Clock Tower, Resident evil* and *Dead rising*. In B. Perron (Ed.), *Horror video games: Essays on the fusion of fear and play* (pp. 238–266). Jefferson, NC: Macfarland.

Weise, M. (2009). The rules of horror: Procedural adaptation in *Clock Tower, Resident Evil* and *Dead Rising*. In B. Perron (Ed.), *Horror video games: Essays on the fusion of fear and play* (pp. 238–266). Jefferson, NC: Macfarland.

Weise, M. J. (2008). *BioShock*: A critical historical perspective. *Eludamos (Göttingen), 2*. Retrieved from http://www.eludamos.org/index.php/eludamos/article/viewArticle/vol2no1-12/65

Weiss, G. (2012). Ayn Rand nation: The hidden struggle for America's soul. New York, NY: St. Martin's Press.

West, S. (2001). *Lara Croft: Tomb raider*. Action, Adventure, Fantasy.

Westwood Pacific [PC]. (2000). *Command & conquer: Red alert 2*. EA Games.

Whalen, Z. (2004). Play along: An approach to videogame music. *Game Studies, 4*(1). Retrieved September 23, 2012, from http://www.gamestudies.org/0401/whalen/

White, H. (2013). Materiality, form, and context: Marx contra Latour. *Victorian Studies, 55*(4), 667–682. doi:10.2979/victorianstudies.55.4.667

Wikimedia Commons. (2012a). *File: École des beaux-arts (from the live).jpg*. Retrieved January 26, 2016, from https://commons.wikimedia.org/wiki/File:%C3%89cole_des_beaux-arts_(from_the_live).jpg

Wikimedia Commons. (2012b). *File:Gustave Courbet - A Burial at Ornans - Google Art Project 2.jpg*. Retrieved January 25, 2016, from https://commons.wikimedia.org/wiki/File:Gustave_Courbet_-_A_Burial_at_Ornans_-_Google_Art_Project_2.jpg – image in the public domain

Wikimedia Commons. (2014). *File: David - The Death of Socrates.jpg*. Retrieved January 26, 2016, from https://commons.wikimedia.org/wiki/File:David_-_The_Death_of_Socrates.jpg

Williams, C. L. (1994). Militarized masculinity. *Qualitative Sociology, 17*(4), 415–422. doi:10.1007/BF02393339

Wishnov, J. (2011). *Batman: Arkham City review*. Retrieved June 1, 2015, from http://www.g4tv.com/games/xbox-360/63090/batman-arkham-city/review/

Wolf, M. J. P. (2001). *Genre and the video game in the medium of the video game*. Austin, TX: University of Texas Press.

Wolf, M. J. P. (2001). *The medium of the video game*. Austin, TX: University of Texas Press.

Wolf, M. J. P. (2012). *Building imaginary worlds: The theory and history of subcreation* (1st ed.). New York, NY: Routledge.

Wolf, M., & Perron, B. (2003). *The video game theory reader*. New York, NY: Routledge.

Wolf, W. (1999). Framing fiction: Reflections on a narratological concept and an example: Bradbury, "Mensonge. In W. Grünzweig & A. Solbach (Eds.), *Grenzüberschreitungen: Narratologie im kontext/Transcending boundaries: Narratology in context* (pp. 97–124). Tübingen, Germany: Gunter Narr Verlag.

Wolf, W. (2006). Introduction: Frames, framings, and framing borders in literature and other media. In W. Bernhart & W. Wolf (Eds.), *Framing borders in literature and other media* (pp. 1–40). Amsterdam: Rodopi.

Wolf, W., & Bernhardt, W. (2006). *Framing borders in literature and other media*. Amsterdam, Netherlands: Rodopi.

Woodroffe, S. (1993). *Simon the sorcerer* [Digital game]. Sutton Coldfield, UK: Adventure Soft.

Woods, G. (1995). Fantasy islands: Popular topographies of marooned masculinity. In D. Bell & G. Valentine (Eds.), *Mapping desire: Geographies of sexualities* (pp. 126–148). London, UK: Routledge.

Word of Warcraft . (2004). Developer and Publisher: Blizzard Entertainment.

World War Z. (2013). Dir. Marc Forster, Prod. Paramount Pictures, Skydance Productions, Hemisphere Media Capital, GK Films, Plan B Entertainment, 2DUX², Apparatus Productions, Latina Pictures. USA.

Worton, M., & Still, J. (1990). *Intertextuality: Theories and practice.* Manchester, UK: Manchester University Press.

Wreden, D., & Pugh, W. (2013). *The Stanley parable* [Digital game]. Galactic Cafe.

Yin, K. (1984). *Case study research: Design and methods.* Newbury Park, CA: Sage.

Yin-Poole, W. (2015, April 3). *Sega adds disclaimer to Aliens: Colonial Marines trailers after admitting they didn't accurately reflect final game.* Retrieved June 22, 2015, from http://www.eurogamer.net/articles/2013-04-03-sega-adds-disclaimer-to-aliens-colonial-marines-trailers-after-admitting-they-didnt-accurately-reflect-final-game

Yoon, T.-J., & Cheon, H. (2013). Game playing as transnational cultural practice: A case study of Chinese gamers and Korean MMORPGs. *International Journal of Cultural Studies, 17*(5), 469–483. doi:10.1177/1367877913505172

Younkins, E. W. (2014). Philosophical and literary integration in Ayn Rand's *Atlas Shrugged. The Journal of Ayn Rand Studies, 14*(2), 124–147. doi:10.5325/jaynrandstud.14.2.0124

Younkins, E. W. (Ed.). (2007). *Ayn Rand's Atlas Shrugged: A philosophical and literary companion.* Burlington, VT: Ashgate Publishing, Ltd.

Zackariasson, P., Styhre, A., & Wilson, T. L. (2006). Phronesis and creativity: Knowledge work in video game development. *Creativity and Innovation Management, 15*(4), 419–429.

Zehnder, S. M., & Lipscomb, S. D. (2006). The role of music in video games. In P. Vorderer & J. Bryant (Eds.), *Playing video games: Motives, responses, and consequences* (pp. 241–258). Mahwah, NJ: Lawrence Erlbaum Associates.

Zemeckis, R. (2000). *Cast away.* Action, 20th Century Fox.

Zipper Interactive [PC]. (2000). *Crimson skies.* Microsoft Game Studios.

Zombieland. (2009). Dir. Ruben Fleischer, Prod. Columbia Pictures, Relativity Media, Pariah. USA.

About the Contributors

Christophe Duret is a PhD candidate in French studies at the Université de Sherbrooke (Quebec, Canada). His research focuses on online role-playing games, using a sociocritical approach. He is the founder and editor of the Éditions de l'Inframince.

Christian-Marie Pons is a Full Professor in the Département des lettres et communications at the Université de Sherbrooke (Quebec, Canada). His teaching and research deal with the emergence of modern communications (XIXth century) and the current deployment of new digital technologies, focusing more specifically on the visual and narrative dimensions of media culture.

* * *

Luke Arnott (MA, Comparative Literature; PhD, Media Studies) is an Assistant Professor in the Faculty of Information and Media Studies at the University of Western Ontario. He teaches courses on representation, popular culture, and video games in FIMS's Media, Information, and Technoculture program. Dr. Arnott's current research is focused on genre theory and the epic, specifically its manifestation in new narrative contexts in media such as video games and comic books; he has also published widely on the relation of space to narrative form in such games as Braid and Metroid, and in comics such as Sin City.

Kristin M.S. Bezio is an Assistant Professor of Leadership Studies at the Jepson School of Leadership Studies at the University of Richmond in Virginia. She is the resident contributing games editor for The Learned Fangirl: A Critical Take on Online Culture and Social Media and has written opinion pieces on violence in games and GamerGate for a variety of news outlets, including the Christian Science Monitor and Seattle Times. Recent academic gaming publications include "Playing (with) the Villain: Critical Play and the Joker-as-Guide in Batman: Arkham Asylum (VG 2009)" in The Joker: A Serious Study of the Clown Prince of Crime, "Maker's Breath: Religion, Spirituality, and the Godless World of Dragon Age II" in Online: Heidelberg Journal of Religions on the Internet, and "Friends & Rivals: Loyalty, Ethics, and Leadership in Dragon Age II" in Identity and Leadership in Virtual Communities: Establishing Credibility and Influence. Her work explores the intersection of popular media – games, film, television, theater, and literature – and questions of leadership and citizenship in both the early modern and contemporary eras.

James Biddle is Senior Lecturer at the Grady College of Journalism and Mass Communication at UGA. His teaching focuses on post-production, audio design and visual storytelling. He is also a certified instructor of Avid Media Composer, Final Cut Pro Ten (X), and Adobe Premiere.

Jamie Burren is a recent graduate of the University of Victoria's teacher education program. Currently he is employed by the Greater Victoria School District as a middle and secondary level English Language Arts Teacher. He has for the past year been working towards my Masters Degree in the Department of Curriculum and Instruction. The current focus of his research is on youth, video games, and literacy.

Daniel Dunne is currently a PhD Candidate at the Swinburne University of Technology. His work focuses mainly upon the combination of both narrative and ludological elements to create a sense of story and place. Previously Daniel has presented on the intersection of narrative, including paratext, multimodality and ergodic literature.

Mike Elrod is a Library Instructor M.A. Media Studies/Design at The New School B.A. Theology from Mercer University Gender Studies Minor.

Hernán David Espinosa-Medina has a B.A. in music with emphasis in audio and production from Universidad de Los Andes, in Bogotá, Colombia, and an M.A. on Screenwriting and Audiovisual Development at Los Andes University, Santiago de Chile. He has taught courses and developed research on sound design, editing, and recording, multimedia product development, screenwriting, transmedia storytelling and cultural and audiovisual and market flows. Currently he is an assistant professor at the Faculty of Communication, Universidad de La Sabana in Chía, Colombia.

Clara Fernández-Vara is a game scholar, designer and writer. She is an Associate Arts Professor at the NYU Game Center. Her area of expertise is narrative in games and how it can integrate with game design, focusing on adventure games. She is particularly interested in applying methods from textual analysis and performance studies to the study of video games and transmedia artifacts. Clara's video-game work is grounded in the humanities, informed by her background in literature, film and theatre. Before joining the NYU Game Center, Clara was a a researcher and game developer at the Massachusetts Institute of Technology (MIT). She holds a Ph.D. in Digital Media from the Georgia Institute of Technology and a Masters in Comparative Media Studies from MIT. Clara has presented her work at various international academic and industry conferences, such as DiGRA (Digital Games Research Association), and Foundations of Digital Games and the Game Developer's Conference (GDC). She has worked both in games for research as well as in the commercial sphere. Her first book, Introduction to Game Analysis, has been published by Routledge.

Claudio Pires Franco is a digital media research professional who works with game developers, media and creative businesses and the public sector by using research to inform the development of digital products and services. Claudio is also finishing a practice-based study towards a Professional Doctorate, which contributes to the UNESCO Chair project Crossing Media Boundaries: New Media Forms of the Book, led by Professor Alexis Weedon at the University of Bedfordshire. Claudio researches digital storytelling in its various shapes, cross-media adaptation, intertextuality, and audience research and participation. His focus is currently on studying the digital book landscape, and the relationships of games with wider media ecosystems.

Michael Fuchs was awarded a doctorate degree in American Studies from the University of Graz in the spring of 2012. Michael has co-edited three books (most recently *ConFiguring America: Iconic Figures, Visuality, and the American Identity*, 2013) and written more than a dozen journal articles and book chapters on adult and horror cinema, American television, and video games. Currently, he is working on three monograph projects on different topics related to horror cinema and in the early stages of co-editing three books, one on video games & intermediality, one on American urban spaces, and one on cityscapes in science fiction & fantasy.

Flávia Garcia de Carvalho was hired as a scientific and artistic illustrator by Oswaldo Cruz Foundation (FIOCRUZ) in 2008. Since 2014 she participates in the research groups "Games and Health" and "Communication and Health" from Brazilian National Council for Scientific and Technological Development (CNPq). She writes and teaches on themes of game studies, game analysis, game culture, graphic design and presentation techniques. In 2016, she received her MS in Sciences from the Institute of Scientific and Technological Communication and Information in Health (ICICT) from Oswaldo Cruz Foundation, researching the meanings of health in digital games. Her research interests are Game Studies, Discourse Analysis and Public Health.

Timothy Frank Hopper is an associate professor in the School of EPHE, Faculty of Education. He received his Masters and PhD from the University of Alberta. Dr. Hopper's scholarly work focuses on teacher education in physical education. His research explores the use of complexity thinking as a theoretical frame. He is currently involved in two externally funded research grants with Dr Kathy Sanford, (1) Electronic-portfolio development in three professional programs, and (2) Youth Civic Engagement: Real Life Learning through Virtual Games Environments.

Maria Katsaridou is a Ph.D. candidate at the Aristotle University of Thessaloniki, Greece. Her fields of study include semiotics, narratology, adaptation theory, animation theory, film and video games. She has participated in various international conferences and has published many articles in academic journals. She has also worked for production companies in the fields of screenwriting and animation.

Julien Lalu, History PhD Student, CRIHAM. In charge of the course "History of the European construction" (University of Poitiers) and president of the A-Kira association.

Andréane Morin-Simard is a doctoral student in film studies at Université de Montréal. Her research focuses on the interaction between popular music and audio-visual media and the effects of intertextuality and interference on the cinematic, televisual and video gaming experience. She has been involved in various research projects on videogame genres within the research team LUDOV (formerly Ludiciné) from Université de Montréal. She is also on the editorial board of the online academic journal Kinephanos, which addresses issues related to popular media.

Theo Plothe is Assistant Professor of Communication at Walsh University. His research investigates the impact of digital media and technologies on communication and culture.

Chris Richardson's research explores representations of crime in contemporary popular culture. He holds a Ph.D. in media studies from Western University, a master of arts in interdisciplinary studies of popular culture from Brock University, and a bachelor of journalism from Ryerson University. Dr. Richardson's work focuses on how media professionals can improve the impact and accuracy of crime coverage by reassessing how they choose sources, establish metaphorical language and reproduce popular crime narratives. He is an executive member of the Popular Culture Association of Canada, a faculty advisor for Lambda Pi Eta, The National Communication Association's undergraduate honors society and the founder and supervisor of the YHC Media Studies Research Collective. His research has appeared in journals such as Popular Music and Society, The Canadian Journal of Criminology and Criminal Justice, and The British Journal of Canadian Studies. In 2012, he published Habitus of the Hood with Dr. Hans Skott-Myhre, interrogating intersections of street culture and popular media.

Kathy Sanford is a Professor in the Faculty of Education at the University of Victoria. Her research interests include teacher education, nonformal and informal adult education, ePortfolios as alternative forms of learning/assessment, gender pedagogy, and multiliteracies. She is currently working on research focused on learning in professional programs, video games and youth civic engagement, museum/library education, and E-Portfolios development in three professional programs.

Marcelo Simão de Vasconcellos is a graphic designer and Communications researcher at Oswaldo Cruz Foundation, the oldest and most important public health institution in Brazil. He holds a PhD in Sciences from the Institute of Scientific and Technological Communication and Information in Health (ICICT) from Oswaldo Cruz Foundation, focusing on the potential of online games for public health communication in Brazil. He is publications chair of the Brazilian Symposium of Games and Digital Entertainment (SBGAMES) and one of the leaders of the research group "Games and Health" from Brazilian National Council for Scientific and Technological Development (CNPq). He also teaches game design disciplines and coordinates a game design team aiming to develop games for health communication. His main research interests are Game Studies, social participation, game design and collective health.

Inesita Soares de Araujo is a senior researcher at Oswaldo Cruz Foundation, working in the Laboratory of Communication and Health (LACES / ICICT), researching Communications and Public Policy. She holds a PhD in Communication and Culture from the Federal University of Rio de Janeiro (UFRJ) and a postdoctoral at the University of Coimbra. She implemented and coordinated the Specialization Course in Communication and Health (2003-2008) and the Graduate Program in Information and Communication in Health (2009- 2012) at Oswaldo Cruz Foundation, where she currently teaches and advises PhD students. She also leads the research groups "Games and Health" and "Communication and Health" from Brazilian National Council for Scientific and Technological Development (CNPq) and coordinates the working group "Comunicación y Salud" from Associación Latinoamericana de Investigadores de la Comunicación (ALAIC). She has two published books: "The reconversion of looking: discursive practices and production of meanings" and "Communication and Health".

Jan Švelch is a Ph.D. candidate at the Institute of Communication Studies and Journalism at Charles University in Prague. He received his B.A. and M.A. in Journalism and Media Studies, respectively. His research focuses on video game paratextuality, glitches, fan communities and fan cultures. His thesis explores the reception of paratextuality in the textual systems of analog and digital games. Besides research, he works as a freelance journalist covering video games for various Czech magazines.

Mattia Thibault is a Ph.D. Candidate in Semiotics at Turin University, in Italy. He is part of CIRCe (the Interdepartmental Centre for Research on Communication) and is enrolled in the SEMKNOW program - the first pan-European doctoral program in Semiotics. For this reason he also spent a semester at Tartu University, in Estonia, in 2014. His main interests are play, games, gamification/ludification, toys, playful behaviours on the Internet and Internet memes. He graduated with an MA thesis on intertextual connections between games and literature in the High Fantasy Genre. He has presented his works during conferences in six different countries and he has published several articles in international academic journals. He is currently editing a book due in 2016 on Urban Gamification. He also has been head or member of the organising committee of several national and international conferences on games, raising the necessary funds for one of them. He designed a few board and card games and has a blog: #Semionerd.

Chris Totten, American University Game Artist in residence, is an independent game developer and founder of Pie For Breakfast Studios. He is also the chair of the Washington DC chapter of the International Game Developers Association. Totten has had articles featured in IGDA Perspectives, GameCareerGuide, and Gamasutra and has written two books on game design: Game Character Creation in Blender and Unity (Wiley 2012) and An Architectural Approach to Level Design (CRC, 2014.) He has also spoken at GDC China, Dakota State University's Workshop on Integrated Design in Games, East Coast Game Conference, Digital Games Research Association (DiGRA) conference, Foundations of Digital Games (FDG), and Games For Change. He has a Masters Degree in Architecture from The Catholic University of America in Washington, DC.

Enrique Uribe-Jongbloed holds a B.A. in Film and Television production from Universidad Nacional de Colombia, an M.A. in World Heritage studies from BTU Cottbus and a Ph.D. in Theater, Film and TV studies from Aberystwyth University. He is currently assistant professor at the Department of Social Communication at Universidad del Norte in Barranquilla, Colombia. He was formerly an associate professor at the Faculty of Communication, Universidad de La Sabana. His research focuses on Cultural Transduction in audiovisual products, including localization, adaptation and translation

Matthieu Weisser is a Musicology PhD Student, CRIHAM and vice-president of the A-Kira association.

Mehdi Debbabi Zourgani, Paris 5 Descartes (mzourgani@gmail.com) Professor/Tutor in psychology Also in charge of the course "Videogames and Culture, videogames and culture" for the third grade students at Eurasiam (http://www.eurasiam.com/). Interdisciplinary course is based on various fields (from Roland Barthes, Frans Mayra, to Ian Bogost). Same goes for the invited speakers and their specialty (arts, litterature, game design, psychology, etc.).

Index

A

B

C

D

E

Printed in the United States
By Bookmasters